Dictionary OF THE Presbyterian & Reformed Tradition in America

GENERAL EDITOR
D. G. HART

CONSULTING EDITOR
MARK A. NOLL

InterVarsity Press
Downers Grove, Illinois

InterVarsity Press
P.O. Box 1400, Downers Grove, IL 60515
World Wide Web: www.ivpress.com
E-mail: mail@ivpress.com

InterVarsity Press® is the book-publishing division of InterVarsity Christian Fellowship/USA®, a student movement active on campus at hundreds of universities, colleges and schools of nursing in the United States of America, and a member movement of the International Fellowship of Evangelical Students. For information about local and regional activities, write Public Relations Dept., InterVarsity Christian Fellowship/USA, 6400 Schroeder Rd., P.O. Box 7895, Madison, WI 53707-7895.

ISBN 0-8308-1453-1

Printed in the United States of America

Library of Congress Cataloging-in-Publication Data

Dictionary of the Presbyterian & Reformed tradition in America / general editor : D. G. Hart; consulting editor : Mark A. Noll.
p. cm.
ISBN 0-8308-1453-1 (paper : alk. paper)
1. Presbyterian Church—United States Dictionaries. 2. Reformed Church—United States Dictionaries. 3. Presbyterian Church—Canada Dictionaries. 4. Reformed Church—Canada Dictionaries. I. Hart, D. G. (Darryl G.). II. Noll, Mark A., 1946- .
BX8909.D53 1999
285'.0973'03—dc21

99-26699
CIP

22 21 20 19 18 17 16 15 14 13 12 11 10 9 8 7 6 5 4 3 2 1
18 17 16 15 14 13 12 11 10 09 08 07 06 05 04 03 02 01 00 99

CONTENTS

PREFACE

The *Dictionary of the Presbyterian & Reformed Tradition in America* is a companion volume to *Dictionary of Christianity in America* (InterVarsity Press, 1990). Like its predecessor, the *Dictionary of Baptists in America* (InterVarsity Press, 1994), *DPRTA* is designed to fill in and flesh out a particular theological and ecclesiastical tradition that *DCA* covered but could not exhaust, in this case the Reformed expression of Christianity in the United States and Canada. As the introduction clarifies, the descendants of the Reformed wing of the Protestant Reformation can be most easily found in the variety of Presbyterian and Reformed denominations that have come to fruition in North America. This is not to deny that the Reformed tradition has not also influenced Congregationalists, Episcopalians and Baptists. But for reasons also spelled out in the introduction, to narrow the Reformed expression of Christianity to Presbyterian and Reformed churches yields precision, aside from keeping this book at a manageable length.

The editors' decision to limit *DPRTA*'s scope to Presbyterian and Reformed should not, however, obscure our simultaneous effort to do full justice to the pluriformity of the Reformed tradition in North America. Typically, church historians have looked primarily at the dominant Anglo-America denominations such as the mainline Presbyterian Church and its dissenting offshoots. But the Reformed tradition does not belong to American Presbyterians alone. It has also received vigorous and careful attention in Dutch-American, German-American and Hungarian-American Reformed communions, as well as in Korean-American and less well-known Scottish-American Presbyterian churches. What is more, mainline American Presbyterianism is not a monolith but has taken different regional forms, from Presbyterians in the southern and northern United States, to the different Presbyterian denominations in Canada. To be sure, the dictum that winners end up writing the history will find support in this volume from the predominance of United States' Presbyterians in the pages that follow. Still, one of our fundamental aims has been to represent the diversity of efforts to propagate, defend and preserve the Reformed tradition in the United States and Canada.

Another editorial decision that should be noted at the outset concerns the subjects chosen and the method used to present and interpret them. Since no reference work can be truly comprehensive, the editors had to make choices about whom and what to include. Our first decision was to highlight individuals and communions while neglecting institutions. Though schools, publications, seminaries and parachurch agencies have been very influential, we believe the lives of individuals and the histories of churches offer a better barometer for reading what it means to be Reformed than do the activities of religious organizations. In addition to featuring individuals and denominations, the editors commissioned several thematic essays that examine the Reformed tradition's influence upon cultural and political life in North America. These essays probably depart from the conventions of most reference works, but in the editors' estimation they also add interpretive depth to the "just-the-facts-ma'am" character of typical dictionary entries. This is just another way of affirming that the primary method for assessing the Reformed tradition in this work is historical. Yet all good history involves interpretation, and in addition to the various perspectives that contributors brought to their subjects, the editors have allowed greater interpretive freedom in the thematic essays.

The editors would like to claim that no work of this kind exists and that *DPRTA* fills a significant gap in historical and theological reference works. But that is a judgment best left to readers. Still, few reference works are such as this, ones that are primarily historical and cover the diversity of Reformed and Presbyterian churches in the United States and Canada. *The Encyclopedia of the Reformed Faith,* edited by Donald K. McKim (Westminster John Knox, 1992) is a very useful guide but is more theological than historical, and its regional coverage is broader than North America. Perhaps the closest competitor to *DPRTA* is Alfred Nevin's *Encyclopedia of the Presbyterian Church in the United States* (1884). But it is over one hundred years old and suffers from being limited to the mainline Presbyterian denominations in the United States. The paucity of similar reference works suggests that *DPRTA* should be a welcome addition to all who are interested in the Reformed tradition as it emerged and developed in the United States and Canada.

In addition to the scholars who contributed to the book, we are indebted to and very grateful for the labors of Peter J. Wallace, now a doctoral student at the University of Notre Dame, who assisted with various administrative and logistical details of the project and contributed directly to the manuscript by revising many of the shorter entries from *DCA* into longer articles with fuller bibliographies. Without Peter's efforts this book would have been much more difficult to complete. Our thanks go as well to Daniel G. Reid at IVP, who gave us good advice and showed remarkable patience throughout the completion of this book.

D. G. Hart
Mark A. Noll

GUIDE TO USING THIS DICTIONARY

Abbreviations

A list of abbreviations used in this dictionary will be found on pages xi-xii.

Authorship of Articles

The authors of articles are indicated by their initials and last name at the foot of each article. A full list of contributors will be found on pages xiii-xiv, in alphabetical order by last name.

Many if not most of the articles within this *dictionary* have been written for this work, but a number have been adapted from the *Dictionary of Christianity in America* (see preface). A symbol immediately following the title of such articles indicates whether material has been deleted (‡) or added (†) to the original article. In either case, the original author's signature has been retained.

Bibliographies

A bibliography has been appended to many of the articles. In the case of biographical articles, bibliographies usually list secondary sources, while important primary sources are listed in the body of the article. Many biographical articles also contain references to articles in important biographical dictionaries and other reference works, which are noted by their standard abbreviations. All bibliographic items are listed in alphabetical order by the author's last name or, in the case of standard reference works, by the abbreviation of that work.

Cross-References

A system of cross-references has been utilized to alert readers to other relevant articles within the *Dictionary*.

1. One-line entries direct the reader to the title of the article where the topic is treated:

Covenanters. *See* REFORMED PRESBYTERIAN CHURCH OF NORTH AMERICA, COVENANTER SYNOD.

2. An asterisk before a word or phrase indicates that further relevant information will be found in an article approximating that title. The *form* of the word asterisked will not always be precisely the same as that of the title of the article to which the asterisk refers. For example, "*pietistic" directs the reader to the article on **Piety, Presbyterian and Reformed.**

3. References such as "(*see* Hodge, Charles)" have been used within the body of articles.

4. Cross-references have been appended to the end of many articles: "*See also* INTELLECTUAL LIFE, PRESBYTERIANS AND."

Introductory Essay

An introductory essay provides a synoptic overview and interpretive perspective on the Presbyterian and Reformed tradition in America. Cross-references to dictionary articles will assist readers who wish to use this essay as a gateway into the articles.

ABBREVIATIONS

General

b.	born
c.	*circa*, about, approximately
d.	died
ET	English translation
vol(s).	volume(s)
?	date uncertain
*	subject included in the *Dictionary of the Presbyterian & Reformed Tradition in America*
†	adapted *DCA* article; material added
‡	adapted *DCA* article; material deleted

Books and Journals

AAP	*Annals of the American Pulpit*, ed. W. B. Sprague, 9 vols.
ANB	*American National Biography*, ed. J. A. Garraty and M. C. Carnes, 24 vols.
AP	*American Presbyterians*
ATR	*Anglican Theological Review*
BRPR	*Biblical Repository and Princeton Review*
CCen	*Christian Century*
CH	*Church History*
CHR	*Canadian Historical Review*
CT	*Christianity Today* (1956-)
*CT**	*Christianity Today*, ed. Samuel G. Craig (published 1930-1949)
DAB	*Dictionary of American Biography*, ed. A. Johnson, D. Malone et al. (vols I-XX, 1892-1974; 1-7, 1944-1988)
DARB	*Dictionary of American Religious Biography*, H. W. Bowden
DCA	*Dictionary of Christianity in America*, ed. D. G. Reid et al.
DCB	*Dictionary of Canadian Biography*, ed. G. W. Brown et al., 14 vols.
DSCHT	*Dictionary of Scottish Church History and Theology*, ed. N. M. de. S. Cameron et al.

EARE	*Encyclopedia of the American Religious Experience*, ed. C. H. Lippy and P. W. Williams, 3 vols.
FH	*Fides et Historia*
HHMBI	*Historical Handbook of Major Biblical Interpreters*, ed. Donald K. McKim
HMPEC	*Historical Magazine of the Protestant Episcopal Church*
IBMR	*International Bulletin of Missionary Research*
JAAR	*Journal of the American Academy of Religion*
JAH	*Journal of American History*
JHI	*Journal of the History of Ideas*
JNH	*Journal of Negro History*
JPH	*Journal of Presbyterian History*
JPHS	*Journal of the Presbyterian Historical Society*
JSH	*Journal of Southern History*
NAW	*Notable American Women: 1607-1950*, 3 vols. (1971)
NAWMP	*Notable American Women: The Modern Period*, 1 vol. (1980)
NCAB	*National Cyclopedia of American Biography*, 55 vols (1892-1974); current series, A-L (1930-1972)
NCHR	*North Carolina Historical Review*
n.s.	new series
PRR	*The Presbyterian and Reformed Review*
PSB	*Princeton Seminary Bulletin*
PTR	*Princeton Theological Review*
RelEd	*Religious Education*
RJ	*Reformed Journal*
RR	*Reformed Review*
SH	*Schapp-Herzog Encyclopedia of Religious Knowledge*, ed. S. M. Jackson
USQR	Union Seminary Quarterly Review
WMQ	*William and Mary Quarterly*
WTJ	*Westminster Theological Journal*

LIST OF CONTRIBUTORS

Adeney, Frances S., University of Southern California.
Anderson, Douglas F., Northwestern College, Orange City, Iowa.
Angell, Stephen W., Florida A & M University, Tallahassee, Florida.
Ashcraft, William M., Truman State University, Kirksville, Missouri.
Balmer, Randall H., Barnard College, New York, New York.
Barker, William S., Westminster Theological Seminary, Philadelphia, Pennsylvania.
Bays, Daniel H., University of Kansas, Lawrence, Kansas.
Beeke, Joel, Puritan Reformed Theological Seminary, Grand Rapids, Michigan.
Bekker, Gary J., Calvin Theological Seminary, Grand Rapids, Michigan.
Bendroth, Margaret Lamberts, Calvin College, Grand Rapids, Michigan.
Benedetto, Robert J., Union Theological Seminary, Richmond, Virginia.
Berk, Stephen E., California State University, Long Beach, California.
Bloesch, Donald G., University of Dubuque Theological Seminary, Dubuque, Iowa.
Boylan, Anne M., University of Delaware, Newark, Delaware.
Bratt, James D., Calvin College, Grand Rapids, Michigan.
Brinks, Herbert J., Calvin College, Grand Rapids, Michigan.
Browning, W. Neal, William Carey International University, Pasadena, California.
Bruins, Elton J., Western Theological Seminary, Holland, Michigan.
Bundy, David D., Christian Theological Seminary, Indianapolis, Indiana.
Buss, Dietrich G., Biola University, La Mirada, California.
Butin, Philip W., Albuquerque, New Mexico.
Buttrick, David G., Vanderbilt Divinity School, Nashville, Tennessee.
Carpenter, Joel A., Calvin College, Grand Rapids, Michigan.
Chesebrough, David B., Illinois State University, Normal, Illinois.
Clarke, Erskine, Columbia Theological Seminary, Decatur, Georgia.
Clutter, Ronald T., Grace Theological Seminary, Winona Lake, Indiana.
Coalter, Milton J., Louisville Presbyterian Theological Seminary, Louisville, Kentucky.
Conn, Harvie M., Westminster Theological Seminary, Philadelphia, Pennsylvania.
Dennison, Charles G. (deceased), Sewickley, Pennsylvania.
Dorsett, Lyle W., Wheaton College Graduate School, Wheaton, Illinois.
Edwards, John H., Woodbridge, Connecticut.
Evans, William B., Erskine College, Due West, South Carolina.
Fisk, William, Muskingum College, New Concord, Ohio.
Fitzmier, John R., Vanderbilt Divinity School, Nashville, Tennessee.
Frantz, John B., Pennsylvania State University, University Park, Pennsylvania.
Fraser, M. Robert, Asia-Pacific Nazarene Theological Seminary, Manila, Philippines.
Freundt, Albert H., Jr., Reformed Theological Seminary, Jackson, Mississippi.
Fry, C. George, Lutheran College, Decorah, Iowa.
Gaffin, Richard B., Westminster Theological Seminary, Philadelphia, Pennsylvania.
Geisler, Norman L., Southern Evangelical Seminary, Charlotte, North Carolina.
Goliber, Sue Helder, Mount St. Mary's College & Seminary, Emmitsburg, Maryland.
Goodpasture, H. McKennier, Union Theological Seminary, Richmond, Virginia.
Graham, Stephen R., North Park Theological Seminary, Chicago, Illinois.
Guelzo, Allen C., Eastern College, St. Davids, Pennsylvania.
Gunter, W. Stephen, Chandler School of Theology, Emory University, Atlanta, Georgia.
Hall, Joseph H., Mid-America Reformed Theological Seminary, Dyer, Indiana.
Hambrick-Stowe, Charles E., Church of the Apostles, Lancaster, Pennsylvania.
Hanko, Herman, Protestant Reformed Seminary, Grand Rapids, Michigan.
Hannah, John D., Dallas Theological Seminary, Dallas, Texas.
Hardesty, Nancy A., Clemson University, Clemson, South Carolina.
Hardman, Keith J., Ursinus College, Collegeville, Pennsylvania.
Harris, William O., Princeton Theological Seminary, Princeton, New Jersey.
Hart, Darryl G., Westminster Theological Seminary, Philadelphia, Pennsylvania.
Heidebrecht, Paul, Immanuel Presbyterian Church, Wheaton, Illinois.
Hesselink, John I., Western Theological Seminary, Holland, Michigan.
Hester, David C., Louisville Presbyterian Theological Seminary, Louisville, Kentucky.
Heuser, Frederick, Jr., Presbyterian Historical Society, Philadelphia, Pennsylvania.
Hoffecker, W. Andrew, Reformed Theological Seminary, Jackson, Mississippi.
Japinga, Lynn W., Hope College, Holland, Michigan.
Johnson, John F., Concordia University, St. Paul, Minnesota.
Johnson, Merwyn S., Erskine Seminary, Due West, South Carolina.
Joy, Mark S., Kansas State University, Manhattan, Kansas.
Kelly, Douglas, Reformed Theological Seminary, Charlotte, North Carolina.
Kemeny, Paul C., Calvin College, Grand Rapids, Michigan.
Kennedy, Earl W., Northwestern College, Orange City, Iowa.
Kling, David W., University of Miami, Coral Gables, Florida.
Lawrence, William G., Owego United Methodist Church, Owego, New

York.
Lee, Sang, Princeton Theological Seminary, Princeton, New Jersey.
Leith, John H., Union Theological Seminary, Richmond, Virginia.
Lewis, Donald M., Regent College, Vancouver, British Columbia, Canada.
Linder, Robert D., Kansas State University, Manhattan, Kansas.
Lippy, Charles H., University of Tennessee, Chattanooga, Tennessee.
Logan, Samuel T., Westminster Theological Seminary, Philadelphia, Pennsylvania.
Longfield, Bradley, University of Dubuque Theological Seminairy, Dubuque, Iowa.
Luidens, Donald Hope College, Holland, Michigan.
Lundin, Roger W., Wheaton College, Wheaton, Illinois.
Macleod, Donald, Princeton Theological Seminary, Princeton, New Jersey.
McKenzie, Brian M., Nobles Memorial Baptist Church, Windsor, Ontario, Canada.
McKim, Donald K., Memphis Theological Seminary, Memphis, Tennessee.
Magnuson, Norris A., Bethel Theological Seminary, St. Paul, Minnesota.
Marsden, George, University of Notre Dame, Notre Dame, Indiana.
Meier, Samuel A., Ohio State University, Columbus, Ohio.
Miethe, Terry L., McMurry University, Abilene, Texas.
Migliore, Daniel L., Princeton Theological Seminary, Princeton, New Jersey.
Moody, Barry M., Acadia University, Wolfville, Nova Scotia, Canada.
Moore, Moses N., Arizona State University, Tempe, Arizona.
Moyer, Albert E., Virginia Polytech Institute and State University, Blacksburg, Virginia.
Mulder, John M., Louisville Presbyterian Theological Seminary, Louisville, Kentucky.
Mullin, Robert B., General Episcopal Seminary, New York, New York.
Nederveen, Gijsbert, Canadian and American Reformed Church, Burlington, Ontario.
Noll, Mark A., Wheaton College, Wheaton, Illinois.
Nordbeck, Elizabeth C., Andover Newton Theological School, Newton Centre, Massachusetts.
Olbricht, Thomas H., Pepperdine University, Malibu, California.
Old, Hughes Oliphant, Center of Theological Inquiry, Princeton, New Jersey.
O'Malley, John S., Asbury Theological Seminary, Wilmore, Kentucky.
Payne, John B., Lancaster Theological Seminary, Lancaster, Pennsylvania.
Phillips, Timothy, Wheaton College, Wheaton, Illinois.
Pierard, Richard V., Indiana State University, Terre Haute, Indiana.
Pointer, Richard W., Westmont College, Santa Barbara, California.
Pronk, Cornelius, Grace Free Reformed Church, Brantford, Ontario.
Reid, Daniel G., InterVarsity Press, Downers Grove, Illinois.
Rennie, Ian, Tyndale College and Seminary, Toronto, Ontario, Canada.
Robert, Dana L., Boston University School of Theology, Boston, Massachusetts.
Rosell, Garth M., Gordon-Conwell Theological Seminary, South Hamilton, Massachusetts.
Ross, Kenneth, Presbyterian Historical Society, Philadelphia, Pennsylvania.
Ruegsegger, Ronald W., Nyack College, Nyack, New York.
Sawyer, Kenneth, McCormick Theological Seminary, Chicago, Illinois.
Scorgie, Glen, North American Baptist College, Edmonton, Alberta, Canada.
Shattuck, Gardiner H., School for Ministries, Episcopal Diocese of Rhode Island.
Shelley, Bruce L., Denver Seminary, Denver, Colorado.
Silva, William A., Trinity College, Hartford, Connecticut.
Smith, Gary Scott, Grove City College, Grove City, Pennsylvania.
Smith, Morton, Greenville Presbyterian Theological Seminary, Greenville, South Carolina.
Smylie, James H., Union Theological Seminary, Richmond, Virginia.
Stackhouse, John G., Regent College, Vancouver, British Columbia, Canada.
Stewart, John W., Princeton Theological Seminary, Princeton, New Jersey.
Stockwell, Clinton E., Chicago Center for Public Ministry, Chicago, Illinois.
Stoeffler, F. E., Temple University, Philadelphia, Pennsylvania.
Strong, Douglas M., Wesley Theological Seminary, Washington, D.C.
Sunquist, Scott W., Pittsburgh Theological Seminary, Pittsburgh, Pennsylvania.
Sweeney, Douglas A., Trinity Evangelical Divinity School, Deerfield, Illinois.
Swierenga, Robert P., Kent State University, Kent, Ohio.
Taylor, Thomas T., Wittenberg University, Springfield, Ohio.
Touchstone, D. Blake, Tulane University, New Orleans, Louisiana.
Toulouse, Mark G., Brite Divinity School, Texas Christian University, Fort Worth, Texas.
Trollinger, William Vance, Jr., University of Dayton, Dayton, Ohio.
Tucker, Ruth A., Trinity Evangelical Divinity School, Deerfield, Illinois.
Van Til, L. John, Geneva College, Grove City, Pennsylvania.
Vaudry, Richard, University of Alberta, Edmonton, Alberta, Canada.
Wade, William J., King College, Bristol, Tennessee.
Wallace, Peter, University of Notre Dame, Notre Dame, Indiana.
Weber, Timothy P., Northern Baptist Theological Seminary, Lombard, Illinois.
Weeks, Louis B., Union Theological Seminary, Richmond, Virginia.
Weir, David A., Centenary College, Hackettstown, New Jersey.
Westerkamp, Marilyn, University of California, Santa Cruz, Santa Cruz, California.
Whiteman, Curtis W., Westmont College, Santa Barbara, California.
Wiers, John R., Kirkwod Community College, Cedar Rapids, Iowa.
Wilshire, Leland E., Biola University, La Mirada, California.
Wilson, Everett A., Bethany Bible College, Scotts Valley, California.
Wilt, Paul C., Westmont College, Santa Barbara, California.
Zuck, Lowell, Eden Theological Seminary, Webster Groves, Missouri.

Introduction

The Presbyterians: A People, a History & an Identity

*To paraphrase Benjamin Breckinridge *Warfield, the rock-ribbed defender of* Presbyterian orthodoxy who taught at Princeton Seminary from 1887 until 1920, when on their knees in prayer all Christians are Calvinists at heart. Non-Calvinists might be inclined to take Warfield's sentiment as a typical display of Reformed condescension toward outsiders. Others, more sympathetic to Warfield, might regard his thought a charitable way of affirming the unity of Christ's body despite its obvious theological diversity. Whatever one's perspective, Warfield's definition of Calvinism will not work for the construction of a historical dictionary on Presbyterians and Reformed in North America. Christians do not remain on their knees all the time and therefore, by Warfield's lights, at some point cease to be Calvinists. This book is about Calvinists on more than their knees. It is about Calvinists on their feet, at repose, at work, at play and in worship.

Historically Presbyterians and Reformed have been known as much for theological convictions as for ancestral origins. Huck Finn's humorous observations about a Presbyterian worship service, for instance, summed up well the reputation of Presbyterians in nineteenth-century America. "It was pretty ornery preaching," he said, "but everybody said it was a good sermon, and they all talked it over going home, and had such a powerful lot to say about faith and good works and free grace and preforeordestination [sic], and I don't know what all, that it did seem to be one of the roughest Sundays I had run across yet." Yet the theological identity of Presbyterians and Reformed in North America is bound up as much with the history of particular ethnic groups and peoples with specific national origins as any of the more apparently nonmainline Protestant churches in

America. Even though Presbyterianism has long been associated with native white Anglo-Saxon Protestantism, its history and identity are embedded in the pattern of immigration, segregation/isolation and assimilation of groups as ethnically and geographically diverse as *Hungarian Reformed and *Korean Presbyterians. To grasp the diversity of Presbyterians and Reformed in North America requires some knowledge of the origins of the tradition in sixteenth-century Europe and the transplanting of Old World beliefs and practices in the New World.

Reformation Origins

All Protestants are indebted to Martin Luther (1483-1546), whose spiritual struggles and biblical exposition led to what Philip *Schaff called the "material principle of the Reformation," the doctrine of justification by faith alone, which in turn precipitated the sixteenth-century division of Western Christianity. Consequently, Presbyterians and Reformed, along with Lutherans, Anglicans and Anabaptists—despite much diversity and disagreement—concur on biblical teaching regarding the nature of human sin and grace in Jesus Christ. Rather than attributing any decisive powers to the individual in the process of salvation or to the mediating structures of the church, early Protestants of almost all stripes confessed along with Luther that God alone is sovereign in the saving of sinners and that Christ's perfect obedience, death, resurrection and ascension alone are sufficient to deliver believers out of the condition of sin and misery. As the *Heidelberg Catechism (1563) puts it so eloquently in its first question and answer, "What is your only comfort in life and death? That I, with body and soul, both in life and death, . . . belong to my faithful Savior Jesus Christ."

Almost simultaneously with Luther's courageous stand against Roman Catholic teaching about sin and grace and the authority of the papacy, other Protestants extended a principle of Luther's—that every matter of Christian faith and practice be tested according to the explicit teaching of the Bible. Following from this impulse to make Scripture the sole standard for the church's witness and work, what Schaff referred to as "the formal principle of the Reformation," was the seed of the Reformed tradition. Thus, in many places throughout Europe, Reformed believers took issue with accepted practices in Roman Catholicism. While many associate the Reformed tradition almost exclusively with John *Calvin's (1509-1564) efforts in the Swiss town of Geneva, the first stages of the Reformation in Switzerland depended also upon the ministry of Ulrich Zwingli (1484-1531) in Zurich. About the same time that Luther reformed the churches in Wittenberg, Zwingli introduced practices that would characterize the religious observances of Presbyterians and Reformed, such as making the sermon central in the *worship service, preaching continuously through a book of the Bible as opposed to following the lectionary, and replacing the ceremonies and holy days of the church year with the weekly sanctification of the Lord's Day.

Despite Zwingli's early efforts at reform, his untimely death in battle against Swiss Catholics (a foreshadowing of the religious wars of the seventeenth century) combined with developments in Geneva to make Calvin the central figure in the origins and history of the Reformed tradition. Born the son of a notary, Calvin prepared for the priesthood at the University of Paris in a college well known for its traditional scholasticism. After a conflict between his father and the local bishop, the young student changed course to prepare for a career in law. Calvin's interest in philosophy and theology remained strong even after completing a degree in law; moreover, his pursuit of humanistic studies brought him into contact with academics and clerics who were critical of the church. The precise date of Calvin's conversion is still much debated, but by 1534 he had been charged with heresy by Roman Catholic authorities and was forced to flee Paris in search of a Protestant stronghold. In 1536 Guillaume Farel, a Reformer in southwest Switzerland, persuaded Calvin to assist in the churches of Geneva. This was the same year as the publication of the first edition of Calvin's *Institutes of the Christian Religion.* The Reformer's initial efforts in Geneva met with opposition and Calvin again had to flee, this time to Strasbourg. But by 1540 city leaders in Geneva recognized their need for Calvin's talents and asked him to return. For the rest of his life Geneva became a place for Calvin to develop and apply the teachings of the Reformed faith.

Though he was never entirely successful in carrying through all of his desired reforms, Calvin had a dramatic influence not just upon the city of Geneva but also upon the Reformed churches throughout western Europe. Calvin expanded the *Institutes* through eight editions, the definitive version being the 1559 edition. During these years Calvin wrote commentaries on many of the books of the Bible, often preached three sermons a week (many of which have not yet been published), penned numerous works establishing the practice of Presbyterian and Reformed churches (the most important of which is *Ecclesiastical Ordinances* [1541]) and defended thoughtfully the Reformed faith (collected in *Tracts and Treatises on the Reformation of the Church,* 3 vols. [1958 (1844)]). Through his writings alone Calvin's influence would have been immense. But Calvin's dominance of church life in Geneva and the influx of Protestant refugees into the city insured that the Frenchman would leave a lasting mark upon churches far beyond either his place of exile or his homeland of France.

Unlike Lutheranism, which depended heavily upon the work of one figure, Reformed churches benefited from the contributions of several important Reformers, making Calvin the first among theological equals in the Reformed branch of Protestantism. Switzerland proved to be fertile soil for the Reformed tradition. John Oecolampadius (1482-1531), an accomplished linguist and humanist who helped to establish the grammatical-historical method of exegeting Scripture among the Reformed, led Protestant efforts at Basel, pastoring St. Mark's Church and teaching at the city's university. Heinrich Bullinger (1504-1575), the chief pastor at Zurich after Zwingli's death in 1531, was a prolific writer and the author of the Second Helvetic Confession (1566). He produced a complete theology in the form of fifty sermons (*The Decades* [1549]), a work especially influential in England, and is often credited with laying the foundation for the Reformed understanding of *covenant theology. Guillaume Farel (1489-1565), in addition to recognizing

Calvin's genius, was in his own right a gifted and courageous evangelist who brought Protestantism to the French-speaking regions of Switzerland. Martin Bucer (1491-1551) led reforms in the city of Strasbourg, labored diligently to overcome differences between Lutherans and the Reformed and developed Reformed polity and worship. Peter Martyr Vermigli (1500-1562), the greatest of the Italian Reformers, wrote able biblical commentaries and elaborated a careful sacramental theology but was forced into exile and ministered most effectively with Bucer in Strasbourg. In England, William Tyndale (1494-1536) would have great influence on English Protestants, even though he lived on the Continent in exile during his most productive years, through his translation of the Bible and his polemics on behalf of the Reformed faith. Thus, while Calvin deserves credit for giving shape to the Reformed tradition, he was by no means the titanic lone authority that Luther was for Lutherans.

Presbyterians and Reformed

The term *Calvinist,* like *Lutheran,* was initially a term of opprobrium. But unlike the movement and communions that trace their origins to Luther and the reforms he achieved in Germany (who call themselves "evangelical"), members of the Calvinist tradition have generally preferred the labels *Presbyterian* or *Reformed.* Generally speaking, little difference exists between Presbyterian and Reformed churches, though in the pages that follow, some of the distinctives of each will emerge such as different confessional standards and divergences in church government. The chief difference between Presbyterian and Reformed is geographical; Calvinist churches in Great Britain have been designated by the term *Presbyterian;* like-minded communions on the Continent have gone by the word *Reformed.* Thus, Presbyterian denominations in North America generally hail from Great Britain while Reformed churches trace their origins to Germany, Switzerland, the Netherlands, France and Hungary.

The word *Presbyterian* specifically designates a pattern of church government, one forged originally by Calvin in his *Ecclesiastical Ordinances.* There is good reason that the Calvinistic churches in Great Britain have gone by the name of the church government under which they operate. While they held to Calvinistic theology, matters of church polity were crucial to their objections to the Church of England and for forming a distinct ecclesiastical identity throughout the British Isles. The English Reformation is at least as complicated as the marital history of Henry VIII, who repudiated the papacy's jurisdiction over church life in England. Yet, whatever the personal and political reasons for Henry's break with Rome, Reformed ideas gained a hearing in England under his son, Edward VI, with the likes of Tyndale, Bucer and Vermigli occupying professorates at Cambridge and Oxford. The influence of Reformed theology, as opposed to Lutheranism, also owes a great deal to the hospitality shown to British Protestant refugees by Reformed centers on the Continent. Bullinger, Zwingli's successor in Zurich, and Calvin in Geneva, as well as Reformed authorities in Frankfurt and Strasbourg, not only offered British Protestants a place of refuge but also instilled the teachings and practice of Reformed theology.

Scotland and Northern Ireland, however, not England, would become the centers of Presbyterian strength in the British Isles. Here the influence of John Knox, especially upon the Scottish Reformation, was crucial. After an extended period of exile on the Continent with a particularly formative stay in Geneva—Knox called Calvin's city "the most perfect school of Christ that ever was in the earth since the days of the Apostles"—he returned to Scotland in 1559 to spearhead the Reformed movement. A year later under Knox's leadership, the Scottish Parliament abolished Roman Catholicism and approved the First Scottish Confession, written by Knox and five other ministers. He went on to produce *A Book of Common Order* (1564), which was based on Calvin's liturgy in Geneva and became the standard for worship in Scotland. When Knox died in 1572, leadership of the Scottish church passed to Andrew Melville, who insisted upon a strict Presbyterian polity and would not compromise with other views—church order stated that the term *bishop* be applied to all pastors. Thus Knox and Melville established by the late sixteenth century a distinctly Presbyterian theology, worship and church government.

Despite the inability of Presbyterianism to gain an official foothold in England, the gathering of the Westminster Assembly during the 1640s, a body called by Parliament to offer guidance about the faith and practice of the Church of England, and the composition of the *Westminster Confession of Faith, Larger and Shorter Catechisms and Directory for Public Worship meant that English Calvinism would leave an indelible imprint upon the development of Presbyterian communions in the English-speaking world. The Westminster Assembly, like many other church bodies of the time, reflected the politics of the surrounding culture. It arose in the context of the English Civil War and drew together a variety of Calvinists, including English Independents (Congregationalists), English Presbyterians and Scottish Presbyterians. Because of Parliament's need for allies, the inclusion of Scottish Presbyterians was key to the success of the Westminster Assembly. Still, though the Scots made significant contributions to the gathering, the Westminster Standards reveal the diversity of Reformed groups in Britain as well as the dominance of English Puritans throughout the proceedings. Historians differ about the theological outlook of the English church during the first half of the seventeenth century. The Church of England was generally Calvinistic, but the Puritan party wanted to reform all of church life according to Scripture. This included worship and church government. Puritanism in England meant something different from its counterpart in New England. While the Puritans who settled in the colonies of Massachusetts Bay and Connecticut followed a Congregationalist form of church government, Puritanism in England included a substantial portion of Presbyterians.[1]

The Westminster Assembly was the crowning achievement of British Presbyterianism. Even though political events in England prevented Presbyterianism from becoming the established order of the national church, the Westminster Standards became the theological norm for Presbyterian churches throughout Anglo-American culture, especially in Scotland, Northern Ireland, the United States and Canada. Though developments among Scottish Presbyterians, especially regarding the relations between state and church, would spawn a variety of denominations, some of which were eventually transplanted in the New World, these churches rarely questioned the basic elements of Presbyterian theology, church polity and spirituality. Thus, by the time the first Presbyterians began to minister in the American colonies at the end of the seventeenth century, the hallmarks of Presbyterian convictions and practice had been well defined and established.

On the other side of the English Channel, where *Reformed* substitutes for *Presbyterian,* cultural and political differences gave communions in the Calvinistic tradition on the Continent greater diversity. Aside from Switzerland, the most important centers for the Reformed tradition were Germany, the Netherlands and France. These countries in turn would be important to the development of the Reformed faith in the New World.

In Germany, Nassau, Bremen and Hesse were significant outposts of Reformed witness, but the city of Heidelberg in the Palatinate emerged as the most important. As was the case with the magisterial Reformation more generally, the success of the Reformed church depended to a great extent upon the elector Frederick III. Unlike most German-speaking Protestants who adopted Lutheran practices, Frederick did not think these reforms went far enough, and while desiring a consensus for Lutherans and Reformed, he brought to his city's university two young Reformed theologians, Zacharias Ursinus and Caspar Olevianus. They were principally responsible for the writing of the *Heidelberg Catechism (1563), a teaching device consisting of 129 questions and answers and divided into 52 parts to facilitate preaching through the catechism over the course of a year. The Heidelberg Catechism quickly became a touchstone for Calvinistic orthodoxy throughout Reformed churches in Europe. After Frederick's death in 1576 his successor, Ludwig VI, reestablished confessional Lutheranism, thus expelling close to six hundred pastors and professors. But his reign lasted only seven years; Ludwig's brother, Johann Casimir, returned Heidelberg to a Reformed bastion, which it remained until the Thirty Years' War.

In France national politics greatly diminished the strength of Reformed Protestantism. French Reformed Christians, known as *Huguenots, endured severe trials throughout most of the sixteenth century. Political repression of French Calvinists could be fierce, the massacre of thirty thousand Huguenots in Paris and other Reformed cities on St. Bartholomew's Day in 1572 being the most notable example. But Calvinists remained a force in French politics, and eventually one of their number was crowned King Henry IV. In order to gain the throne Henry had to convert to Catholicism, but under his administration France granted a measure of toleration to Protestants, especially with the Edict of Nantes in 1598. This toleration, which was never complete, lasted only until 1685, when it was revoked. But this period of relative toleration allowed the French Reformed to be important partners in the witness of international Calvinism.

In the Netherlands the Reformation was again deeply entangled in political struggles. Specifically, for the Dutch the Reformed faith was the chief means of opposing the rule of Catholic Spain. When Guido de Bres wrote the *Belgic Confession (1561), a document that became the doctrinal standard of the Reformation in the Low Countries, he did so in defiance of Spanish authorities. Thus the founding of the Dutch republic was bound up with the reform of Dutch churches. William of Orange, the military commander who led the fight for Dutch independence, embraced the Reformed faith as early as 1573. His son, Maurice, who led Dutch forces to miliary victories over Spanish forces in the late sixteenth and early seventeenth centuries, also put the approval of the republic behind the Reformed cause in the churches. The northern provinces of the Netherlands, where Protestantism was gaining a strong following, eventually formed in 1579 the Union of Utrecht, which in turn led to modern-day Holland. The southern provinces, however, returned their allegiance to Spain and remained Roman Catholic. This area constitutes modern Belgium.

In the seventeenth century Holland became a center of trade and banking. Amid this prosperity some theologians, most notably Jacob Arminius (1560-1609), began to propound beliefs about the relative goodness and moral ability of human nature, beliefs that led to a questioning of Calvinistic teachings concerning human depravity and divine sovereignty in salvation. After Arminius's death the Dutch Reformed churches became embroiled in a controversy over *Arminianism and eventually called a synod at Dort to debate the matter. This body met from 1618 to 1619 and produced the Canons of *Dort. The five points of the canons gave rise to the mnemonic TULIP, a shorthand summary of Calvinist soteriology (see below). The synod also made the Heidelberg Catechism and the Belgic Confession, in addition to its own declarations, the confessional standards for the Dutch Reformed churches, thus establishing the Three Forms of Unity, which continue as the doctrinal norm for Dutch Calvinist denominations in America and around the world.

The New World

The emergence of England as the dominant political and cultural force in the American colonies insured that Presbyterianism would be a large and powerful Calvinistic communion in both the United States and Canada. Nevertheless, the British accent of Presbyterianism over the last two centuries should not be read back into the earliest western European settlements in North America. While Congregationalists in Massachusetts Bay were clearly a strong presence in the New World and outnumbered Presbyterians until 1780, the first congregations in the Reformed tradition on the North American continent were *Dutch Reformed, established in the early seventeenth century in New York, New Jersey and Delaware. The first pastor, Peter Minuit, came in 1628 to shepherd the congregation in New Netherland (New York). The Dutch Reformed churches in the colonies were under the control of the Classis of Amsterdam and would remain so until the eighteenth century, when during the Coetus controversy the Dutch Reformed parishes established their independence, a step that also prompted the formation of their own institution for training ministers (Queen's College, now Rutgers University).

The influence of other Reformed groups from the Continent, the Huguenots and *German Reformed, was not as powerful as the Dutch. French Protestants came to the New World as early as the 1560s, when approximately thirty Huguenot families settled near present-day Charleston, South Carolina. But these efforts at settlement could not withstand Spanish expansion, thus reducing Huguenot influence to a small trickle of immigrants to the colonies over the sixteenth and seventeenth centuries and slightly more during the eighteenth century. Though many French Protestants became important figures in colonial political and cultural life, their religious presence was negligible as they assimilated rapidly into Anglo-American Protestantism, often becoming Episcopalians.

The migration of German Reformed to the American colonies peaked in the mid-eighteenth century. Though they were found also in other colonies, the German Reformed clustered in Pennsylvania because of the policies of religious toleration in that colony. The toll taken on this community in the Old World through the religious wars meant that immigrants were forced to turn to lay leaders for pastoral oversight. One such leader was John Philip *Boehm, who almost single-handedly organized the German Reformed churches under the oversight of the Dutch Reformed through the Classis of Amsterdam. The Dutch provided assistance, sending the able minister Michael *Schlatter, who continued to organize the churches located primarily in the Middle Colonies. By 1791 the German Reformed declared their independence from Dutch oversight and established their own synod.

Though British Presbyterians were among the last to arrive, their ethnic identity positioned them best for growth in the American colonies and nation. Francis *Makemie, the first Presbyterian minister in North America, was ordained in Northern Ireland and in 1683 began ministering in the new world. He was also responsible for organizing the first presbytery in North America, a body that brought together such diverse elements as English Puritans, Scottish Presbyterians, Welsh Calvinists and French Reformed. Still, the largest group was Makemie's own *Scots-Irish, and the settlement throughout the eastern seaboard of immigrants from Northern Ireland provided a powerful impetus for the growth of Presbyterianism in colonial America. Unlike the German and Dutch Reformed communions, Presbyterian churches were much less encumbered by formal ecclesiastical ties to the Old World. This was also true for the other Presbyterian bodies to be established in the eighteenth-century colonies, the Associate Reformed Presbyterians and the Reformed Presbyterians, churches arising from divisions within the Scottish Kirk. The autonomy of American Presbyterianism, therefore, accounts for some of the differences that exist between New World and Old World Presbyterians, especially regarding the relative powers of presbyteries and general assemblies. Unlike the Scottish Kirk, where the highest court (general assembly) oversees in a more direct fashion the activities of lower courts (presbyteries), in the United States the presbyteries have greater sovereignty and independence.

The New Nation and Americanization

While the colonial experience itself demonstrated the difficulties of perpetuating Old World beliefs and practices, the changes associated with the formation and consolidation of a new nation in the nineteenth century compounded the challenges confronting

Presbyterians and Reformed. Religious disestablishment in and of itself meant a break with the Constantinian paradigm in Western Christianity under which most Presbyterian and Reformed churches operated in Great Britain and Europe. To be sure, Presbyterian and Reformed bodies in colonial America rarely achieved the status of the establishment. Yet the Constitution's virtual promise of a religious free market forced European Calvinists to readjust the form and governance of their communions.

The problems posed by the American experiment to Presbyterian and Reformed identity became especially evident with the rise of *revivalism as the dominant form of Protestantism in the new nation. Even the revivals associated with George Whitefield and Jonathan *Edwards posed significant problems for some local ministers committed to Presbyterian forms of church government. But the Second Great Awakening of the early nineteenth century solidified the victory for revivalism that the First Great Awakening had anticipated. Consequently, appeals to individuals to decide or vote for Christ, which echoed the democratic and egalitarian ideology of the new nation, appeared to contradict Calvinism's teaching about divine election and sovereignty in salvation. Also, by establishing an intense religious experience of rational, autonomous individuals (i.e., conversion) as the mark of genuine faith, revivalism called into question Presbyterian and Reformed practices regarding the nurturing of covenant children through infant baptism, catechesis and profession of faith. America's freedom of religion and the opening of the West afforded Presbyterians the opportunity to expand. But Presbyterian growth during the nineteenth century was modest compared to that of Baptists and Methodists and often sacrificed characteristics of Reformed worship and church life.

Consequently, since the beginning of the nineteenth century a constant theme in the history of Presbyterians and Reformed in America has been that of tensions arising from the churches' adaptation to the dominant forms of American religiosity, forms displayed most notably in evangelicalism as defined by the practice and theology of revivalism. Early signs of these tensions emerged within Presbyterian circles when in 1838 the *Presbyterian Church (USA) split, dividing into the *Old School and *New School branches. This division occurred in the wake of the Second Great Awakening and concerned the degree to which Calvinist theology, church government and spirituality should accommodate American assumptions and practices. The Old School party opposed the Arminian theology of revivalists such as Charles Grandison *Finney, cooperation with non-Presbyterians in the work of missions and evangelism, and social reforms in the name of Christ that went beyond the explicit teachings of Scripture. To put a complicated situation simply, the confessional Presbyterians of the Old School stood for Old World patterns of theology and church life while the New School reflected the dominant characteristics of Protestant practices in the new world.

Another example of these tensions, this time on the Reformed side, comes from the founding in 1857 of the *Christian Reformed Church (CRC). An influx of Dutch immigrants during the 1840s brought many strict Calvinists to the upper Midwest, especially Michigan. Initially these Reformed affiliated with the *Reformed Church in

America (RCA), a communion with roots in the Dutch settlements of the seventeenth century. But many in the second wave of Dutch settlers were influenced by Romantic and antirevolutionary sentiments in the Netherlands that prompted a recovery of Reformed confessionalism. Older Dutch-American Reformed churches, however, had not experienced this same impulse to go back to their Calvinist roots. Hence, the new Dutch immigrants were distraught by what they saw as departures from the strict Calvinism to which they adhered in Holland. The specific issues leading to the withdrawal from the RCA and the founding of the CRC were Free Masonry, exclusive psalm singing and Christian education. The CRC prohibited church members from membership in the Masons, held on to the older practice of only singing psalms and established primary and secondary schools that made religious education explicit as opposed to the generic Protestantism undergirding the public schools. Though the CRC remained a small communion until the late nineteenth century, its origins again illustrate the tension between adherence to Old World customs and assimilation to American practices.

Modern America and Modernism

In the late nineteenth century, as America went through the various difficulties associated with modernization, Presbyterians and Reformed again experienced pressures to accommodate the apparently new demands upon the churches. Intellectual challenges from Darwinism (*see* Science, Presbyterians and the) and higher criticism were significant and undermined assumptions, at least among the educated, about the authority and truthfulness of the Bible. The rise of research universities where much of the new scholarship was conducted also meant that the churches slipped a few pegs down the ladder of cultural authority (*see* Intellectual Life, Presbyterians and). Yet the creation of large-scale industrial corporations, the influx of immigrants to work for these business enterprises and the growth of the urban centers where these workers lived and many corporations thrived brought an unparalleled challenge to the church. While new ideas in the academy may have prompted some to ask whether the Bible was true, the new political economy raised the question of whether the *Bible mattered.

In this context Protestant churches pursued *social and economic reforms, perhaps with no more vigor than evangelicals had before the *Civil War but in a manner that broke with older assumptions about the necessity of individual conversion and discipline for social order. Moral persuasion designed to change the minds of significant numbers appeared to be outdated in a time when large bureaucracies swallowed up individual initiative. The Social Gospel, defined in various ways, was a response to this new situation. Presbyterians took the lead in the creation of national organizations dedicated to ameliorating various social ills and through a number of legislative measures called upon government to curb the excesses of capitalism. Of a piece with the goals of the Social Gospel was the ecumenical movement, which generated increasing support during the period between the Civil War and World War I. As churches looked to alleviate the human suffering generated by the new industries and cities, the theological distinctives that defined the various Protestant communions became less important. While Calvinists and Wesleyans may have parted over certain details of social and economic reform, in the main Protestants appealed to general Christian truths to justify their efforts to reform American society. As a result, tensions surfaced in Presbyterian and Reformed communions between those who supported ecumenism and those who desired to preserve denominational autonomy and confessional identity. Much of the history of the Presbyterian and Reformed tradition in the twentieth century can be told around the theme of ecumenism versus sectarianism, that is, of Presbyterians and Reformed willing to cooperate with non-Calvinists for broader purposes and those opposed to cooperation because of theological convictions and ecclesiastical practices.

Several incidents in twentieth-century Reformed and Presbyterian church history illustrate this tension between ecumenism and separatism. On the one hand, this century has seen the mainline Presbyterian church, the Presbyterian Church (USA), incorporate Scottish-American splinter denominations such as the *Cumberland Presbyterians in 1903 and the United Presbyterian Church in 1957 to form the United Presbyterian Church in the United States of America. The greatest example of Presbyterian amalgamation came in 1983 with the reunion of the Northern and *Southern (*Presbyterian Church in the United States) branches of mainline Presbyterianism to form the *Presbyterian Church (USA). On the other hand, the consolidation and bureaucratization of Presbyterianism has resulted in the neglect of theological rigor often in favor of establishing Christian civilization. In protest several new and sectarian Presbyterian denominations have been started. In 1936, for example, a small group of conservative Presbyterians led by J. Gresham *Machen protested ecumenical developments in the Northern Presbyterian Church (PCUSA) and eventually formed a new communion to perpetuate Presbyterian convictions. Though the new denomination, the *Orthodox Presbyterian Church, bore the marks of the *fundamentalist movement that had alerted many to the perils of ecumenism, its early decisions and alliances displayed a pronounced concern for Calvinist orthodoxy and Presbyterian *polity, two concerns rare among mainstream fundamentalism. Similar tensions within the Southern Presbyterian Church (PCUS) during the 1960s and 1970s prompted conservatives to oppose many of the alliances and purposes of mainline Protestantism and to form in 1972 another Presbyterian communion, the *Presbyterian Church in America. As was the case with the earlier split among Northern Presbyterians, the new church was comprised of fundamentalists and conservative Presbyterians. Yet, no matter what the composition of the PCA, its founding represented another effort to preserve Presbyterian distinctiveness in the face of ecumenical ambiguity.

On the Reformed side a similar separatist impulse displayed itself when in 1934 the Eureka Classis of the German Reformed Church (*see* Reformed Church in the U.S.) refused to join in the merger of its denomination with the *Evangelical Synod of North America, a body that was eventually absorbed in 1957 in the United Church of Christ. Again, as in the conservative Presbyterian cases, the Eureka Classis represented the concerns of those Reformed believers who sensed ecumenism would compromise theological convictions and ecclesiastical procedures. Thus, while the mainstream of Presbyterian and Reformed communions in the twentieth century have moved in the direction of consolidation, ecumenical cooperation and denominational federation have also come with a price, namely, the splintering of groups anxious about the compromises often involved in church union.

Central Themes in the Presbyterian and Reformed Tradition

Rivalries between Presbyterian and Reformed have generated some good-natured debates about whether the first question and answer to Westminster's Shorter Catechism or the Heidelberg Catechism summarizes best the heart of the Reformed faith. While Heidelberg properly begins with the work of Christ, the Shorter Catechism begins with what Calvinism has historically stressed, namely, the glory of God—thus the first answer, "Man's chief end is to glorify God and enjoy him forever." Indeed, while critics have faulted Calvinists for neglecting human needs and the created order, Presbyterians and Reformed have been distinguished for endeavoring to give all credit, honor and glory to God rather than humankind or creation for all aspects of life, whether narrowly religious or broadly cultural.

The glory of God is seen most strikingly in the Reformed conception of salvation. Though Calvinists and Lutherans taught similar doctrines of justification by faith, the Reformed spun out a scheme of salvation that highlighted divine sovereignty in all aspects of redemption. This understanding of salvation is best summarized in the famous mnemonic TULIP, derived from the Canons of Dort. This stands for the doctrines of total depravity, unconditional election, limited atonement, irresistible grace and perserverence of the saints. The Reformed churches of the Netherlands spelled out these articles of Calvinism to refute the teachings of Arminianism, and as the five points of Calvinism indicate, the teachings of Arminianism were seen as an assault upon divine sovereignty in salvation. Thus the Reformed tradition has been particularly jealous to deny any contribution from men and women in their salvation and to attribute all aspects of redemption to the sovereign work of God, that is, God the Father who predestines according to his good purpose and for his own glory, God the Son who died for the elect and God the Spirit who works this saving grace in the elect through faith, repentance and sanctification.

But as much as the Reformed tradition is known for what seem to many its arch convictions about salvation—H. L. Mencken, for instance, wrote that Calvinism occupied a place in his "cabinet of private horrors, but little removed from that of cannibalism"—it is marked by other teachings that distinguish it from other Protestant traditions. Here the Reformed doctrine of the regulative principle is one that immediately comes to mind. All Protestants confessed that the Bible alone is authoritative in matters of Christian faith and practice, in contrast to the teachings of Rome, which made the magisterium, or the authoritative instruction of the church, an interpreter of Scripture possessing its own authority. But many of those in Calvinistic communions extended the general Protestant understanding of *sola scriptura* to require the church in its official tasks (word, sacraments and discipline) to do only what Scripture commanded. While this teaching is often attributed to Puritanism, it also finds expression in Calvinism on the Continent, such as in the Belgic Confession, where in Article 32, "The Order and Discipline of the Church," it teaches that discipline must be based on the Word of God and not on "human inventions" or "laws" that would "bind and compel the conscience in any manner." Thus, while Anglicans and Lutherans permitted in church practice whatever was not expressly forbidden in Scripture, Presbyterians and Reformed have endeavored to teach that whatever the church does must be commanded by Christ himself speaking in the Bible.

The Reformed understanding of the regulative principle helps to explain why churches in the Calvinist tradition went further than Lutherans or Anglicans in doing away with the practices of Roman Catholicism. Luther, for instance, stands at the conservative end of the Reformation spectrum, continuing various medieval practices related to the government and worship of the church. But the Reformed, while more conservative than the Anabaptists, were not content with what appeared to be the partial reforms of Lutheranism. And the reason for this reformist impulse is the idea that the church may only do what Scripture commands. Hence, the word *Reformed* itself has always been shorthand for the phrase that the church must "always be reforming itself according to the Word of God." If a practice inherited from Roman Catholicism could not be justified according to biblical teaching, then it had to be abandoned.

One area in which the application of the regulative principle is most obvious is in church government. According to Calvin's interpretation of the New Testament, Christ instituted four separate offices for the oversight of the church: pastors, doctors (i.e., teachers of theology), elders and deacons. Pastors had the responsibility of preaching, administering the sacraments and admonishing the people. Doctors oversaw the purity of doctrine and trained pastors. Elders, who were chosen from the laity, were to watch over the spiritual and moral life of church members. And deacons managed the finances of the church and cared for the needy. According to this system, the word *Presbyterian* takes on added significance. Rather than carrying on the episcopal form of government practiced by Rome as did Episcopalians and (to some extent) Lutherans, Reformed and Presbyterians believed that the teaching of Scripture concerning church polity required a different pattern, one that was less hierarchical and recognized a parity of church officers. The word *Presbyterian* comes from the Greek word for elder, *presbyteros* (Acts 11:30; 14:23; Eph 4:11), a word that the Reformed have used interchangeably with *episkopoi* (Acts 20:17; Titus 1:5-9), the Greek word for bishop. In contrast to those churches that use episcopal forms of government and make a distinction between elder and bishop, thus justifying a hierarchical polity, most Presbyterian communions agreed with Lutherans and Anglicans that authority in the church rested with ordained officers but spread all such authority out to all presbyters, including ministers and ordained laity (elders).

In addition, to instill order and discipline in the church Reformed and Presbyterians use a series of graded representative assemblies, from the lower to the higher, or narrower to broader: the session of the local congregation, which sends delegates to the presbytery, the assembly of a local region, which sends delegates to the synod, the court of a larger region, which sends delegates to the general assembly, the highest judicatory. (Though their polity varies slightly, the Reformed follow the same pattern of graded assemblies, calling them by different names, the consistory for session, the classis for presbytery, and synod or general synod.) While advocates of Reformed polity have argued on the basis of the Pastoral Epistles and the Jerusalem Council in Acts 15 for presbyterian polity, the genius of this form of church government may have more to do with the need to balance order and uniformity in the visible church with what Calvinism teaches about human depravity. By structuring authority in this graded way Presbyterianism provides a system of checks and balances designed to prevent the abuse of power. And by insisting that there be a church court higher than the local congregation (in contrast to Baptists and Congregationalists), Presbyterians strive to heed the teaching of Scripture that the unity of the church be demonstrated beyond the local fellowship of believers.

The application of the regulative principle also made itself evident in the way that the Reformed recast the practice of spirituality (*see* Piety, Presbyterian and Reformed). This is especially true in their behavior on the first day of the week. In *worship on the Lord's Day, what Presbyterians call the Christian sabbath, Calvinists ended many of the elements of Roman Catholic worship, instituting an order of the service that they believed reflected biblical teaching. The most important change was to make the sermon, the proclamation of God's Word, central to worship, a change that yielded as well a different understanding of the sacraments generally and specifically of that sacrament central to the Roman liturgy, which Catholics called the Mass but which Reformed referred to as the Lord's Supper (*see* Sacrament, Presbyterians and the). This meant, despite the arguments of those like Calvin who believed in the weekly observance of Communion, that the administration of the Lord's Supper became subordinate to the sermon and in the end was observed only monthly, quarterly or even less frequently.

Another early characteristic of Reformed worship was the practice of exclusive psalmody. The Psalms have been a further distinctive element of Reformed spirituality. They not only speak to the central impulses of Calvinistic teaching regarding God's sovereignty and covenant with his people, but according to Calvin and other Reformers, the Psalms, as God's own inspired words, provide the best way of praising God in public worship. The case for psalm singing also flowed from the Reformed conviction that this was what Scripture commanded in that the Psalms were the praise Israel sang to God, a practice that the early church did not change. By the mid-eighteenth century some Presbyterian and Reformed communions had added hymns to the Psalms, but a preference for psalm singing remains in virtually all Presbyterian and Reformed churches, a few of which still practice exclusive psalm singing.

One further example of Reformed spirituality and application of the regulative principle was sabbath observance. Presbyterians and Reformed have been rigorous in observing the fourth commandment and therefore trying to abstain from all forms of work or recreation on Sunday, a practice that, like exclusive psalmody, has generally been relaxed in the twentieth century. The practice of sabbath observance also meant the abolition of the church calendar. Whereas Roman Catholics instituted a series of holy days throughout the church year modeled either on the life of Christ or general Christian teaching, the Reformed objected that after the resurrection of Christ the only day that Scripture commanded to be a different or sanctified day was the Lord's Day, when believers celebrated Christ's triumph over sin and death in the resurrection. Thus, Presbyterians and Reformed in their desire to follow Scripture carefully have generally marked the Christian life by observing the weekly sabbath and by refusing to require the human practice of setting apart the holy days of the church year.

Though many of the practices and teachings of Presbyterians and Reformed that set them apart historically from other Christians have been abandoned or significantly diminished by contemporary members of Calvinistic communions and although considerable variety has always existed among Reformed and Presbyterian churches, the Reformed tradition continues to offer a potent antidote to the extremes of formalism on the one side and of experientialism on the other side. Just as Calvin and other leaders of the Reformed tradition tried to steer between the claims of the status quo by Catholics and those of radical reform by Anabaptists, so the Reformed tradition at the end of the twentieth century in its fullest expression is satisfactory neither to those who favor a formal expression of Protestantism, whether liturgical (Anglican or Lutheran) or organizational (mainline Protestant), nor to those in search of an immediate and extraordinary demonstration of God's presence (charismatics and some evangelicals). To those believers outside the tradition, the Reformed unwillingness to veer either to the left or to the right has appeared intransigent and proud. But as Warfield explained, Presbyterians and Reformed have not been narrow and precise merely for the sake of the memory of Calvin or the heritage of the Westminster divines. Rather, as Warfield put it, "Calvinism is . . . that type of thought in which there comes to its rights the truly religious attitude of utter dependence on God and humble trust in his mercy alone for salvation." To be sure, proponents of the Reformed tradition have never been without sin. But in their eagerness and zeal to defend their theological and ecclesiastical convictions they have been motivated to "glorify and enjoy" the triune and sovereign God of the universe. Despite failures in execution, that desire has been the genius and value of the Reformed tradition.

D. G. Hart and Mark A. Noll

---

[1]This explains why the editors have chosen not to include New England Puritanism and Congregationalism in this dictionary. We have taken Presbyterian and Reformed tradition to mean not just Calvinistic theology, which would certainly characterize New England Congregationalists. But we have also included church government in our criteria for designating an individual or institution as Presbyterian or Reformed. Congregationalism, by the nature of the case, falls outside this definition.

A

Abolition, Presbyterians and. By the late 1700s, slavery was recognized by many people as America's great moral problem. How could a nation founded upon the desire for freedom maintain some of its people as slaves? Presbyterian concerns on the issue were debated before the Synod of New York and Philadelphia (the national body) as early as 1774, in response to initiatives by President Ezra Stiles of Yale and Samuel Hopkins, an eminent theologian and Congregational pastor of Newport, Rhode Island. In 1769 Hopkins had persuaded his slave-holding and slave-trading communicants to go on record against human bondage. In 1776 he became the first to advocate colonization of freed blacks to Africa, and increasingly this idea took hold. In 1787 the synod "highly approved" the actions "many of the States have taken in promoting the abolition of Slavery," and in succeeding years similar statements were made in the Presbyterian synod.

Several Protestant denominations made antislavery pronouncements following this. In 1800 the *Reformed Presbyterians ruled that no slaveholder could belong to their communion. Congregationalists and Methodists were almost entirely opposed to slavery. By 1815 there were approximately two hundred thousand freed blacks in America, and the problem was acute. For the purpose of transporting freed blacks to Africa and helping them to build a new life there, the American Colonization Society was organized in 1817. Among its founders was Robert Finley, a Presbyterian clergyman; and its manager was Ralph Gurley, a Presbyterian licentiate for the ministry. The first denomination to give official endorsement to the society was the Presbyterian Church, whose general assembly in 1818 stated, "We recommend to all our people to patronize and encourage the society lately formed, for colonizing in Africa, the land of their ancestors, the free people of colour in our country. . . . [We] exceedingly rejoice to have witnessed its origin and organization among the holders of slaves." The general assembly hoped that other communions would support it as well and called for gradual emancipation of slaves and for kind treatment of those in bondage. The assembly asked Presbyterians not to use the "plea of necessity" for not facing the issue. "It is manifestly the duty of all Christians . . . to use their honest, earnest, and unwearied endeavours, to correct the errors of former times, and as speedily as possible to efface this blot on our holy religion, and to obtain the complete abolition of slavery throughout Christendom, and if possible throughout the world."

Not all Presbyterians agreed with the assembly. In 1816 George Bourne, of the presbytery of Lexington, Virginia, published *The Book and Slavery Irreconcileable,* in which he condemned slavery and colonization on biblical grounds. The presbytery finally deposed him. Free-born blacks increasingly opposed the idea of sending their people back to Africa, citing the mortality rates there and the cruelty of uprooting blacks from their birthplace. Samuel *Cornish (1793-1855), a free-born black from Delaware, became pastor of the First Colored Presbyterian Church in New York City and in 1827 founded the first black newspaper, *Freedom's Journal.* In it he attacked colonization and supported the antislavery societies that were being organized around the nation. Despite this, during the 1820s the colonization movement was favored by such future abolitionists as the Tappan brothers and William Lloyd Garrison and by Southern slaveholders such as John Randolph and Henry Clay, although their reasons differed widely. By 1830, however, the movement was in deep financial trouble.

Meanwhile, the economic situation in the South was changing dramatically. Whereas previously the institution of slavery there was declining, in 1792 the invention of the cotton gin once again made slavery and plantation agriculture profitable. From 1800 to 1860 the number of black slaves rose from 880,000 to almost 4,000,000. Any voluntary movement toward emancipation now seemed impossible. With the Missouri Compromise of 1820, providing for Missouri's admission as a slave state, the national tensions heightened. This brought about the rise of the abolitionist movement, in which Presbyterians were prominent.

Much of the strength and determination of this

movement came from evangelicals of perfectionist tendencies who were also prominent in the revivals and social reforms of the day. Perhaps the best examples of this, among others, were the brothers Arthur (1786-1865) and Lewis (1788-1873) Tappan, wealthy businessmen and prominent Presbyterians in New York City who turned from one benevolent enterprise to the next, generously giving their money to Christian causes. In 1831 Arthur Tappan formed a New York antislavery committee and began to move toward a national organization. In 1832 William Lloyd Garrison (1805-1879) and some Bostonians founded the New England Antislavery Society on a platform of immediatism—that there must be no further delay in freeing all slaves. In 1833 came the British Slavery Abolition Act. Despite fierce opposition, these activists wielded enormous influence during the crucial 1830s, distributing tons of literature, holding innumerable lectures and conferences and knitting together the many reform groups that were springing up everywhere.

For some years the Tappans had been supporting the revival ministry and reform efforts of Charles Grandison *Finney (1792-1875), who had pastored several Presbyterian churches in New York City and had strong antislavery views. The Tappans next turned to the urgent matter of training clergy for the expanding West. Lane Theological Seminary was begun in Cincinnati, Ohio, and in 1830 the most famous pastor in the nation, Lyman *Beecher (1775-1863), was invited to be its first president. Beecher seemed to fill every criterion: he was an abolitionist, a revivalist and something of a scholar and administrator, and he had contacts everywhere. He accepted that office and also the call of Cincinnati's Second Presbyterian Church to be its pastor.

Lane Seminary had attracted numbers of Finney's converts, who were sensitized to reform issues. Among the students was Theodore Dwight Weld (1803-1895), an enormously energetic and influential man who had worked with Finney for several years. In late 1833 Weld, an archfoe of slavery, kept his promise to Arthur Tappan (who was generously supporting the seminary financially) to spread abolitionist ideology among the students. Swinging most of the students to his opinion, Weld felt the time had come to hold debates on slavery, and when they were over, the students voted unanimously for immediate emancipation and began many efforts to help blacks. Fearing reports of radicalism at Lane Seminary, the trustees banned the activities of Weld and the students, upon which they transferred to the new Oberlin College, where Finney was a professor. Oberlin soon won the reputation of being the chief center of abolitionism in the West, sending its students far and wide to spread the message, with Weld leading the van. In 1839 Weld published his greatly influential *Slavery As It Is,* which prompted Harriet Beecher Stowe to write *Uncle Tom's Cabin.*

By the mid-1830s there was much reaction to abolitionism in the North, for many people feared it was a threat to peace. The eminent theologian of Princeton Seminary, Charles *Hodge (1797-1878), wrote in 1836 that abolitionism would increase dissension in the North and promote hatred in the South. Slavery was not condemned as sinful in Scripture, Hodge wrote, but he did hope that it would end as the gradual improvement of the blacks brought it about. By that year, however, tensions were at such a peak everywhere that pleas for moderation were often ignored or shouted down.

Perhaps the event that tipped the scales was the murder of Elijah *Lovejoy, a Presbyterian minister who was working as a journalist. As an antislavery leader, he turned his *St. Louis Observer* into a noted abolitionist paper. Rioters destroyed three of his presses, and he finally moved to Alton, Illinois. There, on November 7, 1837, he was shot to death defending his fourth press, and this sent a jolt across the nation, "a shock as of any earthquake," John Quincy Adams declared. In Boston, at a Faneuil Hall protest meeting that he organized, Wendell Phillips began his sensational career as a radical abolitionist, and clergy everywhere were horrified. By the 1840s, all of this had the effect of transforming a persecuted protest movement into a nationally organized crusade whose momentum could not be stopped.

The Presbyterian Church split into the *Old School and *New School branches in 1837-1838 Slavery was only one issue, for there were also differences over theology and polity. One-third of the Old School's membership was in the South, while the New School's strength was in the North. From 1837 on, the Old School were thus very diplomatic in their dealings with slaveholders, and many petitions against slavery were tabled. In 1845 the general assembly, by a vote of 168 to 13, acknowledged slavery as scriptural and asked slaveholders to treat their slaves as human beings. In 1849 the assembly stated that slavery was a civil institution that should be dealt with by legislatures rather than churches. This timid approach satisfied few but continued through the turbulent 1850s, and after the outbreak of the Civil War, in May 1861 the Old School general assembly in the most compromising of terms expressed its loyalty to the Union. Schism immediately followed. Southern commissioners met in December, stating that slavery was the cause of the schism, publishing a strong defense of slavery and organizing a new Old School denomination.

In 1837 the New School's greatest numerical strength was in areas where abolitionism was strongest, and it had to hew a different path than the Old School. It repeated the position of the assembly of 1818 in 1846 and 1849, and in 1850 it repudiated the idea that slavery was a divinely sanctioned institution. In 1857 the Southern New School presbyteries withdrew to form a separate denomination.

See also CIVIL WAR, PRESBYTERIANS AND THE; SOCIAL REFORM, PRESBYTERIANS AND; SOUTH, PRESBYTERIANS IN THE.

BIBLIOGRAPHY. T. Bender, ed., *The Antislavery Debate* (1992); D. G. Faust, "Evangelicalism and the Meaning of the Proslavery Argument: The Reverend Thornton Stringfellow of Virginia," *Virginia Magazine of History and Biography* 85 (1977) 3-17; E. Fox-Genovese and E. Genovese, "The Divine Sanction of the Social Order: Religious Foundations of the Southern Slaveholders' World View," *JAAR* 55 (1987) 211-33; E. Genovese, *"Slavery Ordained of God"* (1985); J. R. McKivigan, *The War Against Proslavery Religion* (1984); J. H. Moorhead, *American Apocalypse: Yankee Protestants and the Civil War, 1860-1869* (1978); R. B. Mullin, "Biblical Critics and the Battle Over Slavery," *JPH* 61 (1983) 210-26; C. L. Shanks, "The Biblical Anti-Slavery Argument of the Decade, 1830-1840," *Journal of Negro History* 16 (1931) 132-57; T. L. Smith, *Revivalism and Social Reform: American Protestantism on the Eve of the Civil War* (1957); L. E. Tise, *Proslavery: A History of the Defense of Slavery in America, 1701-1840* (1987). K. J. Hardman

Adger, John Bailey (1810-1899).† Presbyterian minister and missionary. Born in Charleston, South Carolina, Adger attended Union College and Princeton Theological Seminary. From 1834 to 1847 he served with the American Board of Commissioners for Foreign Missions as a missionary among the Armenian people in Constantinople and Smyrna (*see* Missions, Presbyterian and Reformed). In 1847 Adger moved back to Charleston, where he organized the Anson Street Chapel, later known as Zion Presbyterian Church, and operated a plantation. Called in 1857 to the faculty of Columbia Theological Seminary, Adger taught church history and church polity until he retired in 1874.

As editor of the *Southern Presbyterian Review* (1857-1874), Adger was a staunch defender of the formation of the Presbyterian Church in the Confederate States of America and strongly criticized the Northern reunion of *Old School and *New School in 1870. In a debate with Charles *Hodge over the spiritual nature of the church, Adger insisted that the Northern body had defected from the traditional Presbyterian doctrine during the war years by deciding the political questions of the day on the floor of the general assembly and by imposing political terms of communion on both ministers and members.

In a Southern Presbyterian dispute over the teaching of evolution Adger sided with James *Woodrow, a faculty colleague who favored the reconciliation of science and theology. Active as a writer and leader in the *Presbyterian Church in the United States (PCUS), Adger helped draft the PCUS *Book of Church Order* (1879).

BIBLIOGRAPHY. *ANB* 1; J. B. Adger, *My Life and Times, 1810-1899* (1899); E. T. Thompson, *Presbyterians in the South,* vol. 2 (1973). L. B. Weeks

Adopting Act (1729). An action of the Synod of Philadelphia whereby the *Westminster Confession of Faith and Catechisms were adopted as the doctrinal position of the Presbyterian Church in colonial America. Subscription to these standards was required of all ministers and ministerial candidates. The synod, created in 1717 out of the Presbytery of Philadelphia, was the highest Presbyterian governing body in America.

Until 1729 American Presbyterianism operated without an official doctrinal standard and without requiring creedal subscription of its ministers. The Adopting Act was the result of a compromise between the dominant Scots and *Scots-Irish party, which desired strict subscription, and those of English and New England background, led by Jonathan *Dickinson, who did not want to see fallible, human documents imposed as tests of orthodoxy and ordination. The act required all ministers and licentiates to subscribe to these doctrinal standards "as being, in all the essential and necessary articles, good forms of sound words and systems of Christian doctrine; and . . . as the confession of our faith." The act provided that one who had scruples regarding one or more of the articles in these standards could still be approved if one's synod or presbytery judged that these differences were over nonessentials. In fact all members of the synod did take exception to the confession's statements on the role and responsibility of the civil magistrate in religious matters.

BIBLIOGRAPHY. G. S. Klett, ed., *Minutes of the Presbyterian Church in America, 1706-1788* (1976);

L. J. Trinterud, *The Forming of an American Tradition: A Re-Examination of Colonial Presbyterianism* (1949). A. H. Freundt

Alexander, Archibald (1772-1851).† First professor at Princeton Theological Seminary and founder of the *Princeton theology. Born in Rockbridge County, Virginia, to a family of *Scots-Irish descent, Alexander grew up in a frontier environment and was converted at the age of seventeen, through the revival preaching of William Graham. Having little formal education, he studied theology with Graham at Liberty Hall Academy (Washington and Lee University). Licensed to preach at age nineteen, he was later ordained as the pastor of two small Presbyterian churches in Virginia. Prior to assuming his duties at Princeton in 1812, Alexander pastored churches, led revivals and served as president of Hampden-Sydney College (1796-1807) in his native Virginia and ministered in the Pine Street Presbyterian Church in Philadelphia (1807-1812). In 1807 he was elected moderator of the general assembly of the Presbyterian Church, and he used this position to promote the establishment of a Presbyterian seminary.

Alexander had become concerned with the state of affairs in theological education in the Presbyterian Church after seeing the serious doctrinal errors that tended to arise from the haphazard system of private instruction, especially in New England. In 1812, when Princeton Theological Seminary emerged as the official Presbyterian seminary in America, he was selected as its first professor, a position he held for more than thirty-eight years, until his death. By his academic diligence, Alexander established Princeton's main themes and set a standard of excellence that his successors at Princeton, Charles *Hodge, Archibald Alexander *Hodge and Benjamin Breckinridge *Warfield, vigorously maintained. Alexander implemented the general assembly's plan that Presbyterian pastors not only experience a call to the ministry but also receive rigorous intellectual training. They should obtain a thorough knowledge of the Bible (including the original languages of Scripture) and be skilled defenders of its content and authority.

To accomplish these ends, Alexander taught Scottish Common Sense philosophy, which he had learned from Graham. Under this school of thought, the defense of Christianity begins with reason judging external evidences for the truthfulness of Scripture: the credibility of its witnesses, fulfilled prophecy and cultural benefits attending the spread of the gospel. But more effective in establishing biblical truth are internal evidences: the self-authenticating purity and sublimity of its content as attested by the Holy Spirit. With this philosophical base, Alexander taught seventeenth-century Reformed theology—the *Westminster Confession of Faith and the work of Swiss theologian Francis *Turretin (1623-1687).

While staunchly defending *Old School Presbyterian doctrines, Alexander was a decided moderate in the Old School-New School debates. Convinced of the need to maintain the unity of the church, he disagreed with the ultra Old School party's desire to oust the *New School, even though he deplored the latter's new measures. Finally in 1837, after seven years of trying to keep the church one, Alexander became convinced that disunion was a sad necessity and joined with the majority of the Presbyterian Church in abrogating the *Plan of Union.

Undergirding Alexander's teaching, preaching and writing was a fervent piety and vital interest in religious experience that had its roots in his revival preaching and continued to be a characteristic feature of the Princeton theology. He died in Princeton.

See also PRINCETON THEOLOGY.

BIBLIOGRAPHY: *AAP* 3; *ANB* 1; J. W. Alexander, *The Life of Archibald Alexander* (1854); *DAB* I; *DARB;* A. W. Hoffecker, *Piety and the Princeton Theologians: Archibald Alexander, Charles Hodge and Benjamin Warfield* (1981); *NCAB* 2; M. A. Noll, ed., *The Princeton Theology, 1812-1921; Scripture, Science, and Theological Method from Archibold Alexander to Benjamin Breckinridge Warfield* (1983). A. W. Hoffecker

Alexander, George (1843-1930). Presbyterian minister and educator. Born in West Charlton, New York, Alexander graduated from Union College in 1866 and Princeton Theological Seminary in 1870. Ordained in 1870, he became the pastor of East Avenue Presbyterian Church in Schenectady, New York. In 1884 he became pastor of the University Place Church in New York City where he gained wide popularity as a preacher. After his church merged with both the Madison Square Church and the First Presbyterian Church in 1918, he became the pastor of the new congregation, which preserved the name of the First Presbyterian Church. Though personally conservative in his theological convictions, Alexander championed the toleration of theological modernism amidst the various theological controversies, such as the trial of Charles A. *Briggs, which rocked the Northern Presbyterian Church (PCUSA) in the 1890s.

In addition to his lifelong pastoral ministry, Alexander was actively involved in a variety of educational and ecclesiastical institutions. He served as president of the Board of Foreign Missions of the Presbyterian Church, U.S.A. from 1903 to 1924 and as president of the Council of the Reformed Churches in America holding the Presbyterian System from 1915 to 1920. From 1877 to 1883 he was a professor of rhetoric and logic at Union College. He also was president of Union College from 1907 to 1909 and chairman of its board of trustees from 1918 to 1930. Among his other educational activities, he was a director of Princeton Theological Seminary from 1884 to 1929, a member of the council of New York University from 1887 to 1930, and president of the New York College of Dentistry from 1897 to 1930. He died in New York City.

Bibliography. *Necrological Report of Princeton Theological Seminary* (1930) 66-67; D. N. Robertson, ed., *In Memory of The Rev. George Alexander, D.D., Minister of The First Presbyterian Church, New York* (1931). P. C. Kemeny

Alexander, James Waddel (1804-1859). Presbyterian minister and educator. Born in Louisa County, Virginia, to Archibald *Alexander, a Presbyterian minister, and Janetta Waddel Alexander, James studied with a private classical tutor as a youth. He graduated from the College of New Jersey in 1820 and remained for two additional years of private study. He attended Princeton Theological Seminary from 1822 to 1824. His father not only had helped to found this institution but also taught as its first faculty member. In 1824 he served as a tutor at the college and in 1825 was licensed to preach by the Presbytery of New Brunswick. He pastored the Presbyterian church in Charlotte County House, Virginia, from 1825 to 1828 and the First Presbyterian Church in Trenton, New Jersey, from 1828 to 1830. He resigned his pastorate in 1830 because of ill health and became the editor of *The Presbyterian,* a religious weekly published in Philadelphia.

Three years later he was appointed professor of rhetoric and belles lettres at the College of New Jersey. Alexander was a capable scholar whose knowledge of Greek, Latin, French, German, Italian and Spanish made him a particularly effective teacher. During this period he also took charge of the African-American Presbyterian Church in Princeton (later known as Witherspoon Street Presbyterian Church). In 1844 he returned to the pastorate at Duane Street Presbyterian Church in New York City to be of more direct service to the Presbyterian church as a pastor. Five years later, however, again because of bad health, he retired. He became the professor of ecclesiastical history and church government at Princeton Seminary, where he thought the more sedentary lifestyle of academia would better suit his frail health. His health improved and in 1851 he again returned to New York City as pastor of the Fifth Avenue Presbyterian Church. He died at Red Sweet Springs, Virginia.

As a pastor in New York City, Alexander played a leading role in the American Sunday-School Union. Founded in 1824, the American Sunday-School Union sought to educate, evangelize and civilize in the principles of democracy the disadvantaged youth of the city. When the *Old School Presbyterians became alarmed about the lack of denominational distinctives taught by this voluntary association as well as by the growing secular character of public schools, Alexander was appointed to head a committee in 1844 to investigate the possibility of establishing Presbyterian parochial schools. Though some parochial schools were founded, Alexander abandoned hopes of seeing such a system established on a wider scale. Instead he worked with the Sunday-School Union and sought to strengthen the teaching of distinctively Christian beliefs and values in the public school system.

Alexander was a disciple of the Old School Presbyterian theology taught by his father and at the seminary with which his family was so closely associated. He was a frequent contributor to the *Biblical Repertory and Princeton Review* with pieces on church history, theology and philosophy. He wrote more than thirty volumes for the American Sunday-School Union and authored a biography of his father, *Life of Archibald Alexander* (1854).

See also Alexander, Archibald; Alexander, Joseph Addison.

Bibliography. *ANB* 1; J. W. Alexander, *Forty Years' Familiar Letters of James W. Alexander* (1860); A. M. Boylan, *Sunday School: The Formation of an American Institution, 1780-1888* (1988); C. Hodge and J. Hall, *Sermons Preached Before the Congregation of the Presbyterian Church . . . in Reference to the Death of their Late Pastor, James Waddel Alexander, D.D.* (1859); A. Nevin, ed., *Encyclopedia of the Presbyterian Church of the United States of America* (1884). P. C. Kemeny

Alexander, Joseph Addison (1809-1861).† Presbyterian educator and biblical scholar. The son of Archibald *Alexander, Joseph was born in Philadelphia and graduated from the College of New Jersey at Princeton at the age of seventeen. A prodigiously gifted linguist, he was instructor of ancient languages and literature at Princeton (1830-1833), studied a year in Europe and taught Old and New Testament (1834-1860) and (after 1851) church history at Princeton Theological Seminary. He published many articles in the *Biblical Repertory and Princeton Review,* which he helped edit, as well as commentaries on Psalms, Isaiah, Matthew, Mark and Acts.

Although Alexander supported *Princeton's Reformed confessionalism and Scottish Common Sense realism and often echoed German biblical scholar E. W. Hengstenberg's attacks on radical biblical criticism, he was the first of the Old Princeton theologians to appreciate fully the historical and critical approach to the Bible, and he cautiously introduced German biblical scholarship into his writings. Appropriating some elements of the more organic model of Romanticism, his articles in the *Biblical Repertory* evidence a keen insight into the literary and historical nature of the Bible. His hermeneutical emphasis on reading the Scripture as both the word of man and the Word of God left a lasting impact on Old Testament scholarship at Princeton.

Alexander took little part in the ecclesiastical debates of his day but was content to continue his scholarly pursuits in the *Old School Presbyterian Church.

See also ALEXANDER, JAMES WADDEL.

BIBLIOGRAPHY. H. C. Alexander, *The Life of Joseph Addison Alexander,* 2 vols. (1870); *DAB* I; J. H. Moorhead, "Joseph Addison Alexander: Common Sense, Romanticism and Biblical Criticism at Princeton," *JPH* 53 (1975) 51-65; M. A. Taylor, *The Old Testament in the Old Princeton School, 1812-1929* (1992). E. W. Kennedy

Alexander, Maitland (1867-1940). Presbyterian minister. Alexander was born in New York City and was reared in Fifth Avenue Presbyterian Church. He graduated from the College of New Jersey (Princeton) in 1889 and from Princeton Seminary in 1892. He was theologically a strict Calvinist and at the same time aggressive in terms of outreach and community involvement. Alexander was important in the *fundamentalist-modernist controversy. He took seriously the *Old School Presbyterian heritage; his grandfather was Archibald *Alexander.

BIBLIOGRAPHY. M. Alexander, *The Burning Heart: Sermons by Maitland Alexander* (1942); *The Great Step* (1915); "The Hierarchy of the Presbyterian Church," *CT** 5 (July 1934) 34.

C. G. Dennison

Alexander, William (1831-1906). Presbyterian educator. Born in Huntington County, Pennsylvania, Alexander graduated from Jefferson (later Washington and Jefferson) College, Pennsylvania, in 1858. Three years later he graduated from Princeton Theological Seminary, and in the following year he was ordained. Between 1860 and 1869 Alexander served as stated supply or pastor to churches in Pennsylvania and Wisconsin. He was also president of Carroll College, Wisconsin, from 1862 to 1864.

In 1869 Alexander moved to California to pastor First Presbyterian Church, San Jose. He left in 1871 to become president of City College, San Francisco, a Presbyterian academy that aspired to be a college. In that same year Alexander, in consultation with William Anderson *Scott, drew up a plan of organization for a theological seminary. The seminary plan was adopted by the Synod of the Pacific in 1871, thereby creating the San Francisco Theological Seminary. Alexander became a member of the founding faculty of the new school, which initially used the City College facilities. In 1874 he resigned from City College to devote his full attention to the seminary. He taught primarily Greek and the New Testament until 1876, when he shifted to church history. While he did not produce any major work of scholarship, Alexander was dedicated in serving his denomination and the school that he helped found. He published numerous sermons and addresses, and for a time he served as an associate editor of the *Presbyterian and Reformed Review.* He also was a member of the Committee on the Revision of the Confession of Faith (1890-1893). He died at his home in San Anselmo, California.

BIBLIOGRAPHY. J. Curry, *History of the San Francisco Theological Seminary* (1907); *NCAB* 5; *Who Was Who in America* 1. D. F. Anderson

Alison, Francis (1705-1779). Presbyterian educator and political theorist. Born in Leck, County Donegal, Ireland, Alison studied at the Royal Academy of Raphoe and Edinburgh University and with the moral philosopher Francis Hutcheson at the University of Glasgow. He arrived in America in 1735 and was soon ordained pastor of a Presbyterian church in New London, Chester County, Pennsylvania (1737-1752). Concerned by the lack of educational opportunities in the Middle Colonies, Alison established New London Academy in 1743 (later relocated to Newark, Delaware, a predecessor of the University of Delaware). In 1752, at Benjamin Franklin's behest, Alison left New London to become rector of the Philadelphia Academy and, later, vice provost and professor at the College of Philadelphia (now the University of Pennsylvania). Concurrently he copastored the First Presbyterian Church of Philadelphia and became a major spokesperson for *Old Side Presbyterianism. A conservative *Calvinist, he was wary of *Arminian tendencies in the *New Side but saw the chief differences in ministerial qualifications and attitudes toward enthusiasm.

In his teaching, Alison trained a whole generation of students in the inductive empiricism of Scottish Common Sense realism, demonstrating the relevance of Scottish academic philosophy to pressing American problems, particularly in political theory. Alison's students, many of whom became prominent political leaders in the Revolutionary era (*see* American Revolution), learned from their mentor concepts such as the right of resistance to tyranny, government by contract and consent and the necessity for balanced forms of government. Alison also actively opposed British encroachments upon American prerogatives, both ecclesiastically and politically.

Bibliography. E. Ingersoll, "Francis Alison, American 'Philosophe' 1705-1779" (Ph.D. diss., University of Delaware, 1974); J. L. McAllister Jr., "Francis Alison and John Witherspoon: Political Philosophers and Revolutionaries," *JPH* 54 (1976) 33-60.

D. M. Strong

Allen, Cary (1767-1795).† Presbyterian revivalist and home missionary. Reared in a large family in Cumberland County, Virginia, Allen attended Hampden-Sydney College and in 1787, while home on vacation, attended a Methodist meeting and experienced a dramatic evangelical conversion. Returning to Hampden-Sydney, he helped precipitate a revival among the students. This revival is now viewed by historians as one of the first fruits of the Second Great Awakening. Allen and many others from the school entered the Presbyterian ministry, spreading this heightened religious interest throughout the South and trans-Appalachian Southwest. Graduating in 1788, he turned to theological study under the direction of Hanover Presbytery.

Licensed in 1790, Allen spent three years as an evangelist for his synod and was a home missionary to various parts of Virginia and Kentucky, eventually settling in Kentucky in 1794, when he married a Miss Fleming of Botetourt. A fiery preacher who denounced universalism, sabbath breaking and the rationalism of Thomas Paine's *Age of Reason,* he called the back country to repentance and faith in Jesus Christ. His message had a socially leveling influence; he even invited black slaves to join their white masters on the equal ground of evangelical Christianity. Blessed with a remarkable speaking ability and an unusually good sense of humor, Allen was a popular preacher. Using his wit to put people at ease, Allen could move an audience from laughter to tears with his bold proclamation of the gospel. He died unexpectedly at age twenty-eight and was buried near Danville, Kentucky.

See also Revivals, Presbyterians and.

Bibliography. W. H. Foote, *Sketches of Virginia, Historical and Biographical,* 2d series (1852).

D. M. Strong

Allis, O(swald) T(hompson) (1880-1973).† Presbyterian clergyman, Old Testament scholar and educator. The son of a Philadelphia medical doctor, Allis was reared in a Presbyterian home. Before taking a Ph.D. in archaeology and Assyriology from the University of Berlin in 1913, he studied at the University of Pennsylvania (A.B.) and Princeton Theological Seminary (B.D.). Beginning in 1910, Allis served as a member of Princeton Seminary's faculty in the Old Testament department for nineteen years, where in addition to teaching Semitic philology he served as an editor of the *Princeton Theological Review.*

In 1929 Allis left Princeton to teach at the newly founded Westminster Theological Seminary in Philadelphia, where he served for six years. Owing to a controversy within the *Presbyterian Church (USA) that implicated Westminster Seminary, Allis resigned in 1935. Freed from the constraints of the teaching schedule and independently wealthy, Allis devoted the rest of his life to writing and editing. In addition to compiling extended studies of English translations of the Bible, Allis focused on the Pentateuch and Old Testament prophecy. In *Prophecy and the Church* (1945) he registered significant objections to dispensational premillennialism, and his *God Spake by Moses* (1951) became a standard defense of the traditional conservative understanding of Pentateuchal authorship. Meanwhile, he served as a contributing editor for *Christianity Today* (Philadelphia) and as an associate editor for the *Evangelical Quarterly* (Edinburgh).

Bibliography. M. A. Noll, *Between Faith and Criticism: Evangelicals, Scholarship, and the Bible in America* (1986); M. A. Taylor, *The Old Testament in the Old Princeton School (1812-1929)* (1992).

D. G. Hart

American Council of Christian Churches. An agency representing separatist *fundamentalists. The American Council of Christian Churches

(ACCC) was founded on September 17, 1941, in New York City in a meeting of the Bible Protestant Church and the *Bible Presbyterian Church. In the years that followed, several other denominations joined the ACCC.

The initial impetus for organizing the group was to witness to Protestant orthodoxy in the face of the modernism represented by the Federal Council of Churches (FCC)—now known as the National Council of Churches (NCC)—and to provide a united organization of separatist churches. Carl *McIntire, a militant defender of orthodoxy, was the first president of the ACCC.

McIntire challenged the right of the FCC to speak for American Protestantism, protesting that the ecumenical movement had compromised the truth of the gospel, was attempting to build a "one-world church" and advocated pacifism and peaceful coexistence with communism. Two early victories for the ACCC were the gaining of free radio time and the granting of a quota of chaplains in the U.S. armed forces, both in addition to what had already been apportioned to the FCC.

The ACCC remains firmly committed to the doctrine of the plenary, verbal inspiration of Scripture as the basis for Protestant orthodoxy and adheres to a separatist doctrine of the church that calls for true believers to depart from what it judges to be apostate denominations. McIntire's strong views regarding separatism and authoritarian leadership inevitably led to clashes within the organization during the 1950s. In 1968 his leadership was rejected by the ACCC, a decision he attempted but failed to reverse in 1970.

In the late 1980s the ACCC reported a total membership of 1.5 million, including denominations, independent churches, associations and individuals. Membership consists of constituent members, who have severed all ties with the NCC, and auxiliary members, who still maintain some ties with the NCC (such as in the case of individuals in denominations that are members of the NCC). The ACCC publishes the *Christian Beacon* and maintains headquarters in Valley Forge, Pennsylvania. It is a member of the International Council of Christian Churches.

BIBLIOGRAPHY. L. Gasper, *The Fundamentalist Movement, 1930-1956* (1963). *DCA* Editors

American Revolution, Presbyterians and the. Presbyterians were fully engaged in the struggle through which the thirteen North American colonies won their independence from Great Britain. Some observers even thought they were the ones most responsible. A Hessian captain, for example, wrote of his experiences in Pennsylvania: "Call this war . . . by whatever name you may, only call it not an American Rebellion, it is nothing more or less than an Irish-Scotch Presbyterian Rebellion." A British colonial minister agreed; he charged in 1777 that "Presbyterianism is really at the Bottom of this whole Conspiracy."

Presbyterians were well positioned to play a leading political role since, of all denominations in the colonies, they were the most widely distributed. The 495 American Presbyterian churches in 1780 included large numbers in New Jersey, southeastern New York, the Philadelphia region and central Pennsylvania. Heavy immigration from the north of Ireland during the generation before the war had also salted considerable numbers of Presbyterians in the back country of Virginia, North Carolina and South Carolina. The colonial history of these Presbyterians contributed to their importance during the Revolution. Presbyterian cosmopolitanism anticipated the process by which individual colonies looking toward London joined with each other to form a new nation. Gilbert *Tennent and other leading revivalists during the Great Awakening also used language that would pave the way for the interchange between religion and politics; their vocabulary would soon be wrenched out of the realm of religion in order to inspire independence.

During the French and Indian War (1756-1763), Presbyterians also contributed to a millennial vocabulary of the sort that would become commonplace in the Revolution. Samuel *Davies in Virginia thought that "the present war" with France might possibly be "the commencement of this grand decisive conflict between the Lamb and the beast, i.e., between the protestant and popish powers," which could, if the cause of right prevailed, "introduce a new heaven and a new earth."

A form of the political philosophy that inspired the American founding fathers was also featured in Presbyterian education of the late colonial period. Both Francis *Alison in Philadelphia and John *Witherspoon, after his migration from Scotland in 1768 to become president of the College of New Jersey, taught their students the moral philosophy of Francis Hutcheson, who made much of the injustice when a mother country restricts the natural growth of a flourishing colony. James Madison's father sent his son to Princeton (where he graduated in 1771) in large part because of Witherspoon's reputation as an advocate of "liberty."

When tensions with Great Britain grew, Presbyterians were often leaders in organizing opposition to the mother country. They helped write new state constitutions in New Jersey, Pennsylvania and North Carolina. At least twelve of the fifty-six signers of the Declaration of Independence were Presbyterians, including the only minister, Witherspoon. Later, ten of the fifty-five delegates who prepared the Constitution were Presbyterians. During the war itself, many Presbyterians enlisted eagerly in the cause. The educational institution with broadest sweep in the colonies was Princeton College, still a thoroughly Presbyterian institution during this period. At least 235 Princeton students rendered some military service for the patriots (about fifty as chaplains). Only thirteen students were known Loyalists.

Presbyterian ministers also rendered vigorous support for the war from their pulpits. Witherspoon, upon first arriving in the colonies, had been criticized for speaking freely of politics. But he was mostly following the habits of his Scottish homeland, where ecclesiastical controversies were also often civil disputes and vice versa. In fact no colonial Presbyterian exploited sermons as freely for political purposes as did their contemporary Congregationalists in New England, where annual rituals like election sermons had been carried on since the early seventeenth century.

In his pronouncements leading up to the conflict, Witherspoon wove together ancient principles of natural law, Whig ideas of natural rights and Scottish Presbyterian ideas about the sacredness of covenant (in this case between a mother country and its colonies). To Witherspoon, as well as to many other Presbyterians, final dominion on earth belonged to God alone. Dominion among men was to be exercised only by mutual consent. British attempts to rule the colonies absolutely, without considering the colonists' legitimate rights and hereditary agreements, violated not just the best human principles of government but also God's rightful place as the Lord of the world. On May 17, 1776, Witherspoon preached a justly famous sermon on "The Dominion of Providence Over the Passions of Men" in which he in effect defended the step he would soon take in Philadelphia: "I do not refuse submission to their unjust claims, because they are corrupt or profligate, although probably many of them are so, but because they are men, and therefore liable to all the selfish bias inseparable from human nature. . . . For these colonies to depend wholly upon the legislature of Great-Britain, would be like many other oppressive connexions, injury to the master, and ruin to the slave." The printed edition of this sermon also contained an address to Witherspoon's fellow Scots in America arguing that, since Britain demanded unconditional colonial submission, the defense of freedom could not be separated from a defense of colonial independence.

Not all Presbyterians, however, were patriots. Loyalism among Presbyterians, as in many other American religious traditions, has become almost invisible because of the commitment of many American churches to the idea that God has specifically ordained the course of the United States, but Presbyterian Loyalists there were.

Scottish settlers in North Carolina, for example, resisted patriotic logic because of the relatively benign treatment they had received from the English. Many of these Scots were Highlanders who had sworn an oath of loyalty to the English king after the last Jacobite Rebellion (1745-1746). Before the Revolution, Highlanders in the Carolina back country had made up part of the Regulator Movement, which organized resistance to the colonial aristocracy of the coast. When that aristocracy opted for the colonial cause during the Revolution, many of the Regulators, including the Scottish Presbyterians, retained their allegiance to King George III.

In what would later be known as Canada, the early leaders of Nova Scotia's fledgling Presbyterian church—Daniel Cock, David Smith and James Murdoch—had been sent out from Scotland's seceding churches. They found republican politics disruptive and seditious and so stood solidly by the imperial government even when many of their Presbyterian coreligionists in the thirteen colonies acted otherwise. After the war, when thirty thousand Loyalists migrated to Nova Scotia, leadership by ministers like George Gilmore, who had been expelled from both Connecticut and New York for his loyalism, set Canadian Presbyterianism on a loyalist, conservative course oriented much more toward the old country than to the new United States.

In summary, despite a Loyalist minority, American Presbyterians provided substantial support for the patriotic cause. Older Presbyterian self-congratulation that the United States federal system arose in imitation of Presbyterian church courts or that the principles of republican democracy were taken directly from John *Calvin are untenable. Yet Presbyterians did contribute to a vigorous defense of liberty—both against what was perceived as the tyranny of Parliament and in situations where colonists restricted freedoms in America (e.g., in Virginia, Presbyterians joined Baptists and other dissenters in petitioning the new state legislature to disestablish the hereditary Church of England).

In the heat of conflict, Presbyterians sometimes lost their sense of priorities, as when a distinguished band of Philadelphia ministers wrote fellow ministers in North Carolina in 1775 that, unless the North Carolinians supported the patriots, "we can have no fellowship with you; our soul shall weep for you in secret, but will not be able any longer to number you among our friends, nor the friends of liberty." The war also disoriented moral sense, as when the Reverend Alexander MacWhorter of Newark preached to George Washington's troops on December 7, 1776, while they retreated from New York toward Philadelphia. MacWhorter's fiery sermon dwelt at great length on the evils of the British and of the "Papist Highland Barbarians" (mostly Presbyterian Scots) whom Britain had enlisted to fight the colonists, while completely avoiding the sins of his American audience that included at least two hundred prostitutes. In addition, the war provided an overwhelming temptation to absolutize the temporal, as when the Pennsylvania Presbyterian Robert Smith proclaimed in 1777 that "the cause of America is the cause of Christ."

Presbyterians provided vital support for the drive toward American independence. Whether they should have, whether the way they did it was in keeping with either general Christian or specifically Presbyterian traditions, or whether the minority of Presbyterian Loyalists had a point worth pondering in the face of the patriot tide are issues strangely neglected in the theology and historiography of American Presbyterian life.

See also Civil War, Presbyterians and the; Politics, Presbyterians and.

Bibliography. M. J. Endy Jr., "Just War, Holy War and Millennialism in Revolutionary America," *WMQ* 42 (January 1985) 3-25; K. L. Griffin, *Revolution and Religion: American Revolutionary War and the Reformed Clergy* (1994); N. O. Hatch, *The Sacred Cause of Liberty: Republican Thought and the Millennium in Revolutionary New England* (1977); J. S. Moir, *Enduring Witness: The Presbyterian Church in Canada* (rev. ed., 1987); M. A. Noll, *Christians in the American Revolution* (1977); "Presbyterians and the American Revolution: A Documentary Account," *JPH* 52 (winter 1974) 303-488; idem, "Presbyterians and the American Revolution: An Interpretive Account," *JPH* 54 (spring 1976) 5-200; *Princetonians: A Biographical Dictionary: 1748-1794,* 5 vols. (1976-1991); J. H. Smylie, "Presbyterian Clergy and Problems of 'Dominion' in the Revolutionary Generation," *JPH* 48 (fall 1970) 161-75; L. J. Trinterud, *The Forming of an American Tradition: A Re-Examination of Colonial Presbyterianism* (1949); B. Wingo, "Politics, Society and Religion: The Presbyterian Clergy of Pennsylvania, New Jersey and New York, and the Formation of the Nation, 1775-1808" (Ph.D. diss., Tulane University, 1976).

M. A. Noll

Anderson, William Madison, Jr. (1889-1935).† Presbyterian pastor and educator. A third-generation Presbyterian minister, Anderson was born in Rock Hill, South Carolina. He received training at Vanderbilt University (1907-1910), Austin College (B.S., 1911) and Austin Theological Seminary (B.D., 1914). Ordained in 1914 to the ministry of the *Presbyterian Church in the United States (PCUS), he pastored the East Dallas Church (1914) before becoming secretary of schools and colleges of the Presbyterian Church in Texas (1915). He served as assistant pastor under his father at First Church, Dallas (1916-1924), becoming senior pastor in 1925, a position he held until his death.

Concern for children resulted in Anderson's establishing the Freeman Memorial Clinic at the church in 1921. His influence on Lewis Sperry *Chafer and his associates resulted in the locating of the proposed Evangelical Theological College (later Dallas Theological Seminary) in Dallas. Convinced of the need for a conservative, dispensationalist seminary that would be academically rigorous, Anderson served that institution from 1924 as its first vice president and professor of homiletics, as well as being elected chairman of the board of trustees in 1926. He remained in all three positions, except for a year's leave of absence from the faculty in 1930-1931 due to the burden of his pastoral ministry, until his death. Through his influence, his father donated his extensive library to be part of the foundation of the new seminary's library, and members of his church constituted about half of the original board of trustees. A pioneer radio preacher in Dallas, he conducted a weekly Bible class that enrolled about thirty thousand members.

R. T. Clutter

Arminianism.† A theological reform movement within the Dutch Reformed Church in the early seventeenth century, Arminianism had considerable influence in Anglo-American theological developments, particularly as it came to be championed by Methodists. The movement is traced to the work of Jacob Arminius (1560-1609). A convinced Calvinist who was educated at the University of Leyden and at

Geneva, he eventually departed from the teachings of John *Calvin on several points of doctrine. Although the movement associated with Arminius came to be synonymous with anti-Calvinism, it was a reaction against an orthodox expression of *Calvinism that was placing particular emphasis on predestination and a cluster of doctrines associated with it.

Arminius was requested by the authorities of the Dutch church to examine and refute what were regarded as the humanist views of Dirck Koornbert, a leader of an anti-Calvinist party in Holland, who objected in particular to the high Calvinist doctrine of predestination. In the course of this investigation, Arminius became convinced of the truth of significant aspects of Koornbert's position. With this altered doctrinal perspective, Arminius began to clash with Franciscus Gomarus (1563-1641), his strict Calvinist colleague on the theological faculty at the University of Leyden. Gomarus's view on predestination, known as supralapsarianism, maintained that God's double decree for the election of some and the reprobation of others was made sovereignly by God before the fall of Adam and Eve rather than as a response to their fall. Hence God permitted the Fall as the event through which he would make effective his eternal decrees. As corollaries of this position, Gomarus held that human nature is totally depraved and that the atoning death of Christ is limited to the elect.

After the death of Arminius in 1609, his theological position was maintained by his successor at Leyden, Simon Bisshop (1583-1643), and consequently Gomarus and his allies began to call for the expulsion of all Arminian teachers from their teaching positions. In response, forty-six pastors signed a document called the *Remonstrance* in 1610, which rejected the supralapsarian doctrine of predestination as well as the alternative infralapsarian view, which held that God's decrees were not eternal but were made after and in light of the Fall. They also rejected the doctrine of limited atonement, which affirmed Christ died only for the elect, and the doctrine of irresistible grace.

The positions stated in the *Remonstrance* were essentially those that had been held by Arminius. In Arminius's view, God's decrees were based on his foreknowledge of the future faith of the elect and not foreordained so as to permit no room for a free human response to God's offer of saving grace. Moreover, this human response was not simply the exercise of free will, which would be to repeat the ancient Pelagian heresy. Arminius maintained that since the human will is enslaved to sin, it is necessary for God to assist people in responding to the invitation to salvation. He does this by providing prevenient grace, so enabling the will to respond freely to God. In his view, God also foreknows who will persevere in their Christian faith after conversion, although once again God's foreknowledge does not mean that he foreordains that they cannot fall from grace if they choose to do so.

A major reason for the Calvinists' opposition to Arminius's position was their desire to uphold at all costs the sovereignty of God, whereby all credit for human salvation rests with God. This view is also called monergism, which indicates that God is the sole party operative to effect human salvation. Arminius's view may be described as synergism, which indicates that God's grace initiates the act of salvation but, to become effective, grace cooperates with the human act of response to grace. For Arminius this meant that "the grace sufficient for salvation is conferred on the Elect, and on the non-Elect; that, if they will, they may believe or not believe, may be saved or not be saved."

The publication of the *Remonstrance* led to a heightening of the controversy, as it now became embroiled in a web of social and political issues. The Arminian position appealed to the growing middle class, especially in the maritime provinces of Holland. However, under the leadership of Maurice of Nassau, the anti-Remonstrant party, also known as the Gomarists, consolidated their position, and at the Synod of Dort in 1618 they secured the condemnation of the Remonstrant tenets. The five principal tenets of the synod are represented in the acronym TULIP—total depravity, unconditional election, limited atonement, irresistible grace and the perseverance of the believer in salvation.

Undoubtedly Arminius and the Remonstrants would have been still perceived as Calvinists by Lutherans and Roman Catholics of their day, particularly given their Calvinist views of the church and sacraments. However, in the course of the succeeding two centuries, their views came to be regarded as distinctly anti-Calvinist, particularly in the Anglo-American context. While the distinguishing mark of Calvinism came to be its focus on God's irresistible grace, for Arminianism the distinguishing feature had come to be a conditional view of grace. Further, while the Arminians of the early seventeenth century tended to place a greater emphasis on God's role in the divine-human synergism, the emphasis on irresistible grace led to a growing ethical emphasis that would merge into a Pelagianism that emphasized human moral effort on the basis of free will. Later

Arminianism also tended to merge into deism or natural religion, where the moral emphasis wholly replaces the theological.

By the eighteenth century Arminianism had become a generic label for a wide variety of moral thinkers who objected to strict Calvinism. The leading representatives of such liberal Arminianism in America were such eighteenth-century Boston clerics as Charles Chauncy at Boston's First Congregational Church and Jonathan Mayhew of Boston's West Church. They were products of a broad latitudinarian culture that was fostered at Harvard, beginning with the presidency of John Leverett in 1707. This anticlerical spirit had merged with a critical attitude toward the Calvinistic tenets of New England Puritanism. These ministers became locked in theological controversy with Jonathan *Edwards, whose leadership in the Great Awakening served to renew the older Calvinist tradition. Yet they were slow to break from the older Calvinists, due to longstanding social and intellectual ties with that heritage. Their successors were to pass over into the ranks of New England Unitarianism amid theological controversy that disrupted the Massachusetts churches between 1805 and 1820.

The original tenets of Arminius enjoyed a restoration in the eighteenth century, emerging with evangelical warmth in the Wesleyan revival. There was probably more affinity between this revived Arminianism and Edwards's defense of Calvinist orthodoxy than there was between the early Methodists and the Arminianism of Chauncy or Mayhew.

Methodism became the largest Protestant denomination within nineteenth-century America, and with it the Arminian ascendancy prevailed in the Second Great Awakening, as well as in numerous other denominations that were divided over the issues of the Awakening (including Presbyterians, Congregationalists, Baptists and, to some extent, the Lutherans, *German Reformed and Mennonites) and still others that were indigenous products of the Awakening (including the United Brethren in Christ, the Evangelical Association, the Restoration Movement or Christian Churches and the Churches of Christ). The Arminian outlook that informed this Methodist age of American Protestantism fit well with the emphasis upon voluntarism and purposiveness that came to characterize American evangelical Protestantism.

See also CALVINISM.

BIBLIOGRAPHY. J. Arminius, *Works*, 3 vols. (1825, 1828, 1875); C. Bangs, *Arminius* (1985); A. W. Harrison, *Arminianism* (1937); J. Miley, *The Atonement in Christ* (1879); A. Outler, ed., *John Wesley* (1964); P. Ramsey, ed., *The Works of Jonathan Edwards: Freedom of the Will* (1957); H. O. Wiley, *Christian Theology*, 3 vols. (1941).

J. S. O'Malley

Armstrong, William Park (1874-1944).† Presbyterian New Testament scholar. Born in Selma, Alabama, Armstrong graduated from Princeton University (B.A., 1894; M.A., 1896), completing his master's degree while attending Princeton Theological Seminary (B.D., 1897). He then studied in Germany (Marburg, 1897; Berlin, 1897-1898; Erlangen, 1898), where more than a thousand Americans were engaged in theological studies at the time. After further graduate studies at Princeton Seminary, in 1899 he was appointed instructor in New Testament at Princeton and then to the chair of New Testament literature and exegesis in 1903. He was ordained in 1900.

Armstrong was on the board of *The Princeton Theological Review* through all its years (1903-1929), did most of the editorial work from 1909 to 1917 and prepared the final index. Armstrong, who was better known for his classroom skills than his written scholarship, published seven articles in the review and several dictionary articles and book reviews, mostly on the Gospels and especially on the resurrection accounts. His response to German biblical criticism was knowledgeable and fair, though he clearly argued for the historicity of the resurrection. He was influential in persuading the young J. Gresham *Machen to teach at Princeton but chose to remain at Princeton Seminary in 1929 when Machen and other colleagues left to form Westminster Theological Seminary. Staunchly conservative himself, he preferred to work for reform from within the church. In 1940, due to failing health, he relinquished his undergraduate duties, remaining as graduate professor of New Testament exegesis until his death.

BIBLIOGRAPHY. *PSB* 38 (1944) 64-66.

T. H. Olbricht

Auburn Affirmation (1924). A document, entitled "An Affirmation," designed to safeguard the unity and liberty of the *Presbyterian Church in the U.S.A. (PCUSA), issued during the *fundamentalist controversy by a group of ministers meeting in Auburn, New York. It was intended as a liberal protest against the Five Point Deliverance of the 1910 General Assembly of the Presbyterian Church in the U.S.A. (reaffirmed in 1916 and 1923), which affirmed biblical doctrines that were "essential and necessary."

The affirmation was published in January 1924 with the signatures of 150 ministers and was reissued in May 1924 with 1,274 signatures. Without denying the particular doctrines, the Auburn Affirmation opposed attempts to make the five points a test for ordination or orthodoxy. They were regarded as theories about facts or doctrines, concerning which other explanations or theories, deduced from Scripture and Presbyterian standards, might be acceptable. The 1926 general assembly opened the way to greater theological pluralism by declaring that Presbyterianism admits a diversity of views, the limits of which the church, rather than the individual, must ultimately decide.

Bibliography. L. A. Loetscher, *The Broadening Church: A Study of Theological Issues in the Presbyterian Church Since 1869* (1954); G. M. Marsden, *Fundamentalism and Modern Culture: The Shaping of Twentieth-Century Evangelicalism, 1870-1925* (1980); E. H. Rian, *The Presbyterian Conflict* (1940).

A. H. Freundt

Auburn Declaration (1837).† A theological statement issued by *New School Presbyterians in August 1837, intended to confirm their Presbyterian orthodoxy. The declaration defended the New School against accusations of heresy made by the *Old School majority at the 1837 General Assembly of the *Presbyterian Church in the U.S.A. (PCUSA). At that assembly, the Old School forced out three New School synods in New York and one in Ohio.

The accusation of the Old School was that theNew School party held to a modified Calvinism or Taylorism that compromised the *Westminster Confession of Faith. A secondary issue was the New School's support of the 1801 *Plan of Union, a cooperative agreement between Presbyterians and Congregationalists by which they would combine their efforts in evangelizing the West and in New School antislavery activity.

The declaration affirmed a moderately orthodox *Calvinism, which its signers believed reflected Presbyterian doctrinal standards. It also denied sixteen accusations alleged against them by the Old School. The 1838 general assembly refused to reconsider its decision, and for a time Presbyterians continued to exist in separate New School and Old School denominations, both claiming the title The Presbyterian Church in the U.S.A. Finally, in 1868 the Old School General Assembly admitted that the Auburn Declaration contained "all the fundamentals of the Calvinistic creed," and in 1870 the Old School/New School schism among Northern Presbyterians was healed. Among Presbyterians in the South, the Civil War facilitated reunion of the two groups in 1864.

Bibliography. "The Auburn Declaration," in *The Presbyterian Enterprise,* ed. M. W. Armstrong et al. (1956); G. M. Marsden, *The Evangelical Mind and the New School Presbyterian Experience: A Case Study of Thought and Theology in Nineteenth-Century America* (1970).

A. H. Freundt

Awakenings. *See* REVIVALS, PRESBYTERIANS AND.

B

Baird, Robert (1798-1863).† Presbyterian minister, ecumenical pioneer and leader of voluntary societies. Born of *Scots-Irish descent in western Pennsylvania, Baird was educated at Washington (1816-1817) and Jefferson (B.A., 1818) colleges and Princeton Theological Seminary (B.D., 1822). He was ordained to the Presbyterian ministry in 1822 and directed the Princeton Academy for the next five years (1822-1828), during which he strongly advocated and influenced public education in New Jersey. He thus launched a career of advocacy not only for public education but also for religious education as an agent of the American Sunday-School Union (1829-1834). Prior to that he was agent for the New Jersey Missionary Society (1828-1829).

In 1834 Baird was appointed as the agent of the French Association, a group that wanted to help the Protestant Church of France, and was sent to Paris under the auspices of the American and Foreign Christian Union in 1835 to become acquainted with the needs of the church there. He quickly became, along with Philip *Schaff, one of the chief interpreters of American religion to Europeans. His concern for temperance took him to many foreign capitals. He became one of the leading advocates of prohibition in Europe, writing a *History of the Temperance Societies in America* (1836) in French. Ardently opposed to the "dreadful evil" of slavery, he advocated gradual emancipation as the only realistic way to bring about its end.

Baird also had an interest in missions and ecumenism. He was a supporter of the Evangelical Alliance and formed his own society, which came to be known as the American and Foreign Christian Union. Traveling all over Europe and America for more than twenty years, at one point he had crossed the Atlantic eighteen times in sixteen years, endeavoring to promote Christian unity across national boundaries. Baird's pioneering work as a leader and shaper of voluntary societies found him drawing support from several denominations while frequently placing them under broad interdenominational governance. His influence on voluntary movements was both seminal and enduring.

A prolific author, Baird charted the movements of voluntary societies, evangelicalism and the American church scene in his classic *Religion in America,* which was published in Scotland in 1843 and was soon translated into French, German, Swedish and Dutch (rev. ed., 1856). While he nowhere strictly defined the nature of the church, the work was deeply sympathetic toward broad American evangelicalism. One of the first significant historians of the American religious experience, he delimited the eras that have largely been followed by historians ever since. Believing that denominations were a healthy expression of genuine evangelical distinctions, he felt that they should not be viewed as barriers to fellowship or common missionary or reform societies. Although Baird was a Presbyterian and considered confessional statements as essential to avoid heresy and error, he was charged by at least one conservative Princeton Seminary faculty member with identifying Presbyterian theology too closely with aberrant New England theology.

Bibliography. J. W. Alexander, "Religion in America . . . by Robert Baird," *BRPR* 17 (January 1895); *ANB* 1; H. M. Baird, *Life of the Reverend Robert Baird, D.D.* (1866); *DAB* I; *DARB; NCAB* 8.

J. H. Hall

Balch, Hezekiah (1741-1810). A pioneer Presbyterian minister in east Tennessee. Born in Maryland, Balch was reared in Mecklenburg County, North Carolina. He graduated from the College of New Jersey and was ordained by Hanover Presbytery in 1770. For some years he was an evangelist in North Carolina and western Pennsylvania, but by 1782-1783 he had moved to Greeneville in northeastern Tennessee, where his Mount Bethel congregation became the largest church in the Holston-Tennessee River Valley.

In 1794 Balch organized Greeneville College and in the following year journeyed to New England in search of funds and library books. At Newport, Rhode Island, he met Samuel Hopkins and was attracted to his New Divinity theology. Introducing these views into east Tennessee, Balch stirred up a fratricidal controversy among Presbyterians, marked by acerbic denunciations in the local press and endless judicial hearings in church courts. In the next few years Balch was attacked by the conservatives led by Samuel *Doak and brought sixteen times before presbytery, four times before synod and once before the general assembly on heresy charges. Despairing of permanent peace, the church courts sought to separate the dissenting brethren by organizing Union (1797) and Greeneville (1800) presbyteries. Balch's introduction of Hopkinsian theology was significant because it led to the growth of liberal currents that spurred large defections of Tennessee Presbyterians into the *New School following the schism of 1837-1838. Balch remained in Greeneville until his death.

See also NEW ENGLAND, PRESBYTERIANS AND.

BIBLIOGRAPHY. *AAP* 3; *ANB* 2. W. J. Wade

Baltzer, Adolf Hermann Franz (1817-1880). Pastor, teacher and executive officer of the *Evangelical Synod. Born in Berlin, Baltzer completed his theological education at the universities of Berlin and Halle and was ordained in 1845 and sent to America by the Bremen Mission Society. He became a frontier Evangelical pastor at Red Bud and Duquoin, Illinois, and joined the Evangelical Church Association of the West in 1846. In 1847 Baltzer moved to St. Louis, where he served as Evangelical pastor at St. Mark's and then St. Paul's.

Baltzer arranged for the printing of a new Evangelical catechism in 1847 at St. Louis, became secretary of the board of the Marthasville, Missouri, Evangelical Seminary in 1849 and from 1850 helped edit the *Friedensbote (Messenger of Peace)*. During eight years as pastor of Friedens Church in St. Charles, Missouri, Baltzer became the organizing father of his denomination. After 1855 he became the first president of the Evangelical Church Association.

Baltzer was named inspector of the abortive German Evangelical Missouri College from 1858 to 1862 and became coprofessor with Andreas *Irion at the Evangelical Seminary (now Eden Theological Seminary) from 1862 to 1865. Between 1866 and 1880 he again served as president of the Evangelical Church Association and its successors, the synods of the West and of North America. Overworked and underpaid, Baltzer died in St. Charles, Missouri.

BIBLIOGRAPHY. D. Dunn et al., eds., *A History of the Evangelical and Reformed Church* (1961); J. W. Flucke, *Evangelical Pioneers* (1931) 99-125; C. E. Schneider, *The German Church on the American Frontier* (1939). L. H. Zuck

Baptism. *See* SACRAMENTS, PRESBYTERIANS AND THE.

Barnes, Albert (1798-1870).† *New School Presbyterian minister. Born in Rome, New York, Barnes graduated from Hamilton College, Clinton, New York (1820) and Princeton Seminary (1824) and was ordained as a Presbyterian minister at Morristown, New Jersey (1825). During his early years in the ministry Barnes shaped a theology compatible with his revivalist preaching in the New School tradition. In a famous sermon entitled "The Way of Salvation" (1829) Barnes contradicted several Old Calvinist doctrines, particularly the doctrines of original sin and the substitutionary atonement, and drew the fire of conservative Presbyterians who questioned his doctrinal soundness. When the First Presbyterian Church, Philadelphia, called Barnes as pastor in 1830, charges were brought against him in the Philadelphia Presbytery, which caused considerable debate in the church courts, but they were ultimately adjudicated by the general assembly of 1831, which merely censured him for "unguarded and objectionable passages."

In 1835 it was alleged in Second Philadelphia Presbytery that his *Notes on Romans* departed from the traditional interpretation of the *Westminster Confession of Faith on essential doctrines such as original sin, justification by faith, the imputation of the guilt of Adam and the righteousness of Christ. This case, too, was appealed to the assembly, which acquitted Barnes and restored him to his pastorate, affirming that Barnes's interpretations, while not "always sufficiently guarded," were "conformable to our standards." Again the *Old School party, which upheld the traditional interpretation of the disputed doctrines, asserted itself and eventually brought about a division of the Presbyterian Church into Old School and New School denominations (1837).

Barnes admitted that he departed from the Westminster Confession on a few points but noted that others in the Presbyterian Church went further than he did. Believing that Adam's sin was not inherited by his posterity, he rejected the doctrines of imputation and original sin. He supported the governmental theory of the atonement, teaching that Christ's death was not a substitute for the sins of the elect but God's way of opening the gates of salvation to any who would believe the gospel.

Barnes supported revivalism and social reform,

including the campaigns against slavery and liquor, and wrote popular biblical commentaries, including the eleven-volume *Notes, Explanatory and Practical, on the New Testament* and his commentaries on four Old Testament books. A prolific author and contributor to the religious journals of the day, his other publications included his autobiography and significant books on revivals, the antislavery issue, the atonement, Christian evidences and the life of Paul. He provided leadership to New School Presbyterianism, strongly supporting the foundation of Union Theological Seminary in New York (1836), while he continued to serve his Philadelphia congregation for thirty-eight years, until his retirement (1868). In his later years he worked hard to see the reunion of the two denominations in the North, which he lived to see (1869-1870).

Bibliography. *ANB* 2; S. J. Baird, *History of the New School* (1868); A. Barnes, *Life at Three-Score and Ten* (1871); *DAB* I; *DARB*; *HHMBI;* G. Junkin, *The Vindication, Containing a History of the Trial of the Reverend Albert Barnes* (1836); G. M. Marsden, *The Evangelical Mind and the New School Presbyterian Experience: A Case of Thought and Theology in Nineteenth-Century American* (1970); *NCAB* 7.

A. H. Freundt

Barnhouse, Donald Grey (1895-1960).† Presbyterian pastor, Bible expositor and editor. Born in Watsonville, California, to devout Methodist parents, Barnhouse enrolled at age seventeen in the Bible Institute of Los Angeles, where he learned dispensational theology under Reuben A. Torrey. After a brief sojourn at the University of Chicago, Barnhouse entered Princeton Theological Seminary in 1915 but left in 1917 to join the Army Signal Corps. Spending six years in Europe after the war, Barnhouse served the Belgian Gospel Mission in Brussels (1919-1921) and then pastored two Reformed churches in the French Alps, also studying at the University of Grenoble. He married missionary Ruth Tiffany in 1922. Barnhouse returned to the United States in 1925 and settled in Philadelphia, where he took graduate courses at the University of Pennsylvania and Eastern Baptist Theological Seminary and pastored the Grace Presbyterian Church.

Barnhouse became the pastor of Tenth Presbyterian Church in 1927 and served there until his death. From that base he began a network radio program in 1928; a monthly magazine, *Revelation,* in 1931 (renamed *Eternity* in 1950); and a circuit of weekly Bible classes. Eventually his tours took him all over the world. As the first Presbyterian minister to broadcast to a national audience, he developed a huge following, with more than four hundred radio stations carrying his "Bible Study Hour" by 1960. Barnhouse published a dozen volumes during his life and produced other material that was posthumously made into books and audio tapes.

Barnhouse combined a mildly dispensational premillennialism with a traditional Calvinist theology emphasizing three fundamentals: the incarnation of the second person of the Trinity in Jesus Christ, the death and resurrection of Christ for lost sinners, and the plenary inspiration of the Bible as God's revelation. Although he argued for Christian liberty in social matters, he had strong personal views that he vigorously promoted. A virulent anticommunist and anti-Catholic, he also spoke out against racism, pointing out that Jesus died for people of all colors.

In doctrine and temperament Barnhouse was a *fundamentalist, but he never fully conformed to the party line. He did not leave the Presbyterian church when many of his allies did, and he criticized them as freely as he did the liberals. Staying within the mainline denomination, he strove to preserve a conservative evangelical and Reformed witness in the face of the liberalizing trends of the day. Always embroiled in controversy, he was censured by his own presbytery in 1930 for slander, and many of his colleagues were uncomfortable with the extent of his influence. His famous resolution in 1953 to be more loving indicated some mellowing, but it was consistent with his earlier independent-mindedness. In 1954 he attended the World Council of Churches meetings in Evanston, Illinois, and expressed his favorable impressions in *Eternity,* but he remained vigorously opposed to outright liberal theology. Accused of treason by fundamentalists, distrusted by liberals and personally distant from other conservatives, Barnhouse was still, in his own way, a leader of the new evangelical movement.

Bibliography. *ANB* 2; M. N. Barnhouse, *That Man Barnhouse* (1983); C. A. Russell, "Donald Grey Barnhouse: Fundamentalist Who Changed," *JPH* 59 (1981) 33-57.

J. A. Carpenter

Barth, Karl (1886-1968).‡ Swiss Reformed theologian. The son of a Reformed minister and professor, Barth attended Berne, Berlin, Tübingen and Marburg universities, studying under Adolf Harnack (1851-1930), Wilhelm Herrmann (1846-1922) and other leading European theologians of his day. In his earlier years, while serving as a village pastor in Safenwil, Switzerland (1911-1921), Barth became convinced of the poverty of his own liberal theology and so began a gradual reorientation that would finally lead him to a renewed theological quest in dialogue with Scripture and Protestant orthodoxy. From the pastorate Barth's career was to take him through a series of academic posts at Göttingen (1921-1925), Münster (1925-1930) and Bonn (1930-1935), Germany, and finally to Basel, Switzerland (1935-1962). Throughout these years he set forth the so-called Barthian theology that would have such an impact on western theology of the mid-twentieth century.

Barth's commentary *The Epistle to the Romans* (1919; rev. ed., 1922) was said to have fallen "like a bomb on the playground of the theologians." Yet it was not translated into English until 1935. The first English translation of Barth's writings was *The Word of God and the Word of Man* in 1928. This volume was widely read and reviewed, but it was not until 1933 that further Barth volumes were translated into English.

American liberal theologians decisively rejected the early Barth. They saw his emphasis on the "infinite qualitative distinction" between God and humanity as making God completely inaccessible and communication about God impossible. By the later 1930s, however, American theologians such as Reinhold *Niebuhr (who later disagreed with Barth), Edwin Lewis and Elmer Homrighausen began to show the influence of Barth in the theologies they produced. But it was not until 1956 that translations of his developing multivolume *Church Dogmatics* (1932-1968; ET, 1936-1969) began to appear regularly in English. Later, English editions would appear soon after the German editions, giving English readers more immediate access to Barth's theology.

Barth's influence in America has extended in a number of directions. His impact on American Protestantism has been strongest in the major Presbyterian traditions. Barth has also had an ongoing impact in American evangelicalism. This is seen in the works of Donald Bloesch and Bernard Ramm and marks a significant change from earlier appraisals of Barth by writers such as Cornelius *Van Til and Charles Ryrie, who from different perspectives rejected Barth's theology as a deviation from orthodoxy.

Though many professional theologians have turned away from Barth, his influence lives in America through those who have continued to do theology in ways similar to what Barth advocated. These include Europeans such as Hendrikus Berkhof, Thomas Torrance and Otto Weber, as well as those who work in America such as Arthur Cochrane and Paul Lehmann. Others such as Robert McAfee Brown, Harvey Cox and Langdon Gilkey also recognize the impact of Barth on their thinking. The Karl Barth Society of North America continues to hold both national and regional meetings. While Barth's theology as a whole may not enjoy a full-scale revival in America, his influence continues in indirect, diffuse and distilled forms.

See also NEO-ORTHODOXY.

BIBLIOGRAPHY. G. C. Bolich, *Karl Barth & Evangelicalism* (1980); E. Busch, *Karl Barth* (1976); D. K. McKim, ed., *How Karl Barth Changed My Mind* (1986); B. Ramm, *After Fundamentalism* (1984); D. N. Voskuil, "America Encounters Karl Barth, 1919-1939," *FH* 12 (1980) 61-74.

D. K. McKim

Bavinck, Herman, Influence of. Herman Bavinck (1854-1921) has been a major influence in North American churches of Dutch Reformed background since the beginning of his ministry in the late nineteenth century. His magisterial work, the four-volume *Gereformeerde Dogmatiek* (1906-1911), has not been translated in its entirety, although one volume, *The Doctrine of God,* was published in English in 1951. Prior to World War II, he also had some influence in American Presbyterian churches, particularly among the Princeton theologians, thanks to his Stone Lectures at Princeton Seminary in 1908-1909. These lectures, *The Philosophy of Revelation,* were reprinted in 1953. Bavinck's most popular work in English has been his one-volume digest of his dogmatics, *Our Reasonable Faith* (original title: *Magnalia Dei).* This was first published in English in 1956 and has been reprinted in a paperback version several times.

Our Reasonable Faith has been widely used in evangelical schools as well as in Reformed institutions of Dutch background. A smaller work, *The Certainty of Faith* (Paideia, 1980), was also translated into English by a Canadian Reformed scholar. One of Bavinck's leading disciples in the United States was Louis *Berkhof, who relied heavily on Bavinck's *Gereformeerde Dogmatiek* in his *Systematic Theology* (1938 and continual reprintings), which has been used in conservative Reformed and evangelical schools until the present. In many ways Bavinck's chief influence in the postwar period was indirect through the "Studies in Dogmatics" of G. C. Berkouwer, professor emeritus of the Free University in Amsterdam, who writes much in the same spirit.

Whereas Bavinck's compatriot and contemporary, Abraham *Kuyper, has had a greater influence in neo-Calvinist circles, particularly in the *Christian Reformed Church (CRC), Bavinck has had a more general appeal. In many ways, he has been the Reformed theologian of the twentieth century. A new impetus to Bavinck studies in North America will be the translation and publication of the complete dogmatics by the recently formed Dutch Reformed Theology Translation Society.

The special appeal of Bavinck's theology has been his faithfulness to Scripture and appreciation of the three Dutch Reformed confessions—the *Belgic Confession, the *Heidelberg Catechism and the *Canons of Dort—along with an impressive knowledge of modern philosophical and religious thought. He also possessed a remarkable knowledge of the history of thought, both Christian and non-Christian. He did not hesitate to engage in dialogue with modern thought but never sacrificed the essentials of the faith. He contributed in various ways to a new understanding of the organic inspiration of Scripture, the doctrine of creation, a mediating position on the doctrine of election and a fresh approach to the *ordo salutis*. One of his major contributions was breaking with the seventeenth-century scholastic approach to theology and the regnant liberalism in the Dutch Reformed Church of his time. In addition, his theology, particularly in *Our Reasonable Faith*, is suffused with a warm piety.

Bavinck was not an innovator, but he does deserve credit for the *aggiornamento* of the historical Reformed faith for the twentieth century. For these reasons it is likely that Bavinck will continue to have some influence not only in North America but also in the larger Christian world.

BIBLIOGRAPHY. J. D. Bratt, *Dutch Calvinism in America: A History of a Conservative Subculture* (1984). I. J. Hesselink

Beecher, Lyman (1775-1863). Congregational and Presbyterian clergyman. A native of Connecticut, Beecher entered Yale College in 1793. During his sophomore year, Yale president Timothy Dwight launched a preaching campaign against religious skepticism among Yale undergraduates. As Beecher later recalled in his autobiography (1865), Dwight led a class disputation on the question "Is the Bible the Word of God?" and soon "all infidelity skulked and hid its head." Beecher himself was "awakened" the following year, during which he began a friendship with Dwight that lasted until the latter's death in 1817.

Although Beecher was licensed a Congregational clergyman in 1798, his first pastoral charge was the East Hampton Presbyterian Church on Long Island. Initially indifferent to his attempts to begin a revival, his congregation was finally stirred by Beecher's "The Remedy for Dueling," a lament delivered in 1806 after Aaron *Burr Jr., fatally wounded Alexander Hamilton in a duel. A subsequent salary dispute led Beecher to accept an offer of the Congregational church in Litchfield, Connecticut, in 1810.

During the Litchfield years, Beecher's reputation as a revivalist, social reformer and political observer grew. As a respected member of the Connecticut Standing Order—a group of conservative clergymen who jealously defended the privileged position of the Congregational church against the more democratic notions of Jeffersonian Baptists—Beecher fought against the disestablishment of Congregationalism in the state. When Connecticut Congregationalism was finally disestablished in 1817, Beecher lamented the loss, believing that the "injury done to the cause of Christ . . . was irreparable." Soon thereafter, however, Beecher realized that disestablishment was, ironically, a positive development. "It cut the churches loose from dependence on state support. It threw them wholly on their own resources and on God." Beecher left Litchfield in 1826 to assume pastoral duties at the Hanover Street Church in Boston. From there he launched his strenuous campaign against New England Unitarianism.

In 1832 Beecher began concurrent terms as president of Lane Theological Seminary and pastor of the Second Presbyterian Church, both in Cincinnati, Ohio. Over the following decade, Beecher discovered that the voluntary efforts of Christian groups organized to resist social ills were extremely useful tools for social reform and revivalism. This discovery led Beecher to reshape his understanding of the doctrine of sin. Having been greatly influenced by Charles Grandison *Finney and Nathaniel W. Taylor, Beecher adjusted the Calvinism of the Puritans and Jonathan *Edwards, a move that stirred resistance among Beecher's ministerial colleagues. In 1835 he was tried for heresy on the grounds that he had departed from the *Westminster Confession of Faith. Efforts to censure Beecher eventually failed, and he was cleared of the charges.

Beecher retired from his pastoral duties in 1843 and from the presidency of Lane Seminary in 1850. The final years of his life were spent lecturing and writing. He died in 1863 and was survived by ten of his eleven children, several of whom, notably Harriet Beecher Stowe and Henry Ward Beecher, played important roles in the continuing development of Christianity in New England.

BIBLIOGRAPHY. *ANB* 2; L. Beecher, *The Autobiography of Lyman Beecher*, ed. B. M. Cross, 2 vols. (1961); M. Caskey, *Chariot of Fire: Religion and the*

Beecher Family (1978); *DAB* I; *DARB*; S. C. Henry, *Unvanquished Puritan: A Portrait of Lyman Beecher* (1973); S. E. Mead, *Nathaniel W. Taylor, 1786-1858: A Connecticut Liberal* (1942); *NCAB* 3.

J. R. Fitzmier

Beecher, Willis Judson (1838-1912).† Presbyterian Old Testament scholar. Beecher was born in Hampden, Ohio, and educated at Hamilton College (B.A., 1858; M.A., 1861). After attending Auburn Theological Seminary in New York during the Civil War and being ordained as a Presbyterian minister in 1864, Beecher pastored a church in Ovid, New York, until 1865. He then taught moral science and belles lettres at Knox College, Illinois (1865-1869), and pastored a church in Illinois (1869-1871) before returning to Auburn Seminary, where he remained until retirement as professor of Hebrew language and literature (1871-1908). Beecher served the wider Christian public as a contributor to the *Sunday School Times.* He delivered the 1902 Stone Lectures at Princeton Theological Seminary and served as president of the Society of Biblical Literature in 1904. He was a member of the Presbyterian Church (USA) Committee on the Revision of the Confession of Faith (1890-1892).

As biblical scholar at a time when European higher-critical theories were beginning to be influential in America, Beecher perceived his task as primarily apologetic in nature, not simply defending orthodox views of the Bible but also articulating them to appeal persuasively to his readers. Challenging the underlying assumptions of the new criticism, Beecher charged that the critics dogmatically asserted that all religion advances through an evolutionary development, without convincing proof. Concentrating his work on the prophets and prophecy, as well as the reliability of the Bible, in *Reasonable Biblical Criticism* (1911) he acknowledged that "my conclusions are simply the old orthodoxy." In this effort he sided with Benjamin Breckinridge *Warfield and William Henry *Green by defending an evangelical view of biblical criticism in the pages of the *Presbyterian Review.* Nonetheless, he did not accept the Princeton doctrine of inerrancy, preferring to allow for slight errors, which could be determined by careful, conservative criticism. Such scholarship, in Beecher's mind, would seek critical neutrality and weigh objectively all evidence by the canons of deductive reason but give higher priority to ancient testimony than to modern theories. He proved to be the last stalwart of conservatism at Auburn, as his successor adopted a more radical stance.

Bibliography. *DARB;* M. A. Noll, *Between Faith and Criticism: Evangelicals, Scholarship, and the Bible in America* (1986).

S. Meier

Beets, Henry (1869-1947). *Christian Reformed Church (CRC) minister. Born in a small Dutch town, Koedyk, the Netherlands, Beets was reared in the established church dominated by liberal theology. He emigrated to the United States in 1886, and while clerking in a general store in Luctor, Kansas, Beets began to attend the services at a local church. He made profession of faith soon thereafter and also experienced a call to the ministry. In 1888 he enrolled at Calvin Seminary and came under the influence of Geerhardus *Vos, who began teaching there the same year. He graduated in 1895 and was ordained the same year. He also married Clara Poel of Grand Haven, Michigan.

For four years, beginning in 1895, Beets ministered in Sioux Center, Iowa, and in 1899 he accepted the call to LaGrave Avenue Christian Reformed Church in Grand Rapids, Michigan, one of the few CRC congregations that worshiped in English exclusively. From 1915 until 1920 he served as pastor of LaGrave's daughter church, Burton Heights.

During this time Beets thrived as writer and editor. He saw the need for Reformed literature in English and wrote commentaries on the *Heidelberg Catechism and *Belgic Confession. Beets also had a great interest in American presidents and wrote biographies of William McKinley and Abraham Lincoln. In 1903 he took over as editor of the religious monthly *The Banner,* which in 1914 became the CRC's denominational magazine. Beets served as its editor until 1928. In all he wrote twenty books and hundreds of editorials and articles. For his literary efforts Muskingum College (Ohio) in 1911 awarded Beets an honorary doctorate. In 1934 Queen Wilhelmina also rewarded Beets with an appointment as Knight of the Orange-Nassau Order.

In addition to his pastoral and literary endeavors Beets rendered important service to the CRC in its denominational offices. From 1902 until 1942 he carried out the responsibilities of the stated clerk, corresponding with other denominations and supplying all manner of information about the CRC. In 1920 he left the parish ministry to become the director of missions, a position he occupied until his retirement in 1939. In this position Beets led the CRC to cooperate with other Reformed denominations, especially the *Reformed Church in America (RCA), in foreign missions. To achieve these goals he coedited the *Missionary Monthly* (1917-1947), a joint CRC-RCA publication. He died at his home in Grand Rapids after suffering a stroke.

Under Beets's leadership the CRC became more fully assimilated in American Protestant circles. He also was responsible for cultivating the denomination's ties to the Netherlands and other Reformed communions around the world.

Bibliography. H. Beets, *Catechism of Reformed Doctrine for Advanced Classes* (1928); idem, *The Christian Reformed Church, Its Roots, History, Schools and Mission Work* (1946); idem, *The Compendium Explained* (1919); idem, *The Man of Sorrows* (1935); idem, *Trolling and Trusting: Fifty Years of Mission Work of the Christian Reformed Among Indian and Chinese* (1940); J. D. Bratt, *Dutch Calvinism in America: A History of a Conservative Subculture* (1984); obituary, *The Banner* (November 1947). D. G. Hart and H. Brinks

Belgic Confession. Composed in 1561, the confession was an attempt to defend the Reformed faith against the charge of sedition and to distinguish it from the "rabble-rousing" views of the Anabaptists. Just as John *Calvin wrote a letter to King Francis I of France with the hope of gaining his approval of the new evangelical faith, so Guido de Bres, its principal author, sent a copy of the Belgic Confession with an accompanying appeal to Philip II of Spain in 1562. The result in both cases was the same: neither king acknowledged the validity of this version of the faith.

De Bres was assisted in the writing of the confession by three Dutch Reformed ministers: H. Modetus, G. Wingan and Adrian Saravia, professor of theology in Leyden. Little is known of de Bres's background and conversion to the evangelical faith. Apparently he had no formal theological training, but he was a knowledgable, gifted scholar who won the respect of Reformed Church leaders in England and France as well as that of Prince William of Orange. A native of the French-speaking part of the Low Countries, he spent much of his latter years as a refugee, and in 1567 he died a martyr's death.

The confession was originally written in French but was soon translated into Dutch and later into Latin, Greek and German. A slightly revised version was adopted at a synod in Antwerp in 1566, the Synod of Wesel in 1571, the Synod of Emden in 1571 and the provincial Synod of Dort in 1574. At the great Synod of Dort in 1619 the French, Latin and Dutch texts were revised, and the confession, along with the *Heidelberg Catechism and the *Canons of Dort, was adopted as one of the doctrinal standards of the Reformed Churches in the Netherlands and Belgium. An English version was published in London in 1640, and in 1768 the confession was again translated into English by John W. Livingston of the (Dutch) *Reformed Church in America (RCA). It continues to be one of the confessional standards of that denomination, the *Christian Reformed Church in North America (CRC) and smaller denominations of Dutch Reformed background.

The Belgic Confession is indebted to and modeled on the French (Gallican) Confession that was published in 1560 and also has some affinity with the Scots Confession of 1560. The topics are traditional, but there are a number of distinctive Reformed accents such as a high view of the authority and interpretation of Scripture, the sovereignty and providence of God, original sin, eternal election (but not an explicit statement of double predestination), the satisfaction view of the atonement, justification by grace through faith, sanctification and good works (the latter also sanctified by God's grace), three marks of the church (discipline being the third), a high view of the sacraments (a genuine partaking of the body and blood of Christ in the Lord's Supper) and an exalted view of the role of civil government.

The last topic has been a controversial one, because Article 36 states that the office of the magistracy is not only to maintain civic order but also to "protect the sacred ministry, and thus remove and prevent all idolatry and false worship." This obviously does not apply in a pluralistic culture where there is a separation of church and state, so the Christian Reformed Church in 1958 adopted a substitute statement for the preceding passage.

Bibliography. A. Cochrane, *Reformed Confessions of the Sixteenth Century* (1966); P. Jacobs, *Theologie Reformierter Bekenntnisschriften* (1959); M. E. Osterhaven, *Our Confession of Faith* (1964 popular exposition); L. Verduin, "Belgic Confession," in *Twentieth-Century Encyclopedia of Religious Knowledge* (1955). I. J. Hesselink

Bell, L(emuel) Nelson (1894-1973).‡ Medical missionary and cofounder of *Christianity Today.* Born in Longsdale, Virginia, Bell was converted at age eleven during an evangelistic service held at his church. Educated at Washington and Lee College (B.A., 1912) and Medical College of Virginia (M.D., 1916), Bell spent twenty-five years as a Southern Presbyterian medical missionary in Tsingkiangpu (now Huaiyin), China (1916-1941). Forced out of China by the Japanese occupation, he took up a medical practice in

Asheville, North Carolina (1941-1956).

A conservative evangelical and devoted churchman, Bell urged other conservatives within the *Presbyterian Church in the United States (PCUS) not to withdraw from the denomination. In 1942 he founded the *Southern Presbyterian Journal* (renamed *The Presbyterian Journal* in 1959) in order to promote evangelical and Reformed orthodoxy within the denomination. Bell successfully led the 1950 struggle against the proposed merger of the PCUS with the *Presbyterian Church in the U.S.A. (PCUSA), a move he believed would dilute the witness of Southern Presbyterians. Bell served on the PCUS Board of World Missions (1948-1966). In 1972 he was elected moderator of the 112th general assembly of the PCUS.

In 1956, along with his son-in-law Billy Graham, Bell founded *Christianity Today.* A member of the journal's board of directors, he managed the production of the periodical, wrote occasional articles on missions in the Far East and wrote a regular column entitled "A Layman and His Faith." As a missionary, churchman and national leader, Bell made a significant contribution to twentieth-century evangelicalism.

BIBLIOGRAPHY. J. C. Pollock, *A Foreign Devil in China: The Story of Dr. L. Nelson Bell* (1971).

L. E. Wilshire

Beman, Nathan S. S. (1785-1871). Presbyterian minister and educator. Born at New Lebanon, New York, of German and Scottish ancestry, Beman graduated from Middlebury College, Vermont, in 1807, after which he taught in Lincoln Academy in New Castle, Maine, and tutored at Middlebury. Ordained to the Presbyterian ministry in 1810, he founded a school in Mt. Zion, Georgia, where he taught until 1823, when he was called to the First Presbyterian Church of Troy, New York. In 1845 he was appointed president of Rensselaer Polytechnic Institute.

Beman's eloquent preaching, his teaching of philosophy and his college administration were all superseded by his influence as national leader of the *New School Presbyterian movement. Elected moderator of the general assembly in 1831, he worked to maintain the looser theological and ecclesiastical arrangements allowed by the *Plan of Union (1801), but he departed with the New School when the plan was abrogated in 1837. His evangelistic and abolitionist fervor, as well as his advocacy of the voluntary movement, placed Beman at the front of the New School. Later he became a signatory of the *Auburn Declaration, a document intending to affirm the New School's genuine Presbyterian heritage. His *Christ the Only Sacrifice: or, The Atonement in Its Relations to God and Man* (1844) stirred opposition from Charles *Hodge, by opposing the doctrine of substitutionary atonement.

While Beman's chief contribution was as a New School Presbyterian leader, he gained some prominence by attacking prelacy in the Episcopal Church and the Roman Catholic Church.

BIBLIOGRAPHY. *ANB* 2; *DAB* I; H. B. Nason, *Biographical Records of the Officers and Graduates of the Rensselaer Polytechnical Institute* (1887); *Proceedings of the Centennial Anniversary of the First Presbyterian Church, Troy* (1891).

J. H. Hall

Bennett, Mary Katharine Jones (1864-1950).† Presbyterian home missions leader. Born in Englewood, New Jersey, Bennett graduated from Elmira College (B.A., 1885) and taught school in Englewood from 1885 to 1894. She became the national secretary for Young People's Work, under the Women's Board of Home Missions for her denomination, the *Presbyterian Church in the U.S.A. (PCUSA) in 1894, serving for four years. In 1898 she married Fred Bennett, a prosperous New York manufacturer. A woman with wide interests and leadership abilities, Bennett served first as a member (1898-1909) and then as president of the Women's Board of Home Missions until its merger with the Presbyterian Board of National Missions in 1923. Although it was intended to bring more equality to the structures of the church, the merger eliminated the only institutions over which women had significant control. Bennett was an influential voice for women during this difficult period of change.

In 1916 Bennett was the first woman to make a board report to the general assembly, and in 1923 she became vice president of the newly created National Board of Home Missions. With Margaret *Hodge, vice president of the Board of Foreign Missions, she compiled a blunt report on the "Causes of Unrest Among Women of the Church" (1927). One of the leading churchwomen of her day, Bennett also represented the denomination in ecumenical causes, including the Council of Women for Home Missions (president from 1916 to 1923). She served with the Federal Council of Churches and the National Committee on the Cause and Cure of War, alongside Carrie Chapman Catt and Jane Addams.

BIBLIOGRAPHY. *ANB* 2; R. Balmer and J. R.

Fitzmier, *The Presbyterians* (1993); L. A. Boyd and R. D. Breckenridge, *Presbyterian Women in America* (1983); *NAW* 1. M. L. Bendroth

Berg, Joseph Frederic (1812-1871). German and Dutch Reformed pastor. Born in Antigua, British West Indies, Berg was the son of Moravian missionaries Christian Frederick Berg and Hannah Robinson Tempest Berg. Educated initially at the Moravian school in Falneck, England, in 1825 Berg came to the United States, where he studied theology at the Moravian Academy at Nazareth, Pennsylvania.

In 1835 Berg was ordained by the Synod of the *German Reformed Church and installed as pastor of the Harrisburg, Pennsylvania, congregation, remaining there for slightly more than one year. He became professor of languages at Marshall College at Mercersburg in 1836 and simultaneously served the Reformed congregation there. A call from the German Reformed congregation on Race Street in Philadelphia brought him to that city in 1837. In 1852 he transferred to the Dutch Reformed Church and assumed the pastorate of its Second Church in Philadelphia. During his ministry in the city, he earned the degree of doctor of medicine at Jefferson Medical College. From 1861 to 1871 he was professor of didactic and polemic theology at the Dutch Reformed Theological Seminary at New Brunswick, New Jersey, and he taught religion at Rutgers College from 1862 until 1867.

During Berg's Philadelphia ministry, he was a vigorous opponent of Roman Catholicism. He edited *The Protestant Banner* (1842-1845), *The Protestant Quarterly Review* (1844-1854) and *The Evangelical Quarterly* (1851-1861) and published his *Lectures on Romanism* (1840), *The Great Apostasy* (1842), *The Jesuits* (1851) and *Papal Usurpation* (1855) as well as other anti-Catholic sermons, lectures, tracts and books. He was a founding member of the American Protestant Association.

Berg died in New Brunswick, New Jersey. He is remembered primarily for his activities in the Protestant-Catholic controversies of the mid-nineteenth century.

Bibliography. *ANB* 2; *DAB* II; *The Fathers of the Reformed Church* IV, ed. D. Y. Heisler (1881); *Historical Directory of the Reformed Church in America,* ed. P. N. Vandenberge (1992); *A Manual of the Reformed Church in America, 1628-1902,* ed. E. T. Corwin (1902); *The Reformed Church Messenger* (July 26, 1871) 4. J. B. Frantz

Berkhof, Louis (1873-1957).† Reformed theologian. He was born in the Dutch province of Drenthe, and Berkhof's parents belonged to the pietist-orthodox Seceder (1834) branch of the Reformed church. (Herman *Bavinck, whose work Berkhof's theology relies on most, shared this regional and religious cast.) The family emigrated to the United States in 1882, settling in Grand Rapids, Michigan, where Louis spent virtually the rest of his life. In 1900 he graduated from the *Christian Reformed Church's Theological School in Grand Rapids and, between two Christian Reformed pastorates, did two years (1902-1904) of graduate work in theology at Princeton Theological Seminary. In 1906 he was appointed to the Grand Rapids (later Calvin) Seminary, where he served the rest of his career as professor of biblical theology (1906-1914), New Testament (1914-1926) and systematic theology (1926-1944). From 1931 to 1944 he served as president of that institution.

In his early years at Calvin, Berkhof followed the lead of the Dutch prime minister and Reformed theologian, Abraham *Kuyper, in his trenchant critique of "revolutionary individualism" and affirmation of the need to fulfill the cultural mandate. Berkhof published several books applying Calvinistic principles to social issues such as industrialism and the impact of redemption on society and culture. While calling for the improvement of culture, he also argued that this needed to be done in separate, distinctly Christian organizations.

Around 1920 Berkhof helped purge the Christian Reformed Church (CRC) of the perceived influx of dispensational *fundamentalism and higher-critical modernism. The latter struck him as the far graver error. Consequently the second half of his career, devoted to articulating a Reformed theological consensus, was marked by a consistent antimodernist agenda. Berkhof produced his monumental works in the early 1930s: *Reformed Dogmatics* (1932; in later editions, *Systematic Theology),* and its popular distillation, *Manual of Reformed Doctrine* (1933). These bear the influence of Berkhof's Princeton mentor, Gerhardus *Vos, and of Bavinck, whose *Gereformeerde Dogmatiek* (1906-1911) Berkhof followed in format, substance and much detail. Throughout, the works show his tradition's taut theocentricity. All initiative, virtue and certainty reside with God; all the opposite, with humanity. Accordingly, the crucial task of life is obedience to divine authority, which is presented for human appropriation in Scripture. For theology in particular, Berkhof insisted that Scripture is the only source and norm. Human reason, experience or church tradition should neither supplement it nor affect its reading. On these bulwarks Berkhof erected his systematics, hewing to a moderate line on the classic issues of Calvinist controversy and reproving modernist proposals.

Berkhof rejected rationalistic strictures on the Bible and orthodoxy yet showed a rationalistic frame of mind himself. Faith alone could appropriate the saving truth of revelation, but reason's job of arraying these truths in systematic unity was vital. Ideas dictated action, and true Christian experience had to follow doctrinal formulations. Thus, after 1920 Berkhof largely gave up his earlier talent for social-cultural commentary and concentrated instead on creating a theological fortress for a beleaguered group facing troubled times. The scope and rigor of his work, as well as its appeal beyond its original audience (particularly among evangelicals of a generally Reformed persuasion), show the strength of his tradition and the talent with which he defended it.

See also Dutch Reformed in America.

Bibliography. *ANB* 2; J. D. Bratt, *Dutch Calvinism in Modern America: A History of a Conservative Subculture* (1984); H. Zwaanstra, "Louis Berkhof," in *Reformed Theology in America,* ed. D. F. Wells (1985). J. D. Bratt

Bertholf, Guiliam (1656-1726). *Dutch Reformed minister. Born in Sluis, in the province of Zeeland, Bertholf emigrated to the Dutch colony of New Amsterdam in 1683 as a farmer and cooper. Although largely self-taught, he was a highly regarded lay reader and read sermons at the Harlem congregation until about 1690, when he purchased a farm in Hackensack, New Jersey. Thereafter (1694-1726) he ministered to the Hackensack and Passaic congregations. He also served as an itinerant pastor to scattered Dutch settlers along the Raritan Valley.

In 1694 Bertholf returned to the Netherlands to be ordained by the Classis of Middleburg, thus avoiding the Amsterdam Classis, which opposed the experiential piety Bertholf practiced because of its apparent anticlericalism. His spiritual mentor, Jacobus Koelman, a well-known pietist with little regard for church rules, had so influenced the character of the Middleburg Classis that Bertholf readily received its acclaim and ordination. Consequently the more regularly ordained and formally trained clergy of New York regarded Bertholf as a disruptive maverick who endangered the influence of New York's ecclesiastical authority throughout New Jersey. However, due to the scarcity of ordained pastors and the complications of colonial-era travel, Bertholf functioned with little interference and was, according to surviving reports, well regarded as a hard-working preacher and counselor. His affinities were with the frontier parishioners and that segment of the *Reformed Church in America (RCA) that favored independence from the Classis of Amsterdam, particularly in the education and ordination of the clergy. Bertholf helped to stamp the Dutch colonial congregations with the pietism and revivalism that the Great Awakening nurtured.

Little is known about the life and death of Bertholf, as is the case with many Dutch pastors of that era. Still, his ministry was crucial to establishing Dutch churches in the new world even as the piety he encouraged would eventually diminish the distinctive old-world beliefs and practices of the Dutch Reformed churches.

Bibliography. *ANB* 2; R. Balmer, *A Perfect Babel of Confusion: Dutch Religion and English Culture in the Middle Colonies* (1989); F. F. De Jong, *The Dutch Reformed Church in the American Colonies* (1978). H. Brinks

Bethune, Joanna Graham (1770-1860). Founder of charitable societies. Born in Canada and reared in Scotland, Joanna Graham came to New York City in 1789 with her widowed mother, the noted Presbyterian laywoman Isabella Graham. After her marriage to Scottish-born merchant Divie Bethune in 1795, Bethune devoted much of her life to educational and philanthropic causes, often in concert with her mother and husband. (She also bore six children, three of whom survived to adulthood.) Among the groups she founded or cofounded were the Society for the Relief of Poor Widows with Small Children (1797), an early Sunday school (1803), the Orphan Asylum Society (1806), a House of Industry (1814), the Female Union Society for the Promotion of Sabbath Schools (1816) and an Infant School Society (1827). During the latter portion of her life, she devoted herself especially to the orphan asylum and to the infant school cause. Before paid careers became available to women, Bethune forged a successful, if voluntary, career in the field of benevolence.

Bibliography. *ANB* 2; G. W. Bethune, *Memoirs of Mrs. Joanna Bethune* (1863); *NAW* 1.

A. M. Boylan

Beveridge, Thomas (1796-1873). *United Presbyterian pastor and seminary and college professor. Born at Cambridge, New York, Beveridge received his training at Union College, New York (1814), and Service Seminary (1819). He then pastored Associate Synod congregations at Sugar Creek and Xenia,

Ohio (1821-1824), and Philadelphia (1827-1835) before being called to serve as professor at Canonsburg Seminary (1835-1855), where he also pastored churches in Washington and Venice, Pennsylvania (1849-1855). He finished his career as professor of church history and biblical criticism at Xenia Seminary from 1855 to 1871.

Beveridge's long service to the church forged enduring links between the old Associate (Seceder) tradition and the United Presbyterian Church. Son of a Scottish immigrant Seceder minister in the upper Hudson Valley, he was one of John Anderson's students in the Service Seminary. Beveridge taught for thirty-six years in the seminaries of the church: in the Associate seminary at Canonsburg and then at Xenia, where the seminary was first an Associate, then a United Presbyterian seminary. Beveridge died at Xenia, Ohio.

BIBLIOGRAPHY. J. McNaugher, *History of Theological Education in the United Presbyterian Church* (1931); J. B. Scouller, *Encyclopedia Manual of the United Presbyterian Church* (1887). W. L. Fisk

Bible, Presbyterians and the. Formal Presbyterian definition concerning the Bible begins with the *Westminster Confession. Once the Westminster Confession, along with the Larger and Shorter Catechisms, came to define Presbyterian confessional identity in Scotland, Ireland and North America, its statements on the Bible became the norm. Modern scholars debate the exact implications of Westminster statements on Scripture, but the main assertions of the confession's first chapter have never been in doubt. Scripture offers especially "that knowledge of God, and of his will, which is necessary unto salvation." "The Bible" means the sixty-six books of the Protestant canon and excludes the Apocrypha. The authority of Scripture does not rest on human testimony "but wholly upon God." Many valid arguments can be mounted to show the inspiration of Scripture, yet "our full persuasion and assurance of the infallible truth, and divine authority thereof, is from the inward work of the Holy Spirit, bearing witness by and with the Word in our hearts." Not everything in the Bible is equally clear, but "the whole counsel of God, concerning all things necessary for his own glory, man's salvation, faith, and life, is either expressly set down in Scripture, or by good and necessary consequence may be deduced from Scripture." In interpreting any one part of Scripture, the most reliable guide is to be found in other parts of Scripture. Finally, for all "controversies of religion," the "Supreme Judge" is "the Holy Spirit speaking in the Scripture."

Before the Era of Criticism. The statements of the Westminster Confession on Scripture gave North American Presbyterians a plumb line for their theology, but they by no means ended debate. Already in the eighteenth century, Presbyterians debated the implications of their confession and have continued to do so ever since. In the 1720s the new church in the American colonies was wracked by the same debate over whether ministers and elders should be required to subscribe the Westminster Confession and Catechisms that beset sister churches in Scotland and especially Northern Ireland at the same time. (In America, however, that debate was not linked, as it was in Ireland, with the drift of some Presbyterians toward Socinianism or Unitarianism.) The *Adopting Act of 1729 represented a compromise tilting toward the conservatives. It required ministers to subscribe as an indication of their belief that the Westminster standards preserved the system of Christian doctrine found in the Bible but allowed prospective ministers to be ordained if they had scruples about parts of the standards that presbyteries ruled did not compromise biblical faith.

During the first three-fourths of the nineteenth-century debate shifted more directly to apologetics and biblical interpretation. At the Presbyterians' first seminary, established at Princeton in 1812, faculty members like Archibald *Alexander and Charles *Hodge mounted an effective defense of the system of biblical doctrine found in the Westminster standards while also moving away from Westminster norms in positioning Scripture over against other authorities. At the same time, Hodge was a particularly effective defender of what Westminster had described as biblical teaching on justification, imputation and the atonement. In 1834 Hodge attacked a commentary on Romans by the *New School Presbyterian Albert *Barnes for letting popular American notions of self-sufficiency, as well as assumptions about the power of human choice rooted in the era's common-sense moral philosophy, overwhelm what the Confession had contended were the Bible's teachings on the sinner's unity with Adam and the redeemed person's unity with Christ. Such debates showed that hereditary Presbyterian traditions on how to put the Bible to use were harder to maintain in the charged ideological atmosphere of the new American nation than was a more simple loyalty to Westminster statements about the Bible itself.

Higher Criticism and After. In the last third of the nineteenth century, Presbyterian debate over Scripture broadened to include consideration of Scripture itself. American reaction to European higher criticism occurred at a time when the American churches were placing ever greater emphasis on the professional education of ministers. So it was that intra-Presbyterian debates over the nature of the Bible were almost always also debates on how far Presbyterians should go in appropriating the new biblical scholarship. To liberal evangelicals, such as Charles Augustus *Briggs of Union Seminary in New York, a cautious acceptance of higher criticism did not overthrow the church's historical trust in Scripture. Where scholars did not rule out the possibility of the miraculous, they could make fruitful use of the newer work since, as Briggs put it, "theories of text and author, date, style, and integrity of writings" cannot establish or undercut the more general confidence in the Bible. Evangelical conservatives, like Archibald Alexander *Hodge and Benjamin Breckinridge *Warfield of Princeton Seminary, however, held that the newer critical views compromised the notion of a divinely inspired Bible. The Scripture's account of itself, which Warfield especially set out as the understanding of the Westminster divines, could still be shown to be true, if only scholars would abandon the prejudices of modern scholarship. This debate was sharp, wide-ranging and decisive. In the short term the more conservative side prevailed, and Briggs and one or two other prominent seminary professors who shared these views were forced out of the Northern Presbyterian church. In the long term the Briggs position won out, and the more conservative Warfield position was left to be defended in small denominations that splintered off from the larger Northern and Southern Presbyterian churches.

The vigor of late nineteenth-century Presbyterian debates obscured an important reality. In the American spectrum of response to biblical higher criticism, most Presbyterians have been close to the middle—adjustors like Briggs far more conservative than radical academic appropriators of higher criticism and conservatives like Warfield far less literalistic than radical *fundamentalist opponents of higher criticism.

After the dust had settled from the intense Presbyterian debate over Scripture that stretched from the early 1880s to the reorganization of Princeton Seminary in 1929, mainstream Presbyterians, namely, theologians and biblical scholars at Princeton Theological Seminary, Union Seminary (Richmond) and Columbia Theological Seminary, anchored the conservative end of the academic mainstream. Presbyterians in the mainline denominations were also leaders in the biblical theology movement of the 1950s and 1960s as well as in more recent proposals to treat the canon of Scripture as the central focus of biblical research (as opposed to the historical process thought to lie behind the canonical developments). *Neo-orthodox influence manifested itself with the Northern Presbyterian Church's Confession of 1967, which stated that "the church has received the books of the Old and New Testaments as prophetic and apostolic testimony in which it hears the word of God and by which its faith and obedience are nourished and regulated."

For conservative Presbyterians, scholars at Westminster Theological Seminary associated with the *Orthodox Presbyterian Church (OPC) have provided leadership in the discussion of Scripture. The seminary's founder, J. Gresham *Machen, was an accomplished New Testament scholar who in major books defended a traditional view of the virgin birth of Christ and the harmony between Jesus and Paul. Machen's successor, Ned B. *Stonehouse, pioneered in showing how a confessionally traditional view of the Bible could be joined to historically sensitive study of the Gospels. At Westminster theologians have also promoted the work of Geerhardus *Vos, who from his post at Princeton Seminary (1893-1932) had urged a consideration of Scripture as progressive unfolding of the divinely sanctioned history of redemption. Presbyterian conservatives from other seminaries and belonging to other denominations joined scholars from Westminster in defending the inerrancy of the Bible during the 1970s and 1980s.

Canada. In Canada the story of Presbyterian engagement with Scripture features the same landmarks as in the United States, only less so. At least three factors have kept *Canadian Presbyterian debate on Scripture more restrained than that in the United States. First, Canadian Presbyterianism remained closely tied to the fortunes of the Scottish Kirk well into the twentieth century and continued to be shaped by events in Scotland. Second, the larger role for tradition in Canadian life more generally meant that in Presbyterian colleges and seminaries less attention has been paid to questions of biblical authority than in the United States. Canadian traditionalism meant that debate over Scripture did not have quite the same all-or-nothing implications that they have had in the United States. Third, Presbyterian contention over joining the United Church of Canada forced attention to issues concerning what it meant to be a Presbyterian more generally rather than to narrower issues concerning the Bible. Both for Presbyterians who joined the United Church, established in 1925, and for those who remained in the continuing Presbyterian church, the Bible, however important, was not the focus of ecclesiastical debate.

The result of this Canadian context was that leading Presbyterians, though their views on Scripture may have closely resembled the views of leading American spokesmen, were never identified so closely with carefully defined positions on the Bible. The spectrum of biblical views among Canadian Presbyterians has probably been somewhat narrower than the spectrum among American Presbyterians. Conservatives have been held close to a moderate center by influences from Scotland and then later from British InterVarsity connections. Liberal evangelicals have been pushed toward the moderate center by similar influences from Scotland and then by the conservative kind of neo-orthodoxy that came to prevail in Canada. And both confessionalists and liberal evangelicals, who may have engaged more actively in debate over the Bible if they had been given the chance, lived in a church preoccupied by a theological agenda defined more by questions not directly touching Scripture—for instance, Scottish inheritance and the needs of Canada—than was the case in the United States.

Conclusion. Within a North American context, Presbyterian engagement with Scripture has been distinct. Unlike Roman Catholics, who, whatever happens in local situations, retain a carefully defined doctrinal authority in the church's magisterium, North American Presbyterians are shaped by an informal confessional tradition with no agreed-upon means of enforcing authority. Unlike university scholars of religion, who, whatever their personal beliefs, tend to follow the trajectory of academic fashion, Presbyterians have tempered their extensive academic work with a confessional tradition. Unlike many popular evangelical groups, who, however they may diverge in practice, speak as one in desiring to shape practice and belief by the Bible alone, Presbyterians have always acknowledged that their loyalty to the Bible is shaped by the Westminster standards as well as by historic Presbyterian efforts to apply or modify the confession. In other words, in their position as confessional as well as Protestant and American, Presbyterians have occupied the same narrow ground held by the German and Dutch Reformed churches, the Lutherans and (with different ecclesiastical arrangements) the Mennonites. If the continuing Presbyterian witness does not demonstrate the truth of what Westminster said about the Bible, it is still convincing evidence that the divines were at least asking the right questions.

Bibliography. M. J. Coalter, J. M. Mulder and L. B. Weeks, eds., *The Confessional Mosaic* (1990); H. M. Conn, ed., *Inerrancy and Hermeneutic* (1988); W. Klempa, ed., *The Burning Bush and a Few Acres of Snow* (1994); B. J. Longfield, *The Presbyterian Controversy* (1991); J. S. Moir, *Enduring Witness* (rev. ed., 1987); M. A. Noll, *Between Faith and Criticism: Evangelicals, Scholarship, and the Bible in America* (rev. ed., 1991); idem, "Presbyterians and Biblical Authority," designated issue of *JPH* 59 (summer 1981) 95-284; J. B. Rogers, *Scripture in the Westminster Confession* (1967); J. B. Rogers and D. K. McKim, *The Authority and Interpretation of the Bible* (1979); J. H. Skilton, ed., *Scripture and Confession* (1973); S. J. Stein, "Stuart and Hodge on Romans 5:12-21: An Exegetical Controversy about Original Sin," *JPH* 47 (December 1969) 340-58.

M. A. Noll

Bible Presbyterian Church.† A Presbyterian denomination born out of the *fundamentalist-modernist controversy. In 1936 the Presbyterian Church of America (later the *Orthodox Presbyterian Church [OPC]) was founded by a group of pastors and elders who left the *Presbyterian Church in the U.S.A. (PCUSA). The immediate cause for this exodus was the suspension of J. Gresham *Machen and J. Oliver *Buswell Jr. from the Presbyterian ministry due to their support of an independent mission board that sought to ensure biblical teaching on Presbyterian mission fields. The newly formed denomination was soon drawn into internal conflict. Differences in doctrine, ethics and church government, coupled with suspicions and disagreements, led Buswell, Carl *McIntire, Allan MacRae, and others to separate and form the Bible Presbyterian Church (BPC) in 1937, taking the Independent Board for Presbyterian Foreign Missions with them.

At its first synod the BPC amended the *Westminster standards to teach premillennialism (although allowing liberty on millennial issues) and included a declaratory statement affirming the universal sufficiency and offer of the atonement and the universal salvation of those dying in infancy. A piety that included abstinence from alcohol was enjoined, and a church government allowing greater freedom to the local church and both independent and church-controlled agencies was established. The chief characteristic was a self-conscious denominational testimony for the Bible and Jesus Christ, which issued in a separatist stance calling for separation from apostasy as well as from those having fellowship with apostates. The new church described itself as "Calvinistic, fundamental, premillennial and evangelistic."

McIntire, the leading figure in the BPC, was the moving force behind virtually every institution in the young denomination. He began the *Christian Beacon* in 1936 and founded Faith Theological Seminary as the rival to Westminster Theological Seminary, which had close ties to the OPC. He was also the primary architect of the *American Council of Christian Churches (ACCC, 1941) and the International Council of Christian Churches (ICCC, 1948) and a vigorous supporter of the Independent Board for Presbyterian Foreign Missions, denying the need for an official denominational missions board.

The separatistic bent, however, proved harmful to evangelistic efforts, and tension grew between various elements in the church. In 1945 the Harvey Cedars Resolutions temporarily assuaged the rising discontent by affirming the need for moral separation from worldly sins such as playing games that normally involved gambling, theater attendance, modern dance, alcohol and tobacco as well as ecclesiastical separation in religious activities from unbelievers and caution when dealing with believers who associated with modernists.

In 1954 several younger ministers, led by Robert G. Rayburn, challenged McIntire's "oligarchical" tendencies and overzealous separatism, arguing that his un-Presbyterian methods were driving the church into congregationalism. In the acrimonious months that followed, MacRae sided with McIntire, and Buswell defended the younger ministers. In response Buswell, Rayburn, and several others were dropped from leadership positions on the Independent Board of Missions and the denomination's educational institutions, which were under McIntire's influence. The majority of the BPC, at the April synod of 1956, voted to withdraw from the ACCC and ICCC, which led to the withdrawal of McIntire and roughly 40 percent of the church to form the Bible Presbyterian Church, Collingswood Synod. This body remains about the same size today as it was in 1956.

The majority, desiring to maintain BPC distinctives such as premillennialism, Calvinism and a milder form of separatism, continued as the Bible Presbyterian Church, Columbus Synod, establishing new institutions: Covenant College (1956) and Covenant Seminary (1957), which attracted most of Faith Seminary's faculty after the split, World Presbyterian Missions and National Presbyterian Missions. Younger voices in the church, such as Francis *Schaeffer and Jay Adams, encouraged the denomination to remember its Presbyterian and Reformed heritage while actively pursuing evangelism and opportunities for church union. Adams reopened the millennial issue by arguing for an amillennial position in a debate with Buswell, a discussion that opened the doors for union proposals with the predominantly amillennialist *Reformed Presbyterian Church in North America, General Synod (RPCNA, GS). In 1958 the synod reaffirmed the 1937 statement on millennial liberty in the church, and in 1961 it effectively neutralized the premillennial clause that they had added to the Westminster standards. It changed its name to the *Evangelical Presbyterian Church (EPC) and four years later merged with the RPCNA, GS, to form the *Reformed Presbyterian Church, Evangelical Synod.

Bibliography. *The Constitution of the Bible Presbyterian Church* (1946); G. P. Hutchinson, *The History Behind the Reformed Presbyterian Church, Evangelical Synod* (1974). J. H. Hall

Biederwolf, William Edward (1867-1939).† Popular Presbyterian evangelist. Born at Monticello, Indiana, Biederwolf was converted as a teenager under the evangelistic ministry of Frank N. Palmer, pastor of the Presbyterian church of Monticello. Biederwolf attended Wabash College, Indiana (1889-1890), and Princeton University, where he received his B.A. (1892) and M.A. (1894). Graduating from Princeton Theological Seminary in 1895, he spent a year in evangelistic work before marrying his high school sweetheart, Ida Casad. He then studied for two years under a Princeton Fellowship at the universities of Berlin and Erlangen and the Sorbonne in Paris. Upon returning to the United States, he accepted a call to the Presbyterian church in Logansport, Indiana (1897-1900), a call that was interrupted briefly by his service as an army chaplain in the Spanish-American War. Growing concerned for the salvation of the lost, he spent several years as an assistant to revivalist J. Wilbur Chapman.

In 1906 Bierderwolf launched out on his own, spending much of the next three decades in evangelistic campaigns, primarily in small towns and medium-sized cities in the United States. Biederwolf combined soul winning with advocacy of civic reform, prohibition and Americanism. Strongly opposed to what he considered the anti-American agitations of the rising labor unions, he advocated in their place a deeper commitment to Christ and country, attacking corruption among employers and employees. His revivals would often include a Civico-Religio-Industrial Parade, which would include community leaders and organizations as well as churches. In his later years premillennialism became a favorite theme. He wrote several books on the topic, including *The Millennium Bible* (1924). He also wrote extensively on doctrine, evangelism and the cults, including several collections of sermons.

Elected president of the Interdenominational Association of Evangelists in 1910 and appointed as executive director of the commission on evangelism of the Federal Council of Churches from 1914 to 1917, Biederwolf promoted a conservative evangelical theology with a strong emphasis on ecumenical endeavors. To combat the negative effects of irresponsible evangelists, he was also active in efforts to reduce corruption among revivalists. He participated in the Men and Religion Forward Movement in 1911-1912, a prime example of his blend between evangelism and the social gospel. During a visit to Asia in the early 1920s, he became an advocate for the lepers of Japan and Korea and was instrumental in raising money for the Biederwolf Home for lepers.

In 1922 Biederwolf became director of the Winona Lake Bible Conference, rescuing it from near-bankruptcy. In 1923 he became director of the Winona Lake Bible School of Theology, a position he held until he became its president in 1933. Later he organized and owned The Winona Publishing Company of Chicago. For his leadership and literary endeavors, he was awarded three honorary doctorates from Northern Baptist Theological Seminary, Bob Jones College and Beaver College. Every winter during his final decade (1929-1939) he also pastored the nondenominational Royal Poinciana Chapel in Palm Beach, Florida, called by some the richest congregation in the world.

Bibliography. *ANB* 2; R. E. Garrett, *William Edward Biederwolf: A Biography* (1948); W. G. McLoughlin Jr., *Modern Revivalism: Charles Grandison Finney to Billy Graham* (1959).

W. V. Trollinger

Blackburn, Gideon (1772-1838).‡ Presbyterian minister, educator and missionary. Blackburn was born in Augusta County, but during his boyhood the family moved to Greene County, Tennessee. He studied theology privately and became a Presbyterian minister in 1792, pastoring churches in New Providence and Eusebia near Knoxville.

Increasingly concerned for missions to the Indians, Blackburn urged the matter before the 1803 general assembly. In 1804 he opened a school for Cherokee youth near Charleston, Tennessee, and in 1805 he added a second in Hamilton County. His curriculum stressed religious instruction, agricultural and mechanical arts and self-government. Exhaustion and unproven charges of illegal whiskey trade with the Indians led to his withdrawal from the work in 1810.

Blackburn moved to Franklin, Tennessee, where he opened Harpeth Academy. He also founded Presbyterian churches in Franklin and Nashville and converted Rachel Jackson, the wife of Andrew Jackson. In 1821 Blackburn became pastor of the Presbyterian church in Louisville, Kentucky, and in 1829 he was made president of Danville (now Centre) College. His outspoken antislavery and *New School views forced his resignation in 1830, and he moved to Carlinville, Illinois, where he founded a Presbyterian church and became active in the formation of the Illinois Anti-Slavery Society. Blackburn was also active in efforts to establish a college in Carlinville, an institution that now bears his name (Blackburn College).

Bibliography. *ANB* 2; *AAP* 4; *DAB* I; *DARB; NCAB* 13.

W. J. Wade

Blair, Samuel (1741-1818). Presbyterian and Congregational minister, college president, school teacher, army chaplain and Congressional chaplain. Blair was born in 1741 at Fagg's Manor, Chester County, Pennsylvania, the son of an Irish immigrant and Presbyterian minister. He received his bachelor's (1760) and master's (1763) degrees from the College of New Jersey, where he served as a tutor from 1761 to 1764. His services as a tutor culminated in *An Account of the College of New Jersey,* the first formal history of the college, published in 1764.

Blair was petitioned to candidate at the Second Presbyterian Church of Philadelphia and was ordained by the Presbytery of New Castle in 1764. By the fall of 1765, however, Blair was candidating for the position of junior pastor to the Reverend Joseph Sewall at Boston's Old South Church. The Boston congregation called him unanimously in the spring of 1766. After returning to Philadelphia to gather his possessions, Blair made his move to Boston by sea. The vessel on which Blair traveled was shipwrecked, and he lost everything.

After marrying Susannah Shippen, whose brother and uncle were trustees of the College of New Jersey, on September 24, 1767, Blair was elected the sixth president of his alma mater in October of the same year. Former president Samuel *Finley had died in July, and John *Witherspoon, the board's first choice, had declined the post. Blair's election resulted in part from an effort to prevent *Old Side Presbyterians from gaining ascendancy in Princeton and caused some dismay among friends of the college. When word spread that Witherspoon might accept the presidency if petitioned again, Blair was encouraged to decline the position. He gracefully obliged and remained in Boston.

As a Boston minister, Blair held a seat on the board of overseers at Harvard College, from which he received a master of arts degree in 1767. In the summer of 1769 he became seriously ill and moved to Philadelphia to recover. While he was there, Sewall died, leaving Blair the only minister of the Old South Church. This brought to the fore a standing disagreement between Blair and his parish over the Half-Way Covenant. The church wanted to retain the practice, but Blair felt that at least one parent ought to be a full member before a child was admitted to baptism. Unwilling to compromise, Blair resigned in September without returning to Boston.

The Blairs moved to Germantown, Pennsylvania, and settled permanently in an august mansion. Samuel opened an elite private school. He also established a Presbyterian church in Germantown, the congregation meeting in his house until its building was completed. In 1774 Blair joined the Synod of Philadelphia and began preaching there against British tyranny. He became an army chaplain during the Revolution. He resigned from the army due to illness in December 1782 and returned to a life of religious and cultural leadership in Germantown.

In July of 1787 Blair shocked his contemporaries by coming out in favor of universalism. He was censured by the Philadelphia Presbytery but awarded a doctorate in sacred theology (S.T.D.) by the University of Pennsylvania in 1790. In the same year the federal government moved to Philadelphia, and Blair was appointed chaplain to the House of Representatives. He served in that capacity for two years. The remainder of Blair's life was relatively uneventful. He devoted himself largely to the welfare of the Presbyterians and others in Germantown and became a stockholder in the Germantown and Perkiomen Turnpike Company. He died at home.

Bibliography. J. McLachlan, *Princetonians 1748-1768* (1976); *Sibley's Harvard Graduates* 4; W. B. Sprague, ed., *AAP,* vol. 3 (1858). D. Sweeney

Blake, Eugene Carson (1906-1985).† Presbyterian minister, ecumenist and civil rights leader. Born in Missouri, Blake majored in philosophy at Princeton University, where he devoted his life to Christian ministry during a student conference at Northfield, Massachusetts (made famous by Dwight L. Moody and Robert *Speer). After teaching for a year at Forman Christian College in Lahore, India (now Pakistan), he attended New College of Edinburgh and Princeton Theological Seminary. Ordained in the *Presbyterian Church in the U.S.A. (PCUSA), he served a short stint as assistant pastor in a church in New York City and in 1935 was called to the pulpit of First Presbyterian Church of Albany, New York, a congregation of twelve hundred members. Five years later he moved to Pasadena Presbyterian Church (thirty-five hundred members) in California before being elected stated clerk of the denomination in 1951. Blake took the clerk's office to new heights of power and influence, ably serving the church in that capacity until 1966 and overseeing the merger of his denomination with *United Presbyterian Church of North America in 1958 to form the United Presbyterian Church in the U.S.A.

From attending the first meeting of the World Council of Churches in 1948 at his own expense to his term as president of the National Council of the Churches of Christ from 1954 to 1957, Blake developed his outline for ecumenical reunion, which he articulated in his famous 1960 sermon, "A Proposal Toward the Reunion of Christ's Church." Blake called all Christians to unite in a church that would be "truly catholic and truly reformed." A truly catholic church would require at least three things: it would have "visible and historical continuity" with the whole church of all ages; it would confess the historic Apostles' and Nicene creeds; and it would be marked by the sacraments of baptism and the Lord's Supper as true means of grace. Likewise, he set forth three aspects of the church's reformed character: it would continually be reforming itself; it would oppose all inequalities in a true democratic spirit, insisting that "all Christians are Christ's ministers"; and it would allow a wide variety of doctrinal and liturgical expression. This sermon was widely publicized and was extremely influential in the organization of the Consultation on Church Union.

From 1966 until 1972 Blake was the general secretary of the World Council of Churches, based in Geneva, Switzerland. In that work he enabled the 1968 assembly in Uppsala to take place, a benchmark gathering for its leadership by churches from emerging nations. An ardent supporter of international ecumenism, he was instrumental in involving Third World churches in the World Council of Churches and worked diligently to include Eastern Orthodox churches from behind the Iron Curtain. Equally fervent in behalf of racial justice, he led many white Protestants in the 1963 March on Washington, where he proclaimed, "We are late, but we are here." Later that summer he was arrested for trying to integrate an amusement park in Baltimore. He remained an active churchman until his death.

Bibliography. *ANB* 2; R. D. Brackenridge, *Eugene Carson Blake, Prophet with Portfolio* (1978).

L. B. Weeks

Boardman, William Edwin (1810-1886). Presbyterian minister and advocate of the higher Christian life. Born in Smithfield, New York, Boardman pursued a number of unsuccessful business ventures and led a restless life until he had a religious experience while working in the small mining town of Potosi, Wisconsin. There he assumed leadership of the small "Plan of Union" church, and by 1843 he had enrolled in Lane Theological Seminary in Cincinnati, where he remained for three years. Ordained a Presbyterian minister, by 1852 he was serving in a *New School Presbyterian church in Detroit, Michigan, where he later served as a missionary of the American Sunday-School Union, eventually moving to their central office in Philadelphia in 1855. After a brief sojourn in California (1859-1862) for the sake of his wife's health, Boardman worked for the United States Christian Commission during the Civil War (c. 1862-c. 1865), serving as its executive secretary. In 1870, after several years in business, Boardman became publicly associated with holiness teachings.

A biography of James Brainerd Taylor had provided Boardman his first acquaintance with the higher life concept, and an itinerant Methodist minister had pointed him to the writings of Charles Grandison *Finney and Asa Mahan. Boardman had read them eagerly, but his Reformed background naturally inclined him to resist Wesleyan terminology in describing the believer's spiritual pilgrimage. Boardman's frequent attendance at Phoebe Palmer's "Tuesday Meetings for the Promotion of Holiness" and his brief term as leader of the Union Holiness Convention reveal how closely he sympathized with the holiness emphasis. His description of his own second conversion reflects the language of second blessing holiness revivalists. The Wesleyan and Oberlin perfectionist teaching and expression that flow through his book *The Higher Christian Life* (1858) combined to produce a statement of the nature and reality of the holy life that was more widely received than were the expositions in the more classic traditions.

Boardman later participated with Robert Pearsall Smith in the English holiness conferences at Brighton and Oxford in 1874 and 1875. After a brief trip to America in June 1875, he returned to England in December 1875 to make his home there. The last years of his life were spent in a healing ministry, reflected in *The Lord That Healeth Thee* (1881).

Boardman's ministry and writings were instrumental in opening the doors of non-Methodist churches to the teachings of the holiness revival. Drawing on his own spiritual pilgrimage and denying any personal theological sophistication, Boardman described in simple language a religious experience characterized by victory over sin.

Bibliography. Mrs. W. E. Boardman, *Life and Labors of the Reverend W. E. Boardman* (1887); M. E. Dieter, *The Holiness Revival of the Nineteenth Century* (1980); B. B. Warfield, *Perfectionism* (1931).

W. S. Gunter

Boehm, John Philip (1683-1749).† *German Reformed pioneer in Pennsylvania. Born the son of a Reformed pastor in Hochstadt, a small town in the German principality of Hesse-Cassel, Boehm served as schoolmaster to Reformed congregations in Worms (1708-1715) and Lambsheim (1715-1720). Because of conflict with town authorities in Lambsheim, Boehm emigrated to southeastern Pennsylvania, arriving with his family in 1720. Settling in the Perkiomen Valley with other German Reformed people, Boehm was soon asked to lead worship services. In 1725 the Reformed settlers north of Philadelphia persuaded Boehm to assume the pastoral office, and the sacrament of the Lord's Supper was first celebrated late that year, a point marking the inception of regular German Reformed worship in Pennsylvania.

The legitimacy of Boehm's ministry was challenged by Georg Michael Weiss, a Heidelberg-educated Reformed minister who arrived in 1727. Denouncing Boehm as "an incompetent preacher," he declared that since Boehm was not ordained, it was illegal for him to administer the *sacraments. In response the congregations served by Boehm appealed to the Classis of Amsterdam of the Dutch Reformed Church, which ruled that Boehm's call was legal, on the condition that he receive ordination. This was agreed upon by Weiss, and Boehm was ordained November 23, 1729. The German Reformed group continued under the oversight of the Dutch church until 1791.

After Weiss's departure in 1730, Boehm immediately faced a challenge from John Peter Mueller, a mystical individualist who opposed the developing relationship with the Dutch Reformed Church. Rejecting the Dutch authorities, he was ordained by the Presbyterian Church and later became a Seventh Day Dunker. Meanwhile, two other German ministers, John Rieger and John Henry Goetschy, interfered in

Boehm's congregations from 1731 to 1739.

The arrival in 1741 of the Moravian leader Count Nicholas von Zinzendorf, whose aim it was to unite all the German sects, represented a more serious threat to the young church's existence. Through much effort Boehm prevented his congregations from joining the Moravians. He was convinced that Zinzendorf's rejection of traditional authority left nothing but an impoverished experiential religion, and he was unwilling to abandon the richness of the *Heidelberg Catechism for the obscure articles of the Synod of Berne or Zinzendorf's own catechism, which made little reference to "the articles of our Christian faith."

Having established nearly a dozen churches, Boehm requested the Dutch Reformed Church to assist him in finding more ministers. In 1746 he was joined by Michael *Schlatter, who was able to relieve the aging Boehm of most of the difficult travel. Realizing the need for permanent ecclesiastical structure, Boehm worked with Schlatter to establish a German Reformed Coetus (Convention) in 1747, which adopted the Heidelberg Catechism and the *Canons of Dort as its confessional standards. Boehm died on April 29, 1749, after twenty-four years of ministry and the founding of twelve congregations.

Bibliography. *ANB* 3; *DAB* I; *DARB;* W. J. Hinke, *Life and Letters of the Reverend John Philip Boehm* (1916); idem, *Ministers of the German Reformed Congregations in Pennsylvania and Other Colonies in the Eighteenth Century* (1951).

W. B. Evans

Bogardus, Everardus (1607-1647).† Dutch Reformed minister. Bogardus studied at Leyden University and ministered briefly in Guinea before being ordained by the Classis of Amsterdam in 1632. He was sent to New Amsterdam the following year to replace Jonas Michaelius as minister of the Dutch Reformed church there, and he married Anneke Jans, a fairly well-off widow. In 1642, during the besotted wedding feast of his stepdaughter, Bogardus secured subscriptions for a new church building, including some rather lavish commitments that he refused later to forgive.

During his career in New Netherland, Bogardus ran afoul of two of the West India Company's directors-general. The dominie criticized Wouter Van Twiller for incompetence, a charge no one was likely to refute. In 1636 the colony's prosecutor brought charges against Bogardus before the Classis of Amsterdam, but he was deemed too valuable to the colony to let him return to the Netherlands to defend himself, so the matter was postponed. When Bogardus condemned Willem Kieft's slaughter of neighboring Indians in 1643, however, he touched off a bitter feud with the director-general, who boycotted Dutch services, instigated others to disrupt them and pressed charges against the dominie. Refusing to settle for arbitration in the colony, both Kieft and Bogardus sailed for the Netherlands in 1647 to resume their quarrel before the classis there. Their boat, however, was shipwrecked off the coast of Wales, and both men perished.

Bibliography. *ANB* 3; *DAB* I; Q. Breen, "Dominie Everardus Bogardus," *CH* 2 (1933) 78-90; E. T. Corwin, *A Manual of the Reformed Church in America* (1879).

R. H. Balmer

Bomberger, John Henry Augustus (1817-1890).† *German Reformed minister. Born in Lancaster, Pennsylvania, Bomberger was the sole member of the first graduating class of Marshall College (1837) and then received his theological training at Mercersburg Theological Seminary (1838), where he studied under Friedrich Augustus *Rauch, the progenitor of the Mercersburg theology. He was ordained that year as pastor of the German Reformed Church in Lewiston, Pennsylvania, and after serving several other pastorates, Bomberger ministered at the prestigious Race Street Church in Philadelphia from 1854 to 1870, where he spun off three daughter churches and became president of the denomination's board of home missions. In 1870 he accepted the position of president and professor of moral and mental philosophy and evidences of Christianity at Ursinus College in Collegeville, Pennsylvania, which he and other conservatives founded to combat the perceived errors being inculcated at Mercersburg. Some of Bomberger's best known writings were penned in opposition to the Mercersburg theology of John Williamson *Nevin and Philip *Schaff.

From 1868 to 1877 Bomberger edited *The Reformed Church Monthly,* which served as the primary organ for his anti-Mercersburg views. A main area of contention was the proposed revision of the liturgy of the German Reformed Church. Nevin was appointed chairman of the revision committee in 1849, and a year later Schaff took over as chairman. Bomberger served on the committee, and work was completed in 1857. In 1861 the committee was again at work considering suggested revisions, but by that time a rift had developed between factions led by Nevin and Bomberger. From that point on Bomberger, who had defended Nevin and Schaff against charges of heresy in 1845, was a vigorous opponent of Nevin and the entire Mercersburg system. In 1867 he published *The Revised Liturgy, a History and Criticism of the Ritualistic Movement in the German Reformed Church* and *Reformed, Not Ritualistic: A Reply to Dr. Nevin's "Vindication."* Other notable publications by Bomberger were two volumes of a condensed translation of Johann Jakob Herzog's *Realencyklopadie* (1856-1860); a revised translation of Johann Heinrich Kurtz's *Textbook of Church History* (1860); *Infant Salvation in Its Relation to Infant Depravity, Infant Regeneration and Infant Baptism* (1859) and *Five Years at the Race Street Church* (1860).

Bomberger served his church as delegate to the 1884 meeting of the Alliance of Reformed Churches in Belfast and was an active member of such voluntary societies as the American Tract Society, American Bible Society and the American Sunday-School Union. An ardent abolitionist, during the Civil War he championed the Christian Commission and energetically joined the chorus of patriotic preachers urging the nation to sacrificial service.

BIBLIOGRAPHY. *ANB* 3; *DAB* I.

S. R. Graham

Boudinot, Elias (Galagina) (c. 1802-1839).† Tribal leader and publisher among the Cherokee Indians. Born near Rome, Georgia, as a young man he was sent to study at the Foreign Mission School at Cornwall, Connecticut. While at the school he converted to Christianity and also took the name Elias Boudinot from a patron of the school. He became widely influential as a Christian leader among his tribe. After his schooling in New England, which included a year at Andover Theological Seminary (1822-1823), he returned to Georgia. A lifelong Presbyterian, in 1826 he married Harriet Ruggles Gold, which caused a furor in the white community. The Boudinots had six children before Harriet died in 1836. His second wife, Delight Sargent, was soon widowed.

Working with missionary Samuel A. Worcester, Boudinot translated a variety of religious and educational literature into the Cherokee language, including portions of the Bible. In 1828, at the direction of the Cherokee National Council, Boudinot began publication of *The Cherokee Phoenix,* the first American Indian newspaper. While most of the articles were in English, at least one-quarter was written in the Cherokee language. He remained editor until 1835, when the Georgia authorities suppressed the paper for its strident criticisms of the government. In 1833 the United Brethren Missionary Society published his first book in his native tongue, *Poor Sarah or the Indian Woman.*

While Boudinot strongly encouraged moral and educational reforms among the Cherokee, he also chastised the government for insensitivity to traditional tribal culture. In his eyes, Christianizing and civilizing his tribe were for the good of his people. Far from absorbing the Indian into American society, he wanted to preserve Cherokee identity while benefiting from the advantages of white civilization. When the removal controversy engulfed the Cherokees, Boudinot first opposed the idea but later advocated emigration to the West as the most prudent alternative and the only way to maintain cultural identity. In 1835, without official authority, he signed the removal agreement (The Treaty of New Echota), thus earning the wrath of the party of Cherokees determined to resist removal. In June 1839, shortly after he had moved to the Indian Territory, he was murdered by embittered opponents of the treaty. His son Elias attempted to continue his father's educational reforms with moderate success.

BIBLIOGRAPHY. *ANB* 3; *DAB* I; *DARB;* R. H. Gabriel, *Elias Boudinot, Cherokee, and His America* (1941); *NCAB* 19; T. Perdue, ed., *Cherokee Editor: The Writings of Elias Boudinot* (1983). M. S. Joy

Bouma, Clarence (1891-1962). *Christian Reformed Church (CRC) professor and journalist. Born in Harlingen, Friesland, the Netherlands, Bouma immigrated to Grand Rapids, Michigan, in 1905. He was educated at Calvin College (B.A., 1914), Calvin Theological Seminary (V.D.M., 1917), Princeton Theological Seminary (B.D., 1918), Princeton University (M.A., 1919) and Harvard Divinity School (Th.D., 1921). After serving a Christian Reformed congregation in Passaic, New Jersey, in 1924 he returned to Calvin Seminary, where he taught systematic theology (1924-1926) and ethics and apologetics (1926-1952). Retiring early because of illness, Bouma died at Grand Rapids on August 12, 1962.

For most of his career Bouma was the CRC's leading voice of *Kuyperian neo-Calvinism, which he adapted to the American setting and propounded through the *Calvin Forum,* a monthly journal he founded and edited from 1935 to 1951. He denounced theological liberalism in the churches and naturalistic and individualistic currents in American society. An outspoken commentator on public affairs, he defended the New Deal at home and vigorously championed internationalism against mainline Protestant pacifism and CRC isolationism.

In all his work Bouma aimed to refurbish Calvinism as a worldview and as a practical program for modern society. He published Reformed voices from around the world and organized aid to the stricken churches of Holland and Hungary after World War II. He was the CRC's chief emissary to postwar neo-evangelicals. Although his ambitions often brought him frustration, Bouma as much as anyone kept alive the cause of integrative neo-Calvinism with its public responsibility and academic rigor.

Bibliography. C. Bouma papers, Calvin College and Seminary archives; J. D. Bratt, *Dutch Calvinism in Modern America: A History of a Conservative Subculture* (1984). J. D. Bratt

Breckinridge, Robert Jefferson (1800-1871). Presbyterian theologian. Born near Lexington, Kentucky, he graduated from Union College in New York, practiced law and served in the Kentucky legislature. After a little theological study at Princeton Theological Seminary, he became pastor of Second Church, Baltimore (1832-1845). From there he became president of Jefferson College in Pennsylvania (1845-1847) and later pastor of First Church, Lexington, Kentucky, and served as state superintendent of public instruction (1847-1853). Breckinridge founded Danville Seminary in Kentucky, where he served as professor of theology for the remainder of his career (1853-1869).

As editor of the *Baltimore Literary and Religious Magazine* (1835-1841), the *Spirit of the Nineteenth Century* (1842-1843) and the *Danville Quarterly Review* (1861-1865), Breckinridge became known as a controversial churchman. He was an outspoken opponent of slavery, intemperance, universalism, sabbath desecration and Roman Catholicism. Within his own church he initiated the Act and Testimony (1834), a statement of the *Old School party in the Presbyterian Church, which led to the denomination's division in 1837. His vigorous insistence that the church declare full allegiance to the federal government during the *Civil War alienated many in the Synod of Kentucky who left the Northern body for the *Presbyterian Church in the Unites States (PCUS) in 1866. Still, his views in favor of the parity of ministers and ruling elders were influential in Southern Presbyterian church *polity. Breckenridge's major theological contribution was a systematic theology in two volumes, *The Knowledge of God, Objectively Considered* (1858) and *The Knowledge of God, Subjectively Considered* (1859).

Bibliography. *ANB* 3; *DAB* I; *Encyclopedia of the Presbyterian Church in the U.S.A.*, ed. A. Nevin (1884); E. C. Mayse, "Robert Jefferson Breckinridge: American Presbyterian Controversialist," (Ph.D. diss., Union Theological Seminary in Virginia, 1974). A. H. Freundt

Briggs, Charles Augustus (1841-1913).† Biblical scholar and Presbyterian minister. A native of New York City, Briggs was educated at the University of Virginia (1857-1860) and Union Theological Seminary in New York (1861-1863) and, after marrying Julia Dobbs in 1865, studied under Isaac Dorner at the University of Berlin (1866-1869). In 1874, after brief service as a Presbyterian pastor in Roselle, New Jersey, he accepted a call to Union Theological Seminary in New York, where in 1876 he assumed the chair of Hebrew and cognate languages.

In 1880 Briggs became coeditor, with Archibald Alexander *Hodge of Princeton Seminary, of the newly founded *Presbyterian Review*. Before long the *Review* proved to be a source of profound tension as Briggs's higher-critical views conflicted sharply with the more traditional Princeton doctrine of Scripture. This, combined with differences over proposed Presbyterian confessional revision (Briggs supported the formulation of a new, simpler creed that could function as the basis for broader church union), led to the dissolution of the journal in 1889.

Throughout the 1880s Briggs published works that championed the higher-critical method and questioned the orthodoxy of *Princeton theology. With his antagonist, Princeton's William Henry *Green, he became one of the leading Old Testament scholars in the country, quickly rising to international prominence. Strong opposition to his positions had been rising in the church, but it was Briggs's inaugural address, "The Authority of Holy Scripture" (1891), delivered upon his induction into the chair of biblical studies at Union, that precipitated one of the most famous heresy trials in American religious history.

In a polemical tone Briggs denied the verbal inspiration, inerrancy and authenticity of Scripture, appeared to place the authority of reason and the church on a par with the Bible and defended the doctrine of progressive sanctification after death. As a result, the 1891 general assembly vetoed Briggs's professorial appointment, the 1892 assembly specifically endorsed the doctrine of biblical inerrancy and, although his presbytery had acquitted him of heresy, the 1893 assembly found him guilty and suspended Briggs from the ministry. In addition, the controversy occasioned the divorce of Union Seminary from the Presbyterian church. Refusing to accept the assembly's verdict, the board of directors retained Briggs at Union and rescinded the assembly's power of veto.

After waiting for several years in hope of restoration to the Presbyterian church, in 1898 Briggs entered the priesthood of the Episcopal church. Despite his acceptance of the higher-critical method, Briggs remained generally conservative in doctrine and was concerned by some of his younger colleagues' rejection of the virgin birth and other traditional doctrines. A scholar with wide and varied interests, his growing concern for church union led him to resign his chair in 1904 to teach symbolics and irenics. Briggs authored more than twenty books, including *General Introduction to the Study of Holy Scripture* (1899). Together with F. Brown and S. R. Driver he edited *A Hebrew and English Lexicon of the Old Testament* (1906), which is still in use, and served as one of the original editors of the prestigious International Critical Commentary series. He died of pneumonia at the age of seventy-two.

Bibliography. *ANB* 3; R. L. Christensen, "Charles Augustus Briggs: Critical Scholarship and the Unity of the Church," *American Presbyterians* (1991); *DAB* II; *DARB;* R. T. Handy, *A History of Union Theological Seminary in New York* (1987); L. A. Loetscher, *The Broadening Church: A Study of Theological Issues in the Presbyterian Church Since 1869* (1954); M. G. Rogers, "Charles Augustus Briggs: Heresy at Union," in *American Religious Heretics,* ed. G. H. Shriver (1966); *NCAB* 7.

B. J. Longfield

Brookes, James Hall (1830-1897).‡ Presbyterian minister. Born in Pulaski, Tennessee, the son of a minister, Brookes was reared by his mother after his father died when Brookes was only three. After attending Stephenson Academy in Ashewood, Tennessee, in 1851 he studied at Miami University in Ohio. Brookes attended Princeton Seminary during the 1853-1854 term but was unable to finish because he lacked funds. Nevertheless, he was ordained in 1854 by the Miami Presbytery and moved to Dayton, Ohio, to begin his first pastoral charge. In 1858 he accepted a call to the Second Presbyterian Church of St. Louis, and six years later he accepted a call to the Sixteenth and Walnut Street Church. There he remained until his retirement. Brookes served as a commissioner to the general assembly in 1857, 1880 and 1893, and he was stated clerk of the Synod of Missouri in 1874.

Brookes was one of the founders of the Niagara Bible Conference, which he presided over until his death. He was also active in the International Prophetic Conferences held in 1878 and 1886. He wrote seventeen books, dozens of sermons and pamphlets, more than 250 tracts and many articles. From 1875 until his death he was editor of *The Truth,* an influential premillennial journal that encouraged conservatives in their battle against liberal Protestantism. Brookes was instrumental in promoting the dispensationalist view that Christ might return at any moment. Among the most notable of his disciples was C. I. Scofield, who would later edit the influential Scofield Reference Bible.

Bibliography. *NCAB* 5; D. R. Williams, *James H. Brookes* (1897).

P. C. Wilt

Brown, Arthur Judson (1856-1963). Presbyterian clergyman and *missions executive. Born in Holliston, Massachusetts, Brown and his family moved to the West after the death of his father. Brown attended Wabash College and Lane and McCormick theological seminaries. In 1883 he was ordained by the *Presbyterian Church in the U.S.A. (PCUSA) and served churches in the West and Midwest. In 1895 the board of foreign missions called him to be an administrative secretary, and he served the board until 1929. Brown traveled extensively for his denomination, guided by his belief in the missionary character of the church, the necessity for Christian co-operation and the call to Christian witness in both word and deed. He was a proponent of self-governing, self-supporting and self-propagating churches around the world.

Brown was a leader and participant in numerous ecumenical endeavors, including the Ecumenical Missionary Conference (New York, 1900), the World Missionary Conference (Edinburgh, 1910) and the International Missionary Council (formed in 1921). He contributed to the development of the World Council of Churches. Brown was drawn into public affairs on various occasions, notably as a member of the Hoover Relief Committee for Europe (1915) and the American Committee on Religious Rights and Minorities (1920). He was also a long-time member of the Church Peace Union. As an author, he interpreted the missionary enterprise through his sixteen books and many reports and pamphlets, including *One Hundred Years: A History of the Foreign Missionary Work of the Presbyterian Church in the U.S.A.* (1936). Brown died at the age of 106.

Bibliography. A. J. Brown, *Memoirs of a Centenarian,* ed. W. N. Wysham (1957); R. P. Johnson, "The Legacy of Arthur Judson Brown," *IBMR* (April 1986) 71-75.

J. M. Smylie

Brown, William Adams (1865-1943).† Presbyterian educator and theologian. Born into a prominent New York family, Brown was educated at St. Paul's

School (Concord, New Hampshire) and received a bachelor of arts degree from Yale College (1886), where he also received a master's degree in economics (1888). At Union Theological Seminary in New York he studied with Charles Augustus *Briggs and Philip *Schaff, receiving his bachelor of divinity degree in 1890. Upon graduation he attended the University of Berlin for two years and there was greatly influenced by Adolf von Harnack (1851-1930) and indirectly by the thought of Albrecht Ritschl (1822-1889). Eventually Brown was to receive his doctor's degree from Yale (1901), but upon returning to New York in 1892 he began teaching at Union Theological Seminary. There he spent his career, first in church history but most significantly as professor of systematic theology (1898-1930) and research professor in the field of applied Christianity (1930-1936).

Throughout his career Brown was a strong advocate of theological liberalism and was particularly concerned with the relationship between the historical and the absolute in Christianity. In *The Essence of Christianity* (1902) he argued that the absolute was to be found in the person of Jesus Christ as revealer of divine sonship and human brotherhood. Concerned over the lack of a theological text that balanced traditional and modern insights, he published his *Christian Theology in Outline* (1906), which traced the history of each doctrine, showing the continuity as well as advance of the church's understanding throughout the ages. Employing a christocentric approach, he again insisted that Jesus Christ is the point of contact between the unchanging revelation of God and contemporary modes of thought.

Brown's Ritschlian sympathies led him to emphasize the importance of the ethical aspect of Christianity in reforming the social order, and he was a strong defender both of the social gospel and the importance of religion in undergirding liberal democracy. During the last twenty years of his life Brown focused on the church as the test for the relevance and practicality of Christian ethics. If the church cannot live Christianly, why should anyone else?

Brown was also actively involved with the Federal Council of Churches, chairing its Department of Research and Education from 1920 to 1938. A key figure in the Universal Christian Conference on Life and Work, which brought Protestants and Orthodox together on an official ecclesiastical level in Stockholm in 1925, he was instrumental in the negotiations to unite the Life and Work movement with the Faith and Order movement, which resulted in the World Council of Churches. Serving as the chairman of the Joint Executive Committee on Life and Work and Faith and Order in North America, he was appointed as one of the eight American members of the Provisional Committee of the World Council of Churches. He died five years before the Amsterdam assembly of 1948 fulfilled his dreams.

Bibliography. *ANB* 3; W. A. Brown, *A Teacher and His Times* (1940); *DAB* 3; *DARB;* S. McC. Cavert and H. P. van Dusen, eds., *The Church Through Half a Century: Essays in Honor of William Adams Brown* (1936). R. B. Mullin

Bryan, William Jennings (1860-1925). Presbyterian layman, politician and antievolutionary leader. He was three times a candidate for president of the United States and served as Secretary of State under Woodrow *Wilson.

Reared in Illinois of Bible-reading parents, Bryan attended school at Illinois College (B.A., 1881) and was admitted to the bar in 1883. He practiced law in Illinois and Nebraska and in 1891 went to Washington for the first time as a thirty-year-old congressman from Lincoln, Nebraska. From 1894 to 1896 he also served as editor of the Omaha *World-Herald.* Bryan adopted the populist creed of the agrarian Midwest that characterized the progressive movement in the region during the decades prior to World War I. He was soon catapulted into the national political arena.

The most controversial election issue in 1896, backed by farmers, was the addition of cheap money (silver) to the American currency. At the Democratic convention Bryan supported silver by delivering his famous "Cross of Gold" speech: "You shall not crucify mankind upon a cross of gold." Although he was only thirty-six years old, Bryan won the presidential nomination, but he lost to William McKinley and sound money in the election.

Chosen as the Democratic nominee in 1900 and again in 1908, Bryan lost both elections. In 1912 Wilson's election brought Bryan to the State Department. Bryan negotiated a series of arbitration treaties with thirty countries, but the crisis of 1914, marked by the sinking of the *Lusitania,* brought a conflict within the administration over the use of the treaties. Bryan resigned in June 1915.

The end of Bryan's political career opened the door for his reforming and religious leadership. He soon threw himself into the prohibition cause and played a significant role in securing the passage of the Eighteenth Amendment outlawing alcoholic beverages across the country after January 1920. The

1920 census, however, revealed that for the first time in American history the majority of the population were living in urban centers. The Eighteenth Amendment had no sooner become law than it was flouted openly. Traditional standards of morality seemed to be crumbling. Bryan saw one of the causes of this moral decline in Charles Darwin's conception of human origin.

In the spring of 1921, Bryan issued a series of attacks on evolution that instantly placed him in the forefront of *fundamentalist forces. The most important of these was his lecture "The Menace of Darwinism." Morality and virtue, he argued, are dependent on religion and a belief in God, and anything that weakens belief in God weakens people and makes them unable to do good. The evolutionary theory robs people of their major stimulus to moral living.

Bryan's last great battle, the Scopes trial, was the consequence of a Tennessee law prohibiting the teaching of evolution by a public school teacher. A young high-school biology teacher in Dayton, John Scopes, was charged with violating the law. He was defended by Clarence Darrow, a well-known lawyer, while Bryan joined the prosecuting team. Darrow argued that nothing less than intellectual freedom was on trial and succeeded in getting Bryan himself on the stand, using Bryan's testimony as evidence of fundamentalist stupidity. Scopes was found guilty and fined a token sum, but Bryan and fundamentalists were ridiculed throughout the country. Five days after the trial, Bryan passed away.

See also Science, Presbyterians and.

Bibliography. *ANB* 3; P. E. Coletta, *William Jennings Bryan: Political Evangelist, 1860-1908* (1964); *DAB* II; *DARB;* P. W. Glad, *The Trumpet Soundeth: William Jennings Bryan and His Democracy, 1896-1912* (1960); L. W. Levine, *Defender of the Faith* (1965); *NCAB* 19. B. L. Shelley

Buck, Pearl Sydenstricker (1892-1973). Author and Presbyterian missionary. Born in Hillsboro, West Virginia, Buck spent her early years in China as the daughter of Presbyterian missionaries. Following graduation from Randolph-Macon Woman's College (A.B., 1914), she returned to China and in 1917 married missionary John Lossing Buck. From 1921 to 1931 she taught at the Kiangan Mission in Nanking. Buck later attended Cornell University (M.A., 1926) and Yale University (M.A., 1933).

Buck completed her first novel, *East Wind, West Wind,* in 1930. Her second novel, *The Good Earth* (1931), gained her international fame, resulting in a Pulitzer prize in 1932. In 1933 she resigned from the Presbyterian Board of Foreign Missions after considerable controversy following her publication of an article the previous year that was highly critical of foreign *mission personnel. Buck returned to the United States in 1934 and obtained a divorce. In 1935 she married her publisher, Richard J. Walsh.

Throughout her writing career, Buck produced more than one hundred books, including *Sons* (1932); *The First Wife and Other Stories* (1933); *The Mother* (1934); *A House Divided* (1935); and *The House of Earth* (1935). Biographies of her father, *Fighting Angel* (1936), and her mother, *The Exile* (1936), contributed to her receiving the Nobel prize for literature in 1938. Known for her novels about China, Buck also published short stories, children's stories and nonfiction, including the autobiographical *My Several Worlds* (1954) and *A Bridge for Passing* (1962).

A renowned humanitarian, Buck's concern for disadvantaged children, particularly fatherless Amerasian children, resulted in the establishment of Welcome House in 1949 and the Pearl S. Buck Foundation in 1964. She died at her home in Danby, Vermont.

Bibliography. *ANB* 3; P. S. Conn, *Pearl S. Buck: A Cultural Biography* (1996); C. Silver, "Pearl Buck, Evangelism and Works of Love: Images of the Missionary in Fiction *JPH* 51 (1973) 216-34; *NAW* 4; *Who Was Who in America,* vol. 5, 1969-1973.

F. Heuser

Bultema, Harry (1884-1952). Pastor, author and founder of Berean Reformed Church. Born in Uithuizen, Groningen, the Netherlands, Bultema was reared in a poor family of farm laborers. Forced to work at an early age, he compensated with a disciplined, voracious course of reading that continued lifelong. On the advice of ministers in his family's (Seceded) Reformed Church, Bultema emigrated to the United States in 1901, settling in Grand Rapids, Michigan, where he took preparatory and seminary education (1904-1912) in the *Christian Reformed Church's (CRC) schools. Bultema was ordained in the Peoria, Iowa, Christian Reformed Church in 1912, and in 1916 he moved to the First Muskegon (Michigan) Christian Reformed Church, where he remained until his death.

Although he never dissented from Dortian Calvinism, Bultema in 1917 published *Maranatha!* which espoused dispensational premillennialism and literal expectations about Old Testament prophecy. His views caused his deposition from the Christian Reformed ministry in 1919. Thereafter he promoted his independent Berean Reformed ministry across Dutch America, most successfully in west Michigan, by warning against modernism, legalism and the inadequacy of formal tradition in the postwar world. His biblical commentaries on Isaiah, Daniel, Revelation and biblical typology taught a pretribulational rapture; denied the significance of creeds, water baptism and Old Testament law; reserved Christ's gospel ethic for the millennial kingdom; and defined the present age as Pauline, to be lived by grace alone.

In the 1930s Bultema's followers joined with other Midwestern *fundamentalists in the Grace Gospel Fellowship, whose publishing house and Grace Bible College, both in Grand Rapids, represent his chief legacy.

Bibliography. T. Boslooper, *Grace and Glory Days* (1990); H. Bultema, *Valiant and Diligent for the Truth* (1986). J. D. Bratt

Burr, Aaron (1716-1757). Presbyterian minister, school teacher and college president. Burr was born in Fairfield, Connecticut. He graduated with a bachelor's degree from Yale College in 1735, whereupon he received one of three Berkeley scholarships that provided for two years of graduate work in New Haven. During his graduate study, in 1736 Burr underwent a conversion experience. "It pleased God, at length," wrote Burr, "to reveal his Son to me in the Gospel, an all-sufficient and willing Saviour." This event not only gave Burr assurance of salvation but also intensified his interest in Christian ministry and led to a shift from *Arminian to *Calvinist theological sentiments. "Before this, I was strongly attached to the Arminian scheme, but then was made to see those things in a different light, and seemingly felt the truth of the Calvinian doctrines."

Licensed to preach in 1736, Burr served brief tenures at churches in Greenfield, Massachusetts, and Hanover, New Jersey, before settling at the First Presbyterian Church in Newark, New Jersey, first as a supply preacher (1736-1738) and later as its full-time pastor (1738-1755). A year later the church found itself in the midst of its first revival under Burr's leadership. Burr became a prominent though moderate proponent of the revivals of the Great Awakening. He developed contacts with George Whitefield, Joseph Bellamy, the *Tennents, and other leading New Lights. His rising popularity led to an offer in 1742 to become associate pastor of the First Church in New Haven. Burr declined the offer and established a successful grammar school in Newark.

In 1748 Burr was appointed the second president of the College of New Jersey. Founded in support of the experimental piety of the Great Awakening and located in Elizabethtown under the administration of founding president Jonathan *Dickinson, the college moved to Newark under Burr. Classes met in the Burr parsonage, and students boarded either with Burr or in the homes of nearby Newark families. Burr married Esther Edwards, daughter of prominent New Light clergyman Jonathan *Edwards, in the summer of 1752, and the two supervised a busy household.

Burr maintained both the presidency of the college and the pastorate of the Newark church until 1755, when Nassau Hall was built and the college moved to its final location in Princeton. While Burr supervised the move to Princeton and oversaw the instruction that began there in the fall of 1756, he fell sick (due in part to exhaustion) and died a year later. He was survived by his wife and two children, Sally and Aaron Burr Jr., who would become vice president of the United States under Thomas Jefferson. He was buried in Princeton and is remembered as the president who did most to lay a firm foundation for the development of the college.

Burr was succeeded in the presidency of Princeton by his father-in-law. Tragically, however, Edwards died from a smallpox inoculation on March 22, 1758, just two months after his arrival in Princeton. The College of New Jersey, now eleven years old, had lost its third president. Brokenhearted over the loss of both her husband and father, Esther Edwards Burr died sixteen days later, only twenty-six years old.

Bibliography. *ANB* 4; R. Balmer and J. R. Fitzmier, *The Presbyterians* (1993); *DAB* III; *NCAB* 5; W. B. Sprague, ed., *Annals of the American Pulpit*, vol. 3 (1858). D. Sweeney

Buswell, J(ames) Oliver, Jr. (1895-1977). Presbyterian educator and organizational leader. Born in Mellon, Wisconsin, Buswell was educated at the University of Minnesota (A.B., 1917), McCormick Theological Seminary (B.D., 1923), the University of Chicago (M.A., 1924) and New York University (Ph.D., 1949). Ordained in the *Presbyterian Church in the U.S.A. (PCUSA) in 1918, he ministered as an army combat chaplain (1918-1919), in a Presbyterian church in Milwaukee (1919-1922) and in a Reformed church in Brooklyn (1922-1926). Buswell was dismissed from the Presbyterian ministry in 1936 for his involvement with a *fundamentalist Presbyterian mission board. He subsequently served with several separatist Presbyterian denominations. He was the author of eleven books and dozens of articles, his most significant contribution being *A Systematic Theology of the Christian Religion* (2 vols., 1962-1963).

As president of Wheaton College in Illinois from 1926 to 1940, Buswell developed the school into a rapidly growing, academically respected, strategic fundamentalist center. After leaving Wheaton, Buswell taught at Faith Theological Seminary in Wilmington, Delaware (1940-1947); was president of the National Bible Institute in New York City and its successor, Shelton College in New Jersey (1941-1955) and taught at Covenant College (1956-1964) and Covenant Theological Seminary (1956-1970) in St. Louis.

A creative developer of conservative Protestant institutions, a distinguished teacher of theology and an ecclesiastical controversialist, Buswell left a legacy that included a vision for a vigorous evangelical intellectual witness and a series of ecclesiastical separations. Both of these helped to shape the neo-evangelical movement that some of Buswell's star pupils led in the 1950s and 1960s.

Bibliography. *Presbyterion: Covenant Seminary Review* 2, nos. 1-2 (1976): J. Oliver Buswell Jr. Commemorative Issue. J. A. Carpenter

Buttrick, George Arthur (1892-1980).† Congregational and Presbyterian preacher and theologian. Born and reared in Northumberland, England, where his father was a pastor in the Primitive Methodist Church, Buttrick underwent a personal religious experience during his grade school years. During his youth he rebelled against the rigid conservatism and organization of the family's denomination, and with his father's help he found his way into the care of the Congregational church and one of its pastors, John Gardner.

After completing high school in Yorkshire, Buttrick sought a career in the British civil service, but he did not pass the qualifying exam. Feeling led toward ordained ministry, he enrolled in a Congregational seminary at Lancashire and took his degree with honors in philosophy in 1915. He took only a minimal amount of work in homiletics and none in theology—both areas where he would distinguish himself in later life. His seminary studies were interrupted by a brief period of service as a military chaplain during the early days of World War I. After ten days as a chaplain he became convinced of his father's pacifism and resigned, moving to America later that year.

Through the assistance of Gardner, who had also come to the United States, Buttrick accepted a call to become pastor of the First Congregational Church in Quincy, Illinois. The following year, 1916, he married Gardner's daughter, Agnes, whom he had met in England. In 1918 he became pastor of the First Congregational Church of Rutland, Vermont, and in 1921 he moved to the First Presbyterian Church of Buffalo, New York. At age thirty-four, Buttrick was named in 1927 to succeed Henry Sloane *Coffin as pastor of Madison Avenue Presbyterian Church, the largest church of its denomination in New York City.

A vigorous supporter of Harry Emerson *Fosdick in the *fundamentalist-modernist conflict, Buttrick was one of the original signers of the *Auburn Affirmation and preached that the Jesus of the Gospels is the highest moral example to which we must strive to attain. Convinced of the evolutionary progress of civilization, he believed that sin is redressed by the atonement of God and people giving of themselves sacrificially for the betterment of humankind. An ardent pacifist, Buttrick pleaded for international reconciliation on the grounds of mutual sympathy, rather than aggression or appeasement.

In his twenty-seven years at Madison Avenue, Buttrick distinguished himself in his preaching and writing. Known in some circles as the preacher's preacher, he twice delivered the Lyman Beecher Lectures on Preaching at Yale and taught homiletics for two decades at Union Theological Seminary in New York. He served as president of the Federal Council of Churches (1939), and he was general editor of *The Interpreter's Bible* (12 vols., 1952-1957) and *The Interpreter's Dictionary of the Bible* (4 vols., 1962).

In 1954 Buttrick went to Harvard as Plummer Professor of Christian Morals and preacher to the university. He retired in 1960, was visiting professor at several theological schools and settled in Louisville, Kentucky, where he died.

Bibliography. J. Sittler, "George Buttrick: A Tribute and Reflection" *CCen* 97 (April 1980) 429-30. W. B. Lawrence

C

Caldwell, David (1725-1824).† Presbyterian minister, educator and physician. A *Scots-Irish immigrant to Pennsylvania, Caldwell began his career as a carpenter, but following a religious awakening he decided to pursue the Presbyterian ministry, studying at the College of New Jersey (B.A., 1761). Ordained in 1765, he was sent to Guilford County, North Carolina, as a missionary. There he founded his Log College in 1767 and become pastor of the Buffalo and Alamance churches in 1768. He tried unsuccessfully to avert the Battle of Alamance in 1771, and he served in the North Carolina constitutional convention of 1776.

Although his support of the Revolution (*see* American Revolution) caused Lord Cornwallis to put a price on his head, after the Battle of Guilford Courthouse (1781) Caldwell, a self-taught physician, helped the British physician tend the wounded. He later discovered that the British army had ransacked his house and farm, destroying all of his papers. After the war he devoted himself to his school, his church and his farm. He served as a delegate to the state convention that refused to ratify the Constitution. Caldwell voted against it, in part on the grounds that it had no religious test for political officeholders. Later he was offered, but declined on account of his age, the presidency of the University of North Carolina. Still, he continued teaching and ministering into the late 1810s, supporting the revivals that swept the state around the turn of the century but disapproving of their excesses. He died at the age of ninety-nine.

Bibliography. *ANB* 4; E. W. Caruthers, *A Sketch of the Life and Character of the Reverend David Caldwell* (1842); B. P. Robinson, "David Caldwell," in *Dictionary of North Carolina Biography*, ed. W. S. Powell, 1:300-302 (1979).

T. T. Taylor

Calvin, John, Influence of. The Presbyterian and Reformed tradition in America derives from the work of Swiss reformer John Calvin (1509-1564), who was instrumental in spreading the Reformed movement throughout Europe. During the seventeenth century, the English *Puritans and the *Scots-Irish transplanted *Calvinism to America. The Puritan and Scots-Irish forms of Calvinism were organized into Congregational, Presbyterian and Baptist churches. *Dutch and *German Reformed immigrants also established American churches.

Calvinism is both a theology and a cultural system. The theological basis of the Reformed tradition is found in Calvin's commentaries, sermons and especially his *Institutes of the Christian Religion* (1559). Calvin's theology was later developed and summarized in several Reformed confessions, including the *Westminster Confession of Faith (1647). These Reformed confessions were adopted by American churches and later modified for the changing theological climate of the new world.

As a cultural system, American Calvinism stresses education, hard work and simplicity of life. The relationship between Calvinism, *capitalism and the Protestant work ethic is a much-discussed topic. Many scholars believe that Calvin's concept of vocation and commitment to worldly activism were factors that encouraged the development of capitalism. Calvin's concepts of law and government as restraining factors in society also influenced the development of the American legal and political system.

The Reformed tradition was the dominant theological tradition in colonial America. In *New England, the Puritans organized a Christian commonwealth. Although their theocratic experiment ended in failure, the movement produced important historical, theological and literary works. Especially noteworthy are the writings of Cotton Mather and Jonathan *Edwards.

The Puritans also established important educational, benevolent and missionary organizations that profoundly influenced American life. The Puritan founders of Harvard (1636) and Yale (1701) universities joined with the Presbyterians and Reformed to organize the American Bible Society (1816), the American Temperance Society (1826) and two mission organizations, the American Board of Commissioners for Foreign Missions (1810) and the American Home Missionary Society (1826).

Presbyterian Scots and Scots-Irish settled in New Jersey and Pennsylvania. John *Witherspoon, a signer of the Declaration of Independence, made a lasting impression on American life by arguing, as Calvin did, against governmental interference in church matters. The Presbyterians established several colleges and seminaries, including Princeton University (1746), Princeton Theological Seminary (1812) and Union Theological Seminary in Virginia (1823). Although plagued by theological controversies and divisions, the Presbyterian churches have also played an active role in American life as important agencies of *education, *social reform, *mission work and ecumenism.

German Reformed immigrants settled in Maryland, eastern Pennsylvania and Ohio. In 1825 the denomination established the Theological Seminary of the Reformed Church. Relocated to Mercersburg in 1837, the seminary attracted John Williamson *Nevin (1803-1886) and Philip *Schaff (1819-1893), who developed a *Mercersburg theology. Other German Reformed denominations were also organized. Eventually these denominations merged into the United Church of Christ.

The Dutch Reformed settled in New York, New Jersey and Delaware and then migrated to the Midwest. The *Reformed Church in America (RCA) organized several educational institutions, including Rutgers University (1766), New Brunswick Theological Seminary (1784) and Western Theological Seminary (1884). In 1857 the Christian Reformed Church in North America* (CRC) was organized in Michigan. The denomination established Calvin College and Calvin Theological Seminary (1876) in Grand Rapids.

See also CALVINISM.

BIBLIOGRAPHY. S. Bercovitch, *The Puritan Origins of the American Self* (1975); W. J. Bouwsma, *John Calvin: A Sixteenth-Century Portrait* (1988); M. J. Coalter Jr. and J. M. Mulder, "Dutch and German Reformed Churches," in *EARE* 1:511-23 (1988); J. H. Leith, *An Introduction to the Reformed Tradition*, rev. ed. (1981); L. A. Loetscher, *A Brief History of the Presbyterians*, 4th ed. (1983); A. E. McGrath, *A Life of John Calvin* (1990); J. T. McNeill, *The History and Character of Calvinism* (1954).

R. Benedetto

Calvinism. A doctrinal tradition originating with the Reformer John *Calvin (1509-1564) and providing the foundational theology of the Congregational, Reformed and Presbyterian churches in America. Calvinism begins with the fundamental principle of the sovereign majesty of God and consequently emphasizes his exclusive initiative in salvation. Otherwise known as Reformed theology (to be distinguished from Lutheran theology, which also originated with the Reformation), Calvinism as it came to America was defined by the tradition's classic confessions such as the *Belgic Confession (1561), the *Heidelberg Catechism (1563), the Thirty-Nine Articles of the Church of England (1562, 1571), the *Canons of the Synod of Dort (1619) and the *Westminster Confession of Faith (1647).

Adhering to the fundamental Reformation principle of *sola scriptura,* Calvinism strives to derive its doctrines entirely from Scripture. Calvin and his successors have believed that Scripture, not reason or church tradition, is the fully trustworthy revelation from God and the only reliable foundation for Christian faith and practice. Hence even Calvinistic doctrinal statements are binding only inasmuch as they reflect the clear teaching of Scripture.

The Synod of Dort (1618-1619) clearly defined in five points the salvific implications of Calvinism over against *Arminianism. These five points, which some scholars believe oversimplify the richness of Calvinist theology and the variety of its historic formulations, nevertheless provide a helpful summary: humanity is by nature totally depraved and unable to merit salvation; some people are unconditionally elected by God's saving grace; God's atonement in Christ is limited in its efficacy to the salvation of the elect; God's transforming grace, ministered by the Holy Spirit, is irresistible on the part of humans; the saints must persevere in faith to the end, but none of the elect can finally be lost. Calvinism at its best has grounded all of these doctrines in the person and work of Christ, but a logical deductivism has at times influenced the tradition.

The doctrine of the sovereignty of God shapes not only Calvinism's understanding of redemption but also its perspective on creation, history, *politics and life in general. Thus the Calvinist worldview has frequently inspired its adherents to engage culture and transform all of life under the mandate of the sovereign rule of God. In addition, Calvinism in America, particularly in its *Puritan strain, has frequently been wedded to a philosophy of history known as covenant theology. This philosophy—encompassing both the sacred and profane, the seed of Adam and the seed of Christ—was to pose its own problems for Calvinist thought and church life.

The most pressing questions within Calvinism in America have revolved around the twin issues of human responsibility and divine sovereignty as they relate to the fall and redemption. These issues, originally pastoral concerns brought into focus by the Great Awakening, set the theme for theological and philosophical reflection and discussion from Jonathan *Edwards through the New England theology of the nineteenth century. The followers of Edwards debated and refined Edward's speculative metaphysic. They were opposed by the Old Calvinists, who called these followers of Edwards "New Divinity Men." The Old Calvinists, in their uneasiness over revivalism, maintained the pre-Awakening Calvinism of the Puritan establishment. Relatively uninterested in the finer points of systematic theology, they stood for the Puritan covenant theology of the past that had assured a stable, orthodox community.

But the movement within Calvinism to modify its understanding of human responsibility and allow for a greater freedom of the will in responding to conversionist preaching provided a theological basis for many American Calvinists to participate in the First and Second Great Awakenings and in American revivalism in general. Among Presbyterians, however, the *Princeton theology of the mid- to late nineteenth century was the most resistant to the modified Calvinism. The Princeton theology has had a continued influence on conservative Presbyterians and other evangelical Calvinists of the twentieth century.

In whatever form it has taken, Calvinism has been a dominant shaping force in American Protestantism and has had a strong influence not only on Congregationalists, Presbyterians and Continental Reformed bodies but also on many Anglicans, Baptists and independent churches. But denominations such as the *Reformed Church in America (RCA) and the *Christian Reformed Church (CRC), as well as a few Presbyterian bodies such as the *Orthodox Presbyterian Church (OPC) and the *Presbyterian Church in America (PCA), would claim to be the faithful conduits of Calvinist orthodoxy in American religious life today.

Bibliography. J. H. Bratt, ed., *The Heritage of John Calvin* (1973); B. Kuklick, *Churchmen and Philosophers* (1985); J. H. Leith, *Introduction to the Reformed Tradition,* rev. ed. (1981); J. T. McNeill, *The History and Character of Calvinism,* rev. ed. (1967); W. S. Reid, ed., *John Calvin: His Influence in the Western World* (1982); B. B. Warfield, *Calvin and Augustine* (1956); D. F. Wells, ed., *Reformed Theology in America* (1985).

The *DCA* Editors

Canada, Presbyterianism in. The Presbyterian tradition in Canada is largely the story of the transplanting to British North America of the main expression of Scottish Christianity.

While Seceder immigrants showed evangelistic and organizational initiative from their beginnings in Nova Scotia with Samuel Kinloch, the moderate religious ethos of the eighteenth-century Church of Scotland was evidently not something to which many immigrating Scots remained passionately committed in their new land. Amid the pressing demands and iconoclastic opportunities of the frontier, religion was soon shown for the peripheral concern it had become for them. Along the St. Lawrence, where French Canada's Roman Catholic Church was showing surprising resilience, Presbyterianism struggled, despite the financial capability of its prominent members, to construct church buildings for congregations that had existed since 1765 in Quebec and since about 1785 in Montreal. And in the Northwest, predominantly Scottish fur traders manifested little religious interest or values through almost two centuries of commerce with aboriginal peoples. Even when Lord Selkirk transplanted a Highland Scots community to the Red River in 1812 (the origins of the modern city of Winnipeg, Manitoba), the settlement was left for decades without a minister.

Still, immigrants (Scots among them) came to British North America only in modest numbers prior to the end of the Napoleonic wars in 1815. Then, with the oceans again safe for British travel and with British energies redirected into the Victorian challenge of building the Second Empire, British North America experienced such a flood of immigrants between 1820 and 1850 as to effectively populate Maritime and central Canada. Scots continued to come, now not only in unprecedented numbers but also with a new religious feeling. For Scotland was at the same time being profoundly affected by the international Second Evangelical Awakening with its powerful blend of streamlined Protestant orthodoxy, personal experience and Romantic feeling.

This new breed of Scottish Presbyterians was associated with both the Established Church of Scotland (the Auld Kirk) and a number of smaller Seceder (dissenting) varieties of Presbyterianism—Relief, Burgher, Anti-Burgher, Secession, to name a few—which, while not matching the Auld Kirk in respectability, showed compensating vigor in more populist evangelistic and church-planting efforts. The divided state of Canadian Presbyterianism was exacerbated by the Scottish Disruption of 1843. A sympathetic reaction in the Canadas, swayed in part by the powerful Free Church ambassador Robert Burns, led to the immediate formation in 1844 of a vigorous colonial counterpart.

Nevertheless, the unitive tendency of shared evangelical priorities and simplified evangelical doctrinal convictions, combined with the leveling influence and urgent spiritual needs of the frontier, led to a series of Presbyterian reconciliations that significantly predated Scottish equivalents. These included a merger of the United Presbyterians (Secession) and Free Church in 1861 as the Canada Presbyterian Church and culminated in the comprehensive Presbyterian Church in Canada reunion (with the Auld Kirk) in 1875. From an ecclesiastical perspective, their united efforts were successful; the census of 1891 showed the Presbyterians to be the largest Protestant denomination in Canada.

Expatriate Scottish Presbyterians present from the beginnings of British North America were steadily joined by others over the years to the point that they constituted something of a social establishment by the mid-nineteenth century when Canada had reached the stage of nation building. A phalanx of Presbyterian politicians (including Oliver Mowat, a premier of Ontario, and Alexander Mackenzie, one of Canada's first prime ministers) worked for a transcontinental nation that would be the "Dominion" of Christ. Thomas *McCulloch in Nova Scotia, William *Dawson of McGill, George Grant of Queen's University in Kingston and Robert *Falconer in Toronto were among the many educators who expressed historic Presbyterian values in building up many of what have become Canada's leading institutions of higher education. George Brown (publisher of the Toronto *Globe),* Ralph Connor (a celebrated author; Charles William *Gordon) and James Redpath (a Montreal industrialist and philanthropist) are among the countless Presbyterians who significantly helped to shape all sectors of Canada in accordance with their religiously rooted vision.

Some strategies for making Canada godly were more attractive to Presbyterians than others. They were solidly behind the temperance movement (with grape juice replacing wine in Presbyterian communion services by the 1880s and the general assembly calling for Prohibition in 1888) and the passage of the Lord's Day Act of 1906, which placed pointed limitations on Sunday activities in Canada. While Presbyterians never embraced the social gospel to the same degree that Methodists did, there was a significant effort between 1875 and 1915 by prominent Presbyterians, dubbed the "Social Uplifters," to balance personal conversion with *social reform. In other instances there was a patent backing off from evangelical priorities in favor of initiatives to transform Canadian culture.

Presbyterian evangelistic vision extended in three principal directions. In order of geographic proximity, it was first extended, largely through the transdenominational French Canadian Missionary Society (1839-1881) and by means of the celebrated and controversial career of Presbyterian convert Father Charles *Chiniquy, toward the conversion of French Canadian Roman Catholics. Second, it was extended, beginning with John Black's arrival in the Red River settlement in the 1850s, in efforts to consolidate the religious loyalties of settlers in the great Northwest (the former Rupert's Land inherited by Canada from the Hudson's Bay Company in 1870). Finally, it was extended overseas, beginning in 1846 with the pioneering efforts of Maritimer Seceder John *Geddie in the New Hebrides and, under the inspiration of missionary statesman Alexander Duff's visit in 1854, soon extending to India, Taiwan, Korea and China.

The Westminster Standards were accorded typical Presbyterian reverence in the earlier part of the nineteenth century in both church and home. However, the Canadian universities were largely founded after the halcyon days of the Scottish Common-Sense philosophical tradition, and consequently they were shaped in the Hegelian atmosphere issuing from Oxford and from the Caird brothers at Glasgow University in the 1870s. Hegelian idealism led a good number to transpose their Presbyterian orthodoxy into a new key. The ferment in the mind of the church uncorked in the celebrated 1876 heresy trial of D. J. MacDonnell, whom the redoubtable Donald Harvey MacVicar ultimately failed to depose for questioning the doctrine of eternal perdition. The delayed effects of British encounters with Continental biblical criticism were eventually felt in Canada as well and were highlighted in the heresy trial of Presbyterian professor John Campbell of Montreal in 1894.

Some Canadian Presbyterians, particularly those associated with Knox College, Toronto, turned to Princeton Seminary in New Jersey (and in the case of A. B. Winchester, to Dallas Theological Seminary, which he helped to found) for conservative alliances. Others, like John McNicol, principal of the Toronto Bible College (1906-1946) and a contributor to *The Fundamentals,* chose to work mainly outside Presbyterian ecclesiastical structures. At the same time a large number of other Presbyterians concluded that the older verities, especially the confidently detailed subordinate standards, were no longer supportable and that the church, unencumbered by creeds, could best demonstrate its usefulness in this world.

Evidence of that usefulness came in 1925 when Presbyterians merged with Methodists and Congregationalists to form the United Church of Canada. At a stroke it became the dominant expression of Canadian Protestantism; its supporters hoped it would also prove a formidable competitor to the Roman Catholic Church for Canadian religious hegemony. In its doctrine, polity and ethos, the new United Church was a synthesis of the uniting traditions. While influenced by Presbyterianism, it effectively absorbed and replaced it.

Approximately one third of Canadian Presbyterians, however, elected to stay out of the United Church. But not until an act of the Canadian Parliament in 1939 did the continuing Presbyterians earn the official right to describe themselves as the *Presbyterian Church in Canada (PCC). The reasons for resisting union were numerous and complex, but among them theological conservativism, Scottish affections and *Calvinist loyalties figured large.

The 1925 divorce was devastating. While the continuing PCC has declined less rapidly, numerically speaking, than the more inclusive United Church, the median age of its membership is the oldest of all Canadian churches. It has had limited success in retaining its younger generation, despite an ambitious goal to double in the 1980s. In 1966 it began to ordain women, and in 1982 it took the equally debated further step of prohibiting its ministers, scruples of conscience notwithstanding, from declining to participate in such ordination services. Some dissidents have joined Canadian extensions of the *Presbyterian Church in America (PCA), although this group still has only a minuscule presence (thirteen congregations, six hundred active members) in Canada. The venerable Knox Church, Toronto, and the more recent Presbyterian Renewal Fellowship are leading champions of evangelical interests in the church. In membership the church has held its own since 1925, though Canada's population has grown greatly during the same years. Between three and four percent of Canadians now identify at least nominally with the Presbyterian church. In terms of communicant membership, Presbyterians now rank seventh among Canadian churches.

The figure of the staunch and industrious Presbyterian, ubiquitous in Canadian history and literature, still looms large in the anglophone Canadian cultural memory. The contemporary secular Canadian ethos has been shaped in part by a brooding dissatisfaction with a caricatured god of damnation and control who was honored for a time in the land north of summer. Today some secularized Canadians carelessly assume that the PCC's chief reason for continued existence is to promote the interests of such a deity. Since 1925 the PCC has not recovered a robust sense of identity and vision. The rejuvenation of the Presbyterian tradition in Canada will depend upon the church's ability to recoup those positive and large-hearted themes and practices that have been so profoundly life-giving in Canada's past.

See also PRESBYTERIAN CHURCH IN CANADA.

BIBLIOGRAPHY. *Acts and Proceedings of the 120th General Assembly of the PCC* (1994); N. K. Clifford, *The Resistance to Church Union in Canada* (1985); B. Fraser, *The Social Uplifters: Presbyterian Progressives and the Social Gospel in Canada, 1875-1915* (1988); W. Klempa, ed., *The Burning Bush and a Few Acres of Snow: The Presbyterian Contribution to Canadian Life and Culture* (1994); J. McNeill, *The Presbyterian Church in Canada* (1925); D. E. Meek, "Canada," in *DSCHT*, 131-33; J. Moir, *The Enduring Witness: A History of the Presbyterian Church in Canada* (2d ed., 1987); idem, "Presbyterian and Reformed Churches," in *The Canadian Encyclopedia* (1985); W. S. Reid, ed., *Called to Witness* (2 vols., 1975, 1980); J. G. Stackhouse, "Presbyterian Church in Canada," in *DCA*, 930; R. W. Vaudry, *The Free Church in Victorian Canada* (1989).

G. G. Scorgie

Canadian and American Reformed Churches. A small confederation of churches whose doctrinal standards include the Nicene Creed, the Apostles' Creed and the Athanasian Creed as well as the *Belgic Confession (1561), the *Heidelberg Catechism (1563) and the *Canons of Dort (1618-1619). These latter three statements of faith from the Reformation era are known as the Three Forms of Unity.

Specific developments in the Reformed churches in the Netherlands during the 1940s led to the formation of the Canadian and American Reformed Churches (CARC) when a schism took place primarily because of church political dealings. The Reformed churches, by mutual agreement, had promised to abide by church order, a set of rules for the regulation of church life locally and federatively. One of the rules stated that a synod ceases to exist once its agenda is completed. The 1939 synod, however, took upon itself powers that made it a self-perpetuating body that went far beyond its jurisdiction. This breach of church order led to a hierarchical form of church government. Synod also made binding the teaching of presumptive regeneration, a doctrine to which many ministers and church members could not ascribe. Further, synod deposed several professors and ministers, an act that lies beyond its powers. The rift that resulted from these actions could not be healed and occasioned the institution of the Reformed Churches Liberated in 1944.

When the first wave of immigrants from the Liberated churches came to North America in the late 1940s, they sought to join the *Christian Reformed Church (CRC). The CRC maintained official relationships with the churches in the Netherlands and sided with the churches loyal to synod. The CRC did not allow discussion of the recent developments that had taken place and so effectively closed the door for dialogue and the possibility of union. (In 1963 and 1977, synods of the Canadian Reformed churches would again send appeals to the CRC to discuss the differences and come to a possible union, but these overtures were of no avail.) Dutch immigrants from the Reformed Churches Liberated also sought the possibility of joining with the *Protestant Reformed Churches in America (PRC), but these efforts were also unsuccessful. The PRC, which maintained that God made his covenant with the elect only, was not an acceptable doctrinal position to the CARC.

The first Canadian Reformed church was instituted in Coaldale, Alberta, on April 16, 1950. The first American Reformed church was instituted in Grand Rapids, Michigan, on September 25, 1955.

The Canadian Reformed churches hold the Bible as the inspired Word of God, a completely reliable and trustworthy account of God's dealings with humankind. The Bible is received for the regulation, foundation and confirmation of our faith. The CARC also professes the need to seek unity in the faith with fellow Christians.

Worship services are held twice on the Lord's Day under the supervision of the overseers. Ordinarily in the afternoon service the Heidelberg Catechism is expounded. Every congregation is involved in outreach within the community. Many churches also support the radio ministry called *The Voice of the Church.* Missions among the natives in northern British Columbia as well as five missionary posts in Brazil and Irian Jaya are supported by a concerted effort of several neighboring congregations. The churches also maintain a theological college in Hamilton, Ontario, for the training of ministers.

BIBLIOGRAPHY. C. Van Dam, ed., *The Liberation: Causes and Consequences, the Struggle in the Reformed Churches in the Netherlands in the 1940s* (1995); W. W. J. VanOene, *Inheritance Preserved: The Canadian Reformed Churches and the Free Reformed Churches of Australia in Historical Perspective,* rev. ed. (1991); idem, *With Common Consent* (1990); W. W. J. VanOene, ed., *1995 Yearbook* (1995).

G. Nederveen

Capitalism, Presbyterians and. Enthusiastic supporters, outspoken critics, successful practitioners, destitute victims—Presbyterians in America have functioned in all of these roles and more in relation to the capitalist economic system that emerged in the colonial era and has ever since held sway in the United States. Alongside countless other citizens, Presbyterians have reaped the rewards and endured the hardships of an American capitalism premised on the notion that a free exchange of goods and services within the marketplace will serve best to ensure the economic health of the nation and its people.

Whether Presbyterians and other Calvinistically inclined Protestants were especially instrumental in promoting the rise of capitalism has aroused much debate ever since German sociologist Max Weber put forward that thesis in the early part of the twentieth century. He argued for a close connection between the spirit of capitalism and the work ethic of Protestants in the sixteenth and seventeenth centuries. Specifically, the Protestant emphases upon fulfilling one's earthly calling diligently and practicing a strict asceticism in the use of worldly goods supposedly proved ideal for both capital accumulation and the mentality necessary for the development of modern capitalism. After nearly a century of scholarly reaction and discussion, it appears that Weber's thesis might apply especially well to two groups of seventeenth-century Protestants vitally important for later American Presbyterianism, English *Puritans and Scottish Presbyterians. Their concern to glorify God in all human activities and to confirm their divine election through abiding by a strict Calvinist code of ethics may have enhanced an intellectual and moral climate conducive to capitalist enterprise.

Once in the new world, Presbyterians promoted a set of economic virtues that in theory squared with Christian teaching and in practice generated wealth. Honesty, sobriety, industriousness, frugality, discipline—these were the marks of the conscientious Christian steward who used God's resources wisely. Presbyterian laymen found that these virtues paid off, and by the middle of the eighteenth century some Presbyterian businessmen had joined the ranks of the colonial elite in cities like Philadelphia and New York. At the same time, the unfettered pursuit of happiness carried on by many provincials undoubtedly bothered certain Presbyterians who shared fellow colonial Calvinist Jonathan *Edwards's suspicion of individual acquisitiveness. He warned against the corrupting influence of wealth and urged colonial Christians toward more organized efforts on behalf of the poor, a call Presbyterians heeded in 1757 with the creation of The Corporation for Relief of Poor and Distressed Ministers' Wives and Children.

The *American Revolution and its aftermath unleashed a set of economic forces that brought a national market economy and liberal values firmly into place in the new nation by the first decades of the nineteenth century. Presbyterians joined in the frenzied quest to take advantage of the economic opportunities available in frontier regions like western New York and the Ohio valley. Denominational leaders expressed occasional complaints in the late 1700s about the selfish pursuit of profit, especially when it did not even subside on the sabbath. But more often they and other Presbyterians found themselves echoing the sentiments of minister Samuel Miller, who at the turn of the century hailed America's commercial prospects as the brightest in the world.

Enterprising capitalism expanded rapidly in antebellum America transforming city and countryside alike. While some historians have suggested that the evangelicalism of *New School Presbyterians was particularly accommodating to the new economic order, all Presbyterians continued to espouse the traditional set of economic virtues and to denounce their opposites—idleness, intemperance, prodigality, sloth, extravagance. They also wrestled to work out a broader economic ethic that supported the market economy without sacrificing the distinctions or integrity of their religious convictions. The result was an economic perspective characterized by a series of tensions: people were responsible to practice the virtues that brought success, but any success achieved was to be understood as wholly the gift of God; people were to be content in all things, but economic ambition was a positive good; economic gain was both valuable and vain; Christian piety was a defense against selfish materialism, but it was also an essential asset for achieving economic success; and wealth was not to be interpreted as a sure sign of individual salvation or God's blessing, yet wealthy laymen were disproportionately selected for positions of congregational leadership. The latter tendency especially rankled Stephen *Colwell, Philadelphia industrialist, *Old School layman and author of *New Themes for the Protestant Clergy* (1851), a sweeping call for greater Christian attention to the plight of the poor in America. Colwell attacked the wage slavery created by Northern industrial capitalism and warned against the church's too easy embrace of the morality and methods of American business. His work stands out as the most telling Presbyterian critique of American capitalism before the Civil War.

Echoes of Colwell's arguments could be heard from divergent Presbyterian voices in the postbellum era, when the pace of industrialization and urbanization only quickened. At one end of the spectrum there was unreconstructed Southern theologian Robert Lewis *Dabney, who condemned virtually all features of industrial society, including the corporate form, and yearned to hold onto the agrarian ways of an older South. On the other end there were proponents of Christian socialism like California minister J. E. Scott, who repudiated capitalist competition and advocated a gradualist socialism based on the Golden Rule. Neither of these extremes appealed to the vast majority of Presbyterians. Nor did many of them go to another kind of extreme and embrace the uncritical marriage of Christianity and capitalism embodied in the gospel of wealth. Instead, most endorsed the free market system that was turning the United States into an economic giant but expressed greater or lesser degrees of concern about growing social and economic ills that accompanied the nation's capitalist development in the late nineteenth and early twentieth centuries.

Labor-management conflict, monopolistic business practices, unsafe working conditions, increasing urban poverty and widespread intemperance were just some of the evils that gained Presbyterian attention. More socially conservative Presbyterians such as Princeton professor William B. Greene and minister Charles Rosenbury *Erdman usually insisted on individual conversion and Christian charity as the keys to social improvement. More progressively inclined Presbyterians joined the ranks of the social gospel movement and began to advocate a broader range of political and social solutions. They saw evil structures and evil environments, not just evil people, and they believed that the compassion of the church and the power of the state were both needed to effect *social reform. A high point of the movement within Presbyterianism came in 1910 when the general assembly of the Northern church adopted the social creed that two years later became the hallmark of the Federal Council of Churches. The creed called for better working conditions for women, an end to child labor, workmen's compensation, greater equality of wealth, a more reasonable work week, higher wages for industrial workers and the elimination of poverty. Some of those same causes were taken up by Presbyterian layman and president of the United States Woodrow *Wilson during his first administration (1913-1916).

Theological conflict and economic crisis plagued Presbyterians in the interwar years. Those drawn to more liberal doctrinal positions seem also to have been those most often drawn politically leftward in the face of the Great Depression. Their sentiments increasingly influenced the economic witness of the *Presbyterian Church in the U.S.A. (PCUSA) in the 1930s. Pronouncements of the general assembly more vigorously supported the rights of labor and more rigorously challenged the existing social order. And new denominational agencies were created to assist churches in fulfilling their Christian call to combat economic evils. Still, the 1944 general assembly claimed that the church had "signally failed to speak and to act in matters of economic and industrial relations."

The last half of the twentieth century saw Southern and Northern Presbyterians address a host of economic concerns through a myriad of boards, committees, study groups and departments within and beyond denominational boundaries. Hunger, poverty, welfare reform, labor equality, food policy, urban renewal, workplace discrimination and unemployment are problems related to modern American capitalism that have generated Presbyterian action. Presbyterian responses during these decades often reflected the latest theological impulses so that the influence of *neo-orthodoxy, the biblical theology movement and liberation theology may be seen in both the issues confronted and the perspectives adopted. For example, liberation theology's rise in the 1970s pushed many Presbyterians toward greater consideration of American capitalism's global effects, particularly the plight of Third World nations struggling to gain a larger share of the world's riches. Even with this heightened global awareness, however, today's Presbyterians, like their predecessors, undoubtedly spend most of their daily energies trying to secure their own place within the American capitalist system while remaining faithful to their understanding of the Christian gospel. That task is no easier now than it was for those colonial Presbyterians who originally helped set America on its capitalist course.

See also SOCIAL REFORM, PRESBYTERIANS AND.

BIBLIOGRAPHY. D. Irvin, "Social Witness Policies—A Historical Overview," *JPH* 57 (fall 1979) 353-403; G. Marshall, *Presbyteries and Profits* (1980); R. W. Pointer, "Philadelphia Presbyterians, Capitalism and the Morality of Economic Success, 1825-1855," *Pennsylvania Magazine of History and Biography* 112 (July 1988) 349-34; G. S. Smith, *The Seeds of Secularization* (1985); R. H. Tawney, *Religion and the Rise of Capitalism* (1926); M. Weber, *The Protestant Ethic and the Spirit of Capitalism* (1930).

R. W. Pointer

Carrick, Samuel Czar (1760-1809). Presbyterian minister and educator. Carrick was born in York (now Adams) County, Pennsylvania, but as a youth he moved to the Shenandoah Valley in Virginia. A member of the first graduating class of Liberty Hall Academy, he was ordained to the Presbyterian ministry in 1783. During the next few years he began occasional missionary tours into the Tennessee country and in 1791 settled near the forks of the Holston and French Broad rivers, establishing Lebanon Church. One year later he organized a congregation at nearby Knoxville, the newly established capital of the Tennessee territory.

In 1793 Carrick opened in his home a seminary, offering instruction in ancient languages, English, geography, logic and philosophy. In 1794 the school was chartered as Blount College, a nondenominational school named in honor of the territorial governor, Carrick becoming its president. The college admitted young women to its classes and was arguably the first such coeducational institution in America. During its first years enrollments were low and finances uncertain, and in 1807 the institution was renamed East Tennessee College to take advantage of a promise of Congressional land-grant support. After the Civil War it would become the University of Tennessee. Carrick died unexpectedly in August 1809 and was memorialized in the Knoxville Gazette as "a much-needed man of culture in a pioneer community, a gentleman of commanding appearance, of great urbanity."

BIBLIOGRAPHY. *AAP* 3; *ANB* 4; *DAB* II; E. W. Crawford, *An Endless Line of Splendor* (1983); W. H. Foote, *Sketches of Virginia, Historical and Biographical* (1856).

W. J. Wade

Caven, William (1830-1904).‡ Canadian Presbyterian leader. Born in the southwest of Scotland, Caven's faith and life were nurtured among the Seceders or United Presbyterians who had left the Church of Scotland in the eighteenth century to preserve their evangelical witness. At seventeen he migrated with his family to the Galt area of Ontario, began studies soon after at the Secession Seminary in London, Ontario, and then pastored for more than a decade. In 1861 the Free Church and Secession joined in Ontario and Quebec to form the Canada

Presbyterian Church. Its theological institution was Knox College, Toronto, and Caven was appointed to its chair of exegetical theology in 1865. He was to remain there for the remainder of his life, becoming principal in 1873.

Caven was a typical nineteenth-century evangelical Presbyterian of the Secession heritage, akin in outlook to James *Orr. He was staunchly conservative yet without confessional rigidity, greatly interested in social questions, thoroughly committed to *missions and fearful of church and state too readily transgressing each other's boundaries. An active churchman, he was moderator of the Canada Presbyterian Church in the year prior to the Presbyterian union of 1875. Caven was interested in church union, partly out of fears of Roman Catholicism, but not at the expense of doctrinal consensus. A number of his writings were posthumously published under the title *Christ's Teaching Concerning the Last Things* (1908). Caven also contributed to *The Fundamentals* (1910-1915).

Bibliography. J. A. Macdonald, "A Biographical Sketch" in W. Caven, *Christ's Teaching Concerning the Last Things* (1908). I. S. Rennie

Chafer, Lewis Sperry (1871-1952).‡ Presbyterian minister and founder of Dallas Theological Seminary. Born into the home of a Congregational pastor in Rock Creek, Ohio, Chafer was reared in a stable home that was sadly disrupted by the death of his father in 1882. Chafer and his siblings were educated at nearby New Lyme Institute and Oberlin College, where he studied for three semesters in the Conservatory of Music.

In the early 1890s Chafer supplemented the family's income by joining Arthur T. Reed, an evangelist with the Young Men's Christian Association in Ohio. In 1899 Chafer became an assistant in the First Congregational Church, Buffalo, New York. In early 1901 Chafer's center of activity shifted to Northfield, Massachusetts, where he traveled widely in evangelistic work during the winters and assisted in the music ministry of Dwight L. Moody's famous summer conferences. His encounter with C. I. Scofield in the fall of 1901 redirected his life. He became an extension teacher for Scofield's Bible correspondence school and traveled extensively throughout the South. In 1907 he transferred his ministerial credentials to the *Presbyterian Church in the United States (PCUS).

Chafer gained prominence in the Bible conference movement. While pastoring Scofield's former church in Dallas and directing a mission Scofield had established in 1890, Chafer founded the Evangelical Theological College in 1924 (since 1936, Dallas Theological Seminary) and served as its president and professor of systematic theology until his death.

Chafer would eventually emerge as a champion of the premillennial and dispensational movement. In addition to numerous books, which include *Satan: His Motive and Methods* (1909), *True Evangelism* (1911), *The Kingdom in History and Prophesy* (1915), *Salvation* (1917), *He That Is Spiritual* (1918), *Grace* (1922) and *Major Bible Themes* (1926), he published his magnum opus, a multivolume *Systematic Theology*, in 1948.

Bibliography. *ANB* 4; J. D. Hannah, "The Social and Intellectual History of the Evangelical Theological College" (Ph.D. diss., University of Texas at Dallas, 1988). J. D. Hannah

Chalmers, Thomas (1780-1847). Scottish Presbyterian theologian, pastor and apologist. Chalmers was born at Anstruther and began his ministry in 1803 in the village of Kilmany. From 1815 to 1823 he served successive parishes of the Church of Scotland in Glasgow. He then accepted the chair of moral philosophy at St. Andrews. In 1828 he moved to Edinburgh University as the professor of theology. For the decade before 1843, he led the battle to secure the Church of Scotland's control over its own affairs, but when that effort failed he led the Free Church of Scotland out of the established Kirk in 1843, and he was the Free Church's guiding spirit until his death in his sleep on the night of May 30-31, 1847. Chalmers's renown rested on his power as a preacher and his efforts in Glasgow to address problems of urban poverty through a voluntary system featuring the communal spirit of an idealized rural parish. With a life-long interest in liberal arts and sciences, he was also a leading apologist (as in his "Astronomical Discourses" in Glasgow and his "Bridgewater Treatise" on Natural Theology in 1833) defending the harmony of traditional Christianity and the most reliable results of modern science.

Chalmers's works were published in the United States almost as soon as they first appeared in Scotland. By the time of his death, over seventy editions (some in many volumes) had appeared in America. When he died, he was eulogized in America as Protestantism's "brightest earthly light" (New England Congregationalist Bela Edwards) and as "the most important author who flourished in the first part of the nineteenth century" (New Jersey Presbyterian Archibald *Alexander).

Chalmers's voluntary, church-centered response

to the rising problem of urban poverty made him an exemplary figure for Americans with the same goals. When in the late 1820s some New Yorkers assisted Charles *Finney in founding nontraditional churches, leaders like businessmen Lewis *Tappan and the Dutch Reformed minister James C. Bliss followed Chalmers in creating "free churches" (i.e., no pew rents) that could evangelize the urban poor as well as ease the conditions of poverty. Shortly thereafter, Dr. John Backus, a leading Presbyterian from Baltimore, visited Chalmers in Scotland and came away with a copy of his *Christian Economics.* He also left with a resolve to see Baltimore churches institute the plan of voluntary "systematic benevolence" that Chalmers had practiced in his St. John's charge in Glasgow. Into the twentieth century, Chalmers was invoked by Social Gospel advocates like Charles Richmond Henderson of Chicago and sociologists like Mary Richmond for his Christian efforts against urban poverty.

Chalmers's apologetics had considerable impact on moderate Presbyterians in Canada and the United States. Particularly important was his two-pronged strategy for the great questions being thrown up by nineteenth-century scientists and philosophers. One the one hand, performances like his lectures on astronomy and his Bridgewater Treatise de-fanged the new science by showing that nothing in the new perspective, when properly considered, detracted from traditional Christian teachings on God's providential lordship over the material world. On the other hand, Chalmers did not invest as much in his scientific apologetics as did many American Reformed theologians in their advocacy of Newton and Bacon. It was, Chalmers held, the history of consciousness rather than the study of nature that opened most clearly to Christian teachings on sin and redemption. Much of modern science and philosophy could be enfolded in traditional Calvinism, but Chalmers felt no urgency about demonstrating the truth of Christianity according to the canons of modern science.

Bibliography. *Biblical Repertory and Princeton Review* (various articles by A. Alexander, J. W. Alexander and C. Hodge) 13 (1841) 30-54; 14 (1842) 562-83; 19 (1847) 360-78; 20 (1848) 529-42; S. J. Brown, *Thomas Chalmers and the Godly Commonwealth in Scotland* (1982); B. B. Edwards, *Discourse on the Life and Character of Thomas Chalmers* (1847); M. Gauvereau, *The Evangelical Century* (1991).

M. A. Noll

Chamberlain, Jacob (1835-1908). Dutch Reformed missionary. Born in Sharon, Connecticut, and reared in Hudson, Ohio, Chamberlain graduated from Western Reserve College in 1856 and studied theology at Union Theological Seminary, New York, and the Dutch Reformed Theological Seminary in New Brunswick, New Jersey. Following his seminary graduation he studied medicine at the College of Physicians and Surgeons in New York City. On taking his medical degree in 1859, he was ordained a missionary by the Reformed Protestant Dutch Church (now the *Reformed Church in America [RCA]). In April 1860 he arrived at the site of his life's work, the Arcot Mission in the Madras Presidency of South India.

After studying Tamil and then Telugu, Chamberlain engaged in extensive evangelistic tours. Utilizing his medical skills, he established two hospitals that ministered to thousands of Indians. As a linguist he was instrumental in producing a Telugu translation of the Bible. His concern for the education of Christian leaders led in 1887 to his founding at Madanapalle what is reputed to be the first theological seminary on the mission field. There he taught and later served as principal from 1891 to 1902. Chamberlain also worked to unify the Presbyterian and Reformed churches in India and played a principal role in the establishment of the Reformed Synod of South India in 1902, of which he was elected the first moderator.

Afflicted by recurring illness, Chamberlain was forced to spend a total of more than ten years in America and the West, an opportunity he took to promote the cause of *missions. Chamberlain's writings include *The Bible Tested in India* (1878), *The Religions of the Orient* (1896) and *The Kingdom in India, Its Progress and Its Promise* (1908). In 1878 his denomination honored him by making him president of the General Synod of the Reformed Church in America. He died on March 2, 1908, at his home in Madanapalle in South India.

Bibliography. H. N. Cobb, "A Biographical Sketch," in J. Chamberlain, *The Kingdom in India: Its Progress and Its Promise* (1908); *DAB* II; *Missionary Review of the World* (August 1908).

D. G. Reid

Chapman, J(ohn) Wilbur (1859-1918).† Presbyterian pastor and evangelist. Born in Richmond, Indiana, Chapman studied at Oberlin College in Ohio (1876-1877) and graduated from Lake Forest College in Illinois (B.A., 1879). While attending Lane Theological Seminary in Cincinnati, Ohio (B.D., 1882), Chapman was licensed by the Presbytery of Whitewater in April 1881. His first charge was a two-church circuit, consisting of a rural church in College Corner, Ohio, and a village church in Liberty, Indiana. In subsequent years he served the Old Saratoga Dutch Reformed Church of Schuylerville, New York (1883-1885), the First Dutch Reformed Church of Albany (1885-1890), Bethany Presbyterian Church of Philadelphia (1890-1893, 1896-1899) and Fourth Presbyterian Church of New York (1899-1902). After 1890 Chapman became increasingly involved in evangelistic endeavors and assisted Benjamin F. Mills, a close friend from college days, in the Cincinnati-Covington and Minneapolis campaigns of 1892, and Dwight L. Moody in the Chicago World's Fair campaign of 1893.

In 1901 Chapman was appointed corresponding secretary of the Presbyterian General Assembly Committee on Evangelism, where he came in contact with John H. Converse, president of Baldwin Locomotive Works, to whom Chapman acknowledged a great debt, not only for his financial support but also for his zeal for lay evangelism. After 1903 Chapman devoted himself full-time to evangelistic work. Teamed with musician Charles Alexander, he conducted meetings across the United States and around the world, with outstanding success in Boston (1909) and Chicago (1910). In 1912 Chapman left on a fourteen-month tour of Australia and New Zealand, introducing his team-style evangelism with impressive results.

Utilizing social gospelers to preach to union workers, former alcoholics to preach in the red-light district (including nightclubs), women to preach to ladies' meetings, and a variety of other evangelists, Chapman introduced the method of the simultaneous campaign into urban evangelism. In addition to the central meeting, numerous other meetings would take place in various parts of a target city, using evangelists and musicians to attract and influence people of various classes. Chapman's demeanor was far from the flamboyance associated with many revivalists, including his protege Billy *Sunday. Rather he was a gentleman preacher who avoided controversy and aimed instead for people's heartstrings. His own social concerns were mostly limited to personal morality and social evils such as alcohol, sabbath breaking, dancing, gambling and immorality, and he preferred to focus on the message of the gospel, blending Reformed doctrines, such as total depravity, with Keswick emphases on full surrender to God by yielding to the power of the Holy Spirit.

Chapman was also a founder and the first director of the Winona Lake Bible Conference in Indiana. He was the author or editor of thirty books and many tracts and pamphlets. In addition, he authored several hymns and gospel songs and compiled a number of hymn books. In 1917 he was elected moderator of the Presbyterian general assembly. After his term as moderator he served his denomination with the National Service Commission and the New Era Forward Movement. Chapman died after emergency surgery on Christmas Day, 1918.

See also PRESBYTERIAN CHURCH (USA).

BIBLIOGRAPHY. *ANB* 4; *DAB* II; *DARB;* J. C. Ramsey, *John Wilbur Chapman: The Man, His Methods and His Message* (1962); D. E. Soden, "Anatomy of a Presbyterian Urban Revival: J. W. Chapman in the Pacific Northwest," *AP* 64 (1986) 49-57.

P. C. Wilt

Chavis, John (c. 1763-1838). African-American Presbyterian minister, missionary and educator. Little is definitely known of Chavis's early life. He was born free around 1763 and grew up in Granville County, North Carolina. After service in the Revolutionary War, he attended Washington Academy (Washington and Lee University) and reportedly studied for the ministry under John *Witherspoon at Princeton.

In 1800 Chavis was licensed to preach by the Presbytery of Lexington. He subsequently came to the attention of the Presbyterian general assembly and in 1801 became the first African-American commissioned by the Presbyterian Church to work among Southern slaves. From 1801 to 1807 he was active in Virginia's Lexington and Hanover presbyteries while serving as a missionary to slaves in Maryland, Virginia and North Carolina. After settling in North Carolina in 1807, Chavis joined the Orange Presbytery and ministered to both blacks and whites in Granville, Orange and Wake counties.

His ministry was complemented by an interest in education that led Chavis to establish a school in North Carolina where he taught blacks and whites. In correspondence and writings such as *Letter Upon the Atonement of Christ* (1837), Chavis displayed theological and political conservatism. He opposed the *abolition of slavery and consequently enjoyed the support of influential Southern whites. However, in 1832 Chavis was barred from continuing his public ministry as a result of increased restrictions upon black ministers occasioned by the Nat Turner revolt. His last years were spent as an educator, his meager income supplemented until his death by assistance from the Orange Presbytery. Despite the restrictions imposed upon his ministry, Chavis is hailed as a pioneer of African-American Presbyterianism.

Bibliography. *ANB* 4; R. Balmer and J. R. Fitzmier, *The Presbyterians* (1993); M. B. DesChamps, "John Chavis as a Preacher to Whites," *NCHR* 32 (April 1955) 65-72; *Dictionary of North Carolina Biography* I; E. W. Knight, "Notes on John Chavis," *NCHR* 7 (July 1930) 326-45; W. S. Savage, "The Influence of John Chavis and Lunsford Lane on the History of North Carolina," *JNH* 25 (January 1940) 14-24; G. C. Shaw, *John Chavis, 1763-1838, A Remarkable Negro* (1931). M. Moore

Chiniquy, Charles (1809-1899). French Canadian Roman Catholic priest and temperance advocate cum Presbyterian evangelist and polemicist. Born in Kamouraska, Lower Canada, and ordained a Roman Catholic priest in 1833, Chiniquy, whose childhood had been scarred by the alcohol-related death of his father, found his vocation in fighting the ravages of alcohol. He organized Quebec's first temperance society in 1840 and preached temperance and abstinence throughout French Canada with considerable effect. By 1851 his spectacular preaching methods had helped more than half of all French Canadians to take the pledge.

At the same time Chiniquy's job security was undermined by his insubordination and outrageous comments. Rumors of sexual promiscuity also dogged him, and in 1851 he was dismissed by Ignace Bourget, bishop of Montreal. Chiniquy relocated to the French Catholic parish of Ste-Anne-de-Kankakee, Illinois, but chronic patterns of behavior led to his excommunication by the bishop of Chicago in 1856. He founded (briefly) the Catholic Christian Church and then, upon testimony to evangelical conversion, became a Presbyterian minister in 1860. When difficulties with the Presbytery of Chicago led to his suspension (1862), he and his large Ste-Anne congregation were enthusiastically accepted into the Canada Presbyterian Church. In 1864, at age fifty-four, he finally married.

Chiniquy then embarked, under the auspices of the Canada Presbyterian Church and with the same energy and style he had shown in his earlier temperance campaigns, on a second crusade: the conversion of French Canadians to Protestantism. During the ensuing years he and the Catholic bishops of Quebec waged unrelenting war. His oratorical talents made him a formidable foe at the popular level. His polemical writings included *The Priest, the Woman and the Confessional* (1875), a widely circulated and lurid assault on the morality of Catholic priests and the confessional system. He also wrote two volumes of combative memoirs that were extensively translated and circulated worldwide: *Fifty Years in the Church of Rome* (1885) and *Forty Years in the Church of Christ* (1900). He received an honorary doctorate from Presbyterian College, Montreal (1893). It has been estimated that his evangelistic efforts prompted several thousand Québecois to change their religious allegiance. Recently some Quebec historians have shown sympathy towards Chiniquy as an early champion of anticlericalism. His career continues to be highly controversial.

Bibliography. *DCB* 12; J. Noel, "Dry Patriotism: The Chiniquy Crusade," *CHR* 71, 2 (1990) 189-207; M. Trudel, *Chiniquy* (1955). G. G. Scorgie

Christian Reformed Church in North America.† A Reformed denomination, principally of Dutch descent, centered in the American Midwest. The Christian Reformed Church (CRC) grew out of the later (1840s-1920s) wave of Dutch immigration to the United States. The roots of the CRC may be found in the Secession of 1834 from the National Reformed Church in the Netherlands, when a substantial minority of orthodox Reformed pietists became disillusioned with the inroads of French Revolutionary ideology into the National Church. Complaining that the confessional standards of the church were being weakened and protesting the aristocratic control of the state church, the original Secession drew primarily from the lower classes.

In the United States, the Dutch Protestant Reformed Church in America (later, the *Reformed Church in America [RCA]) had been primarily an English-speaking church since before the American Revolution, and most Seceder immigrants became uncomfortable with the degree of Americanization that had occurred. Although the first arrivals affiliated with the RCA, some seceded in 1857 to form the True Dutch Reformed Church. The group became a viable enterprise only around 1880 with the resurgence of Dutch immigration and a second defection from the RCA, this time over the issue of Freemasonry. For the next fifty years, the church, now called the Christian Reformed Church, continued this strategy of absorbing the disaffected (in New Jersey) and the recently immigrated (extending to the west coast). It moved into Canada with the post-World War II Dutch migration there. More recent additions have come from outside the Dutch circle, consisting of many African-Americans but largely Korean-Americans.

During the 1920s the church was rocked by controversies over the issues of biblical criticism and common grace. Affirming a position on biblical inspiration similar to that of Princeton Seminary's Benjamin Breckinridge *Warfield, the general synod deposed Ralph Janssen for heresy and insubordination in 1922. His chief foe, Herman *Hoeksema (founder of the *Protestant Reformed Churches in America), was deposed three years later for denying that God shows any grace to the reprobate. These two cases illustrate the strict confessionalism that dominated the CRC during the first half of the twentieth century, refusing both modernization and Americanization on the one hand and extreme *fundamentalism on the other.

While the language change from Dutch to English was completed in the 1930s—having been spurred on by anti-Germanic sentiment surrounding World War I—the movement toward Americanization did not accelerate until the second half of the twentieth century. Once again the issue of common grace proved to be the touchstone for the debate. Many of the younger Dutch-American theologians emphasized common grace over/against the traditional antithesis between regenerate and unregenerate thinking, but a new wave of conservative immigration from the Netherlands, primarily to Canada in the 1940s and 1950s, insisted upon maintaining the antithesis, both in thinking and in separate institutions. These confessionalists were organized by Evan Runner (who was not Dutch but a convert from *Old School Presbyterianism), a philosophy professor hired at Calvin College in 1951. Uncomfortable with an undue emphasis on common grace, Runner encouraged his constituency to maintain separate Christian institutions and advocated the formation of a distinctly Christian political party. In recent years the CRC has struggled with further issues of Americanization and modernization, wrestling with such questions as evolutionary theory and women's ordination. This has led to significant unrest and the departure of dozens of more traditional churches.

Still, the CRC has been consistently defined by traits from its Netherlandic past. It stresses heartfelt conversion and piety, although cast in covenantal rather than revivalistic terms; confessionalism and orthodoxy, as set by its three standards—the *Belgic Confession, the *Heidelberg Catechism and the *Canons of Dort; and Christian cultural engagement. The last emphasis was enunciated by the Dutch neo-Calvinist forebear Abraham *Kuyper and is exemplified in the denomination's longstanding Christian day school system as well as its academic and political leadership in recent American evangelicalism. One of the few evangelical denominations to encourage and sustain careful Christian scholarship across a broad spectrum of disciplines, Christian Reformed influence may be seen in the renewed interest in the life of the mind in some evangelical circles.

See also CANADIAN AND AMERICAN REFORMED CHURCHES; DUTCH REFORMED IN AMERICA; PROTESTANT REFORMED CHURCHES IN AMERICA, THE.

BIBLIOGRAPHY. J. D. Bratt, *Dutch Calvinism in Modern America: A History of a Conservative Subculture* (1984); P. De Klerk and R. R. De Ridder, eds., *Perspectives on the Christian Reformed Church* (1983); J. H. Kromminga, *The Christian Reformed Church* (1949). J. D. Bratt

Church Government. *See* POLITY, PRESBYTERIAN.

Civil War, Presbyterians and the. The Civil War, the bitter struggle that split the United States between 1861 and 1865, proved as divisive of the American Christian community (and especially the Presbyterian church) as it was of the country as a whole. Several decades before the fighting began, the Presbyterian, Methodist and Baptist denominations broke apart along sectional lines, beginning with the Presbyterian *Old School-*New School rift in 1837. During the conflict itself, Christians in the United States and the Confederacy both claimed God's favor on their cause and prayed for military victory. The Civil War era so profoundly shaped American religious life that by the end of the nineteenth century, despite the healing of political divisions between North and South, the Protestant denominations rent prior to 1861 remained separated on regional grounds.

The morality of slavery was the critical issue that divided Northern and Southern Christians. Northerners attacked the South as a barbarous region morally blighted by the odium of the "peculiar institution"; Southern whites replied that the Northern churches put more faith in social experimentation than in the Bible, thus repudiating God's Word, which blessed slavery. Although the 1818 Presbyterian general assembly declared that slavery was inconsistent with the gospel and called upon Christians to abolish "this blot on our holy religion," most Presbyterians in the South disagreed. They touted the evangelistic work of clergymen like Charles Colcock *Jones of Georgia, known popularly as the apostle to the blacks. A slaveholder committed to leaving the system itself untouched, Jones sought to mitigate some of its harshness by bringing religious instruction to slaves on plantations in his area.

The national debate over slavery played a crucial

role in the Presbyterian schism of 1837-1838. After the Second Great Awakening, a New School party had been formed by Presbyterians (located mainly in New York and Ohio) open to innovative practices and ideas, including *abolition and other *social reform movements. The traditionalist Old School coalition, whose strength lay in Pennsylvania, New Jersey and throughout the South, resisted the liberalizing tendencies the New School championed. After Old School forces gained control of the general assembly in 1837, they proceeded to remove the four major New School synods from the denomination's rolls. Concerned about the antislavery sentiments of many New School adherents, Southern delegates to the general assembly wholeheartedly supported the expulsion of those synods. When a separate New School denomination was formed in 1838, most Presbyterians in the South remained part of the Old School body.

The growing sectional crisis of the 1850s further exacerbated the divisions within Presbyterianism. The few Southern presbyteries that joined the New School Presbyterian Church found themselves continually at odds with Northern members over the slavery issue. When the 1857 general assembly overwhelmingly condemned a Mississippi presbytery's declaration that slaveholding was their "Biblical right," twenty-one presbyteries in the Southern and border states withdrew in protest. Meeting at Knoxville, Tennessee, in 1858, representatives of the New School in the South organized themselves as the United Synod of the Presbyterian Church in the U.S.A.

The coming of the Civil War completed the rupture of American Presbyterianism. Despite the harmony that existed at the Old School general assembly of 1860, feelings aroused by the election of Abraham Lincoln in the fall imperiled the denomination's unity. As a prominent South Carolina clergyman declared, the Union had become "synonymous with oppression, with treachery, with falsehood, and with violence" in the minds of many of his people. When the Old School assembly next convened in May 1861, hostilities between the Union and the Confederacy had already begun. Some conservatives led by Charles *Hodge of Princeton Seminary, who had consistently advised silence on political matters, urged their denomination to ignore the war the nation was facing. But when Gardiner *Spring, a New York City pastor also long opposed to antislavery agitation, moved that the church offer its support of the Union, the general assembly enthusiastically affirmed him.

The reaction in the South to the assembly's action was predictable: "A platform has been erected upon which no place has been left for a southern man to stand," the *Southern Presbyterian* concluded. Old School leaders began to organize their own church, gathering for their first general assembly in Augusta, Georgia, in December 1861. In his "Address to All the Churches of Jesus Christ throughout the Earth," theologian and proslavery advocate James Henley *Thornwell, who had formulated the "doctrine of the spirituality of the church" in the 1850s as an intellectual bulwark against abolitionism, justified the formation of the new Presbyterian Church in the Confederate States of America. Thornwell argued that, if Northern Presbyterians had not meddled in political matters, the ecclesiastical division would not have been necessary. Now, Southern Christians might rightly fight both to defend the God-given institution of slavery and to preserve their churches from unwarranted interference by the North.

Northern Presbyterians, no less than their white Southern counterparts, were convinced that their country's military cause was holy and just. Since the Northern Old School church still possessed a strong element in slaveholding border states that remained loyal to the Union, it at first condemned the South's rebellion against the United States government without mentioning the slavery issue. However, at the 1864 general assembly, when the Union's emancipation policy had become unmistakable, Northern Old School Presbyterians announced that "the time has at length come, in the providence of God, when . . . every vestige of human slavery among us should be effaced." New School Presbyterians were even more confident than the Old School in the North about the religious meaning of the Civil War. Philadelphia pastor Albert *Barnes, for example, maintained that the conflict was a divinely appointed method of purging the nation of the sin of slavery. And the 1862 New School general assembly identified the Union war effort with the redemption of humankind, calling the United States "one of the great sources of hope, under God, for a lost world."

The Civil War furnished Presbyterians with an occasion not only for patriotic pronouncements but also for practical demonstrations of support of their national causes. In the North, regulations allowed each of the army's thousand-man regiments to elect an ordained Christian minister as its chaplain, and approximately twenty-three hundred chaplains eventually served in the Union ranks. Methodists sent the most clergy into service, while Presbyterians ranked second, supplying about one-fourth of all the Union chaplains. Northern Presbyterians were also actively involved in the operation of the United States Christian Commission. Organized in 1861 under the leadership of the New York Young Men's Christian Association and Philadelphia merchant and Presbyterian lay leader George H. Stuart, the Christian Commission evangelized the Union armies by helping chaplains lead worship and distributing religious tracts among the soldiers. Commission agents also discovered opportunities to minister to the physical needs of the troops, acting as nurses on battlefields and in hospitals.

In the Confederate states, where many aspects of political life were poorly organized or left to individual initiative, the military chaplaincy was not well supported by the government. The contributions of white Presbyterians to the Southern war effort, therefore, had to be made principally through unofficial channels. For instance, after the 1863 general assembly of the Southern Old School church resolved to direct its primary evangelistic efforts at its nation's soldiers, the denomination appointed special commissioners to oversee religious efforts in each of the largest armies of the Confederacy. These clergy functioned both as chaplains and as intermediaries between soldiers and the central denomination. A number of Southern generals, moreover, were noted for their piety and willingness to promote worship and religious instruction among their men. Generals Stonewall *Jackson, a teacher in a sabbath school for slaves before the war, and D. H. Hill, a lay theologian, were frequently extolled by their fellow Presbyterians as exemplars of Christian martial valor.

Despite the heroism Presbyterians in the South endeavored to foster, Confederate military forces surrendered to the North in 1865. In the wake of this failure, many Southern Christians sought spiritual lessons to alleviate the pain of their defeat. Virginia Presbyterian minister John Miller believed the war's disastrous outcome might be "the very impress of a Father's loving kiss"—a distinctive mark of God's chastening but enduring love. Like the early church martyrs who had also experienced suffering, he said, Southerners ought to recognize how the war was a providential opportunity for receiving divine grace. And as Moses Drury *Hoge, pastor of the Second Presbyterian Church in Richmond, argued in 1865, if Christians embraced hardship with the proper religious attitude, God might transform the South's defeat into a means of moral purification. While misfortune alone would not sanctify the South, the acceptance of "sanctified affliction," Hoge thought, could lead Southern Christians into closer communion with God.

The Civil War had a significant institutional as well as spiritual impact upon Southern Presbyterianism. During the war, the Old School-New School division lost its former raison d'être, and the practical advantages of merger overrode whatever theological differences still troubled Presbyterians in the South. Following Old School theologian Robert Lewis Dabney's* meeting with representatives of the United Synod, the 1864 general assembly of the Presbyterian Church in the Confederate States adopted a merger plan. When the next meeting of the United Synod accepted the Old School's proposal, the two Southern Presbyterian bodies united in a new denomination that after 1866 adopted the name the *Presbyterian Church in the United States (PCUS).

The Old School and New School churches in the North stayed separate during the Civil War, but the political issues that divided them in the 1830s ceased to have meaning once slavery was destroyed. Although theological disagreements continued to be significant and negotiations about reunion lasted for three years, these problems were finally resolved. In 1869 the general assembly of each church overwhelmingly approved their merger.

When the first united general assembly in the North met in 1870, it expressed a wish to eliminate the remaining schism and reestablish cordial relations with the Southern church. This effort, however, proved unsuccessful, for animosity between the North and the South was still strong throughout the Reconstruction period. After rebuffing initial overtures about reunion, representatives of the Southern church met with negotiators from the North in 1875. The Northerners said they knew no reason why the two bodies could not come back together. The Southerners stoutly disagreed and proceeded to list the invectives the Northern general assembly had hurled against the South during the war. Memories of decades of antagonism persisted for the rest of the century. Although the organization of the *Presbyterian Church in the U.S.A. (PCUSA) in 1983 eventually healed the breach, the division of Presbyterians into Northern and Southern branches was one of the most enduring religious legacies of the Civil War.

See also Abolition, Presbyterians and; South, Presbyterians in the.

Bibliography. D. C. Chesebrough, ed., *God Ordained This War* (1991); J. T. Davis, "The Presbyterians and the Sectional Crisis," *Southern Quarterly* 8 (1970) 117-33; J. O. Farmer, *The Metaphysical Confederacy: James Henley Thornwell and the Synthesis of Southern Values* (1986); C. C. Goen, *Broken Churches, Broken Nation: Denominational Schisms* *and the Coming of the American Civil War* (1985); J. P. Maddex, "From Theocracy to Spirituality: The Southern Presbyterian Reversal on Church and State," *JPH* 54 (1976) 438-57; G. M. Marsden, *The Evangelical Mind and the New School Presbyterian Experience: A Case Study of Thought and Theology in Nineteenth-Century America* (1970); J. R. McKivigan, *The War Against Proslavery Religion: Abolitionism and the Northern Churches 1830-1865* (1984); J. H. Moorhead, *American Apocalypse: Yankee Protestants and the Civl War, 1860-1869* (1978); G. H. Shattuck, *A Shield and Hiding Place: The Religious Life of Civil War Armies* (1987); M. Snay, *Gospel of Disunion* (1993); E. T. Thompson, *Presbyterians in the South: Religion and Separatism in the Antebellum South* 3 vols. (1963-1973); L. G. Vander Velde, *The Presbyterian Churches and the Federal Union* (1932). G. H. Shattuck

Clark, Gordon Haddon (1902-1986). Calvinist philosopher. Born in Philadelphia, Clark graduated from the University of Pennsylvania (B.A., 1924), where he also did his graduate work in philosophy (Ph.D., 1929). During his years as a graduate student and for several years thereafter, Clark was an instructor (1924-1936) at the University of Pennsylvania and at the nearby Reformed Episcopal Seminary (1932-1936). He also studied at the Sorbonne in Paris during 1931. In 1936 he was a visiting professor at Wheaton College, Illinois, where he joined the faculty the following year. There Clark had a decisive influence on the minds of a number of future evangelical intellectual leaders, most notably E. J. Carnell and Carl F. H. Henry.

Within a *fundamentalist institution that had not yet achieved intellectual depth, Clark stood out as a profound and rigorous thinker whose philosophical rationalism challenged both modernism and the unexamined thoughts of students raised on popular fundamentalism. For these students, Clark provided their first encounter with an intellectually respectable Christianity. But however much devotion he evoked from his students, Clark's *Calvinism was an intolerable challenge to the *Arminianism that prevailed on Wheaton's campus, and at the end of the 1942-1943 school year, Wheaton's president, V. Raymond Edman, let him go. By 1945 Clark was teaching on the faculty of Butler University, where he came to chair the department of philosophy for twenty-eight years. From that secular campus he continued to exert a notable influence on the evangelical intellectual world, and the Reformed sector in particular, through more than thirty publications. Most notable were *A Christian Philosophy of Education* (1946), *A Christian View of Men and Things* (1951) and his history of Western philosophy, *Thales to Dewey* (1956). In the early years of *Christianity Today,* he served as a contributing editor.

In 1943, during his hiatus between Wheaton and Butler, Clark sought ordination in the *Orthodox Presbyterian Church (OPC). Having passed the examinations and received ordination, Clark was challenged on doctrinal grounds having to do with his understanding of the role of logic, particularly the law of noncontradiction, in theology and apologetics. This conflicted with the *presuppositionalism of Cornelius *Van Til and his definition of the incomprehensibility of God, which was influential within that denomination. Clark's teaching that human knowledge could be identical to God's knowledge troubled many on the faculty of Westminster Theological Seminary who agreed with Van Til that human knowledge must always be analogical to God's knowledge. The controversy, which was long remembered on both sides, ended when Clark left the denomination and joined the *United Presbyterian Church (UPCNA) in 1948. Nine years later, when the UPCNA voted to merge with the *Presbyterian Church in the U.S.A. (PCUSA), Clark decided that he could not join a modernist denomination and transferred his credentials to the *Reformed Presbyterian Church, General Synod (RPC, GS). Through his writing and speaking, he played an important role in the life of the church, continually calling it to maintain a distinctive Reformed presence. Some within the wider evangelical intellectual world concurred with Carl Henry's assessment that Clark was "one of the profoundest evangelical Protestant philosophers of our time."

Bibliography. R. H. Nash, ed., *The Philosophy of Gordon Clark* (1968). D. G. Reid

Coffin, Henry Sloane (1877-1954).‡ Presbyterian minister and educator. Born in New York City, Coffin was educated at Yale, Edinburgh, Marburg and Union Theological Seminary (New York). Following his ordination in the *Presbyterian Church in the U.S.A. (PCUSA, 1900), he founded and served in a Presbyterian mission in the Bronx. After pastoring the Bedford Park Presbyterian Church (1900-1905), he was called to the prestigious Madison Avenue Presbyterian Church in New York City (1905-1926), where he became known as one of America's great preachers. During this pastorate he also served as professor of practical theology at Union Theological Seminary, eventually serving as president and professor of homiletics (1926-1945).

Throughout his career, Coffin championed liberal causes. He opposed American entry into World War I and become a liberal leader during the *fundamentalist controversy within the Presbyterian church. As a signer of the *Auburn Affirmation he advocated an inclusivist church. In the heated general assembly of 1925 he defended the New York Presbytery's liberal ordination practices. Calling himself an "evangelical liberal," Coffin attempted to find a mediating position between conservative and liberal positions.

Always the committed churchman, Coffin worked to make Union Seminary a training ground for pastors as well as scholars. He became well known as a liturgist (*The Public Worship of God,* 1946), a hymnologist (*Hymns of the Kingdom,* 1910) and an ecumenist, and he served as moderator of the PCUSA in 1943-1944.

Bibliography. *ANB* 5; *DAB* 5; *DARB; NCAB* E; B. J. Longfield, *The Presbyterian Controversy: Fundamentalists, Modernists, and Moderates* (1991); M. P. Noyes, *Henry Sloane Coffin: The Man and His Ministry* (1964). T. P. Weber

Colwell, Stephen (1800-1871). Lawyer, iron manufacturer and social reformer. Colwell was born in Brooke County, Virginia (now West Virginia). After graduating from Jefferson College (Penn.) in 1819, Colwell studied law with Judge Halleck of Steubenville, Ohio, and then practiced law in St. Clairsville, Ohio, and in Pittsburgh. In 1836 Colwell became an iron merchant. Operating first out of Weymouth, New Jersey, and later establishing himself on the outskirts of Philadelphia, Colwell spent the last twenty-five years of his life manufacturing iron, reflecting on the economic and ethical implications of the laws and practices governing American industry and contributing both time and talent to various *social reform efforts. A Presbyterian elder, Colwell is perhaps best known for his anticipation of the ideals and commitments of the social gospel movement in America. Colwell accused the churches of doctrinalism and clericalism and castigated his fellow Christians for their neglect of the poor and the oppressed. Among other works such as *Charity and the Clergy* (1853) and *The Position of Christianity in the United States* (1854), his *New Themes for the Protestant Clergy* (1851) heralded a kind of social Christianity that would not gain wide scale acceptance until the turn of the twentieth century.

Colwell served on the boards of directors of three railroads and on the trustee boards of both the University of Pennsylvania and Princeton Seminary, where he helped establish a chair of Christian ethics. He was a member of the United States Revenue Commission and was an active proponent of the colonization of slaves. He contributed to the Union cause during the Civil War, working with both the Sanitary and Christian Commissions visiting battlefields and hospitals. He also proved a strong supporter of the Freedmen's Aid Society. Colwell died in Philadelphia.

See also Social Reform, Presbyterians and.

Bibliography. *DAB* IV. D. Sweeney

Confession of 1967.† Most recent theological standard of the *Presbyterian Church in the U.S.A. (PCUSA). At the 1958 general assembly, which merged the *United Presbyterian Church of North America (UPCNA) and the PCUSA, a committee was commissioned to draft a brief contemporary confession of faith. In 1965 the committee presented a draft of the confession, along with a proposal to create a Book of Confessions, to the general assembly. A revised draft of the confession was submitted in 1966. By June 1967 the Confession of 1967 had been ratified by all but 19 (who rejected it) of 184 presbyteries. The confession and Book of Confessions were accepted by the 1967 general assembly.

The confession has its roots in the late nineteenth century, when several presbyteries requested the general assembly of the PCUSA to work toward creedal revision and/or a briefer, contemporary statement of faith. After revising the *Westminster Confession, the assembly of 1903 declined to adopt the new statement of faith. The twentieth century brought several changes in the theological atmosphere of the Presbyterian church, which brought the church to the realization that the Westminster standards no longer adequately reflected its beliefs. Most significant among these were the increased appreciation for biblical criticism and the newer biblical theology movement, a fuller appropriation of the social gospel, the ecumenical movement and the *neo-orthodoxy of Karl *Barth and H. Richard *Niebuhr and Reinhold *Neibuhr.

The preface of the Confession of 1967 acknowledges the historical particularity of all creeds and singles out eight earlier church statements to serve with it as the theological guides of the church: the Apostles' Creed, the Nicene Creed, the Scots Confession, the *Heidelberg Catechism, the Second Helvetic Confession, the *Westminster Confession and Shorter Catechism and the Theological Declaration of Barmen. The confession's overriding theme is Christian reconciliation, the "peculiar need" of its generation. Four contemporary situations are pinpointed as urgently requiring such reconciliation: the discrimination dividing the family of humanity, conflict between nations, "enslaving poverty" in an affluent world and male-female relations. The confession regards the Bible as "the witness without parallel" yet in the "words of men" and so approachable only "with literary and historical understanding." It also notes that the church universal organizes its ministry with a variety of acceptable forms, though the presbyterian *polity is especially suited to promote "the responsibility of all members for ministry," to foster "the organic relation of all congregations in the church" and to protect against "exploitation by ecclesiastical or secular power and ambition."

Conservatives, who formed Presbyterians United for Biblical Concerns and Presbyterian Laymen, Inc., resisted the confession on a number of counts, including what they determined to be a weakening of the orthodox view of the authority of Scripture and the deity of Christ, an absence of reference to the virgin birth, a discarding of the doctrine of predestination and a possible compromise of Presbyterian polity. Questions were also raised regarding the role of the church as an agent of reconciliation in the social and political arena.

Bibliography. E. A. Dowey Jr., *A Commentary on the Confession of 1967 and an Introduction to the "Book of Confessions"* (1968); J. B. Rogers, *Presbyterian Creeds: A Guide to the Book of Confessions* (1985). M. J. Coalter

Confessions and Catcheisms. *See* Adopting Act (1729); Belgic Confession; Confession of 1967; Dort, Canons of; Heidelberg Catechism; Westminster Confession of Faith.

Congregationalism. A Protestant tradition of ecclesiology and church government, Congregationalism maintains that local congregations, consisting of men and women who acknowledge the lordship of Jesus Christ and seek his will, can minister and govern themselves through congregational vote, covenant and participation. Congregationalists view this polity as a more complete fulfillment of the Reformation principle of the priesthood of all believers. Although there are specific Congregational denominations, this type of church government can also be found in many other churches and denominations in America, particularly among Baptist and independent churches. Here we focus on historic Congregationalism in America.

Historic Congregationalism came to America with the Separatist Pilgrims of Plymouth and the Puritans of the Massachusetts Bay Colony. Congregationalism originated in English Puritanism, being the more radical wing of a Reformed movement that believed it impossible to renew the Church of England from within. Choosing rather to form "gathered" congregations bound by a covenant between God and believers, these nonconformists came into conflict with the Anglican Church, including Anglicans of Puritan persuasion. By 1608 a group of Separatists had taken refuge from persecution at Leiden in the Netherlands. In 1620 a band of Pilgrims settled in Plymouth, Massachusetts. In 1629 the nonseparatist English Puritans, fleeing persecution under Archbishop William Laud (1573-1645) in England, established settlements around Boston, Massachusetts. These American Puritans ordained their ministers congregationally, even when the latter had already been ordained episcopally in England. In the rigorous living conditions of New England, the two groups found themselves cooperating with each other and agreeing on the central points of Calvinism as it was mediated by the English Puritan divines.

From 1646 to 1648, the religious leaders of New England met several times in a synod at Cambridge, Massachusetts, and there decided to accept the Westminster Confession of Faith as their doctrinal statement. They also drafted and adopted the "Platforme of Church Discipline"—better known as the "Cambridge Platform"—defining their polity. Codifying the "mixed" polity of Puritan theorists, they described a government of local, independent churches that was shared by church members and church officers. It is the earliest document setting forth American Congregational faith and church government and served as the constitution of the "Congregational Way" well into the nineteenth century.

The Great Awakening, which peaked in the years 1740-1742 and spread throughout the colonies, had a great impact on New England Congregationalism. On the one hand there was the revival of a heartfelt religion that was profoundly evangelical in character. The Congregationalist minister and theologian of the movement, Jonathan *Edwards, was perhaps the greatest intellect early American Congregationalism produced, and he set the agenda for the tradition of New England Theology that was carried on well into the nineteenth century. On the other hand, a significant number of Congregational clergy opposed the revivals, and a rift developed that was to seriously divide Congregationalism into liberal and evangelical wings and profoundly affect American religious and political life in general.

This liberalism, centered in eighteenth-century Boston, was fueled by Enlightenment ideas and manifested itself first in a liberalized Calvinism and then in an Arian or Socinian view of the person of Christ. The chief leaders of this movement were the Congregational ministers Charles Chauncy and Jonathan Mayhew. The appointment of Unitarian Henry Ward to the chair of divinity at Harvard in 1803, the publication of William E. Channing's manifesto, *Unitarian Christianity,* in 1819 and the Dedham Decision of 1820 in which the Massachusetts Supreme Court awarded the property of a trinitarian congregation to a Unitarian parish, were all landmarks in the gradual move toward the founding of a separate American Unitarian Association in 1825.

In the nineteenth century, Congregationalism was again influenced by theological liberalism, the leading voice being that of Congregational minister Horace Bushnell, called by some "the father of American religious liberalism." His controversial views on the Trinity, the atonement, conversion and the nature of religious language were widely influential, first in the seminaries and then in the pulpits. Other influential liberal ministers of late nineteenth-century Congregationalism were Henry Ward Beecher and Washington Gladden, the latter developing Bushnell's romantic notions of evolutionary progress into the Social Gospel. Liberalism has continued to hold a prominent place in twentieth-century Congregationalism, though in recent decades it has traded its earlier optimism for a more chastened mood.

Although the modified Calvinism of colonial times was intentionally left behind by the Congregational mainstream, evangelicals and evangelical theology has maintained a presence within Congregationalism. The Congregational "Burial Hill Declaration" (1865) proclaimed, "With the whole church we confess the common sinfulness and ruin of our race, and acknowledge that it is only through the work accomplished by the life and expiatory death of Christ that believers in Him are justified before God, receive the remission of sins, and through the presence and grace of the Holy Comforter are delivered from the power of sin and perfected in holiness." These beliefs are echoed in the contemporary United Church of Christ's Statement of Faith (1959) when it speaks of confessing a belief in God who seeks "in holy love to save all people from aimlessness and sin" and in Jesus Christ "conquering sin and death and reconciling the world to Himself." Although a minority, evangelical churches and individuals continue within contemporary Congregational fellowships and denominations, with notable evangelical leaders such as Harold John Ockenga (1905-1985) and theologian Donald G. Bloesch (1928-) representing this tradition.

Concern for the proclamation of the gospel has always been present in Congregationalism, and early Congregational Puritans were concerned to take the gospel to the Native American Indian population. The Protestant foreign mission movement in America arose among Congregationalists when in 1810 the American Board of Commissioners for Foreign Missions (ABCFM) was organized. In 1812 the ABCFM sent out five missionaries, two of whom had dedicated themselves to missionary service in the "Haystack Prayer Meeting" of 1806. While the ABCFM was originally predominantly Congregational, a number of other Reformed denominations used it until they had formed their own agencies.

In 1801, under the *Plan of Union, Congregationalists cooperated with Presbyterians in frontier missionary work. Finding that Congregationalism was being swallowed up in Presbyterianism, however, the Congregationalists repealed the agreement at the Albany convention of 1852. One of the fruits of this earlier cooperative spirit was the American Home Missionary Society, which was established in 1826 in conjunction with the Presbyterians, but after 1861 became the church planting agency of the Congregational churches. In 1846 the American Missionary Association was established. Committed to evangelism to nonwhites and strongly *abolitionist, after the Civil War it carried out a noble effort to educate former slaves. Currently the United Church of Christ carries out its mission work through the Board of World Ministries and the Board of Homeland Ministries, the successors of the earlier boards, along with mission work done by the other Congregational denominations and fellowships.

Feeling the need to organize and work with each other in wider ministries, American Congregational churches from their inception have formed fellowships beyond the local church. Starting first with the colonial consociations and associations, by 1822 the first state conference was held in Maine. In 1871 the National Council of Congregational Churches was formed, serving the interests of the churches in national, international and other delegated tasks. In 1913, meeting in Kansas City, the National Council was given a broader mandate in the work of the

Church. A general secretary was chosen to represent the churches before other groups. The present United Church of Christ actively continues programs and agencies on a national level.

In the late nineteenth century, Congregationalists began to consider whether their fellowship might not extend beyond their National Council. As early as 1871 the National Council at Oberlin produced a "Declaration on the Unity of the Church" and began consultations with other denominations, many of which were unsuccessful. Two consultations did, however, lead to later developments. Talks with a Restorationist group, the Christian Connection, were carried out in 1890 and again in 1923, finally leading to a merger of the two bodies in 1931 when they formed the General Council of Congregational and Christian Churches.

In 1938 a union of the General Council of Congregational and Christian Churches with the Evangelical and Reformed Church was proposed, but it was not until 1957 that a body of delegates from both denominations, meeting at Cleveland, Ohio, elected a constitutional committee. In July 1961, in Philadelphia, a constitution was adopted and the United Church of Christ was established. Consultations with the Disciples of Christ, which broke down in 1895, were again revived in 1977. In the late 1980s the two denominations were actively exploring avenues of cooperation.

Congregational polity continued to be modified as it developed in American history. The "Statement of Congregational Principles" or "Boston Platform" (1865) superseded the Cambridge Platform and proclaimed three affirmations: (1) the local church derives its power and authority directly from Christ; (2) there must be duties of respect and charity included in a communion of churches; and (3) the ministry implies "no power of government." In contemporary practice, ministers are ordained and installed by the local church but "ministerial standing" is held by associations (sometimes by conferences) that cooperate in the ordination or installation. Organizations beyond the local church (associations, conferences, general synod) speak for themselves but not for the local churches. The constitution and bylaws of the United Church of Christ further define this relationship of both mutual cooperation and congregational independence.

Other Congregational churches and fellowships of churches in the Congregational tradition continue to exist apart from the United Church of Christ. These have either remained independent or have joined the loose fellowships of the National Association of Congregational Churches (noted for its "referendum council," which allows local churches to modify any act of national bodies) and the Conservative Congregational Christian Conference (noted for its mutual confession of a more comprehensive and conservative doctrinal statement). The United Church of Christ, along with these other fellowships, have appropriated, each in its own way, various strands of historic American Congregationalism.

Bibliography. G. G. Aktins and F. L. Fagley, *History of American Congregationalism* (1942); D. Horton, *The United Church of Christ: Its Origins, Organization and Role in the Church Today* (1962); M. L. Starkey, *The Congregational Way: The Role of the Pilgrims and Their Heirs in Shaping America* (1966); W. W. Sweet, *The Congregationalists* (1939); W. Walker, *The Creeds and Platforms of Congregationalism* (1893) L. E. Wilshire

Cornish, Samuel Eli (1795-1858). African-American Presbyterian minister, evangelical activist and pioneer journalist. Cornish was born to free black parents in 1795 in Sussex County, Delaware. Moving to Philadelphia around 1815, Cornish came under the influence of John Gloucester, pastor of Philadelphia's First African (Presbyterian) Church. Trained for the ministry by Gloucester and members of the Philadelphia Presbytery, he was licensed and commissioned in 1819 to serve as a missionary among the slaves of Maryland. This experience made Cornish a lifelong opponent of slavery "for the Gospel's sake." Recruited and employed by a New York City society for missionary work among the city's growing black population, Cornish established First Colored Presbyterian Church and was installed as its pastor in 1824. He intermittently served other black Presbyterian congregations in Newark, New Jersey (1843), and New York (1845-1847).

Committed to evangelical activism, Cornish played a leading role in the struggle against racism and slavery and held membership in a variety of evangelical reform organizations such as the American Bible Society, American Moral Reform Society, American Anti-Slavery Association and American and Foreign Anti-Slavery Society. As pioneer journalist and founding editor of *Freedom's Journal* in 1827 (the first black newspaper), *The Rights of All* in 1829 and *The Colored American* in 1837, he gave editorial voice to the concerns and needs of the black community. He and Theodore *Wright authored *The Colonization Scheme Considered, In Its Rejection by the Colored People* (1840).

After the schism of the Presbyterian church in

1837 Cornish remained loyal to the *Old School wing of the Presbyterian church, which he believed to be "orthodox in faith" but "despotic and anti-Christian" in some of its practices. Unable to endorse the tactics of the more radical generation coming to the fore of the reform crusade and antislavery struggle, he became estranged from the movement and suffered ridicule as "an Old School Man." He died in New York in 1858, an all but forgotten champion of evangelical reform and the struggle against racism and slavery.

BIBLIOGRAPHY. *ANB* 5; R. Balmer and J. R. Fitzmier, *The Presbyterians* (1993); W. T. Catto, *A Semi-Centenary Discourse: Delivered in the First African Presbyterian Church, Philadelphia* (1857); A. E. Murray, *Presbyterians and the Negro—A History* (1966); J. H. Pease and W. H. Pease, "The Negro Conservative: Samuel Eli Cornish," in *Bound with Them in Chains: A Biographical History of the Anti-Slavery Movement* (1972); D. E. Swift, *Black Prophets of Justice: Activist Clergy Before the Civil War* (1989); idem, "Black Presbyterian Attacks on Racism: Samuel Cornish, Theodore Wright and Their Contemporaries," *JPH* 51 (1973) 433-70.

M. Moore

Corwin, Edward Tanjore (1834-1914). *Reformed Church in America (RCA) pastor and historian. Born in New York City, he received his education at the College of the City of New York and the New Brunswick Theological Seminary, from which he was graduated in 1856. After a year of graduate study, he served Reformed church congregations in Ridgewood (1857-1863) and Millstone, New Jersey (1863-1888), and Greenport, New York (1895-1897). He served as rector of Hertzog Hall at the New Brunswick Theological Seminary from 1888 to 1895. He died in North Branch, New Jersey.

Shortly after beginning his first pastorate, Corwin published *The Manual of the Reformed Protestant Dutch Church* in 1859, a compilation of all Dutch Reformed Church pastors and congregations beginning with the Reverend Jonas Michaelius and the first Dutch Reformed Church in 1628. The manual was expanded and republished in 1869, 1879 and 1902. In 1895 his history of the denomination was published in the American Church History series. He was coeditor of the *Centennial of the Theological Seminary of the Reformed Church in America* (1884). In 1906 he published *A Digest of Constitutional and Synodical Legislation of the Reformed Church in America,* which summarized all official actions of the denomination from 1738 to 1906.

The collection of colonial Dutch Reformed records Corwin obtained in the Netherlands during 1897-1898 were published in the six-volume *Ecclesiastical Records, State of New York,* 1901-1916. Corwin's publications continue to provide the basic knowledge of the RCA from the early seventeenth century through the nineteenth century.

BIBLIOGRAPHY. *ANB* 5; "The Amsterdam Correspondence," *American Society of Church History,* vol. 7; "The Ecclesiastical Conditions of New York at the Opening of the Eighteenth Century," *Papers of the American Society of Church History,* 2d series, vol. 3 (1912).

E. J. Bruins

Covenant Theology. A doctrine or system of theology explaining the relationship between God and humankind in terms of a compact, or covenant; also called federal theology. Theologians who have taught the covenant doctrine have based it on biblical themes, especially God's covenant with Israel as recorded in the Old Testament.

Although the concept of covenant is ancient, the rigorous development of an overall, systematic covenant theology grew out of the Protestant Reformation. The concept of a "covenant" (Latin *foedus,* from which is derived "federal theology"), as it was generally understood at the time of the Reformation, meant a compact between two or more parties by which they solemnly obligated themselves to each other to accomplish a particular task. This concept was utilized as a theological construct by sixteenth-century Reformed theologians, particularly John *Calvin (1509-1564), Ulrich Zwingli (1484-1531) and Johann Heinrich Bullinger (1504-1575). Anabaptists also developed a doctrine of covenant, primarily referring to the union of believers with each other.

Reformed covenant theology has taught that God offers grace and salvation to humankind. To those who by faith accept God's offer of salvation—on his terms—he assuredly grants salvation. Thus humankind gains assurance from its covenant relationship with God. Although there are many variations, theologians have discerned three covenants in Scripture: The Covenant of Works (offered to Adam, which he failed); the Covenant of Grace (offered after the Fall of Adam, again to Abraham and renewed in Christ); and, for some theologians, the Covenant of Redemption (the eternal promise of God's salvation underlying the Covenant of Grace).

The covenant approach to theology strongly affected English Puritanism, and through Puritanism's influence in the New World it came to have a significant influence in America. One of the trademarks of Puritan theology, it is evident in the writings of such Puritan giants as William Perkins, Dudley Fenner, Richard Sibbes, John Preston, William Ames and the separatist Robert Browne. The appeal of the covenant among Puritans of England and America was varied, but most noteworthy was its rational and easily understood organizational structure. The doctrine offered absolute assurance of God's eternal graciousness. Moreover, since many English and American Puritans were involved in the commercial and political world with its many "compacts" and "contracts," the preacher's use of "covenant" contextualized theology in terms of their everyday world and spoke to them in a special way. Although Puritans did not invent covenant theology, they did make good use of it.

The writings of William Ames, the English Puritan theologian and university professor, were an important means for spreading the covenant method of theology in both England and America. His *Medulla Theologiae* (1627, known in many English editions as *The Marrow of Sacred Divinity)* and his *De Conscientia* (1630) present nearly the entire scope of theology within the framework of covenants. In dealing with "intelligent creatures" (i.e., man and woman), God governs in a moral, intelligible way through covenants. "This covenant is, as it were, a kind of transaction of God with the creature whereby God commands, promises, threatens, fulfills; and the creature binds itself in obedience to God so demanding." First God covenanted with Adam in the covenant of creation, saying: "Do this and you will live; if you do it not you shall die." Adam failed, but then in the very dawn of human history (Gen 3), God made his second covenant, the unconditional covenant of grace. The history of the new covenant is the story of salvation.

Not all theologians developed the covenant idea in exactly the same way as Ames, but his exposition illustrates the main lines of the doctrine. Although European rather than American, Ames helped to mold American Puritan thought, and he was one of the forerunners of American *Congregationalism. Many American settlers praised him as the "learned doctor," and his *Medulla* and *De Conscientia* had a wide readership, with the *Medulla* long serving as a textbook at Harvard and Yale.

Through the English Puritan writers, covenant theology entered New England Congregationalism. American versions of it can be found in the writings of John Cotton, Thomas Hooker, Thomas Shepard, Peter Bulkeley and many others. *Scottish Presbyterians also brought their distinctive covenant doctrine to America. Another source of the covenant ideal is the *Westminster Confession of Faith (1647), a theological creed revered by Congregationalists, Presbyterians and Baptists in both England and America. Outside of the Reformed tradition, however, the covenant concept was not nearly as prominent. Some Anabaptist groups, namely Amish, Hutterites and Mennonites, drew upon their own understanding of covenant in forming communal and mutual aid groups.

Covenant Theology and the Church. Although rooted in theological speculation, the covenant ideal had many applications in America. American Congregationalists wanted to organize churches pleasing to God and free from all episcopal trappings. From the individual covenant of grace, they deduced the corporate church covenant, whereby the believers would band together to carry out their covenant responsibilities. According to Perry Miller, the church covenant "was held to be a miniature edition of the divine covenant." The local congregation was to be composed only of truly godly people, so-called visible saints. To gain membership in the church, the Christian believer had to testify to his or her faith and conversion; moreover, the believer promised to covenant with fellow believers in fruitful church fellowship. A congregation was "a society of believers joined together in a special bond. . . . This bond is a covenant." A very early American version of the church covenant at Salem, Massachusetts, read: "We Covenant with the Lord and one another; and doe bynd ourselves in the presence of God, to walke together in all his waies, according as he is pleased to reveale himself unto us in his Blessed word of truth."

This type of covenanted church had been occasionally practiced in English churches in the Netherlands before 1620. It functioned, to an extent, surreptitiously in England, and then became the norm for American Congregationalist churches. In addition to the Salem covenant, other church covenants were enacted very early in Charleston (1630) and at Watertown (1630).

When religious zeal waned, as it did within a few decades, the problem of maintaining pure, saintly churches became a dilemma. Many respectable citizens, baptized as infants into the church, could not as mature persons point to a particular experience of true conversion. Thus, they were not allowed to take up active membership in the church. To solve this dilemma, the New England Congregationalists created the policy of the Half-Way Covenant (1662). This allowed persons without, or unassured of, conversion to have a minimal "half-way" participation in the church, including baptism for their children. Regarded as a compromise measure, the Half-Way Covenant was, nevertheless, accepted as a practical solution in a society no longer in tune with the ideological fervor of its founding fathers.

Covenant Theology and Public Life. Just as God had covenanted with humankind in salvation and in gathering churches, so groups within society were to covenant with one another as they carried out their ordinary affairs. In fact, the seventeenth century was an age of compacts, contracts and secular covenants, through which the public business was transacted. Theological covenants and social-political covenants sprang out of the same milieu in America, and overlapped with one another. The Mayflower Pilgrims formed themselves into a "civil Body Politick" by means of a covenant, the Mayflower Compact (1620). Roger Williams founded Providence in Rhode Island by a compact (1636); the Fundamental Orders of Connecticut (1639) created government by covenant, and such practice prevailed throughout the towns of New England.

In a larger sense the Puritan leadership envisioned the entire people of Christian New England as forming a covenanted people in compact with God, a kind of national covenant. They were a New Israel. Governor John Winthrop preached a sermon on shipboard while sailing to America, in which he promised that by "mutual consent" they would establish their own "due form of Government both civil and ecclesiastical." The founding of America, in Puritan eyes, was a mission world witness accomplished by covenant. "Thus stands the cause between God and us; we are entered into Covenant with him for this work. . . . We shall be as a City upon a Hill" (1630). Covenant theology was one important ingredient, although not the only one, in developing the American ideal of political compact and contract so prominent in its great public documents. H. Richard Niebuhr has suggested the likelihood of an enduring connection between "The Idea of the Covenant and American Democracy."

The reign of covenant theology began to fade in the late eighteenth century; its greatest day was in the early history of America. Nevertheless, the covenant ideal, with its teaching about mutual obligation and communal responsibility, continued to influence American life, although in evermore secularized forms. Moreover, the pervasive ideal that America has a moral mission in the world, beyond the mundane, owes much to covenant theology.

BIBLIOGRAPHY. S. E. Ahlstrom, *A Religious History of the American People* (1972); P. Y. De Jong, *The Covenant Idea in New England Theology, 1620-1847* (1945); P. Miller, *The New England Mind: The Seventeenth Century* (1939); H. R. Niebuhr, "The Idea of Covenant and American Democracy," *CH* 23 (1954) 126-35; R. G. Pope, *The Half-Way Covenant* (1969); W. Roth and R. R. Ruether, *The Liberating Bond: Covenant—Biblical and Contemporary* (1978); K. L. Sprunger, *The Learned Doctor William Ames* (1972).

K. L. Sprunger

Craig, John (1710-1774).† Pioneer Presbyterian minister in western Virginia. Originally from County Antrim, Northern Ireland, Craig attended Edinburgh University in Scotland and immigrated to Maryland in 1738. Licensed by the Presbytery of Donegal in Pennsylvania (August 1738), he was encouraged by John *Thomson to serve as a supply preacher in Opequhon, Irish Tract and other places in western Virginia. In September 1740 he was ordained and went on to organize the Augusta Stone Church and Tinkling Spring Presbyterian Church. The first Presbyterian minister in western Virginia, Craig was joined by Thomson in 1744, as the *Scots-Irish Presbyterians kept pushing back the frontier.

Craig's parish extended over more than six hundred square miles at first, and today thirteen Presbyterian churches owe their origin to his missionary activity. Retiring from Tinkling Spring in 1754, Craig continued to serve the Augusta church until he died. Known for his long sermons and tireless efforts in the rugged back country of Virginia, he ministered primarily among the Scots-Irish settlers on the frontier. During the French and Indian War, he encouraged his people to remain in the valley of Virginia, declaring that their bravery and "noble Christian dependence on God" would remain a testimony to their posterity. He worked side by side with his members in fortifying the church building against Indian attacks. One of the early bearers of confessional *Calvinism in colonial America, he sided with the *Old Side in the split of 1741, and with Samuel *Davies he helped form a distinctive American Presbyterian consciousness in Virginia.

BIBLIOGRAPHY. H. A. White, *Southern Presbyterian Leaders* (1911). L. B. Weeks

Craig, Samuel G. (1874-1960). Presbyterian minister, editor, publisher and author. Craig was born in DeKalb County, Illinois, and educated at Princeton University (A.B., 1895; A.M., 1900) and at Princeton Seminary (1900). He later studied in Berlin (1910, 1911). He pastored two congregations: First Presbyterian at Ebensburg, Pennsylvania (1900-1910), and

North Church in Pittsburgh, Pennsylvania (1912-1915).

Craig came to prominence as an editor and publisher. From 1915 to 1930 he held a number of editorial positions with *The Presbyterian,* the independently run paper that represented the conservative cause within the *Presbyterian Church in the U.S.A. (PCUSA). In 1925 Craig became editor in chief and consistently defended the *Old School forces at Princeton Seminary and in the denomination. With Princeton's reorganization in 1929, Craig threw his support to J. Gresham *Machen and to Westminster Seminary, which he believed would carry on the Princeton tradition. His service on Westminster's board and his views placed him at variance with the paper's board of directors, and he was fired.

Craig organized the Presbyterian and Reformed Publishing Company in 1930, a company committed to the promotion of a scholarly and popular defense of historic *Calvinism. Through this company Craig published *Christianity Today,* which he edited from 1930 to 1949. The new paper defended the conservative and Calvinist position and especially Machen and Westminster. However, when Machen refused to comply with denominational directives regarding his involvement in the Independent Board for Presbyterian Foreign Missions, Craig and Machen parted company. Machen began *The Presbyterian Guardian* in 1935 and was instrumental in the organization of the *Orthodox Presbyterian Church (OPC) in 1936. Craig remained with the PCUSA.

Christianity Today appeared intermittently until 1949, when Craig stopped its publication. In 1956 its name was revived by the efforts of the neo-evangelicals associated with Fuller Seminary and Billy Graham. Craig died in Princeton, New Jersey.

Bibliography. S. G. Craig, *Christianity Rightly So Called* (1946); idem, *Jesus of Yesterday and Today* (1956); F. H. Stevenson, "Samuel G. Craig, Editor of *Christianity Today,*" *CT** 4 (May 1933) 4-14.

C. G. Dennison

Craig, Willis Green (1834-1911). Presbyterian pastor and educator. Born in Danville, Kentucky, Craig graduated from Centre College in Kentucky in 1852 and from Danville Theological Seminary in 1860. Ordained to the Presbyterian ministry in 1862, Craig spent the next twenty years pastoring the First Presbyterian Church of Keokuk, Iowa. From 1882 until 1891 he served as professor of biblical and ecclesiastical history at McCormick Theological Seminary in Chicago. Craig assumed the seminary's chair in didactic and polemic theology in 1891, a position he held until his death. For many years he oversaw the field education of McCormick students in evangelism and city missions.

In the years following 1885 Craig chaired the board of trustees of the Church of the Covenant and led a campaign to build one of Chicago's largest church sanctuaries for this rapidly growing congregation. A staunch theological conservative who was committed to federal theology, plenary inspiration and strict subscription to the Westminster standards, Craig strongly opposed efforts of other faculty to introduce progressive orthodoxy at McCormick in the late nineteenth and early twentieth centuries. Highly respected by many members of his denomination for his Christian character, keen intellect, stimulating teaching and sound scholarship, Craig was elected moderator of the *Presbyterian Church in the U.S.A. (PCUSA) General Assembly in 1893. He died in Chicago.

Bibliography. L. J. Halsey, *A History of the McCormick Theological Seminary of the Presbyterian Church* (1893); L. A. Loetscher, *The Broadening Church: A Study of Theological Ilssues in the Presbyterian Church Since 1869* (1957).

G. S. Smith

Cumberland Presbyterian Church.† Presbyterian denomination with churches predominantly in the South and West. An outgrowth of the frontier revivals of 1800 in Kentucky, this denomination originated in 1810 in Dickson County, Tennessee, with the formation of an independent Cumberland Presbytery by Finis *Ewing, Samuel King and Samuel *McAdow. This followed a lengthy controversy between the more Arminian and revivalist elements of Cumberland Presbytery and the *Presbyterian Church in the U.S.A. (PCUSA) over subscription to the *Westminster Confession's teaching on predestination, educational requirements for ministers and the extent of synodical authority over presbyteries.

In 1805 a group of ministers from the Cumberland Presbytery were suspended by the Synod of Kentucky for teaching contrary to the Westminster Confession of Faith. Claiming to be the rightful heirs of the *Tennents' Log College and the Great Awakening, Ewing and his colleagues argued that their reservations about certain parts of the confession should not debar them from the ministry. Faced with the requirement of unqualified subscription, they were forced to start the Cumberland Presbyterian Church (CPC). Four years later the church produced an appropriately modified version of the Westminster Confession.

Attempting to bridge the gap between *Calvinism and *Arminianism, the "medium theology" of Ewing and Robert Donnell tried to rid the confession of all "fatality" but also weakened the effects of the fall on humanity, expanded human freedom and heightened humanity's natural ability to ready itself for conversion. Instead of the old Calvinist belief that salvation is wholly a work of God, the Cumberland theology considered it a cooperative effort. Self-consciously modeling doctrine in accordance with the mood of the newly formed republic, Ewing insisted that people determine their own destiny, and Donnell proclaimed that their church's emphasis on liberty gave it the right to be "properly called an American church." Still based on the federal or covenant theology of the seventeenth century, the modified Confession of 1814 started from the sinfulness of humanity and the wrath of God and taught that God's grace in the sacrificial death of Jesus Christ removes the penalty of the law, giving people the chance to choose salvation freely.

The church enjoyed rapid growth on the frontier with the establishing of the Cumberland Synod in 1813 and the formation of a general assembly in 1829. Growing fivefold between 1835 and 1860, the predominantly rural denomination established congregations from Pennsylvania to California. By the 1840s, stirrings arose from certain corners of the church that felt that the trappings of Calvinism had not yet been sufficiently removed. To counter these trends Milton Bird founded the *Theological Medium* in 1845, which was continued under various names through the end of the century, and Richard Beard, professor of theology at Cumberland University, wrote his three-volume *Lectures on Theology* (1860, 1869, 1870), which became the standard of conservative Cumberland theology. Nevertheless, the forces for change were irresistible, and in 1883 Stanford Burney, Beard's successor, successfully guided the revision of the confession to affirm the complete autonomy of humanity, rejecting the last vestiges of federal Calvinism, including the substitutionary atonement. No longer was salvation both the gift of God and the choice of people but the act of people in choosing to believe and obey God.

Partially due to the church's strength in the border states, the Civil War did not result in a formal split. Instead, after the war the Cumberland Presbyterians helped establish the Colored Cumberland Presbyterian Church (1869) (*see* Cumberland Presbyterian Church in America). In 1880 it applied to the World Association of Reformed Churches but was denied membership because of its rejection of certain Reformed doctrines. Ironically, it was accepted four years later, even after the drastic confessional revision of 1883.

Following the revision by the PCUSA of the Westminster Confession's teaching on divine sovereignty, a merger of the two denominations was approved in 1906, on the condition that the existing Cumberland presbyteries be allowed to remain segregated. A continuing Cumberland Presbyterian Church was perpetuated, however, by a sizable minority—both on the conservative and liberal wings—which feared that doctrinal harmony between the two churches had not been achieved.

Standing self-consciously between Calvinism and Arminianism, Cumberland Presbyterians have held to a medium theology that affirms an unlimited atonement, universal grace, conditional election, the eternal security of the believer and the salvation of all children dying in infancy. The denomination supports Bethel College in McKenzie, Tennessee, and Memphis Theological Seminary. Close ties are maintained with the predominantly African-American Cumberland Presbyterian Church in America (formerly Second Cumberland Presbyterian Church), which subscribes to the Cumberland Presbyterian confessional standards.

See also CUMBERLAND PRESBYTERIAN CHURCH IN AMERICA.

BIBLIOGRAPHY. B. M. Barrus, M. L. Baughn and T. H. Campbell, *A People Called Cumberland Presbyterians* (1972); T. H. Campbell, *Studies in Cumberland Presbyterian History* (1944).

W. B. Evans

Cumberland Presbyterian Church in America. Predominantly African-American Presbyterian denomination with churches located in the Southern and central United States.

Initially known as the Colored Cumberland Presbyterian Church, the denomination was formed during Reconstruction in the wake of the American Civil War as Southern whites and the newly emancipated African-Americans sought to define a new social order. Prior to the Civil War, some estimates had placed African-American membership in the *Cumberland Presbyterian Church (CPC) as high as twenty thousand persons. Realizing that the African-American Cumberland Presbyterian members would not be accorded equality in worship and membership in the church courts and desiring to minister effectively to the African-American population, a convention of African-American ministers in 1869 petitioned the Cumberland Presbyterian general assembly to allow the formation of "presbyteries of colored ministers."

Fearful of racial integration, the white general assembly then authorized the formation of separate presbyteries and synods for its African-American members. The first presbytery was formed in 1869; a synod followed in 1871, and by 1874 a formal and complete separation of the two churches was effected. Thus the division into two distinct churches resulted both from the desire of the former slaves for autonomy and from the white church's fear of racial integration.

The first general assembly of the Colored Cumberland Presbyterian Church was formed in Nashville, Tennessee, on May 1, 1874. At this time the church comprised forty-six ministers and approximately three thousand communicant members. Early leaders included Alfred Barnett, John Humphrey, Hampton Jones, Alfred McCaulley, Lewis Neal and Moses T. Weir.

The Colored Cumberland Presbyterian body grew significantly, and by 1895 the church claimed approximately fifteen thousand members in twenty-two presbyteries. Realizing the need for ministerial training, the church founded a number of educational efforts during the late nineteenth and early twentieth centuries. Schools were established at Bowling Green, Kentucky (c. 1885), Springfield, Missouri (1895), Huntsville, Alabama (1898), and Milan, Tennessee, all of which eventually closed due to the chronic scarcity of funds.

Relations with other Presbyterian bodies, including the white Cumberland Presbyterian Church with which the group shares a common confessional heritage, were limited during the early years of the denomination. Financial and educational assistance from the white Cumberland Presbyterian body was minimal. For several decades after 1906, when a majority of the CPC merged with the *Presbyterian Church in the U.S.A. (PCUSA), the Colored Cumberland body received some financial support and recognition from the much larger and primarily northern Presbyterian body.

In the late 1930s ties between the Colored Cumberland and Cumberland churches began to grow stronger, due in part to the efforts of Colored Cumberland church minister S. A. Nelson and Cumberland Presbyterian minister Alba Bates. A cooperative education program involving both churches began to take shape by 1947, and Colored Cumberland students were admitted to the Cumberland Presbyterian Theological Seminary in 1953 and Bethel College in 1961. In 1957 committees were formed to plan and negotiate a merger of the two denominations. A plan of union was approved by both general assemblies in 1966, but the proposed merger failed to win approval from the required twelve out of sixteen African-American presbyteries. While formal merger was not approved, significant cooperation in denominational activities has been achieved, particularly with the Federated Board of Christian Education formed in 1972 (now known as the United Board for Christian Discipleship).

For much of its history the church was known as the Colored Cumberland Presbyterian Church. After the reception of the Presbytery of Liberia, West Africa, in 1949, the denomination's name was changed to Colored Cumberland Presbyterian Church in the U.S.A. and Liberia, Africa (the relationship with the Liberian church was dissolved in 1960). In 1960 the church's name was changed to Second Cumberland Presbyterian Church, and in 1992 the name Cumberland Presbyterian Church in America was adopted.

The majority of Cumberland Presbyterian Church in America churches are located in Alabama, Tennessee, Texas and Kentucky, and the denominational headquarters is located in Huntsville, Alabama. A monthly denominational periodical, *The Cumberland Flag,* is published.

See also CUMBERLAND PRESBYTERIAN CHURCH.

BIBLIOGRAPHY. B. M. Barrus, M. L. Baughn and T. H. Campbell, *A People Called Cumberland Presbyterians* (1972); T. H. Campbell, *One Family Under God* (1982); J. Jenkins, *Souvenir History of Colored Cumberland Presbyterian Church* (1905).

W. B. Evans

Curtis, Edward Lewis (1853-1911). Presbyterian pastor and seminary professor. He was born in Ann Arbor, Michigan, to William Stanton Curtis, a Presbyterian pastor who subsequently was a philosophy professor at Hamilton College and president of Knox College in Illinois, and to Mary Leach Curtis, who graduated from and eventually taught at Mount Holyoke Seminary. After graduating from Yale in 1874 and from Union Theological Seminary in New York City in 1879, Curtis studied Old Testament at the University of Berlin from 1879 to 1881. In 1881 he was appointed an instructor in Hebrew and Old Testament at McCormick Theological Seminary in Chicago. Ordained to the Presbyterian ministry in 1883, Curtis was promoted by McCormick to professor of Old Testament literature and exegesis in 1886 in recognition of his excellent scholarship and teaching.

Curtis's reputation as a Hebrew linguist and his numerous periodical articles led to his selection as the Holmes Professor of Hebrew Language and Literature at Yale University in 1891, a position he held for the next twenty years. Despite suffering from angina pectoris and from a stroke he experienced in 1906 that significantly impaired his eyesight, Curtis managed to complete his major scholarly work, *A Critical and Exegetical Commentary on the Book of Chronicles,* which was published in 1910 in the International Critical Commentary series. Respected by both colleagues and students as an Old Testament scholar and as a caring teacher, Curtis died on board a boat traveling between Castine, Maine, and Boston. After Curtis's death, his former student, Albert Madsen, who had assisted Curtis with his commentary, completed Curtis's manuscript on *The Book of Judges,* which was issued in 1913 as part of the Bible for Home and School series.

Bibliography. *DAB* XI; L. J. Halsey, *A History of the McCormick Theological Seminary of the Presbyterian Church* (1893); *Biblical World* 38 (October 1911) 279.

G. S. Smith

D

Dabbs, James McBride (1896-1970). Southern Presbyterian civil rights advocate. Born in Hayesville, South Carolina, and reared on a large cotton plantation, Dabbs attended the University of South Carolina, Clark University and Columbia University. After teaching briefly, Dabbs farmed for a living and wrote about the South until his death. A fervent Christian, he brought faith to bear on issues of importance for the region. His books include *The Southern Heritage* (1958), *Who Speaks for the South* (1964) and *Haunted by God* (1972).

Dabbs helped form the Fellowship of Southern Churchmen and served as president of the Southern Regional Council, a civil rights organization. Theologically Dabbs reiterated classic themes of Reformed tradition: the sovereignty of God over the affairs of the world, the universality of human sinfulness, the need for Christian proclamation of the gospel and the responsibility of Christians for others in every aspect of life. L. B. Weeks

Dabney, Robert Lewis (1820-1898).† Southern Presbyterian theologian and educator. Born in Louisa County, Virginia, Dabney studied at Hampden-Sydney College (1836-1837). Following a stint as a school teacher (1838-1839) he continued his education at the University of Virginia (1842) and Union Theological Seminary in Virginia (1846). Dabney began his ministerial career as a rural missionary but soon became pastor of Tinkling Spring Church, Virginia (1847-1853), and headmaster of a classical academy. In 1853 Hampden-Sydney awarded him an honorary doctorate, and he was called to Union Seminary, then located at Hampden-Sydney, as professor of church history and *polity. From 1859 to 1883 he taught theology and simultaneously served much of that time as copastor of Hampden-Sydney College Church (1858-1874). He declined the chair of church history at Princeton Seminary in 1860, preferring to remain in the South. In 1870 he was elected moderator of the Southern Presbyterian Church. In 1883 Dabney left Virginia for health reasons and became professor of philosophy at the University of Texas (1883-1894), where he helped found the Austin Theological Seminary and also served on its faculty (1884-1895). By 1890 Dabney was in ill health and had suffered a total loss of his eyesight, yet always a man of intense energy and conviction, he continued to lecture.

Prior to the *Civil War Dabney opposed secession, but he soon became a strong advocate of the Southern cause. When war interrupted his academic profession Dabney served as a chaplain (1861) in the Confederate army and, in 1862, as an officer under General Stonewall *Jackson. A loyal Southerner, Dabney never wavered from his belief that the cause of the South was right and would eventually be vindicated. Embittered by Reconstruction policies, he vigorously opposed reunion with the Northern Presbyterians. Despite his regional loyalties, he was nevertheless a perceptive social critic of post-Civil War industrial *capitalism, secular materialism and powerful centralized government.

An active churchman, Dabney worked to promote the union of the Presbyterian Church in the Confederate States of America (*Old School) with the United Synod of the South (*New School). Believing that the great majority of Southern New School men were doctrinally sound, he realized that the only way to prevent the spread of the New School theology was to ensure that all Southern ministers were trained in Old School seminaries. Later, in the evolution debates surrounding James *Woodrow, Dabney argued that the naturalism that pervaded nineteenth-century science would spread through the church as well, if Woodrow's views were accepted.

A man of wide and detailed learning, Dabney taught with great intensity and clarity of insight, and he was recognized as the leading Southern Presbyterian theologian after the Civil War. His theology was the moderate but consistent *Calvinism of the *Westminster Confession and Catechisms and was comparable to that of other nineteenth-century Old School Presbyterian theologians such as Charles *Hodge. Convinced of the authority and infallibility of Scriptures, Dabney took W. Robertson *Smith to task for abandoning the authority of Scripture for the authority of Julius Wellhausen. Like the Princeton theologians, Dabney was influenced by Francis *Turretin and the Scottish Common-Sense philosophy, but he avoided speculation and deplored some of the traditional theological distinctions, regarding them as overrefinements and undue subtleties.

Dabney's style was terse, powerful and fresh. Interested in practical matters, he was concerned to apply Christian faith not only to religious topics but also to moral and social philosophy. Because of his willingness to wrestle with difficult theological issues and make his own critical observations, some have regarded Dabney's systematic theology as more profound than that of Charles Hodge. His many writings include *Life and Campaigns of Lieut-General Thomas J. Jackson* (1866), *A Defense of Virginia, and Through Her of the South* (1867), *Sacred Rhetoric* (1870), *Systematic and Polemic Theology* (1871), *The Sensualist Philosophy of the Nineteenth Century* (1875), *Christ Our Penal Substitute* (1897), *The Practical Philosophy* (1897) and articles on a wide range of topics in *Discussions* (4 vols., 1890-1897).

As a defender of the South and its institutions, Dabney's influence for most of his lifetime did not extend outside of his region. At war with most of the developments of the latter half of the century and inflexible in resisting change, he lived to see many of the issues he had championed fall from favor within his denomination. Recent reprints of several of his books have given him a larger reading public than he enjoyed even during his lifetime.

BIBLIOGRAPHY. *ANB* 5; *DAB* III; *DARB;* T. C. Johnson, *The Life and Letters of Robert Lewis Dabney* (1903); D. F. Kelly, "Robert Lewis Dabney," in *Reformed Theology in America,* ed. D. F. Wells (1985); *NCAB* 2; D. H. Overy, *Robert Lewis Dabney: Apostle of the Old South* (1967). A. H. Freundt

Davies, Samuel (1723-1761).† Presbyterian minister and educator. Born in Delaware and of Welsh lineage, Davies grew up with parental expectations that he would serve the Presbyterian Church. After studying with Samuel *Blair in Pennsylvania, he was licensed to preach there in 1746 and was ordained as an evangelist to Virginia for the Synod of New York (*New Side Presbyterian) the following year. Moving with his new bride in April of 1747, he served as an evangelist and organizer of dissenting congregations that had been meeting informally. Less than six months after his arrival he became so ill that he had to return to Delaware, where in the fall of 1747 his young wife died. Returning to Virginia in 1748, Davies remarried and continued his fledgling ministry.

In Virginia Davies had to overcome the suspicion and hostility of Anglican officials who had the power to authorize and bar assemblies by religious dissenters. Soon, in part due to his winsome manners and clear arguments, he was conducting worship services over a five-county area. In his struggle to gain licenses for his congregations Davies became known as an advocate of civil liberties. Eventually, arguing against the king's attorney general that the Toleration Act of 1689 applied to the colonies as well as the British homeland, Davies was able to secure enough toleration to allow open evangelism and organization of dissenting churches. For his evangelical zeal for preaching Davies gained the reputation of fomenting a Southern Great Awakening during colonial times, including a notable ministry to the slave population. In 1755 he was instrumental in organizing the Presbytery of Hanover, the first in Virginia.

In 1753 the Synod of New York commissioned Davies and Gilbert *Tennent to conduct a campaign in England and Scotland for two years to raise support for the fledgling College of New Jersey (later named Princeton University). While in England, Davies received an official declaration from the king confirming his claim that the Toleration Act did indeed apply to Virginia. Establishing an international reputation as a preacher during the tour, Davies was particularly successful among the Scottish Presbyterians, and the pair returned with a large endowment for the college.

Following the unexpected deaths of presidents Aaron *Burr and Jonathan *Edwards, Davies was elected president of the College of New Jersey in 1758. Initially Davies declined the position due to his desire to remain in Virginia, but he was prevailed upon by the joint request of the trustees of the college and the Synod of New York the following year. Taking office in July 1759, he initiated a promising series of educational reforms before dying of pneumonia eighteen months after taking office. A model preacher and intellectual leader, Davies has been remembered for his skill as an orator, for his academic leadership at the College of New Jersey and as a champion of religious freedom who helped break the grip of established religion in the colonies.

BIBLIOGRAPHY. *AAP* 3; *ANB* 6; *DAB* III; *NCAB* 4; G. W. Pilcher, *Samuel Davies: Apostle of Dissent in Colonial Virginia* (1971); G. W. Pilcher, ed., *The Reverend Samuel Davies Abroad* (1967).

L. B. Weeks

Dawson, John William (1820-1899). Presbyterian scientist and educator. Regarded as Victorian Canada's foremost natural scientist, Dawson was educated at Thomas *McCulloch's Pictou Academy and the University of Edinburgh, where he studied under Robert Jameson. His interest in geology and natural history had begun while he was a schoolboy in his native Nova Scotia but was given considerable impetus when in 1842 he accompanied Charles Lyell, probably the most important geologist of his day, on a tour of Nova Scotia coal fields. The two remained lifelong friends, and Lyell became a mentor to Dawson.

Until his appointment as principal of McGill College, Montreal, in 1855, Dawson had worked at a number of jobs in his native Nova Scotia: surveying mineral deposits for the provincial government, teaching at both Pictou Academy and Dalhousie College and ultimately serving as provincial superintendent of education. In 1854 he was elected a fellow of the Geological Society of London, and in the following year he published his first major geological work, *Acadian Geology* (final, expanded ed., 1891). In 1854 Lyell recommended Dawson for the recently vacated chair of natural history at the University of Edinburgh. Dawson did not receive the Edinburgh chair, but to his surprise he was offered the principalship of McGill, having been proposed by Governor-General Sir Edmund Head. He remained at McGill until his retirement in 1893. Under Dawson's leadership the college was rescued from the brink of ruin and established as a world-class institution.

Dawson was a renowned geologist and natural scientist. He was the first president of the Royal Society of Canada and the only person to serve as president of both the American and British Associations for the Advancement of Science. He was also acclaimed as the most scholarly critic of Darwin in the Anglo-American world. He opposed Darwinism on scientific, philosophical and theological grounds, seeing it as a rejection of design and as undermining religion and morality. He was a proponent of the day-age theory of creation and was committed to a Baconian/inductive scientific methodology, though toward the end of his life he may have become less hostile to certain conceptions of theistic evolution. His reputation as an anti-Darwinian led to his being offered the chair of geology at Princeton (a position to be combined with a special lectureship at Princeton Seminary on the relationship of religion and science). Dawson declined this offer, however, in order to remain in Montreal and serve the interests of Protestantism against the perceived threat from ultramontanism. Dawson wrote prolifically (more than four hundred books and articles) on scientific subjects and on the relationship of Christianity to *science. A lifelong Presbyterian, Dawson was continuously active in church affairs and also served as president of the Dominion [of Canada] Evangelical Alliance. He was knighted in 1884.

See also SCIENCE, PRESBYTERIANS AND.

BIBLIOGRAPHY. *DCB* 12; W. Dawson, *Fifty Years of Work in Canada* (1901); D. N. Livingstone, *Darwin's Forgotten Defenders: The Encounter Between Evangelical Theology and Evolutionary Thought* (1987); C. F. O'Brien, *Sir William Dawson* (1971); R. W. Vaudry, "Canadian Presbyterians and Princeton Seminary, 1850-1900," in *The Burning Bush and a Few Acres of Snow: The Presbyterian Contribution to Canadian Life and Culture,* ed. W. Klempa (1994).

R. W. Vaudry

Day, Thomas Franklin (1852-1943). Presbyterian home missionary and seminary professor. Born in Allegheny City, Pennsylvania, Day and his family moved to Ohio in 1858. In 1876 Day graduated from Ohio University. He then attended Union Theological Seminary in New York from 1877 to 1880, where his lifelong interest in the Hebrew language and the Old Testament was sparked by Charles Augustus *Briggs.

Ordained in 1881 by the Presbytery of Utah, Day was a home missionary in the presbytery from 1880 until 1890. In the summer of 1888, he pursued Hebrew and Old Testament studies with William Rainey Harper at the University of Chicago. Due in part to the recommendation of Harper, Day was invited in 1890 to join the faculty of the San Francisco Theological Seminary in California. Day taught Old Testament and Hebrew at the seminary until his forced resignation in 1912.

Despite the controversy surrounding his mentor Briggs and the dissatisfaction of some students with his higher-critical views of the composition of the Old Testament, the 1890s passed with no formal action taken against Day. Opposition may have been forestalled due to Day's deep and fervent evangelical spirituality and to the tenuousness of the seminary's existence. Whatever the explanation, pressure from within the Synod of California to investigate Day became open in 1906. Militant conservatives, most numerous in the Presbytery of Los Angeles but with vocal supporters in other presbyteries, forced a synod vote in 1910 on the written answers Day provided to questions regarding his views on the Old Testament. Six answers were accepted, six were rejected, and two were rejected in part.

Day had in the meantime published *The New*

Bible-Country (1910), a booklet expressing his firm yet irenic commitment to the "new country" of biblical criticism. He and his supporters refused to concede that Day was answerable to the synod, and Day sought to mollify his critics by revamping his teaching to feature conservative views in addition to his own. By 1912 the pressure against Day had not diminished, and he reluctantly resigned from the seminary. After travel abroad and a year of teaching at Olivet College, Michigan, Day completed a doctoral degree at Syracuse University in 1916. Thereafter he lived in active retirement in San Anselmo until his death.

Bibliography. D. F. Anderson, "Modernization and Theological Conservatism in the Far West: The Controversy Over Thomas F. Day, 1907-1912," *FH* 24 (summer 1992) 76-90; C. B. Day, "The Thomas Day Heresy Case in the Synod of California," *JPH* 46 (1968) 79-106; Thomas F. Day Papers, San Francisco Theological Seminary, San Anselmo, California. D. F. Anderson

Demographics, Presbyterianism and. For much of its history, Presbyterianism in the United States rode a rising wave of demographic growth. Despite periodic schisms that rent the denominational fabric, the overall membership trends were favorable ones to the mid-twentieth century. However, beginning in the 1960s, all previous patterns of growth halted, and for the first time the Presbyterian tradition experienced significant decline in membership. The early growth and the subsequent decline have been related to a variety of sociodemographic factors.

The earliest records (in 1690) of Presbyterians in the future United States count eighteen churches served by ten pastors. Together these congregations numbered one thousand parishioners. By 1717 three thousand colonists counted themselves Presbyterians, and this rose to eighteen thousand by the time of George Washington's first inauguration. Presbyterians represented about .4 percent of the European residents of the colonies, a proportion that they maintained for the next generation.

However, with the growing immigration of Scottish and Irish settlers in the early decades of the nineteenth century, the proportion of Americans who were Presbyterians began to rise. By 1835, on the eve of the first of the great Presbyterian schisms (between *New and *Old Schools), more than 234,000 Americans were Presbyterians; this represented approximately 1.6 percent of the country's population.

The initial growth in Presbyterian membership was largely fueled by selective migration patterns from the British Isles and by internal retention of children of the faithful; these forces for growth were to obtain for almost two centuries.

The New School/Old School controversy revolved around sundry issues, one component of which was the emerging note of evangelicalism that swept through the frontiers of the growing nation. The revivalist fervor that marked Methodist and Baptist appeals to pioneer families was echoed in the Presbyterian community through New School preachers who worked outlying New York and New England communities. With the flow of migrants from those regions down the Appalachian range into the Piedmont and the Blue Ridge Mountains, the New School had a short decade of dramatic growth following its founding in 1838, but then it plateaued at about 140,000 until after the *Civil War.

Meanwhile, the Old School branch maintained a steady growth from 128,000 in 1839 to a high of 303,000 in 1861-1862. It continued to welcome newcomers from Europe, immigrants who found New School enthusiasms unfamiliar and unappealing. With the onset of the Civil War, the Old School suffered precipitous membership loss, as it was well established in the South. Roughly a quarter of the Old School's members left between 1861 and 1862 to form the *Presbyterian Church in the United States (PCUS), sometimes called the Southern Presbyterian church.

At the conclusion of the Civil War, the Old and New School branches in the North overcame their differences. For the next ninety years, the principal branch of Presbyterianism in the northern states was the *Presbyterian Church in the U.S.A. (PCUSA). Picking up with a growth trajectory that had been in place prior to the 1838 schism, this church grew steadily until its merger in 1958. Indeed, not only did its numbers grow (from under half a million in 1870 to almost 2.8 million in 1958), but so did its share of the American population. In 1870, the PCUSA represented just over 1.11 percent of the population; by 1858 that had grown slowly and steadily to 1.61 percent.

Meanwhile, in the Southern states, the PCUS experienced similar patterns of growth, although on a somewhat reduced scale. Beginning in 1863 with fewer than 73,000 members, the PCUS grew uninterruptedly until the 1960s when it counted 960,000 parishioners; by the time of its merger to form the *Presbyterian Church (United States of America) in 1983, the PCUS had dropped to just over 800,000. During the twentieth century, the proportion of Americans in the PCUS rose slowly from about .21

percent in 1863 to a high in 1968 of .48 percent.

In the Northern states the *United Presbyterian Church of North America (UPCNA) drew together Scottish Covenanters and Seceders who migrated together in the 1840s and 1850s. While strictly presbyterian in their *polity, they were strongly individualistic in their personal pieties—patterns that they brought to the new world. The UPCNA began to number its flock in the 1880s, when it had 83,000 members (.16 percent of the population). The UPCNA was never able to make inroads into the United States population nor into succeeding waves of immigrants; while the numbers grew steadily, growth was largely internally generated. At the time of the UPCNA merger with the PCUSA in 1958, the UPCNA still represented about .15 percent of the population, or about a quarter of a million members.

The PCUSA, PCUS and UPCNA represented the principal carriers of Presbyterianism in the United States for the latter half of the nineteenth and first half of the twentieth centuries. Together they grew from 590,000 members, or 1.5 percent of the population in 1870, to 3.9 million members, or 2.2 percent in 1958. By the 1980s, when the three had merged in the Presbyterian Church (United States of America), the numerical downturn was well underway. Around them swirled a profusion of smaller denominations, none of which approached them in size.

Doctrinal or ecclesiastical schisms produced a number of splinter denominations since colonial times. Prominent among these was the *Cumberland Presbyterian Church (CPC), founded by mid-Appalachian Presbyterians in the wake of the Great Revival of the early 1800s. By the mid-century, the CPC counted just over 100,000 adherents, with that figure rising steadily after the Civil War, reaching 150,000 at the turn of the twentieth century. Two-thirds of the CPC merged with the PCUSA in 1906. Since then, the remnant has grown slowly, peaking at just under 100,000 members in 1983 (in the wake of recent arrivals disenchanted with the PCUS and UPCUSA merger).

Another significant splinter from the mainstream of the Presbyterian tradition came in the 1930s with the formation of the *Orthodox Presbyterian Church (OPC). Founded by Carl *McIntire and J. Gresham *Machen with a great deal of fanfare in the wake of the *fundamentalist-modernist controversy, the OPC began with roughly five thousand members and grew slowly to a peak of nineteen thousand in 1987. In the early 1990s the OPC has lost one thousand members. A telling factor in the life of the OPC is that from the outset, it was composed of a disproportionate number of older members. This has been reflected in a Sunday school enrollment that has not kept pace with its overall membership, hitting its high point in the early 1970s.

In terms of numerical growth, the most successful breakaway branch of Presbyterianism has been the *Presbyterian Church in America (PCA). Begun in reaction to alleged liberalism in the larger Presbyterian denominations, the PCA grew from 41,000 members in 1973 to more than 230,000. This growth has been enhanced by merger in 1979 with the Reformed Presbyterian Church, Evangelical Synod (which brought 27,000 members) and by defectors from the other Presbyterian branches in the wake of the merger that created the PC(USA). In the mid-1990s, with twelve hundred congregations and more than two thousand clergy, the PCA seemed well positioned to continue this initial growth. On a cautionary note, the principal growth of the PCA has been due to entire congregations leaving the main Presbyterian communions; that may be an increasingly difficult source of future members since the window of opportunity for such movements was closed in the 1980s.

At the beginning of the nineteenth century, .38 percent of those living in the United States counted themselves Presbyterians. That proportion grew for the next century and a half, through 1.50 percent in 1850, 1.98 in 1900, to 2.21 in 1950. However, since the 1950s the share of the American populace who count themselves Presbyterians has declined by more than a third to 1.31 percent. This reflects massive changes in both of the engines that drove Presbyterian growth: the patterns of immigration have shifted dramatically away from western Europe since the 1960s, and birth rates have plummeted in the constituency that makes up the Presbyterian communions. A third factor, reflecting wider cultural shifts toward greater privatism in matters of faith, exacerbated the issue among the baby boom generation. This generation has remained away from the church in unprecedented numbers, reflecting an individualized religion that is not bound to ecclesiastical institutions.

As a result of these three factors, the numbers tell a tale of overall Presbyterian membership stagnation: in 1950 all branches of Presbyterianism counted roughly 3.33 million members; forty years later the number is 3.25 million. Despite the intervening decades of membership surge and decline—and of denominational mergers and schisms—Presbyterianism stands in numeric terms where it did at mid-century. But its mood has changed profoundly. In this context the measures of the church's faithfulness have subtly shifted from personal and communal witness and service to data sheets and contribution flow charts; these ledgers are inevitably grim given the larger sociodemographic changes going on. Perhaps it is time to ask again: What should be the measures of Presbyterian faithfulness?

Bibliography. D. R. Hoge, B. Johnson and D. A. Luidens, *Vanishing Boundaries: The Religion of Mainline Protestant Baby Boomers* (1994); D. A. Luidens, "Numbering the Presbyterian Branches: Membership Trends Since Colonial Times," in *The Mainstream Protestant "Decline,"* ed. M. J. Coalter, J. M. Mulder and L. B. Weeks (1990); *Statistical Abstracts of the United States: 1991;* H. C. Weber, *Presbyterian Statistics Through One Hundred Years, 1826-1926* (1927).

D. A. Luidens

DeWitt, John (1842-1923). Presbyterian minister and educator. Born in Harrisburg, Pennsylvania, the son of a *New School Presbyterian minister, DeWitt entered the College of New Jersey as a sophomore in the fall of 1858. He was graduated in 1861 and entered Princeton Theological Seminary in the spring of 1862. He was licensed two years later by the First Presbytery of New York (*Old School), studied an additional year at Union Theological Seminary (1864-1865) and was ordained by the Third Presbytery of New York (New School) the following year as the minister of the Irvington, New York, Presbyterian Church (1865-1869), the first of three notable pastorates. He served the Central Congregational Church, Boston (1869-1876), and the Tenth Presbyterian Church, Philadelphia (1876-1882), before he was called as professor of ecclesiastical history at Lane Theological Seminary (1882-1888), professor of apologetics at McCormick Theological Seminary (1888-1892) and finally as professor of church history at Princeton Theological Seminary (1892-1912).

DeWitt taught church history as the story of God's redemption of creation, which he interpreted as the story of the spiritual progress of human society. This study, in his view, included the whole history of western civilization, its arts, literature, science and law. He was editor of the influential *Princeton Theological Review* (1902-1907) and served on two important *Presbyterian Church in the U.S.A. (PCUSA) general assembly committees: the committee on the revision of the *Westminster Confession of Faith (final action, 1903) and the committee that prepared the Book of Common Worship (1906).

Bibliography. F. W. Loetscher, "John DeWitt," *PTR* 22 (1924) 177-234; *PSB* 17, 3 (1923) 14- 17.

K. J. Ross

Dickinson, Jonathan (1688-1747).† Presbyterian minister and theologian. Born at Hatfield, Massachusetts, he graduated from Yale College (1706). After receiving his master of arts degree from that institution, Dickinson studied theology independently (1706-1708) before becoming a pastor and practicing medicine in Elizabethtown, New Jersey. There Dickinson was to minister the rest of his life (1709-1747).

In 1717 Dickinson persuaded his Congregational church to join the Presbytery of Philadelphia, where their pastor would gradually exert his influence in shaping colonial Presbyterianism. A strong Calvinist, he was nonetheless opposed to the rigid confessionalism of *Scots-Irish Presbyterians who wished to impose full subscription to the *Westminster Confession of Faith and Catechisms as a test of orthodoxy. As a leader of the antisubscriptionists, Dickinson argued for the strict examination of the ministerial candidate's religious experience. In the end he helped negotiate an uneasy peace through the *Adopting Act of 1729, which required ministerial candidates to accept the Westminster standards "as being in all the essential and necessary articles, good forms of sound words and systems of Christian doctrine, and . . . as the confession of our faith." The emphasis upon "essential" articles, as well as its allowance for mental reservations, marked a victory for Dickinson's party.

However, this victory was not to last. The Great Awakening divided Presbyterians over the issue of *revivalism and drove the wedge deeper yet between subscriptionists and antisubscriptionists. Although he sought to hold the *Old Side and *New Side together, Dickinson's sympathies were clearly with the New Side Presbyterian revivalists. After failing to reconcile the parties at the May 1741 meeting of the Synod of Philadelphia, Dickinson led in the formation of the rival Synod of New York (1745).

Dickinson provided colonial Presbyterians with leadership through several controversies: defending *Calvinism against *Arminianism and deism, presbyterianism against episcopacy and nonconformity against Anglicanism. His training in the classics of *Puritan and Presbyterian theology and *piety led him to strongly criticize the excesses of the revivalist movement, insisting on proper discipline, both ecclesiastical and personal. He refused to be carried away by the extremes of the day and taught that vibrant religion does not need to be disorderly. Arguing that enthusiasm and deism alike lead to antinomianism, he inculcated the Reformed doctrine that sanctification is the true and necessary fruit of justification by faith. In 1740 his church experienced an intense but subdued revival, marked by a lack of emotionalism as well as by lasting changes in his parishioners.

Dickinson's published works included *The Reasonableness of Christianity* (1732), *A Display of God's Special Grace* (1742) and *Sermons and Tracts* (1793). His most famous work was *Five Points: The True Scripture-Doctrine Concerning Some Important Points of Christian Faith* (1741). He was arguably the most distinguished Presbyterian minister in the colonial period, with an international reputation as a theologian second only to that of Jonathan *Edwards, who like him defended the Great Awakening while criticizing revivalistic excesses.

In 1746 the College of New Jersey, otherwise know as the Log College, was opened in Dickinson's home. The college was established for the training of prorevivalist ministers, and Dickinson served as its first president (1746). He died before it moved to Princeton.

Bibliography. *AAP* 3; *ANB* 6; H. C. Cameron, *Jonathan Dickinson and the College of New Jersey* (1880); *DAB* III; K. J. Hardman, *Jonathan Dickinson and the Course of American Presbyterianism, 1717-1747* (1971); *NCAB* 5; B. F. LeBeau, *Jonathan Dickinson and the Formative Years of American Presbyterianism* (1997); L. E. Schmidt, "Jonathan Dickinson and the Making of a Moderate Awakening," *AP* 63 (1985) 341-53. A. H. Freundt

Doak, Samuel (1749-1830).† First Presbyterian minister to settle in Tennessee. Born in August 1749 to *Scots-Irish immigrants in Augusta County, Virginia, Doak sought an education, following a profession of religion at age sixteen, and offered to surrender his patrimony for the privilege. He graduated from the College of New Jersey in 1775 and, returning to Virginia, studied theology under John Blair Smith and William Graham while he tutored at Hampden-Sydney College. He was ordained by the Hanover Presbytery.

Shortly before 1780 Doak removed to the frontier settlements along the Holston River in northeastern Tennessee, establishing the first Presbyterian congregations in that territory. In spite of his reputation as a scholarly pastor and teacher, Doak was known to cut his sermons off abruptly when word came of an Indian raid, sometimes leading the pursuit himself. In 1784 he participated in the convention that framed the state constitution. Settling in Washington County, Tennessee, Doak founded Martin Academy in 1785, chartered ten years later as Washington College and the first institution of higher learning west of the Appalachians. In 1818 Doak moved once more to Greene County, where, with his son Samuel W. Doak, he founded Tusculum Academy and College near Greeneville. A man of sober and even grave disposition, Doak was nevertheless irenic and well-disposed toward moderate revivals, and the early success of Presbyterianism in east Tennessee is largely attributable to his skill and indefatigable labors. In the New Divinity controversies he was a vigorous leader of the orthodox party.

Bibliography. *AAP* 3; *ANB* 6; J. E. Alexander, *A Brief History of the Synod of Tennessee* (1890); *DAB* III. W. J. Wade

Dooyeweerd, Herman (1894-1977).† Dutch Reformed educator. A leading Christian philosopher of the twentieth century, Dooyeweerd built on the foundations laid by Groen Van Prinsterer (1801-1876) and Abraham *Kuyper (1837-1920) in developing the core ideas of Dutch neo-Calvinism into a wide-ranging, tightly argued, well-nuanced system, known as the philosophy of the cosmonomic idea. Dooyeweerd spent his entire academic career (1926-1965) at the (Calvinist) Free University of Amsterdam, where he had received his doctorate in 1917 and in whose environs he had been born and reared. As professor of legal philosophy he remained involved in the political and religious life of the Netherlands long after his retirement.

Dooyeweerd's North American influence rose with the post-1945 Dutch immigration to Canada and the subsequent building there of political, labor and especially academic (the Institute for Christian Studies in Toronto) institutions bearing his inspiration. In this context "Dooyeweerdian" implies the conviction that religion is at the heart of every human enterprise; that Christians are called above all to forceful, reformatory social-cultural engagement; that these efforts are to be guided by God's creation ordinances or norms more than by the Bible alone; and that human activity and natural being are to be respected and encouraged in all their diversity. Following John *Calvin's lead, Dooyeweerd affirmed that a radical Christian philosophy must be biblically directed and have a fundamentally religious starting point. His ideas have been made available to English readers in *A New Critique of Theoretical Thought* (4 vols., 1953-1958), *The Twilight of Western Thought* (1960) and *Roots of Western Culture* (1979).

Bibliography. L. Kalsbeek, *Contours of a Christian Philosophy* (1975); C. T. McIntire, ed., *The Legacy of Herman Dooyeweerd: Reflections on Critical Philosophy in the Christian Tradition* (1986). J. D. Bratt

Dort, Canons of. Composed at the international Synod of Dort (1618-1619) to respond to the challenge to Reformed orthodoxy by the Remonstrants. The Remonstrants were followers of Jacobus Arminius (d. 1609), (*see* Arminianism) professor of theology at the University of Leyden. The key issue was the doctrine of sin and grace. The position of the Remonstrants was semi-Pelagian, although with a distinctive Reformed coloring. Arminius himself denied that his views were Pelagian, and he was willing to subscribe to the *Belgic Confession and *Heidelberg Catechism.

Arminius's chief disciple, Simon Episcopius, drew up five objections to Reformed orthodoxy, focusing on the doctrine of predestination, in a *Remonstrance* published in 1610. The positions taken therein have a Reformed ring to them but represent a subtle softening of the classic Augustinian-Calvinist theology of the radicality of sin and grace, God's gracious election and the inability of the human will in regard to salvation.

As a result, the States General of the Netherlands convened an international synod that met periodically in the city of Dordrecht from the fall of 1618 until the spring of 1619. This was not simply a Dutch national synod, for there were delegates from England (Anglicans), Germany and Switzerland. The French Reformed Church also appointed delegates, but they were prevented from attending by King Louis XIV. The result of the debates was the condemnation of the Remonstrants and the formulation of the so-called five points of Calvinism: unconditional election, limited atonement, total depravity, irresistible grace and the perseverance (or preservation) of the saints—in that order. The popular acronym for these five points, TULIP, is misleading because it begins with total depravity (an expression not used in the canons), thus starting on a negative note.

The canons have often gotten a bad press, even in Reformed circles, for three reasons: their allegedly rationalistic orthodox character; the doctrine of reprobation; and the phrasing of certain tenets such as limited atonement. Taking these objections in reverse order, it should be kept in mind that the atonement is not limited in its scope. Christ's death is sufficient to cover the sins of the world, but it is efficacious only for the elect.

The canons indeed teach double predestination and reprobation, that is, that God has condemned the nonelect to eternal punishment for their sins. This was also taught by Augustine, Martin Luther (in *The Bondage of the Will)* and John *Calvin, but the Canons of Dort are sometimes alleged to have gone beyond them. There is, however, no equal ultimacy in the canons, as far as election and reprobation are concerned, and the dominant motif in the First Head of Doctrine, "Divine Election and Reprobation," is on God's gracious election to salvation. Only two of the eighteen articles in this first section deal with reprobation (6 and 15), in which it is stated that "not all, but some only, are elected, while others are passed by in the eternal decree."

Concerning the scholastic character of the canons, it must be granted that they occasionally reflect the scholastic approach characteristic of that period. However, the canons are also replete with biblical references and are remarkably pastoral and eloquent. An illustration of that is found in III/IV, 12:

> This is the regeneration, the new creation, the raising from the dead, and the making alive so clearly proclaimed in the Scriptures, which God works in us without our help. But this certainly does not happen only by outward teaching, by moral persuasion, or by such a way of working that, after God has done his work, it remains in man's power whether or not to be reborn or converted. Rather, it is an entirely supernatural work, one that is at the same time most powerful and most pleasing, a marvelous, hidden, and inexpressible work, which is not lesser than or inferior in power to that of creation or of raising the dead, as Scripture . . . teaches. . . . And then the will, now renewed, is not only activated and motivated by God but in being activated by God is also itself active. For this reason, man himself, by that grace which he has received, is also rightly said to believe and to repent.

BIBLIOGRAPHY. The Canons of Dort in *Ecumenical Creeds and Confessions* (1988); P. Y. De Jong, ed., *Crisis in the Reformed Churches: Essays in Commemoration of the Great Synod of Dort* (1968); M. E. Osterhaven, "Dort, Synod of," in *Evangelical Dictionary of Theology,* ed. W. A. Elwell (1984); J. Pelican, *The Christian Tradition: Reformation of the Church and Dogma (1300-1700)* (1984).

I. J. Hesselink

Dowey, Edward A., Jr. (1918-). Presbyterian theologian and educator. Born in Philadelphia, Dowey grew up in the manses of the Presbyterian churches his father served. He began his undergraduate studies at Keystone (Junior) College, La Plume, Pennsylvania, with the intention of going into the ministry, but philosophical questions led him to question his belief in God. He finished his undergraduate work at Lafayette College, where he graduated summa cum laude in philosophy in 1940.

During his senior year at Lafayette, Dowey was greatly impressed by a lecture given by John Alexander *Mackay, president of Princeton Theological Seminary, and as a result he decided to reconsider formal theological studies. He entered Princeton Theological Seminary in the fall of 1940. While there Dowey encountered the theology of Karl *Barth, where he found the means to recover his belief in God.

Dowey was ordained by the *Presbyterian Church in the U.S.A. (PCUSA) in 1943. After three years in the navy chaplaincy during World War II, Dowey continued graduate studies at Columbia University and Union Theological Seminary in New York City. He completed the doctor of theology degree in 1949 at the University of Zurich under the supervision of Emil Brunner. Dowey's dissertation, *The Knowledge of God in Calvin's Theology,* has been published and reprinted several times, and it has come to be regarded as an important and helpful introduction to the study of John *Calvin.

After teaching at Lafayette College, Columbia University and McCormick Theological Seminary, Dowey returned to Princeton Theological Seminary in 1957, where he was a member of both the theology and church history departments for more than thirty years, enjoying great respect, influence and popularity.

Dowey is best known for his work as chairman of the Special Committee of the General Assembly of the United Presbyterian Church in the USA on a Brief Contemporary Statement of Faith from 1958 to 1966. Under his leadership, the church adopted the work of that committee, the *Confession of 1967, as one of its confessional standards. The committee also recommended, and the *United Presbyterian Church in the U.S.A. (UPC) approved, the creation of the Book of Confessions as the confessional basis of the church. This Book of Confessions included not only the *Westminster Confession of Faith, the church's doctrinal basis from 1789, but also six other historic creedal statements as well as the Confession of 1967. Dowey later published *A Commentary on the Confession of 1967 and an Introduction to the Book of Confessions.*

As a theologian, historian, educator and churchman, Dowey's impact on contemporary church life has been widespread and had enduring consequences.

BIBLIOGRAPHY. E. A. Dowey Jr., *The Knowledge of God in Calvin's Theology* (1965); idem, *A Commentary on the Confession of 1967 and an Introduction to the Book of Confessions* (1968); E. A. McKee and B. G. Armstrong, eds., *Probing the Reformed Tradition: Historical Studies in Honor of Edward A. Dowey Jr.* (1989); D. L. Migliore, "A Conversation with Edward Dowey," *PSB* 9, 2 (1988) 89-103.

W. O. Harris

Duffield, George (1732-1790). Presbyterian clergyman. Born in Lancaster County, Pennsylvania, the son of George and Margaret Duffield, who had migrated from Ireland shortly before his birth, Duffield descended from Huguenot stock.

Graduating from the College of New Jersey in 1752, Duffield studied theology for two years, and in 1754 he returned to his college to become a tutor. In that same year he married Elizabeth, daughter of Samuel *Blair, who died within a year. Five years later Duffield married Margaret Armstrong, a sister of General John Armstrong. Duffield was an ardent *New Side (prorevival) man, and in 1757 he was called to the church at Carlisle, Pennsylvania, where he became embroiled in a protracted controversy with a local *Old Side pastor. The terms of the reunion in 1758 left New Side and Old Side Presbyterians in constant conflict, and this was reflected in Duffield's pastorates.

In 1766 the Synod of New York and Philadelphia sent Duffield and Charles Beatty on a mission of exploration into the Indian country of the Ohio Valley. The next year they reported that "they found on the frontier numbers of people earnestly desirous of forming themselves into congregations." Encouraged by this, the Presbyterian Church sent several ministers to serve on the frontier.

In 1762 the Second Church of Philadelphia called Duffield to be assistant to the aging pastor, Gilbert *Tennent, but Duffield's presbytery refused to let him accept the call. In 1772 he accepted the call of the newly formed Third, or Pine Street, Church of Philadelphia. By then war sentiments against Britain were rising, and Duffield allied himself with the most outspoken advocates of independence, bringing Tory hatred. Old Side men were also furious at his call to Third Church, appealed to the courts and lost. They finally tried to bar the congregation and Duffield from the church by force. The king's magistrate had him arrested for starting a riot. However, Duffield attracted many supporters and soon made his church one of the greatest of the denomination. By the time of the Revolution, he was the dominant Presbyterian leader in Pennsylvania.

During the sessions of the Continental Congress, a number of the delegates sat under Duffield's patriotic sermons, and he served as chaplain to the Congress for a time. He also served as chaplain to the Pennsylvania militia and was so effective in stirring patriotic zeal that the British promised a reward of fifty pounds for his death or capture. After the war he became the first stated clerk of the general assembly, and he served Third Church until his death. His remains are buried in the basement of the church, which still stands.

Bibliography. *AAP* 3; *ANB* 7; *General Catalog of Princeton University, 1746-1906* (1908); H. O. Gibbons, *A History of Old Pine Street Church* (1905); L. J. Trinterud, *The Forming of an American Tradition: A Re-Examination of Colonial Presbyterianism* (1949). K. J. Hardman

Dulles, John Foster (1888-1959).† Secretary of State and Presbyterian layman. Born in Washington, D.C., Dulles grew up in a Presbyterian manse in Watertown, New York, where he early learned to appreciate the importance of religious convictions. His father, Allen Macy Dulles, a respected liberal Presbyterian minister, practiced a home devotional life emphasizing for his children the importance of a pious and educated commitment to the principles of Scripture.

Named valedictorian at his graduation from Princeton University (1908), Dulles also earned the highest honors in the philosophy department, including a scholarship to the Sorbonne in Paris, where he studied briefly with philosopher Henri Bergson. Upon his return from France, he studied law at George Washington University Law School and took the New York State bar exam in 1911. He accepted a job as a law clerk with the Wall Street law firm of Sullivan and Cromwell, and by the time he was thirty-nine he had become head of the firm. In 1917 he accepted an assignment by President Woodrow *Wilson to Central America, the beginning of a career in public service that climaxed in his role as Secretary of State (1952-1959) under the Eisenhower administration.

Throughout these years, Dulles remained active in the life of the church. Not only did he serve as an elder in his local congregation but also in 1924 he represented the New York Presbytery before the Presbyterian general assembly, defending the presbytery's ordination of ministers who would not affirm the virgin birth.

Dulles worked in ecumenical church circles as well. Beginning in 1921, he became closely associated with the Federal Council of Churches of Christ in America (now the National Council of the Churches). His most significant contribution to ecumenical Protestantism resulted from his leadership as chair of the Commission on a Just and Durable Peace. Formed by the Federal Council of Churches in 1941, during World War II, the commission was to mobilize Christian support for a peace consonant with Christian principles. Among its members were notable church leaders such as John R. Mott, Reinhold *Niebuhr, Charles Clayton Morrison and Harry Emerson *Fosdick. Dulles served as chair for the full five years of the commission's work. The commission's influential support for the development of a United Nations organization marks an important point in American Protestantism.

Dulles's political thought, which always rested on his belief in a divine moral order, shifted after World War II. Prior to the war, he argued that this was a transcendent order that could not be aligned with the cause of any one nation. This led him to affirm that international conflicts must be resolved by mutual accommodation and compromise. In the face of a belligerent Soviet foreign policy, Dulles became disillusioned with such optimism and became convinced that there was an immanent moral order that could be appealed to as the standard for international law and justice. Increasingly he identified this order with the policies of the free nations, especially the United States.

Bibliography. *ANB* 7; *DAB* 6; J. M. Mulder, "The Moral World of John Foster Dulles," *JPH* 49 (summer 1971) 157-82; R. W. Pruessen, *John Foster Dulles: The Road to Power* (1982); M. G. Toulouse, *The Transformation of John Foster Dulles: From Prophet of Realism to Priest of Nationalism* (1985).
M. G. Toulouse

Dutch Reformed in America. Dutch Calvinists arrived in North America in the same decade as did the Pilgrims and earliest *Puritans. From that venerable beginning their institutions have come down to the present in an unbroken line and with a persistent ambivalence. In theology and ethics the Dutch have shared much with the Puritan/Congregational and Presbyterian traditions; yet, perhaps from the same instinct that prompted the Pilgrims to leave the Netherlands, the Dutch have resisted melting into America, even into its other Reformed streams. Their fairly small numbers have made them conservative, lest new ventures alienate too many of their members, so they have not fostered as many departures to the left and right as have British-descended Reformed bodies. Rather, the Dutch have demonstrated a strong historical and confessional sense at once mediated by and reconfirming group loyalties.

From the start the group seems to have fared better under pressure than in power. Their first congregation was founded on Manhattan in 1628; others followed Dutch settlements up the Hudson River valley and onto Long Island. But as New Netherland never pretended to be anything but a commercial venture, the church had to fight apathy and materialism among its patrons as well as its populace. In contrast, after the English conquest of the colony in 1664, high fertility rates and cultural tenacity kept the Dutch presence strong. The Reformed Church reinforced both these proclivities and became a home of Dutch identity, while its religious integrity attracted French and German Calvinist immigrants into its fold.

This harmony was shattered in the Leisler uprising of 1688-1691, the beginning of an eighty-year period of creativity and strife. In the Leisler episode itself, the New York City clergy opposed the popular will and thereafter became beholden to their fellow English elite and agents of commercial prosperity. Many of the commoners who had supported Leisler and after 1700 pursued their land hunger into New Jersey adopted a more turbulent piety. Like the Reformed pietists emerging simultaneously in the Netherlands, they resented formalism and elite control and supported some leaders of ardent conviction if dubious credentials. Their champion appeared with the 1720 immigration of Theodorus *Frelinghuysen, who provoked the Raritan Valley congregations with his moral strictures and demands for experiential conversion. Frelinghuysen looms large in the prehistory of the First Great Awakening, and his program echoed that of his neighbor, Gilbert *Tennent, also in his call for stronger local (i.e., colonial) initiatives in clerical education and ordination.

These proposals fueled the coetus party that emerged in denominational councils in the 1740s. The opposition, centered in New York City, formed the conferentie, championing order and dignity. The rift endured for decades (during the Revolution, for instance, coetus churches tended Patriot; conferentie, either neutral or Loyalist) but was formally healed in 1772 under the leadership of the American-born, Netherlands-ordained John *Livingston. His plan of union won Amsterdam's assent to local autonomy but on the basis of the traditional Netherlandic standards. The two sides agreed as well upon perpetuating Dutch language in worship and rigorous pastoral education. The War for Independence, much of which was fought in Dutch Reformed precincts, severely tested the church but also confirmed its status, as its new constitution of 1792 attested.

In the young republic the Dutch Reformed suffered with other venerable churches as more populist fellowships rode the democratic tide. The Dutch responded by undertaking rapid language change, building educational institutions (Queens, later Rutgers, College and New Brunswick Theological Seminary) to provide their own leadership and participating in the broader Protestant benevolent empire of Bible, tract and *mission societies. They consistently took the *Old School side in these agencies' disputes and, perhaps accordingly, adopted foreign missions as their favorite cause. By the *Civil War the Dutch had fields in India, China and Japan; by century's end, another notable enterprise in Arabia. Domestically their extension efforts were constricted by their theological requirements and ethnic air and proved successful only when a locality had a Dutch-descended coterie to build on. Over the nineteenth century, then, the group showed a triple aspect: progressive American abroad, generically Protestant against "threats" (Catholic, Mormon and alcoholic) at home, but at bottom both clannish and genial, more demanding theologically but less behaviorally than other evangelical Protestants.

This settled order was challenged by a new immigration (1840s-1920s) from the Netherlands. Though flowing with the business cycle, the migration was heavily weighted with orthodox Reformed believers. Indeed, ministers who had seceded from the Netherlands Reformed Church in 1834 founded the key colonies in western Michigan and southeastern Iowa around which the enduring Dutch Midwestern network was built. The whole community was thus colored with Seceder tones of strict orthodoxy and sober conversion; its social, cultural and political issues were negotiated in terms of Reformed theology. While the new arrivals first affiliated with the East Coast denomination (after 1867, the *Reformed Church in America [RCA]), some thought that body lax and complacent and in 1857 withdrew to form the *Christian Reformed Church (CRC). Disputes over Freemasonry, which the RCA tolerated but the CRC forbade for its anticlericalism, widened the breach in 1880. Thereafter, a sizable majority of the immigrants joined the younger denomination.

By one measure all this recapitulated the RCA's eighteenth-century quarrels, with migrant commoners rebelling against perceived New York elitism. Seen another way, the two groups were following the lessons of their own experience, reading each other, their own ideals and American realities in that light and diverging accordingly. In any case the disputes that the new immigration wrought between and within the two denominations worked a renewal of Reformed consciousness and a pluralization of group options that endured long after the original recriminations had died out.

The options the CRC offered were defined by its overriding hostility to modernism, a label that entailed secularism and liberalism of every sort. The Secession of 1834 had been triggered by laxer doctrine and tighter bureaucracy in the Netherlands Reformed Church, and the Christian Reformed measured the American scene by that standard. They cultivated Reformed consciousness in their young by rigorous catechesis and a complete Christian day school system. Their piety required intent grappling with the issues of personal salvation and sacrificial charity for the sick and suffering. But another attitude arose under the inspiration of the Netherlands' neo-Calvinist movement (1880-1920). Led by Abraham *Kuyper, neo-Calvinists aimed to bring orthodox commitments out of the shelter of church and home into every domain of public life, and so they built distinctively Christian institutions in *politics, mass communications, labor relations and higher *education. Kuyper's American followers found Calvinistic consciousness easier to build than separate organizations but on that basis bred a systematic and often prescient critique of American society.

The two models usually coexisted but sometimes conflicted, particularly under the intrusive nationalism of the world wars. A doctrinal dispute in the 1920s left the pietist-confessionalists in control of the CRC for a generation, suspicious of doctrinal development, worldly behavior and ecumenical ventures. Fundamentalist as this regime appeared, its Reformed convictions resisted the dispensationalism, *Arminianism and revivalistic spirituality of the broader American type. The context of the 1950s, by contrast, gave command to progressive neo-Calvinists and more optimistic, outgoing pietists. Thus Christian Reformed figures loomed large in the post-1945 neo-evangelical movement, particularly on issues of politics, social ethics and educational philosophy. The CRC itself worked at ethnic diversification, adding African-, Korean- and generically American congregations to its mix.

Over the twentieth century the CRC has moved from suspicion of to engagement with the American environment. The RCA's direction has been more complex. By World War I it had come to complete identification with the cause of Protestant America, endorsing Prohibition, the public schools and Anglo-conformity for immigrants. The 1920s and again the 1960s struck hard at this ideal, triggering a twofold response in the denomination. Voices largely out of the Midwest called for renewal of Reformed distinctives; the East Coast sector suggested merging with Presbyterian bodies and participating in the Federal/National and World Councils of Churches. The RCA rejected the second but creatively combined the first and third proposals. Thus it has followed a mainline trajectory. It expanded rapidly in the 1950s' community church boom but since 1965 has lost many of those accessions so that today historically Dutch elements constitute an increasing percentage of its membership.

If their histories have brought the two denominations closer together, they also present a miniature of *Calvinism's fortunes in America at large. The RCA and CRC have both spun off small sects within the Reformed ambit and lost members to less exacting bodies without. They have concentrated on retaining their children through the ministrations of a covenantal community, imbued with sober piety, confessional clarity and a keen sense of public responsibility. They have been perennially uneasy with being just Dutch but suspect that a broader casting of their tradition might cost it the virtues that make it worthy. Thus they live in the tensions of faith in a sovereign God whose workings cannot finally be held to human account but nonetheless merit trusting obedience.

Bibliography. R. H. Balmer, *A Perfect Babel of Confusion: Dutch Religion and English Culture in the Middle Colonies* (1989); H. Beets, *The Christian Reformed Church* (1923); J. D. Bratt, *Dutch Calvinism in Modern America: A History of a Conservative Subculture* (1984); E. T. Corwin, *A History of the Reformed Church, Dutch* (1895); G. F. De Jong, *The Dutch Reformed Church in the American Colonies* (1978); P. De Klerk and R. De Ridder, eds., *Perspectives on the Christian Reformed Church: Studies in Its History, Theology, and Ecumenicity* (1983); H. G. Hageman, *Two Centuries Plus* (1984); J. Tanis, *Dutch Calvinistic Pietism in the Middle Colonies: A Study in the Life and Theology of Theodorus Jacobus Frelinghuysen* (1967); J. J. Timmerman, *Promises to Keep* (1975); J. W. Van Hoeven, ed., *Piety and Patriotism: Bicentennial Studies of the Reformed Church in America, 1776-1976* (1976); D. F. Wells, ed., *Dutch Reformed Theology* (1989); H. Zwaanstra, *Reformed Thought and Experience in a New World: A Study of the Christian Reformed Church and Its American Environment, 1890-1918* (1973).

J. D. Bratt

E

Education, Presbyterians and. The seeds for what has been an intimate connection between Presbyterians and education in America were carried to the colonies in the seventeenth century by two groups of Calvinists. The *Puritans brought their commitments to Reformed faith and life principally to the New England colonies, while *Scots-Irish Calvinists shaped the Middle Colonies with theirs. In the new nation these two Reformed voices were joined in the eighteenth century to form a distinctly American Presbyterian church. Like their Reformed forbearers, the American church valued education highly, not only for its clergy but for the public as well.

Reformed theology virtually required commitment on the part of its adherents both to obtain an education for themselves and to make it available for others in society. Fundamental to Reformed faith is the affirmation of the sovereignty of God over all things, including civic behavior and institutions and the life of the individual mind. The mind, the whole life of the person and the life of a community have the same purpose and goal: to serve God by obedience to God's will and thereby to glorify God in all things. In Reformed perspective, learning becomes a duty necessary to understanding the will of the sovereign God manifest in human history in order to serve God faithfully in the whole of life.

The Reformers advocated an education not only in the languages of the Bible and the history and doctrines of the church but in the liberal arts as well. The liberal arts provided insight into the contemporary culture, with which the message of the Bible was necessarily in conversation if it were to be interpreted meaningfully. Moreover, studying the liberal arts developed skills of reason and logic, writing and speaking—all of value to the theological task of making clear the message of the Bible. Finally, the original languages of the Bible, Hebrew and Greek, were part of a liberal education and essential knowledge to Reformed believers called upon by their theology to be able to read the Bible for themselves.

Presbyterians in America insisted on the same high educational standards for clergy and held the same high regard for lay education as did their Continental predecessors. The critical difference was that in colonial America, the establishment of educational institutions to accomplish these tasks was still to be done. Presbyterians lent themselves energetically and impressively to the task.

A first answer to the educational needs of Presbyterian clergy in the colonies was provided by log colleges, the most famous of which was founded by Presbyterian minister William *Tennent Sr. near Neshaminy, Pennsylvania, around 1735. Followers of this pastor-teacher in turn founded the College of New Jersey in 1746, which later became Princeton University. This pattern was repeated regularly throughout the Middle Colonies and again as Presbyterians moved beyond the Alleghenies. In the period prior to the *Civil War, Presbyterians built forty-nine colleges, Congregationalists twenty-one, German Reformed four and Dutch Reformed one. The founding of these institutions to teach liberal arts to citizens and church members alike has been a lasting inheritance from the Reformed churches in America.

The nineteenth-century experience added a new dimension: the Sunday school. Sunday schools first appeared in the 1790s in the United States. They were formed on the British model as schools for poor working children that served the dual purpose of providing a rudimentary education and of keeping the children, free from their labors, profitably occupied and off the streets. In the United States, however, they soon lost their role of teaching reading and writing and civic virtues to the growing number of free charity schools provided by the city. The Sunday school was left to another purpose: namely, teaching the values and perspectives of the evangelicalism that arose from the Second Great Awakening and spread everywhere in American society. The evangelicals believed that knowledge of evangelical doctrines prepared children for the necessary conversion experience and at the same time established the desirable habits of self-discipline, honesty and hard work. In this way, the Sunday schools served the public good.

Presbyterians were involved here too from the beginning. Sharing the doctrinal convictions of evangelicalism while divided on the style of revival preaching and the appropriate role of believers in the process of conversion, Presbyterians founded Sunday schools as places for inculcating students with the seriousness of sin, their dependence upon the grace of God for regeneration and the need to live a moral, chaste life of obedience and duty to avoid as much as humanly possible the temptations to sin all around them.

The Sunday-school movement led in 1824 to the founding of the American Sunday-School Union. Presbyterians were among the prominent leaders of this effort, providing, with Episcopalians, most of the early managers for the organization. The avowed purpose of this group was missionary: to establish a sabbath school in every place in need of evangelical education and to provide literature for a wide, general readership that would keep the evangelical perspective in view. Union missionaries, some supported by the Presbyterian Board of Missions, journeyed to frontier communities, established a sabbath school, equipped it with Union literature—a library of pamphlets and tracts—and moved on to another community, checking on the established school periodically. The sabbath schools were often the only schools in the community initially and served to teach reading and writing as well as religion, using the Bible as a textbook.

The American Sunday-School Union retained its religious education influence throughout the first half of the nineteenth century. Denominational Sunday schools participating in the Union began enrolling more of their own members' children, as tax-supported schools became increasingly available for the general public. An informal division of labor began to emerge: common or public schools took responsibility for general education in an atmosphere intended to be nonsectarian, in accordance with the Constitution's first amendment. Sunday schools took responsibility for the nation's religious education, which was both evangelical and denominational.

In the post-Civil War period, to the end of the nineteenth century, however, the Union's influence gave way to Sunday-school conventions aimed not at promoting a united evangelical perspective but at improving the educational quality of the Sunday schools, now largely denominational in identity, by offering conventions for teachers to learn better teaching skills and methods.

Perhaps the crowning achievement of this effort was the interdenominational curriculum that emerged from the 1872 national convention as "the uniform lesson plan," a sequence of Bible lessons covering a period of years by which the Bible could be studied in an orderly and informed fashion. While denominations shared the basic plan, individual differences could be honored as the denomination set the content of the lesson. This curriculum is still in use, a testimony to the lasting influence of the Sunday school conventions and the American Sunday-School Union.

The focus of Presbyterians on education through the twentieth century has continued to be on the Christian education of members and their children. The most common setting for such education has remained the Sunday or church school. But Presbyterians have continued to provide leadership in public education as well, serving as college presidents in church-related schools or as chaplains and campus ministers at Presbyterian colleges and state-supported colleges and universities.

Religious influence on modern college campuses has diminished considerably since the nineteenth and early twentieth centuries. At the beginning of the twentieth century, a college that was distinctly Christian reflected that emphasis not only in curricular requirements but also in the college's influence over student behavior and extracurricular activities. At the end of the twentieth century, what being a distinctly Christian college means is far less clear. In 1988 sixty-nine colleges or universities were related to the Presbyterian church. In most cases, required chapel attendance is gone, a curriculum significantly influenced by Christian commitments is gone, and control over student extracurricular activities is gone. What remains is a largely historic connection between the church and the college, with Presbyterian presence largely dependent upon campus ministries, a church on campus and Presbyterians among a diverse faculty and student body. The campus is a mirror of late twentieth-century secular and pluralistic society in America, with mainstream Protestant religion, including Presbyterianism, playing largely an individualistic and privatized role in people's lives.

See also INTELLECTUAL LIFE, PRESBYTERIANS AND.

BIBLIOGRAPHY. A. M. Boylan, *Sunday School: The Formation of an American Institution* (1988); M. J. Coalter et al., eds., *The Pluralistic Vision: Presbyterians and Mainstream Protestant Education and Leadership,* vol. 6 in *The Presbyterian Presence: The Twentieth-Century Experience* (1992); L. A. Cremin, *Traditions of American Education* (1976); D. C. Hester, "The Use of the Bible in Presbyterian Curricula, 1923-1985," in *The Pluralistic Vision: Presbyterians and Mainstream Protestant Education and*

Leadership, ed. M. J. Coalter, J. M. Mulder, L. B. Weeks (1992); P. C. Kemeny, *Princeton in the Nation's Service: Religious Ideals and Educational Practice, 1868-1928* (1998); J. H. Leith, *Introduction to the Reformed Tradition* (1977); M. A. Noll, *Princeton and the Republic, 1768-1822: The Search for a Christian Enlightenment in the Era of Samuel Stanhope Smith* (1989); "Report and Recommendations of the Standing Committee on Christian Education: The Church and Public Education," *Minutes of the General Assembly of the United Presbyterian Church in the USA* (1969); W. W. Sweet, *Religion on the American Frontier, 1783-1840,* vol. 2, *The Presbyterians* (1964); L. B. Weeks, "Presbyterians," in *EARE* (1988). D. C. Hester

Edwards, Jonathan (1703-1758).† Colonial Congregational preacher and theologian. Born in East Windsor, Connecticut, and educated at Yale College (B.A., 1720, M.A., 1722), Edwards apprenticed for two years under his grandfather, Solomon Stoddard, and in 1729 he became the sole preacher of the Congregational church in Northampton, Massachusetts.

Edwards's reputation as an influential preacher was fixed in 1734-1735, when a sermon on justification caused a widespread awakening among his congregation. Edwards published a description of the Northampton conversions in *A Faithful Narrative* (1737), which turned out to be a pattern for revivals that swept through the colonies in the next few years. His congregation encouraged him to publish some of the more effective sermons, and in 1738 the five discourses headed by *Justification by Faith Alone* were widely received in England and America.

Edwards continued to preach in Northampton and became active in publishing defenses of the colonial revivals. *The Distinguishing Marks* was distributed in 1741 after Edwards had delivered the controversial address at the Yale College graduation. This defense of the results of the revivalists' activities as a true work of the Spirit of God established Edwards as the leading spokesman against the established clergy who found the revivals disruptive and too emotional. He revised and refined his arguments for the Awakening in *Some Thoughts Concerning the Revival,* published in 1743. Here he struck a moderate pose, criticizing those who were overzealous in favor of the revivals as well as those who opposed it outright. Three years later he wrote the *Treatise on Religious Affections,* further evidence of Edwards's intellectually demanding style and determination to defend the centrality of the "affections" in religious experience.

Though he was a thoughtful advocate for revivalism, preaching was Edwards's primary vehicle of expression. Throughout his career he penned more than twelve hundred sermons, of which only a small percentage were published. Still, the sermons lived on through the theological treatises that grew out of his preaching and were widely disseminated to laypeople and scholars alike.

The notoriety of Edwards's preaching and writing on revivals placed him in the forefront of American Christianity just prior to the Great Awakening and made him a figure well-known among Presbyterians in *New England and the Middle Colonies. Though formal ties did not exist, *New Side Presbyterians who advocated revivals looked to Edwards for leadership and sustenance. When in 1758 the trustees of the College of New Jersey, an institution dedicated to New Side Presbyterianism, needed a new president, they asked Edwards to preside over the Princeton school. In 1748 Edwards had left his congregation in Northampton because of opposition from church members to his exclusion from the Lord's Supper those who had not experienced conversion. When called to be president of the College of New Jersey Edwards was working at a mission to Native Americans in Stockbridge, Massachusetts, where he spent more time writing than preaching and was able to write *Freedom of the Will* (1754) and *Original Sin* (1758). Shortly after arriving in Princeton, however, Edwards died of a smallpox inoculation. Though his work at the college was shortlived, Edwards's influence on Presbyterians was great through his writings and through the networks established between his theological descendants in New England and like-minded Presbyterians to the *South.

To be sure, Edwards had the greatest impact upon New England theology and Congregationalism. After the split in 1837 between *Old School and *New School branches of the Presbyterian Church, Presbyterians became less dependent on New England and Edwards. Still, his status as one of America's greatest theologians and philosophers ensured that nineteenth-century Presbyterians would always have to reckon with the incomparable President Edwards in every theological discussion of consequence.

Bibliography. *AAP* 1; *ANB* 7; *A. V. G. Allen, Jonathan Edwards* (1889); C. C. Cherry, *The Theology of Jonathan Edwards: A Reappraisal* (1966); *DAB* III; *DARB;* P. Miller, *Jonathan Edwards* (1949); *NCAB* 5; M. A. Noll, "Jonathan Edwards and Nineteenth-Century Theology," in *Jonathan Edwards and the American Experience,* ed. N. O. Hatch and H. S.

Stout (1988); O. E. Winslow, *Jonathan Edwards, 1703-1758* (1940). J. H. Edwards

Elders. *See* POLITY, PRESBYTERIAN.

Election. As a biblical term, *election* refers to God's choosing a particular people to receive his salvation from sin, guilt and condemnation. Classic Pauline passages teaching this doctrine are to be found in Ephesians 1 and Romans 9. The *Westminster Confession of Faith of 1647, which expressed this doctrine for American Presbyterians, *Congregationalists and the large number of Baptists who were represented by the Philadelphia Confession of 1707, declared in Chapter III, 5: "Those of mankind that are predestinated unto life, God, before the foundation of the world was laid, according to his eternal and immutable purpose, and the secret counsel and good pleasure of his will, hath chosen in Christ, unto everlasting glory, out of his mere free grace and love, without any foresight of faith or good works, or perseverance in either of them, or any other thing in the creature, as conditions, or causes moving him thereunto; and all to the praise of his glorious grace."

This was in accord with the *Calvinistic teaching of the sovereignty of God's grace in unconditional election as set forth by the Synod of Dort in 1619 in answer to the five articles of the *Arminian *Remonstrance* of 1610, which taught that God's election was conditional, based on foreseen faith and perseverance.

*Puritanism in both England and America wrestled with the question of how one can be assured of salvation since it is based alone on the grace of God in the Holy Spirit's work of regeneration producing faith and repentance. In New England the majority of Puritan leaders favored a scheme of steps of preparation for grace, whereby an individual might gain assurance of salvation. "Preparationism," by focusing on the subjective experience of salvation, helped open the way for increasing Arminianism in the eighteenth century. Such leaders of the Great Awakening as Jonathan *Edwards and George Whitefield, however, were Calvinists who reasserted the traditional understanding of God's sovereignty in election.

In the nineteenth century the *New School theologians like Congregationalist Nathaniel Taylor again accommodated orthodox Calvinism to meet the needs of the revivals of the Second Awakening. Baptists also were divided between Particular (Calvinistic) and General (Arminian) Baptists.

By the twentieth century, *revivalism's emphasis on freedom of the will and the individual's role in making a decision for Christ had caused Arminianism to prevail in America over the Calvinistic understanding of unconditional election.

BIBLIOGRAPHY G. M. Marsden, *The Evangelical Mind and the New School Presbyterian Experience: A Case Study of Thought and Theology in Nineteenth-Century America* (1970); P. Schaff, *The Creeds of Christendom,* 3 vols. (1877).

W. S. Barker

Ely, Ezra Stiles (1786-1861). Presbyterian minister and controversialist. Born in Lebanon, Connecticut, and educated at Yale (1803), Ely embodied the antithesis of his namesake, Yale's irenic Old Light president, Ezra Stiles. Ely's first pastorate at the Colchester Congregational church (1806-1810) ended in dispute over efforts to excommunicate nonattending but influential members. From 1810 to 1813 he served as stated preacher to the Almshouse and Hospital of New York City. His sympathy for the young victims of prostitution led to false accusations of consorting with prostitutes. In 1813 he was invited to pastor Old Pine Church in Philadelphia (the *Presbyterian Church in the U.S.A. [PCUSA]), but his installation was delayed until 1814 due to the stir he created by a savage written attack on New Divinity theology in "A Contrast Between Calvinism and Hopkinsianism" (1811).

One of the most controversial episodes in Ely's career occurred with the publication of a sermon on "The Duty of Christian Freemen to Elect Christian Rulers" (1828). Anticipating later efforts by evangelicals to advance moral objectives through political means, Ely called for a Christian party in politics. Detractors within and without the evangelical community accused Ely of abusing his office and proposing a *Calvinist theocracy. Of greater political consequence was a letter Ely wrote in 1829 to his friend President Andrew Jackson, wherein he relayed unsubstantiated rumors about the sexual improprieties of Peggy Eaton, the wife of John H. Eaton, who was Jackson's Secretary of War. The resulting furor led to the resignation of Jackson's entire cabinet.

In 1835 Ely left Pine Street Church to join the faculty of newly established Marion College in northern Missouri. This antislavery institution and Ely himself were soon embroiled in controversy in this proslavery state. More problematic was Ely's speculation in western lands, particularly an ill-fated investment in the creation of a Presbyterian utopia in Marion. The ensuing Panic of 1837 financially ruined Ely. Charged with illegal banking, embezzlement and cheating investors, Ely eventually returned to Philadelphia and pastored the First Presbyterian Church of Northern Liberties from 1844 until a paralytic stroke in 1851 forced his retirement.

Controversies aside, Ely distinguished himself during his tenure at Pine Street. He served as stated clerk of the Presbyterian general assembly (1825-1836) and as moderator (1828). Marrying into wealth, he donated more than fifty thousand dollars to his own church, and in 1827 he supplied the funds for building Jefferson Medical College. In addition, from 1816 to 1828 he published seven books, and from 1829 to 1836 he edited the Presbyterian weekly, *The Philadelphian.*

Bibliography. *Biographical Sketches of the Graduates of Yale College,* ed. F. B. Dexter, 5:647-51; C. Dahl, "The Clergyman, the Hussy and Old Hickory: Ezra Stiles Ely and the Peggy Eaton Affair," *JPH* 52 (1974) 137-55. D. W. Kling

Erdman, Charles Rosenbury (1866-1960). Presbyterian clergyman and educator. Born in Fayetteville, New York, the son of premillennialist leader William Jacob *Erdman, Charles Erdman was raised in a *New School Presbyterian environment. After graduating from Princeton University and Princeton Theological Seminary, Erdman served churches in Overbrook and Germantown, Pennsylvania. In 1906 he assumed the chair of practical theology at Princeton Seminary, which he held until his retirement in 1936. He pastored the First Presbyterian Church of Princeton from 1924 to 1934.

In 1925, at the height of the *fundamentalist-modernist controversy in the Presbyterian Church U.S.A, Erdman won election as moderator of the general assembly. Though a self-described fundamentalist, he believed that the unified evangelical mission of the church was more important than precise doctrinal agreement. At a crucial moment in the general assembly, when fundamentalists were apparently succeeding in forcing liberal Presbyterians into doctrinal conformity, Erdman referred the issue to a committee and so broke the momentum of the fundamentalist exclusivists. Erdman was also a major voice for inclusivism in an extended feud among Princeton faculty that led to the reorganization of the seminary and the exodus of some faculty to form Westminster Theological Seminary in 1929. He also sat on the Presbyterian Board of Foreign Missions from 1906 to 1942 and was president of the board from 1926 to 1940. Erdman wrote more than thirty books, most of which were biblical commentaries, and contributed to *The Fundamentals.* He numbered Woodrow *Wilson, Grover Cleveland and Billy *Sunday among his friends.

Bibliography. *ANB* 7; *DAB* 6; C. T. Fritsch et al., "In Memoriam," *PSB* 54 (1960) 36-39; L. A. Loetscher, *The Broadening Church: A Study of Theological Issues in the Presbyterian Church Since 1869* (1957); B. J. Longfield, *The Presbyterian Controversy: Fundamentalists, Modernists and Moderates* (1991). B. J. Longfield

Erdman, William Jacob (1834-1923).† Presbyterian pastor. Born in Allentown, Pennsylvania, Erdman was educated at Hamilton College and Union Theological Seminary. He was ordained in the First Presbyterian Church of Philadelphia in 1860 and ministered in a number of Presbyterian and Congregational churches in Ontario, Minnesota, New York, Michigan, Indiana and Boston. Most notable was his association with Dwight L. Moody and his ministry in Moody's Chicago Avenue Church (1875-1878).

Erdman was a premillennialist and closely associated with the Niagara Conference. He and a number of fellow premillennial ministers, including Nathaniel *West and Henry Martyn *Parsons, gathered in 1876 for Bible study and fellowship in what they called the Believers' Meetings for Bible Study. Within two years this dispensational study group had organized what would later be called the Niagara Bible Conference, the prototype of Bible and prophecy conferences in America. He was often featured as a Bible expositor at the conference and served as its secretary throughout its existence. In the theological controversy that brought the conference to its end, Erdman came to reverse his own position and joined the dissenters in denying the secret rapture of the church. He presided over a discussion of the points at issue in 1900, but without success.

Erdman also served as a consulting editor for the Scofield Reference Bible. He wrote several books, many pamphlets and scores of articles in religious and Bible study journals. His son, Charles Rosenbury *Erdman, was a professor at Princeton Theological Seminary and a controversial figure in the *fundamentalist-modernist debate within the Presbyterian Church.

Bibliography. *ANB* 7; E. R. Sandeen, *The Roots of Fundamentalism: British and American Millenarianism, 1800-1930* (1970). P. C. Wilt

Erskine, Ebenezer (1680-1754) and Ralph (1685-1752). The Erskine brothers, Ebenezer and Ralph, were devout, learned and able ministers in the Church of Scotland. Their stance on four basic issues put them at odds with the general assembly from 1720 to 1740. First, the gospel, centered on Jesus Christ as Savior, Lord and head of the church, set them over against the Arian and unitarian tendencies of the time. Second, they held a Reformation accent on grace (starting with law and gospel, the basis of justification by grace through faith), which led them to oppose the moralism and rationalism of the day. Third, while affirming predestination, they insisted that the gospel call to Christian faith should be openly spoken to all and not limited to the elect. Fourth, they insisted that a minister should be elected by the congregation he would serve rather than selected by wealthy landlords of the district (patronage).

A conflict between the Erskines and the Church of Scotland emerged when Ebenezer objected to patronage. Clearly the controversy involved other issues as well. By all accounts, the Scottish general assembly handled the Erskine group badly, denying them due process, deposing them from their parishes and refusing effectual reconciliation at the highest levels. With strong, steady support from their congregations, they and a handful of other ministers seceded and formed an "Associate" Presbytery (Gairney Bridge, 1733), the name indicating neither an intentional separation from the Church of Scotland nor a new denomination. Finalized in 1740, the Secession spread through Scotland but soon (1747) split again into Burgher and Anti-Burgher factions. The Seceder factions in Scotland eventually reunited with each other (1820) and with the Church of Scotland (1929 and 1956).

The dates of the Secession coincide closely with the Great Awakening in North America (from c. 1730) and the *New Side/*Old Side division among American Presbyterians (1737-1758). Indeed, the Erskines and Gilbert *Tennant corresponded with each other in 1738 and the years following. The great revivalist George Whitefield visited Scotland in 1741 and embraced the Erskines' cause but refused to limit himself to their group. Lay Seceders asked for ministers in North America as early as 1742. When Seceder ministers came to North America in 1753, however, they were rudely received by the settled Presbyterians and had to proceed on their own. They did so, and they flourished wherever *Scots-Irish immigrants settled.

In 1782 the majority of American Seceders (Associate Presbyterians) and Covenanters (Reformed Presbyterians, dating back to 1638) united to form the Associate Reformed Church of America. The church led a stormy life until 1820-1822 and then divided along geographical lines. The Southern portion continues as the Associate Reformed Presbyterian Church. The Northern and Western portions reunited in 1858 as the *United Presbyterian Church of North America (UPCNA). The Seceders held to the *Westminster Confession and Catechisms in theology and the Presbyterian form of *polity. They affirmed the verbal inspiration of Scripture; the supreme authority of the Bible, even over the nation; the evil of slaveholding; the inconsistency of Christian faith with the codes of secret societies; the practice of closed communion; the moral duty of political involvement as God's purposes may require at the time; and the exclusive use of psalms in worship.

The Restoration, or Campbellite, movement owes a debt to the Erskines' influence. Thomas Campbell (1763-1854) came from Northern Ireland to America as an Anti-Burgher minister in 1807. When the Associate Synod of North America censured him for laxity in admitting people to the Lord's Supper, Campbell withdrew. Campbell and his son Alexander (1788-1866) soon emerged as the principal leaders in the Restoration movement (Christian Church, Disciples of Christ and Churches of Christ). While the Campbellites drew from sectarian sources other than the Erskines, the impact of the Seceder movement cannot be denied. And in some impulses and practices such as exclusive psalmody, unaccompanied singing and closed communion, the more strict Churches of Christ bear a certain resemblance to churches of the Seceder movement.

Bibliography. *DSCHT;* R. A. King, *A History of the Associate Reformed Presbyterian Church* (1966); R. Lathan, *History of the Associate Reformed Synod of the South* (1882); A. R. MacEwen, *The Erskines* (1900); J. M'Kerrow, *History of the Secession Church* (1841); A. P. F. Sell, "The Message of the Erskines for Today: A Published Address" (1987). M. S. Johnson

Eucharist. *See* SACRAMENTS, PRESBYTERIANS AND THE.

Evolution. *See* SCIENCE, PRESBYTERIANS AND.

Evangelical Presbyterian Church. A Presbyterian denomination organized in March 1981 by churches that had withdrawn from both the *United Presbyterian Church (UPCUSA) and the *Presbyterian Church in the United States (PCUS) in protest over theological pluralism in those denominations. A constituting convention in St. Louis launched a conservative Presbyterian body equally committed to Reformed theology and evangelical witness. The first general assembly of the EPC convened in September 1981 and counted thirty-seven ministers and thirty-eight ruling elders representing twelve churches.

The precipitating issue that led to the formation of the EPC was the controversy surrounding the admission of United Church of Christ minister Mansfield Kasemann into the UPCUSA's National Capitol Union Presbytery in 1980. Kasemann was unable to state without qualification that Jesus is the Son of God. Already displeased with the mainline bodies' lack of commitment to evangelism and their predilection for left-wing social and political causes, significant numbers of conservative churches began to withdraw. Some, like Philadelphia's Tenth Presbyterian Church, joined the *Presbyterian Church in America (PCA), which had been formed in 1973 by dissenting PCUS congregations.

However, several withdrawn churches had women elders and deacons and were unwilling to relinquish this practice, as the PCA demanded. Also, the strong charismatic presence in some congregations (sometimes known as the freedom of the Holy Spirit in *worship) proved a potential barrier to joining existing conservative Presbyterian denominations. Led by such conservatives as Bartlett Hess of Ward Presbyterian Church in Detroit and Andrew Jumper of Central Presbyterian Church in St. Louis, a network of evangelical Presbyterians determined to form a centrist, moderate alternative.

A 1978 Supreme Court ruling on local church property, which deprived the mainline Presbyterian bodies of their presumed claim to ownership, created an opening for churches to leave with their property. Some two hundred churches departed the UPCUSA and PCUS between 1978 and 1982, when general assembly action made denominational control explicit. In 1983, when the UPCUSA and the PCUS merged, an eight-year period of grace known as Article 13 was given to former PCUS congregations to leave with property. Fifty-five churches moved into the EPC during this time.

The EPC adopted a modern-language version of the *Westminster Confession as well as a contemporary rendering of the Shorter Catechism. The Book of Government and Worship was compiled by denominational founders while the Book of Discipline was adapted from the PCA's Rules of Discipline. In addition, the denomination at its first assembly affirmed a statement of "Essentials of the Faith," which outlined the theological truths on which unity was to be expected. Considered nonessential and open to differences of opinion and liberty of conscience were such matters as eschatology, the gifts of the Holy Spirit and the ordination of women. Ironically, these latter issues have kept the EPC from membership in the North American Presbyterian and Reformed Council (NAPARC), though the denomination is an active member of the National Association of Evangelicals (NAE) and the World Alliance of Reformed Churches.

Furthermore, the assembly identified certain rights held in perpetuity by the congregation, including choice of officers and control of property and benevolence funds. The intended effect of these structural decisions was to curb the centralization of denominational power. The EPC also took steps in its early years to guard against clergy domination by providing for a 2:1 parity of ruling elders to ministers in all presbytery and general assembly meetings.

While refusing to make political endorsements, the EPC has developed position papers on various issues such as abortion and homosexuality. These documents, though not binding on church members, represent the denomination's theological reflection and its desire to speak from a Reformed perspective.

The EPC has grown steadily since its inception, much of it due to the church-planting efforts of its larger churches (twelve EPC congregations have more than one thousand members). The denomination is well-established in metropolitan areas like Detroit, St. Louis and Denver. About half of the EPC's 175 churches are located in the South. An Argentinean presbytery was added in 1987, and a fraternal relationship was started with an association of Puerto Rican pastors in 1992.

By 1993 it had grown to 175 churches, 375 ministers and 52,360 members. The general assembly office is located in Livonia, Michigan.

P. Heidebrecht

Evangelical Synod of North America. Predecessor denomination of the Evangelical and Reformed Church and the United Church of Christ. By the opening of the nineteenth century in Germany, Enlightenment criticism and pietist inwardness brought about both conflict between religious groups and new possibilities for church union. In Prussia, King Frederick William III united the Lutheran and Reformed churches in the Evangelical Church of the Prussian Union (1817). The spirit of union was undergirded by a strong pietistic emphasis upon practical Christianity, which aided the founding and development of missionary societies in Basel, Switzerland, and Barmen, Germany.

The Evangelical Synod derived from European pietistic mission efforts combined with the nonpolemical spirit of the German union churches. This new church formed the only American denomination patterned on the German Prussian Union Church. Most of its members settled in Missouri, Illinois and neighboring states. In response to the desire of immigrants for union churches, six mission pastors from Basel and Barmen organized the German Evangelical Church Association of the West (Kirchenverein des Westens) in 1840 at Mehlville (St. Louis), Missouri.

The six founders, led by Hermann Garlichs, Louis *Nollau and Georg Wall, drew up a simple confessional paragraph acknowledging the symbolic books of the Lutheran and Reformed churches (the Augsburg Confession and Luther's and the *Heidelberg Catechisms). The founders believed that behind the symbols was the Word of God, and above the Word was the reality of God's redeeming love through Jesus Christ.

The noncontroversial spirit of the founders did not indicate indifference to theological training. By 1850 a seminary was opened at Marthasville, Missouri, predecessor of the present Eden Theological Seminary, and a unifying church journal, the *Friedensbote (Messenger of Peace),* was first issued in the same year. Andreas *Irion, president of the seminary between 1857 and 1870, was the leading early Evangelical theologian, making use of a catechetical method to teach irenic pietistic Lutheranism.

In 1847 the founders had published their own Evangelical Catechism (modeled on Luther's and the Heidelberg), still in print in a shortened form. Ten years later they approved their own worship book (Agende), and by 1862 a new Evangelical hymnal, largely derived from the German choral tradition, began a successful life.

After 1855 Adolf *Baltzer, a university-trained immigrant pastor/teacher, strengthened the synod organizationally as its first full-time president. By 1866 the church association had grown sufficiently so that it then took the name German Evangelical Synod of the West. In 1872 the synod adopted its definitive name German Evangelical Synod of North America (dropping the word *German* in 1927), after it had united with a smaller United Synod of the East and a United Synod of the Northwest, the latter adding what is now Elmhurst College, as a preseminary preparatory school.

For a long time, parochial schools were part of most Evangelical congregations. An extensive diaconal movement began in 1847, when Nollau organized the Good Samaritan Hospital at St. Louis. His pioneer work developed into an extensive deaconess movement, with homes, hospitals and other institutions such as orphanages in Cleveland, Evansville, Detroit, Chicago and other places.

The most important twentieth-century American theological family included Reinhold, H. Richard and Hulda *Niebuhr, who were born into, educated by and members of the Evangelical Synod and its successors.

The early *mission orientation of the Evangelical Synod expanded to include special projects at home for Native Americans, German/Russian immigrants, seamen, islanders, mountain people and underprivileged city folk. Abroad Evangelicals carried on extensive missions in India and Honduras. Establishing churches was a prominent Evangelical program: half of the congregations within the Evangelical Synod had received denominational home missions aid. The need for centralized integration of these activities led to the adoption of a new constitution in 1927, blending presbyterian with congregational and episcopal elements. The ecumenical interests of the synod were reawakened by participation of its leaders in worldwide conferences beginning with Stockholm and Lausanne in 1925 and 1927. Louis W. *Goebel, vice president of the Evangelical Synod, aided in moving church union conversations among Evangelicals with German Reformed churches. In 1928 President Samuel D. Press of Eden Seminary began conversations with President George Richards of the Lancaster Reformed Seminary, and under the influence of H. Richard Niebuhr as committee chairman, dialogues were begun from which emerged the 1934 Evangelical and Reformed Church.

See also GERMAN REFORMED IN AMERICA.

BIBLIOGRAPHY. E. J. F. Arndt, *The Faith We Proclaim: The Doctrinal Viewpoint Generally Prevailing in the Evangelical and Reformed Church* (1960); D. Dunn et al., eds., *A History of the Evangelical and Reformed Church* (1961); H. Kamphausen, *Geschichte des religioesen Lebens in der Deutschen Evangelischen Synode von Nord Amerika* (1924); A. Muecke, *Geschichte der Deutschen Evangelischen Synode von Nord Amerika* (1915); C. E. Schneider, *The German Church on the American Frontier: A Study in the Rise of Religion Among the Germans of the West* (1939). L. H. Zuck

Evans, Louis Hadley (1897-1981). Presbyterian minister. Born in Goshen, Indiana, and educated at Occidental College in Los Angeles (A.B., 1919) and McCormick Theological Seminary in Chicago (B.D., 1922), Evans was ordained to the ministry in 1922. During his long career, he served the *Presbyterian Church in the U.S.A. (PCUSA) at both the congregational and national levels.

Evans pastored the First Presbyterian Church in Westope, North Dakota (1922-1925); Calvary Presbyterian Church in Wilmington, California (1925-1928); First Presbyterian Church in Pomona, California (1928-1931); Third Presbyterian Church in Pittsburgh, Pennsylvania (1931-1941); and First Presbyterian Church in Hollywood, California (1941-1952). From 1953 to 1962 he served as associate general secretary and minister-at-large for the Board of National Missions. Renowned for his powerful preaching, he traveled extensively throughout the United States and was a popular inspirational speaker at military camps, colleges and universities and on radio and television.

During the 1950s Evans was associated with the Broadcasting and Film Commission of the National Council of Churches of Christ, where he participated in a highly personal series of television talks directed to the needs of the average person. Designed to help viewers apply the basic principles of Christianity to the problems of everyday life, the talks were planned specifically for a television audience.

Evans wrote several books, including *Youth Seeks a Master* (1941), *This Is America's Hour* (1952), *The Kingdom Is Yours* (1952), *Life's Hidden Power* (1958), *Your Marriage, Duel or Duet* (1962, 1975) and *Make Your Faith Work* (1957). He retired from active ministry in 1963 and died at his home in Pasadena, California.

BIBLIOGRAPHY. J. H. Smylie, *American Presbyterians: A Pictorial History* (1985); *Who Was Who in America*, vol. 9, 1985-1989. F. Heuser Jr.

Ewing, Finis (1773-1841). Principal founder of the *Cumberland Presbyterian Church (CPC). Born into a Presbyterian family in Virginia, Ewing moved to Logan County, Kentucky, in 1795 and was converted during the Great Revival under the exhortations of Southern Presbyterian leader James *McGready. Ewing was ordained to the Presbyterian ministry by prorevivalists, though his education and theological convictions did not qualify him in the eyes of antirevival Presbyterians.

In 1810, while in the throes of a lengthy dispute between revival and antirevival Presbyterians, Ewing and two others started the CPC. The primary cause of the schism was the revivalists' repudiation of central Calvinistic convictions. Ewing specifically moderated the teachings of the *Westminster Confession to give greater place to the human will in conversion. He was one of the chief proponents of this modified *Calvinism, which in a number of parallel forms became the new evangelical orthodoxy of the Second Great Awakening.

Ewing published his views in *A Series of Lectures on the Most Important Subjects of Divinity* (1827). He held that God offers himself to all humanity through rational law and not to a limited elect through seemingly arbitrary and inscrutable decrees. In keeping with the growing democratic ideals of the new nation, he emphasized that God gives every person full opportunity to repent. Ewing added an egalitarian frontier theme to a developing *New School Presbyterianism, modifying predestinarian Calvinism in order to make it compatible with the frontier camp meeting. The Cumberland doctrine fit well with the pragmatic revivalism of Charles Grandison *Finney and the benevolent movement that played such a strong role in antebellum evangelism.

BIBLIOGRAPHY. *ANB* 7; B. M. Barrus, M. L. Baughn and T. H. Campbell, *A People Called Cumberland Presbyterians* (1972); *DAB* III; E. T. Thompson, *Presbyterians in the South*, vol. 1 (1963).

S. E. Berk

F

Falconer, Sir Robert Alexander (1867-1943). Canadian Presbyterian educator. Born in Charlottetown, Prince Edward Island, into a Free Church heritage, Falconer was reared in the missionary community of Trinidad. He enrolled at the University of London (B.A., 1885) and the University of Edinburgh (M.A., 1889; B.D., 1892) and engaged in further studies at Leipzig, Berlin and Marburg. Falconer was ordained in 1892 and the same year chosen as lecturer in New Testament at Pine Hill Divinity Hall, Halifax. His ability was recognized by his appointment as professor in 1895 and principal in 1904. He was an outstanding example of the new generation of *Canadian Presbyterian scholars who espoused a moderate liberal evangelicalism.

In 1907 Falconer became president of the University of Toronto, where he would remain for twenty-five years, inaugurating the tradition of Maritime scholars moving westward to give leadership in Canadian education. The great Canadian university experiment, in which denominational liberal arts and theological colleges federated into the provincial university, was beginning to unravel at its fountainhead in Toronto, and Falconer successfully reordered the institution so that it came to have the largest student body in the British Commonwealth and to achieve something akin to Ivy League status.

In his public capacity as a speaker and writer Falconer stressed the British connection, the place of the Bible and morality in national character and the foundation of the humanities for higher education. At the center of Canada's intellectual life, he and his brother-in-law Alfred Gandier, principal of the Presbyterian Knox College, exerted influence on the ecumenical experiment that gave birth to the United Church of Canada in 1925.

Falconer was a distinguished representative of the last generation of Presbyterians who exercised a measure of ascendancy in Canadian culture. He died at Toronto.

BIBLIOGRAPHY. R. Falconer, *Idealism in National Character* (1920); M. Gauvreau, "Presbyterianism, Liberal Education and the Research Ideal: Sir Robert Falconer and the University of Toronto, 1907-1932," in *The Burning Bush and a Few Acres of Snow: The Presbyterian Contribution to Canadian Life and Culture,* ed. W. Klempa (1994).

I. S. Rennie

Finley, Samuel (1715-1766).† *New Side Presbyterian minister and fifth president of the College of New Jersey (later Princeton University). Born in Ireland, Finley was a pious, intellectually precocious youth who immigrated to Philadelphia at age nineteen. He probably attended William *Tennent's Log College in Neshaminy, Pennsylvania, and thus cast his lot with those Presbyterians who became supporters of the Great Awakening and favored an active, experimental *piety. In 1742 he was ordained and enjoyed success as an itinerant evangelist in the Middle Colonies, despite one foray into Connecticut where he was arrested for vagrancy because he attempted to preach at an unrecognized society. He quickly made a reputation as a controversialist, defending infant baptism, attacking the Moravians and repudiating the pacifism of the Quakers, in which he magnified the role of the *Scots-Irish during the French and Indian War.

In 1744 Finley accepted a call to Nottingham, Maryland, and there he remained for seventeen years, founding his own small but distinguished academy to prepare young men for the Presbyterian ministry. As a scholar, teacher and one of the most successful and respected of the New Side Presbyterians, Finley was a logical choice for the presidency of the College of New Jersey, chartered in 1746 as a successor to Tennent's primitive college. Finley served from 1761 to 1766, his term (like those of his four predecessors) cut short by death. Although he published several sermons and essays, Finley left no significant theological work of any size.

BIBLIOGRAPHY. *AAP* 3; *ANB* 7; A. Alexander, *Biographical Sketches of the Founder and Principal Alumni of the Log College* (1845); *DAB* III.

E. C. Nordbeck

Finney, Charles Grandison (1792-1875). Presbyterian revivalist and educator. Finney, who would one day be known as the father of modern revivalism, was born in Warren, Litchfield County, Connecticut, the seventh child of farming parents, Sylvester and Rebecca (Rice) Finney. With land increasingly scarce and costly in Connecticut, in 1794 the Finneys joined with many other young families in the great westward migrations of post-Revolutionary America. Settling in Hanover (now Kirkland), Oneida County, New York, following a brief stay in the village of Brothertown, Charles first attended a nearby common school, then the Hamilton Oneida Academy in Clinton. While there he came under the influence of Principal Seth Morton, who taught the popular, six-foot-two-inch Finney the basics of classical education, singing and the cello.

In 1812 Finney returned to Connecticut to attend the Warren Academy in preparation for further studies at Yale College. Persuaded against attending Yale, Finney then spent two years teaching in New Jersey. In 1818 his mother's illness forced him to return to New York, where he began the study of law, entering the office of Judge Benjamin Wright in Adams as an apprentice. Although it is uncertain whether Finney was formally admitted to the bar, he did regularly argue cases in the local justice's court of Adams.

Finney's remarkable religious conversion on October 10, 1821, however, dramatically changed the direction of his life. Leaving a promising legal career, claiming he had been given "a retainer from the Lord Jesus Christ to plead his cause," he sought entry into the Presbyterian ministry. Taken under care by the St. Lawrence Presbytery in 1823, he studied theology with George Gale, his Princeton-trained pastor in Adams, was licensed to preach later that year and was subsequently ordained in 1824. Hired by the Female Missionary Society of the Western District, he began his labors as a missionary to the settlers of upstate New York in the spring of 1824.

Under Finney's preaching, a series of *revivals broke out in a number of villages throughout Jefferson and St. Lawrence counties, places such as Evans Mills, Antwerp, Brownville and Gouverneur. By 1825 his work had spread to the towns of Western, Troy, Utica, Rome and Auburn. These so-called western revivals (centered in Oneida County), in which Finney exercised "*new measures" such as the anxious seat, protracted meetings, allowing women to pray in public and the like, brought Finney national fame.

Not all were pleased with his success. Yale-trained revival leaders such as Lyman *Beecher and Asahel Nettleton, troubled by false reports of alleged excesses, joined with other evangelical leaders from the Northeast at the village of New Lebanon in the summer of 1827 to discuss their differences. It was at that meeting that Finney emerged as the new leader of evangelical revivalism. This leadership was consolidated from 1827 to 1832 as Finney's revivals swept urban centers such as New York City, Philadelphia, Boston and Rochester. Although Finney was involved in promoting revivals throughout his lifetime, even traveling to England for that purpose in 1849-1850 and again in 1859-1860, these early years were the high water mark of his revival career.

Forced in 1832 to curtail his travels, having contracted cholera in addition to the recurrent respiratory illnesses that troubled him throughout most of his lifetime, Finney became pastor of the Chatham Street Chapel (Second Free Presbyterian Church) in New York City. He subsequently held pastorates at the Broadway Tabernacle of New York City (1836-1837) and the First Congregational Church of Oberlin, Ohio (1837-1872). In 1835 he accepted an appointment as professor of theology at the newly formed Oberlin Collegiate Institute in Ohio (now Oberlin College). He later served as president of Oberlin College from 1851 until 1866.

Theologically Finney can best be described as a *New School *Calvinist. His preaching and teaching—always pointed and dramatic—stressed the moral government of God, the ability of people to repent and make themselves new hearts, the perfectibility of human nature and society and the need for Christians to apply their faith to daily living. For Finney, this included the investment of one's time and energy in establishing the millennial kingdom of God on earth by winning converts and involving oneself in social *reform (including *abolition, temperance, and the like).

Throughout his lifetime Finney produced a variety of books, sermon collections and articles. Among the more important were his *Lectures on Revivals of Religion* (1835), a kind of manual on how to lead revivals. He wrote: "It [a revival] presupposes that the church is sunk down in a backslidden state, and a revival consists in the return of the church from her backslidings, and in the conversion of sinners. . . . A revival is nothing else then a new beginning of obedience to God." His *Lectures on Systematic Theology* (1846) reflect his special brand of "arminianized Calvinism." His *Memoirs* (1876) recount his remarkable involvement in the great revivals of the first half of the nineteenth century.

Bibliography. *ANB* 7; R. Carwardine, *Transatlantic Revivalism: Popular Evangelicalism in Britain and America, 1790-1865* (1978); *DAB* III; *DARB*; R. A. G. Dupuis and G. M. Rosell, eds., *The Memoirs* *of Charles G. Finney* (1989); C. E. Hambrick-Stowe, *Charles G. Finney and the Spirit of American Evangelicalism* (1996); K. J. Hardman, *Charles Grandison Finney (1792-1875): Revivalist and Reformer* (1987); W. G. McLoughlin Jr., ed., *Lectures on Revivals of Religion* (1960); *NCAB* 2.

G. M. Rosell

Fisher, Samuel Reed (1810-1881). *German Reformed pastor, editor and publisher. Born and reared in Norristown, Pennsylvania, Fisher attended local common schools and studied with the Reverend George Wack, pastor of Boehm's Reformed Church in nearby Blue Bell. In 1829 he enrolled in the preparatory department of Jefferson College, Cannonsburg, Pennsylvania, and graduated from the college in 1834. Between 1834 and 1836, Fisher attended the Theological Seminary of the German Reformed Church at York, where he was instrumental in the school's founding and wrote the constitutions of the Diognothean and Goethian literary societies.

Fisher was licensed to preach and ordained in 1836. He served the Reformed church's Emmitsburg, Maryland, charge of six congregations from 1836 until 1839. Thereafter he became the general business manager of the denomination's Office of Publications in Chambersburg, Pennsylvania, until the Confederates burned the town in 1864 during the Civil War, and then in Philadelphia until 1875. He became a member of the seminary's board of visitors in 1838, stated clerk of the denomination's synod in 1840 and treasurer of its board of education.

In addition Fisher was a prolific writer. As editor of the denomination's periodical, *The Reformed Church Messenger,* until 1875, he wrote editorials and obituaries of pastors. He contributed articles to *The Guardian* and *The Mercersburg Review,* published sermons on *The Moral Power of the Christian Ministry* (1843) and *Ministerial Fidelity* (1843), and wrote a *History of the Publication Efforts of the Reformed Church in the United States* (1885).

Stricken while en route to a meeting of the general synod in Tiffin, Ohio, Fisher died there. He was buried in the cemetery of Zion's Reformed Church in Chambersburg, Pennsylvania. His work as editor and publisher was most significant in that he provided the church's members with news of developments within their own denomination and in the church at large.

BIBLIOGRAPHY. H. Harbaugh and D. Y. Heisler, *The Fathers of the Reformed Church in Europe and America,* vol. 4, ed. W. M. Dietrick (1888).

J. B. Frantz

Foreign Missions. *See* MISSIONS, PRESBYTERIAN AND REFORMED.

Forman, Charles William (1821-1894). Presbyterian missionary. Born in Washington, Kentucky, Forman graduated in 1844 from Centre College in Danville, Kentucky. During his college days he had an evangelical conversion experience and made a public profession of faith in the Presbyterian church of Washington, Kentucky. Upon graduation, he attended Princeton Theological Seminary from 1844 to 1847. Licensed in the *Old School Presbytery of New Brunswick in 1846 and ordained an evangelist by the Old School Presbytery of Ebenezer in 1847, Forman set sail for India, where he spent his life as a missionary for the Presbyterian Church in India.

In the wake of the Second Great Awakening, many American Protestants, like their counterparts in Great Britain and on the Continent, gained a renewed interest in foreign missions. After the schism with *New School Presbyterians in 1837, Old School Presbyterians severed their ties with the American Board of Commissioners for Foreign Missions. Forman was among the earliest Old School Presbyterian missionaries sent abroad under the direction of the newly formed Board of Foreign Missions of the Presbyterian Church. Presbyterian missionary activity in India had been established in the decade before Forman arrived with the the founding in 1834 of a mission station in Ludhiana, in the Punjab. At the close of the first Sikh war, Presbyterian missionaries soon expanded into the Punjab, which had been recently annexed by the British government, and then throughout the United Provinces. Forman was part of a second wave of Presbyterian missionaries who worked in the frontier regions of the Punjab.

In 1849 Forman was sent to Lahore, where he played a formative role in the missionary work in the region as an educator. He served as superintendent of the Lahore missionary schools from 1849 to 1866. In 1853 the school took residence in the old Rang Hahal place. Forman helped to cultivate a generation of indigenous teachers who worked predominately among Bengali Christians. In 1866 he became pastor of the Lahore church and served as secretary of the Punjab Bible and Tract Society. He published in Hindustani "The Christian Sword and Shield" and various Christian tracts that reached editions of ten thousand each. He returned as superintendent of the Lahore Missionary Schools in 1869. He also helped to found the Lahore Mission College, which was open from 1864 to 1866. When the institution reopened in 1886, Forman served as its principal until 1888. The school was later renamed Forman Christian College in his honor. In addition, he was appointed by the Indian government to the Punjab Text and Book Committee and the Punjab Educational Conference. He died at Kassauli, India.

Forman had six sons and three daughters. Five of his sons served as foreign missionaries. One son, John R. Forman, a graduate of the College of New Jersey and Princeton Seminary, played a leading role in the early work of the Student Volunteer Movement for Foreign Missions before returning to India as a missionary with the Northern Presbyterian Church.

Bibliography. *Encyclopedia of Missions* (1975) 239; K. S. Latourette, *A History of the Expansion of Christianity*, vol. 6 (1944); *Necrological Report Presented to the Alumni Association of Princeton Theological Seminary at Its Annual Meeting May 7th, 1895* (1895) 315-16; J. Richter, *A History of Missions in India* (1908).

P. C. Kemeny

Fosdick, Harry Emerson (1878-1969).† Liberal Baptist preacher. Born in Buffalo, New York, Fosdick was educated at Colgate University (B.A., 1900), where he was mentored by William Newton Clarke, the foremost Baptist liberal theologian of the period. Ordained to the Baptist ministry, Fosdick's first pastorate was Montclair Baptist Church, Montclair, New Jersey (1904-1915). During 1918 he served as a chaplain in France and then became pulpit minister at First Presbyterian Church in New York City (1918-1925).

There Fosdick gained national attention on May 21, 1922, when he preached his most famous sermon, "Shall the Fundamentalists Win?" Ivy Lee, a Presbyterian layman, published and distributed the sermon under the title "The New Knowledge and the Christian Faith." Fosdick suggested that belief in the virgin birth was unessential, belief in the inerrancy of the Bible was incredible to the modern mind and the literal second coming of Jesus Christ was outmoded and needed rethinking. The sermon made Fosdick the focal point of controversy within the *Presbyterian Church in the U.S.A. (PCUSA). In 1924 he was asked to become a member of the Presbyterian church; however, being a Baptist minister, he declined, thereby resigning his ministry at First Presbyterian Church.

At the urging of James C. Colgate and John D. Rockefeller Jr., Fosdick became pastor of Park Avenue Baptist Church (1925-1930). By 1930 the congregation had erected a new building named Riverside Church.

Fosdick was a renowned pulpiteer and for years preached his message of Christian personalism to millions of listeners via a radio program entitled *National Vespers*. His writing ministry also reached millions through works such as *The Meaning of Prayer* (1915), *The Meaning of Faith* (1917), *The Meaning of Service* (1920) and *The Modern Use of the Bible* (1924). Fosdick was also professor of practical theology at Union Theological Seminary.

Bibliography. *ANB* 8; *DAB* 8; *DARB;* H. E. Fosdick, *The Living of These Days: An Autobiography* (1969); R. M. Miller, *Harry Emerson Fosdick* (1985); *NCAB* E.

C. W. Whiteman

Free Reformed Churches. A small Reformed denomination, started by post-World War II immigrants from the Netherlands. Its congregations are mainly confined to the provinces of Ontario and British Columbia, Canada, where these immigrants, mostly members of the Christelijke Gereformeerde Kerken in the Netherlands (CGKN, a secession church dating to 1834) and members of the Reformed Alliance (a conservative organization within the Dutch Reformed state church) settled. The beginnings of the FRC were small, and the denomination has remained that way because many of the immigrants who came from these two Reformed churches, especially in the early 1950s, joined the existing *Christian Reformed Church (CRC) and the *Reformed Church of America and Canada. Two other independent Reformed congregations in the states of Michigan and New Jersey and a home mission station in Washington also became part of the FRC.

The FRC hold to the Three Forms of Unity for Reformed churches: the *Heidelberg Catechism, the *Belgic Confession and the *Canons of Dort. It aims to live by the faith of Scripture, upholding its doctrines and world-and-life view, emphasizing personal experience. Consquently the FRC seeks to regulate its congregational life in harmony with the classic Reformed tradition.

The ministers who first served FRC congregations came from the CGKN, but most of them now have been trained at seminaries in North America. Although the denomination does not operate its own seminary, it closely controls and supervises the training of its ministers. The FRC meets annually for synod meetings, is active in missionary outreach, supports mission and translation work among the Achi Indians in Guatemala and sponsors a radio ministry, *The Banner of Truth Radio Broadcast,* which may be heard in various parts of Canada and the United States. Its congregational life is structured around preaching, catechetical instruction and Christian education for its youth and Bible study for members all ages. Various outreach activities are undertaken at the local level. The FRC publishing committee oversees the publication of its official organ, *The Messenger,* and offers church education materials. Printed sermons, taped sermons and a youth publication are also available.

The FRC is a member of the International Council of Reformed Churches, in full corresponding relationship with the CGKN, and has a looser relationship with several independent Reformed churches. It also sends observers to the meetings of the Association of Reformed Churches, an organization that consists of congregations that have seceded from the CRC during debates over the ordination of women.

BIBLIOGRAPHY. *Yearbook of the Free Reformed Churches of North America* (1995). C. Pronk

Frelinghuysen, Theodorus Jacobus (1691-c. 1747).† Dutch Reformed minister. Born to a Westphalian German Reformed pastor on the Lower Rhine, Frelinghuysen studied at Hamm before attending the University of Lingen and was deeply influenced by pietistic followers of Gisbertus Voetius. After fourteen months pastoring in East Friesland, a hotbed of radical Dutch-German pietism, he immigrated to America. When Frelinghuysen arrived in New York in 1720, his contumacious behavior immediately aroused the suspicions of the more formalistic Dutch ministers there. A fervent pietist, Frelinghuysen chided his clerical colleagues for their personal vanity and for their use of the Lord's Prayer in worship.

Frelinghuysen quickly settled in the Raritan Valley of New Jersey, where he enjoyed considerable success among the Dutch. He flouted ecclesiastical conventions and excoriated the Dutch Reformed hierarchy in Amsterdam for failing to send pietist ministers to the new world. In New Jersey his pietistic scruples demanded the exclusion of sinners (i.e., the unconverted) from the Lord's table, but his rather arbitrary enforcement of that discipline provoked bitter recriminations from some of the more affluent church members, who published an extensive bill of particulars, called the *Klagte,* against him. Frelinghuysen, however, refused to relent, sometimes taunted his ecclesiastical opponents and, though plagued by recurrent, debilitating bouts of mental illness, continued to demand high standards of morality from his congregants.

Following the Dutch pietists Voetius, Herman Witsius and Willem à Brakel, Frelinghuysen emphasized "experimental divinity," focusing on the experiential aspect of faith. Starting with the insignificance and abject sinfulness of human beings before a righteous God, he insisted upon the necessity of heartfelt repentance and faith, resting upon the grace of God in Christ, as signs of true conversion that would naturally overflow in joy, peace and obedience. Naturally his emphasis on the wickedness and insignificance of man appealed more to the underside of society than to the wealthy. Although he affirmed the strong doctrine of predestination of the Synod of *Dort, in practice Frelinghuysen tended to push aside the doctrine of election in the fear that it would undermine the necessity of obedience.

Frelinghuysen's evangelical fervor and his itinerancy contributed to the onset of the Great Awakening in the Middle Colonies. Gilbert *Tennent, who often shared Frelinghuysen's pulpits, acknowledged that Frelinghuysen had taught him much about *piety and *revival, and his famous sermon, "On the Danger of an Unconverted Ministry," echoed many of his mentor's sentiments toward his own colleagues. Both Jonathan *Edwards and George Whitefield also spoke highly of Frelinghuysen's ministry, the latter even claiming that he had garnered several homiletic insights from Frelinghuysen's preaching.

Among Frelinghuysen's contributions to the Dutch Reformed Church in America was his effort to establish greater autonomy by seeking approval from the Classis of Amsterdam for the organization of a coetus in America. The coetus was approved in 1747, but Frelinghuysen did not live to see the fruit of these labors.

BIBLIOGRAPHY. *AAP* 9; *ANB* 8; R. H. Balmer, "The Social Roots of Dutch Pietism in the Middle Colonies," *CH* 53 (1984) 187-99; *DAB* IV; *DARB; NCAB* 12; J. R. Tanis, *Dutch Calvinistic Pietism in the Middle Colonies: A Study in the Life and Theology of Theodorus Jacobus Frelinghuysen* (1968); idem, "Frelinghuysen, the Dutch Clergy and the Great Awakening in the Middle Colonies," *RR* 38 (1984) 109-18. R. H. Balmer

Froeligh, Solomon (1750-1827). Dutch Reformed minister. Born in Red Hook, New York, Froeligh was the oldest son of a farming family. At the age of fourteen he sensed a call to the ministry under the influence of the local minister, Johannes Schuneman. In 1771 he was married to Rachel Vanderbeck of Hackensack, New Jersey. Over the next ten years he studied classics and theology with local ministers in New Jersey, and by 1774 he successfully completed licensure and ordination exams. The same year Froeligh was ordained by the general convention of the Dutch churches and received the master of arts degree from the College of New Jersey.

In 1775 Froeligh began to pastor four congregations on Long Island until British occupation the following year. His ardent patriotism forced him to return to Hackensack, where he served as chaplain to Continental soldiers. From 1777 until 1786 he ministered in a series of congregations, at Fishkill, New York, at Poughkeepsie, New York, and at Hillsborough, New Jersey. His most significant years as a minister were spent in Hackensack (1786-1822). He also taught theology at Queens College in New Brunswick, New Jersey (1797-1822), and in 1811 Froeligh received an honorary doctorate in divinity from Queens College.

The work in Hackensack led to a church split that had been building for years. The congregation had been divided between those who favored an American church and their opponents who preferred Amsterdam's ecclesiastical authority. The Great Awakening was another factor dividing the loyalties of Hackensack's parishioners. When Froeligh could not unite the factions he became increasingly partisan. By 1822 he and several committed traditionalists vigorously defended double predestination and experiential *piety. He preached and published his view that the Dutch Reformed churches had become excessively tolerant of heresy, especially the teaching of Hopkinsianism. Consequently the Dutch Reformed Church synod of 1822 deposed Froeligh and stripped him of his assistant professorship in theology. This precipitated Froeligh's secession from the *Reformed Church in America (RCA) into the True Reformed Protestant Dutch Church. In 1822 it consisted of approximately twenty-five congregations. Eventually these churches either disbanded or fused with other denominations by the end of the nineteenth century.

Toward the end of his life one friend suggested Froeligh rest from his labors, to which he replied he would "rather wear out than rust away." He died on a Monday, after having preached the previous day. A stalwart defender of traditional *Calvinism in an era when *Arminianism was said to be invading the RCA, Froeligh combined traditional Calvinism with pietism much in the manner of Theodorus *Frelinghuysen.

Bibliography. A. E. Brouwer, *Reformed Church Roots* (1977); W. C. Kiessel Jr., "Solomon Froeligh, D.D.," *RJ* 4 (July-August 1954) 11-13; A. C. Lieby, *The United Church of Hackensack and Schraalenburgh* (1976).

D. G. Hart and H. Brinks

Fundamentalist-Modernist Controversy.† The fundamentalist-modernist controversy was an extended conflict in the Protestant churches and American society at large between religious liberals, who sought to preserve Christianity by accommodating the traditional faith to modern culture, and militant theological conservatives determined to save evangelical Christianity and American civilization from the advances of modernism and Darwinism. It proved especially divisive in the Northern Presbyterian Church (PCUSA).

In 1865 most Americans thought of their country as a Christian nation and looked on evangelical Protestantism as the national religion. Though the evangelical establishment was marked by denominational rivalries and marred by divisions between Northern and Southern churches, it demonstrated an impressive unity of beliefs and values. In the years between the *Civil War and World War I, this consensus dissolved. Differing responses to the profound intellectual and social changes of the late nineteenth and early twentieth centuries produced sharp divisions in American Protestantism that, in the wake of World War I, erupted in the fundamentalist-modernist controversy.

A revolution in thinking challenged traditional Christianity in the years after Appomattox. The publication of Charles Darwin's *Origin of Species* in 1859 and the subsequent rise of evolutionary philosophy attacked dearly held beliefs about the accuracy of the Bible and God's providential design. Additionally, changes in the study of history, sociology, psychology and world religions and the Bible questioned the possibility of absolute religious and moral truth. Profound social changes added to the cultural turbulence. Immense immigration, rapid urbanization and industrialization and the gradual secularization of society all presented formidable challenges to America's churches.

Presbyterians responded to these changes in different ways. Many, accepting the advances in science, history and biblical studies, set out to save Christianity by adjusting the traditional faith to modern intellectual trends. These liberals, or so-called modernists, built on the foreign philosophical tradition of Immanuel Kant (1724-1804) and German Idealism and the religious thought of Friedrich Schleiermacher (1768-1834) and Albrecht Ritschl (1822-1889). In addition, they were heavily influenced by Unitarianism, Transcendentalism and the religious thought of Horace Bushnell. By the 1880s an identifiable movement known as the New Theology had arisen. Pastors such as Theodore Munger and theologians like William Newton Clarke worked to accommodate the old faith to new ways of thinking. By the end of World War I liberals were well entrenched in the Northern Presbyterian Church, dominating many of the seminaries and a sizeable number of pulpits especially in New York.

Liberal theology placed particular stress on the idea of divine immanence. Enamored of evolutionary thought, modernists insisted that God revealed himself through the progress of history. This affirmation led to an optimistic worldview manifested in an irrepressible faith in the goodness and freedom of humankind and the inevitable movement of history toward the fulfillment of the kingdom of God on earth.

Experience provided the final religious authority for modernists. Doctrines were seen as tentative and historically conditioned accounts of unchanging religious feelings. This emphasis allowed liberals to endorse wholeheartedly the findings of biblical higher criticism. Since the Bible was only a historically limited record of the progressive self-revelation of God to Israel, historical or scientific difficulties could be overlooked as anachronistic expressions of abiding religious experience.

Finally, ethics became the test of religious truth. In liberal circles concern for life here eclipsed interest in the life hereafter. The divinity of Jesus was commonly attributed to his ethical and religious perfection, and the church was understood to be an agency for moral action and development. Many liberals, insisting that the purpose of Christianity was to transform society into God's kingdom, became vocal proponents of the social gospel.

While liberals were making peace with modernity by adjusting Christianity to culture, some conservatives engaged in theological innovations that would influence the fundamentalist movement of the 1920s. Most significant was the development of dispensational premillennialism, primarily by the Englishman John Nelson Darby. Popularized in America by Bible and prophecy conferences, the Scofield Reference Bible (1909) and numerous Bible institutes, dispensationalism was a complex method of literal biblical interpretation that divided history into seven eras, each marked by a different covenant between God and humanity. According to this scheme, the present age was destined to irreversible spiritual decline that would end only with the supernatural personal return and millennial reign of Christ. The dispensationalist view of the Bible as divinely inspired and without error found contemporary scholarly support in the doctrine of scriptural inerrancy formulated by nondispensationalist Presbyterian conservatives, most notably Benjamin Breckinridge *Warfield at Princeton Theological Seminary.

Around the turn of the twentieth century, conservative Protestants tried to forge alliances to defend supernatural Bible-based Christianity against the advances of liberal theology. The clearest manifestation of this effort was the publication of twelve paperback volumes entitled *The Fundamentals* (1910-1915), which affirmed the authority of the Scriptures against the claims of modern *science and higher criticism.

In the heat of the cultural crisis that gripped the United States after World War I, the lines between modernists and fundamentalists emerged more clearly than they had before. As the controversy intensified, theological moderates moved to one extreme or the other, thus polarizing church and society. The battle was waged on two fronts: the churches and the culture at large. In the *Presbyterian Church in the U.S.A. (PCUSA), conservatives sought to halt liberalism by requiring subscription to traditional doctrines of supernaturalist Christianity, such as the inerrancy of Scripture, the virgin birth, substitutionary atonement, bodily resurrection and miracle-working power of Christ. J. Gresham *Machen's *Christianity and Liberalism* (1923) articulated the conservative claim that modernism was not Christianity and that liberals therefore ought to withdraw from the churches. Liberals, led by Henry Sloane *Coffin and Harry Emerson *Fosdick, insisted that they were evangelical Christians and appealed to the American sense of liberty and tolerance. By 1926 the liberal appeal to tolerance had essentially succeeded. To the dismay of the fundamentalists, the church refused to drive modernists from its ranks.

In the culture generally, a variety of interdenominational groups, such as the World's Christian Fundamentals Association and a host of fundamentalist stars—William Bell Riley, John Roach Straton and J. Frank Norris—led by three-time presidential candidate and Presbyterian layman William Jennings *Bryan, sought to save American civilization from the effects of Darwinism. Bryan, for instance, concluded that German military atrocities, biblical higher criticism, modernist theology and the revolution in morals of the 1920s were all directly attributable to the spread of atheistic evolutionary philosophy. Darwinism, by sanctioning the law of hate, paralyzed the Christian conscience and threatened American democracy. To halt this apostasy a number of Southern states had by the mid-1920s passed laws banning the teaching of organic evolution in the public schools. This movement resulted in the famous Scopes trial of 1925, when Bryan and agnostic lawyer Clarence Darrow faced off in Dayton, Tennessee. Though John Scopes was convicted of teaching biological evolution in a local school, the Eastern press coverage, which characterized fundamentalists as ignorant hicks, and Bryan's simplistic defense of the Bible under Darrow's cross-examination did irreparable damage to the fundamentalist cause. With Bryan's death five days after the trial, fundamentalism lost its most conspicuous leader.

In the 1930s the controversy moved into the arena of foreign *missions. In response to an interdenominational report on American Protestant foreign missions, *Rethinking Missions* (1932), conservatives led by Machen called for the missions officials of the PCUSA to repudiate the book's denial of Christianity's uniqueness and substitution of humanitarianism for evangelism. When efforts to reform the official board failed, conservatives in 1933 founded the Independent Board for Presbyterian Foreign Missions. Denominational leaders regarded the new agency as a breach of Presbyterian law and ratified the Mandate of 1934, which called for the members of the Independent Board to resign or face trial. Conservatives refused, and several Independent Board members were tried and suspended from the ministry. In 1936 they founded the *Orthodox Presbyterian Church (OPC).

See also Intellectual Life, Presbyterians and; Science, Presbyterians and.

Bibliography. W. B. Gatewood Jr., ed., *Controversy in the Twenties: Fundamentalism, Modernism and Evolution* (1969); D. G. Hart, *Defending the Faith: J. Gresham Machen and the Crisis of Conservative Protestantism in Modern America* (1994); W. R. Hutchison, *The Modernist Impulse in American Protestantism* (1976); B. J. Longfield, *The Presbyterian Controversy: Fundamentalists, Modernists and Moderates* (1991); G. M. Marsden, *Fundamentalism and American Culture: The Shaping of Twentieth-Century Evangelicalism, 1870-1925* (1980); E. R. Sandeen, *The Roots of Fundamentalism: British and American Millenarianism, 1800-1930* (1970); F. M. Szasz, *The Divided Mind of Protestant America: 1880-1930* (1982).

G. M. Marsden and B. J. Longfield

G

Garnet, Henry Highland (1815-1882).† African-American Presbyterian preacher and abolitionist. Born in slavery on a Maryland farm, at age nine Garnet fled to New York City along with his parents and sister. Three years later slavecatchers invaded Garnet's home, destroyed the family's household possessions and forced the family to split up. His parents and sister only narrowly escaped being returned to slavery. Garnet was educated in New York City schools operated by black Presbyterian ministers, in the abolitionist-sponsored Noyes Academy in New Hampshire and in Oneida Theological Institute in New York (1840). While in school he and his fellow students started the first antislavery society in New York State in 1834.

Ordained by the Presbytery of Troy in 1842, Garnet served Presbyterian churches in Troy, New York; Stirling, Jamaica; New York City; and Washington, D.C. Involving himself with the politically active wing of the antislavery movement, he campaigned at various times for the Liberty, Free Soil and Republican parties prior to 1865. In 1843, in his most famous speech, later published as *An Address to the Slaves of the United States of America,* Garnet exhorted slaves not to submit voluntarily to the degradation of bondage. Instead, he said, "let your motto be resistance! resistance! RESISTANCE!" White abolitionists frequently objected to his blacks-only conventions, which they claimed damaged the cause of *abolition by stirring up fear and suspicion among Northern whites. During the *Civil War, Garnet helped to recruit black troops. In 1881 Garnet accepted an appointment as United States minister to Liberia, and he died shortly after his arrival there.

BIBLIOGRAPHY. *ANB* 8; *DAB* IV; J. Schor, *Henry Highland Garnet: A Voice of Black Radicalism in the Nineteenth Century* (1977). S. W. Angell

Geddie, John (1815-1872).† Canadian Presbyterian missionary. Born in Banff, Scotland, Geddie immigrated with his parents to Nova Scotia, Canada the following year. He received his academic preparation and theological education at Dalhousie College under Thomas *McCulloch and was ordained by the Seceder Presbyterian Church of Nova Scotia in 1838. Motivated by his parents' *piety, he pursued mission service, though he had to stir other Presbyterians to support foreign missions while he was a pastor in Cavendish and New London on Prince Edward Island.

Having studied printing and medicine, Geddie and his family sailed for the South Seas in 1846 and settled on Aneitium Island in the New Hebrides two years later. There, despite cultural blunders and harassment from white traders and native leaders alike, he won the confidence of the people and their chiefs by learning the language and ministering through word, print and medicine. In 1852 a church was established at Aneitium with fifteen members, and a school was begun to train indigenous church officers and missionaries. In 1859 the whole population became Christian, and Geddie started a new mission station on Efate with native missionaries. When at home on furlough in the 1860s he was honored with a doctorate from Queen's University at Kingston and was appointed moderator of the synod of the Presbyterian Church, although he declined the responsibility. He died while on a trip to Melbourne, Australia, in 1872, where he was guiding his translation of part of the Old Testament through publication.

BIBLIOGRAPHY. G. Patterson, *The Life of John Geddie* (1882). J. H. Smylie

General Synod of the Associate Reformed Presbyterian Church.† Presbyterian denomination deriving mainly from Scottish Seceder heritage. The Associate Reformed Presbyterian Church (ARPC) members migrated to the American colonies in the 1700s. In 1742 the several societies jointly requested the parent body in Scotland (the Anti-Burgher Synod) to send Associate Presbyterian ministers, a petition that finally was answered in the persons of Alexander Gellatly and Andrew Arnot in 1753, who promptly constituted the Associate Presbytery of Pennsylvania. After a period of steady growth, predominantly through immigration and organizing congregations among the *Scots-Irish, the Presbytery of New York was formed. These two Seceder presbyteries, in opposition to the wishes of the mother synod in Scotland, formed the ARPC in 1782 through union with the smaller Reformed, or covenanting, Presbytery, with John Mason presiding as moderator. In 1799 the synod adopted the *Westminster Confession and Catechisms as the doctrinal standards of the church.

The new church grew to establish four synods by 1803, and in 1804 the first general synod was formed. In 1805 the general synod established a theological seminary in New York, with Mason as sole professor. This institution was maintained until 1821, when controversies involving Mason's receiving communion in a *Presbyterian Church in the U.S.A. (PCUSA) congregation and singing unapproved versions of psalms led to synodical defections. Convinced that Mason's party controlled the general synod, the synods of the West and South departed in 1820 and 1822 respectively. Mason and the majority of the Synod of Pennsylvania voted to join the PCUSA, merging the ARP seminary with Princeton Seminary. The Synod of the West, after a period of rapid growth, reunited with the remaining Associate Presbyterian Synod of New York in 1855, forming the Associate Reformed General Synod. Three years later this denomination merged with the Associate Synod (another Seceder body), forming the *United Presbyterian Church in North America (UPCNA). Only the Synod of the Carolinas and a very small Associate Church minority remained outside the union.

The Synod of the Carolinas (or Synod of the South) continued the heritage of the ARPC. It grew slowly at first due to mistrust of the general synod from likeminded Presbyterians and migration of its antislavery members to the North. In 1837 Erskine College was established, primarily to train pastors. Erskine Seminary was officially founded in 1858, and the following year a women's college was added. Growth was stabilized, in part due to home *mission emphases sometimes involving a colonizing method whereby a part or the whole of a congregation would move to a new settlement. Requirements for membership in the ARP hindered rapid growth, since they required acceptance of the standards of the church. In 1839 a foreign missions committee was started, but due to the ARP's small size little work was begun until the 1880s. From 1843 to 1851 *The Christian Magazine of the South* functioned as the denominational monthly, but in 1850 the *Erskine Miscellany* (later known as *Associate Reformed Presbyterian)* became established as the primary organ of the church. Known as the Associate Reformed Presbyterian Church since 1858, in 1935 the term *general synod* was added (GS, ARPC).

The late nineteenth and early twentieth centuries saw membership more than triple. Simultaneously the church began to relax the traditional principles of closed communion, starting in 1899 when they permitted all members in good standing of evangelical churches to receive the Lord's Supper. Other trends included the introduction of certain *revivalist practices (such as itinerant evangelists), and the gradual disappearance of church discipline. By the 1920s the strict sabbath observance of previous generations had diminished, and in 1946 the general synod allowed the singing of "acceptable" hymns. While some ministers had sympathies for the *neo-orthodox theologians Karl *Barth and Emil Brunner in the 1930s and 1940s, the theological commitments of the ARP remained basically conservative and Reformed, as evidenced by the addendum to the Westminster Confession, which added chapters on the Holy Spirit and the gospel.

Genuine *piety, an increasing emphasis on local church government and allegiance to the Westminster standards—maintained with varying degrees of firmness—characterize the GS, ARPC. While most of the church moved toward congregationalism, several ministers began to call the church back toward its Presbyterian roots. In the late twentieth century the church was stirred by issues of separatism, inerrancy and women's ordination, currently holding moderately conservative conclusions.

Bibliography. R. A. King, *A History of the Associate Reformed Presbyterian Church* (1966); R. Lathan, *History of the Associate Reformed Synod of the South* (1882); L. Ware, *The Second Century: A History of the Associate Reformed Presbyterians, 1882-1982* (1983). J. H. Hall

Gerhart, Emanuel Vogel (1817-1904). *German Reformed theologian and educator. Educated by his father, himself a German Reformed minister, Gerhart graduated from Marshall College in Mercersburg, Pennsylvania (1838), and Mercersburg Theological Seminary (1841), where he studied with Frederick Augustus *Rauch and John Williamson *Nevin. After pastoring a German Reformed congregation in Gettysburg, Pennsylvania (1843-1849), Gerhart then worked briefly as a *missionary among German immigrants in Cincinnati. For the next five years he served as president and professor of theology at his denomination's Heidelberg College in Tiffin, Ohio. From 1855 to 1866 he was president and professor of moral philosophy at the newly merged Franklin and Marshall Colleges in Lancaster, Pennsylvania. After relinquishing the presidency to his former professor, Nevin, Gerhart later accepted a position as professor of systematic and practical theology at the Reformed Church Seminary in Mercersburg, where he was made president of the faculty. While teaching there from 1868 to 1904, he successfully moved the seminary to Lancaster and contributed many articles to periodicals and from 1857 helped edit the *Mercersburg Review.*

Believing that American Protestants, both liberal and conservative, had fallen prey to a "subjectivistic rationalism," Gerhart joined the *Mercersburg theologians in their attempt to form a christocentric theology that allowed all other doctrines to flow logically from christology. His theological contribution is seen in his *Philosophy and Logic* (1891) and two-volume *Institutes of the Christian Religion* (1891, 1894). Along with Philip *Schaff and Nevin, Gerhart helped shape the direction and theology of the German Reformed Church during the second half of the nineteenth century.

Bibliography. *ANB* 8; *DAB* IV; C. Yrigoyen, "Emanuel V. Gerhart: Apologist for the Mercersburg Theology," *JPH* 57 (1979) 485-500.

G. S. Smith

German Reformed in America. German Reformed churches, organized in the Middle Colonies as a coetus (association) in 1747 and in a synod in 1793, united as the Reformed Church in the United States under a general synod in 1863. Comprised predominantly of immigrants from the Rhineland and German-speaking Swiss territories, German Reformed believers were linked by their early use of the Palatinate Liturgy (1563) and their abiding allegiance to the *Heidelberg Catechism (1563). They shared in the pietism that characterized other German religious groups, but a churchly spirit made them wary of sectarianism and *revivalism. Through much of the nineteenth century, influenced by brilliant Mercersburg Seminary theologians John Williamson *Nevin and Philip *Schaff, the church was embroiled in controversy over how to be such a catechetical and liturgical church in evangelical America.

Strongest in Pennsylvania, Maryland, the Shenandoah Valley, North Carolina, Ohio and the upper Midwest, by 1934 this Reformed church was organized in 6 regional synods, divided into 58 classes and posted a membership of 348,189 communicants in 1,675 congregations with 1,332 ordained ministers. In that year it joined with the *Evangelical Synod of North America, a Lutheran-Reformed unionist group that also embraced the Heidelberg Catechism (as well as the Augsburg Confession and Luther's Small Catechism), to form the Evangelical and Reformed Church. Since the 1957 merger with the Congregational Christian Churches, the German Reformed tradition has continued as one element in the life of the United Church of Christ.

Early settlers from the Rhineland in the seventeenth and early eighteenth centuries scattered from the Hudson Valley to the Carolinas, but with a dearth of pastors most were absorbed into Dutch and English churches. Lay leaders with some European training, like tailor Conrad Templeman and schoolmaster John Philip *Boehm, conducted services and gathered the first congregations in Maryland and southeastern Pennsylvania in the 1720s and 1730s. Boehm emerged as a great founder, drawing up a constitution of church ordinances and a "written Confession of Faith" (no longer extant) that identified the Heidelberg Catechism and the *Canons of the Synod of Dort as normative. Boehm contended, he wrote, against "all sorts of errorists" in "this wretched country so full of sects." In 1725, pressured by spiritually hungry believers, he began to administer the sacraments. When Georg Michael Weiss, a recently arrived minister, objected to this irregularity, the churches appealed to the Reformed Church in the Netherlands (the church in Germany being weak), and Boehm was ordained by Dutch Reformed ministers in New York in 1729.

The Dutch Reformed Church took the German Reformed under its wing until after the Revolution. A turning point came in 1746, when the synod in Holland sent Michael *Schlatter, an energetic Swiss-born and Netherlands-trained young pastor, to Pennsylvania. In one year Schlatter toured the churches, distributed Bibles, formalized church membership according to "pure Reformed doctrine," arranged congregations into thirteen charges, forged unity among four pastors, assumed the pastorate of the Germantown-Philadelphia charge and established the coetus of Pennsylvania (1747). The 1748 Kirchen-Ordnung was an updated version of Boehm's 1725 constitution, with churches governed by elders and deacons in consistory.

Schlatter returned to Europe in 1751 and motivated six more pastors to emigrate, but the clergy shortage persisted. Some were even drawn off by more radical pietist groups such as the Ephrata Brethren, Count Zinzendorf's Moravians and, in the case of Philip William *Otterbein, the United Brethren. Coetus leaders insisted that Reformed doctrine differentiated the church from the broad heart religion of pietism and American evangelicalism. The 1793

Constitution of the Synod of the German Reformed Church established independence from Amsterdam and the authority to ordain its own clergy. The ministry was to stress "the evangelical plan of salvation" and "a practical Christian life." Cooperation with the Lutherans, themselves in an evangelical mood in the new republic, enabled a burst of church building, plans for a joint hymnal and the founding of Franklin College (1787).

For ordinary German Reformed believers—farmers and workers—*piety, church life and the catechism gave life meaning within the larger society. From 1827 on the popular *Weekly Messenger* bound the German Reformed family together with a common source of information, devotional material and opinion.

Beginning in 1819 the synod organized regional classes, only to have the Ohio Classis separate and become an independent synod in order to ordain its own clergy. As the first German Reformed seminary was founded in 1825 tension and schism began to mark the church's life. Antiseminary sentiment in 1822 prompted a number of churches in eastern Pennsylvania to follow the Reverend Dr. L. F. Herman, whose training of clerics had been forbidden by synod, and form a separate Free Synod (which rejoined fifteen years later). John Winebrenner in Harrisburg adopted the methods of "new measures" *revivalism and preached against infant baptism. Censured by synod, he split from the Reformed church and established the Churches of God. The appointment of Nevin in 1840 and Schaff, a brilliant young theologian from Berlin, in 1844 as professors at the seminary, then in Mercersburg, sparked a golden age of German Reformed theology and tension within the church. Their high conception of the church and emphasis on formal liturgy conflicted with America's prevailing spirit of revivalism. The language issue was part of the debate, with evangelicals worshiping in English and Mercersburg proponents preferring German. A number of Pennsylvania congregations split over these matters. The Ohio Synod, part of the anti-Mercersburg coalition, suffered schism in 1846 when the Columbiana Classis under Peter Herbruck withdrew to protest compromise with Ohio's Methodist and Finneyite ethos (rejoining the Ohio Synod eight years later).

At Mercersburg Nevin wrote against revivalism in *The Anxious Bench* (1843) and on Christ's real presence in the sacrament in *The Mystical Presence* (1846). Schaff's inaugural lecture, *The Principle of Protestantism* (1845), brought heresy charges from Joseph F. Berg of the Philadelphia Classis, but Schaff was overwhelmingly vindicated by synod. Through *The Mercersburg Review* the theologians continued their incisive critique of subjectivism, individualism and voluntarism. No mere association of likeminded believers, the church is the body of Christ, created in heaven and developed historically by the Holy Spirit. Salvation comes not with a quick decision but by a steady process of discipleship. With its attack on sectarianism, its catholic ecclesiology and its appreciation of the historical development of theology and liturgy, Mercersburg embraced an ecumenical vision.

Mercersburg critics, predominantly in Philadelphia (the Old Reformed), Ohio and North Carolina, charged the movement with Romanizing, elevating tradition over Scripture and sacramental efficacy over personal faith. The issue came to a head over a proposed book of worship. The "Provisional Liturgy" of 1857 contained too much ritual for many, and the 1866 *Revised Liturgy* was no better. John H. A. *Bomberger attacked and Nevin defended the liturgy in print. In Ohio, where the synod adopted its own worship book, Jeremiah H. *Good at Heidelberg College led the opposition. In Pennsylvania, the Old Reformed gathered at the Myerstown Convention in 1867, published a magazine and founded Ursinus College and a seminary with Bomberger as president. The North Carolina Classis seceded from the synod in 1853, not over slavery as did other churches but over "the heresies of Mercersburg." They returned after Appomattox, grateful for Northern aid but determined "to fight, to contend for the faith of our fathers."

German Reformed unity came only too slowly. In 1863 the Eastern and Ohio synods joined in a new general synod. The three hundredth anniversary of the Heidelberg Catechism that year, during the nation's *Civil War, fostered a yearning for harmony within the church. But hostility reached fever pitch in 1866 over the *Revised Liturgy,* and it was not until 1878 that the general synod established a peace commission. The commission's minutes record that "during the addresses many wept," and when its report was adopted at general synod in 1881 delegates rejoiced that their "common prayer . . . was heard—that we all may be one." The Heidelberg Catechism was upheld as the basis of unity, but "freedom in scriptural and theological investigation" was affirmed. The various liturgies and hymnals already in use were allowed, though the 1866 worship book generally prevailed.

Most significant, the Reformed Church in the United States was able to devote its attention to expansion and *mission. Home missions focused on the Winnebago of the upper Midwest, while foreign missions were undertaken in Japan, China and Mesopotamia (Iraq). New settlements of German Reformed people in Wisconsin had led to the creation of the Sheboygan Classis in 1854. Mission House seminary in Wisconsin, founded in 1862, trained pastors to serve the new wave of German immigrants in the Midwest. New classes were organized in Iowa, Nebraska, Minnesota, the Dakotas, Canada and the West Coast. For a time new parallel German-language synods existed alongside the older synods, now operating in English, but these were merged after World War I. The Reformed Church in the United States, true to its Heidelberg and Mercersburg heritage, pioneered in the ecumenical movement of the early and mid-twentieth century, leading to denominational mergers that culminated in the United Church of Christ.

Bibliography. D. Dunn et al., *A History of the Evangelical and Reformed Church* (1961, 1992); J. I. Good, *History of the Reformed Church in the United States* (1899); idem, *History of the Reformed Church in the United States in the Nineteenth Century* (1911); L. H. Gunneman, *The Shaping of the United Church of Christ* (1977); E. C. Jaberg et al., *A History of Mission House-Lakeland* (1962); J. H. Nichols, *Romanticism in American Theology: Nevin and Schaff at Mercersburg* (1961); W. T. Parsons, *German Reformed Experience in Colonial America* (1976); G. W. Richards, *History of the Theological Seminary at Lancaster, Pennsylvania* (1952); G. H. Schriver, *Philip Schaff: Christian Scholar and Ecumenical Prophet* (1987).

C. E. Hambrick-Stowe

Girardeau, John Lafayette (1825-1898). Presbyterian minister and theologian. He was born in 1825 on James Island, near Charleston, South Carolina, and dramatically converted while a student at the College of Charleston at age fifteen. He received his ministerial education at Columbia (South Carolina) Theological Seminary from 1845 to 1848, where he was influenced by James Henley *Thornwell (then president of South Carolina College) and by Benjamin Morgan *Palmer, famous preacher of First Presbyterian Church: both strong Calvinists with evangelistic spirits. During these years he conducted mission services in the Columbia slums, reaching many destitute persons for Christ.

After graduation Girardeau considered *mission service abroad but decided he was called to minister to the numerous black population of his native Low Country South Carolina. For about five years he served as preacher and pastor to the slave community around rural Wilton Church in Colleton County. He systematically visited the slaves on the surrounding plantations, and hundreds attended his Sunday preaching, which exalted the gospel of Christ. Conversions and the growth of spiritual life in the community were notable.

In 1854 Girardeau became pastor of Zion Presbyterian in Charleston, at that time a small mission church of thirty-six black members. By 1860 there were more than six hundred members, with a regular sabbath attendance of some fifteen hundred (about 90 percent black and 10 percent white). After several months of prayer meetings, this congregation experienced a powerful revival in 1858 that lasted several weeks and converted hundreds, both black and white. In addition to effectively preaching the doctrine of the sovereign grace of God, Girardeau divided his congregation into small groups, or weekly class meetings, with fifty or fewer people in each class. The object was (according to Rule 7 of the Zion bylaws), "to promote mutual acquaintance and brotherly love . . . to apprise them of one another's sickness and need; to acquaint the leaders with the same; and to further the growth of the members in Christian knowledge and experimental religion." These small groups were led by blacks (unusual in pre-1860 South Carolina) and did much to develop Christian leadership among them in the hard years to follow. During the *Civil War, Girardeau served as chaplain in the Confederate army and was noted for his compassionate ministrations to Northern as well as Southern soldiers who had been wounded on the battlefield.

After the war Girardeau was elected moderator of the Southern Presbyterian Church (*Presbyterian Church in the United States [PCUS]) and was chosen as professor of systematic theology in Columbia Seminary. There he combined deep personal *piety, eloquent preaching (considered by many comparable to that of Charles Spurgeon), a philosophic interest and a wide range of theological knowledge. Perhaps his greatest theological contribution was in the unfolding of the doctrine of adoption in his *Discussion of Theological Questions*. He died in Columbia.

Bibliography: *ANB* 9; J. L. Girardeau, *Calvinism and Evangelical Arminianism* (1890); idem, *Discussion of Theological Questions* (1905); idem, *Sermons* (1907); D. Kelly, *Preachers with Power: Four Stalwarts of the South* (1992). D. Kelly

Gloucester, John (1776-1822). Presbyterian minister and founder of the first African-American Presbyterian church. Born a slave in Kentucky and converted by the preaching of a Presbyterian minister, Gideon *Blackburn, Gloucester began to receive training for the ministry when Blackburn purchased him and took him to his home in Tennessee for instruction in Presbyterian divinity. After Gloucester preached to the nearby Cherokees, Blackburn advocated in 1807 that the Presbytery of Union license him to preach. At the same time, Archibald *Alexander, then pastor of Third Presbyterian Church in Philadelphia, who met Gloucester at the 1807 general assembly, asked him to go North for the purpose of serving in the Evangelical Society, an agency that evangelized blacks in Alexander's hometown. Blackburn agreed to free Gloucester to comply with Alexander's request. Gloucester's preaching led in May 1807 to the organization of the First African Presbyterian Church of Philadelphia. He was finally licensed to preach in 1810 by the Presbytery of Union and a year later transferred his credentials to the Presbytery of Philadelphia.

In addition to pastoral duties and overseeing a sabbath school and a day school, Gloucester traveled frequently to raise funds for the manumission of his wife and four children. In 1818 he went as far as England to secure the remainder of the fifteen hundred dollars he needed. His trip was successful, and upon his return to Philadelphia he was reunited with his family. Gloucester's two sons, Stephen and James, followed in their father's footsteps, the former founding the Central Presbyterian Church of Philadelphia in 1844 and the latter organizing the Siloam Presbyterian Church of Brooklyn in 1849. Gloucester's admirers remembered him as an excellent preacher and an even better singer. Consumption contributed to his death.

Bibliography. *Encyclopedia of African-American Religions*, ed. L. G. Murphy (1993).

D. G. Hart

Goebel, Louis W. (1884-1973). *Evangelical Synod minister and president of the Evangelical and Reformed Church. Born at Carlinville, Illinois, Goebel graduated from Elmhurst College (B.A., 1903) and from Eden Theological Seminary (B.D., 1906). Ordained in 1907, Goebel became pastor of St. John's Evangelical Church, Bellevue, Kentucky, between 1907 and 1911, and he was minister of the First Evangelical Church in Chicago from 1911 to 1938.

A pioneer in the Protestant ecumenical movement, Goebel was in the forefront of negotiations that led to the 1957 union of his denomination and the Congregational Christian Churches to form the United Church of Christ. He also participated in earlier efforts that in 1934 resulted in the union of the *Evangelical Synod of North America and the Reformed Church in the United States. Goebel served as the first full-time president of the Evangelical and Reformed Church between 1938 and 1953.

Having traveled to twenty-six countries while he was president of the Evangelical and Reformed Church, Goebel was a member of the Central Committee of the World Council of Churches (1948-1954). The Federal Republic of Germany in 1953 bestowed on him the Commander Cross of the German Order of Merit for his postwar denominational relief efforts. He also served on the general board of the National Council of Churches. Goebel died at Webster Groves, Missouri.

Bibliography. F. S. Buschmeyer, "L. W. Goebel: Ecumenical Pioneer," *United Church Herald* (August 1, 1964) 20-21; L. W. Goebel, "Twenty-fifth Anniversary of the E & R Church," *United Church Herald* (June 18, 1959) 18-19. L. H. Zuck

Goforth, Jonathan (1859-1936).‡ Canadian Presbyterian missionary. Reared in the Presbyterian heartland of western Ontario, upon his conversion in 1877 Goforth devoured the writings of Robert M. McCheyne, Charles H. Spurgeon and the *Puritans. Soon he committed himself to evangelistic *missionary service. While studying at Knox College, Toronto, he engaged in intense evangelistic activity in the poorest parts of the city. In 1888 he and his bride, an artist, left for China.

Goforth was a deeply spiritual person and a man of iron determination and indefatigable activity. He regarded Hudson Taylor as a mentor in the Spirit, while Charles Grandison *Finney's writings encouraged the development of his evangelism into mass *revivalism. For years the Goforth family lived lives of almost constant itinerant evangelism, a ministry that widened after his leadership in the Manchurian revival of 1907. When on furlough his powerfully direct preaching style made him one of the best-known missionaries of his generation. Goforth's book, *By My Spirit* (1912), promoted the cause of missions in China.

A strenuous opponent of theological liberalism, Goforth refused to enter the United Church in 1925 and in his old age pioneered work for the Presbyterians in Manchuria. Appropriately, his funeral service was held in Knox Presbyterian Church, Toronto, where he and his wife had been married and sent on their way to China.

Bibliography. A. Austin, *Saving China: Canadian Missionaries in the Middle Kingdom, 1888-*

1959 (1986); R. Goforth, *Goforth of China* (1937).

I. S. Rennie

Good, James Isaac (1850-1924). *German Reformed pastor and historian of the Reformed Church in the United States. Born in York, Pennsylvania, he was reared in Reading, Pennsylvania, and was educated at Lafayette College (A.B., 1872; A.M., 1875).

Good was ordained upon his graduation from Union Theological Seminary in New York City in 1875. From 1875 to 1877 he served Heidelberg Church, York; 1877 to 1890, Heidelberg Church, Philadelphia; and Calvary Church, Reading, from 1890 to 1905. Simultaneous with his pastorate in Reading, he became professor of church history at Ursinus College and Seminary in 1890, transferring to dogmatics and pastoral theology in 1893. In that year, he was appointed dean of Ursinus Theological Seminary and was instrumental in its move from Collegeville to Philadelphia in 1898. When the Ursinus and Heidelberg seminaries merged in 1907 to become Central Theological Seminary, he moved to its location in Dayton, Ohio, where he was professor of Reformed church history and liturgies until his death in 1924.

Prominent in denominational affairs, Good held numerous offices, including president of the board of foreign missions (1893-1924); president of the general synod (1911-1914); vice president of the World Alliance of Reformed and Presbyterian Churches and cochairman of the committee that prepared *The Hymnal of the Reformed Church,* published jointly in 1920 by the Reformed Church in the United States (German) and the *Reformed Church in America (RCA; Dutch). In addition he was elected to the executive council of the Presbyterian Historical Society in 1899 and 1902 and was a vice president from 1917 to 1923.

Good is best known for his studies in the history of the German Reformed church. Beginning in 1879, he made more than fifty trips to Europe, where he secured a "large number of historical books," approximately four thousand pages of transcripts, one thousand photographic copies of manuscripts and numerous prints and etchings. In the archives of the Dutch Reformed Church at The Hague in the Netherlands, he discovered letters from the "Pioneer German [Reformed] Pastor" John Philip *Boehm (1683-1749) and the "Minutes and Letters of the Coetus of the German Reformed Church in Pennsylvania" that previously were unknown to American scholars. He searched also the archives of the RCA at New Brunswick, New Jersey, and obtained Henry *Harbaugh's collection of historical documents from Harbaugh's widow.

Good used these sources and illustrations for numerous publications, which include *The Origin of the Reformed Church in Germany* (1887), *Rambles Around Reformed Lands* (1889), *The Reformed Church of Germany, 1620-1890* (1894), *Historical Handbook of the Reformed Church* (1897), *History of the Swiss Reformed Church Since the Reformation* (1913), *The Heidelberg Catechism in Its Newest Light* (1914), *The Reformed Reformation* (1916) and *Famous Reformers of the Reformed and Presbyterian Churches* (1917). His most significant works were the *History of the Reformed Church in the United States, 1725-1792* (1899), which covered the denomination's early development in America, and the *History of the Reformed Church in the U. S. in the Nineteenth Century* (1911), in which he expressed his anti-Mercersburg interpretation of the controversies that afflicted the denomination during that period. Good died in Philadelphia.

Bibliography. *ANB* 9; W. J. Hinke, "The Contributions of Dr. James I. Good to Reformed Church History," *The Reformed Church Review* 3 (April 1924) 152-67; idem, "Reverend Professor James I. Good, D.D., LL.D., 1924," *Journal of the Presbyterian Historical Society* 12 (October 1924) 65-81.

J. B. Frantz

Good, Jeremiah H. (1822-1887). *German Reformed pastor. Born in Rehrersburg and reared in Reading, Pennsylvania, he enrolled in Marshall College, Mercersburg, Pennsylvania, in 1838 and graduated as class valedictorian four years later. He taught in the college's preparatory department while attending the Theological Seminary of the Reformed Church at Mercersburg.

Following his graduation from the seminary in 1846, Good was ordained and installed as pastor of the Reformed church in Lancaster, Ohio. In 1848 he founded and until 1853 edited *The Western Missionary* under the auspices of the Ohio Synod. In 1849 Good moved to Columbus, where he served a small Reformed congregation and instructed students for the ministry. When in 1850 the Ohio Synod established what became Heidelberg College and Theological Seminary at Tiffin, he became professor of mathematics and mechanical philosophy. He was instrumental in the institution's early development, chairing the committee that was charged with selecting the site and planning the buildings. In 1869 he became the seminary's president and professor of dogmatic and practical theology, remaining in that position until ill health forced his retirement in 1887.

During his tenure at the college and seminary, Good served his denomination in various other ways. He was president and long-time treasurer of its Ohio Synod, assisted in the preparation of its liturgy and hymnal and was a member of the peace commission that met in 1879 to resolve liturgical, ecclesiological and theological issues that threatened to rupture the Reformed church. He published numerous articles in *The Western Missionary;* with Henry *Harbaugh, he made an annotated translation into English of the *Heidelberg Catechism (1849) and several devotional guides. Good died in Tiffin, Ohio.

Bibliography. *ANB* 9; W. M. Deatrick, ed., *The Fathers of the Reformed Church in Europe and America* IV (1888); A. S. Zerbe, *The Life and Labors of Reverend Jeremiah Haak Good* (1925).

J. B. Frantz

Gordon, Charles William (1860-1937). Canadian Presbyterian minister and novelist, writing under the name of Ralph Connor. Born in Glengarry County, eastern Ontario, he was raised in the intense *piety of his father's Highland Scots Free Church congregation. He was educated at the University of Toronto (B.A., 1883), studied theology at Knox College, Toronto, and completed his training at the University of Edinburgh, where he encountered Henry Drummond, the liberal evangelical evangelist, whose vision of cosmic spiritual evolution made a profound impact. After four years of ministry among ranchers, lumbermen and miners in the foothills of the Rockies, where he saw the need of a manly Christianity, he moved in 1894 to St. Stephen's Church, Winnipeg, strategically situated on the main street of the burgeoning prairie center. Here he was greatly influenced by the bold leadership of James *Robertson, the superintendent of home *missions in the West, and by the vision of his father-in-law, John Mark *King, principal of Presbyterian Manitoba College. But he did not adhere to the Old Princeton theology of the one or the Secession evangelicalism of the other. Drummond was his mentor, and his theology was in the social gospel mold, governed by self-sacrifice and open to modernity.

Amid his pastoral responsibilities Gordon began to churn out his novels, which sold in the millions: *Black Rock* (1898), *Sky Pilot* (1899), *Man from Glengarry* (1901), *Glengarry School Days* (1902), *Prospector* (1904) and a number more. A well-known chaplain in World War I, he raised the ire of T. T. Shields by seeming to preach in his Toronto Baptist pulpit that the supreme sacrifice on the Western Front merited heaven. He was elected moderator of the *Presbyterian Church in Canada (PCC) in 1921 and was a leading advocate of the movement that produced the United Church of Canada in 1925. As a result of the congregational amalgamations that followed church union, the building of Gordon's old congregation became the home of Elim Chapel, one of the outstanding conservative evangelical congregations of Winnipeg. He died in the city that had so long been his home.

Bibliography. D. B. Mack, "Modernity Without Tears: The Mythic World of Ralph Connor," in *The Burning Bush and a Few Acres of Snow: The Presbyterian Contribution to Canadian Life and Culture,* ed. W. Klempa (1994).

I. S. Rennie

Graham, Sylvester (1794-1851). Presbyterian minister and health reformer. The youngest of seventeen children, Graham was born in West Suffield, Connecticut, to John, a Presbyterian minister and physician, and Ruth Graham, just two years prior to John's death at the age of seventy-four. Graham's health suffered as he lived with a series of relatives and worked as a farmhand, clerk and teacher. He studied for a time in 1823 at Amherst Academy in Massachusetts but left after students circulated reports that defamed his character. He then suffered a nervous breakdown but met his wife, Sarah Earle, one of two nurses who cared for him during this time. They were married in 1826.

Graham's whereabouts are uncertain for the next few years, but by 1831 he was preaching as stated supply in Morris County, New Jersey. About the same time the Pennsylvania Temperance Society appointed him as its general agent. To carry out his duties for the society Graham studied human physiology, diet and exercise. He reported his findings in an 1830-1831 lecture series in Philadelphia and repeated the series in New York a few months later. This launched a speaking and writing career that championed the consumption of healthy foods and pure water, the correct way to sleep, regular exercise, loose-fitting clothes and cheerfulness at meals, what Graham called the science of human life. Some of his more representative titles were *The Young Man's Guide to Chastity* (1834), *Treatise on Bread and Breadmaking* (1837) and *Lectures on the Science of Human Life* (1839). His frank discussion of temperance, sexual moderation and vegetarianism prompted controversy from audiences who were shocked by Graham's indelicacy or from bread makers whom he accused of making an unhealthy product. Ralph

Waldo Emerson dubbed him the "poet of bran bread and pumpkins."

Despite his critics, Graham attracted many disciples, from such popular figures as Horace Greeley, Arthur Tappan and William Lloyd Garrison to the students at Oberlin College, Williams College and Wesleyan University. His reforms also led to the establishment of Graham hotels and boarding houses in many towns. Graham's system also found regular expression in the *Graham Journal of Health and Longevity*, published from 1837 to 1839. The peak of his popularity came in 1840. He spent the last years of his life tending his vegetable garden and writing lectures on the Bible. He died at his home in Northampton, Massachusetts, despite a dose of Congress water and a cold bath.

Bibliography. *ANB* 9; R. Balmer and J. Fitzmier, *The Presbyterians* (1993); *DAB* VII; *NCAB* 5; J. A. Sokolow, *Eros and Modernization: Sylvester Graham, Health Reform and the Origins of Victorian Sexuality in America* (1983). D. G. Hart

Grant, George Monro (1835-1905). Canadian presbyterian educator. Born in a Scottish immigrant community in Nova Scotia, Grant's early experiences of warring religious factions gave him a deep hostility toward any form of sectarianism. In 1853 Grant went to study at the University of Glasgow, returning home in 1861 as an ordained Church of Scotland missionary.

Grant was deeply influenced by the Scottish thinkers John Caird (1820-1898) and Edward Caird (1835-1908), as well as by the English philosopher, T. H. Green (1836-1882), all of whom stimulated his interest in Kantian and Hegelian philosophy. German biblical scholarship also influenced him, as did romantic idealists like Coleridge and Carlyle. In 1877 he became principal of Queen's University in Kingston, Ontario, and had a powerful impact on fellow Presbyterian clergy through an annual theological conference held at Queen's.

Relentlessly optimistic, Grant pioneered the social gospel in Canada and interpreted the Christian message in terms of active social service, moral elevation and opposition to secularism. A popularizer rather than a systematic thinker, he was arguably the most influential Canadian clergyman in the last two decades of the nineteenth century.

Bibliography. W. Christian, *George Grant: A Biography* (1993); W. L. Grant and F. Hamilton, *Principal Grant* (1904); D. B. Mack, *George Monro Grant: Evangelical Prophet* (1992).

D. M. Lewis

Green, Ashbel (1762-1848). Presbyterian minister and educator. Green was born to the Reverend Jacob and Elizabeth Pierson Green. Green's father had been converted under George Whitefield and was himself a multitalented preacher, important supporter of Princeton College and significant figure in New Jersey Revolutionary history. In 1783 Green graduated from the College of New Jersey (later Princeton University), where he came under the influence of John *Witherspoon. Although he absorbed Witherspoon's combination of traditional *Calvinist *piety and hearty promotion of the Scottish Enlightenment, it was the pious part of Witherspoon's legacy that shaped Green most. After brief service teaching at Princeton, he was ordained in 1787 as copastor of Philadelphia's Second Presbyterian Church. From 1792 to 1800 he also served as cochaplain of the United States Congress.

During the first decade of the new century Green corresponded with Samuel *Miller of New York and others about the need for a theological seminary and also took steps, as a trustee of the College of New Jersey, to tighten its discipline and reform the teaching of President Samuel Stanhope *Smith, another Witherspoon student who carried Witherspoon's scientific commitments further than Green felt Christian orthodoxy allowed. Matters on both fronts came to a head in the summer of 1812, when Green was named to replace Smith as president of the college and when he was also elected president of the board of the Presbyterians' new seminary at Princeton. He served as college president until 1822 and led the seminary's board until he died.

After leaving the college in 1822 due to a misunderstanding with the trustees, Green returned to Philadelphia, where for twelve years he edited *The Presbyterian* (later *The Christian Advocate)*, a widely ranging periodical. In an active retirement, Green published *Lectures on the Shorter Catechism*, wrote an informative biography of Witherspoon (not published until 1973) and was a leading *Old School polemicist in the struggles that eventually divided the church. Although dizziness in the pulpit afflicted him most of his adult life, he still preached regularly, especially to African-American congregations, until shortly before his death.

Bibliography. *AAP* 4; *ANB* 9; J. H. Jones, ed., *The Life of Ashbel Green . . . Begun to Be Written by Himself* (1849); J. McLachlan, "Ashbel Green," in *Princetonians 1776-1783* (1981); M. A. Noll, *Princeton and the Republic, 1768-1822: The Search for a Christian Enlightenment in the Era of Samuel Stanhope Smith* (1989). M. A. Noll

Green, William Henry (1825-1900).† Presbyterian biblical scholar and educator. Educated at Lafayette College (A.B., 1840) and Princeton Theological Seminary (1846), Green joined the Princeton faculty in 1851, where he taught Old Testament and Semitic studies for fifty years. He wrote extensively and almost exclusively in his field of specialization and until his death was chairman of the Old Testament section of the committee that produced the American Revised Version (1901) of the Bible. In 1868 he was elected president of Princeton University but declined to accept. In 1891 he served as the moderator of the General Assembly of the *Presbyterian Church in the U.S.A. (PCUSA).

Like his other Old Princeton colleagues, Green was firmly committed to the divine inspiration and inerrancy of Scripture. He was resolute in his opposition to the mounting influence of biblical criticism in America. Among his contemporaries he took the lead in refuting the documentary hypothesis of the origin of the Pentateuch. These emphases were reflected in his two-volume *General Introduction to the Old Testament* (1898) and *The Higher Criticism of the Pentateuch* (1895).

A frequent contributor to the *Biblical Repertory and Princeton Review* and its successors, Green chastised his fellow conservatives for not taking the human aspects of Scripture seriously while blasting the liberal critics for ignoring the divine side. He was a prominent figure in the ecclesiastical trial of Charles Augustus *Briggs and was the foremost conservative Old Testament scholar in North America until his death.

Bibliography. *DAB* IV; M. A. Noll, *Between Faith and Criticism: Evangelicals, Scholarship, and the Bible in America* (1986); "The Jubilee of Professor William Henry Green," *PRR* 7 (1896) 507-21; M. A. Taylor, *The Old Testament in the Old Princeton School (1812-1929)* (1992).

R. B. Gaffin

Grimké, Francis James (1850-1937). African-American Presbyterian minister and activist. Grimké, nephew of *abolitionists Sarah Grimké and Angelina Grimké, was born in the vicinity of Charleston, South Carolina, to a slave and her owner. Upon the close of the *Civil War, Francis attended Lincoln University in Pennsylvania, where he graduated at the head of his class.

After an aborted study of law at Lincoln and Howard universities, Grimké began theological studies at Princeton Seminary in 1875. Although he was trained in the *Princeton theology, Grimké's mature theology was broadly evangelical and moderate. Thus he successfully steered a path between an emergent theological liberalism and the *fundamentalist reaction. His theology would also inspire an uncompromising ethical earnestness that would earn him the title "Black Puritan."

Upon successfully completing his studies at Princeton in 1878, Grimké accepted a call to the Fifteenth Street Presbyterian Church in Washington, D.C. After a brief pastorate in Jacksonville, Florida, at the Laura Street Church (1882-1883), he returned to Fifteenth Street Church, where he served as pastor until his retirement in 1925 and as pastor emeritus until his death.

Grimké vigorously used pulpit and pen to inspire the black community to moral righteousness and to protest increasing racism in the Presbyterian Church and the wider American community. He led efforts to prevent the Presbyterian Church's acquiescence to segregated judicatories as occasioned by its union with the *Cumberland Presbyterian Church (CPC) in 1905, and in 1910 he played a prominent role in the formation of the National Association for the Advancement of Colored People (NAACP). A collection of the massive corpus of articles, letters and sermons that chronicle his life and expansive ministry fills four volumes of *The Works of Francis J. Grimké,* edited by Carter G. Woodson (1942).

Bibliography. *ANB* 9; R. Balmer and J. R. Fitzmier, *The Presbyterians* (1993); H. J. Ferry, "Francis J. Grimké: Portrait of a Black Puritan" (Ph.D. diss., Yale University, 1970); H. T. Kerr, ed., *Sons of the Prophets: Leaders in Protestantism from Princeton Seminary* (1963); A. E. Murray, *Presbyterians and the Negro—A History* (1966).

M. Moore

Guldin, Samuel (1664-1745). Swiss Reformed pastor. Born in Berne, Switzerland, the third child of John Joachim Guldin and Anna Maria Koch, he was enrolled in the Latin School in Berne in 1679. Between 1689 and 1692 Guldin studied in Geneva, Lausanne and the Netherlands. In 1692 he began to serve the Stetten parish, near Berne. Within a year doubts about his salvation threatened to end his ministry. An intense religious experience relieved his anxiety and enabled him to become a popular preacher and effective pastor. He became assistant at the prestigious minster in Berne in 1696. His powerful sermons were intended to effect the conversion of the large crowds who heard them.

Guldin's style of ministry produced charges of pietism that led to his removal in 1699. Responding to pressure from his family, he promised to conform in doctrine and practice as directed by Bernese authorities. In 1701 he was assigned to Boltigen, south of Berne. Uneasy because of his submission, he soon asked to be released. Consequently he was defrocked and forced to leave Switzerland.

After a respite in German provinces, Guldin emigrated in 1710 to Pennsylvania. He settled on a large tract in Philadelphia County, along Wissahickon Creek, but he bought and sold land elsewhere as well. Although he preached at least occasionally to the Reformed congregation in Germantown, there is no evidence that he ever preached anywhere else or served as pastor of any congregation in America.

In 1718 Gulden published a *Kurtze Apologie oder Schutz-Schrift der unschuldig verdächtig gemachten und verworffen Pietisten zu Bern in der Schweiz* (Short Apology or Defense of the Unjustly Suspected and Condemned Pietists of Berne, Switzerland) and a *Kurtze Lehr und Gegensätze in Erlauterung und Rettung der göttlichen Wahrheit (Short Thesis and Counterthesis in Explanation and Defense of Divine Truth).* In 1743 and 1744 he published two editions of *Unpartheyisches Zeugnüss Veter Die Neue Vereinigung Aller Religions—Partheyen In Pens Sylvanien (Nonpartisan Witness About the New Union of All Religious Parties in Pennsylvania),* in which he claimed that only Christ, not the Moravians, could unite the churches.

Guldin died in Philadelphia. His promising ministry that was cut short in Europe could have been fulfilled in America but was not. Nevertheless he was well-known and respected as a pious observer and commentator if not an active participant in the German settlers' religious development.

Bibliography. J. H. Dubbs, "Samuel Guldin: Pietist and Pioneer," *Reformed Church Quarterly Review* 39 (1892) 309-25; C. H. Glatfelter, *Pastors and People,* vol. 1 (1980); J. I. Good, *History of the Reformed Church* (1899); G. W. Richards, ed., *Ministers of the German Reformed Congregations in Pennsylvania and Other Colonies in the Eighteenth Century* (1951). J. B. Frantz

Gunnemann, Louis H. (1910-1989). Pastor, theological educator and interpreter of the United Church of Christ. Born in Indianapolis, Indiana, Gunnemann was a graduate of Lakeland College, Wisconsin (B.A., 1932), Mission House Theological Seminary (B.D., 1935), a seminary of the former Reformed Church in the United States in Plymouth, Wisconsin, and Princeton Theological Seminary (Th.M., 1953). He was pastor first of St. John's Evangelical and Reformed Church, Tipton, Iowa (1935-1941), then of Salem Reformed Church, Lafayette, Indiana (1941-1950), and of Immanuel United Church of Christ, a merger of Salem Reformed Church with St. John's Evangelical Church (1950-1952).

In 1953 Gunnemann became professor of practical theology and dean of Mission House Theological Seminary. He was a leading force in the negotiations that brought about in 1960 the union of Mission House with Yankton Divinity School, South Dakota, to form United Theological Seminary of the Twin Cities, New Brighton, Minnesota. He served as dean and then as vice president for academic administration of this institution from 1962 until his retirement in 1976. He was secretary of the Association of Theological Schools from 1964 to 1966.

Gunnemann served the United Church of Christ in various capacities. He was assistant moderator of the general synod (1973-1975), chairman of the commission on worship (1961-1973), a member of the commission that created the Statement of Faith of the United Church of Christ (1957-1959), a member of the hymnal committee (1967-1974) and a member of the Board for Homeland Ministries (1961-1969).

In the latter part of his career, after his retirement from seminary teaching and administration, Gunnemann devoted himself to interpreting the United Church of Christ to its own members as well as to the larger public in two books: *The Shaping of the United Church of Christ* (1977) and *United and Uniting: The Meaning of an Ecclesial Journey* (1987). Author of numerous articles for church and theological education journals, he also wrote *The Life of Worship* (1966) and was coeditor of *Prism: A Theological Forum for the United Church of Christ* (1985-1888). He died in Minneapolis, Minnesota. J. B. Payne

H

Hall, John (1829-1898).† Presbyterian minister. Born in County Armagh, Ireland, of *Scots-Irish descent, Hall received his education at the Royal College, Belfast, graduating in 1845, and he received his theological training at the Irish Presbyterian general assembly's seminary, graduating in 1849. From 1849 to 1852 he was a "student's missionary" in County Connaught, Ireland, where the rampant alcoholism turned him into a fervent temperance advocate. His growing reputation as a preacher led to a call in 1852 to the First Presbyterian Church of Armagh, where he remained until 1858, when he moved to Mary's Abbey Presbyterian Church in Dublin. Hall remained in Dublin until 1867, when as a fraternal delegate to the General Assembly of the *Presbyterian Church in the United States (PCUS), he received a call to the Fifth Avenue Presbyterian Church in New York City. It grew to become the largest congregation in the city, and Hall remained there until his death.

Hall was a gifted preacher, but he was especially noted for his pastoral labors, including an extensive program of regular visitation to each family in his large congregation. His theology was conservative, affirming a strict doctrine of biblical inspiration and upholding the theology of the *Westminster Confession and Catechisms, which led to opposition from a minority in his church during his latter years. In 1875 he delivered Yale's Lyman Beecher Lecture, published as *God's Word Through Preaching* (1875). From 1882 to 1891 he was chancellor of the University of the City of New York. Hall published a number of sermons and several other devotional books, and he was a regular contributor to religious periodicals.

Bibliography. *DAB* IV; T. C. Hall, *John Hall, Pastor and Preacher* (1901). J. R. Wiers

Harbaugh, Henry (1817-1867). *German Reformed pastor, theologian and historian. Born in Franklin County, Pennsylvania, the tenth child of George and Anna Snyder Harbaugh, he received his early education at the local school. Frustrated with local prospects, he moved as an adolescent to the Massilon area of Ohio, where while engaging in manual labor he improved himself by attending lectures, debates and political forums and by enrolling in the New Hagerstown Academy.

In 1840 Harbaugh returned to Pennsylvania to attend Marshall College and the Theological Seminary of the Reformed Church in Mercersburg. Upon his graduation in 1843, he became the pastor of Lewisburg, Pennsylvania, a charge that consisted of two and later three congregations with others in the vicinity to be served irregularly. In 1850 he accepted the call to the large and prestigious Lancaster congregation. After a ten-year pastorate there, he moved to Lebanon, where he served the newly organized St. John's Church. In 1863 he returned to the Theological Seminary of the Reformed Church as professor of didactic and practical theology, a position that he held until his death.

During his Lewisburg pastorate, Harbaugh began to submit articles to *The Reformed Church Messenger* and to edit and publish *The Guardian,* a magazine that he hoped would guide and enlighten young people. With Jeremiah H. *Good, he translated and published the *Heidelberg Catechism, adapted for use in catechetical instruction (1849).

While in Lancaster, Harbaugh began his research on the early leaders of the German Reformed Church in this country, publishing *The Life of Michael Schlatter* (1857) and the first two volumes of *The Fathers of the Reformed Church in Europe and America* (1857, 1858). His most profound historical work was his "Creed and Cultus: With Special Reference to the Relation of the Heidelberg Catechism to the Palatinate Liturgy," published in the *Tercentenary Monument in Commemoration of the Three Hundredth Anniversary of the Heidelberg Catechism* (1863). Harbaugh was also the founder of the Historical Society of the Reformed Church in 1863.

In numerous other publications, he reflected and disseminated the *Mercersburg theology of John Williamson *Nevin and historian Philip *Schaff, emphasizing christology, the continuity of church history and liturgical worship. His first books were a trilogy on a Christian understanding of life after death: *The Sainted Dead* (1848), *Heavenly Recogni-*

tion (1851) and *The Heavenly Home* (1853). *The Golden Censor* (1860) became a devotional guide for the youth of the church. A thoughtful writer on worship, Harbaugh also served on the church's liturgical committee that prepared the "Provisional Liturgy" (1857) and the "Revised Liturgy" (1866). His hymn "Jesus, I Live to Thee" appeared in hymnals not only of the Reformed church but also of Episcopalians, Methodists, Baptists and Presbyterians.

Equally if not more important than his historical and theological publications were Harbaugh's pioneering study of the Pennsylvania German dialect, which, prior to Harbaugh, was spoken by many of his countrymen, written by few and published by practically no one. To this end he wrote poems and stories that appeared initially in *The Guardian*. Among the best-known are the nostalgic "Das Alt Schulhaus an der Krick" (The Old Schoolhouse by the Creek), "Die Alte Feierheerd" (The Oldtime Hearthfire) and "Heimweh" (Homesickness).

Following a brief illness, Harbaugh died in 1867. After his death, his close friend Benjamin Bausman gathered fifteen of his compositions and published them as *Harbaugh's Harfe* (1870).

Bibliography. *ANB* 10; G. Allen, "The Pennsylvania Dutch Poets—Part 1, Henry Harbaugh," *The American German Review* 8 (August 1942) 10-12; H. Harbaugh, *Fathers of the Reformed Church in Europe and America* 4, ed. D. J. Heisler (1872) 355-78; L. Harbaugh, *Life of the Reverend Henry Harbaugh, D.D.* (1900); E. C. Kieffer, "Henry Harbaugh: Pennsylvania Dutchman, 1817-1867," *Proceedings and Addresses of the Pennsylvania German Society* 51 (1945) 7-358; idem, "Henry Harbaugh in Lancaster," *Lancaster County Historical Society* 45 (1941) 57-83; J. Spangler Kieffer, "Recollections of Dr. Harbaugh," *The Reformed Church Review,* 4th series 21 (October 1917) 427-45; R. E. Wentz, "Henry Harbaugh, Quintessential 'Dutchman,'" *Pennsylvania Folklife* 41 (autumn 1991) 36-47.

J. B. Frantz

Harlan, John Marshall (1833-1911). Jurist and Presbyterian elder. Harlan was born to James Harlan, a prominent member of the Kentucky bar. Graduated in 1850 from *Old School Presbyterian-related Center College in Danville, Kentucky, the young Harlan studied law at Transylvania University and with his father before being admitted to the bar in 1853.

Although himself a slaveholder, Harlan was a conservative Whig and antislavery on religious and philosophical grounds. A reluctant Republican in the 1850s, he was driven by national events into support for the Union. He served as a colonel in the Union army and was a leader in Kentucky Republican politics in the years that followed. Nominated to the Supreme Court by President Rutherford B. Hayes, he was seated December 11, 1877, and served as associate justice for a third of a century. He died in Washington, D.C.

A frequent dissenter from the majority, Justice Harlan had an almost religious reverence for the Constitution, which he believed balanced a concern for the public welfare with individual rights. He denounced the court's slow retreat from the defense of equal rights for black Americans. In his lone dissent in *Plessy v. Ferguson* (1896), the decision that set "separate but equal" as the pattern for racial segregation in America, he protested, "our Constitution is color-blind."

An elder in the New York Avenue Presbyterian Church in Washington, D.C., Harlan taught a weekly Bible class and served on the *Presbyterian Church in the U.S.A. (PCUSA) general assembly committee on the revision of the *Westminster Confession of Faith (final action, 1903).

Bibliography. *ANB* 10; *DAB* VIII.

K. J. Ross

Harrison, Everett Falconer (1902-1999). Presbyterian clergyman and biblical scholar. Born to missionary parents serving in Alaska, he was reared in the course of his father's later prestigious pastorates in Seattle, Washington; St. Louis, Missouri; and Minneapolis, Minnesota. Harrison received his education at the University of Washington (B.A., 1923), the Bible Institute of Los Angeles, Princeton University (M.A., 1927), Princeton Theological Seminary (Th.B. 1927), Dallas Theological Seminary (Th.D., 1939) and the University of Pennsylvania (Ph.D., 1950). He taught at Dallas Theological Seminary from 1927 to 1947 in the departments of Old Testament studies (1927-1935) and New Testament studies (1935-1940, 1944-1947), though he took two extended leaves. The first (1930-1932) was to teach at the Hunan Bible Institute, Changsha, China (the fulfillment of an undergraduate vow when in the Student Volunteer Movement), and during the second (1940-1944) he pastored the Third Presbyterian Church in Chester, Pennsylvania, while doing graduate studies in Hellenistic Greek at the University of Pennsylvania.

In 1947 Harrison became a part of the original faculty of Fuller Theological Seminary in Pasadena, California, and served as professor of New Testament until his retirement in 1973. His major publications include *Introduction to the New Testament* (1964) and *A Short Life of Christ* (1968). He served as an editor of the *Wycliffe Bible Commentary, Baker's Dictionary of Theology* and the revision of *The International Standard Bible Encyclopedia,* as well as on the translation committees of two Bibles, the New American Standard Version and the New International Version. In both institutions he distinguished himself by his godly demeanor and the academic brilliance that characterized his defense of traditional evangelical views.

Bibliography. G. M. Marsden, *Reforming Fundamentalism* (1987); M. A. Noll, *Between Faith and Criticism* (1986). J. D. Hannah

Hastings, Thomas (1784-1872). Presbyterian hymn writer. Born in Litchfield County, Connecticut, the son of a physician/farmer, in his teens Hastings moved with his family to Oneida, New York, and further developed an interest in music. By 1806 he was leading the village choir and teaching music. Ten years later he collaborated with Solomon Warriner on *Musica Sacra; or Springfield and Utica Collections United,* a book consisting of psalms, hymn tunes, anthems and chants that stayed in print until 1836. In 1822 he married Mary Seymour in Buffalo, New York. A year later he became editor of *The Recorder,* a religious periodical published in Utica, New York. Hastings oversaw that publication for nine years before returning to teaching and composing. Meanwhile he produced two more hymnals, *The Union Minstrel, for the Use of Sabbath Schools* (1830), and with Lowell Mason, *Spiritual Songs for Social Work* (1831).

In 1832 twelve churches in New York City called Hastings to be their musician. For the next forty years he served in this capacity, and for a brief time he was employed by the Bleecker Street Presbyterian Church as its choirmaster. During this time he was incredibly prolific in compiling a variety of hymnals such as *The Christian Psalmist, or Watts Psalms and Hymns* (1836), *The New York Collection* (1837) and *Church Melodies* (1858). He also wrote several books about hymns and sacred music such as *Dissertation on Musical Taste* (1822, 1853) and *Sacred Praise* (1856).

Though a lover of all kinds of music, Hastings had definite ideas about the kind appropriate for worship and believed that sacred music should be distinct from forms used in other settings. In addition to writing and teaching about hymnody and choral music, he composed approximately six hundred hymns, many of them published. The better known of his texts were "How Calm and Beautiful the Morn," "Hail to the Brightness of Zion's Glad Morning," "Jesus, Merciful and Mild" and "Come Ye Disconsolate." He also wrote numerous tunes, many of which survive in twentieth-century hymnals, such as Ortonville, Hastings, Zion, Retreat and perhaps the best known of all, Toplady, the tune to which the hymn "Rock of Ages" is usually sung. Hastings, known for his great knowledge of the Bible, also collected various editions of the sacred writings. His son, Thomas, became a highly acclaimed architect. Hastings died of natural causes at the age of eighty-seven, still active in his musical and literary efforts.

Bibliography. *ANB* 10; *DAB* VIII; A. Nevin, ed., *Presbyterian Encyclopedia* (1884).

D. G. Hart

Hays, Will H. (1879-1954). Presbyterian layman, lawyer and political activist. Hays was an excellent partisan strategist, capable of marshaling powerful rhetorical skills and abundant financial resources on behalf of the Republican causes and denominational projects. From a base in central Indiana politics, Hays became the chair of the Indiana Republican Party in 1914, then joined in national politics as the chair of the Republican National Committee from 1918 to 1921. Consolidating Republican gains in the 1918 congressional elections, Hays coordinated attacks on President Woodrow *Wilson and his policies, increasing the agitation for change in the 1920 election and setting the stage for the rejection of the Versailles Treaty. Having managed the successful presidential campaign of Warren G. Harding, Hays was named Postmaster General, introducing labor reforms and technical innovations in his single year of service. Though he would later be questioned concerning irregularities in raising funds to liquidate Republican party debts, Hays was held in high esteem as being somehow above the political fray.

During the mid-1920s, against a backdrop of denominational in-fighting to which he appears to have been indifferent, Hays organized a successful fundraising drive to provide for *Presbyterian Church in the U.S.A. (PCUSA) church-related employees through the Presbyterian Pension Fund.

In 1922 Hays left partisan politics and accepted appointment as the president of the Motion Picture Producers and Distributors of America (MPPDA) at a salary of $100,000 per year. His task as movie czar was to promote a voluntary code of restraint, analogous to the self-regulation imposed by the Office of Commissioner of Baseball. Hays sought to prevent further legislative efforts to regulate the movie industry, whether federal or local. The formation of the Production Code Administration in 1934 was the result of a working alliance between the MPPDA and those who advanced the Roman Catholic Legion of Decency. Under the direction of Hays, the standards for motion picture production, distribution and advertisement maintained a steady focus on family films throughout the years of the Depression and World War II, before yielding to a new era of popular entertainment in the United States.

Bibliography. *ANB* 10; R. J. Cinclair, "Will H. Hays: Republican Politician" (Ph.D. diss., Ball State University, 1969); W. S. Freeman, "Will H. Hays and the League of Nations" (Ph.D. diss., Indiana University, 1967); W. H. Hays, *The Memoirs of Will H. Hays* (1955); C. A. Ross, "A Presbyterian Elder, a Church Crusade and the Period of 'Family Movies,'" *FH* 24 (1993) 80-90; S. Vaughn, "Morality and Entertainment: The Origins of the Motion Picture Production Code," *JAH* 77 (1990) 39-65. K. S. Sawyer

Heidelberg Catechism.† A German Reformed catechism published in 1563. Frederick William III, elector of the Palatinate, commissioned the principal formulators of the Heidelberg Catechism, Casper Olevianus (1536-1585) and Zacharius Ursinus (1534-1583), to create a work that would bridge the divisions among Lutheran, *Calvinist and Zwinglian disciples during the Reformation. The historian Max Goebel characterized the resulting catechism as a harmonious blend of "Lutheran inwardness, Melanchthonian clearness, Zwinglian simplicity, and Calvinistic fire."

Opening with the famous question "What is your only comfort in life and in death?" the catechism is divided into three parts, which parallel the path to salvation. The catechism begins with humanity's guilt and misery before the unreachable perfection of God's law and then focuses on redemption through Christ's suffering and resurrection for all who repent and believe. Christ's exemplary righteousness and sacrificial satisfaction for manifold human transgressions are emphasized along with the doctrine of providence. But the catechism avoids discussion of predestination, reprobation and limited atonement, and it recognizes in the Lord's Supper both the Zwinglian recall of Jesus' suffering in humanity's behalf and the mystical union of the earthbound redeemed and the ascended redeemer found in *Calvin's theology. The catechism concludes with a section on the human joy and gratitude arising from the reception of divine grace. It acknowledges good works as the fruits of saving faith, views the Ten Commandments as a summary of the ethical Christian life and declares prayer the "chief part of the gratitude which God requires."

Question 80, on the difference "between the Lord's Supper and the Popish Mass," was not included in the first edition of the catechism but was added to the second edition by command of the Elector Frederick III, likely as a response to the Council of Trent. The final form of this question appeared in the third edition, where the Mass is explicitly denounced as "an accursed idolatry." Still, Ursinus devotes seven pages to expounding this question in his commentary, claiming that "This Question is necessary on account of the errors, and horrid abuses which the Mass has introduced into the Church." This editing, although approved by the author, stirred up a significant controversy in the nineteenth century, particularly in the *German Reformed community (Reformed Church in the United States), partly due to the Roman Catholic drift in the *Mercersburg theology of John Williamson *Nevin.

This catechism was the first Protestant confession to be brought to America by Europeans, when the *Dutch Reformed arrived on Manhattan Island (1609). It has been the most widely accepted doctrinal standard among Reformed denominations in America up to the present day. Formally adopted in 1792 at the formation of the *Reformed Church in America (RCA), it has remained a creedal statement for all America Reformed bodies that stem from Germany or the Netherlands, including the *Christian Reformed Church (CRC), the *Reformed Church in the United States (Eureka Synod) and the *Protestant Reformed Churches. It was also sanctioned for use in the reunited *Presbyterian Church in the U.S.A. (PCUSA) in 1870, but it became only a formal creedal statement for that denomination in 1967.

Bibliography. J. W. Nevin, *History and Genius of the Heidelberg Catechism* (1847); P. Schaff, *A History of the Creeds of Christendom* (1877); Z. Ursinus, *Commentary on the Heidelberg Catechism*, trans. G. W. Williard (1954). M. J. Coalter

Hendry, George S. (1904-1993). Presbyterian minister and professor of systematic theology. A native of Aberdeenshire, Scotland, Hendry was born in the village of Meikle Wartle on March 20, 1904. He graduated from Aberdeen University with first-class honors in classics and received his bachelor of divinity degree from the University of Edinburgh. After serving as the minister of Holy Trinity Parish Church at Bridge of Allan, Scotland, from 1930 to 1949, he was called to Princeton Theological Seminary as the Charles Hodge Professor of Systematic Theology, a position he occupied with distinction from 1949 to his retirement in 1973.

In 1935 Hendry was the Hastie Lecturer at the University of Glasgow, in 1951 the Croall Lecturer at Edinburgh University and in 1978 the Warfield Lecturer at Princeton Theological Seminary. He served as secretary of the Joint Committee on a New Translation of the Bible that supervised the preparation of the New English Bible (published in 1961), and he was a member of the committee that drafted the *Confession of 1967 of the *Presbyterian Church in the U.S.A. (PCUSA).

A cofounder of the *Scottish Journal of Theology* and a frequent contributor to *Theology Today* and other theological journals, Hendry's major publications were *God the Creator* (1938), *The Holy Spirit in Christian Theology* (1956; rev. ed., 1965), *The Gospel of the Incarnation* (1958), *The Westminster Confession for Today* (1962) and *The Theology of Nature* (1980). Hendry was an eloquent twentieth-century voice of Reformed theology and a creative interpreter and critic of the theology of Karl *Barth. Admired by both students and colleagues as a master lecturer and preacher, he died in Princeton.

D. L. Migliore

Henry, Joseph (1797-1878). Physical scientist and science administrator. The son of Scottish immigrants, Henry was born in Albany, New York, and baptized at Albany's First Presbyterian Church. When he began to talk, his mother taught him a paraphrase of the closing verse of Psalm 23 that he remembered into his old age. When Henry was almost fourteen, his father died of alcoholism, an event that probably contributed to Henry's later advocacy of temperance. As his interest in science developed, he was exposed to natural theology—the popular belief that science augments Christian religion and that the study of design in nature can reveal God's existence. He gained an international reputation through research done on electricity and magnetism while teaching at the Albany Academy in Albany, New York (1826-1832), and the College of New Jersey in Princeton (1832-1846). He then became the first director of the newly created Smithsonian Institution in Washington, D.C., serving from 1846 until his death. Also, he became a leader in the newly founded American Association for the Advancement of Science and the National Academy of Sciences.

While he was at Princeton, Henry solidified his Presbyterian convictions through close relationships with theologian Charles *Hodge and other colleagues; he also served as a trustee of the Princeton Theological Seminary and joined Princeton's First Presbyterian Church. Moving to Washington, Henry, his wife and children became stalwarts of the New York Avenue Presbyterian Church, an institution that included in its congregation President Abraham Lincoln. He also participated at the national church level, for example, serving on the Presbyterian board of publication.

Henry stands out in the mid-nineteenth-century United States as the foremost practitioner of experimental physics and one of the nation's most influential builders of science's institutional framework. In addition, he swayed the practice of science on a more personal and individual level. Through his initiatives as a teacher, mentor and colleague, he fostered the careers of a wide range of men and women who emerged as America's next generation of scientific leaders. Also, as Smithsonian director and the most visible representative of the nation's scientific community, he formed deep personal bonds with a broad spectrum of political officials and civic leaders. Henry's nurturing actions, along with public-spirited deeds and principled declarations, contributed to an image of the man that, during his later years and after his death, symbolized the ideal scientist and even American science itself. Central to this vision was the notion of Henry being a Christian philosopher. Thus Henry helped catalyze an ideology of science in the United States having distinct Christian overtones.

In his personal outlook, Henry was neither doctrinaire nor concerned with theological minutia. He was reluctant to discuss his faith publicly but loyally followed essential Presbyterian teachings and rejected anti-Christian aspersions of scientific skeptics. Convinced of the compatibility of Christian religion and science, he could, for example, openly profess the *Westminster Confession of Faith while being privately sympathetic to Darwin's theory of evolution. He died in Washington, D.C.

See also SCIENCE, PRESBYTERIANS AND.

BIBLIOGRAPHY. *ANB* 10; *T. D. Bozeman, Protestants in an Age of Science: The Baconian Ideal and Ante-Bellum Religious Thought* (1977); *DAB* VIII; J. H. Finley, *The Scientific Writings of Joseph Henry,* 2 vols. (1886); C. Hodge, "Joseph Henry," *BRPR: Index Volume from 1825-1868* 194-200; *A Memorial of Joseph Henry* (1880). A. E. Moyer

Hepburn, James Curtis (1815-1911).† Presbyterian missionary to Japan. Born in Milton, Pennsylvania, of *Scots-Irish and English ancestry, Hepburn was brought up by earnest Christian parents, joining the Presbyterian church at the age of nineteen. He graduated from the College of New Jersey (now Princeton University) in 1832 and received his medical degree from the University of Pennsylvania in 1836. He practiced medicine for several years and married in 1840. Accompanied by his wife, he served as a medical missionary under the American Board of Commissioners for Foreign Missions between 1841 and 1845, first in Singapore and then in Amoy (now Xiamen), China.

Because of poor health, the Hepburns returned to New York, where he practiced medicine until they went to Japan in 1859. Upon his arrival in Kanagawa, near the present port of Yokohama, Hepburn immersed himself in the study of the language. Soon he opened a dispensary, and while carrying on medical work he also trained young Japanese men in medical science and taught English and mathematics. He was one of the founders and the first president of what is now Meiji Gakuin. Hepburn became proficient in Japanese at all levels of usage.

This facility enabled Hepburn to make contributions in Japan that rivaled his medical work. He compiled the first Japanese-English dictionary, had a key role in translating the Bible into Japanese and produced a Bible dictionary in Japanese. He used and popularized a system of romanizing Japanese that in modified form is still in use. The Hepburns returned to the United States in 1892, living in retirement in New Jersey.

BIBLIOGRAPHY. *ANB* 10; E. R. Beauchamp, "Hepburn, James Curtis," *Kodansha Encyclopedia of Japan* (1983); *DAB* IV; W. E. Griffis, *Hepburn of Japan* (1913). W. N. Browning

Higher Education. *See* EDUCATION, PRESBYTERIANS AND.

Hillis, Newell Dwight (1858-1929).‡ Presbyterian and Congregationalist clergyman. Born in Magnolia, Iowa, Hillis at the age of seventeen joined the American Sunday-School Union (ASSU) and spent approximately five years organizing Sunday schools and ASSU churches in Nebraska, Utah and Wyoming. A graduate of Lake Forest College, Illinois (B.A., 1884), he also studied at McCormick Theological Seminary (B.D., 1887).

Following Presbyterian ordination in 1887, Hillis pastored the First Presbyterian Church, Peoria, Illinois (1887-1890), and First Presbyterian Church, Evanston, Illinois (1890-1894), before moving to the independent Central Church in Chicago (1894-1899). There he established his reputation as a preacher and lecturer. In 1899 he moved to the Plymouth Church of Brooklyn, New York (1899-1924), following in the line of distinguished preachers Henry Ward Beecher and Lyman Abbott.

Hillis became an immensely popular preacher in both the United States and Great Britain. His style was described as "brilliant, original and pictorial." He also developed an interest in urban planning. His illustrated lecture "A Better America" was used by the United States government during and following World War I. During the war Hillis spoke across the nation, advocating the Allies' cause and vilifying Germany.

Hillis wrote about twenty-five books, including *Great Books as Life Teachers* (1899), *Great Men as Prophets of the New Era* (1922) and *A Man's Value to Society* (1896), as well as a compilation, *Lectures of Henry Ward Beecher* (1913). For many years his sermons were transcribed and published in Chicago and Brooklyn newspapers (one thousand sermons in twenty-five years).

BIBLIOGRAPHY. *ANB* 10; R. H. Abrams, *Preachers Present Arms* (1933); *DAB* V. D. Macleod

Hodge, A(rchibald) A(lexander) (1823-1886).‡ Presbyterian minister and theologian. Born the eldest son and successor of Princeton theologian Charles *Hodge, he was educated at Princeton (1841) and Princeton Seminary (1846) and came to defend Calvinist theology in the tradition begun by Archibald *Alexander, after whom he was named. Upon graduating from seminary, Hodge and his family went to Allahabad, India, as Presbyterian missionaries. Forced to return for reasons of health, Hodge was a pastor in Maryland, Virginia and Pennsylvania for several years (1851-1862). In 1864 he became professor of systematic theology at Western Theological Seminary, Allegheny, Pennsylvania, and in 1878 he accepted the chair of didactic and exegetical theology at Princeton Theological Seminary, a position he held until his death in 1886.

His *Life of Charles Hodge* (1880) was not merely an adulatory biography of his father. It reveals characteristics of evangelical *piety that motivated all Princetonians—the role of conversion in religious experience and the necessity of balancing a vital devotional life with orthodox doctrinal belief. In *Outlines of Theology* (1878), Hodge responded to liberals who used a naturalistic worldview to interpret Scripture. To critics who claimed contradictions existed in the biblical text and between the Bible and what scientists have found in nature, the younger Hodge made explicit Princeton's doctrine of plenary and verbal inspiration. While difficulties in interpretation and apparent irreconcilable statements exist, no proved discrepancies have been found. Since God's works in nature and his Word are both revelation, scientific research can never ultimately conflict with biblical teaching. Hodge reaffirmed his views on inerrancy in an article, "Inspiration," written with Benjamin Breckinridge *Warfield in 1881 for the *Presbyterian Review.* His denomination adopted Princeton's view of the Bible as its official teaching in the *Portland Deliverance (1892), and the Five Point Deliverance (1910), which influenced the *fundamentalist-modernist debate.

After the Civil War, Hodge led evangelical resistance to mounting secularism. At the First General Council of the World Alliance of Reformed Churches in 1877, he denounced attempts to replace biblical theism with naturalism as the philosophical foundation of education, law, politics and other public institutions. Arguing against secularist claims that religion applies only to private morality and that public life should be neutral, Hodge contended that God holds both nations and individuals accountable for implementing biblical principles in public life. He believed church and state should be separate, but as an ardent postmillenialist he also thought religion must be closely integrated into American political, economic and social institutions.

In *Popular Lectures on Theological Themes,* published posthumously in 1887, Hodge called for a revitalization of *Calvinism. He contended that only the Reformed worldview, because it seeks the glory of God in all areas of life, is sufficiently broad to provide a biblical basis for the family, law, education and economics.

See also PRINCETON THEOLOGY.

BIBLIOGRAPHY. *ANB* 10; *DAB* V; L. A. Loetscher, *The Broadening Church: A Study of Theological Issues in the Presbyterian Church Since 1869* (1954); M. A. Noll, *The Princeton Theology 1812-1921: Scripture, Science, and Theological Method from Archibald Alexander to Benjamin Breckinridge Warfield* (1983); C. A. Salmond, *Princetonia: Charles and A. A. Hodge* (1888); G. S. Smith, *The Seeds of Secularization: Calvinism, Culture, and Pluralism in America, 1870-1915* (1985). W. A. Hoffecker

Hodge, Charles (1797-1878). Presbyterian theologian, churchman and educator. Arguably the premier Reformed (i.e., *Calvinistic) theologian of America's nineteenth century, Hodge was called in 1822 by the Presbyterian Church as the third professor to teach at Princeton Theological Seminary. Excellence of training, breadth of interests, warmth of personality, comprehension of intellectual, political and cultural issues, commitment as a churchman and gifts as a seminary teacher all combined to propel Hodge into a front-rank status as an American theologian, a rank he held for the more than fifty years he taught at Princeton Seminary.

Known in the English-speaking world for his popular *Way of Life* (1841) and his monumental *Systematic Theology* (3 vols., 1872-1873), Hodge and his thought are better explored in the prestigious *Biblical Repertory and Princeton Review,* a journal he edited for nearly forty years and to which he contributed more than 140 articles, some of which exceed one hundred pages. While many of these articles concentrate on biblical and theological issues of his day, many others address social, scientific, political and ecclesiastical controversies in antebellum America. In these and other ways, Hodge and his colleagues interpreted the Augustinian/Calvinistic tradition to American life and culture and thereby shaped the *Princeton theology, a nineteenth-century style of theological thought that excelled in scriptural faithfulness, scholarly acumen and cultural discourse. Few topics in American life and faith in the mid-nineteenth century escaped Hodge's comment and stout confessionalism. Some of these essays are reprinted in *Theological Essays* (1846) and *Essays and Reviews* (1857).

Always personable and engaging, Hodge was reared by his widowed mother in the cultural milieu of Philadelphia. In 1812 she moved to Princeton so she could more easily finance the education of her two sons at the College of New Jersey (later Princeton University). Graduating in 1815 from the college, the adolescent Hodge came under the mentoring of Archibald *Alexander, the first professor of Princeton Seminary. Hodge enrolled at the seminary in Princeton in 1816 and graduated in 1819. Alexander served until his death in 1851 as a surrogate father and confidant for the young theologian. Hodge married Sarah Bache, a great-granddaughter of Benjamin Franklin, and together they parented eight children. Sarah Hodge died in 1849, and Hodge married Mary Hunter Stockton, a widow from a prominent family in Princeton, in 1852. The Hodge household was a gathering place for countless friends and visitors and often served as a classroom when Hodge's lifelong struggle with a painful and defective hip hindered his ability to walk.

Ordained by New Brunswick Presbytery in 1821,

the young Hodge discovered he was ill-suited for preaching and pastoral work and turned to more scholarly endeavors. Alexander invited him to teach the biblical languages at the seminary, and in 1822 Hodge was appointed by the Presbyterian general assembly as professor of oriental and biblical literature. Until his retirement in 1878, Hodge held several chairs in biblical studies and theology. Few persons in antebellum America exceeded Hodge's training for a career as a theologian. Not only did he benefit from the John *Witherspoon pedagogical tradition at Princeton, but also he was one of the first American scholars to attend Continental universities for advanced studies in Semitic languages, biblical criticism and the history of doctrine. He studied with August Tholuck and Wilhelm Gesenius at Halle, listened to Friedrich D. E. Schleiermacher preach and lecture in Berlin and dutifully attended lectures at the Royal Academy of Science in Berlin to keep abreast of science.

In the following decades as a professor at the seminary in Princeton, Hodge's work centered on biblical studies and theological discourse. He published several New Testament commentaries on Romans (1835, 1864), Ephesians (1856) and 1 and 2 Corinthians (1857). A leader in the *Old School wing of American Presbyterianism, Hodge published a *Constitutional History of the Presbyterian Church in the United States of America* (1840) to explain the origins of Presbyterian *polity and the Old School justification for the denomination's split in 1837. Hodge's articles and editorial policies in the *Biblical Repertory and Princeton Review* are the best indicators of his range, erudition and wit. In addition to issues in biblical scholarship, doxological science, an emerging American literature, ecclesial proceedings, philosophical issues and, of course, theological controversies, Hodge was also an acute political commentator. His articles on slavery, *abolitionism, Jacksonian democracy and the Civil War are especially insightful. In his seventies Hodge published two works that would insure his prominence in American theology. The first was his *Systematic Theology* and the other a famous monograph, *What Is Darwinism?* (1874). One indispensable source for understanding Hodge's personal faith is *Conference Papers* (1879).

Not only was Hodge's legacy imprinted on nineteenth-century theology through his scholarly works, but also it was carried on through the three thousand pastors, teachers and missionaries he taught while at Princeton. He served on many civic, interdenominational and college boards, and his leadership in Presbyterian ecclesial affairs was often sought. His voluminous, extant letters unveil a rich and varied circle of friends and colleagues in North America and abroad. Few Reformed scholars were better known in Victorian America.

See also Hodge, A. A.; Princeton Theology.

Bibliography. *ANB* 10; *DAB* IX; *DARB*; *HHMBI*; A. A. Hodge, *Life of Charles Hodge* (1880); W. A. Hoffecker, *Piety and the Princeton Theologians: Archibald Alexander, Charles Hodge, and Benjamin Warfield* (1981); M. A. Noll, ed., *Charles Hodge, The Way of Life* (1987); idem, *The Princeton Theology: Scripture, Science, and Theological Method from Archibald Alexander to Benjamin Breckinridge Warfield* (1983); M. A. Noll and D. N. Livingstone, eds., *Charles Hodge, What Is Darwinism?* (1995). J. W. Stewart

Hodge, Margaret E. (1869-1943).† Presbyterian *missions leader. Elected a member of the Philadelphia branch of the Woman's Board of Foreign Missions (*Presbyterian Church in the U.S.A. [PCUSA]) in 1899, Hodge served as president from 1910 to 1917. In 1917 she became executive secretary of the denomination's six regional women's foreign mission boards, and three years later, president of the Woman's Board of Foreign Missions, which consolidated all six groups.

Hodge was a forceful advocate for women's interests after the denomination reorganized its mission boards in 1923, absorbing the independent Women's board into its own board of foreign missions. The move was designed to end the segregation of "woman's work" from the activities of the male-run boards, but since women had previously had complete control over their own agencies, many women were concerned that they would now have even less input. As a vice president of the new organization, Hodge voiced the growing discontent of Presbyterian women, coauthoring with Mary Katharine Jones *Bennett an influential report on the "Causes of Unrest Among Women of the Church" (1927). Stating that most women were more interested in missionary endeavors than "freedom and equality," the report showed that the dissolution of the women's boards had stifled women's ability to be involved significantly in the broader work of the church.

Hodge also served on two specially appointed committees to respond to the report, where she and Bennett pressed the denomination to consider wider equality for women in all aspects of church life. Their efforts were continually frustrated by theoretical egalitarians like Robert Elliott *Speer, whose support for equality led them to reject any distinctively women's work.

Bibliography. L. A. Boyd and R. D. Brackenridge, *Presbyterian Women in America* (1983).

M. L. Bendroth

Hoeksema, Herman (1886-1965). Pastor, theologian and leader of the *Protestant Reformed Churches (PRC). Hoeksema was born in the city of Groningen, the Netherlands, to a family soon deserted by its dissolute father. Himself a youthful vagrant, Hoeksema was converted in his teens to a rigorous *Calvinism and, after emigrating (1904) to Chicago, won endorsement for formal training at Calvin Theological Seminary. Upon graduation in 1915, he undertook a five-year pastorate in Holland, Michigan, made notable by his defiance of the town's wartime patriotism.

In 1920 Hoeksema took over the Eastern Avenue Christian Reformed Church (CRC) in Grand Rapids, the denomination's largest congregation. He led successful battles against dispensationalism and alleged higher-critical tendencies at Calvin Seminary, but his own denial of the doctrine of common grace brought him rebuke by the CRC synod of 1924 and his formal deposition in 1925. Hoeksema led his followers from across the Dutch-American network into the Protestant Reformed denomination (*see* Protestant Reformed Churches in America). Virtually until his death he edited its magazine, taught in its theological seminary and pastored its flagship congregation, the First Protestant Reformed Church of Grand Rapids.

Hoeksema's theology began from the doctrine of election—understood as double predestination and the linchpin of divine sovereignty—and eventuated in a radical antithesis between church and world. He was ever adamant against *modernism, worldliness and any perceived compromise of Calvinist consistency. Notable among his many publications are *The Heidelberg Catechism* (1943-1956), *The Protestant Reformed Churches in North America* (1947) and *Reformed Dogmatics* (1966).

Bibliography. A. C. DeJong, *The Well-Meant Gospel Offer* (1954); G. Hoeksema, *Therefore I Have Spoken* (1975).

J. D. Bratt

Hoge, Moses Drury (1819-1899).† Presbyterian minister. Hoge was born at Hampden-Sydney, Virginia, the son of a Presbyterian minister, and the grandson of Moses Hoge, president of Hampden-Sydney College (1807-1820). Most of his early childhood was spent in Ohio. Hoge attended Hampden-Sydney College, graduating with distinction in 1839, and Union Theological Seminary of Virginia, graduating in 1843. He went to First Presbyterian Church of Richmond, Virginia, as assistant to William S. Plumer. When a mission church (Second Presbyterian) was started in 1845, Hoge became the pastor, remaining there until his death. He also taught school for a few years, and from 1854 to 1859 he served as coeditor of the *Central Presbyterian*. He turned down several offers to other pulpits and college presidencies, preferring to remain for more than fifty years in the church that he had helped plant.

Although originally he was opposed to secession, like many Virginians Hoge came to believe that constitutional liberty was at stake. While he did not consider slaveholding to be inherently sinful, he did offer freedom to his own slaves, but only one took him up on the offer. During the Civil War he was honorary chaplain for the Confederate Congress, as well as a volunteer chaplain to the Confederate soldiers stationed nearby, preaching at least twice a week, often to large crowds. In addition to his pastoral labors, he was involved in running the Union blockade during the Civil War to procure Bibles from England. In the midst of the wreck of the South at the end of the war, Hoge worked for the reconciliation of North and South, seeing the opportunity to proclaim the hope of the gospel to the disillusioned population of Richmond.

As moderator of the Presbyterian Church, U.S., general assembly in 1875, Hoge worked for reconciliation with the Northern church and played a key role in the establishment of fraternal relations between the two bodies. Hoge defended the orthodoxy of the Northern church against those who used charges of heterodoxy as the main reason for the continued existence of the Southern church, and he argued that the points of disagreement between the two denominations were not significant enough to impair fellowship.

Hoge was a frequent delegate and speaker at the Evangelical Alliance, as well as the Alliance of Reformed Churches. At the 1884 Evangelical Alliance meeting at Copenhagen, his address "On Family Religion" stimulated the crown princess of Denmark to invite him to teach her how to provide religious training for her own family.

Considered by many in his own day to be the finest preacher in America, Hoge pastored a church that became one of the largest and most influential Presbyterian churches in all the South. An orthodox *Calvinist, he preached the grace of God with great force and power. In 1890 the people of Richmond declared him to be the first citizen of the city. He was seriously injured in a streetcar accident in November 1898 and died two months later.

Bibliography. *ANB* 11; *DAB* V; P. H. Hoge,

Moses Hoge, His Life and Letters (1899); J. M. Wells, *Southern Presbyterian Worthies* (1936).

J. R. Wiers

Hoy, William Edwin (1858-1927). Reformed Church in the United States (*German Reformed) missionary. Born near Mifflinburg, Pennsylvania, Hoy briefly attended Mercersburg Academy in Mercersburg, Pennsylvania, before transferring to Franklin and Marshall College in Lancaster, Pennsylvania, from which he graduated in 1882. After graduating from the Theological Seminary of the Reformed Church in Lancaster in June 1885, Hoy was ordained and commissioned as a missionary to Japan on October 15 of that year by the Eastern Synod of the Reformed Church in the United States.

Upon reaching Tokyo in December 1885, Hoy soon met the evangelist Masayoshi Oshikawa, who was seeking a missionary to join him in establishing a school in Sendai. In 1886 Hoy and Oshikawa founded Sendai Training School for ministers in a rented house. The school was eventually expanded to include a preparatory school and a college, and it became known as Tohoku Gakuin (North Japan College). In 1887 Hoy married Mary B. Ault, one of the women sent by the board of foreign missions of the Reformed Church to establish a girl's school in Sendai, which would be named Miyagi Gakuin.

Though Hoy was not the first missionary of the Reformed Church in the United States to Japan, he can be regarded as the most important pioneer of its work in that country. Supremely dedicated and enthusiastic for the missionary cause, he persuaded a reluctant board of foreign missions to adopt an educational rather than an evangelistic focus for its mission and to move the center of its operations from Tokyo to Sendai. In 1893 Hoy initiated the publication of the journal *The Japan Evangelist.* Even after Hoy ceased to be the editor, the journal continued until 1927, when its name was changed to *The Japan Christian Quarterly.*

Because he suffered from asthma in the damp cold of northern Japan, Hoy sought the more favorable climate of China for his missionary work. Transferring to China in 1899, he founded the China Mission of the Reformed Church at Yochow City in Hunan province, and he remained its primary leader until his departure in 1927. There he established Huping Christian College, a hospital, a Bible training school for women and a number of churches. In 1927 Hoy had to flee China with his wife and daughter, Gertrude, because of a communist uprising against foreigners. He died at sea. Both his wife and daughter would return to China to carry on the mission.

Bibliography. C. W. Mensendiek, *Not Without Struggle: The Story of William E. Hoy and the Beginnings of Tohoku Gakuin* (1986).

J. B. Payne

Huguenots.‡ The popular name for the Calvinist French Protestants, officially the Reformed Church of France. An epithet of uncertain origin, the word was often used to describe the French Protestants as both a religious movement and a political faction. Under the intellectual and spiritual leadership of their exiled countryman, John *Calvin, and with the help of missionary pastors dispatched from Geneva, French Protestants grew rapidly in numbers from about 1540 to 1560. During these decades many French nobles, including the powerful House of Bourbon, embraced the evangelical Calvinist faith and began to fuse the movement with political goals. Efforts to suppress the French Reformed Church led to a series of ferocious, complex and inconclusive wars of religion in France between 1562 and 1598. A resolution of the civil conflict came when the Huguenot leader Henry of Navarre, of the House of Bourbon, succeeded to the throne as Henry IV (1509-1610), declared himself a Catholic and in 1598 issued the Edict of Nantes. The edict granted the Protestants religious toleration, full civil liberties, control of the education of their children and the right to fortify certain Protestant towns. In many ways, it allowed the Huguenots to exist as a state within a state.

However, during the reigns of the next two kings these rights would be undone. Military and political prerogatives were removed under Louis XIII (1610-1643), beginning under the direction of Cardinal Richelieu (minister, 1624-1642), then almost completely in 1629 following the Protestant defeat at La Rochelle. The Huguenots' religious rights were gradually withdrawn early in the reign of Louis XIV (1643-1715) and abolished in 1685 with the revocation of the Edict of Nantes. With Protestantism illegal in almost all of France, more than four hundred thousand of the more than two million Huguenots immigrated to Prussia, the Netherlands, Switzerland, the British Isles and North America.

A Huguenot presence had been established in America as early as 1562, when Jean de Ribault along with thirty Huguenot families settled in Port Royal, near present-day Charleston, South Carolina. But the colony disintegrated when de Ribault was hastily called home because of the religious civil wars. Two years later, René de Laudonnière with about two hundred Huguenots colonized the same general area. They founded Fort Caroline near the mouth of the St. Johns River, not far from the modern city of Jacksonville, Florida, but in 1565 the settlement was annihilated by a Spanish strike. Only about thirty survivors returned to France.

Huguenot immigration to British North America between 1565 and 1685 consisted mostly of families and small groups, probably numbering no more than five thousand in all and coming mainly by way of the Netherlands and England. In the sixty-five years following the revocation of the Edict of Nantes, about fifteen thousand more Huguenots immigrated to America. Most of them settled in and around Charleston, but large numbers also landed in Pennsylvania, Virginia, New York, Rhode Island and Massachusetts. The story of Huguenot community migration to America came to an end when in 1712 Madame Marie Ferée founded a plantation in Lancaster County, Pennsylvania. Though small in numbers, the Huguenots wielded a considerable influence in colonial life because of their skills as merchants, bankers, craftsmen, lawyers and physicians. They also dotted the landscape of fame in America with French Huguenot surnames: Paul Revere, John C. Frémont, Matthew Vassar, James Bowdoin, Thomas Hopkinson Gallaudet, Henry David Thoreau, Henry Wadsworth Longfellow and John Greenleaf Whittier, to name a few.

The story of the Huguenots in America constitutes one of the great mysteries of ethnic assimilation in American history. Like so many other immigrants in the colonial period, they came to find religious freedom and to better themselves economically. However, by 1750, as a group they had largely assimilated almost flawlessly into Anglo-American culture. It may be that assimilation occurred easily because the Huguenots did not immigrate en masse. Also, they may have been especially eager to forget their recent past in France. Moreover, most of the American-bound Huguenots migrated by way of another country, which helped to make a second adjustment easier. Perhaps most of all, the very fact that the Huguenots' primary identity was religious rather than French allowed them to assimilate more easily and more rapidly into the evangelical Protestant ethos of colonial America.

BIBLIOGRAPHY. J. Butler, *The Huguenots in America: A Refugee People in New World Society* (1983); J. G. Gray, *The French Huguenots: Anatomy of Courage* (1981); R. M. Kingdon, *Geneva and the Consolidation of the French Protestant Movement* (1967); idem, "Why Did the Huguenot Refugees to the American Colonies Become Episcopalian?" *HMPEC* 49 (1980) 317-35; G. E. Reaman, *The Trail of the Huguenots in Europe, the United States, South Africa and Canada* (1963). R. D. Linder

Hungarian Reformed Church in America. An ethnic Reformed denomination that uses the *Heidelberg Catechism and the Second Helvetic Confession as its doctrinal standards, and practices a combination of Presbyterian and Reformed church *polity that was developed in eighteenth-century Hungary. The church took shape as the result of Hungarian immigration throughout the nineteenth and early twentieth centuries to the United States. Because the migration of Hungarians was sporadic, the establishment of Hungarian Reformed congregations at Pittsburgh and Cleveland in 1890 was initially under the oversight of the Reformed Church in the United States (*German Reformed; RCUS). As more Hungarians of a Reformed background came to America, other congregations were also formed but affiliated with the *Presbyterian Church in the U.S.A. (PCUSA).

By 1904 Hungarian congregations associated with the RCUS withdrew from that communion and formed with recently established ethnic churches a classis under the direct supervision of the Reformed Church in Hungary. Hungarian immigration to America just prior to World War I enabled the Hungarian Reformed Church to grow considerably and necessitated the formation of a second classis. With the demise of the Austro-Hungarian empire and hardships suffered by the Reformed Church in Hungary during wartime and after, the mother church advised the Hungarian Reformed in America to affiliate with a denomination in the United States. Efforts to join the PCUSA in the 1920s failed because Hungarian Reformed wanted to continue as ethnic classes within the American church. Older associations as well as the existence of some Hungarian congregations still with the RCUS made possible the Tiffin Agreement of 1921, which arranged the Hungarian Reformed (both outside and within the RCUS) into four ethnic classes. These churches in 1934 became part of the Evangelical and Reformed Church when the RCUS merged with the *Evangelical Synod of North America. When in 1957 the Evangelical and Reformed Church joined the United Church of Christ, some Hungarian Reformed churches remained separate.

The churches that go by the name Hungarian Reformed Church trace their denominational origins to seven Hungarian Reformed congregations that were dissatisfied with the Tiffin Agreement, remained independent and in 1924 formed their own communion, the Free Magyar Reformed Church in America. In 1928 the church was comprised of two classes. Thirty years later the denomination adopted its present name. A small denomination of roughly ten thousand members, the Hungarian Reformed Church has congregations scattered throughout the United States and Canada. Though for one year during the 1950s the denomination joined the *fundamentalist International Council of Christian Churches, the Hungarian Reformed Church has developed ecumenical ties more typically with mainline Protestant communions, holding membership in the National Council of Churches, the World Council of Churches and the World Alliance of Reformed Churches.

Bibliography. *Handbook of Denominations in the United States* (1985); A. C. Piepkorn, *Profiles in Belief: The Religious Bodies of the United States and Canada,* vol. 2 (1978). D. G. Hart

I

Intellectual Life, Presbyterians and. In the 1992 film *A River Runs Through It,* the father, a Presbyterian pastor in early twentieth-century Montana, remarks that "a Methodist is a Baptist who can read." The comment, a conventional one at that time, suggests both the Presbyterian identification with higher education and why Presbyterians were far outnumbered by their populist competitors. Presbyterians' insistence on an educated clergy ensured that they would have an appeal particularly among the literate and hence that Presbyterians would play a disproportionate role in American intellectual life. However, even though at the time of the American *Revolution Presbyterianism seemed poised to become America's leading denomination, their insistence on an educated clergy limited their popular base as the nation expanded.

Particularly important to Presbyterian intellectual leadership was their early alliance with evangelical Congregationalists of *New England. During at least the first century of British settlements in North America, New Englanders had a virtual monopoly on American intellectual life. The Great Awakenings of the eighteenth century generated mission-minded intercolonial consciousness among New Light Congregationalists who, when they moved south or west of Connecticut, typically allied themselves with Presbyterianism. The major intellectual manifestation of this alliance was the establishment of the College of New Jersey at Princeton in 1746. This enterprise, originally dominated by *New Side Presbyterians, attracted America's premier intellect, Jonathan *Edwards, to its presidency in 1758. After Edwards's early death, his most illustrious successor was Scotland's John *Witherspoon, who during his years at Princeton (1768-1793) was widely regarded as America's leading scholar. Under Witherspoon Presbyterians helped forge an intellectual alliance among evangelical *piety, Enlightenment confidence in science grounded on Scottish Common-Sense philosophy and republican virtues. This combination, which played a major role in American intellectual life until the era of the Civil War, provided a basis for an era of substantial Presbyterian influence as well.

During the early national era much of the Presbyterian impact on intellectual life came through college building. Between 1780 and 1829 Presbyterians founded one-third of America's forty new colleges. By the eve of the Civil War the number of Presbyterian colleges had risen to forty-nine. Much of this growth was related to the expansion of Scottish and *Scots-Irish influences, especially in the *South. Often invigorated by religious *revivals, Presbyterians pursued an aggressive program of culture building. When in the early 1820s Thomas Jefferson laid his plans for the establishment of the University of Virginia as the model nonsectarian university, he saw Presbyterians as his principal opponents. While Jefferson argued that state universities should be religiously neutral, the Presbyterians countered that they would be essentially establishments for teaching Jeffersonian unitarian moralism. Presbyterians were largely responsible for thwarting most attempts at establishing state universities on Jeffersonian Enlightenment principles and played major roles in the founding or early control of the universities of Georgia, North Carolina, Tennessee, Delaware, South Carolina, Illinois and California.

During the first half of the nineteenth century American intellectual life, such as it was, was not usually centered in the fledgling colleges and universities, even though they provided basic classical training for most of the nation's intellectuals. In an era before American graduate schools and specialized journals, the strongest intellectual centers were the theological seminaries and divinity schools. Of these the Presbyterians' Princeton Theological Seminary, founded in 1812, was one of the earliest and most influential. Union Theological Seminary in New York City, established by *New School Presbyterians in 1836, became a formidable rival. These schools and their counterparts, especially among Congregationalists, attracted many of the best academic minds of the era. The faculties of the schools published scholarly theological reviews that were some of the most important American resources for keeping up with current intellectual trends, both

American and from abroad. Of the Presbyterian theologians, Archibald *Alexander and Charles *Hodge of Princeton and Henry Boynton *Smith of Union were the best known. As late as 1879 G. Stanley Hall complained that in American colleges many teachers of philosophy were trained primarily in theology so that their students were more familiar with theologians such as Hodge than they were with Plato, Leibniz and Kant.

During the first half of the nineteenth century much of American intellectual life took place not in formal academic institutions but among talented gentlemen scholars. The principal Presbyterian manifestation of this tendency was the presence of gentlemen theologians in many Presbyterian parishes. Such pastors were often the best educated persons in town.

Antebellum Southern culture, which was more solidly Protestant than was the North, supported a number of major Presbyterian theologians and cultural leaders. James Henley *Thornwell of Columbia Theological Seminary was an important defender of the Southern cause. After the Northern invasion and defeat of the Confederacy, Robert Lewis *Dabney, who spent most of his career at Union Theological Seminary in Virginia, was a leading defender of the lost cause.

In the North after the Civil War the strength that Presbyterians had built in the nation's intellectual life began to erode. The professionalization of newer academic disciplines led to a revolution that by the early twentieth century displaced theology and theological schools to the periphery of American intellectual life. New intellectual trends, especially Darwinism and biblical criticism, helped undermine the trust in biblical revelation on which much of Presbyterian intellectual life had been built. Presbyterians played prominent roles in the debates over these issues. James *McCosh, the Scottish-born president of the College of New Jersey, was one of the most prominent reconcilers of a theistic version of biological evolution and traditionalist trust in the Bible. Charles Hodge, however, strongly opposed Darwinism on the ground that Darwin himself presupposed a universe without God. In the South James *Woodrow lost his job at Columbia Theological Seminary in 1886 for holding views similar to those of McCosh. In the area of biblical criticism the Presbyterian debates centering on the trials of Charles Augustus *Briggs of Union Theological Seminary in New York received national attention. Although Briggs was defrocked by the Presbyterian general assembly in 1893, both he and his seminary simply withdrew from the *Presbyterian Church in the U.S.A. (PCUSA).

These episodes were important symptoms of larger trends that were forcing distinctive Presbyterian concerns out of the mainstream of American intellectual life. By the first decades of the twentieth century, dominant academic opinion would be agreed that theological considerations should be excluded from the respectable academy, excepting theological schools. The emphasis in Christian education would be more exclusively on morality and service, ideals that seemed less likely to divide. Woodrow *Wilson, president of Princeton University from 1902 to 1910, exemplified these ideals. Although a pious Presbyterian himself, Wilson in his academic applications of Christianity had little to do with specific theological concerns.

During the first half of the twentieth century much of Presbyterian theological education itself turned from exclusive focus on the Reformed doctrinal heritage toward more openness to contemporary theological trends, including theological modernism. In the 1920s Presbyterian debate over such issues provided the principal intellectual dimension of the *fundamentalist-modernist controversy. Princeton theologian J. Gresham *Machen, who accused modernists of abandoning the essence of Christianity, was widely recognized as one of the formidable intellectuals of the era. Nonetheless the overwhelming national intellectual trends were against Machen and others who spoke for a specifically Presbyterian intellectual outlook.

At the same time Presbyterianism's longstanding commitment to systematic thought meant that there were still many Presbyterians who were contributing to American intellectual life. The *neo-orthodox revival of the 1930s to the 1950s was an intellectual's movement and was particularly strong among Presbyterians. Neo-orthodoxy revived concern to relate theological perspectives to other dimensions of thought. Presbyterian theological seminaries (including Union Theological Seminary in New York, which still had many Presbyterian ties) were leading centers for such concerns. Some lay academics, such as historian E. Harris Harbison of Princeton University, shared similar ideas.

The major Presbyterian denominations also still had many of their own colleges, which by midcentury faced major questions concerning their continuing church identity. In 1950 Howard Lowry, president of Wooster College and a spokesperson for neo-orthodoxy, published *The Mind's Adventure,* which called for a revival of Christian intellectual life, particularly at church-related colleges. While such proposals gained considerable attention during the 1950s, they were difficult to implement in the face of strongly secular trends in American higher education. After the 1960s and the countercultural attacks on the Protestant establishment, most such concerns were abandoned. The academic perspectives of the vast majority of Presbyterian colleges closely resembled those found at their formally secular counterparts. Traditions of solid Christian scholarship at most Presbyterian theological seminaries did continue. Presbyterian leadership in the religion programs of the Lilly Foundation in Indianapolis played a major role in sustaining theological and historical scholarship during what might otherwise have been very lean years. Elsewhere, however, calls for distinctively Christian intellectual life (let alone distinctively Presbyterian) were becoming rare. The major exceptions were among some intellectually vigorous evangelicals and separatist Presbyterians, most of whom traced their immediate intellectual lineage back to Machen and/or to *Dutch Reformed thought in the tradition of Abraham *Kuyper.

See also SCIENCE, PRESBYTERIANS AND.

BIBLIOGRAPHY. T. D. Bozeman, *Protestants in an Age of Science: The Baconia Ideal and Ante-bellum American Religious Thought* (1977); B. Holifield, *Gentlemen Theologians: American Theology in Southern Culture, 1795-1860* (1978); H. Hovenkamp, *Science and Religion in America, 1800-1860* (1978); B. Kuklick, *Churchmen and Philosophers: From Jonathan Edwards to John Dewey* (1985); M. J. Lacey, ed., *Religion and Twentieth-Century American Intellectual Life* (1989); G. M. Marsden, *The Soul of the American University: From Protestant Establishment to Established Nonbelief* (1994); and M. A. Noll, *Princeton and the Republic, 1768-1822: The Search for a Christian Enlightenment in the Eras of Samuel Stanhope Smith* (1990).

G. M. Marsden

Irion, Andreas (1823-1870). *Evangelical Synod educator. Born in Germany, Irion studied at the Basel Mission House in Switzerland between 1846 and 1851, where he was influenced especially by the pietist Wolfgang Friedrich Gess.

Repudiated by the Russians as a missionary to Germans in Caucasia, Irion was sent instead to America. Louis *Nollau in St. Louis persuaded the board of the three-year-old Evangelical Seminary in Marthasville, Missouri (now Eden Theological Seminary), to engage Irion as a professor, where he assisted Wilhelm Binner from 1853 to 1857, becoming head of the school when Binner resigned in 1857. Irion continued in that post until his early death.

Irion supervised quarrying stones and erecting new seminary buildings with the aid of students, all accomplished without a building or finance committee or an architect. For ten years Irion exerted great influence on Evangelical churches through his editing of the *Friedensbote (Messenger of Peace).*

Irion became especially influential through his work as a teacher and theologian. He revised what became the Small Evangelical Catechism of 1862, making use of it in his lectures. His teaching was characterized as pietistic, Lutheran, speculative, logical and orthodox.

BIBLIOGRAPHY. J. W. Flucke, *Evangelical Pioneers* (1931); H. Kamphausen, *Geschichte des religioesen Lebens in der Deutschen Evangelischen Synode von Nord-Amerika* (1924); C. E. Schneider, *The German Church on the American Frontier* (1939).

L. H. Zuck

Irish Presbyterians. *See* SCOTS-IRISH AND IRISH PRESBYTERIANS IN AMERICA.

J

Jackson, Samuel Macauley (1851-1912).† Presbyterian educator and author. Born in New York City, where his father was an Irish immigrant businessman, Jackson was educated at the College of the City of New York, graduating with distinction (A.B., 1870; A.M., 1876). He studied theology at Princeton Theological Seminary (1870-1871) and Union Theological Seminary of New York (1871-1873), where Philip *Schaff and Henry Boynton *Smith awakened his interest in church history. Following his graduation, he did further study at the universities of Leipzig and Berlin in Germany (1873-1876). During this period he also traveled in Palestine.

Returning to the United States, Jackson was ordained and served as pastor of the Presbyterian Church in Norwood, New Jersey (1876-1880). Finding himself unsuited to the pastoral ministry because of his retiring temperament, he became involved in charitable work and historical scholarship. He served on the board and held positions with such organizations as the Charity Organization Society and the Prison Association of the State of New York, but his most famous work was as editor of standard reference works, including several with his mentor, Schaff, such as *A Dictionary of the Bible* (1880) and *A Religious Encyclopedia* (1882-1884). He later edited the thirteen-volume compendium, the *New Schaff-Herzog Encyclopedia of Religious Knowledge* (1907-1911), as well as *Johnson's Universal Cyclopedia* (1893-1895, 1897). He also edited and contributed the volume on Zwingli to the series *Heroes of the Reformation* (1899) and served as secretary for the American Society of Church History for many years. In 1895 he became professor of church history at New York University, where he remained until his death.

Bibliography. *ANB* 11; *DAB* V.

J. R. Wiers

Jackson, Sheldon (1834-1909).† Presbyterian missionary. Born in Minaville, New York, Jackson attended Union College in Schenectady (B.A., 1855) and Princeton Theological Seminary (B.D., 1858), was ordained by the Presbytery of Albany a week after graduation and was married within weeks. Influenced by the revival of student interest in *missions during the fall of his senior year at Princeton, Jackson applied for overseas work with the Presbyterian Church and was appointed by the Foreign Board to teach Choctaw Indians at Spencer Academy in the Indian Territory. Unhappy, both because of health problems and his desire to preach more, Jackson was reassigned under the home board to La Crescent, Minnesota (1858).

From 1859 until 1863 Jackson labored in western Wisconsin and southern Minnesota, beginning his long career of pioneering Presbyterian work on the Western frontier. In 1863 he served briefly as an agent of the United States Christian Commission with the Union army before being called back to Minnesota for a five-year pastorate in Rochester. During the decade of the 1860s, he helped organize twenty-three churches and secured twenty new ministers from seminaries in the East. By 1869 Jackson had worked to secure a call from the Synod of Iowa to superintend its regional home missions. Later the denominational board appointed him to oversee the Presbyterian work from Canada to Mexico and from Nebraska to Nevada. From 1872 to 1882 he edited the *Rocky Mountain Presbyterian* (later the *Presbyterian Home Missionary),* a journal designed to promote the interests of home missions and bring coherence to his widespread missionary empire. In 1877 he first visited Alaska, establishing what would become his most notable missionary venture.

Jackson's consistent concern for the social improvement of people, both native and settler, led to his 1879 appointment by the United States government to head a special commission "to investigate the conditions of the natives in S.E. Alaska." In 1884 he was appointed the first superintendent of public instruction for Alaska, a post he held until his death in 1909. He carefully documented the corruption of the government agents, who were frequently little better than robber barons. Concerned for the plight of the Eskimos as well as the settlers, he tirelessly worked to improve economic conditions and educational possibilities. Despite the federal government's early reticence, Jackson raised funds and personally directed the introduction of domestic reindeer from Siberia to Alaska (1891) to prevent either the starvation or forced removal of the Eskimos to reservations.

Jackson, known as the Bishop of All Beyond (or Apostle to Alaska), was tireless in his efforts to establish the American frontier as a Christian society. His pioneering efforts often caused friction with his own church and government, but these efforts also founded more than 150 churches, Westminster College in Salt Lake City, the *North Star* newspaper in Sitka, Alaska (1887), The Alaska Society of Natural History and Ethnology (1887) and The Women's Executive Committee of Home Missions (1878; later called The Women's Board of Home Missions). For his outstanding efforts in establishing a Presbyterian presence in the Northwest, he was elected moderator of the *Presbyterian Church in the U.S.A. (PCUSA) in 1897. He remained active in his efforts on behalf of his beloved Alaska until his death in 1909.

BIBLIOGRAPHY. *ANB* 11; A. K. Bailey, "Sheldon Jackson: Planter of Churches," *JPHS* 27 (1948) 120-48, 193- 214; *JPHS* 28 (1949) 21-40; N. J. Bender, *Winning the West for Christ: Sheldon Jackson and Presbyterianism on the Rocky Mountain Frontier, 1869-1880* (1996): *DAB* V; *DARB;* J. A. Lazell, *Alaska Apostle* (1960); *NCAB* 9; R. L. Stewart, *Sheldon Jackson: Pathfinder and Prospector of the Missionary Vanguard in theRocky Mountains and Alaska* (1908).

S. Sunquist

Jackson, Thomas Jonathan ("Stonewall") (1824-1863).† Confederate general and Presbyterian layman. Born in Clarksburg, Virginia (now West Virginia), Jackson barely passed the entrance examination at West Point, though he achieved seventeenth place in his graduating class (1846). He was an officer in the Mexican War, where he first exhibited his military talents. In 1851 he resigned his commission and began a ten-year position as an instructor of artillery tactics and natural philosophy at the Virginia Military Institute. During this decade he married the daughter of a Presbyterian minister, Eleanor Junkin (1853), who died the following year in childbirth. In 1857 he married Mary Anna Morrison, also a daughter of a Presbyterian minister.

Sometime after the Mexican War, in the late 1840s, Jackson began a serious study of religion, beginning with Roman Catholicism, then developing a private code of morals and finally affiliating with the Presbyterian Church in 1851. As a deacon in the Presbyterian Church in Lexington, Virginia, Jackson taught a Sunday school for blacks, which remained a chief concern for him even during the war years. He believed that everything in life should be a religious act, and Southern preachers often referred to him as a prophet-warrior. He consistently observed the sabbath, studied the Bible and was in the habit of rising for prayer several times during the night on the eve of battle. A personal friend of the Southern Presbyterian theologian Robert Lewis *Dabney (who served on Jackson's staff), he frequently sought Dabney's company and enjoyed discussing theology.

During the Civil War Jackson distinguished himself as an outstanding Confederate officer. He had hoped that war could be avoided but answered the call to defend his native state. At the first battle of Bull Run, his stout resistance to Union advances earned him the nickname "Stonewall," a moniker he insisted rightfully belonged to his whole brigade, not just himself. Other battles that gave evidence of his tactical genius were the Seven Days' battles, the Shenandoah Valley campaign, Cross Keys, Port Republic, the second battle of Bull Run and Fredericksburg. Considered by many to be one of the finest strategists in American military history, Jackson believed that his successes and failures were primarily due to God's providence. Convinced that the spiritual well-being of his troops was essential, he encouraged chaplains and evangelists to preach the Word of God on any suitable occasion, and he supported the formation of the Chaplains' Association in his army, providing for more effective unity and co-operation between chaplains.

In the battle of Chancellorsville, Jackson was caught in the confused fire of his own men on May 2, 1863. His left arm was amputated, and he began to improve. Then pneumonia set in, and he died on May 10, at the age of thirty-nine. His dying words were "Let us cross over the river, and rest under the shade of the trees." His commanding officer, General Robert E. Lee, mourned the loss of his "right arm."

BIBLIOGRAPHY. *ANB* 11; *DAB* V; R. L. Dabney, *Life of Lieut.-Gen. Thos. J. Jackson,* 2 vols. (1864-1866); G. F. R. Henderson, *Stonewall Jackson and the American Civil War,* 2 vols. (1898); J. P. Smith, *Religious Character of Stonewall Jackson* (1897); F. E. Vandiver, *The Mighty Stonewall* (1957).

D. B. Chesebrough

Jellema, William Harry (1893-1982). *Christian Reformed philosopher and professor. Jellema was born in a Dutch immigrant part of Chicago and was reared there and in Holland, Michigan. He drew particular influence from his maternal grandmother, who embodied the *piety of the orthodox *Dutch

Reformed tradition. At Calvin College (1910-1914) he absorbed as well the neo-Calvinism of Abraham *Kuyper. He wedded that to the idealist philosophy he learned from Robert Wenley at the University of Michigan (B.A., (1915; M.A., 1916; Ph.D., 1922), writing his dissertation on Josiah Royce.

In 1920 Jellema returned to Calvin, where he founded the philosophy department and set an enduring stamp upon its labors. Among the hundreds of students he taught in his two tenures there (1920-1935; 1947-1963) were Cornelius *Van Til, William Frankena, Alvin Plantinga, Peter Kreeft and Nicholas Wolterstorff. From 1935 to 1947 he taught at Indiana University, where his students included Carl F. H. Henry. Jellema was thus dean of the Reformed *presuppositionalist school of Christian philosophy that has registered heavily in the field since 1945.

Jellema was a legendary teacher, inspiring his students with the vision that philosophy articulates the deepest spirit of its age, never proceeds from purely rational or neutral assumptions and so is a vital calling for Christian believers. Jellema's idealism later modulated under the neo-Thomist influence of Etienne Gilson. Jellema worked the two together against the pragmatic naturalism he lamented in twentieth-century culture. He championed classic liberal-arts education at Calvin and as a founding faculty member at Grand Valley State University, where he taught from 1963 to 1978. Jellema died at Grand Rapids.

Bibliography. W. H. Jellema papers, Calvin College archives; J. E. Tomberlin and P. Van Inwagen, eds., *Alvin Plantinga* (1985) 3-33.

J. D. Bratt

Jessup, Henry Harris (1832-1910).† Presbyterian *missionary. Born in Montrose, Pennsylvania, Jessup was educated at Yale College (B.A., 1851) and Union Theological Seminary in New York (B.D., 1855). Ordained as a missionary in 1855 by the *Presbyterian Church in the U.S.A. (PCUSA), he was sent to Syria by the American Board of Commissioners for Foreign Missions (ABCFM) and arrived in Beirut in 1856.

After four years of language study and ministry in Tripoli, Jessup returned to Beirut, where for thirty years he was pastor of the Syrian church in that city and head of its school. Jessup quickly became fluent in Arabic, and his ministry led him to associations with the journal *El-Neshrah,* a hospital for the emotionally disturbed and a leading role in the establishment of the Syrian Protestant College in 1866, now known as the American University of Beirut.

Although he is best known for his *Fifty-three Years in Syria*—a history of the mission as well as an autobiography—Jessup also wrote concerning Arab women, Arab family life and the relations between Greek Christians and Protestant missions. The Board of Foreign Missions of the Presbyterian Church in the U.S.A. took over the work of the ABCFM in 1870. In 1879 the general assembly of that denomination elected Jessup moderator when he was in the United States on furlough. Declining several prominent appointments, including the ambassadorship to Persia, which would have taken him away from his adopted home, he remained in Syria until his death.

Bibliography. *ANB* 12; *DAB* V; H. H. Jessup, *Fifty-three Years in Syria,* 2 vols. (1910); J. H. Smylie, "Henry Harris Jessup: Mission in the Land of the Bible," in *Go Therefore: 150 Years of Presbyterians in Global Mission,* ed. J. H. Smylie et al. (1987).

J. H. Smylie

Johnson, Herrick (1832-1913). Presbyterian pastor and educator. Born in Kaughnewaga, New York, to a wealthy merchant family, Johnson graduated from Hamilton College in 1857 and from Auburn Theological Seminary in 1860. He quickly began work as the assistant pastor to Nathaniel *Beman, a prominent *New School promoter of *revivalism and *education, at the First Presbyterian Church of Troy, New York. In 1863 Johnson accepted a call to pastor the influential Third Presbyterian Church of Pittsburgh. During the Civil War Johnson ministered to many sick and wounded soldiers under the auspices of the United States Christian Commission, headquartered in Pittsburgh. In 1868 he succeeded another renowned New School leader, Albert *Barnes, as pastor of the prestigious First Presbyterian Church of Philadelphia. Johnson strongly supported the reunion of the *Old and New Schools, which occurred in 1869.

In 1874 Johnson accepted the chair of homiletics and rhetoric at Auburn Theological Seminary. Six years later he moved to Chicago to pastor the Fourth Presbyterian Church and to teach a course in sacred rhetoric at McCormick Theological Seminary. In a series of lectures delivered at Farwell Hall in Chicago and published in 1881 as *Christianity's Challenge,* Johnson presented the claims of the Bible to be God's revelation and examined biblical teaching about Christ, human nature, the afterlife, pleasure, business and women. In 1882 the *Presbyterian Church in the U.S.A. (PCUSA) selected Johnson to be the moderator of its general assembly. During the early 1880s he also wrote *Revivals— Their Place and Power* (1882) and *Plain Talks About the Theater* (1883). When the combined responsibilities of his church and the seminary proved to be too great, Johnson returned in 1883 to his greatest passion—teaching—as the occupant of the chair of homiletics and pastoral theology at McCormick. Remaining in this position until 1905, Johnson trained a generation of ministers how to preach the gospel persuasively and powerfully.

From 1880 to 1913 Johnson played a leading role in the PCUSA. He founded the Presbyterian Board of Aid for Colleges and Academies in 1883 and for the next twenty years served as its president. He chaired the committee that prepared a new statement of doctrine in conjunction with the revision of the *Westminster standards the denomination adopted in 1903. That same year his *Sermons from Love to Praise* were published. More significantly, Johnson reworked his lectures on preaching given during his twenty-five years at McCormick into *The Ideal Ministry* (1908), a volume that explained the functions, aims and themes of preaching as well as how to prepare, construct and deliver sermons. An outstanding preacher himself, Johnson was one of the most respected teachers of homiletics and pastoral theology during his era. A pastor to pastors, he was a spiritual guide and a mediating force in his denomination. He died in Philadelphia.

BIBLIOGRAPHY. Dick Bolton and Barbara Bolton, eds., *A File of Shepherds: In Commemoration of the 150th Anniversary of Third Presbyterian Church* (1983); E. Y. Hill, "In Memoriam: The Reverend Herrick Johnson" (1914); *NCAB* 10; C. E. Robinson, *Herrick Johnson: An Appreciative Memoir* (1914); "A Valiant Captain of the Lord's Host," *The Continent,* November 27, 1913. G. S. Smith

Jones, Charles Colcock (1804-1863). Presbyterian minister. Born into a prominent family in Liberty County, Georgia, and educated at Andover and Princeton seminaries, Jones entered the ministry in 1830. He served the First Presbyterian Church of Savannah (1831-1832), taught ecclesiastical history and church polity at Columbia Theological Seminary in South Carolina (1837-1838; 1848-1850) and was corresponding secretary of the Board of Domestic Missions of the Presbyterian Church in Philadelphia (1850-1853). But Jones is best known as the devoted apostle to the blacks.

Although he impugned slavery while studying in the North (1825-1830), upon returning to his family's plantations, Jones joined Southern clergymen in biblically defending the peculiar institution. Despite ill health, he developed a system for evangelizing slaves and convinced masters in Liberty County and throughout the South to adopt it. Jones wrote such widely used texts as *A Catechism of Scripture, Doctrine and Practice . . . for the Oral Instruction of Colored Persons* (1837; 1843), *The Religious Instruction of the Negroes in the United States* (1842) and *A History of the Church of God* (1867). Jones did not view his mission as a threat to the institution of slavery, believing that slaves must be transformed into a "civilized people" before they could commend themselves to their masters as worthy of freedom.

BIBLIOGRAPHY. *ANB* 12: E. Clarke, *Wrestlin' Jacob: A Portrait of Religion in the Old South* (1979); D. G. Mathews, "Charles Colcock Jones and the Southern Evangelical Crusade to Form a Biracial Community," *JSH* (1975) 299. B. Touchstone

K

Kellogg, Samuel Henry (1839-1899).† Presbyterian missionary and pastor. Born at Quoque, Long Island, Kellogg received his early education at home, except for about six months at Haverstraw Mountain Institute. He briefly attended Williams College in 1856 and graduated from Princeton College in 1861 with high honors. Completing his studies at Princeton Theological Seminary in 1864, he also served as an instructor in mathematics at the college from 1862 to 1864. In 1864 he was ordained as a missionary to India by Hudson Presbytery and married to Antoinette Hartwell. In that same year Kellogg and his wife set sail for Calcutta. After six years of ministry in Barhpur, North India, Kellogg spent about five years teaching and writing at the Theological School at Allahabad.

In 1875 Kellogg completed a monumental grammar of the Hindi language. Following the death of his wife in 1876, he returned with his four children to America and remarried in 1879. Kellogg served as pastor of the Third Presbyterian Church in Pittsburgh and as professor of systematic theology at Western Seminary in Allegheny, Pennsylvania (1877-1885). From 1886 to 1892 he was pastor of St. James Square Presbyterian Church in Toronto. In 1892 he returned to India to assist in revising the Hindi Old Testament. He died there, following a bicycle accident.

An accomplished linguist as well as a missionary, Kellogg wrote nine books and numerous pamphlets and articles in scholarly journals. He was a member of the American Society of Orientalists as well as the Victoria Institute of England and an associate of the Philosophical Society of Great Britain.

Bibliography. *ANB* 12; *DAB* V; H. H. H. Holcomb, *Men of Might in India Missions* (1901).

P. C. Wilt

Kerr, Hugh Thomson (1871-1950). Presbyterian pastor. Born in Ontario, Canada, Kerr earned his bachelor of arts degree at the University of Toronto in 1894, his master of arts degree there in 1895 and his bachelor of divinity degree at Western Theological Seminary in Pittsburgh in 1897. Following his ordination by Pittsburgh Presbytery in 1897, he pastored *Presbyterian Church in the U.S.A. (PCUSA) congregations in Pittsburgh (1897-1901), Hutchison, Kansas (1901-1907), and Chicago (1907-1913). While in Chicago he also taught courses in systematic theology and religious education at McCormick Theological Seminary. In 1913 Kerr returned to Pittsburgh to become the senior minister of the Shadyside Presbyterian Church.

While overseeing the many programs of one of the city's largest and most influential congregations until his retirement in 1946, Kerr became highly respected for his eloquent, well-reasoned sermons, his leadership roles in the PCUSA, his educational endeavors, his many publications and his numerous contributions to Pittsburgh. As a consequence of serving for fifteen years as president of the denomination's board of Christian education and as moderator of the general assembly in 1930, Kerr had the opportunity to preach in Presbyterian pulpits throughout the United States. Thousands of people heard his sermons, which for twenty-five years were broadcast on KDKA radio. Kerr founded and for many years led discussion groups with students at the University of Pittsburgh and Carnegie Institute of Technology. He also served as a lecturer in homiletics and worship at Western Theological Seminary.

Twenty books and hundreds of articles flowed from Kerr's pen. Many of his books were collections of sermons either for adults or for children, perhaps most notably *Design for Christian Living* (1953). His Stone Lectures at Princeton Theological Seminary were published in 1935 as *A God-Centered Faith: Studies in the Reformed Faith. Preaching in the Early Church* (1942) was based upon his Moore Lectures delivered at San Francisco Theological Seminary. He authored *A Year in the Bible,* a guide for daily Bible reading, which was widely used for four decades.

Kerr played an active role in numerous organizations that worked for civic betterment in Pittsburgh, including the Association for the Improvement of the Poor and Pittsburgh Hospital.

From 1946 until his death Kerr served as pastor emeritus of the Shadyside Church. During these years he helped to raise twenty-seven million dollars for the restoration fund of the church, chaired the Alliance of Reformed Churches and acted as the executive secretary of the Pitcairn-Crabbe Foundation, one of Pittsburgh's most important charitable trusts. A man of many talents, Kerr left his imprint on his congregation, denomination and city.

Bibliography. S. Belfour, *Centennial History of the Shadyside Presbyterian Church* (1966); D. C. Kerr, "A Brief Biographical Sketch," in *Design for Christian Living: Sermons by Hugh Thomson Kerr* (1953); J. Van Trump, "The Mountain and the City: The History of Shadyside Presbyterian Church," *Western Pennsylvania Historical Magazine* 44 (1961) 21-34; "Hugh Thomson Kerr," in F. C. Harper, *Pittsburgh of Today,* vol. 5 (1932).

G. S. Smith

Kerr, Hugh Thomson, Jr. (1909-1992). Presbyterian minister, theologian, teacher and editor. Kerr's father, Hugh Thomson *Kerr Sr., was a prominent Presbyterian minister of the first half of the twentieth century. He became the pastor of Shadyside Presbyterian Church in Pittsburgh and wrote the well-known hymn "God of Our Life Through All the Circling Years."

Born in Chicago, the younger Kerr grew up in Pittsburgh, graduated from Princeton University in 1931 and received masters' degrees from the University of Pittsburgh and Western Theological Seminary (now Pittsburgh Seminary). He studied at Tübingen University and earned his doctoral degree from the University of Edinburgh in 1936.

Kerr taught at Louisville Presbyterian Theological Seminary from 1936 to 1940, when he joined the faculty of Princeton Theological Seminary. There he became the Benjamin B. Warfield Professor of Theology in 1950. Though he retired from the faculty in 1974, he continued to offer courses at Princeton Seminary until his death.

In 1944 *Theology Today* was launched by Princeton's president, John Alexander *Mackay, as a prominent Reformed theological voice amid the turmoil of World War II. Although Mackay was initially listed as editor, Kerr was responsible for the journal from its inception. He became editor in 1951 and was active in guiding the journal until he died. Under his leadership, *Theology Today* became a barometer of twentieth-century theological changes and the most widely circulated quarterly journal of theology in the world. Kerr and *Theology Today* gradually moved from a *neo-orthodox position to a recognition of the ecumenical theological context of the late twentieth century.

As a teacher, Kerr was known for his clarity and innovations in the classroom, particularly in the use of media. He was a prolific writer and editor, ranging from a collection of John *Calvin's writings to his last work, *A Simple Gospel* (1991). He was known to millions of church members through his annual devotional manual, *A Year with the Bible,* a publication begun by his father. He served on numerous church committees and ecumenical task forces, especially ones dealing with religion and art and women's rights. He was married to Dorothy DePree. They had one son.

Bibliography. T. W. Gillespie, "Memorial: Hugh Thomson Kerr (July 1, 1909-March 27, 1992)," *Princeton Seminary Bulletin* 22 (1992) 325-32; "In Memoriam: Hugh Thomson Kerr, 1909-1992," *Theology Today* 49 (1992) 147-51; obituary, *New York Times,* March 28, 1992.

J. M. Mulder

King, John Mark (1829-1899). Presbyterian minister, theologian and educator. Born at Yetholm in the Scottish border country, King was educated at Edinburgh University (M.A., 1854), the United Presbyterian Divinity Hall and at Halle, Germany, and was nurtured in a Secession Presbyterian tradition.

King came to Canada as a United Presbyterian missionary in 1856 and was ordained in 1857. In 1863 he became pastor of Toronto's Gould Street United Presbyterian Church (cum St. James Square Presbyterian in 1878), a congregation that under his leadership grew to become one of the strongest in Canada. He was awarded the first doctor of divinity degree conferred by Knox College (1882) and was elected moderator of the general assembly (1883).

In 1883 King chose to leave his sphere of urban influence to become the first principal and professor of theology at Manitoba College, the Presbyterians' new training center in western Canada. He righted the college's perilous financial condition and began preparing ministers for church-planting tasks in the western Canadian prairies. While carrying a full load of teaching, King managed to keep abreast of theological developments elsewhere.

His theology was more derivative than creative, but King made a thoughtful, informed and influential case for the central themes of evangelical orthodoxy. A number of his essays, public lectures and sermons were published, including *Education Not Secular nor Sectarian but Religious* (1889), *The Purely Ethical Gospel Examined* (1897) and *A Critical Study of [Tennyson's] "In Memoriam"* (1898). *A Theology of Christ's Teaching* (1903), a posthumous publication of King's theology lectures, is the most extensive expression of his thought.

King's death in Winnipeg was mourned by the entire province of Manitoba. King's son-in-law, the novelist Charles *Gordon (Ralph Connor), was a leader among those of King's proteges who subsequently embraced a more liberal evangelical outlook.

BIBLIOGRAPHY. *DCB* 12; G. Harland, "John Mark King: First Principal of Manitoba College," in *Prairie Spirit,* ed. D. Butcher et al. (1985).

G. G. Scorgie

Kirk, Edward Norris (1802-1874). Congregationalist and Presbyterian evangelist and pastor. Born in New York City, Kirk graduated from the College of New Jersey (B.A., 1820) and went on to study law in New York (1820-1822). However, his conversion turned his attention to the ministry, and he returned to Princeton to study at the seminary (1822-1826).

Six years later Kirk became pastor of the Fourth Presbyterian Church in Albany, New York, a congregation organized in response to his revival messages. Within eight years, more than one thousand new members had been added. But amid this success Kirk went to Great Britain, where his protracted meetings enhanced his reputation as a polished and powerful preacher and opened the door for evangelistic campaigns in several major Eastern cities upon his return to America. His success in Boston led to the formation of Mt. Vernon Congregational Church, where he pastored from 1842 to 1871. During his long ministry there and even before, Kirk combined his evangelism with antislavery, temperance, *educational and other reform activities, personally embodying the strong links between *revivalism and social *reform within antebellum evangelicalism.

Proof that nineteenth-century revivalism was as popular in urban as in rural areas, Kirk's evangelistic preaching held great appeal for middle-class Presbyterians and Congregationalists in cities on both sides of the Atlantic Ocean. Kirk tailored the revivalism of Charles Grandison *Finney to fit the urbane tastes of his audiences in Boston, New York and London. In so doing, he made revivalism far more respectable and set the stage for the businessmen's-style evangelism of his most famous convert, Dwight L. Moody.

BIBLIOGRAPHY. *ANB* 12; R. Carwardine, *Transatlantic Revivalism: Popular Evangelicalism in Britain and America, 1790-1865* (1978); *DAB* V; *DARB;* D. O. Mears, *Edward Norris Kirk* (1877); *NCAB* 6; T. L. Smith, *Revivalism and Social Reform: American Protestantism on the Eve of the Civil War* (1957).

R. W. Pointer

Korean-American Presbyterianism. Protestant Christianity began spreading in Korea in the 1880s through the efforts of Korean converts and American missionaries. It was not too long after the arrival of American missionaries in Korea that the first significant Korean immigration to America occurred. The first ship with 101 Korean immigrants on board landed in 1903. By 1907 the Korean population in Hawaii was 7,226. It was only after the Immigration and National Act of 1965, however, that large numbers of Koreans began coming to the United States, averaging 25,000 Korean immigrants per year throughout the 1970s and 1980s.

From the beginning of the Korean immigration, there was a preponderance of Christians among those who came. The first Korean Presbyterian church in the United States was founded in Los Angeles in 1906. The large presence of Christians among Korean immigrants has continued, with one study estimating 51 percent of Korean new arrivals to be Christians.

The strong presence of Christians among Korean immigrants, as well as the uprooted first-generation immigrants' need for fellowship with other Koreans, are among the most important reasons for the central role that the church has always played in Korean-American communities. A 1979 study showed that almost 70 percent of Korean immigrants in the United States were affiliated with Korean ethnic churches. Of those who reported as church-affiliated, 52.8 percent were Presbyterian. The 1995 estimate of all Korean immigrant churches in this country is somewhere between 2,500 and 3,000, with the largest and one of the best known being the Young Nak Presbyterian Church of Los Angeles with a membership of 6,000. The greatest number of these churches are in the Los Angeles area, with an estimated 800 churches, followed by the greater New York area with about 400.

Some of the Korean immigrant congregations to which those Presbyterians belong have become part of American Presbyterian denominations. As of 1995, 297 Korean-American Presbyterian congregations are members of the *Presbyterian Church in the U.S.A. (PCUSA), and many of these ministers had previous affiliation with two of the major Presbyterian denominations in Korea: the Presbyterian Church of Korea (Tong Hap), which has a centrist Reformed theological outlook, and the Presbyterian Church of the Republic of Korea (Ki Jang), which is known as a progressive church. Another American denomination, the *Presbyterian Church in America (PCA), has 112 Korean-American congregations.

Some Korean-American Presbyterians have elected to organize their own denominations. The three major ones are the Korean Presbyterian Church in America (272 congregations) with some in Canada and Central and South America. Most of the clergy of this denomination have backgrounds very similar to that of the Korean-American clergy in the PCUSA. The other two larger Korean denominations are more conservative. The Korean-American Presbyterian Church, which draws many of its clergy from the Hap Tong tradition in Korea (associated with the present-day Chong Shin Theological University in Sa-Dang-Dong, Seoul), has 295 congregations, including churches in Canada, Central and South America and Germany. The other major Korean-Presbyterian denomination is one with the same English name as one of the above, the Korean Presbyterian Church in America, and claims more than fifty congregations, seven of which are in Canada and Central and South America. The clergy of this last denomination consist mainly of those with the Ko Shin Presbyterian background, which is associated with the former Korea Theological Seminary.

There are several other Korean Presbyterian denominational bodies in the United States. There are also many independent Korean-American Presbyterian congregations. At the same time, many Korean immigrants who were Presbyterian in Korea attend churches of other denominations in America. The denominational crossing is quite frequent among Korean immigrant Christians, because their need to belong to their own ethnic group in many cases overrides denominational distinctions.

The vast majority of Korean immigrant Presbyterians are characterized by fervent *piety and a strong commitment to the church. Their churches have a strong Bible study program throughout the church year. Worship services are usually held three times on Sundays: in the predawn hours, in the morning and again in the evening. Most churches also hold services on Wednesday evenings. The predawn prayer service is a longstanding tradition of Korean Protestant Christianity. Even if only a small number attend, it is usually deemed a necessary aspect of the church's life. Korean-American Presbyterians are also strong in their stewardship. Many Korean-American churches typically commit a significant portion of their financial resources to world mission usually by giving partial support to a Korean missionary in some part of the world. Many Korean-American churches have been able either to build or acquire their own places of worship while others resort to meeting in an American church building.

There are some ways in which Korean-American Presbyterian churches as immigrant churches in America have a special role and face unique challenges. The first has to do with the highly important social role of immigrant churches. Unlike European immigrants, Korean-Americans face a racial barrier and have difficulties in achieving a complete social and structural assimilation into mainstream America. The only community in which Korean immigrants feel accepted is in the ethnic church. While this fact makes Korean immigrant churches indispensable, it also puts a terrible burden on them. Korean immigrants come to their churches craving social recognition as well as spiritual nourishment.

Korean-American Presbyterians, as an ethnic minority group, also face a challenge to affirm their particularity on one hand and their spiritual and sociopolitical need to be open and inclusive on the other. Korean-American Presbyterian denominations that are unrelated with American denominations, therefore, face the danger of isolation from the larger church and society. But those Korean-American Presbyterians who are part of an American denomination may suffer from the lack of a meaningful participation and fellowship.

The PCUSA, for example, deals with this dilemma of minority groups by establishing ethnic caucuses or councils that are fellowship groups without any judicatory powers. In the same denomination, Korean-Americans of the entire church as well as on regional basis meet as the Korean Presbyterian Councils for fellowship and for discussion of issues of particular concern. The PCUSA, like many other American denominations, has also established the offices of Korean-American consultants who act both as resource persons for Korean-American congregations and as facilitators of the Korean-American churches' fuller participation in the life of the denomination.

Some Korean-American Presbyterians in the PCUSA have also organized their own Korean "language presbyteries" consisting only of Korean-American churches. Such ethnically particular presbyteries as well as ethnic councils are all attempts to meet the particular needs of Korean-American Presbyterians and at the same time to remain related with the larger American church and society.

Perhaps the greatest challenge facing the Korean-American Presbyterians at the end of the twentieth century has to do with the ministry to future generations. With the exception of a small group of second and later generation Korean-American adults in places like Hawaii, the Korean immigrant church is still a first-generation church consisting largely of those who were brought up in Korea and thus tend to be Korean in cultural outlook. But the younger generation is acculturated and often has little or no proficiency in its parents' language. Many Korean-American congregations have separate Sunday services in English to meet the needs of the younger generation. Some independent English-speaking Korean-American churches, including some Presbyterian, are beginning to emerge here and there. And some promising young Korean-American Presbyterian men and women are studying at various seminaries for English-speaking Korean-American ministries of the future.

Bibliography. W. M. Hurh and K. C. Kim, *Korean Immigrants in America* (1984); S. H. Lee and J. V. Moore, eds., *Korean-American Ministry* (1993).

S. H. Lee

Kuiper, Rienk Bouke (1886-1966). *Christian Reformed and *Orthodox Presbyterian pastor, professor and author. Born in a country manse in the province of Groningen, the Netherlands, Kuiper emigrated with his family to the United States in 1891 and was reared in Grand Haven, Michigan, and Chicago. He was educated at the University of Chicago (B.A., 1907), Indiana University (M.A., 1908), Calvin Theological Seminary (1908-1911) and Princeton Theological Seminary (B.D., 1912). Kuiper then spent eighteen years as a pastor in western Michigan, mostly in Christian Reformed congregations in Grand Rapids. His progressive spirit, unquestioned orthodoxy and able leadership brought him prominence in denominational affairs, capped by his appointment to the presidency of Calvin College in 1930.

Kuiper actively supported the conservatives in the Presbyterian controversies of the 1920s and in 1933 accepted a professorship in practical theology at Westminster Theological Seminary. He served there until 1952, a voice for the classic Reformed stance in Orthodox Presbyterian Church (OPC) affairs and, after 1936, as head of the seminary faculty. In 1953 he took on his third presidency, this time of Calvin Seminary. After smoothing the wake of controversy there, he retired in 1956.

Although he was a gifted teacher and administrator, Kuiper gained greatest renown as a powerful preacher and uncompromising advocate of traditional Reformed doctrine. He wrote ten books, often in a semipopular vein, that registered significantly in his denomination's debates. He died at Grand Rapids.

Bibliography. J. D. Bratt, *Dutch Calvinism in Modern America: A History of a Conservative Subculture* (1984); E. Heerema, *R. B.: A Prophet of the Lord* (1986).

J. D. Bratt

Kuizenga, John E. (1876-1949). *Dutch Reformed pastor and theologian. Born in Muskegon, Michigan, Kuizenga grew up in the conservative wing of the *Reformed Church in America (RCA) and attended one of its institutions, Hope College, receiving a bachelor of arts degree in 1899. Upon graduating he began his long teaching career, first at Northwestern Classical Academy in Iowa (1900-1903), where he taught English. During this time he was married in 1901 to Anna J. Mulder, who died in 1939. Kuizenga then taught at Western Theological Seminary in Holland, Michigan, for one year prior to his ordination as a minister and taking a call to a congregation in Graafschap, Michigan.

In 1906 Kuizenga returned to the classroom, this time at his alma mater, and would stay there until 1915. While teaching at Hope College Kuizenga studied at the University of Michigan, completing a master of arts degree in philosophy, and also at the University of Chicago Divinity School. From 1916 to 1930 he taught at Western Theological Seminary, first practical theology (1916-1928) and then systematic theology (1928-1930). In 1924 Kuizenga added to his duties the presidency of the seminary. He received an honorary doctorate in divinity from Hope in 1916. In 1924 he was elected president of the general synod of the RCA. In response to administrative changes and the departure of conservatives to found Westminster Theological Seminary, Princeton Theological Seminary appointed Kuizenga in 1930 to teach apologetics and ethics. He did so until 1940, when he became the Charles Hodge Professor of Systematic Theology. After the death of his first wife, Kuizenga was married in 1944 to Elsie C. Foster. Upon his retirement in 1947 he returned to his home in western Michigan, where he taught in an emeritus capacity at Hope College for the last two years of his life. Kuizenga had one daughter by each of his wives.

Though his writings were sparse, Kuizenga provided astute leadership both to the RCA and to Princeton Theological Seminary by insisting on the verities of Reformed orthodoxy even as those truths were being questioned within Reformed and Presbyterian churches.

Bibliography. "Faculty Memorial Minutes," *Princeton Seminary Bulletin* 43 (1949) 46-47.

D. G. Hart and H. Brinks

Kuyper, Abraham (1837-1920).† Dutch Calvinist theologian and statesman. Born in Maassluis, the Netherlands, Kuyper was brought up in an orthodox Reformed household, his father being a minister in the Reformed Church. A brilliant student, Kuyper took both his undergraduate and doctoral degrees in theology at Leyden (1855-1862), where he imbibed the growing liberalism of mid-nineteenth-century Europe. His encounter with the staunchly conservative parishioners of his first country church drove him back to study the sixteenth-century Reformers, which led him to return to the confessional roots of his Reformed heritage. In 1870 he was called to a large Amsterdam congregation, where he rallied the conservative forces that had been forming in the state church. Two years later he became editor of the daily newspaper *De Standaard,* which enmeshed him in the political front of the growing Dutch neo-Calvinist movement (1875-1925).

As founder and leader of this wide-ranging movement, Kuyper worked to mobilize the conservative Reformed sector of the Dutch population against the theological and cultural *modernism ascendant at the time. This required the development of a Calvinistic world-and-life view, which Kuyper advanced through his voluminous writings; and of a full set of separate institutions through which the Reformed could take forceful action.

After becoming a member of the Dutch parliament in 1873, Kuyper collapsed beneath the strain of his hectic schedule. Reducing his involvements, he directed his prodigious energy toward the foundation and organization of three institutions: the Antirevolutionary political party (1877), a Christian school association (1878) and the Free University of Amsterdam (1879). The conservative *Calvinism of the movement caused tension and eventually a split in the National Reformed *(Hervormde)* Church in 1886, and Kuyper and his followers eventually merged with an older secession group to form the Gereformeerde Kerken in 1892. Due to its institutional breadth, the neo-Calvinist movement spread its influence throughout society. Kuyper was even influential in the foundation of a Calvinistic labor union. But the pinnacle of the political success of the neo-Calvinists was in Kuyper's term as prime minister of the Netherlands from 1901 to 1905.

Kuyper's influence in North America has descended chiefly along Dutch immigrant lines, especially those connected with the *Christian Reformed Church (CRC), but has been negligible among the wider spectrum of evangelicals. In the United States the strategy of separate institutions went forward only in the *educational realm, but there it has produced a full system of Christian schools and concerted leadership in Christian scholarship nationwide. Kuyper's Canadian descendants have had some success as well in labor and politics. Kuyper's legacy consists chiefly in a *presuppositional approach to philosophy and apologetics and in the drive to engage every domain of society and culture from a distinctly Christian point of view. Cultural analysis accordingly aims at uncovering the worldview behind a movement or a text, while social engagement proceeds under a principled pluralism toward a biblical concept of justice, out of the conviction that Christian models in both realms offer the best solution to modern problems.

See also DUTCH CALVINISM.

BIBLIOGRAPHY. J. D. Bratt, *Dutch Calvinism in Modern America: A History of a Conservative Subculture* (1984); P. S. Heslam, *Creating a Christian Worldview* (1998); D. W. Jellema, "Abraham Kuyper's Attack on Liberalism," *Review of Politics* 19 (1957) 472-85; A. Kuyper, *Lectures on Calvinism* (1898); idem, *A Centennial Anthology,* ed. J. D. Bratt (1998).

J. D. Bratt

Kyle, Melvin Grove (1858-1933).† Presbyterian *fundamentalist educator and biblical archaeologist. Born in Cadiz, Ohio, Kyle graduated from Muskingum College (1881) and Allegheny Theological Seminary (1885) before entering the United Presbyterian ministry. In 1908 Kyle began his long tenure as professor of biblical archaeology (1908-1921) and then president (1921-1929) at Xenia Theological Seminary, located at Xenia, Ohio, and later at St. Louis, Missouri. Kyle brought the seminary into national prominence by his archaeological research, writing and training of scores of Presbyterian pastors. During this most productive period of his life Kyle helped to found the Bible League of North America, was a prominent speaker on the Winona Bible Conference circuit, was active in establishing the League of Evangelical Students (a forerunner of InterVarsity Christian Fellowship) and encouraged the support of fundamentalist missions under the umbrella of the Bible Union.

Following the lead of his friend and fellow archaeologist George F. Wright, Kyle edited (1922-1933) the respected theological journal *Bibliotheca Sacra* just prior to its 1934 removal to the new dispensationalist seminary in Dallas, Texas (later Dallas Theological Seminary). After overseeing the merger of Xenia and Pittsburgh theological seminaries in 1929, he retired and became a visiting lecturer in archaeology at Dallas. Kyle was also known for his books and articles, most notably for his contribution to *The Fundamentals* (1910), entitled "The Recent Testimony of Archaeology to the Scriptures." He asserted that archaeology is "exactly in harmony" with the biblical narrative and believed that the eventual collation of archaeological evidences would discredit Julius Wellhausen's documentary hypothesis and all higher criticism. D. M. Strong

L

Leiper, Henry Smith (1891-1975).† Presbyterian missionary and ecumenist. Born in Belmar, New Jersey, Leiper was educated at Amherst College, Columbia University and Union Theological Seminary in New York. During his student days he became involved with the Student Volunteer Movement and committed himself to go into *mission work. He was ordained by the *Presbyterian Church in the U.S.A. (PCUSA) in 1915 as an assistant pastor in a Presbyterian church for a short while, though he later became a Congregationalist (1922). After doing relief work in Siberia, Leiper served as a missionary with the American Board of Commissioners of Foreign Missions in China (1918-1922) and became assistant secretary of the ABCFM upon his return to the United States. He was also a pastor in Paris to Americans living abroad (1932).

Leiper's interests led him to increasing involvement in national and world ecumenical agencies. From his early involvement as associate secretary of the Congregational National Commission on Missions (1923-1930), he began to branch out into broader ecumenical endeavors. He was foreign secretary of the Federal Council of Churches (1930-1948) and associate general secretary of the World Council of Churches (1938-1952), returning to denominational affairs as executive secretary of the Missions Council of the Congregational Christian Churches (1952-1959), though continuing to remain active in the international field. Leiper wrote *World Chaos or World Christianity* (1938) and edited a survey of the contemporary state of the church entitled *Christianity Today* (1947). He also wrote on racism, nationalism and church-state relations, issues that came to the fore through his involvement with Dietrich Bonhoeffer and the Confessing Church in Germany.

Bibliography. W. J. Schmidt, *What Kind of a Man? The Life of Henry Smith Leiper* (1986).

J. M. Smylie

Leitch, Addison H. (1909-1973). United Presbyterian college and seminary professor and seminary president. Born in Ben Avon, Pennsylvania, he received the bachelor of arts degree from Muskingum College in 1931, the bachelor of theology and master of theology degrees from Pittsburgh-Xenia Seminary, and the doctoral degree from Cambridge University. For the next several years he taught at Assiut College in Egypt and Pikeville and Grove City colleges in the United States. From 1946 to 1955 he served Pittsburgh-Xenia Seminary, first as professor of philosophy of religion and religious education, then in the chair of systematic theology. He was called to the presidency of the seminary in 1955.

The first president of the seminary with an earned rather than honorary doctorate, Leitch directed the seminary more forcefully than ever before into the world of university *education. An excellent publicist, he masterfully set forth the claims of the seminary and church colleges in denominational publications. His administration saw the liquidation of all debts incurred in the relocation of the seminary from Allegheny to East Liberty.

Feeling growing discomfort with the plans for merger of Pittsburgh-Xenia and Western theological seminaries, he resigned as president in 1959, remaining on staff until 1961. He then served for several years as director of church relations at Tarkio College.

Leitch's ability to transmit his views of the church clearly to its constituencies and his grasp of the essence of issue tensions and conflicts in ministerial education made him one of the great spokesmen for the mission of the church in mid-twentieth-century America.

Bibliography. R. L. Kelley Jr., "Pittsburgh-Xenia Seminary," in *Ever a Frontier: The Bicentennial History of the Pittsburgh Theological Seminary*, ed. J. A. Walther (1994); A. H. Leitch, *Beginnings in Theology* (1957); idem, *Interpreting Basic Theology* (1961).

W. L. Fisk

Liturgy. *See* WORSHIP, PRESBYTERIANS AND.

Livingston, John Henry (1746-1825). *Dutch Reformed pastor and educator. Born in Poughkeepsie, New York, into the aristocratic Livingston clan, he graduated from Yale (B.A., 1762) and briefly studied law (1762-1764) before illness precipitated his conversion and call to the ministry in the Reformed Dutch church. Livingston studied theology at the University of Utrecht (S.T.D., 1770) and was licensed and ordained by the Classis of Amsterdam. He returned to America in 1770 as pastor of the Dutch Reformed Church of New York City, a charge he served for forty years.

Livingston's lineage, education and irenicism equipped him to assume leadership in the struggling Reformed Dutch denomination. In 1772 he repaired the bitter division between the church's coetus and conferentie parties, a mid-eighteenth-century schism rooted in the controversy over whether the American church should become self-sufficient or remain dependent upon Holland. Following the dislocation of the American *Revolution (a patriot, Livingston fled New York during British occupation), he resumed his pastorate and decisively influenced the formation of an independent Reformed Dutch Church in America by compiling its constitution (published 1793), preparing several hymnbooks and educating students for ministry.

With his 1784 appointment as professor of theology by the Classis of Amsterdam, Livingston became the first theological educator in America under the direct aegis of a denomination. In the next forty years, Livingston prepared 120 men for the ministry, first as an independent professor in New York and Long Island and then, following the merger of his theological school with Queen's College (now Rutgers University), as president and professor of theology from 1810 to 1825. Livingston is recognized as the father of the Reformed Dutch Church in America.

BIBLIOGRAPHY. *AAP* 9; *ANB* 13; *DAB* VI; *DARB*; A. Gunn, *Memoirs of the Reverend John H. Livingston* (1829). D. W. Kling

Livingston, William (1723-1790). Presbyterian layman, lawyer and governor. Born in Albany, New York, William was the son of Philip, second lord of Livingston manor. He graduated from Yale (B.A., 1741) and then went to New York, where he apprenticed in law and affiliated with the Presbyterian Church. Put off by the extremes of *Old Side and *New Side Presbyterianism (at Yale, he had felt the same about Old and New Lights), Livingston embraced a noncreedal, inclusive Christianity. Following his admittance to the bar in 1748, he joined forces with two other lawyers, William Smith Jr. and John M. Scott, and formed the powerful triumvirate of New York politics against the equally powerful De Lancey party.

A prolific writer and polemicist, Livingston initiated the trio's publication of *The Independent Reflector* (1752-1753), New York's first magazine and the earliest expression of radical Whig ideas by American writers. Thus, with a strong aversion to hierarchy and centralized authority of any kind, Livingston attacked clerical pretensions in general and Anglicans in particular who sought to establish King's College (Columbia) as an arm of the Church of England. In this context he championed religious pluralism as a means of assuring religious freedom, even calling for the complete separation of church from state. Livingston's expressions of hostility to clerical power signaled a trend of laicization that would profoundly shape American religion.

In 1772 Livingston retired to New Jersey, but he was soon drawn into the whirl of public events surrounding the *Revolution. Rising to positions of leadership, Livingston attended the Continental Congresses, commanded the New Jersey militia and served as governor (1776-1790).

BIBLIOGRAPHY. *ANB* 13; *DAB* VI; *NCAB* 5; J. Mulder, "William Livingston: Propagandist Against Episcopacy," *JPH* 54 (1976) 83-104.

D. W. Kling

Long, George A. (1884-1969). *United Presbyterian (UPCNA) pastor and seminary president. Born at Greenville, Pennsylvania, he received the bachelor of arts degree from Westminster College in 1909 and graduated from Pittsburgh Theological Seminary in 1912. He then pastored Second United Presbyterian Church, Allegheny (1912-1921), and Homewood church in Pittsburgh (1921-1942) before being called to the presidency of Pittsburgh-Xenia Seminary in 1943, where he remained until his retirement in 1955.

Long's pastorates were marked by striking growth in the number of communicants. As an active member of the board of directors of Pittsburgh-Xenia Seminary he obtained a strong grasp of the administrative policies of the seminary between 1930 and 1943. As president he directed numerous changes, most prominent of which were the reopening of the graduate department, a new emphasis on continuing education, including the institution of summer workshops for clergy in the church colleges, and the creation of a Christian education department directed toward enlarging the role of women in the church.

Widely credited with being a good administrator, Long presided over the planning for the relocation of the seminary from the Allegheny site in Pittsburgh's north side to a new and less crowded site in East Liberty. Here Long directed the building of commodious and attractive quarters. The new campus was completed in 1954, and his last year as president was the first year the new buildings were occupied.

Bibliography. R. L. Kelley Jr., "Pittsburgh-Xenia Seminary," in *Ever a Frontier: The Bicentennial History of the Pittsburgh Theological Seminary,* ed. J. A. Walther (1994). W. L. Fisk

Lord's Supper. *See* SACRAMENTS, PRESBYTERIANS AND THE.

Lovejoy, Elijah Parish (1802-1837). Presbyterian minister and *abolitionist martyr. Born in Albion, Maine, into a Congregational minister's family of *Puritan heritage, Lovejoy attended Waterville (now Colby) College and then journeyed west to teach school in Missouri. Settling in St. Louis in 1827, he bought into and began editing a local newspaper.

The seeds of faith and his later radical abolitionism were planted when Lovejoy experienced conversion under the preaching of an antislavery evangelist, David Nelson. Deciding to enter the ministry, Lovejoy attended Princeton Seminary and then returned to St. Louis, where he was called to edit a Presbyterian newspaper. Lovejoy initially devoted far more space to attacking Roman Catholics, Baptists and Campbellites than slaveholders.

Gradually Lovejoy grew convinced of the evils of slavery and moved toward the radical position of immediate abolition. Increasingly unwelcome in St. Louis, he moved his paper to Alton, Illinois, in 1836. There he again met with hostility. Mobs destroyed his press on three occasions, and Lovejoy, who had defended a black man burned at the stake by a mob, was accused by a judge of inciting slaves to revolt. Ever more outspoken in his condemnation of slavery, he portrayed a host of slaveholders' abuses and accused them of raping slave women as a matter of course. He was finally shot down in an encounter between his small band of followers and a mob seeking to burn down his warehouse. An early and well-publicized abolitionist martyr, Lovejoy in his death played a notable role in galvanizing antislavery sentiment.

Bibliography. *ANB* 14; *DAB* VI; M. L. Dillon, *Elijah P. Lovejoy, Abolitionist Editor* (1961); F. H. Dugan, "An Illinois Martyrdom," *Papers in Illinois History and Transactions* (1938); J. C. Lovejoy, *Memoir of the Reverend Elijah P. Lovejoy* (1970).

S. E. Berk

M

Macartney, Clarence Edward Noble (1879-1957).† Presbyterian minister. Coming from a line of Scottish Covenanters, Macartney entered the Presbyterian ministry after earning degrees from the University of Wisconsin, Princeton University and Princeton Theological Seminary. He served churches in Paterson, New Jersey (1905-1914), Philadelphia (1914-1927) and Pittsburgh (1927-1953). In 1925 he declined an appointment to the chair of apologetics at Princeton Seminary.

In 1922 Macartney led the conservative response to Harry Emerson *Fosdick's famous sermon "Shall the Fundamentalists Win?" and in 1924 won election as moderator of the general assembly. A steadfast opponent of liberal theology, he supported the formation of Westminster Theological Seminary after the Princeton reorganization in 1929. In the 1930s, when his most militant colleagues seceded, Macartney chose to maintain a conservative witness within the denomination, believing that he could have more impact in a larger denomination.

True to the old Princeton tradition, Macartney preached a blend of Reformed confessionalism and Common-Sense realism, emphasizing the traditional *Calvinism of the *Westminster standards. Agreeing with J. Gresham *Machen, he argued that liberalism contradicted the truth of Christianity, creating a new religion in its place. He wrote fifty-seven books, most of which were collections of sermons, and traveled widely at home and abroad. Concerned with the moral decline of family and society, he was a vocal opponent of sabbath desecration, divorce, liquor and birth control. Macartney was a popular lecturer and preacher at colleges and seminaries.

BIBLIOGRAPHY. *ANB* 14; B. J. Longfield, *The Presbyterian Controversy: Fundamentalists, Modernists, and Moderates* (1991); C. E. Macartney, *The Making of a Minister: The Autobiography of Clarence E. Macartney,* ed. J. C. Henry (1961); C. A. Russell, *Voices of American Fundamentalism: Seven Biographical Studies* (1976). B. J. Longfield

MacGregor, James Drummond (1759-1830).† Presbyterian missionary. MacGregor was raised in St. Fillans, County of Perthshire, Scotland, in a strict Anti-Burgher secessionist Presbyterian family. He studied classics and theology at Edinburgh University and was ordained by the Associate Presbytery of Glasgow. In 1786 he accepted a call to aid the struggling Highland Scottish Presbyterians of Nova Scotia and emigrated almost immediately. MacGregor settled at Pictou; using that as his home base, he itinerated on numerous missionary trips. Thus he was the first Presbyterian minister to visit Prince Edward Island (1791), the Miramichi area of New Brunswick (1797) and Cape Breton Island (1798). Later journeys solidified this earlier Presbyterian work throughout the region.

The sole Anti-Burgher minister in Canada for nine years, MacGregor was briefly associated with the Burgher Presbytery of Truro. Finally the parent body in Scotland heeded his requests for assistance and sent Duncan Ross. The two men formed the Associate Presbytery of Nova Scotia in 1795, and, after considerable growth, the united secessionist Presbyterian Synod of Nova Scotia in 1817, an independent judicatory autonomous of Scotland. MacGregor has consequently been dubbed the father of Presbyterianism in the Maritimes. His indefatigable labors for forty-five years under harsh conditions earned him one of the first doctor of divinity degrees in British North America. Besides his ecclesiastical work, MacGregor published a volume of sacred poems in Gaelic, denounced slavery and intemperance, encouraged improved agricultural and health-care methods and assisted Thomas *McCulloch in the formation of Pictou Academy.

BIBLIOGRAPHY. *DCB* 6; G. Patterson, *Memoir of the Reverend James MacGregor, D.D.* (1859).

D. M. Strong

Machen, J(ohn) Gresham (1881-1937).‡ Presbyterian clergyman, New Testament scholar and educator. Born the second of three sons to a prominent Baltimore lawyer, Machen was reared in an *Old School Presbyterian home of genteel tastes. Remaining in Baltimore for his undergraduate education, Machen majored in classics at Johns Hopkins University and graduated in 1901. He stayed at Hopkins for another year to undertake graduate study with the renowned American classicist Basil L. Gildersleeve.

Machen enrolled at Princeton Theological Seminary the following year. At Princeton he earned a master's degree in philosophy (1904) from the university while completing the requirements for the bachelor of divinity degree at the seminary (1905). There Machen was greatly influenced by Benjamin Breckinridge *Warfield. Machen's interests in Greek literature, however, did not subside. In the fall of 1905, Machen left to study at the German universities in Marburg and Göttingen. One year later he returned to Princeton to become an instructor in the New Testament department (1906-1914), a position he held until his ordination, at which time he became assistant professor.

Aside from some early studies of the birth narratives in the Gospels, the apostle Paul absorbed most of Machen's scholarly interests as a young man. After a year of service in the Young Men's Christian Association during World War I, he devoted three years of research to *The Origin of Paul's Religion* (1921), a work intended to answer critics in establishing the continuity between Jesus and Paul. From his study of Paul, Machen returned to his early interest in the New Testament accounts of Christ's birth, with the publication of *The Virgin Birth of Christ* (1930). These studies were marked by the careful conservative scholarship that had typified the Princeton tradition.

Machen was best known for his participation in the *fundamentalist-modernist controversy. In *Christianity and Liberalism* (1923) Machen argued that liberalism and historic Christianity are two distinct religions. The logic of Machen's opposition to liberalism led to confrontation both within Princeton Seminary and in the *Presbyterian Church in the U.S.A. (PCUSA). In 1929, when Princeton Seminary was reorganized to ensure a more inclusive theological spectrum, Machen and a core of conservative faculty members withdrew from Princeton to found Westminster Theological Seminary at Philadelphia.

With increasing suspicion of liberalism on the *mission field, Machen led other conservative Presbyterians in the formation of the Independent Board for Presbyterian Foreign Missions in 1933. When the general assembly proscribed this board in 1934, Machen refused to sever his connections with the board and was tried and suspended from ministry in the Presbyterian church in 1935. After appealing the verdict in 1936, Machen played a central role in founding a new denomination, the Presbyterian Church of America (later the *Orthodox Presbyterian Church [OPC]). On a trip to Bismarck, North Dakota, to rally support for the new denomination, Machen contracted pneumonia and died.

Bibliography. *ANB* 14; *DAB* 2; *DARB;* D. G. Hart, *Defending the Faith: J. Gresham Machen and the Crisis of Conservative Protestantism and Modern America* (1994); G. M. Marsden, "J. Gresham Machen, History and Truth," *WTJ* 42 (1979) 157-75; W. S. Reid, "J. Gresham Machen," in *Reformed Theology in America,* ed. D. F. Wells (1985); C. A. Russell, *Voices of American Fundamentalism: Seven Biographical Studies* (1976); N. B. Stonehouse, *J. Gresham Machen: A Biographical Memoir* (1954).

D. G. Hart

Mackay, John Alexander (1889-1983). Presbyterian minister, ecumenist and *educator. Born in Inverness, Scotland, Mackay studied at the University of Aberdeen (M.A., 1912) and then traveled to America, where he attended Princeton Theological Seminary (B.D., 1915). The following year he studied at the University of Madrid, Spain, where he came under the influence of the great mystic and philosopher Miguel de Unamuno.

In 1916 Mackay was ordained a minister of the Free Church of Scotland and soon appointed an educational missionary by that church and sent to Lima, Peru, where he founded the Anglo-Peruvian College and served as its principal (1916-1925). From 1925 until 1932 Mackay served as a writer and evangelist for the South American Federation of the Young Men's Christian Association with occasional posts in Uruguay and Mexico. In 1932 he returned to the United States to be secretary for the Latin American division of the board of foreign missions of the *Presbyterian Church in the U.S.A. (PCUSA). A pioneer in the ecumenical movement, Mackay was a central figure in founding the World Council of Churches and chairman of the Joint Committee of the World Council of Churches and the International Missionary Council (1948-1954).

In 1936 Mackay became president of Princeton Theological Seminary, where he served until 1959. At Princeton he was able to restore stability to a faculty that had recently undergone a struggle over *fundamentalism and the departure of the conservative element that formed Westminster Theological Seminary in 1929. During his years at Princeton, Mackay founded the theological quarterly *Theology Today* (1944), for which he served as editor from 1944 to 1951. He also served as moderator of the general assembly of the PCUSA (1953) and president of World Presbyterian Alliance (1954-1959).

Mackay authored several books, some of which were written in Spanish. His study of the spiritual history of Spain and Latin America was translated into English as *The Other Spanish Christ* (1933). Other publications included *A Preface to Christian Theology* (1941), *God's Order* (1953) and *Ecumenics: The Science of the Church Universal* (1964).

BIBLIOGRAPHY. *ANB* 14; *The Annual Obituary 1983* (1984); E. J. Jurji, ed., *The Ecumenical Era in Church and Society* (1959). D. Macleod

Mackie (Macky), Josias (John) (?-1716).† Presbyterian minister. Mackie was one of the first Presbyterian clergy to come to America, but little is known of his early life except that he originated from St. Johnstone, County Donegal, Ireland, the son of Patrick Mackie. He evidently had a classical education, since it is known that his library was particularly well-stocked with Greek and Latin works for someone in the American wilderness.

Mackie may have immigrated as early as 1684; he was in Virginia by 1692. In that latter year it is recorded that he received permission from the commonwealth to preach at certain designated places. The locations Mackie selected to conduct Presbyterian worship were along the Elizabeth River in Norfolk and Princess Anne counties, so far from the Presbytery of Philadelphia that they remained practically independent. As the pastor of these struggling dissenting churches, Mackie was probably the successor of Francis *Makemie, the early Presbyterian pioneer. Also following Makemie, there are strong indications that Mackie was employed as a planter and merchant in order to supplement his meager resources as a pastor. He owned a substantial amount of land, and his will indicates that he maintained a fair amount of commerce. Due to the long distance from any other Presbyterian support, Mackie's work was difficult, and by 1712 the Presbytery of Philadelphia, the nearest judicatory, reported that he was laboring under "melancholy circumstances." Little is known about the circumstances of his death.

BIBLIOGRAPHY. *AAP* 3. D. M. Strong

Mackinnon, Clarence D. (1868-1937). Canadian Presbyterian minister and educator. Born in Hopewell, Pictou County, Nova Scotia, where his father was a Presbyterian minister, Mackinnon was educated in Scotland, first at George Watson's College and afterward at the University and New College, Edinburgh. At the university he imbibed the evolutionary thinking of John George Romanes, and at New College he came under the influence of Marcus Dods and A. B. Davidson. He was also influenced by Henry Drummond. In all this Mackinnon was fairly typical of a significant group of Canadian Presbyterian progressives who exercised increasing influence within the Presbyterian Church of Canada. Mackinnon was ordained a minister in the Presbyterian Church of Canada in 1892 and served a number of congregations in Nova Scotia and Manitoba before succeeding Robert *Falconer as principal of Presbyterian College, Halifax (later renamed Pine Hill Divinity School) in 1909. He served as chaplain during World War I and took an active part in the establishment of the Khaki University. He was a strong supporter of the church union movement that resulted in the formation of the United Church of Canada in 1925, and he continued as principal of its theological seminary at Halifax (Pine Hill) until his death.

BIBLIOGRAPHY. *The Canadian Who's Who, 1936-1937*; N. K. Clifford, *The Resistance to Church Union in Canada, 1904-1939* (1985); B. J. Fraser, *The Social Uplifters: Presbyterian Progressives and the Social Gospel in Canada, 1875-1915* (1988); C. D. Mackinnon, *Reminiscences* (1938).

R. W. Vaudry

MacLaren, William (1828-1909). Presbyterian minister, theologian and educator. Regarded by some as the finest systematic theologian Canada ever produced before the late twentieth century, MacLaren was born and reared in eastern Ontario among Free Church Presbyterians. He received his early education in Ottawa and Toronto before attending the Free Church's Knox College in Toronto for both his arts and theological education. He was ordained in the Free Church in 1853 and spent the next twenty years ministering to congregations in Ontario and, briefly, in Boston, Massachusetts. In 1873 he was appointed to Knox College, where he remained until his retirement in 1908, serving as professor of systematic theology and later as principal. MacLaren was also an active churchman outside the classroom. He served for more than fifteen years as convener of the Presbyterian Church's committee on foreign missions and in 1884 was elected moderator of the general assembly. He was also involved with the American Bible League, serving on the editorial board of the *Bible Student and Teacher.*

MacLaren's appointment to Knox College came at a critical juncture in the history of *Canadian Presbyterianism. In 1875 the four branches of Canadian Presbyterianism joined to form the national communion, the *Presbyterian Church of Canada. At the same time the winds of theological and philosophical change were beginning to be felt, both in the general culture and in the Presbyterian church. A new generation of Presbyterian progressives, accommodating to evolutionary thinking, idealism and higher criticism, were making their presence known in the church. MacLaren, however, represents an older, more conservative, less accommodating, more confrontationist tradition within the Presbyterian church. He was a confessionalist who was determined in his opposition to organic union with the Methodist and Congregationalist churches (which occurred in 1925 with the formation of the United Church of Canada). MacLaren was also one of the principal Canadian exponents of the *Princeton theology, commonly associated with Charles *Hodge and Benjamin Breckinridge *Warfield.

Bibliography. N. K. Clifford, *The Resistance to Church Union in Canada, 1904-1939* (1985); B. J. Fraser, *The Social Uplifters: Presbyterian Progressives and the Social Gospel in Canada, 1875-1915* (1988); R. W. Vaudry, "Canadian Presbyterians and Princeton Seminary, 1850-1900," in *The Burning Bush and a Few Acres of Snow: The Presbyterian Contribution to Christian Life and Culture,* ed. W. Klempa (1994).

R. W. Vaudry

Makemie, Francis (1658-1708). Presbyterian missionary, apologist and founder. Often acknowledged as the father of American Presbyterianism, Makemie was born in County Donegal, Ireland, and educated at the University of Glasgow because Trinity College, Dublin, was closed to dissenters. He was ordained in Ulster as a missionary by the Irish Presbytery of Laggan in 1682 and migrated to Maryland the following year. He immediately began a far-ranging career as an itinerant evangelist in North Carolina, Virginia and Maryland, including a two-year stint in Barbados (1696-1698). Makemie returned to Virginia in 1699, received a license to preach and settled in Accomack County, where he operated a mercantile business, his wife's inheritance. This business supported his preaching forays.

Makemie wrote a catechism, no longer extant, in defense of *Calvinistic doctrines and the *Westminster standards. When George Keith, the Quaker (and, later, Anglican) missionary, challenged that apology, Makemie issued a vigorous defense, *An Answer to Keith's Libel,* in which he called Keith "a most Arrogant Spirit" and attacked Quakers and "Papists." Makemie's rejoinder, published in Boston in 1694, won recognition and praise from Increase Mather. After organizing various congregations in the Chesapeake region, Makemie turned his efforts to the formation of the Presbytery of Philadelphia in 1706, the first such presbytery in America, which promptly named him moderator and thereby secured his place in history as father of American Presbyterianism.

Makemie can also claim a role in the evolution of religious liberty in America. In 1707 Edward Hyde, Viscount Cornbury, the transvestite governor of New York, imprisoned Makemie and his colleague John Hampden for preaching without a civil license, a tactic that Cornbury employed on various occasions as a means of promoting the Church of England in the colony. Hampden was soon released, but Makemie, labeled a "Disturber of Governments" by Cornbury, spent six weeks in jail and was brought to trial. Although he prevailed in court by demonstrating his compliance with the Act of Toleration, Makemie was assessed court costs as well as the costs of the prosecution. After his acquittal, Makemie publicized his ordeal and argued for religious toleration in *A Narrative of a New and Unusual Imprisonment of Two Presbyterian Ministers and Prosecution of Mr. Francis Makemie.* The case embarrassed Cornbury, contributed to his recall and helped to shape the arguments for religious liberty in America.

Bibliography. *AAP* 3; *ANB* 14; R. Balmer and J. R. Fitzmier, *The Presbyterians* (1993); L. P. Bowen, *The Days of Makemie* (1885); *DAB* XII; *DARB; NCAB* 11; I. M. Page, *The Life Story of Reverend Francis Makemie* (1938); *SH* 7.

R. Balmer

Marquis, David Calhoun (1834-1912). Presbyterian minister and theologian. Born in Lawrence County, Pennsylvania, he was educated at Jefferson College, Canonsburg, Pennsylvania (A.B., 1857) and Western (Pittsburgh) Theological Seminary, Pennsylvania, and Presbyterian Theological Seminary of the Northwest (McCormick), Chicago (B.D., 1863). Marquis pastored Presbyterian churches in Decatur, Illinois (1863-1866), Chicago (1866-1871), Baltimore (1871-1878) and St. Louis (1878-1883). After declining twice, he accepted a call as professor of New Testament literature and exegesis at his seminary alma mater, McCormick Theological Seminary, in 1883.

In the struggle for denominational leadership after the Civil War, Marquis used his pulpit to oppose the *New School theology and social agenda. As a member of the seminary's board of directors (1867-1871) he fought theological innovation within the Chicago seminary, which was renamed after its Presbyterian benefactor, Cyrus Hall *McCormick, with whom Marquis shared conservative convictions. Marquis edited McCormick's submissions in a vituperative war of letters in the *Northwestern Presbyterian* after the appointment of Willis Lord, a New Schooler, to the chair of theology in 1867.

Marquis was among three professors called in 1881 as part of the seminary's reorganization designed to solve the seminary's financial and theological instability. His advocacy of traditional views such as verbal inspiration helped postpone until the 1920s the seminary's drift to a more liberal position. Marquis served as moderator of the Presbyterian general assembly in 1886. He retired from his duties in 1908.

BIBLIOGRAPHY. L. A. Loetscher, *The Broadening Church: A Study of Theological Issues in the Presbyterian Church Since 1869* (1954); W. T. Hutchinson, *Cyrus Hall McCormick*, 2 (1935).

W. A. Hoffecker

Marshall, Catherine Wood (1914-1983). Presbyterian writer. Born in Johnson City, Tennessee, Marshall grew up in Presbyterian manses in Canton, Mississippi, and Keyser, West Virginia. She graduated from Agnes Scott College in 1936. While in college she met Peter *Marshall, twelve years her senior and pastor of Westminster Presbyterian Church in Atlanta. They were married on November 4, 1936, and moved to Washington, D.C., where he became pastor of New York Avenue Presbyterian Church and chaplain of the United States Senate. They had one son, Peter John.

From March 1943 to the summer of 1945 Catherine was bedridden with tuberculosis; she considered her disease spiritual as well as physical. When Peter died abruptly of a heart attack at the age of forty-six in January 1949, Catherine collected his sermons and prayers into *Mr. Jones, Meet the Master*, which became an instant bestseller. In 1951 she published a biography of her late husband entitled *A Man Called Peter: The Story of Peter Marshall*. The book was three years on the bestseller list and was made into a successful movie in 1955. Her other books included *To Live Again* (1957); *Beyond Ourselves* (1961); a novel, *Christy* (1967); *Something More* (1974); *Adventures in Prayer* (1975); and *The Helper* (1978). On November 14, 1959, she married Leonard E. LeSourd, executive editor of *Guideposts* magazine, and became an editor of the magazine herself in 1961. Together they published Chosen Books. She died March 18, 1983.

BIBLIOGRAPHY. *ANB* 14; C. Marshall, *Meeting God at Every Turn* (1980). N. A. Hardesty

Marshall, Peter (1902-1949).† Presbyterian minister and chaplain of the United States Senate. Born in Coatbridge, Scotland, Marshall studied in Coatbridge Technical School and Mining College (1916-1921) and was a machine operator and foreman in a tube mill in Scotland, actively involved in the Congregational church. Deeply influenced by Eric Liddell's exploits in the 1924 Olympics, he committed himself to *missionary service. Unable to afford theological training in Britain, in 1927 he immigrated to the United States with the assistance of an American cousin. After about a year of employment spent largely in Elizabeth, New Jersey, and Birmingham, Alabama, he enrolled in Columbia Theological Seminary in Decatur, Georgia, graduating in 1931, despite the fact that he had never received an undergraduate degree. Ordained to the Presbyterian ministry that same year, he served pastorates in Covington (1931-1933) and Atlanta, Georgia, with phenomenal results.

In 1937 Marshall accepted a call to the eighteen hundred-member New York Avenue Presbyterian Church in Washington, D.C., becoming a United States citizen the next year. With a growing reputation as a fine preacher, in 1947 Marshall was elected chaplain of the senate by the Republican majority, amid charges of partisan politics. The charges were proved irrelevant by the Democratic majority the following year, which unanimously reelected him. In that position he became widely known for his brief and memorable prayers, which often had an uncanny relevance to the issues being debated on the floor and were said to influence the direction of the day's business. Through this position, Marshall called the senators to seek the wisdom of God in their decision making in great and small matters alike. Many, even among the more secular-minded senators, quickly came to appreciate the warmth and sincerity of his ministry.

An eloquent speaker whose sermons were marked by relevance to life, he made a special impact upon the large number of young people who attended his churches in Atlanta and Washington. He impressed his hearers with the reality of the presence of God in worship and the living character of the Word of God. While he was in Washington, his church regularly turned away large numbers of people who could not fit into the sanctuary when he preached. His ability to communicate effectively with people of all ages apparently carried over even to infants, none of whom, according to lore, cried in his arms during baptism.

In 1946 he suffered his first heart attack, taking

six months to recuperate. Once back in the pulpit, however, Marshall refused to let the fear of death cut back on his preaching engagements and wholehearted commitment to his ministry. Three years later, he died of another heart attack at the age of forty-six.

His wife, Catherine Wood *Marshall, whom he married in 1936, wrote his best-selling biography, *A Man Called Peter* (1951), and compiled several books of his sermons, among them *Mr. Jones, Meet the Master* (1949) and *John Doe, Disciple* (1963), as well as *The Prayers of Peter Marshall* (1954).

BIBLIOGRAPHY. C. W. Marshall, *A Man Called Peter: The Story of Peter Marshall* (1951).

N. A. Magnuson

Mason, John Mitchell (1770-1829). Associate Reformed minister and educator. Born in New York City, the son of a Scottish Presbyterian minister, Mason was educated at Columbia College (1789) and Edinburgh (1792). Mason pastored two Associate Reformed congregations in New York City (1793-1821). He delivered the municipal commemorative oration at George Washington's death and ministered to the dying Alexander Hamilton after his duel with Aaron Burr.

In 1805 Mason established a biblical and theological school for training pastors of the Associate Reformed Synod. It was the prototype for the American seminary. He was its sole professor through its closing in 1821. Concurrently he was a trustee and later provost (1811-1816) of Columbia College. He elevated its academic standards, enhanced its financial position, helped acquire the property for its present campus and taught classics and apologetics.

Mason helped found the New York Missionary Society (1790) and the American Bible Society (1816). Many of his most influential writings were published a chapter at a time in the *Christian's Magazine,* which he established and edited. *Letters on Frequent Communion* (1798), *Essays on the Church of God* (1807-1809) and *A Plea for Sacramental Communion on Catholick Principles* (1816) reflect his concerns for sacramental reform and Christian unity. Mason exemplified these convictions, practicing intercommunion with American Presbyterians, working for the formal merger of his denomination with the *Presbyterian Church in the U.S.A. (PCUSA) and eventually joining the latter's Presbytery of New York during his presidency of Dickinson College in Carlisle, Pennsylvania (1821-1824).

BIBLIOGRAPHY. *AAP* 4; *DAB* VI; J. H. M. Knox, "John M. Mason, S.T.D.," *Columbia University Quarterly* 3 (December 1901) 26-34; E. Mason, ed., *Mason's Works,* 4 vols. (1832); F. D. McCloy, "John Mitchell Mason: Pioneer in American Theological Education," *JPH* 44,3 (1966) 141-55; J. Van Vechten, *Memoirs of John M. Mason* (1856).

P. W. Butin

Mateer, Calvin Wilson (1836-1908).† Presbyterian missionary. Born near Harrisburg, Pennsylvania, Mateer attended Jefferson College (later Washington and Jefferson; B.A. 1857) and Allegheny (Western) Theological Seminary (B.D., 1861). Ordained in 1861, he pastored a Presbyterian church in Delaware, Ohio (1861-1863), while waiting for the necessary funds from the Presbyterian board for foreign missions. Finally he set sail as a Presbyterian missionary to China in 1863.

Mateer spent his entire career in Shantung province, north China, traveling extensively and planting numerous churches. Based at Tengchow, in the 1860s he established a boys' school (later known as Shantung Christian) that eventually became one of the best Christian colleges in nineteenth-century China, remaining president until 1895. Insisting upon teaching in Chinese rather than English, he also developed a museum of Western technology to train the Chinese in science. Mateer was a man of great energy, determination and all-around skill: a fine teacher and schoolmaster, he was also an indefatigable writer, organizer, publicist and promoter. His language texts were used for decades, and no school taught science better than did his. One of the editors of the revised Mandarin Bible, he also served as chairman of the committee on textbooks of the Missionary Conference. His strong personality made him a formidable adversary, however. After 1900 Mateer was a missionary statesman, well known among American Presbyterians as a successful missionary. His wife, Julia, was more visible than were most missionary wives and was herself the author of several works in Chinese.

BIBLIOGRAPHY. *ANB* 14; *DAB* VI; D. W. Fisher, *Calvin Wilson Mateer, Forty-five Years a Missionary in Shantung* (1911); I. T. Hyatt, *Our Ordered Lives Confess: Three Nineteenth-Century American Missionaries in East Shantung* (1976).

D. H. Bays

Matthews, Mark Allison (1867-1940).‡ Presbyterian minister. Born in Calhoun, Georgia, Matthews attended Calhoun Academy and later graduated from Gordon County University (1887). He studied theology privately under J. B. Hillhouse, professor at Calhoun Academy and minister of Calhoun's Presbyterian church. Converted at thirteen, Matthews was ordained at the age of twenty in the *Presbyterian Church in the U.S. (Southern; PCUS). Matthews succeeded Hillhouse as pastor. He then pastored at Dalton, Georgia (1893-1896), Jackson, Tennessee (1896-1902), and First Presbyterian Church of Seattle, Washington (1901-1940).

A *Calvinist premillennialist, Matthews eschewed professional evangelists, leading his own *revivals. In 1917 he founded the Bible Institute of Seattle. He also began the first church-owned and operated radio station in the country (KTW) and helped to establish a major hospital. His pulpit pronouncements on social issues were wide-ranging. He supported socialized medicine and mandatory agricultural education for young men and argued for coeducational instruction. At the same time he opposed suffrage and women's ordination. As an American patriot, Matthews enthusiastically supported the first and second world wars.

Matthews's Seattle congregation grew to become the largest Presbyterian church in the country, with nine thousand members. He combined a personal pulpit flair, strong executive ability and a *fundamentalist theology (save for his disbelief in hell as a state or place of literal fire). Matthews participated actively in the civic and political life of Seattle and was recognized for his contributions by a bronze bust erected in his honor.

Bibliography. *ANB* 14; C. A. Russell, *Voices of American Fundamentalism: Seven Biographical Studies* (1976). C. A. Russell

McAdow, Samuel (1760-1844). Early *Cumberland Presbyterian minister. McAdow was born in Guilford County, North Carolina. Educated initially by the local Presbyterian minister, David Caldwell, and later at Mecklenburg College, McAdow operated the family farm after his father's death. He married Henrietta Wheatly in 1788.

Sensing a call to the ministry, McAdow then studied divinity at Caldwell's Log College and was licensed in 1794 by the Presbytery of Orange. Sometime later he was ordained and served the Hopewell church in Orange County, North Carolina. After his wife's death in 1799, McAdow moved west to Kentucky, where he engaged in itinerant preaching and participated in frontier *revivals. In 1800 he married Catherine Clark, who died in 1804.

Early in his ministry in North Carolina, McAdow had expressed reservations regarding what he took to be the *Westminster Confession's fatalistic teaching on divine sovereignty. Upon moving to Kentucky, he soon became embroiled in the lengthy controversy between the prorevivalist Cumberland Presbytery and the antirevivalist Synod of Kentucky over subscription to the Westminster Confession's teachings on predestination, the extent of synodical authority over presbyteries and ministers and educational requirements for ministers.

After marrying Hannah Cope in 1806, McAdow moved to Dixon County, Tennessee. When the revivalist ministers of Cumberland Presbytery found they could not resolve the conflict with the synod, three Cumberland Presbytery ministers—Finis *Ewing, Samuel King and McAdow—formed an independent Cumberland Presbytery on February 4, 1810, at McAdow's house in Dixon County. This event marks the founding of what became the *Cumberland Presbyterian Church (CPC).

McAdow took little part in subsequent Cumberland Presbyterian activities. He moved to Jackson County, Tennessee, in 1815. In 1828 he moved to Illinois, apparently because of his opposition to slavery.

Bibliography. B. M. Barrus, et al., *A People Called Cumberland Presbyterians* (1972); R. Beard, *Brief Biographical Sketches of Some of the Early Ministers of the Cumberland Presbyterian Church,* 2d series (1874). W. B. Evans

McAfee, Cleland Boyd (1866-1944). Presbyterian minister and theological educator. McAfee was born into a family of educators. His father was president of Park College, where Cleland and his brother *Joseph spent years as students and teachers. Both Cleland and Joseph combined sincere interest in domestic and foreign *missions with a willingness to serve in a variety of denominational and cooperative efforts. After studies at Park College (A.B., 1884; A.M., 1888), Union Seminary (1888) and Westminster College (Ph.D., 1892), McAfee taught at Park College from 1888 to 1901, served pastorates in Chicago and Brooklyn and then served as professor of systematic theology at McCormick Theological Seminary (1912-1930). Following his term as moderator of the General Assembly of the *Presbyterian Church in the U.S.A. (PCUSA) from 1929 to 1930, McAfee served as secretary of the Presbyterian Board of Foreign Missions until 1936. Following his official retirement, McAfee taught at McCormick and elsewhere and remained active in church service until his death. McAfee wrote the well-known hymn "Near to the Heart of God."

McAfee's years as a pastor were formative. His practical pastoral focus is shown in publications throughout his career. He held to practical and irenic evangelical views, eager to promote the mission of the church. His appointment to teach theology at McCormick allowed him to combine his practical theological focus with his interests in missions on a wider field. Given the rising levels of conflict within the PCUSA as the focus of contention shifted to foreign missions budgets, personnel and doctrine, McAfee was a good choice as secretary of the board of foreign missions. McAfee was a target of J. Gresham *Machen and others who felt that the denomination's own missions staff were conceding too much to contemporary critics who were too ready to cut the nerve of foreign missions. McAfee's irenic temper and his deep commitment to world evangelism lowered the temperature of the debates in the 1930s, but there was no doubting that the denomination would not allow Machen or anyone else to challenge its control of missions.

Bibliography. C. B. McAfee, *Changing Foreign Missions* (1927); idem, *The Foreign Missionary Enterprise and Its Sincere Critics* (1935); idem, *The Uncut Nerve of Missions* (1932). K. S. Sawyer

McAfee, Joseph Ernest (1870-1947). Presbyterian educator and *missions leader. Born in Louisiana, Missouri, McAfee received his bachelor of arts degree from Park College in 1889. After studying at both Union and Auburn seminaries in New York, he took his bachelor of divinity degree from Princeton Seminary in 1896. He taught Greek at Park throughout the 1890s and in 1900 became chaplain and professor of religion. In 1906 McAfee began fourteen years of full-time service in the home missions movement, serving as associate secretary (1906-1914) and general secretary (1914-1917) of the Presbyterian board of home missions, and then as the secretary of the American Missionary Association (1918-1920). At the age of fifty-one McAfee became a community counselor at the University of Oklahoma (1921-1923) and finished his career as the director of community service at the Community Church of New York (1924-1932). He died in Princeton, New Jersey, after fifteen years of active retirement.

Throughout his career, McAfee articulated and exemplified an increasing concern among America's mainline Protestants to expand their traditional missions strategy and include both spiritual and social services. McAfee thought conservatives promulgated a narrowly spiritual and other-worldly type of evangelization and thus ignored the physical and social needs of congregations and communities. While personal *piety remained an important concern, McAfee stressed the importance of recent advances in social theory and of understanding society's vast structural problems in his effort to develop an effective missions strategy for the modern world. His publications included *Missions Striking Home* (1908), *World Missions from the Home Base* (1911) and *College Pioneering* (1938).

Bibliography. R. H. Balmer and J. R. Fitzmier, *The Presbyterians* (1993); *DARB.* D. A. Sweeney

McCord, James Iley (1919-1990). Presbyterian minister, theological educator and ecumenical leader. Born in Rusk, Texas, McCord was graduated from the University of Texas at the age of nineteen and received a master's degree from the University of Texas in 1942. He studied at Harvard University, the University of Edinburgh (New College) and Union Theological Seminary in New York before receiving his bachelor of divinity degree from Austin Presbyterian Theological Seminary in 1942.

After serving congregations in Manchester, New Hampshire, and Austin, Texas, he became dean and professor of systematic theology at Austin Seminary in 1952. He assumed the presidency of Princeton Theological Seminary in 1959 and became a central figure in that institution's history. During his presidency, McCord substantially strengthened Princeton by vastly increasing its endowment, establishing the Center of Continuing Education (the first at any seminary in the United States), expanding the library, broadening the faculty and increasing the number of students.

McCord was deeply involved in the ecumenical movement, primarily in the World Alliance of Reformed Churches, which was formed under his leadership. He served as president of the World Alliance from 1977 to 1982. He took an especially keen interest in the churches of eastern Europe, where he traveled extensively during the Cold War.

McCord was a perceptive theologian and read widely and deeply in historical and contemporary theology. He deplored what he called the "theological amnesia" of his generation, and after the heyday of *neo-orthodoxy he declared that theology was "a shambles." To rejuvenate theological awareness, he founded the Center of Theological Inquiry in Princeton. Upon his retirement in 1983, he became its chancellor and chairman of its board until 1989. In 1986 he received the Templeton Prize for Progress in Religion.

McCord died in Princeton. He was married to Hazel Thompson, and they had three children.

Bibliography. *ANB* 14; T. W. Gillespie, "A Memorial Tribute to the Reverend Dr. James Iley McCord," *PSB,* n.s. 11 (1990) 121-27; obituary, *New York Times,* February 21, 1990; R. C. White Jr., "President James I. McCord: The Measure of His Leadership," *Princeton Seminary Bulletin,* n.s., 4 (1983) 137- 39. J. M. Mulder

McCorkle, Samuel Eusebius (1746-1811).† Presbyterian minister and educator. After graduating from the College of New Jersey (B.A., 1772), he prepared for the ministry with his uncle, Joseph Montgomery of Delaware and Pennsylvania, and thereafter served as pastor of Thyatira Church in Rowan County, North Carolina, from 1776 until his death, also teaching at Salisbury Academy and his own Zion-Parnassus Academy.

A firm believer in the interrelationship between the religious and civic well-being of a nation, McCorkle worked for the unity of the Presbyterian Church and the education of the backcountry of North Carolina. As a trustee at the young University of North Carolina, he tried unsuccessfully to mold that school in the likeness of John *Witherspoon's College of New Jersey. Believing that a classical education was essential for the foundation of virtue, he promoted a curriculum that would emphasize ancient languages, religious training and mandatory chapel attendance. McCorkle vocally opposed the modern scientific program instituted by William R. Davie, but his own views triumphed only after his death.

In the 1790s McCorkle published doctrinal works on deism, communion, sabbath observance, sacrificing and charity in order to raise funds for the university. He addressed broader social and political themes in *A Sermon on the Comparative Happiness and Duty of the United States Contrasted with . . . the Israelites* (1795), *The Work of God for the French Republic* (1798) and *True Greatness: A Sermon on the Death of General George Washington* (1800). His cautious appraisals of the *revivals of 1802 were published by James Hall. His brother-in-law was the noted Federalist congressman John Steele.

Bibliography. *ANB* 14; W. F. Craven, "Samuel Eusebius McCorkle," in *Princetonians 1769-1775: A Biographical Dictionary,* ed. R. Harrison (1980); T. T. Taylor, "Samuel E. McCorkle and a Christian Republic, 1792-1802," *American Presbyterians* 63 (1985) 375- 85. T. T. Taylor

McCormick, Cyrus Hall (1809-1884).† Presbyterian philanthropist. Born in Rockbridge, Virginia, to a planter and mechanical genius, McCormick built on the labors of his father. In 1831 he invented the mechanical reaper, a machine that revolutionized farming in the American plains and made the United States the world's leading producer of wheat. His organizational and business skills enabled McCormick to accumulate a fortune through his manufacturing of reapers, headquartered in Chicago. In 1858 he married Nancy Maria Fowler.

A devout *Old School Presbyterian, McCormick used his wealth to fund educational enterprises, influencing Presbyterianism in both the North and South. His financial gift helped to establish a seminary in Chicago in 1859 that eventually took his name. Disturbed by the harshness of Reconstruction after the Civil War, as well as what he considered the radical stance of the seminary he had so liberally endowed, McCormick turned his benevolence toward his native state, contributing significant sums to Washington and Lee University and Union Theological Seminary, single-handedly salvaging the seminary from financial collapse after the war.

Under his control during the 1870s, *The Interior* of Chicago strongly promoted Presbyterianism in the old Northwest. Before the war he had worked to hold the Old School Presbyterian Church together, and after the war he advocated their reunion with the New School. An influential Democrat, he supported a peaceful resolution to the issues surrounding the Civil War. Staunchly conservative both theologically and socially, McCormick vigorously opposed efforts to depart from or modify Old School *Calvinism within American Presbyterianism.

Bibliography. *ANB* 14; H. N. Casson, *Cyrus Hall McCormick: His Life and Work* (1909); *DAB* VI. G. S. Smith

McCosh, James (1811-1894).† Presbyterian minister, philosopher and educator. Born in Scotland and educated at the universities of Glasgow (1824-1829) and Edinburgh (M.A., 1834), McCosh served as a Presbyterian minister from 1835 to 1852. As such, he sided with Thomas Chalmers and the insurgent evangelical party in the Disruption of 1843, leading to the creation of the Free Church of Scotland. The second phase of his career began in 1852 when McCosh became professor of logic and metaphysics at Queen's College in Belfast, Ireland (1852-1868). For the next sixteen years he was immersed in the leading philosophical debates of his age.

Widely regarded as the last major voice of the philosophical realism of the Scottish Enlightenment, McCosh attempted throughout his diversified career to fuse the best modern thinking with a lively evangelical faith. Influenced by Sir William Hamilton's restatement of Scottish Common-Sense realism in a neo-Kantian framework, McCosh's own "intuitional realism" labored to counteract German idealism, David Hume's skepticism and John Stuart Mill's sensationalism. His most significant philosophical contributions came in *The Intuitions of the Mind* (1860) and *The Scottish Philosophy* (1875).

After attending the *Old School general assembly as a fraternal delegate from the Free Church in 1866, McCosh became enamored with the vitality of American Christianity. In 1868 he was appointed president of the College of New Jersey, thus culminating his career in the United States. During his two-decade tenure (1868-1888) at Princeton he helped transform a fledgling, parochial college into a national university.

In 1870 McCosh proposed the idea of an international Presbyterian Alliance designed to promote Reformed ecumenicity, combat the inroads of German idealism into the British and American intellectual communities and to rejuvenate the evangelical Reformed presence on the Continent. Convinced by his experience in the Disruption, as well as his favorable impressions of American Protestantism, he was convinced that state control of the church led to a decline of both doctrine and *piety. Fearing that a "new Moderatism" was infiltrating the English-speaking world, McCosh worked tirelessly to unite the international Reformed community.

Five years later McCosh was elected president of the formational meeting of the World Alliance of Reformed Churches holding the Presbyterian System, and he was commissioned to prepare the statement of principles for the Edinburgh Conference of 1877. Convinced that evangelical reunion needed to start with the major theological traditions, McCosh also supported the work of the Evangelical Alliance.

McCosh regarded the training of the intellect as the primary method for transforming society. Viewing philosophy as the fountain of societal development, he believed that as philosophical convictions spread to theology, they impact the church, which in turn shapes society and culture. Though McCosh was an early advocate in America for reconciling Christian orthodoxy and Darwinism, an ardent defender of *revivalism and a tireless academic reformer and administrator, his legacy nonetheless was not successful in preserving a role for Scottish realism among American intellectuals or in maintaining Princeton's evangelical heritage.

Bibliography. *ANB* 14; *DAB* VI; *DARB;* J. D. Hoeveler Jr., "Evangelical Ecumenism: James McCosh and the Intellectual Origins of the World Alliance of Reformed Churches," *JPH* 55 (spring 1977) 58-73; idem, *James McCosh and the Scottish Intellectual Tradition: From Glasgow to Princeton* (1981); *NCAB* 5; W. M. Sloane, ed., *The Life of James McCosh: A Record Chiefly Autobiographical* (1896).

S. R. Pointer

McCulloch, Thomas (1776-1843).† *Canadian Presbyterian minister and educator. Born in Scotland, McCulloch was educated at the University of Glasgow and received his theological training at the Secession Divinity Hall (Anti-Burgher) in Whitburn. Ordained a Presbyterian minister in 1799, he served the Seceder congregation at Stewarton for four years before being sent as a *missionary to British North America in 1803. Intending to minister on Prince Edward Island, he was prevailed upon to settle instead in Pictou, Nova Scotia, where he immediately turned his attention to education. Deploring the low level of instruction available and the Anglican control of higher education in the colony, he founded a grammar school in 1805 as a preliminary step. In a compromise agreement with the Anglican authorities, who refused to allow a dissenter college in the colony, he established his Pictou Academy in 1816, which despite the restrictions imposed was soon recognized as one of the finest schools in British North America. Here McCulloch took the first important steps to educate a native Presbyterian clergy and laid the foundations in 1821 for what would eventually become Pine Hill Divinity College in Halifax, Nova Scotia. The success of his teaching is shown by three members of his first class of graduates from the divinity school who received their master of arts in theology from the University of Glasgow.

McCulloch emphasized the classics less than many educators of his day, stressing a more scientific education, including a strong emphasis on theology. He also agitated for the rights of dissenters throughout Nova Scotia and wrote extensively, significantly influencing the direction of political change in the colony. Opposed only to Roman Catholics and the Church of Scotland, he worked to build a coalition of dissenters and even supplied the pulpit of the Granville Street Baptist Church in Halifax for a short time in 1839.

In addition, McCulloch wrote extensively, using the pen to instruct and to promote social change. His best-known work, *The Stepsure Letters,* established him as the founder of modern Canadian humor. A pioneer Canadian scientist, he maintained an active interest in natural philosophy and natural history, giving the first public lectures on chemistry in the colony.

During the 1820s and 1830s, ministers from the Church of Scotland incessantly attacked Pictou Academy because it was producing a steady stream of Secessionist ministers, and McCulloch received no support from the Anglican authorities, who saw Pictou Academy as a serious rival to their own King's College. After the Anglicans expanded the board of trustees in 1831 to include several ministers of the Church of Scotland, McCulloch accepted an appointment in 1838 as the first principal of Dalhousie College, Halifax. Lord Dalhousie had originally planned in 1819 for it to be a nonsectarian college under Anglican auspices, but after twenty years of inaction, the board of governors finally turned to McCulloch as the best educator in Nova Scotia. After five years as principal, McCulloch died at the age of sixty-seven.

B. M. Moody

McCurdy, James Frederick (1847-1935). Presbyterian educator and biblical scholar. Called the father of biblical studies in Canada, McCurdy was born in Chatham, New Brunswick, where his father was a Presbyterian minister. He was educated at the local Presbyterian Academy and at the University of New Brunswick (B.A., 1866). He spent a year as a school principal in New Brunswick before continuing his studies at Princeton Theological Seminary.

After he completed his theological course, McCurdy remained in Princeton for a further eleven years, acting as assistant to William Henry *Green, professor of Old Testament, and teaching oriental languages. Princeton awarded him an honorary doctorate in 1878. In 1882 he went to Germany, where he studied at Göttingen and Leipzig under Franz and Friedrich Delitzsch, E. Schrader and P. A. de Lagarde. During this time his views seemed to be undergoing a number of changes, and he came to accept Julius Wellhausen's position on Pentateuchal criticism. McCurdy returned to Canada in 1885 and the following year received an appointment as tutor in oriental languages at University College, Toronto. In 1886 he gave the Stone Lectures at Princeton Seminary, and in 1888 he was appointed as professor and head of the department of oriental languages at University College. From this position he exercised a significant influence on the rising generation of biblical scholars in Canada and was one of the first to introduce higher criticism into the country.

In 1911-1912 McCurdy was director of the American School of Oriental Research at Jerusalem. Between 1894 and 1901 he published his three-volume magnum opus, *History, Prophecy and the Monuments.* Besides writing a number of Old Testament commentaries, he wrote the biography of his friend and pastor, D. J. Macdonnell of St. Andrew's Church, Toronto, the only Presbyterian leader to stand trial for heresy in the Canadian church. McCurdy was also a member of the Society for Psychical Research.

Bibliography. J. S. Moir, *A History of Biblical Studies in Canada: A Sense of Proportion* (1982); *Who's Who in Canada,* 1934-1935.

R. W. Vaudry

McGee, J(ohn) Vernon (1904-1988). Radio evangelist. Born and reared in the South, McGee received his bachelor of divinity degree from Columbia Theological Seminary in Decatur, Georgia, and graduate degrees from Dallas Theological Seminary in Dallas, Texas. He was ordained to the ministry in 1933, serving Presbyterian churches in the South until 1941, when he became the pastor of a Presbyterian church in Pasadena, California. During this pastorate he began a weekly radio program called *The Open Bible Hour.*

In 1949 McGee became the pastor of an interdenominational congregation, The Church of the Open Door in Los Angeles, California. To increase church attendance, he began the radio program *Through the Bible,* teaching the books of the Bible consecutively. Every five years he completed a series of programs from Genesis through Revelation. He retired from the pastorate in 1970 but continued to broadcast his Bible lessons as well as weekly sermons. Beginning in 1973, *Through the Bible* was aired in Spanish over the transmitters of Trans World Radio. In the years following, McGee's program was broadcast in many other languages. His ministry has also provided tapes of his radio programs and Bible study books through the mail.

Bibliography. J. V. McGee, *Through the Bible Radio Ministry 40th Anniversary* (1981).

W. M. Ashcraft

McGiffert, Arthur Cushman (1861-1933).‡ Presbyterian and Congregational church historian and educator. Born in Sauquoit, New York, McGiffert was educated at Western Reserve University (B.A., 1882) and Union Theological Seminary in New York (B.D., 1885) and pursued graduate studies in Germany, France and Italy. He received his doctoral degree at the University of Marburg (1888), where he developed a close friendship with Adolf Harnack (1851-1930). McGiffert taught at Lane Theological Seminary from 1888 until 1893, when he succeeded Philip *Schaff as Washburn Professor of Church History at Union Theological Seminary in New York. Denominational heresy charges following publication of *A History of Christianity in the Apostolic Age* (1897) led McGiffert from the Presbyterians to the Congregationalists in 1900. As president of Union Seminary from 1917 until 1926, McGiffert sought closer association with Columbia University, eased the seminary's financial plight through successful fund raising and supervised the renovation of the curriculum. He served as professor emeritus at Union until his death.

McGiffert's methodological allegiances were with the scientific historians, and his clear theological convictions were with Harnack and Albrecht Ritschl (1822-1889) in the advancement of Protestant liberalism. He grafted liberalism to his historical studies, but by the end of his life he denied any meaningful continuity in Christian history. McGiffert's published titles included *The Apostles' Creed* (1902), *Martin Luther* (1911), *The God of the Early Christians* (1924) and *A History of Christian Thought* (2 vols., 1931-1933). His theological commitments and prominent position at Union Seminary made him one of America's foremost theological liberals.

BIBLIOGRAPHY. *DAB* I; *DARB; NCAB* 24.

K. S. Sawyer

McGready, James (c. 1758-1817).‡ Presbyterian revivalist. McGready came from *Scots-Irish stock in Pennsylvania, but as a child he moved with his family to western North Carolina. He studied theology under a Princeton Seminary graduate named John McMillan. After a bout with smallpox he converted. In 1788 he was licensed to preach by the presbytery of Redstone, in western Pennsylvania.

Returning to North Carolina, McGready preached the wrath of God so vigorously that he ignited *revival fires that drove penitents to faith in Jesus. One of these was Barton W. Stone, who later led the Cane Ridge camp meeting. In 1796 he preached in the southwestern corner of Kentucky to three small congregations in Logan County, notorious for its lawlessness. Surprisingly, however, the backwoodsmen responded enthusiastically to McGready's vivid preaching.

In July 1800, after an original revival at Red River, McGready decided to send out advance notice of the next communion service at the Gasper River church. When the word spread through the settlements, scores of pioneers headed for Gasper River. They came from as far away as one hundred miles, prepared to stay several days. This was probably the first camp meeting in American history. Such revivals spread to many other settlements throughout the South and Midwest. The most famous camp meeting was at Cane Ridge, in Bourbon County, Kentucky, in August 1801. McGready's last days were spent preaching in northern Kentucky and southern Indiana.

BIBLIOGRAPHY. *ANB* 15; C. C. Cleveland, *The Great Revival in the West, 1797-1805* (1916); *DAB* V; *DARB;* C. A. Johnson, *The Frontier Camp Meeting: Religious Harvest Time* (1955); B. A. Weisberger, *They Gathered at the River: The Story of the Great Revivalists and Their Impact upon Religion in America* (1978).

B. L. Shelley

McIntire, Carl (1906-). Presbyterian minister. Born in Ypsilanti, Michigan, the son of a Presbyterian minister, McIntire graduated from Park College, Parkville, Missouri, in 1927, and attended Princeton Theological Seminary, where he was a devoted student of J. Gresham *Machen. When Machen and a group of conservatives left Princeton to form Westminster Theological Seminary in 1929, McIntire followed and graduated from Westminster in 1931. McIntire was an ordained minister of the *Presbyterian Church in the U.S.A. (PCUSA) until he was defrocked in 1935 for membership on the conservative Independent Board for Presbyterian Foreign Missions.

In 1936 McIntire joined Machen in the newly founded church that eventually became known as the *Orthodox Presbyterian Church (OPC). One year later McIntire led a group to form the Bible Presbyterian Church. The headquarters for this movement was Collingswood, New Jersey, where McIntire also pastored the local Bible Presbyterian Church. With Allan A. MacRae and J. Oliver *Buswell Jr. he founded Faith Theological Seminary in 1937. In 1941 McIntire founded the *American Council of Christian Churches as a counter to the Federal Council of Churches. In 1948 he formed the International Council of Christian Churches to provide an international association of *fundamentalists.

Through his *Twentieth-Century Reformation Hour,* a daily half-hour radio broadcast begun in 1957, and his publication, *Christian Beacon* (1936-), McIntire disseminated militant fundamentalism. By the 1980s his views had fallen out of favor even among devoted fundamentalists, and his institutions, notably Shelton College in Cape May, New Jersey, had run afoul of tax officials. McIntire, however, still claims the loyalty of a core of devoted followers.

Bibliography. L. Gasper, *The Fundamentalist Movement, 1930-1956* (1963); J. D. Woodbridge, M. A. Noll and N. O. Hatch, *The Gospel in America* (1979). R. H. Balmer

McKelway, Alexander Jeffrey (1866-1918). Presbyterian minister and political activist. Although he was born in Pennsylvania, McKelway's family background and education (at Hampden-Sydney College and Union Theological Seminary in Richmond) were Southern. McKelway served as a Presbyterian pastor in North Carolina (1891-1897). He then became editor (1898-1905) of the *Presbyterian Standard,* the denomination's periodical in North Carolina. During this time he developed an interest in social-justice issues, particularly child-labor reform. Consequently, in 1909 McKelway moved to Washington to lobby for federal legislation under the auspices of the National Child Labor Committee. Soon McKelway became convinced that his fellow former Southerner, Presbyterian and moderate progressive Woodrow *Wilson would be well suited for the presidency.

When Wilson decided to run in 1912, McKelway urged him to state explicitly his progressivism in order to keep *social reformers from voting for Theodore Roosevelt. When Wilson sought reelection in 1916, McKelway was even more involved, especially since the final drive for the passage of the federal Child Labor Bill coincided with the campaign. Several months before the election McKelway persuaded Wilson to intervene with Congress on behalf of the legislation. After the bill's passage, McKelway turned his full energies toward the reelection campaign. He drafted the labor and welfare planks of the Democratic platform and founded the Democratic Bureau of Education and Social Service, an organization that made direct appeals for Wilson to voters interested in social reform. McKelway was one of the few Southern churchmen whose concerns matched those of the social gospel advocates of the North.

Bibliography. *ANB* 15; B. J. Brandon, "A Wilsonian Progressive—Alexander Jeffrey McKelway," *JPH* 48 (1970) 2-17; H. J. Doherty, "Alexander J. McKelway: Preacher to Progressive," *JSH* 24 (1958) 177-90. D. M. Strong

McNaugher, John (1857-1947). United Presbyterian professor and seminary president. Born at Allegheny, Pennsylvania, he attended Westminster College, Pennsylvania, and after graduation (1880) studied theology at Xenia Theological Seminary (1884). He served as professor of New Testament at Allegheny Seminary (renamed Pittsburgh Seminary in 1912 and merged with Xenia Seminary in 1930) from 1886 to 1943 and as president from 1909 to 1943. He served as president of the World Alliance of Reformed Churches, moderator of the General Assembly of the *United Presbyterian Church of North America (UPCNA) and chairman of the commission on a new confessional statement for the denomination.

McNaugher was the author of three books on theology, edited two editions of the psalter hymnal plus five other collections of religious music, and strongly defended the preeminence of the psalms in Christian worship.

Widely respected for the gifts of the intellect he manifested both as a speaker and writer, McNaugher epitomized for many the *intellectual life of the denomination. In his fifty-seven years at the seminary he left an indelible conservative imprint on both the thought and style of the seminary and its students. McNaugher died at Pittsburgh, Pennsylvania.

Bibliography. R. L. Kelley Jr., "Pittsburgh-Xenia Seminary," in *Ever a Frontier: The Bicentennial History of the Pittsburgh Theological Seminary,* ed. J. A. Walther (1994); H. A. Kelsey, *The United Presbyterian Directory* (1958); J. McNaugher, *The History of Theological Education in the United Presbyterian Church* (1931); idem, *Jesus Christ, The Same Yesterday, Today and Forever* (1947); idem, ed., *The Psalms in Worship* (1907). W. L. Fisk

McQuilkin, Robert Crawford (1886-1952).† Presbyterian educator. Born in Philadelphia, Pennsylvania, McQuilkin made profession of faith at age twelve in the *United Presbyterian Church (UPCNA). Following high school, he worked at William Steele and Sons, Philadelphia, as a clerk and estimator (1902-1911). After a spiritual experience (1911) at the New Wilmington Missionary Conference under the ministrations of Charles G. Trumbull, he became associate editor (1912-1917) of Trumbull's *The Sunday School Times* and married Marguerite Lambie (1912). After graduating from the University of Pennsylvania (1917), he studied theology privately under Melvin G. *Kyle, professor of theology at Xenia Seminary and archaeological editor of *The Sunday School Times,* and was ordained in the UPCNA.

The McQuilkins were among the initiators of the Victorious Life conferences (1913-1923). First held at Oxford, Pennsylvania, for several years the conferences were held at Princeton, New Jersey (1914-1918), before moving to Stonybrook, Long Island (1919-1922), and finally Keswick Grove, New Jersey. After leading a Bible conference in Columbia, South Carolina, McQuilkin became founding president at Columbia Bible School (1923-1952), which was the first Bible school to grant the bachelor of arts degree, becoming accredited in 1929. Seven years later they started giving graduate degrees, developing the Graduate School of Missions in 1947. For several years McQuilkin preached regularly in a nearby Baptist church. Starting with just eight students, the school grew quickly under his leadership. From 1926, he taught the weekly Business Men's Bible class in Columbia, with attendance peaking at more than four hundred. He preached regularly at Bible conferences around the country, receiving an honorary doctor of divinity from Wheaton College after leading the annual evangelistic services there for five years.

McQuilkin was active in *missions, but his own attempt to become a missionary to Africa in 1917 was foiled by his inability to secure passage, through numerous mishaps over a span of two years. Nonetheless more than three hundred of his students, including his daughter, went into foreign missions throughout the world due to his influence. The Victorious Life conferences supported missionaries, including Ralph Norton of the Belgian Gospel Mission. McQuilkin also served as director of the Latin American Mission and the Mexican Indian Mission. In 1928 McQuilkin founded the Ben Lippen Conference Center in Asheville, North Carolina, and in 1940 the Ben Lippen School. Both became institutions of national importance. Efforts to improve evangelical education resulted in the Evangelical Teacher Training Association with McQuilkin as president (1931-1941).

Strongly supportive of the discipline of the church but not particularly bound to Presbyterian *polity, McQuilkin withdrew from the Southern Presbyterian Church in 1951 and helped in the formation of the Fellowship of Independent Evangelical Churches. Among his publications were *Studying Our Lord's Parables* (1925), *The Baptism of the Spirit: Shall We Seek It?* (1935), *The Lord Is My Shepherd* (1938), *The Message of Romans: An Exposition* (1947) and *Victorious Life Studies* (1918). During World War II, he received sharp criticism from pacifists for his booklet "Why It Is Right for a Christian to Fight." In addition, he continued his relationship with *The Sunday School Times,* writing the weekly lessons from 1931 to 1937. McQuilkin's role in promoting Victorious Life teachings was to have a significant effect in shaping the spirituality of a large sector of *fundamentalism and evangelicalism.

Bibliography. M. McQuilkin, *Always in Triumph: The Life of Robert C. McQuilkin* (1955).

D. D. Bundy

Mears, Henrietta Cornella (1890-1963).† Presbyterian *educator. Born in Fargo, North Dakota, and educated at the University of Minnesota, Mears inherited the zeal and devotion of her energetic and pious mother. After graduation, she became a high school principal in Beardsley, Minnesota, where she also taught chemistry, speech and dramatics, moving later to North Branch and eventually Minneapolis, teaching Sunday school wherever she went. In Minneapolis, she served as a Sunday school teacher at William B. Riley's First Baptist Church in Minneapolis, where she saw her class of eighteen-year-old girls grow from five to five hundred. Among her most successful ventures was a mentoring program between young married women and the teens.

In 1928 Mears and her sister Margaret moved to southern California, where Mears became director of Christian education at Hollywood Presbyterian Church. Under her leadership the church's entire Sunday school grew from 450 to more than 4,000 in less than three years. Within a year she had despaired of finding a biblically sound and educationally effective curriculum, so she began writing her own. Due to the simplicity and excellence of the material, she soon became swamped with requests from other churches, and in 1933, the first year of publication, more than 130 Sunday schools were using her curriculum. By 1940 the number of churches had topped 2,000. Her emphasis on presenting conservative Bible teaching in a manner that was appealing to children and youth quickly caught on, and in 1938 Mears began training seminars for Sunday school teachers, traveling around the United States and Canada.

A highly respected Bible teacher, Mears had a powerful impact on college-age young men and is said to have encouraged about five hundred men to enter the ministry—making her one of the most significant shapers of West Coast Presbyterianism. Many later recalled that her encouragement and teaching—and frequently her direct challenge—spurred them into the pastorate. Convinced of the absolute truth of Scripture, she used her scientific training to deal fairly with the intellectual objections of "her collegians" but emphasized that these questions could ultimately be solved only by a change of heart. Among her proteges were Bill Bright, founder of Campus Crusade for Christ; Richard Halverson, chaplain of the United States Senate; and Louis H. Evans Jr., pastor of National Presbyterian Church, Washington D.C. Mears was also noted for her influence on Hollywood personalities such as Dale Evans and Roy Rogers.

Mears was cofounder of Gospel Light Publications (1933) and the Hollywood Christian Group, as well as Forest Home, a Christian conference center in the San Bernardino Mountains. She never married, choosing rather to devote her life to her varied ministries. Though she did not openly espouse women's rights, she served as a strong role model for evangelical women in ministry. The late Clarence Roddy, homiletics professor at Fuller Theological Seminary, often referred to her as the best preacher in southern California.

Bibliography. E. M. Balwin and D. V. Benson, *Henrietta Mears and How She Did It* (1966); G. M. Marsden, *Reforming Fundamentalism: Fuller Seminary and the New Evangelicalism* (1987).

R. A. Tucker

Meckelenburg, Jan van (Megapolensis, Johannes) (1603-1669).‡ *Dutch Reformed minister. Born in Koedijk, the Netherlands, of Roman Catholic parents, he converted to the Reformed church at age twenty-three and was disinherited. After serving several pastorates and marrying Machtelt Steengen, in 1642 he moved to Rensselaerswyck (now Albany) with his wife and four children. He struggled to build a congregation among farmers and artisans and evangelized the neighboring Mohawk Indians.

In 1649 Meckelenburg planned to return to the Netherlands, but Peter Stuyvesant prevailed on him to accept the more prestigious pastorate of New Amsterdam. He is best known for the defense of the historic principle of "religious uniformity in a civil commonwealth," which in New Netherland protected the Reformed church. But the colony's owners, the West India Company directors, wished to encourage colonization of foreigners and non-Reformed Hollanders. Meckelenburg thus lost the struggle for religious conformity.

When the English fleet of conquest arrived in 1664, Meckelenburg prevailed on the fiery Stuyvesant to surrender and avoid bloodshed, believing resistance to be futile. The West India Company directors and his superiors in the Classis of Amsterdam castigated him for being "chicken-hearted" and withheld his salary. Meckelenburg died discouraged and in poverty six years after the English conquest, but his selfless service planted the seeds of the *Reformed Church in America (RCA).

Bibliography. *AAP* 9; *ANB* 15; *DAB* VI; *DARB;* G. F. De Jong, "Dominie Johannes Megapolensis: Minister to New Netherland," *New York Historical Society Quarterly* 52 (1968) 6-47; *NCAB* 12.

R. P. Swierenga

Mercersburg Theology.† The christocentric theological system developed at the *German Reformed seminary in Mercersburg, Pennsylvania, under the leadership of the theologian John Williamson *Nevin and the church historian Philip *Schaff. Utilizing insights of the philosopher/psychologist Frederick Augustus *Rauch, their predecessor at Marshall College and Mercersburg Seminary, Nevin and Schaff formulated a theological system based on the incarnation and the continuation of the life of Christ in his church. This they hoped would be a corrective to the *revivalism and sectarianism that prevailed in mid-nineteenth-century American Christianity. Strongly influenced by the romanticism, idealism and pietism of the mediating (or evangelical) school of German theology, they sought to make American Christianity more historical, in contrast to the neglect of the history of the church by many American denominations; more organic and churchly, in contrast to the revivalist focus on individual salvation; more sacramental, in contrast to the nearly total preoccupation of American (*Puritan) emphasis on the sermon; and more ecumenical, in contrast to American sectarianism. The Mercersburg theology emphasized development in doctrine and the value of the Protestant Reformation in contrast to both Roman Catholicism and the tractarian movement.

The doctrines of the movement were set forth in a journal created by Nevin and Schaff, the *Mercersburg Review,* as well as in major theological and historical works they produced. Nevin's most important works were *The Anxious Bench* (1843), a critique of new measures *revivalism, and *Mystical Presence* (1846), in which he reaffirmed the *Calvinistic doctrine of the spiritual presence of Christ in the Eucharist against both Lutheran and the more common memorialist ideas. Schaff contributed to the movement with his *Principle of Protestantism* (1845), a manifesto that pointed out weaknesses in American Christianity and emphasized the value of every era of church history, and *What Is Church History?* (1846), in which he vindicated the concept of development in doctrine.

The movement may be divided into three periods of somewhat different emphases. The first (1836-

1843), under the leadership of Rauch, emphasized philosophy. The second (1843-1858), comprising the main work of Nevin and Schaff, dealt with the church question. The third (1858-1866) dealt with questions of liturgy and liturgical reform, particularly within the German Reformed Church, although it touched off similar questions in other traditional denominations.

The period of strongest influence in American theology was the second, while Nevin and Schaff worked together in Mercersburg. This was also the period of their most heated controversies with the broader evangelical world, including their skirmishes with Charles *Hodge and the *Princeton Review.* Nevin left Mercersburg in 1853, and Schaff moved to New York in 1865. After they left, a number of their students, including Emanuel Vogel *Gerhart, carried the standard of the Mercersburg theology, but none of them had the creative gifts of the founders of the movement, and it gradually fell from prominence in American theology. There was renewed interest in the Mercersburg theology in the 1930s due to widespread concern for the themes of christocentrism and ecumenism. The Mercersburg theology continues to experience revivals of interest because of the continuing importance of the issues it addresses.

BIBLIOGRAPHY. L. J. Binkley, *The Mercersburg Theology* (1953); J. H. Nichols, *Romanticism in American Theology: Nevin and Schaff at Mercersburg* (1961); J. H. Nichols, ed., *The Mercersburg Theology* (1966).

S. R. Graham

Michaelius, Jonas (1577-?).† *Dutch Reformed minister. Born in Grootebroek, in the province of Holland, he graduated from the University of Leyden in 1605 and was probably licensed by the Classis of Enkhuysen. After ministering in Holland and Brabant for around twenty years, he requested a transfer to the Dutch colony in Brazil, leaving in 1625. The Portuguese victory over the Dutch, however, was completed before he had reached South America. Turning to new frontiers, Michaelius arrived in New Amsterdam on April 7, 1628, to become the first minister of the Dutch Reformed Church in North America. Michaelius is best known for a rather lugubrious letter he sent to Adrian Smoutius in Amsterdam, dated August 11, 1628, that provides a glimpse into the early days of New Netherland.

Michaelius wrote of the death of his wife seven weeks after he had arrived in New Amsterdam. He reported that he had fifty Walloon and Dutch communicants at the first administration of the Lord's Supper in New Amsterdam. Although he described the climate as "good and pleasant," Michaelius lamented the state of civil government, the barbarity of the natives and the lack of provisions. Zealous for the conversion of the native Americans and the reform of the local leadership of the West India Company, he was generally unsuccessful on both counts and quickly made several enemies. Michaelius left New Netherland in 1632 to make his accusations in person, but when the Classis of Amsterdam recommended that he return to America in 1637, the directors refused.

BIBLIOGRAPHY. *ANB* 15; E. T. Corwin, *Manual of the Reformed Church in America,* 5th ed. (1922); *DAB* VI; M. Kammen, *Colonial New York* (1975).

R. H. Balmer

Miller, Samuel (1769-1850).† Presbyterian minister and educator. Born near Dover, Delaware, where his father was a Presbyterian pastor, Miller graduated from the University of Pennsylvania in 1789 and studied theology at Dickinson College with Charles Nisbet. He served in the New York City Presbyterian collegiate pastorate (1793-1813), where he made his name with his 1,054-page *A Brief Retrospect of the Eighteenth Century* (1803) and opposition to high church episcopacy. Soon elected moderator of the Presbyterian general assembly (1806), he was a vigorous supporter of the need for more regular theological *education and became a founder of that denomination's theological seminary at Princeton (1812) and professor of ecclesiastical history and church government there from 1813 until his death.

Miller's move from New York to Princeton coincided with his development of a new aspect of his thinking on church government. Whereas he had formerly seen the dangers of episcopacy as his first threat, now he claimed that the democratic tendency in congregationalism was equally problematic. In his 1831 *Essay on the Warrant, Nature and Duties of the Office of the Ruling Elder in the Presbyterian Church,* he argued for a "Presbyterian Republicanism," where the ruling elder, as a layman, is a representative of the people, prohibiting the mob rule of the masses while at the same time functioning as a check against clerical power. His evolving view of the role of the ruling elder and his growing suspicion of New England theology helped nudge Princeton Seminary into *Old School Presbyterianism in the 1830s.

BIBLIOGRAPHY. *ANB* 15; DAB VI; B. C. Lane, "Miller and the Eldership: A Knickerbocker Goes to Nassau," *PSB* 6, no. 3 (1985) 211-24; S. Miller, *The Life of Samuel Miller,* 2 vols. (1869).

E. W. Kennedy

Missions, Presbyterian and Reformed. Like other churches in the post-Reformation era, those in the *Calvinist tradition did little to reach people beyond Europe. However, Sidney Rooy shows the roots of the modern missionary movement were in Reformed theology because it emphasized a genuine concern for the conversion of souls, expansion of the church and establishment of the kingdom of God. Also, *Puritanism in North America had a formative impact on mission outreach. According to Andrew Ross, four elements distinguished missionary enterprise in the Reformed tradition: a stress on the highest levels of *education for clergy and laity alike as an inherent good; church-centeredness, that is, the new Christians should as soon as possible form self-supporting, self-governing and self-propagating churches, and missions should be the activity of churches in the sending countries rather than independent societies; indigenization, as shown by the emphasis on vernacular Bible translation and literature and desire to develop an educated ministry and laity; and the creation of deep local loyalties among the new Christians.

The task of planting new churches on the frontier and renewing the older ones hindered the growth of mission outreach in North America, but a group of students at Andover Seminary committed themselves to overseas service and persuaded the Massachusetts Congregationalists to organize the American Board of Commissioners for Foreign Missions (1810). The first workers left for India in 1812, and in subsequent years endeavors were launched in Ceylon, China, Japan, Hawaii, Turkey, Syria, southern Africa, and elsewhere. Other Reformed bodies sent out workers under the ABCFM, but gradually they formed their own boards, and by 1913 the ABCFM had become "the agency of the Congregational churches for Christian work abroad," answerable to the denomination's general council.

The *Presbyterian Church in the U.S.A. (PCUSA) appropriated money for home mission work, and in 1802 a standing committee on missions was named. In 1812 the general assembly decided that to form a separate agency that would be an integral part of the church's program was "extremely inconvenient at this time" and gave its backing to the ABCFM. In 1816 the general assembly agreed to create a board of missions and authorized the formation of auxiliary societies at local levels to aid in raising funds and extending the board's operations. In 1817 the *Presbyterian Church in the U.S. (PCUS) joined with the *Dutch Reformed and Associate Reformed Churches to establish the United Foreign Missionary Society, whose object was "to spread the Gospel among the Indians of North America, the inhabitants of Mexico and South America, and in other portions of the heathen and anti-Christian world." Soon the United Society's leaders realized that the ABCFM's work was thriving and the two were appealing to the same constituency, and in 1826 they voted to merge with the ABCFM.

Meanwhile, sentiment in the Presbyterian church was growing for a separate agency, and in 1831 the Pittsburgh Synod formed the Western Foreign Missionary Society. Its leading light was Elisha B. Swift, who originally had planned to go out under the ABCFM, and it sent workers to Turkey and India. In 1837 it was expanded to become the Presbyterian Foreign Missionary Society, and the headquarters were moved to Philadelphia. Foreign missions were an issue in the schism between the *Old and *New School that occurred at this time. The Old School supported the new board of foreign missions while the New School continued an affiliation with the ABCFM. After the reunion in 1869 several ABCFM works were transferred to the Presbyterian board, and the era of Reformed interdenominational cooperation in sending missionaries ended.

When the Southern Presbyterians (PCUS) separated in 1861, they created a foreign mission board, but wartime conditions permitted them only to conduct Indian missions. In 1867 the denomination posted its first missionary to China, and in subsequent years it expanded the work there and launched significant endeavors in Korea, Japan and the Belgian Congo (Zaire). It even sent some black missionaries to the Congo, but the Belgian authorities halted this practice. In Asia it engaged in cooperative efforts with other denominations, but this proved to be divisive. In 1924, the peak year, 514 served under the Southern Presbyterian board. After World War II it emphasized moving the mission field bodies closer to the national churches, an action that was particularly effective in Taiwan.

By the time the two main Presbyterian bodies merged in the 1980s, their missionary forces had declined drastically. Those in the PCUS who opposed the merger formed the *Presbyterian Church in America (PCA) in 1973, and its board (Mission to the World) soon became the largest Presbyterian denominational agency, with more than 536 workers in 50 countries.

The smaller Presbyterian bodies have also been active. The *United Presbyterian Church of North America (UPCNA), a union of two Scottish Covenanter and Seceder groups in 1858, continued the labors of its predecessors in India and the Middle East. These grew into the significant Punjab mission in India and Coptic mission in Egypt. In 1912 Samuel *Zwemer, a veteran Dutch Reformed missionary and noted Islamicist, came to Cairo and began training church leaders to reach Muslims. The American University at Cairo, founded in 1920, took over this function, and although it was an ecumenical enterprise, the United Presbyterians played the key role in staffing it.

The Associate Reformed Presbyterian Church established a Board of Missions in 1839 and sent workers to Liberia, Egypt and India, but its major field today is Mexico, where it has labored among the Indian population and formed an indigenous church. Another small Covenanter body is the five-thousand-member *Reformed Presbyterian Church of North America, which maintains active works in the Mediterranean region and Japan. The *Evangelical Presbyterian Church, an evangelical denomination formed in 1981, supports a missionary staff of 35 people, while the *Cumberland Presbyterian Church (CPC) has a small program as well.

Missions were a major issue in the *fundamentalist controversy that rent the Northern Presbyterian church after World War I. In 1933 J. Gresham *Machen and his associates created the Independent Board for Presbyterian Foreign Missions in 1933 and sent its first missionary couple to India in 1934. When they refused to dissolve the independent board, the general assembly suspended them from the ministry, and they formed a new denomination. However, a rift opened among the dissidents over the issue of independency, and the *Orthodox Presbyterian Church (OPC, as it was renamed in 1939) set up its own agency to carry out mission work in Japan and Korea. Carl *McIntire and his Bible Presbyterians now controlled the independent board, and for a time it was quite active. However, after a schism in the 1950s most of its staff transferred to other conservative boards.

The Dutch Reformed Church (now *Reformed Church in America [RCA]) as early as 1784 decided to engage in church extension, and it cooperated in reaching Indians through the New York Missionary Society as well as took part in the short-lived United Foreign Missionary Society. The first work of its more conservative counterpart, the *Christian Reformed Church (CRC), was an Indian mission in New Mexico in 1896. After World War I fields were opened in China and Nigeria, and later in Japan, Taiwan, Sri Lanka, Argentina and Brazil. The most important effort was in Nigeria under the Sudan United Mission. In 1939 the CRC board took over the enterprise directly and later added some institutional ministries of the South African Dutch Reformed Church, including a theological school.

The *German Reformed Church functioned as a separate entity under the jurisdiction of the Church of Holland but in 1793 declared its independence. Officially renamed the General Synod of the Reformed Church in the United States in 1863, it financially supported a missionary in Turkey under the ABCFM from 1838 to 1866. While looking for a field of its own, the church gave money to the independent German Evangelical Mission Society of the U.S. When the society got into difficulties, it invited the *Evangelical Synod of North America (as it was named in 1877) to take over the work that it did in 1883-1884. It gave considerable money to the Basel and Barmen missions in Germany as well as to the American society. The Evangelical Synod then established a Board of Missions to administer the work in India and a new field, which was opened in Honduras in 1921.

Meanwhile, the Reformed Church in the U.S. created a board under denominational control and sent the first missionary to Japan in 1879. This was followed by a mission in China's Hunan province in 1900 and a United Mission in Mesopotamia in 1923 with the RCA and Northern Presbyterians. In 1934 the two German-American denominations merged to create the Evangelical and Reformed Church, and the mission agencies united two years later to form the Board of International Missions for the new group, although for a time afterward they still functioned separately. Finally it joined in the United Church of Christ merger and in 1961 became part of the United Church Board for World Ministries.

Four bodies united in 1875 to form the Presbyterian Church in Canada, but its predecessors had already been involved in mission. The Secession Synod of Nova Scotia in 1846 sent missionaries to the New Hebrides Islands and a few years later began works in Trinidad and British Guiana. In 1871-1872 the celebrated Canadian [Free] Presbyterian Church missionary George Leslie Mackay went to Formosa (Taiwan) and launched a major effort that resulted in a strong church in the northern part of the island, and in the 1950s it became an integral part of the autonomous Presbyterian Church of Formosa.

Presbyterians took the lead in women's missionary work as well. While on home leave from China in 1834, David Abeel called for single women to minister in Asia. Sarah Doremus, wife of a well-to-do businessman and member of a Dutch Reformed

Church, responded enthusiastically and began organizing a women's group, but the leader of the American Board thwarted her efforts. Still, Doremus remained committed to the idea and in 1860 organized the interdenominational Woman's Union Missionary Society, which sent out its first worker to Burma in 1861. Presbyterian women in Canada formed regional societies in 1876 and 1885. The movement spread throughout the Protestant denominations, and at least thirty-five boards were created which raised large amounts of money and sent out women to the mission fields.

Bibliography. R. P. Beaver, *American Protestant Women in World Mission* (1980); E. E. Elder, *Vindicating a Vision: The Story of the American Mission in Egypt* (1958); M. D. Hoff, *The Reformed Church in America: Structures for Mission* (1985); *MARC Mission Handbook, 1993-95* (1993); J. E. Mitchell, *The Associate Reformed Presbyterian Church of Mexico* (1970); J. S. Moir, *Enduring Witness: A History of the Presbyterian Church in Canada* (1975); S. H. Rooy, *The Theology of Missions in the Puritan Tradition* (1965); A. Ross, "Missionary Expansion," in *Encyclopedia of the Reformed Faith*, ed. D. K. McKim (1992); W. S. Rycroft, *The Ecumenical Witness of the United Presbyterian Church in the U.S.A.* (1968); E. H. Smith, *Nigerian Harvest* (1972); W. E. Strong, *The Story of the American Board* (1910); *Yearbook of American and Canadian Churches* (1993). R. V. Pierard

Modernists. *See* FUNDAMENTALIST-MODERNIST CONTROVERSY.

Moffett, Samuel Austin (1864-1939). Pioneer Presbyterian *missionary to northern Korea. Born in Madison, Indiana, Moffett studied chemistry at Hanover College (A.B., 1884; M.S., 1885) and attended McCormick Seminary (B.D., 1888). Under the influence of the Young Men's Christian Association, Dwight L. Moody and the Student Volunteer Movement, Moffett committed his life to Christian missions in 1886. In 1889 Moffett sailed for Korea with the Presbyterian Mission Board, arriving in the port city of Chemulpo on his twenty-sixth birthday, January 25, 1890.

By 1893 Moffett had moved to Pyongyang, the ancient capital city, and became in effect the first Protestant missionary to take up residence in inland Korea. Initially Moffett met with violent opposition, but he immediately began catechism classes and by 1895 had purchased 110 acres inside the city that soon became the theological and medical center of Presbyterian missionary labors in Korea. In large part because of Moffett's initiative, four Presbyterian churches formed the Korean Presbyterian Church in 1907, with Moffett as its moderator.

Influenced by John Livingston *Nevius, American missionary to China, Moffett adopted Nevius's three-self principle, concerned with building strong indigenous churches and well-trained leaders. In his forty-six years in Korea, Moffett cofounded Union Christian College (now Soong Jun University), founded the Presbyterian Theological Seminary and encouraged the young Korean Presbyterian Church to form its own mission board. For his foresight and ceaseless initiative in establishing new churches, Moffett's Korean friends named him the Looking-up-the-Road Man. Forced out of Korea by the Japanese in 1936, Moffett died three years later in Monrovia, California.

Bibliography. M. Seth, "The Looking-up-the-Road Man," *Presbyterian Life* 7 (July 24, 1954) 10-13, 26; R. E. Shearer, *Wildfire: Church Growth in Korea* (1966). S.W. Sunquist

Montgomery, Lucy Maude (1874-1942). Canadian Presbyterian author. Born at Clifton (now New London), Prince Edward Island, she was reared by grandparents in the nearby Cavendish area before earning a teacher's certificate at Prince of Wales College, Charlottetown (1893-1894), and then studying English literature at Dalhousie College, Halifax, for a year. She taught in rural schools on Prince Edward Island (1894-1898) and was employed briefly (1901) by the *Daily Echo* newspaper in Halifax, but otherwise she resided in Cavendish, where she attended her grandmother and developed her freelance writing.

Montgomery's first book, *Anne of Green Gables* (1908), introduced readers to "one of the immortal children of fiction"—the feisty, romantic orphan Anne Shirley. Its success prompted an immediate sequel, *Anne of Avonlea* (1909), and eventually a series of seven "Anne" books. From 1908 to 1939 Montgomery wrote twenty-four books, mainly children's literature, including an autobiographical "Emily" trilogy, a personal memoir, *The Alpine Path* (1917), and two works of adult fiction: *The Blue Castle* (1926) and *A Tangled Web* (1931). Her work has been the stimulus for numerous plays, musicales and movies, as well as a popular weekly television series. In 1923 she became the first Canadian woman Fellow of the (British) Royal Society of Arts (F.R.S.A.), and in 1935 she was awarded the Order of the British Empire. Combining a celebration of life and adolescent experience, Montgomery's work effectively marginalized Presbyterian convictions in favor of larger conceptions of virtue and feeling. Despite misgivings about Christianity's long-term viability, she kept her opinions private.

Montgomery married Ewan Macdonald, a Presbyterian minister, in 1911, and permanently moved from her beloved Prince Edward Island to accompany him to the Ontario communities of Leaskdale (1911-1925) and Norval (1925-1935) and eventually to retirement in Toronto. Her husband's longstanding nervous instability added considerable stress to her life. She died in Toronto. Her body was returned for burial to Cavendish, Prince Edward Island, where a national park now celebrates her literary legacy.

BIBLIOGRAPHY. M. Gillen, *The Wheel of Things* (1975): H. Ridley, *The Story of L. M. Montgomery* (1956); J. Sorfleet, ed., *L. M. Montgomery* (1976); W. Toye, ed., *The Oxford Companion to Canadian Literature* (1983). G. G. Scorgie

Moore, George Foot (1851-1931). Old Testament scholar. Born in Pennsylvania, Moore received much of his early education through private study and tutoring by his father, a Presbyterian minister. Graduating second in his class from Yale (B.A., 1872), Moore studied for the ministry at Union Theological Seminary (B.D., 1877) and received Presbyterian ordination (1878). After pastoring in Zanesville, Ohio (1878-1883), Moore became successively professor of Old Testament at Andover Theological Seminary (1883-1902) and professor of the history of religion at Harvard (1902-1928) until his retirement. At Harvard Moore served as a member of both the faculty of arts and sciences and the faculty of divinity.

Moore's numerous publications gained him international recognition as a critical scholar in Hebrew and Old Testament. His classic commentary on Judges was published early in his career (1895). Having studied and taught in Germany (1885; 1909-1910), Moore's work reflected German scholarship, which he was instrumental in introducing into America. In addition to serving as assistant editor of *The Andover Review* (1884-1903) and editor of the *Harvard Theological Review* (1913- 1924), his publications on the Old Testament were complemented by significant contributions to the history of religions and early Judaism, as seen in his two-volume *History of Religions* (1913-1919) and the three volumes of *Judaism in the First Centuries of the Christian Era* (1927-1930). Moore's broad interests and expertise are likewise reflected in the societies that he served as president: the American Academy of Arts and Sciences, the Massachusetts Historical Society, the American Oriental Society and the Society of Biblical Literature and Exegesis.

BIBLIOGRAPHY. *ANB* 15. S. Meier

Moorehead, William Gallogly (1836-1914).† Presbyterian minister and educator. Born near Rix Mills, Ohio, Moorehead graduated from Muskingum College (B.A., 1858), before attending Allegheny and Xenia theological seminaries (B.D. from the latter, 1862). After ordination in 1862 he served seven years in Florence and Sienna, Italy, as a *United Presbyterian Church (UPC) *missionary under the auspices of the American and Foreign Christian Union. Upon his return he served as pastor of First United Presbyterian Church, Xenia, Ohio (1870-75). In 1873 he accepted an appointment to Xenia Seminary as professor of New Testament literature and exegesis, which he taught until 1908, when he became professor of English Bible and biblical theology. He became president of the seminary in 1899 and would remain Xenia's president and professor until his death. He also continued to pastor local churches until 1885.

Moorehead was prominent among American premillennialists, speaking frequently at Bible institutes and Bible and prophecy conferences. He also served as a longtime leader of the Niagara Conference, an interdenominational summer prophecy conference that became a popular forum for the rising dispensational theology. In the 1890s he modified his eschatology, joining some other Niagara leaders in asserting that the rapture of the church would occur after (as opposed to before) the tribulation. The theological conflict that ensued helped bring the Niagara conferences to an end in 1900. Moorehead also wrote eight books, including a firm defense of the Mosaic authorship of the Pentateuch. A prominent leader in the UPC, he represented the denomination in a number of national and international organizations.

BIBLIOGRAPHY. E. R. Sandeen, *The Roots of Fundamentalism: British and American Millenarianism, 1800-1930* (1970); *Testimonial and Memorial to William Gallogly Moorehead for Forty-one Years Professor in the Xenia Theological Seminary* (1915). W. V. Trollinger

Morgan, Joseph (1671-1749?). Presbyterian minister. Born at Preston, Connecticut, Morgan studied at Yale College (B.A., 1702; honorary M.A., 1719) and served Congregational churches in Greenwich, Fairfield County, Connecticut. From 1700 to 1704 he was pastor of the Bedford, Eastchester and Westchester churches, composed of settlers from Connecticut, in Westchester County, New York. The governor, Lord Cornbury, tried to make the *Puritan churches and ministers part of the Anglican establishment. Many churches lost their buildings and the pastors their manses.

Morgan returned to Greenwich and ministered there until 1708. In 1709 he settled into a twenty-year pastorate in the Presbyterian church in Freehold, New Jersey, and preached the ordination sermon of Jonathan *Dickinson. He was received into the Philadelphia Presbytery in 1710, being one of many colonial Congregationalists who entered the Presbyterian denomination when they moved out of *New England. In 1721, along with other ministers of New England origin, Morgan protested a proposal to strengthen the powers of the synod and the presbyteries and to threaten the rights of conscientious dissent. Around 1731 he moved to the Maidenhead and Hopewell churches in New Jersey. He was moderator of synod in 1731. In 1737 he was temporarily suspended from the ministry for drunkenness.

Morgan had a reputation for gentleness and tolerance and was not a strict denominationalist. Although he was a *Calvinist, he opposed Great Awakening *revivalism. The Philadelphia presbytery sought in vain around 1739 to restore him to his former Hopewell congregation, over the objection of the prorevival congregation. As an amateur scientist, inventor and philosopher he frequently corresponded with the Royal Society in London. Several of his sermons, a utopian novel and tracts against deism, Socinianism, *Arminianism and antipaedobaptists were published.

Bibliography. W. J. Bell Jr., "The Reverend Mr. Joseph Morgan, An American Correspondent of the Royal Society, 1732-1739," *Proceedings of the American Philosophical Society* 95 (June 1951) 254-61; L. J. Trinterud, *The Forming of an American Tradition: A Re-Examination of Colonial Presbyterianism* (1949); R. Webster, *History of the Presbyterian Church in America* (1857).

A. H. Freundt Jr.

Morris, Edward Dafydd (1825-1915).† Presbyterian minister and theologian. Born in Utica, New York, Morris graduated from Yale in 1849, where he became involved in the politics of the Free-Soil party and Auburn Theological Seminary in 1852. Of Welsh extraction, he occasionally preached or lectured in the Welsh language throughout his life. Ordained in the *New School Cayuga Presbytery later that year, he pastored the Second Presbyterian Church of Auburn, New York (1852-1855), and the Second Presbyterian Church of Columbus, Ohio (1855-1867). In 1867 he moved to Lane Theological Seminary in Cincinnati, Ohio, teaching church history there until 1874 and systematic theology from 1874 to 1897. He served as a trustee of Lane from 1863 to 1867, and again in 1870, in order to serve as treasurer and superintendent of the seminary.

An evangelical, ecumenical, New School *Calvinist, both his teaching and many periodical articles and books—most importantly, *Theology of the Westminster Symbols* (1900)—displayed clarity of thinking, the broad range of his interests, his irenic and friendly spirit and his fervent commitment to the theology and mission of his denomination, broadly interpreted. Deeply involved in the successful negotiations to reunite the *Old and New Schools of the *Presbyterian Church in the U.S.A. (PCUSA) in the 1860s, Morris's efforts were rewarded by his election as the moderator of the general assembly of the reunited PCUSA in 1875. He later served on the committee charged with revising the *Westminster Confession in the 1890s, making substantial contributions in the revision process.

Bibliography. *ANB* 15; *DAB* VII.

G. S. Smith

Moss, Robert Verelle, Jr. (1922-1976). Second president of the United Church of Christ, ecumenical leader, educator and New Testament scholar. Born in Wilson, North Carolina, Moss was baptized and confirmed into the Corinth congregation (Hickory, North Carolina) of the former Reformed Church in the United States (Southern Synod) and was ordained at his home church in 1946, which was then a part of the Evangelical and Reformed Church. He was educated at Franklin and Marshall College (A.B., 1943) and Lancaster Theological Seminary (B.D., 1945), both schools in Lancaster, Pennsylvania, and the University of Chicago (Ph.D., 1954). He taught in the department of religion of Franklin and Marshall College before becoming professor of New Testament at Lancaster Theological Seminary (1951-1957). Even after becoming president of that institution (1957-1969), Moss continued as professor of New Testament. From 1969 until his death Moss served as the second president of the United Church of Christ, which had been formed in 1957 by a merger of the Evangelical and Reformed Church with the Congregational-Christian Churches.

During his tenure as president of the United Church of Christ Moss was deeply engaged with the social issues that confronted the church in the late 1960s and early 1970s. Even though one of his sons was wounded in the Vietnam war, he was a strong advocate of amnesty for Vietnam war resisters. Moss was likewise an avid proponent of racial justice. He gave active support to the decision to use denominational funds for the legal defense of the Reverend Benjamin Chavis and the Wilmington Ten, who were accused of stirring up racial violence in Wilmington, North Carolina, in 1971. Early in his presidency he urged the churches to work toward the elimination of cultural and institutional sexism and to name women to "highly visible" positions of responsibility.

Moss was a leader in the ecumenical movement. He served on the Central Committee of the World Council of Churches and the executive committee of the National Council of Churches. He was an official observer at the Second Vatican Council in 1962, a delegate to the Third Assembly of the World Council of Churches in New Delhi in 1961 and the Fifth Assembly in Nairobi in 1975. He was cochairman of the Roman Catholic-Presbyterian and Reformed Dialogue group from 1966 to 1968. It was largely due to his initiative that the United Church of Christ began conversations with the Christian Church (Disciples of Christ) in 1977 toward possible union.

During his period as president of Lancaster Theological Seminary, Moss assumed a leadership role in theological education. He served as chairman of the Commission on Accrediting for the American Association of Theological Schools (1964-1966) and then as president of the latter organization.

Moss was the author of three books, *The Life of Paul* (1955), *We Believe* (1957) and *As Paul Sees Christ* (1958), as well as numerous articles in professional journals and magazines. He died in Montclair, New Jersey. J. B. Payne

Murray, John (1898-1975).† Presbyterian minister and theologian. Reared in the Free Presbyterian Church of Scotland, Murray studied theology at Princeton Theological Seminary (Th.M., 1927). In 1930, after fulfilling a commitment to teach one year at Princeton (1929-1930), he joined his former professor, J. Gresham *Machen, on the faculty of the newly formed Westminster Theological Seminary in Philadelphia. There he taught systematic theology until his retirement in 1966. Seeing the need for a conservative Reformed journal to continue the theological scholarship of the defunct *Princeton Theological Review,* he became one of the founding editors of the *Westminster Theological Journal* in 1938. A minister in the *Orthodox Presbyterian Church (OPC), he was deeply involved in the life of the church on both sides of the Atlantic throughout his career. Following retirement, he preached and lectured extensively throughout Great Britain until shortly before his death.

In a remarkable way Murray combined a systematizing bent with superior exegetical gifts, fused by deep *piety. Influenced especially by Benjamin Breckinridge *Warfield and Geerhardus *Vos, he sought to apply the biblical-theological method and insights of Vos to systematic theology, perhaps seen best in his development of his mentor's insights regarding the covenant in *The Covenant of Grace* (1953). While he did not produce a major work in systematic theology, relying largely on Charles *Hodge's *Systematic Theology,* his commentary, *The Epistle to the Romans* (2 vols., 1960, 1965), was well received. Through his lecturing and numerous books and articles (accessible in the *Collected Writings of John Murray,* 4 vols., 1976-1983) he brought fresh exegetical depth to many areas of classical Reformed theology, to which he remained firmly committed.

Bibliography. I. H. Murray, "The Life of John Murray," in *Collected Writings of John Murray,* vol. 3 (1976). R. B. Gaffin

N

Neo-orthodoxy. Protestant theological movement of the twentieth century. Neo-orthodoxy in America became an important force in the 1930s when a number of theologians became increasingly dissatisfied and disillusioned with the liberal theology in which they had been trained. As the works of Europeans such as Karl *Barth and Emil Brunner became known, their views came to have an increasing effect on American theologians and in mainline American churches. This influence was strongest from the late 1930s to the 1950s. After that, neo-orthodoxy maintained a following, though its theological force among ministers and theologians abated.

Neo-orthodoxy is also sometimes called neo-reformation theology, neo-Calvinism or neo-liberalism. From one perspective, neo-orthodoxy was a rediscovery of central theological themes of the Protestant Reformation, so it represented an attempt to restate these doctrines in a contemporary fashion. Insofar as major proponents of neo-orthodoxy were Reformed, as opposed to Lutheran, in their commitments, the movement had a strong *Calvinistic flavor. Since many American theologians identified with neo-orthodoxy were former theological liberals, there is also a sense in which the movement represented a renovation or revision of liberalism. Thus a plurality of labels is appropriate. *Neo-orthodoxy* as a term designated a basic commitment to orthodox doctrine as the normative expression of Christian faith. Some American theological conservatives, however, opposed the reformulations of neo-orthodoxy and stated that neo-orthodoxy was actually no-orthodoxy.

The Failure of Liberalism. The beginnings of American neo-orthodoxy can be traced to the 1930s, when the full effects of World War I, coupled with the Great Depression in America, began to take their toll on American theologians. These events led them to question and reject the basic tenets of liberal theology. Liberalism stressed a basic continuity between human beings and God. This orientation expressed itself in an emphasis on the immanence, rather than the transcendence, of God, the belief that humanity is inherently good and morally perfectible and thus the view that religious knowledge comes through the use of reason and religious experience. Liberalism, therefore, was compatible with the empirical methods of natural science in which observation and experimentation were key ingredients.

From the liberal perspective, the Bible is to be subjected to the latest in literary and historical research. It is regarded as the record of the religious experiences of ancient peoples that could be repeated again and again in each generation. The religious truths of these "abiding experiences" are always developing. The task of theologians is to construct categories to describe religious experience in light of contemporary science and culture. These perspectives of liberalism were influenced by the principles of continuity, autonomy and dynamism. In emphasizing these, the formative forces of liberal thought stood in dramatic contrast to traditional Christian orthodoxy.

The Swiss theologian Karl Barth was led to reject liberal theology through his renewed study of Scripture, first expressed in his *Commentary on Romans* (1919; 2d ed., 1922). Barth, however, was also shaken when his former theological professors, who had taught him the principles of liberal theology, uncritically supported the kaiser's policies when World War I broke out. These included the historian of dogma Adolf von Harnack (1851-1930), the major liberal theologian of the day. Harnack had popularized the views of Albrecht Ritschl (1822-1889), who, along with Friedrich Schliermacher (1768-1834), had laid the foundations of liberal theology.

The American Movement. In 1939 *The Christian Century,* America's leading liberal theological journal, published a series of autobiographical reflections by American mainline church leaders. This series, known as "How My Mind Has Changed," has been an occasional feature of the journal ever since. The 1939 articles revealed a significant theological shift overtaking American theologians. Thirty-two of the thirty-four contributors noted the emerging "theology of crisis" proposed by Barth and Brunner. Throughout the 1930s books and articles by liberal Protestants questioned the viability of liberalism.

Henry P. *Van Dusen wrote of "The Sickness of Liberal Religion" (1931), Wilhelm Pauck asked "What Is Wrong with Liberalism?" (1935) and Henry Sloane *Coffin questioned "Can Liberalism Survive?" (1935). In 1935 Harry Emerson *Fosdick preached a sermon entitled "Beyond Modernism," which was published in *The Christian Century.* There he claimed the church must not accommodate itself to modern culture but challenge it.

Early neo-orthodox proponents in America included Walter Lowrie, H. Richard *Niebuhr, Pauck, George W. *Richards, Edwin Lewis and Elmer Homrighausen. While they did not necessarily follow Barth's theological method, they did take note of Barth and his critique of liberalism. For instance, Reinhold *Niebuhr, in *Moral Man and Immoral Society* (1932), emphasized the neo-orthodox theme of the radical nature of human sinfulness and recognized the unrealistic optimism of Protestant liberalism, which was incapable of dealing effectively with the social conditions of the times. Later, however, Niebuhr joked that an even better title for his volume would have been *Immoral Man and Even More Immoral Society.*

Neo-orthodoxy came to prominence in the wake of World War II. During the 1940s and 1950s, neo-orthodoxy's realism was welcomed by many in mainline Protestant denominations. As an alternative to liberalism and *fundamentalism, it offered a fresh means of hearing the gospel. By locating the focus of revelation in Jesus Christ, to whom Scripture witnesses, neo-orthodoxy seemed to offer a way of allowing the Bible to serve as a source of doctrine without demanding literary or historical perfection. Neo-orthodoxy was particularly strong in the *Presbyterian Church in the U.S.A. (PCUSA). There it affected the church's ministers, its doctrinal deliberations and the church-school curriculum. The denomination's Princeton Theological Seminary, under the leadership of John Alexander *Mackay, became a major center for neo-orthodox theology. The *Confession of 1967, adopted as part of the church's confessional standards, shows a number of neo-orthodox emphases.

However, as America moved into an era of progress and increasing prosperity in the decades following World War II, neo-orthodoxy began to wane as a dominant theological force. Some have noted that whereas neo-orthodoxy had chastised liberalism for only reflecting its culture's optimism, neo-orthodoxy was reflecting its culture's despair. When America moved into better times, the appeal of neo-orthodoxy lessened. By the 1960s theology had become issue-oriented in response to powerful forces of secularism. During the 1970s and 1980s process theology and liberation theology became major theological movements, gradually eclipsing the influence of neo-orthodoxy.

As a theological position, however, neo-orthodoxy maintains strong individual adherents. Its emphases on the transcendence of God coupled with a strong sense of human sin has been a part of many of the theologies of evangelicalism in America. In particular, a number of prominent American theologians have noted the impact of Barth's theology on their own theological formation. In that sense, neo-orthodoxy still exerts an influence, and its perspectives continue to shape American Christian thought.

See also BARTH, KARL.

BIBLIOGRAPHY. S. E. Ahlstrom, "Continental Influence on American Christian Thought Since World War I," *CH* 21 (1958) 256-72; K. Cauthen, *The Impact of American Religious Liberalism* (1962); W. Hordern, *The Case for a New Reformation Theology* (1959); D. K. McKim, ed., *How Karl Barth Changed My Mind* (1986); D. N. Voskuil, "America Encounters Karl Barth, 1919-1939," *FH* 12 (1980) 61-74; idem, "American Protestant Neo-Orthodoxy and Its Search for Realism (1925-1939)," *Ultimate Reality and Meaning* 8 (1985) 277-87; H. A. Warren, *Theologians of a New World Order* (1997).

D. K. McKim

Netherlands Reformed Congregations of North America. A conservative *Calvinistic denomination with roots in the Netherlands. The mother denomination in the Netherlands, the *Gereformeerde Gemeenten* (Reformed Congregations), was officially organized in 1907 under the leadership of G. Hendrik Kersten (1882-1948) and Nicolaas H. Beversluis (1850-1931) as a result of a merger between the *Gereformeerde Kerken onder het Kruis* (Reformed Churches under the Cross; established in 1839 after breaking away from the Secession congregations that seceded from the Reformed State Church in 1834) and the *Ledeboeriaanse gemeenten* (Ledeboerian congregations; established in 1841 under the leadership of Lambertus G. C. Ledeboer [1808-1863], who seceded from the Reformed State Church). Both the Reformed Churches under the Cross and the Ledeboerian congregations were heavily influenced by the Dutch *Nadere Reformatie* (Dutch Second Reformation), a primarily seventeenth- and early eighteenth-century movement that sought to apply Reformation truths to daily life and heart experience. The *Nadere Reformatie* is the Dutch counterpart to English *Puritanism and in some senses to the Scottish Covenanters.

Though the ties between the *Gereformeerde Gemeenten* and the Netherlands Reformed Congregations of North America (NRC) are close, the NRC is a distinct denomination with roots dating back to the mid-1850s. The NRC's oldest congregations were organized in 1865 (South Holland, Illinois) and 1870 (Grand Rapids, Michigan). Most of the members of the nineteenth-century congregations destined to join the NRC after 1907 were Dutch immigrants from either the Reformed Churches under the Cross or the Ledeboerian congregations. These congregations were usually called "Nederduitsch" Reformed Congregations or Old Reformed Congregations.

In 1910 the NRC (then called *Gereformeerde Gemeenten in Amerika)* held its first synod, representing seven congregations in Michigan, New Jersey, Illinois and Wisconsin. Throughout the twentieth century the NRC have slowly expanded primarily through immigration and internal growth. In the 1950s a wave of immigrants from the Netherlands came to Canada and formed new congregations.

Since 1975 the NRC have been active in Christian education. Every congregation with a membership that exceeds 150 has its own Christian school. By 1994 the Netherlands Reformed Christian Education Association (organized in 1982) included eleven elementary schools, seven high schools, 155 teachers (mostly NRC) and 2,658 students.

In 1993 the denomination underwent a split when the synodical body deposed the consistory of its largest and oldest Grand Rapids congregation on the supposed ground of schism because the consistory stated it would obey synod unconditionally in all matters, providing synod did not make decisions contrary to Scripture or church order. The substantive, underlying issue was the preaching of an unconditional offer of grace—the same issue that split the mother denomination in the Netherlands in 1953. The split resulted in the establishment of the Heritage Netherlands Reformed Congregations (1994), which view themselves as continuing the authentic NRC tradition that supports an unconditional offer of grace.

Both the NRC and HNRC believe Scripture to be the infallible and inerrant word of God. Both use the King James Version in worship services. Singing is always congregational and limited to psalmody with an organ accompaniment. The focus of worship services is on preaching. Sermons underscore the vertical line of the gospel, stressing that a right relationship with God is indispensable for proper horizontal, person-to-person relationships. Also accented is the need for personal conversion, which results in experiencing the reality of the guilt of sin; deliverance in Christ; and gratitude for the electing love of the Father, redeeming love of the Son and sanctifying love of the Spirit.

True conversion is never presumed—also not in children. The child growing up in the church receives the outward benefits of the covenant, but the covenant's essence can be received only by regeneration. Several NRC congregations left the *Christian Reformed Church (CRC) after that denomination adopted Abraham *Kuyper's doctrine of presupposed regeneration.

The NRC and HNRC subscribe to three Continental Reformed doctrinal standards: the *Belgic Confession of Faith (1561), *Heidelberg Catechism (1563) and *Canons of Dort (1618-1619). The Heidelberg Catechism is preached weekly except on church feast days.

A biblically conservative life is emphasized as an outgrowth of bowing gratefully under divine lordship. The Christian must maintain the church's antithetical heritage of being in but not becoming of the world. Consequently television, dancing, theater attendance, overindulging in sports and modern fashions and all that tends to promote fleshly lusts are viewed as hindrances to the Christian's godly walk.

Church government is presbyterial, with classes held twice a year; synods meet biannually. Each church, however, holds title to its own properties.

The official periodical for the NRC is *The Banner of Truth;* for the HNRC, *The Banner of Sovereign Grace Truth.* Both denominations have active book and tape ministries and are becoming more involved in mission work.

Bibliography. J. R. Beeke, "Our NRC's 80th Anniversary," *Banner of Truth* 53, no. 8 (Aug. 1987) 202-4; 53,9 (Sept. 1987) 230-31; Z. Crum et al., *'k Zal Gedenken: Portret van 75 jaar Gereformeerde Gemeenten* (1981); C. de Jongste, *Klacht en Jubel: facetten uit de 'kleine kerkhistorie' rondom Ds. Nicolaas Hendrik Beversluis* (1983); G. H. Kersten and J. Van Zweden, *A Brief Historical Survey of the Reformed Congregations in the Netherlands and the United States of America* (1951). J. R. Beeke

Nevin, Alice (1837-1925). A leading female voice in the late-nineteenth-century *German Reformed Church, known for authorship and composition of hymns. Nevin was born in 1837, when her father, John Williamson *Nevin, was professor at the Presbyterian Theological Seminary near Pittsburgh. The family moved to Mercersburg in 1840 as her father transferred to the German Reformed Church and the faculty of its small seminary. The theology associated with John Williamson Nevin and Philip *Schaff incorporated a high Christ-centered ecclesiology, deep sense of history and formal liturgy.

In 1851 a fatigued Nevin resigned his professorship and moved to Lancaster. Alice Nevin and her four siblings finished growing up on the family estate, Caenarvon Place, adjacent to that of President James Buchanan. The family continued in the German Reformed Church, with the father teaching at Franklin and Marshall College from 1861, serving as president from 1866 to 1876, and much involved in the liturgical controversy that grew out of the *Mercersburg theology. In 1871 the seminary moved to Lancaster, sharing facilities with the college for twenty years. The Nevin children absorbed their father's theological perspective, as two of them became prominent Episcopalians and Alice exhibited a high liturgical commitment in her work as a church musician.

Nevin's education centered on literary and musical studies. Her artistic sensibilities were elevated during visits with her sister Blanche (who became a nationally-known artist and sculptor) to Italy, where her brother Robert was rector of the Episcopal church in Rome. After the organization of St. Stephen's Church at Franklin and Marshall College (1865), Alice Nevin served for many years as organist and choir director. This was a significant position in the German Reformed Church, for these were the years of struggle over the proposed, highly liturgical Order of Worship (1866). The college church was in effect the stage on which the liturgy was most carefully performed. Nevin authored and composed many original hymns for adults and children, some of which appeared in the denomination's *Weekly Messenger.* She published a book of *Hymns and Carols for Church and Sunday School* (1879), which was widely used in German Reformed churches. This collection of classic and new music, including some of her own, is notable for its sophistication, as she abhorred "the jingling rhymes and melodies, called Sunday-school hymns and songs, with which the country is flooded." She believed that even music for the church's infant school could have dignity, while music for "children from ten to sixteen years of age, can be used equally well in the service of the church."

Nevin assumed a major role as a civic leader and philanthropist in Lancaster. Three years before her death she published a small book of *Poems* (1922). One of these, "God's Will," concludes with a succinct expression of the theology she shared with her father: "When one with Thee, my life shall be / Attuned to gladsome melody."

See also MERCERSBURG THEOLOGY; NEVIN, JOHN WILLIAMSON.

BIBLIOGRAPHY. A. Nevin, *Hymns and Carols for Church and Sunday-School* (1879).

C. E. Hambrick-Stowe

Nevin, John Williamson (1803-1886).† Reformed theologian and educator. Born near Shippensburg, Pennsylvania, Nevin was reared and educated as a Presbyterian, graduating from Union College (B.A., 1821) and Princeton Theological Seminary (1826), where he studied with Charles *Hodge and later substituted for Hodge as instructor of Bible and oriental languages (1826-1828). When Hodge returned from his studies in Europe, Nevin accepted a post at Western Theological Seminary near Pittsburgh, where he taught for a decade. By 1840, when Nevin was called to Mercersburg Seminary of the *German Reformed Church, he had come strongly under the influence of the writings of German theologians such as Isaac A. Dorner (1809-1884) and Johann A. W. Neander (1789-1850). For a period of more than three years, Nevin served as the sole professor at the seminary while also holding (1841-1853) the position of president of Marshall College. With the added stimulus brought by the coming of Philip *Schaff to Mercersburg in 1844, the work of Nevin and Mercersburg Seminary began to rise in prominence.

Just one year earlier, Nevin demonstrated his gift for controversy with his critique of American new measures *revivalism, *The Anxious Bench* (1843). American revivalistic individualism and sectarianism, said Nevin, violated a true sense of the church and seriously devalued the *sacraments. As an alternative, he advocated a system of nurture based on catechetical instruction. Nevin's fully developed understanding of the Lord's Supper appeared in 1846 as *The Mystical Presence: A Vindication of the Reformed or Calvinistic Doctrine of the Holy Eucharist.* Nevin argued that the Reformed churches in America had lost the essential position of John *Calvin on the Eucharist in favor of a Zwinglian memorialist doctrine. This volume kicked off a wide-ranging, thirty-year theological battle with his former mentor, Hodge, who believed that Nevin had capitulated to the liberalizing trends of German idealism. Nevin responded by charging Hodge with a rationalistic systematizing that ignored the organic dimension of Scripture.

From 1849 to 1852 Nevin served as primary contributor and editor of the *Mercersburg Review*, the chief organ for disseminating the *Mercersburg theology. During much of that period, Nevin and Schaff were involved in the often acrimonious debates within the German Reformed Church over the relationship between Protestantism and Roman Catholicism. In his zeal to defend the church of Rome against what he perceived to be unfair attacks by Protestants, and due to his own intensive study of the church fathers, Nevin developed deep sympathy for Roman Catholicism. Indeed, for a time in 1852 it appeared that Nevin might ally himself with the church of Rome, but after a period of retirement and convalescence Nevin emerged as a defender of Protestantism. Nevin lectured at Franklin and Marshall College from 1861 to 1866 and served as president of that institution from 1866 to 1876. The last decade of his life was spent in retirement.

Nevin's most important contributions to theology and church life in America were his critique of the "sect spirit" and the excesses of revivalism and his emphasis on the importance of tradition and the church. He was one of the most influential and controversial figures in the German Reformed Church in America.

See also MERCERSBURG THEOLOGY.

BIBLIOGRAPHY. *ANB* 16; T. Appel, *The Life and Work of John Williamson Nevin* (1889); *DAB* VII; *DARB; NCAB* 5; S. Hamstra and A. J. Griffioen, eds., *Reformed Confessionalism in Nineteenth-Century America: Essays on the Thought of John Williamson Nevin* (1995); J. H. Nichols, *Romanticism in American Theology: Nevin and Schaff at Mercersburg* (1961); R. E. Wentz, *John Williamson Nevin: American Theologian* (1997). S. R. Graham

Nevius, John Livingston (1829-1893).† Presbyterian *missionary. Born near Ovid, New York, Nevius attended Union College, Schenectady, (B.A., 1848) and, after teaching school in Georgia for a year, Princeton Theological Seminary (B.D., 1853), where he decided to become a missionary. Ordained by the Presbytery of New Brunswick that May and married the following month, he and his bride set sail in September for China. Assigned to Ning Po, China, under the Presbyterian Mission Board, he was there for several years (1854-1859) and then spent a brief period in Japan (1859-1861), where he worked on a *Compendium of Theology* for the Chinese church. Two more terms were spent in Shantung province at Tungchow (1861-1864) and Chefoo (1871-1893).

Nevius objected to the conventional practice of mission boards paying national evangelists for their services. On the occasion of a visit to Korea in the early 1880s, he formulated what he believed to be the biblical view of church planting based on 1 Corinthians 7:20, "Let every man abide in the same calling wherein he was called" (AV). Missionary churches should be self-supporting, self-propagating and self-governing units, Nevius concluded. His treatise, published in China in 1885, appeared in book form the following year and appeared in two successive editions by 1889. In 1890 missionaries in Korea invited Nevius as a consultant to review their field, after which the Korean Presbyterian Church experienced extraordinary growth. From one hundred communicant members at that time, the church grew to thirty thousand in 1910 and one hundred thousand in 1933. When his *Planting and Development of Missionary Churches* was issued in a fourth edition after World War II, the Korean Presbyterians reported eight hundred thousand communicants (*see* Korean-American Presbyterians).

Nevius also applied his principles with notable success in his work in central Shantung. Nevius's theories were required for study by missionary candidates and had an obvious influence on subsequent theories of church planting and growth. Despite the widespread acceptance of his methods, however, Nevius faced resistance from contemporaries who questioned the arbitrariness of paying foreign workers and insisting on self-support for national ministers, as well as the criticism that after Nevius left Shantung, the church there failed to exhibit the characteristics he expected. Later studies, moreover, suggest that rapid church growth in Korea resulted as much from fortuitous circumstances as from the application of Nevius's methods.

A prolific author in both Chinese and English, Nevius described and analyzed the "strange psychical phenomena" that he encountered in the orient in *Demon Possession and Allied Themes* (1894), which challenged the widespread belief, even among evangelicals, that demon possession no longer occurred. Widely reviewed in both Christian and scientific journals, the book proved to be highly influential among missionaries who often encountered similar phenomena throughout the world, but it was generally scorned by the medical journals. Nevius cautiously suggested that wherever the gospel was first proclaimed, demonic activity would manifest itself in a similar manner to that recounted in the Christian Gospels. Refraining from directly casting the demons out, Nevius admonished demon-possessed people to trust in Christ, claiming that once people became Christians, the demons inevitably left them alone. Nevius died peacefully in his home near Chefoo a few months before the book was published.

Bibliography. *ANB* 16; C. Clark, *The Korean Church and the Nevius Methods* (1930); *DAB* VII; H. S. C. Nevius, *The Life of John Livingstone Nevius: For Forty Years a Missionary in China* (1895).

E. A. Wilson

New England, Presbyterians and. Throughout the colonial period and well into the nineteenth century, a lively and complex history characterized the relationship between Presbyterians and New England. The source of this relationship was the Reformed tradition mediated through *Puritanism in England and Presbyterianism in Scotland and Ireland and given written expression in the *Westminster Confession of Faith (1648).

Presbyterian Influences in New England. The Puritans who settled New England in the 1620s and 1630s—both the separatist Pilgrims of Plymouth Plantation and the nonseparatists of the Massachusetts Bay Colony—overwhelmingly supported a congregational form of church government over against the episcopacy of the Church of England. However, despite the identification of the New England Way of church government with autonomous, covenanted, lay-ruled congregations, both Presbyterians and their form of *polity penetrated New England. Many Puritans held to mild Presbyterianism in the administration of the internal affairs; that is, they embraced government by a board of elders with the sanction of the lay brethren of the individual church, but they rejected the Presbyterian model of the power of synods over churches.

Because New England's earliest churches never precisely settled the question of the proper relationship of one church to another, it was inevitable that problems would arise. In light of the controversies over Anne Hutchinson and Roger Williams, the continued pressure from Presbyterian-minded laity and clergy in New England and the rising Presbyterian party in England, New England ministers met to codify principles of Congregational church government. The Cambridge Platform (1648) defined the polity of Congregationalism in great detail. The platform affirmed the autonomy of the local church, but at the same time it embodied some presbyterian ideals. The office of the ruling elder was recognized, ordination by other ministers was allowed and the usefulness of councils and synods whose authority was advisory and admonitory, though not judicially binding, was acknowledged.

Despite such efforts to clarify the New England Way, the subsequent history of colonial New England religious life, especially in the Connecticut River Valley, was punctuated with strife over strict Congregational versus Presbyterian forms of church polity. In the seventeenth century, Connecticut's controversy over presbyterianism culminated in the Toleration Act of 1669, which granted toleration to Presbyterians. In western Massachusetts, Solomon Stoddard at Northampton urged the churches of the Bay Colony to develop a Presbyterian or connectional plan in order to prevent local churches from deviating from orthodoxy. In yet other instances during the colonial period, disaffected church members at Milford, Connecticut, and at Easton, Massachusetts, briefly joined nearby presbyteries as a form of protest against unfavorable decisions in internal disputes.

By 1700 strict Congregationalism prevailed in Massachusetts, whereas in Connecticut authorities favored closer relations among churches. Here, a modified form of Presbyterianism was introduced with the Saybrook Platform (1708). Formulated to address "defects in the discipline of the churches," as well as to arrest a perceived decline in lay *piety, the platform devised a unique "presbygational" polity. It provided for county ministerial associations and a colony-wide general association, though their duties were not clearly defined. The most explicit Presbyterian feature of the platform was its formation of all churches into county consociations of ministers and laymen whose decisions in local disputes were binding.

New England and Colonial Presbyterianism. Because the *Scots-Irish came to dominate American Presbyterianism following the *Revolution, New England influences are often overlooked. In point of fact, no other group exerted such a definitive influence during the colonial period. Beginning with the first organized presbytery in 1706—the official formation of the Presbyterian Church in America—New England connections were manifest. Three of the seven organizers had New England roots, and a fourth, Francis *Makemie, the oft-cited father of the American Presbyterian church, turned to New England to supply vacant Presbyterian pulpits. From 1706 to 1738, twenty-one of the more than eighty ministers who served the Presbyterian church came from New England.

The Great Awakening accelerated interaction between New England and Presbyterians. Itinerant evangelists such as George Whitefield and Gilbert *Tennent moved freely about the colonies. In 1741

Whitefield cooperated with Presbyterians in Boston and later founded the Old South Presbyterian Church in Newburyport. When the Presbyterian Tennent toured New England, he was warmly received by a large portion of the New England clergy.

More enduring than the brief forays of itinerants was the influence of Jonathan *Edwards and his disciples upon Presbyterian life during the last half of the eighteenth century. New Light Edwardseans and *New Side Presbyterians (which included the New England-born element and Scots-Irish Log College men) found common cause in their shared theology, piety and defense of *revivals. Edwards was the great magnet of attraction. Jonathan *Dickinson, a New Englander and the greatest intellectual among colonial Presbyterians, maintained a regular correspondence with Edwards. Aaron *Burr, the guiding light of New Jersey Presbyterianism, converted during an Edwardsean revival in Connecticut and later married Edwards's daughter. David Brainerd, Edwards's protege, died a martyr to missions among the Indians of New Jersey. Edwards's disciples, Joseph Bellamy and Samuel Hopkins, continued the Edwardsean influence among Presbyterians through their published writings and correspondence with New Side leaders. So attractive were Edwards, Bellamy and Hopkins that all three were invited (but declined) to pastor Presbyterian churches.

In yet other ways New England ministers influenced the form and spirit of colonial Presbyterianism. Under their sway a carefully crafted qualification of the Westminster Confession became part of the *Adopting Act of 1729, whereby individual ministers were granted the right to reject any portion of which they felt they could not in conscience accept. As long as a minister's disavowal did not affect an "essential" doctrine of the Presbyterian creed, he was accepted. Moreover, in church government, the New England party affirmed a decentralized system by which the basic authority of the church lay in presbyteries and not, as eventually prevailed, in the general assembly or in the general synod.

Presbyterian ministerial training was also shaped decisively by New England clergy. Given the absence of an American Presbyterian college, New England provided the New Side party with a large percentage of graduates of Yale (less so of Harvard) who entered the ministry. By the 1758 reunion of New and *Old Side parties, the majority of clergy serving the Presbyterian church came from New England. In addition, when New Side Presbyterians founded the College of New Jersey (Princeton) in 1746, the institution bore the unmistakable imprint of New England influences. The college's first five presidents were either New Englanders or sympathizers of Edwards, who himself presided briefly over the college.

During the last two decades of the eighteenth century, however, countervailing forces checked Edwardsean influences within Presbyterianism. Wave after wave of Scots-Irish immigrants transformed the character of the Presbyterian church and thus seriously eroded the New England influence. John *Witherspoon, recruited from Scotland to preside over Princeton, was cool to Edwardsean theological refinements, and he succeeded in purging the college of this so-called New Divinity. The New Divinity theological agenda as a moving force within Presbyterianism was mitigated though by no means expunged. During the first third of the nineteenth century the Presbyterian church was racked with controversy in its churches and seminaries over New Divinity Hopkinsianism.

Formal Cooperative Endeavors. The dynamic interchange resulting from the Great Awakening, as well as the close resemblance in Connecticut to Presbyterian polity, encouraged formal cooperative endeavors between Congregationalists and Presbyterians. During the colonial period, their shared fear of the introduction of an Anglican bishop in the colonies (and with it, an Anglican establishment) led to an exchange of correspondence and the establishment of an annual joint convention of representatives of the New Side Presbyterian Synod of New York and Philadelphia and the Association of Connecticut. This body met from 1766 to 1775 and resumed in 1790, following the American Revolution and the reorganization of Presbyterian church.

In this atmosphere of harmony, it was a natural step to begin efforts to unify missionary work, both at home and abroad. The Second Great Awakening provided the impetus for renewed missionary zeal and the formation of a united evangelical front that continued cooperation between Presbyterians and Congregationalists. Among the scores of voluntary societies that emerged during the heat of revival, the American Board of Commissioners for Foreign Missions, the American Home Missionary Society, the American Bible Society and the American Tract Society were led and staffed by New England Congregationalists and Presbyterians.

Perhaps the most explicit scheme devised to bring Presbyterians and New Englanders together was the *Plan of Union of 1801. The plan involved cooperative endeavors between Congregationalists and Presbyterians in planting churches in the frontier, west of the Hudson River. The plan was intended to eliminate duplicated efforts and needless conflict in the newly settled regions of New York, the Ohio River Valley, and beyond. The arrangement lasted until 1837, when Presbyterian *Old School conservatives revoked the plan. Fifteen years later Congregationalists followed suit by dissolving the union at the Albany Convention.

See also SOUTH, PRESBYTERIANS IN THE; WEST, PRESBYTERIANS AND THE.

BIBLIOGRAPHY. J. M. Bumsted, "Presbyterianism in Eighteenth-Century Massachusetts: The Formation of a Church at Easton, 1752," *JPH* 46 (1968) 243-53; A. C. Guelzo, *Edwards on the Will: A Century of Theological Debate* (1989); P. R. Lucas, "Presbyterianism Comes to Connecticut: The Toleration Act of 1669," *JPH* 50 (1972) 129-47; idem, *Valley of Discord* (1976); E. R. MacCormac, "The Development of Presbyterian Missionary Organizations: 1790-1870," *JPH* 43 (1965) 149-73; P. T. McClurkin, "Presbyterianism in New England Congregationalism," *JPH* 31 (1953) 245-56; 32 (1954) 109-14; L. J. Trinterud, *The Forming of an American Tradition: A Re-Examination of Colonial Presbyterianism* (1949); W. Walker, *The Creeds and Platforms of Congregationalism* (1893).

D. W. Kling

New Measures. This style of revivalism espoused by Charles G. *Finney highlighted the place of human effort in obeying divine laws to promote religious awakenings. Finney started his revivalist work in the "Burned-Over District" of western New York in the mid-1820s. He was ordained by the Presbyterians and had studied law. Since his primary purpose was multiple individual conversions, he used some highly criticized methods (or measures) to achieve results. Exerting direct and often public pressure on individuals, sometimes by name, he pressed for an immediate decision about conversion. Other innovations included sustained prayer, women praying in mixed groups, encouragement of lay participation and the mourner's bench. These means reflected a conviction that it was possible for any human to choose to make a commitment by faith. Revival would occur whenever Christians utilized the proper God-given means. Influential laypersons supported Finney and his successful methods, but prominent clergymen Lyman Beecher and Asahel Nettleton confronted Finney in 1827. While Beecher (and many others) soon relented in their attack, Nettleton, who typified "old measures" revivalism with its emphasis on the divine initiative, never withdrew from his attack.

Finney did not invent these measures. For over two decades the Methodists had been using equivalent measures, adapting the measures used in the Cane Ridge revival to both urban and rural settings with little controversy. In their case, the measures were compatible with their theology and mission.

BIBLIOGRAPHY. R. Carwardine, *Transatlantic Revivalism, Popular Evangelicalism in Britain and America, 1790-1865* (1978); K. J. Hardman, *Charles Grandison Finney, 1792-1875* (1987).

M. R. Fraser

New School Presbyterians and Theology.‡ New School Presbyterianism was the prorevivalist wing of nineteenth-century Presbyterianism with ties to New England theology, and for the middle third of the century it existed as a separate denomination. Its origins lay in the evangelical awakening of the early nineteenth century, especially enhanced by the *Plan of Union of 1801 that created a working alliance between Presbyterians and Congregationalists in upstate New York and the Midwest.

New School Presbyterianism, however, was not perceptively different from the broader evangelical movement that nurtured it until it was attacked by *Old School Presbyterians in the 1830s. Until then, it was part of an evangelical phalanx that shared a common commitment to evangelism through *revivals and to christianizing America through moral *reform. Perhaps the best early representative of the New School spirit was Lyman *Beecher. His easy movement between Congregationalism and Presbyterianism, support of revivalism, moral absolutism in reforming the nation and relative laxity in adhering to the *Westminster standards were all indicative of the New School mentality.

Growing apprehension among Presbyterians over the innovations of Samuel Hopkins and Nathaniel Taylor paved the way for denominational schism in 1837-1838. Taylor's reinterpretation of original sin and his affirmation of unregenerate people's "power to the contrary" in resisting sin and choosing good were especially alarming.

Between 1831 and 1836 the Old School party brought heresy charges against Albert *Barnes (twice), George *Duffield (1794-1868) and Beecher, only to have the defendants acquitted in each case. Frustrated, Old School partisans mustered a majority at the 1837 general assembly, where they abrogated the Plan of Union of 1801 and eliminated four synods formed under the plan. That action cut the strength of the New School in half. The 1838 general assembly completed the schism by refusing to acknowledge the New School representatives from the deposed synods.

In assessing the causes of the division, theological differences were primary. New School toleration of theological diversity was a reality, but it is questionable how prevalent the New Haven theology was among Presbyterians. Old School Presbyterians also favored a stricter understanding of the *Westminster Confession and a more rigorous form of church discipline than did the New School. Moreover, Old Schoolers were wary of Presbyterian participation in parachurch voluntary societies. New School zeal for interdenominational cooperation and its endorsement of the theology and practice of Charles Grandison *Finney's new measures also greatly troubled Old School Presbyterians. Finally, *abolitionism contributed to the division, with New Schoolers opposing slavery more zealously than did Old Schoolers.

From 1837 until the reunion in 1869, New School Presbyterians existed as a separate denomination, and a discernible shift in spirit occurred. New Schoolers became more doctrinally vigilant, more distinctly Presbyterian and hence more narrowly denominational. Cooperative ventures with Congregationalists steadily declined, and by 1852 the Plan of Union had been terminated. The New School sustained its own theological periodicals (e.g., *American Biblical Repository, Presbyterian Quarterly Review* and the *American Presbyterian and Theological Review)* and supplied ministers through its own seminaries (e.g., Auburn, Lane and Union in New York City). Henry Boynton *Smith emerged as a major American theologian and the preeminent leader of the New School.

The experience of the Civil War hastened Presbyterian reunion as both Old and New Schools realized the previous causes for separation had largely dissipated. When a compromise was reached concerning the meaning of subscription to the Westminster Confession, formal reunion took place in 1869.

By almost any indicator, New School Presbyterianism stood near the center of American culture, and its near fusion of Christian and American values contributed to both its success and its failure. New Schoolers combined a pietist/revivalist emphasis with the cultural mandate of making America a Christian nation. In the half century after reunion, however, these twin strands unraveled under the pressures of modern America. Thus nineteenth-century New School Presbyterianism would have historical ties with both twentieth-century theological liberalism and *fundamentalism.

Bibliography. S. J. Baird, *A History of the New School* (1868); G. M. Marsden, "Reformed and American," in *Reformed Theology in America,* ed. D. F. Wells (1985); idem, *The Evangelical Mind and the New School Presbyterian Experience: A Case Study of Thought and Theology in Nineteenth-Century America* (1970); idem, "The New School Heritage and Presbyterian Fundamentalism," *WTJ* 32 (1970) 129-47; L. A. Pope, "Albert Barnes, *The Way of Salvation* and Theological Controversy," *JPH* 57 (1979) 20-34.

S. R. Pointer

New Side Presbyterians.† The first Presbyterian clergy in the American colonies were Scottish and *Scots-Irish ministers sent to preach to Presbyterian immigrants in Pennsylvania and Maryland. These were joined by Presbyterian-minded *Puritans from *New England, who differed from the immigrant ministers over the degree of adherence to the *Westminster Confession of Faith and the relative importance and place of presbyteries and synods. The New Side consisted of two distinct groups: the Presbytery of New York, who were predominantly from New England; and the Presbytery of New Brunswick, who were centered around the Scots-Irish Tennents and their Log College. The New Englanders were strongly influenced by their Puritan origins, while the Log College men blended that with the Continental pietism they encountered in the *Dutch Reformed pastor Theodore *Frelinghuysen, but both regarded personal religious experience more highly than did their *Old Side counterparts as the primary qualification for church membership and ordained ministry.

The conflict arose first in 1728-1729 over the *Adopting Act, which demanded strict subscription to the confession and was resisted by the New Englanders led by Jonathan *Dickinson but supported by the Tennents. Contention broke out anew in 1738 over the standing of candidates for ordination graduated from the Log College, a strongly pietistic school operated by William *Tennent in Neshaminy, Pennsylvania, and in 1739 over the action of the New Brunswick, New Jersey, presbytery in ordaining a Log College graduate, John *Rowland, without synodical review. Further strife was generated by Gilbert *Tennent's support of itinerant evangelists and lay exhorters who sometimes invaded the parishes of settled ministers. Tennent justified these tactics in a sensational sermon preached on March 8, 1740, in Nottingham, Pennsylvania, "The Danger of an Unconverted Ministry." There Tennent urged laypeople to abandon "the ministry of Natural men" and follow the itinerants. Dickinson's Presbytery of

New York generally opposed such extremes and tended to vote with the majority of the synod for restrictions on such violations, but since they supported a moderate *revivalism, they were sympathetic to the Tennents as well.

The Synod of Philadelphia censured Tennent and his associates, and in June 1741, Tennent's critics presented a "Protestation" that forced the withdrawal of Tennent and the New Brunswick presbytery from the synod. The ejected members organized their own so-called New Side jurisdiction, which was joined by the Presbytery of New York in 1745 to form the New Side Synod of New York. Under the influence of Dickinson, the newly formed synod carefully regulated the extremes of the Great Awakening, but since the Tennents were confident that their brethren from New York supported the revivals in general, they willingly acquiesced.

Upon his arrival in Philadelphia in 1739, George Whitefield made the acquaintance of William and Gilbert Tennent and, finding their revival in motion, quickly allied himself with their cause. With Whitefield's sympathetic interest and assistance, the New Side assumed a leading place in the overall Great Awakening of the 1740s, and its influence was carried into Pennsylvania and Virginia by Samuel *Finley, Samuel *Davies and Samuel *Blair. A famous Indian mission was undertaken in New Jersey and Pennsylvania under David Brainerd. Whitefield credited Gilbert Tennent for helping him develop his theological understanding of *Calvinism and requested the Presbyterian revivalist to take his place on a preaching tour of New England. The work of the Log College was continued in Elizabethtown and Princeton, New Jersey, where the College of New Jersey (Princeton University) was organized under Dickinson and Aaron *Burr. Jonathan *Edwards was briefly the president of the College in 1758 and addressed the New Side Synod in 1752.

As early as 1742, Gilbert Tennent began to express regret that his actions had been so violent, but the publication of his *Irenicum Ecclesiasticarum* (1749) did little at first to convince his New Side colleagues that they had been too extreme, nor did it assure the Old Side that the New Side was truly repentant. Nonetheless, it eventually opened the way to restoration of fellowship between the New Side and Old Side synods in 1758. But the tension between the confessional and pietist factions in the Presbyterian Church was never healed. As the minority partner in the united church, the Old Side felt slighted and mistreated by the New Side majority, while the New Side remained suspicious of the Old Side and refused to allow them any significant role in the *education offered at Princeton. Predictably, these issues remained submerged during the national crisis of the *Revolutionary era, only to surface again in the schism between the *New School and the *Old School in 1837.

Bibliography. A. Alexander, *The Log College* (1851); A. Heimert and P. Miller, eds., *The Great Awakening* (1967); G. S. Klett, ed., *Minutes of the Presbyterian Church in America, 1706-1788* (1976). L. J. Trinterud, *The Forming of an American Tradition: A Re-Examination of Colonial Presbyterianism* (1949).

A. C. Guelzo

Nichols, Robert Hastings (1873-1955). Presbyterian minister and educator. Born in Rochester, New York, Nichols earned degrees at Yale University (B.A., 1894; Ph.D., 1896) and Auburn Theological Seminary (B.D., 1901) and studied at Oxford University (1900-1901). Ordained in the *Presbyterian Church in the U.S.A. (PCUSA) in 1901, he pastored churches in Unadilla, New York (1901), and in South Orange, New Jersey (1902-1910). He became a professor of church history at Auburn Seminary in 1910 and at Union Theological Seminary in New York after Auburn associated with that institution in 1938. Among his many ecclesiastical activities, he was stated clerk of the Synod of New York (1922-1951). His publications included *The Growth of the Christian Church* (1914), *The Ancient Church* (1922) and *Medieval Christianity* (1925). He also served as secretary of the American Society of Church History (1921-1950) and as editor of *Church History* (1932-1948). He retired in 1944. His son, James Hastings Nichols, was a noted church historian.

During the *fundamentalist/modernist controversy, Nichols played a leading role in the liberal party. In protest to the Five Point Deliverance of the 1910 general assembly (reaffirmed in 1916 and 1923), Nichols prepared the first draft of what became known as the *Auburn Affirmation. The affirmation (1924) opposed the fundamentalists' attempt to make subscription to certain doctrines essential for ordination and differentiated between the facts of religion and the theories developed to interpret those facts. It also called for an inclusive church in which doctrinal differences could be tolerated. After the five points were deemed unconstitutional by 1925 general assembly, the inclusive position endorsed by the affirmation triumphed in the church.

Bibliography. C. E. Mathews, "Minute on the Death of Professor Robert Hastings Nichols," *USQR*

11 (1955) 45-46; J. T. McNeill, "In Memoriam," *CH* 25 (1956) 191-92; *NCAB* 42; C. E. Quirk, "Origins of the Auburn Affirmation," *JPH* 53 (1975) 120-42.

P. C. Kemeny

Niebuhr, H(elmut) Richard (1894-1962).‡ Protestant theologian. Born in Wright City, Missouri, Niebuhr was the youngest son of German immigrant Pastor Gustav and American-born Lydia Niebuhr. Niebuhr graduated from Elmhurst College (1912) and Eden Theological Seminary (1915). Ordained in the *Evangelical Synod of North America (1916), Niebuhr held a pastorate in St. Louis until 1918, when he began his academic career by teaching at Eden Theological Seminary (1919-1922). Niebuhr earned the bachelor of divinity (1923) and doctor of philosophy (1924) degrees from Yale University Divinity School. He was president of Elmhurst College (1924-1927), dean of Eden Theological Seminary (1927-1931) and professor of Christian ethics at Yale Divinity School, where he remained from 1931 until his death.

Niebuhr's broad interests included a lifelong concern for the relationship of the church and the modern world. He analyzed the sociological and historical roots of denominational divisions in *The Social Sources of Denominationalism* (1929). He studied the influence of the idea of the kingdom of God on American culture in *The Kingdom of God in America* (1937). And his typology of church-world interaction in *Christ and Culture* (1951) has become a classic. Niebuhr also figured prominently in the merging of the Congregational Christian and the Evangelical and Reformed Churches that formed the United Church of Christ in 1957.

Niebuhr's theological work centered on questions of unity and diversity, the shape of knowledge of objective truth in a relativistic framework and the nature of faith in modern life. In *The Meaning of Revelation* (1941) Niebuhr argued that knowledge of universal truth can be gained only partially through historical traditions. Revelation occurs within particular communities and is limited by historical relativism, yet what is revealed is universal and objective, the sovereign God of history.

Niebuhr's *Radical Monotheism and Western Culture* (1960) was a theological response to pluralism and the problem of faith in the twentieth century. Beyond the many religions and centers of value held by humans is one God. Faith, a relation of trust and loyalty among the self, others and a common cause, should be directed toward that One. However, often faith in finite centers of value, such as *capitalism, American nationalism or church-centeredness, rivals genuine faith in God. Niebuhr attempted to focus on God as the object of faith and avoid absolutizing any relative conceptions of God by developing a confessional stance toward theology and ethics.

Niebuhr's posthumous work, *The Responsible Self* (1963), outlined a dispositional ethic oriented toward God and communal life. Values are relational; ethical action is the response of a social self to a center of value in which one trusts and to which one is loyal. Natural humanity, sinful and fearful of death, develops an ethic of survival. Transformation to a life-affirming ethic can occur only as dependence upon God is recognized and the goodness of God is apprehended in all actions upon one. The "fitting response" results from learning to respond to God as friend in the inevitable ethical dilemmas of life.

See also NIEBHUR, REINHOLD.

BIBLIOGRAPHY. *ANB* 16; *DAB* 7; *DARB;* J. Diefenthaler, *H. Richard Niebuhr: A Lifetime of Reflections on the Church and the World* (1986); J. W. Fowler Jr., *To See the Kingdom: The Theological Vision of H. Richard Niebuhr* (1974); L. A. Hoedemaker, *The Theology of H. Richard Niebuhr* (1970); *NCAB* 47; P. Ramsey, ed., *Faith and Ethics* (1957).

F. S. Adeney

Niebuhr, Reinhold (1892-1971).† Ethical theologian. Born in Wright City, Missouri, Niebuhr graduated from his denomination's Elmhurst College (1910) and Eden Seminary (1913) before attending Yale Divinity School (B.D., 1914) and Yale University (M.A., 1915).

Niebuhr and his younger brother and theological counterpart, H. Richard *Niebuhr, grew up in the *Evangelical Synod of North America, a church tracing its origin to the Church of the Prussian Union in Germany, which combined Lutheran and Reformed congregations. It united with the Reformed Church in the United States in 1934 to become the Evangelical and Reformed Church, which in turn became part of the United Church of Christ in 1957. Niebuhr's theology shows the influence of both Reformed and Lutheran motifs, but the latter is dominant.

Niebuhr pastored Bethel Evangelical Church in Detroit, Michigan, for thirteen years, during which he wrote his first book, *Does Civilization Need Religion?* (1927). In 1928 he moved to Union Theological Seminary in New York, where he would spend the rest of his career, first as associate professor of philosophy of religion (1928-1930) and then as professor of applied Christianity (1930-1960). He was the founder and editor (1941-1966) of *Christianity and Crisis,* a magazine bringing religion to bear on critical social issues. During his years at Union, Niebuhr wrote several significant books, including his highly influential *Moral Man and Immoral Society* (1932) and his two-volume theological exposition, *The Nature and Destiny of Man* (1941-1943). He spent most of 1958 at the Institute for Advanced Study in Princeton, writing *The Structure of Nations and Empires,* which analyzed the lessons of history for the struggles of the Cold War.

Politically Niebuhr was at first supportive of socialism and was a Socialist Party candidate for congressional office in 1930, but by 1940 he had come to favor the mixed economy of Franklin Delano Roosevelt's New Deal, criticizing the socialist faith of Norman Thomas as irrelevant to the American situation.

Theologically Niebuhr was deeply influenced by social gospel liberalism, but his theological reflection and pastoral experience in Detroit, where he gained firsthand experience with Ford auto workers involved in labor disputes, transformed his optimism into a "Christian realism." Increasingly pessimistic regarding human possibilities, Niebuhr began to see the hope of the world in the coming kingdom of God that stands in judgment over all human endeavors and achievements. Love—no longer a simple possibility—became an "impossible possibility" breaking into human life in moments of faith and surrender, but never as a political strategy. It is the suprahistorical norm that guides us in our struggle for social justice.

Niebuhr sought to relate love and justice dialectically. Love represents both the fulfillment and negation of every stride toward a more just society. Yet all progress toward social justice invariably falls drastically short of the ideal of love, which sporadically appears in history but is never an ongoing reality in history. Whereas justice employs coercion, love represents suffering passivity, the power of powerlessness. The highest holiness is the holiness of God's love, which overcomes evil by bearing the pain of evil in vicarious identification with a suffering humanity.

Niebuhr's Christian realism seeks to unite the ultimate norm of pure love with the rational norm of justice in order to maintain social relevance. The Christian realist acknowledges the ambiguity and paradox in all human ethical decision making, poignantly aware that we are often confronted by two evils and must then choose the lesser in a spirit of penitence. Our hope is in the divine grace that enables us to live with our ambiguity rather than in human perfectibility.

While Niebuhr has often been associated with *neo-orthodoxy, his basic methodology remained liberal. He saw revelation as the inner awakening to the reality of suffering love and theology as the elucidation of religious experience. The Bible is an indispensable aid in understanding the divine purpose in history but is not itself God's revelation to us in the form of human words. Jesus is the crowning exemplification of the moral ideal of sacrificial love but not God incarnate in human flesh.

Niebuhr is best understood as an apologetic theologian who sought to validate the claims of the Christian faith to the secular world. His apologetics proceeded by exposing the contradictions in human existence and showing that only the love of the cross, which represents the divine forgiveness, can be the answer to human sin and despair.

After his retirement from Union in 1960, Niebuhr continued to teach seminars on political theory and social ethics at Union, Harvard, Princeton and Barnard College. He supported Martin Luther King's application of his social ethic in the civil rights movement and opposed the increasing American involvement in Vietnam.

See also NIEBUHR, H. RICHARD.

BIBLIOGRAPHY. *ANB* 16; *DARB;* G. Fackre, *The Promise of Reinhold Niebuhr* (1970); R. W. Fox, *Reinhold Niebuhr: A Biography* (1986); G. Harland, *The Thought of Reinhold Niebuhr* (1960); R. Harries, *Reinhold Niebuhr and the Issues of Our Time* (1986); D. W. Kegley and R. W. Bretall, eds., *Reinhold Niebuhr: His Religious, Social and Political Thought* (1956); *NCAB* G; R. H. Stone, *Reinhold Niebuhr: Prophet to Politicians* (1972). D. G. Bloesch

Nollau, Louis Eduard (1810-1869). Father of the *Evangelical Synod of North America. Born in Prussia, Nollau while in military service decided to become a foreign *missionary. He studied at the Rhenish Mission Society in Barmen, Germany. In 1837 the Barmen society sent Nollau and Tilman Niess to North America to establish a mission in Oregon to the Flathead Indians. On the way Nollau and Niess stopped at St. Charles, Missouri, where the latter died. The Indian mission was aborted.

Nollau then accepted an Evangelical pastorate at Gravois Settlement, Missouri (now St. John's United Church of Christ, Mehlville), serving there from 1838 to 1841, when he returned to Germany to marry. With five other pastors, Nollau led in the formation of the Evangelical Church Association of the West.

This predecessor of the Evangelical Synod of North America was organized in his parsonage in 1840. Nollau's life was closely bound up with this church body, although he served as a missionary from 1846 to 1849 with the Barmen society in Capetown, South Africa.

Returning to Missouri, Nollau pastored St. Peter's Evangelical Church, St. Louis, from 1852 until his early death. From his St. Louis congregation Nollau founded in 1857 the Good Samaritan Hospital, patterned after Theodore Fliedner's pioneer deaconess work at Kaiserswerth, Germany, begun in 1836. Nollau also organized the German Evangelical Orphans Home in St. Louis. Out of his work has come an extensive diaconal ministry supported by former Evangelical churches in the Midwest, continued now in the United Church of Christ.

Bibliography. J. W. Flucke, *Evangelical Pioneers* (1931); C. E. Schneider, *The German Church on the American Frontier: A Study in the Rise of Religion Among the Germans of the West* (1939).

L. W. Zuck

O

Occom, Samson (1723-1792).† Presbyterian evangelist. A Mohegan Indian born near New London, Connecticut, Occom converted to Christianity about 1740 during the Great Awakening. Later (1743-1747) he studied at Moor's Charity School at Lebanon, Connecticut, where his success inspired his teacher, Eleazar Wheelock, with the idea of training young Indians as evangelists. After teaching school in New London in 1748, Occom moved to Long Island to teach his fellow Indians. He was licensed by the Congregationalists and began preaching to several tribes in New York and Connecticut. In 1759 he received ordination as a Presbyterian minister.

Occom became an influential preacher and tribal leader among the Indians in the Northeast, traveling widely in southern New England, Long Island and the New York region. In 1764 he accompanied Nathaniel Whitaker on a successful two-year trip to England, preaching three hundred to four hundred sermons in eighteen months, raising funds for Wheelock's mission. Upon his return, Occom disagreed strongly with Wheelock's decision to start a mission college (Dartmouth) and left to become an itinerant preacher.

After the American *Revolution, in 1785 Occom led several of his followers from Connecticut to a new settlement, Brothertown, in western New York, hoping to avoid white encroachment. There he continued his evangelistic work until late in life. Although little is known about the doctrinal nature of his preaching, he was considered a more powerful and dynamic preacher among Native Americans than among whites, and he was perhaps the most significant Native American evangelist of his era.

Bibliography. *AAP* 3; H. W. Blodgett, *Samson Occom* (1935); *DAB* VII; *DARB;* W. D. Love, *Samson Occom and the Christian Indians of New England* (1899); L. B. Richardson, *An Indian Preacher in England* (1933). M. S. Joy

Ockenga, Harold John (1905-1985).‡ Presbyterian and Congregational minister and neo-evangelical leader. Born and reared in Chicago in a Methodist family, he attended Taylor University, and in 1927 he enrolled at Princeton Theological Seminary. Ockenga was among the student followers of J. Gresham *Machen. When Machen protested changes at Princeton and founded Westminster Theological Seminary in Philadelphia in 1929, Ockenga left Princeton and graduated from Westminster the following year.

After pastoring two Methodist churches in New Jersey, Ockenga accepted an invitation in 1931 to assist Clarence *Macartney, who was pastor of the First Presbyterian Church of Pittsburgh. Later that year Macartney and Machen recommended Ockenga for the pastorate of the Point Breeze Presbyterian Church in suburban Pittsburgh. While at that church, Ockenga completed a doctoral degree in philosophy at the University of Pittsburgh (1939) and met Audrey Williamson, who in 1935 became his wife.

In 1936 A. Z. Conrad, a *fundamentalist leader in Boston, chose Ockenga to succeed him as pastor of Park Street Congregational Church. Ockenga soon exercised his talents in wider circles. In 1940 and 1941, he planned and promoted the National Association of Evangelicals (NAE) and served until 1944 as its first president. In 1947 Charles E. Fuller, the famous radio *revivalist, invited Ockenga to be founding president of Fuller Theological Seminary in Pasadena, California. Ockenga helped lead the evangelical resurgence in other ways by promoting and teaming up with a young evangelist named Billy Graham and by assisting Graham in the founding of *Christianity Today* in 1956.

Bibliography. *ANB* 16; H. C. Englizian, *Brimstone Corner* (1968); H. Lindsell, *Park Street Prophet: A Life of Harold John Ockenga* (1951); G. M. Marsden, *Reforming Fundamentalism: Fuller Seminary and the New Evangelicalism* (1987).

J. A. Carpenter

Old School Presbyterians.† During the 1730s and 1740s several colonial denominations suffered internal divisions over questions regarding the theological legitimacy and ecclesiastical propriety of the Great Awakening in New England and the Middle Colonies. New England Congregationalism was rent asunder as two parties—the New Light pro-Awakening party and the Old Light anti-Awakening group—sought to impose their respective views on the denomination. Colonial Presbyterians were also of two minds about the Awakening. Under the leadership of Gilbert *Tennent, *New Side Presbyterians labored to advance the Awakening against the objections of *Old Side traditionalists. Although the *New Side/Old Side division nearly effected a permanent schism within colonial Presbyterianism, the contending parties were finally reconciled in 1758. The rapproachement favored the New Side party, who had consolidated their gains by installing a series of pro-Awakeners (Jonathan *Dickinson, Aaron *Burr, Jonathan *Edwards, Samuel *Davies and Samuel *Finley) in the presidency of the fledgling College of New Jersey at Princeton, New Jersey. Building on Princeton's impressive New Side intellectual tradition, its next president, John *Witherspoon, made Princeton the center of Presbyterian thought in America.

Witherspoon's presidency effected a new balance in the New Side/Old Side animosities. A Scot, he represented thousands of Scots and *Scots-Irish Presbyterians who had immigrated to the new nation long after the Awakening. These new Americans, accustomed to the more traditional Presbyterianism of the Scottish Kirk, rapidly became the dominant force in American Presbyterianism, and a gradual shift away from New Side sentiment took place. This movement is best seen in the career of Archibald *Alexander. Reared in Virginia, Alexander served a Presbyterian church in Philadelphia, from where he successfully led the effort to form Princeton Theological Seminary in 1812. As the seminary's first professor, Alexander formed a distinct version of Presbyterian theology that found its genesis in older, European formulations of *Calvinism. Alexander eschewed the nuanced American versions of Reformed thought found in the *Puritans and their latter-day heirs, Edwards and Nathaniel W. Taylor. Using Francois *Turretin's *Institutio Theologiae Elencticae* and demanding strict adherence to the *Westminster Confession of Faith, Alexander formed what became known as the Old School theology.

Under Alexander's direction and due in great measure to the efforts of his colleague Charles *Hodge, Princeton Seminary became the intellectual center of Old School Presbyterianism. The Old School opposed many of the popular emphases of nineteenth-century American Protestantism. In matters ecclesiastical, the Old School affirmed Presbyterian *polity (with its hierarchical system of presbyteries, synods and general assemblies) as the most accurate, biblical form of church polity. Old School theologians were assiduous in their opposition to several nineteenth-century attempts to unite American Presbyterians and Congregationalists into a single ecclesiastical body. Nor were they interested in the myriad of interdenominational efforts (voluntary societies concerned with *abolition, temperance or foreign *missions) that were popular in antebellum America. From the Old School perspective, such efforts threatened the purity of the church and hence were suspect.

The Old School found the *revival tactics of the Second Great Awakening similarly distasteful. As Charles Grandison *Finney promulgated his new measures for evangelism, and as Methodists, Baptists and some Presbyterians on the frontier experimented with camp meeting revivalism, Old School thinkers criticized these new phenomena as doctrinally shallow. When Lyman *Beecher and Taylor formulated their New Haven theology, largely in defense of the new revivalism, the Old School responded predictably. Princeton theologians decried Taylor's progressive view of human depravity as a heretical denial of the classic Calvinistic doctrine of the imputation of sin. Beecher fared little better at the hands of the Old School. In 1835, after becoming president of Lane Theological Seminary, a Presbyterian institution in Cincinnati, he was tried and later acquitted on the charge that he had abandoned the central tenets of the Westminster Confession.

Despite the fact that Princeton Seminary served as the chief intellectual center of the Old School through much of the nineteenth century, many Old School congregations were located in slaveholding states. Conversely, much of the New School strength was located north of the Mason-Dixon line. In 1837 Old School forces managed to expel four Northern New School synods from the denomination on theological grounds, an event that led to the creation of two competing denominations. Despite this apparent Old School victory, however, the tumultuous slavery issue continued to threaten the unity of the Old School and the New School alliances. Notwithstanding strenuous efforts to maintain unity within each of the competing groups, the New School body divided over the slavery issue in 1857, and the Old School divided soon after Confederate forces attacked Fort Sumter in 1861. The New School/Old School schism in the North was healed during 1868 to 1870, while Presbyterians in the South reunited in 1864, facilitated by the crisis of the Civil War.

See also NEW ENGLAND, PRESBYTERIANS IN; NEW

SCHOOL PRESBYTERIANS; SOUTH, PRESBYTERIANS IN.

BIBLIOGRAPHY. S. E. Ahlstrom, *A Religious History of the American People* (1972); L. A. Loetscher, *A Brief History of the Presbyterians* (1978); E. T. Thompson, *Presbyterians in the South,* 3 vols. (1973). J. R. Fitzmier

Old Side Presbyterians.† Conservative party within eighteenth-century Presbyterianism. Presbyterianism was planted in the Middle Colonies by Francis *Makemie in the 1690s. Although the original intention was to organize Scottish and *Scots-Irish immigrants along with presbyterian-minded *Puritans from *New England under an authoritative synodical government, it proved difficult to recruit clergy from Scotland or Ulster. Since the only colonial colleges were based in Congregational New England, their graduates tended to import notions of Congregational polity and pietist evangelicalism into the Presbyterian churches and rather loosely held to the *polity of the *Westminster Confession. This posed a serious challenge to traditional Presbyterian order, especially after 1735, when William *Tennent organized a theological school, the Log College, that espoused pietist principles, including a strong emphasis on *revivalism and the conversion experience. The two issues that troubled the majority of the synod were that the revivals Tennent and his students had started in the mid-1730s led overly enthusiastic ministers and supporters to denounce all who were not wholeheartedly behind the revival movement; and the education that Log College graduates were receiving was proving to be significantly inferior to that of the New England colleges.

In an effort to preserve conservative Presbyterian order, the majority of Scottish and Scots-Irish clergy, known as the Old Side, responded to the New England influence by passing three acts in the Synod of Philadelphia: forbidding pastors from "intruding" into another minister's congregation as the revivalists had done; requiring Log College graduates to submit their credentials to a synodical examination committee before licensure and ordination; and censuring the New Brunswick, New Jersey, presbytery in 1739 for ordaining a Log College graduate, John *Rowland, in defiance of the synod's examination act.

These tactics provoked fiery protest from Gilbert *Tennent, who accused the Old Side of being unregenerate in his famous 1740 sermon, "The Danger of an Unconverted Ministry." Other members of the revivalist party continued their practices and were charged with intruding into other pastors' congregations, but they refused to accept the discipline of their presbytery. The Synod of Philadelphia responded by rebuking Tennent, and under the terms of a "Protestation" Tennent and the New Brunswick presbytery were ejected from the synod in 1741.

The *New Side and Old Side factions then engaged in a protracted pamphlet war debating the merits of revivals, itinerant preaching and the Great Awakening of the 1740s. Significant spokesmen for the Old Side were Francis *Alison, John *Thomson and John Ewing, who argued against the New Siders' "disorderly Way, contrary to all Presbyterian Rules," criticized the psychology of revival and attacked the New Siders' association with George Whitefield, who they believed was misleading people by his overemphasis on conversion, to the detriment of sanctification, and his constant accusations against "unregenerate ministers" whom he had never met. Jonathan *Dickinson and the Presbytery of New York attempted to moderate between the factions, but after four futile years of negotiations, they received permission to join the excluded Presbytery of New Brunswick to form the Synod of New York in 1745.

The Old Siders, however, were unable to compete against the greater zeal and finances of the New Siders and the mobility of New Side itinerant preachers, and so Old Side arguments failed to win a popular following. Due to the general poverty of the Scots-Irish immigrants to whom they chiefly ministered, the effort by Alison to organize a rival college failed to gain the necessary financial support to equal the New Side college at Princeton. Therefore, while the Old Side continued to expand among the Scots-Irish immigrants in Virginia and Carolina under the ministry of Thomson, the prospects for the future looked bleak.

The New Side and Old Side jurisdictions were eventually reunited in 1758. Some historians have argued that Old Side principles continued to command significant loyalty within Presbyterian education, especially under John *Witherspoon at the College of New Jersey (Princeton) after 1768, but others have suggested that Witherspoon snubbed such Old Side luminaries as Alison and promoted an essentially New Side agenda. The relationship between New England Congregationalism and Scots-Irish Presbyterianism, however, remained critical as it played an important, if not the dominant, role in the *Old School-New School division of 1837. In the years leading up to the schism, Archibald *Alexander and Charles *Hodge of Princeton Theological Seminary believed themselves to be in direct succession to the revivalists of the New Side, although Hodge later recognized that his sympathies were split between New and Old Side perspectives.

See also NEW SIDE PRESBYTERIANS.

BIBLIOGRAPHY. C. Hodge, *The Constitutional History of the Presbyterian Church in the United States of America,* 2 vols. (1851); E. A. Ingersoll, "Francis Alison: American 'Philosophe,' 1705-1779" (Ph.D. diss., University of Delaware, 1974); E. I. Nybakken, "New Light on the Old Side: Irish Influences on Colonial Presbyterianism," *JAH* 68 (1981-82); L. J. Trinterud, *The Forming of an American Tradition: A Reexamination of Colonial Presbyterianism* (1949).

A. C. Guelzo

Orr, James (1844-1913).† Scottish Presbyterian theologian, educator and minister. Born in Glasgow, Scotland, Orr studied at the University of Glasgow and The Theological Hall of the United Presbyterian Church of Scotland in Edinburgh. He then pastored a U.P. church in Hawick (1874-1891) before becoming professor of church history in the United Presbyterian Theological College (1891-1901). After coconvening the committee that joined the United Presbyterians with the Free Church, he was appointed professor of apologetics and theology at United Free Church College in Glasgow (1901-1913). He established himself as an expert in German philosophy and theology with the Edinburgh Kerr Lectures, published as *The Christian View of God and the World* (1893), and volumes on *The Supernatural in Christianity* (1894) and *The Ritschlian Theology and the Evangelical Faith* (1897). Essays entitled *The Bible Under Trial* (1907), *The Virgin Birth* (1907) and *The Resurrection of Christ* (1908) achieved his reputation as an orthodox opponent of *modernism. These works, along with contributions to *The Pulpit Commentary,* made him known to conservatives in the United States and Canada, resulting in invitations to lecture at Chicago, Auburn, Princeton and Toronto. His last contribution (as editor), *The International Standard Bible Encyclopedia* (4 vols., 1915), was a reference work of enduring value.

Although he promoted modified subscription to the *Westminster Confession, Orr remained committed to evangelical *Calvinism. Asserting the necessity of doctrinal development and growth, he believed that John *Calvin had misplaced his emphasis by subordinating the love of God to his sovereignty and holiness. While emphasizing continuity with the past, Orr sought to build on that foundation rather than remain tied to it. Orr's biblical studies were generally conservative, though he could not affirm the doctrine of inerrancy as formulated by the *Princeton theologians, and he insisted on toleration for critical positions. Amid a controversy involving Glasgow's George Adam Smith, Orr defended the right of his colleague to teach an essentially documentary hypothesis, even though he personally disagreed with his conclusions, as long as Smith maintained an evangelical doctrine of Scripture. Five years later Orr published *The Problem of the Old Testament* (1906), taking a traditional stand on the essential Mosaic authorship of the Pentateuch and other issues in higher criticism. He argued that the documentary hypothesis rested upon naturalistic assumptions that were inconsistent with Christian supernaturalism. Rejecting Charles Darwin's theory of human origins for similar reasons, he nonetheless allowed for the possibility of at least some evolutionary activity. In *God's Image in Man* (1905), he insisted that both the human body and soul must have been supernaturally produced.

Because of his reputation as a defender of orthodoxy, Orr was one of a small number of British theologians invited to participate in *The Fundamentals* project (1910-1915). He contributed essays on "The Virgin Birth of Christ" (vol. 1), "Science and Christian Faith" (vol. 4), "The Early Narratives of Genesis" (vol. 6) and "Holy Scripture and Modern Negations" (vol. 9). Orr's background and scholarly erudition made him particularly attractive to American conservatives who were watching their seminaries move further and further to the left, and his work made significant contributions to the issues and structures of fundamentalist apologetics in the United States.

BIBLIOGRAPHY. *DSCHT;* E. R. Sandeen, *The Roots of Fundamentalism: British and American Millenarianism, 1800-1930* (1970); G. G. Scorgie, *A Call for Continuity: The Theological Contribution of James Orr* (1988).

D. D. Bundy

Orthodox Presbyterian Church.† A small Presbyterian denomination with roots in the *fundamentalist-modernist controversy. The Orthodox Presbyterian Church (OPC) was founded on June 11, 1936, in the aftermath of the fundamentalist-modernist controversy that in 1929 had seen a group of professors at Princeton Theological Seminary, led by J. Gresham *Machen, leave that seminary to establish Westminster Theological Seminary.

Paramount among the reasons for that action was the conviction of Machen and his colleagues that Princeton and the *Presbyterian Church in the U.S.A. (PCUSA), of which Princeton was the leading seminary, had departed from historic Christianity. The particular matters at issue were their adoption of a weak view of the authority of Scripture and rejection of significant doctrines such as the virgin birth of Christ and the substitutionary atonement. The seven years between 1929 and 1936 saw increasing friction between the majority in the Presbyterian church and the minority led by Machen, with the result being the foundation of a new denomination. Originally calling itself The Presbyterian Church of America, the new body was forced by court action to discontinue use of that name in 1939, and it adopted in its place the name Orthodox Presbyterian Church.

After Machen's death in 1937, the young denomination split over the question of whether it would maintain a traditional *Calvinist theology, Presbyterian *polity and Reformed *piety or move in the direction of American fundamentalism. The latter party, under the leadership of Carl *McIntire and J. Oliver *Buswell Jr., wanted the OPC to tolerate the dispensational premillennialism of the Scofield Reference Bible, encouraged more congregational independence and pushed for a fundamentalist ethic that included abstinence from alcohol and tobacco. As early as 1923, Machen had called dispensationalism "a false method of interpretation of God's Word" and had opposed prohibition as a violation of Christian liberty. The majority of the OPC agreed with Machen, and after a short but vigorous debate, McIntire and his party departed to form the Bible Presbyterian Synod (later *Bible Presbyterian Church).

In 1943 the prominent philosopher Gordon H. *Clark sought ordination in the OPC, which stirred up a controversy over the incomprehensibility of God and the noetic effects of redemption. Clark's teaching that human knowledge could be identical to God's knowledge troubled many on the faculty of Westminster Seminary who agreed with Cornelius *Van Til that human knowledge must always be analogical to God's knowledge. Before the matter reached closure, Clark left the OPC and joined the *United Presbyterian Church in 1948. This debate centered around the question of whether the OPC would embrace a rationalistic Enlightenment concept of intellectual neutrality or would attempt to articulate a confessional theology that recognized the full extent of the noetic effects of sin and redemption.

During the same period the OPC clarified its position in relationship to the neo-evangelical movement. In 1943 it declined the invitation to join the National Association of Evangelicals (NAE), stating that the NAE was inconsistent in its stance against modernism. Yet the chief objections were the weak theological position that the organization was forced to hold by the diversity of its membership and the NAE's plans to engage in *missions and evangelism—functions that Orthodox Presbyterians believed were the task of the visible church, not to be run by parachurch groups which lacked biblical authority. Recognizing that non-Reformed denominations were "manifestations of Christ's body," the OPC nonetheless declined active involvement in broadly evangelical movements, joining instead with Reformed churches around the world in the *Reformed Ecumenical Synod in 1948, finally withdrawing in 1988 due to liberal trends in member churches. Since the 1940s the OPC has considered merger with several conservative Reformed churches. Since 1975 it has been a member of the North American Presbyterian and Reformed Council, an association designed to facilitate fraternal relations between like-minded denominations.

The OPC has since its inception been best known for its vigorous affirmation of the truths of historic Christianity and Reformed orthodoxy as they are expressed in the *Westminster Confession of Faith and Catechisms. The denomination utilizes three standing committees representing the fundamental emphases within the OPC: world missions, home missions and Christian education. Recognizing its emphasis on traditional Reformed orthodoxy, Reformed denominations in Third World countries have recently requested pastor-professors from the OPC to come train indigenous ministers.

Bibliography. C. G. Dennison, ed., *The Orthodox Presbyterian Church, 1936-1986* (1986); C. G. Dennison and R. C. Gamble, eds., *Pressing Toward the Mark: Essays Commemorating Fifty Years of the Orthodox Presbyterian Church* (1986); D. G. Hart and J. R. Muether, *Fighting the Good Fight: A Brief History of the Orthodox Presbyterian Church* (1995); N. B. Stonehouse, *J. Gresham Machen: A Biographical Memoir* (1954). S. T. Logan

Otterbein, (Philip) William (1726-1813).† *German Reformed pastor, cofounder and bishop of the United Brethren in Christ. Born to Daniel and Henrietta Otterbein in Dillenburg, the county seat of Nassau, Germany, William, as well as his father and all five surviving brothers, prepared themselves for the German Reformed ministry at the academy of Herborn (near Dillenburg), the intellectual center of German Reformed pietism. After his ordination in 1749 and a brief pastorate at Ockersdorf, Otterbein fell afoul of the liberal leadership in the region, and so he found it wise to become one of Michael *Schlatter's six recruits for service in the American colonies. He returned to visit relatives in Germany once, briefly, in 1770-1771.

Arriving in the colonies in 1752, Otterbein served a series of German Reformed congregations: Lancaster, Pennsylvania (1752-1758); Tulpehocken (1758-1760); Frederick, Maryland (1760-1765); York, Pennsylvania (1765-1774); and the Second Evangelical Reformed Church in Baltimore (1774-1813). He married Susan Le Roy of Lancaster in 1762; she died six years later, leaving Otterbein a widower for the rest of his life. During his early days in the colonies, he traveled widely under the auspices of the coetus, the first supervising body of the German Reformed congregations in America, thus playing a role among the German Reformed somewhat similar to Henry Melchoir Muhlenberg's role among the Lutherans. Conservative in his social views, he opposed the use of organs in worship, Christian participation in Masonic lodges and patronage of the theater.

While he was pastor at York, Pennsylvania, Otterbein met the Mennonite Martin Boehm, who had developed the custom of holding evangelistic meetings *(Grosse Versammlungen),* one of which was in progress in Isaac Long's barn north of Lancaster. After the sermon, the learned Otterbein and the lay preacher Boehm, sensing a kinship of spirit, embraced each other, saying "Wir sind Brüder" ("We are brethren"). Subsequently they engaged in preaching tours together. Out of their joint endeavors came the United Brethren in Christ in 1789. Otterbein's ecumenical ventures included taking part in the consecration of his friend Francis Asbury as superintendent of American Methodism in 1784. Traveling widely throughout Maryland, Pennsylvania and Virginia, Otterbein promoted the United Brethren on the class basis, similar to the Wesleyan approach in England, refusing to organize it as a separate denomination. His only known published work is *Die heilbringende Menschwerdung und der herrliche Sieg Jesu Christi* (1763), but he is also credited with the confession of faith of the United Brethren (1789).

At the newly formed group's first conference, both Otterbein and Boehm were elected bishops (1800). Thus during his later years Otterbein served in the dual relationship of bishop of the United Brethren in Christ and pastor of a Baltimore congregation loosely associated with the German Reformed Church, remaining a member in good standing of the German Reformed coetus. After 1805, his health prohibited him from traveling as widely, and seven weeks before his death he finally ordained three of his assistants as the first ministers of the United Brethren. This action was widely disputed for fifty years, since he had previously refused to establish the Brethren as an independent denomination. He died in 1813 and was buried in the churchyard of his church in Baltimore.

BIBLIOGRAPHY. *ANB* 16; J. B. Behney and P. H. Heller, *The History of the United Brethren Church* (1979); A. C. Core, ed., *Philip William Otterbein* (1968); *DAB* VII; *DARB;* A. W. Drury, *The Life of Philip William Otterbein, Founder of the United Brethren in Christ* (1884); *NCAB* 10; J. S. O'Malley, *The Pilgrimage of Faith: The Legacy of the Otterbeins* (1973).

F. E. Stoeffler

P

Palmer, Benjamin Morgan (1818-1902).† Southern Presbyterian pastor. Born in Charleston, South Carolina, Palmer graduated from the University of Georgia (1838) and Columbia Theological Seminary (1841). He pastored congregations in Savannah, Georgia (1841-1843), and Columbia, South Carolina (1843-1856), in addition to teaching church history and *polity at Columbia Theological Seminary (1853-1856). Palmer helped found *The Southern Presbyterian Review* in 1847 and thereafter served as editor and frequently contributed to the journal. In 1856 Palmer became the minister of the First Presbyterian Church of New Orleans, a position he held for more than forty-five years.

One of the most outstanding Southern pulpit orators during 1850 to 1900, Palmer generally preached without notes for about an hour, often drawing as many as fifteen hundred people to his church. An *Old School *Calvinist to the core, his sermons focused on the great doctrines of the Bible. During the *Civil War he served as a short-term minister to both the Army of the West and the Army of Tennessee, and he was appointed commissioner to the Army of the West, organizing and recruiting chaplains and ministers for the long-term spiritual needs of the soldiers.

Elected moderator of the first General Assembly of the Presbyterian Church in the Confederate States of America, after that body split from the Old School Presbyterian Church in 1861, Palmer articulated the doctrine of the sole kingship of Christ over his church. Along with James Henley *Thornwell, he believed in the spirituality of the church, the doctrine that the institutional church is exclusively spiritual and as an organization should not take any political positions.

He perhaps was most famous for his 1861 sermon in which he declared that it was the God-given duty of the Southern Presbyterian Church to "conserve and perpetuate" the institution of slavery. Palmer argued that slavery did not need to be abolished but reformed, and that this task could be done only if Christianity was allowed to permeate all of Southern society. His sermon was frequently quoted by Northern antagonists as an example of Southern extremism and bigotry.

Rejecting reunion with the Northern church after the Civil War, Palmer argued that it would bring ruin to Southern congregations. In the pastoral letter that was approved by the general assembly of 1870, he argued that since the Northern church had declared the Southern church apostate, there could be no reconciliation until they repented of that declaration. Beyond that, he claimed that the Spring resolutions of 1861 had subordinated the church to the state and that the reunion of the *Old School and *New School Presbyterian bodies in 1869 had fatally compromised the doctrinal integrity of the Northern church.

A social and theological conservative, Palmer opposed racial integration during Reconstruction, arguing that blacks should be allowed to maintain their own educational and ecclesiastical institutions. He waged a campaign in New Orleans for strict sabbath observance and worked to keep his denomination from accepting theistic evolution, a position espoused by James *Woodrow of Columbia Theological Seminary.

Bibliography. *ANB* 16; *DAB* VII; T. C. Johnson, *The Life and Letters of Benjamin Morgan Palmer* (1906); E. T. Thompson, *Presbyterians in the South,* vol. 2 (1973). G. S. Smith

Parkhurst, Charles Henry (1842-1933). Presbyterian minister. Parkhurst studied at Amherst (B.A., 1866) and then taught in *New England between two extended study periods at Halle and Leipzig between 1867 and 1873. He served as pastor in Lenox, Massachusetts (1874-1880), before his appointment as pastor of the Madison Square Presbyterian Church in New York City in 1880. Parkhurst is best known for his involvement in exposing and opposing public corruption in New York City. As pastor of Madison Square Presbyterian Church, Parkhurst's social activist preaching attracted the attention of civic reformers. Following his rapid advancement in 1890 to the presidency of the Society for the Prevention of Crime, Parkhurst helped galvanize popular opinion concerning public corruption. His accusations from the pulpit were challenged as anecdotal and moralistic. Parkhurst substantiated his charges by his own investigations of cronyism and corruption, prompting prosecutorial attention to the patronage and graft systems of the Tammany Hall political machine. His efforts advanced a broad alliance that inaugurated an era of reform politics. Throughout his public ministry, Parkhurst patrolled the boundaries between public service and private enrichment, always calling for higher standards in government and greater involvement by educated citizens.

Bibliography. *ANB* 17; *DAB* VII; *DARB; NCAB* 11; C. H. Parkhurst, *My Forty Years in New York* (1923); idem, *Our Fight with Tammany* (1895).

K. S. Sawyer

Parsons, Henry Martyn (1828-1913).† *Canadian Presbyterian minister. Born in East Haddam, Connecticut, Parsons graduated from Yale College (1848) and Connecticut Theological Institute (1854). He then served churches in Springfield and Boston, Massachusetts, and Buffalo, New York. In 1880 he accepted the pastorate of Knox Presbyterian Church in Toronto, a position he held until his death. Involved in Toronto social service, Parsons helped establish the Toronto Mission Union and served as a board member of the Toronto Home for Incurables.

Prominent in the millenarian movement, Parsons was a long-time leader of the Niagara conferences and a thoroughgoing dispensationalist. He was one of the original members of the Believers' Meeting in 1876, which two years later was responsible for establishing the first International Prophecy Conference in America. He also helped organize and lectured at the 1885 Niagara Prophecy Conference, a crucial event in the spread of premillennialism in Canada. In the same vein, Parsons was a board member of the Toronto Willard Tract Depository, a publishing company that promoted dispensational premillennialism. He also wrote a number of books and articles, primarily on premillennialism, and served as an instructor at the Toronto Bible Training School. In the 1890s a theological debate over the traditional Niagara teaching that Jesus could return at any moment brought the conference to its end. Parsons held to the traditional teaching of the secret rapture of the church, disagreeing with his long-time colleagues Nathaniel *West and William *Erdman, who had come to reverse their former endorsement.

Bibliography. C. N. Kraus, *Dispensationalism in America* (1958); R. G. Sawatsky, "'Looking for that Blessed Hope': The Roots of Fundamentalism in Canada, 1878-1914" (Ph.D. diss., University of Toronto, 1986).

W. V. Trollinger

Patton, Francis Landey (1843-1932).‡ Presbyterian clergyman, educator and theologian. Never a citizen of the United States, Patton was born in Bermuda, where he also died. Before graduating from Princeton Theological Seminary in 1865, he also attended Knox College in Toronto and the University of Toronto. In 1865 Patton was ordained, and for the next seven years he held pastorates in the vicinity of New York City.

Between 1872 and 1881 he served as professor of theology at the Presbyterian Theological Seminary of the Northwest (now McCormick Seminary) in Chicago. During these years Patton gained national attention as prosecutor in the heresy trial of David *Swing. Princeton Seminary hired him in 1881 to teach apologetics, and in 1883 Patton began lecturing in ethics at the College of New Jersey. In 1888 the college chose Patton to succeed James *McCosh as president of the institution.

Though Patton was known as a defender of theism and Christian ethics, as well as for his personal charm, many supporters of the college doubted his administrative abilities. He successfully restructured the college to become Princeton University in 1896. Yet, never comfortable with presidential duties, he resigned in 1902 and nominated Woodrow *Wilson as his successor. In that same year, Princeton Seminary created the office of president. Patton assumed that position and continued to lecture on ethics in the university until he retired to his home in Bermuda in 1913. His publications included *The Inspiration of the Scriptures* (1869), *A Summary of Christian Doctrine* (1898) and *Fundamental Christianity* (1926).

Bibliography. *DAB* VII; *DARB;* P. C. Kemeny, *Princeton in the Nation's Service: Religions Ideals and Educational Practice, 1868-1928* (1998); *NCAB* 5.

D. G. Hart

Peale, Norman Vincent (1898-1993).‡ Reformed minister and promoter of positive thinking. After graduating from Ohio Wesleyan University in 1920, Peale pursued a career in journalism but decided to prepare for the ministry. Upon graduating from Boston University in 1924 (B.S.T., M.A.) he was appointed to a small congregation in Brooklyn, New York, which by 1927 had grown from forty to nine hundred members. His next pastorate, University Methodist Church in Syracuse, New York, also flourished. In 1932 he accepted a call to Marble Collegiate Church in New York City, a move that required him to join the *Reformed Church in America (RCA). Peale spent the remainder of his career at Marble Collegiate, a congregation dating back to 1628 and said to be the oldest Protestant church in continuous use in the United States.

Peale's message was a combination of psychological themes and therapeutic prescriptions drawn loosely from Scripture and expressed in everyday language. Many have criticized his message of positive thinking as a reduction of Christian theology to American notions of self-reliance and materialism. Peale clearly staked his place in the tradition of American harmonial religion, which stresses spiritual composure, physical health and even economic well-being as stemming from rapport with the cosmos. Arguably the post-World War II economic affluence and the accompanying anxieties of modern urban living contributed to build a religious atmosphere primed to receive a gospel promising confident living and peace of mind. But whatever the reasons for his success, Peale became one of the most prominent religious figures of the postwar decades.

Bibliography. *ANB* 17; *Current Biography* (1974) 306-9; A. Gordon, *Norman Vincent Peale* (1958); D. Meyer, *Positive Thinkers* (1988); C. Westphal, *Norman Vincent Peale* (1964). D. G. Reid

Peck, Thomas Ephraim (1822-1893). Presbyterian minister and educator. Born in Columbia, South Carolina, Peck graduated from the College of South Carolina in 1840. He prepared for the ministry by studying privately with James Henley *Thornwell, a Presbyterian minister and professor of metaphysics at his alma mater. He was licensed to preach by the Charleston Presbytery in 1844. He provided pulpit supply to Presbyterian churches in Salem and Jackson, South Carolina, and at the Second Presbyterian Church of Baltimore before he became the pastor of the Broadway Street Presbyterian Church in Baltimore in 1846. In 1857 he became the pastor of the Central Presbyterian Church in the same city. Two years later he declined a position as professor of ecclesiastical history and church government at Union Theological Seminary in Virginia but accepted the following year. In 1883 Peck succeeded Robert Lewis *Dabney as professor of theology. Peck served as moderator of the General Assembly of the *Presbyterian Church in the U.S.A. (PCUSA) in 1878. He died in Richmond, Virginia.

As a disciple of Thornwell and a successor to Dabney, Peck's distinctive contribution to American Presbyterianism came in his vigilant defense of the *Old School Presbyterian theology and the Southern Presbyterian ecclesiology. Through his classroom teaching and his writings, he advocated the *Calvinism of the *Westminster Confession and the inerrancy of the Scriptures as the church's sole rule of faith and practice. He also espoused *jure divino* Presbyterianism, which held that the church's government and rule are limited to the Bible's teachings.

Bibliography. *ANB* 17; DAB XIV; T. C. Johnson, ed., *Miscellanies of Reverend Thomas E. Peck,* 3 vols. (1895-1897); T. E. Peck, *Notes on Ecclesiology* (1892). P. C. Kemeny

Pidgeon, George Campbell (1872-1971).‡ Canadian Presbyterian minister. Born in a Scottish community on the south shore of the Gaspé Peninsula in eastern Quebec, Pidgeon absorbed many of the qualities of late nineteenth-century Presbyterianism. He was conservative in theology, stressed personal conversion, embodied *piety, gave leadership in movements of moral *reform and sought interdenominational cooperation.

Pidgeon graduated from Presbyterian College in Montreal, pastored in Quebec and Ontario, was professor of practical theology at Westminster Hall, Vancouver (1909-1915), and then came to Bloor Street Church in Toronto, where he would remain until 1948. Toronto was one of the preaching centers of the Protestant world when Pidgeon arrived, but Pidgeon readily held his own. He spent a period as first convener of the Board of Moral and Social Reform of the *Presbyterian Church in Canada.

In 1917 Pidgeon became convener of the board of home missions, with its particular responsibility for western Canada. The scarcity of population particularly impressed upon him the need of church union, and in 1921 he became the convener of the committee working toward that end. He was chosen as moderator of the Presbyterian general assembly in 1925, and when on June 10 of that year the Methodists, the Congregationalists and two-thirds of the Presbyterians joined to form the United Church of Canada, he was chosen as moderator. Upon his retirement the tradition of Bloor Street changed radically with the coming of the brilliant theological liberal E. M. Howse.

Bibliography. J. W. Grant, *George Pidgeon* (1962). I. S. Rennie

Pierson, A(rthur) T(appan) (1837-1911). Presbyterian minister, mission theorist and Bible expositor. Born in New York City, Pierson attended Hamilton College (B.A., 1857) and studied theology at Union Seminary, New York (B.D., 1860). His career as a Presbyterian minister first took him to Waterford, New York (1863-1869), to Fort Street Presbyterian Church, Detroit (1869-1882) and then briefly to Second Presbyterian Church, Indianapolis (1882-1883). Afterward he pastored the nondenominational Bethany Tabernacle in Philadelphia (1883-1889) and later served briefly at Spurgeon's Tabernacle in London (1891-1893).

The 1880s and 1890s were Pierson's most productive years as a mission theorist. As head of the missions committee of the Philadelphia Presbytery, he wrote "The Problem of Missions," in which he argued for Christian colonies of mission workers. In 1886 he wrote *The Crisis of Missions,* a best-selling book that put the issue of missions before the American people in a vivid way. Throughout his career he was to author over fifty books, five of which covered recent mission history and were entitled *The Miracles of Missions.* He became editor of *The Missionary Review of the World,* and in his twenty-five years of service he transformed it from a small venture into the major American missions periodical of the period, published monthly and surveying the work of all Protestant missions around the world.

Pierson delivered the Alexander Duff Lectures and the Nathan Graves Lectures—two of the major mission lectureships antedating the establishment of chairs of missions in theological seminaries. In speaking and writing, Pierson promoted the Student Volunteer Movement (SVM), the Laymen's Missionary Movement and women's work in missions. He helped to found the Africa Inland Mission and addressed the ecumenical missions conferences of 1888 and 1900. In 1893 he succeeded A. J. Gordon as president of Gordon's Missionary Training School, now known as Gordon College.

Pierson's greatest theoretical contribution to missions stemmed from his premillennialism. In 1886 he delivered a speech at the International Prophetic Conference entitled "Our Lord's Second Coming as a Motive to World-Wide Evangelization." In it he argued that the hope of Christ's Second Coming was the greatest motivation for world evangelization, defined as offering the good news to every person. Pierson did not believe that the world would be converted before Christ returned, but the world evangelization was a prerequisite to this return. For Pierson, then, the motivating force of the SVM watchword (which was credited to him)—"the evangelization of the world in this generation"—was its implicit belief that Christ would return once world evangelization was complete.

In his later years Pierson's piety and biblical conservatism brought him into demand as a Bible expositor. He spoke at new Bible training schools, such as Moody Bible Institute, Biblical Seminary, Nyack Missionary Training Institute and "higher life" gatherings, such as Keswick conferences. He contributed to *The Fundamentals* and was an original editor of the Scofield Reference Bible. Most of his later works were on biblical or spiritual themes.

In his lifetime Pierson was a controversial figure. His piety and premillennialism alienated some people, while his tendency to cooperate across confessional lines for the sake of world evangelizationa lienated others. And yet Pierson was the leading American spokesperson for foreign missions in the late nineteenth century. Under his influence people such as John Mott, Robert *Speer, Samuel *Zwemer, Henry Frost and many others were propelled into work for foreign missions. After he died, admirers established in his honor Pierson Bible College in Seoul, Korea.

BIBLIOGRAPHY. *DAB* VII; D. L. Pierson, *Arthur T. Pierson* (1912); *The Missionary Review of the World* (1886- 1912); D. L. Robert, "Arthur Tappan Pierson and Forward Movements of Late-Nineteenth-Century Evangelicalism" (unpublished Ph.D. dissertation, Yale University, 1984); D. L. Robert, "The Legacy of Arthur Tappan Pierson," *IBMR* (July 1984) 120-25. D. L. Robert

Pierson, Lydia Jane (1802-1862). Lay theological and devotional writer for the *German Reformed Church *Weekly Messenger* from 1837 to 1842. Writing under the name Lydia Jane, she represents dozens of women who contributed to this widely-read periodical that gave the denomination identity and cohesion.

Born Lydia Jane Wheeler in Middletown, Connecticut, she moved at sixteen with her family to central New York. She taught school until 1821, when she married widower Oliver Pierson and resettled in Tioga County, Pennsylvania. Despite hardship from her husband's business disasters, she became a regional writer of note, publishing poetry and topical pieces in many Pennsylvania newspapers. Thaddeus Stevens became her patron after admiring her article in favor of free public education. He covered her sons' college tuition and arranged publication of two books of poetry, *Forest Leaves* (1845) and *The Forest Minstrel* (1846).

Pierson's affiliation with a nearby Lutheran-Reformed union church led to her lively contribution to the German Reformed Church through its *Weekly Messenger.* Her work, including the genres of devotional poetry, prose meditation, biblical exposition, short story and prophetic exhortation on church political issues, is of high literary quality. Though some of her poetry is sentimental, many of her pieces are boldly written and powerful. She put forth a broadly evangelical faith, fervent *piety, deep sympathy for human suffering and impatience with religious conflict. Her family moved to Michigan in 1853, where she died.

Bibliography. C. E. Hambrick-Stowe and B. Brown Zikmund, eds., *The Living Theological Heritage of the United Church of Christ,* vol. 3, *Colonial and National Beginnings* (1998).

C. E. Hambrick-Stowe

Piety, Presbyterian and Reformed. Piety is a matter of how one lives the Christian life. The focus of Reformed piety is found in Christ's summary of the Decalogue, that is, love of God and love of neighbor.

Reformed piety springs from a sense of awe before the grace of God. God's love toward us is revealed in Jesus Christ, "who at the cost of his own blood has fully paid for all my sins and has completely freed me from the dominion of the devil" (Heidelberg Catechism, Q&A 1). The Christian experience of God is trinitarian. It knows the love of the Father in the life of the Son through the enlightening power of the Spirit. "Therefore, by his Holy Spirit, he assures me of eternal life, and makes me wholeheartedly willing and ready from now on to live for him" (Heidelberg, Q&A 1). God's mighty works of creation and redemption are so wondrous that we can only bow in *worship before him. If "man's chief end is to glorify God and to enjoy him forever" (Westminster Shorter Catechism, Q 1), then serving God's glory in worship is of the greatest possible importance. By worshiping God we express our love toward him. This is done in the assembling of the congregation for public worship as well as in the worship of the family circle and the secret worship of the individual. From this sense of awe before the grace of God the worship of Presbyterian and Reformed churches has a sense of solemnity and dignity. Because glory is to be given to God alone, it is conducted in simplicity and humility rather than with theatrical pomp or ostentation.

A Reformed piety is one that is reformed according to Scripture. Not only does the Bible guide the Christian life, but also it is the means of bringing us into fellowship with God. Both in public worship and in private devotion the contemplation of the Word of God is an important means of experiencing the presence of God. As one finds in the biblical commentaries of Charles *Hodge, the learned study of Scripture is not merely scholastic; it is devotional as well. "The Spirit of God makes the reading, but especially the preaching, of the word an effectual means of convincing and converting sinners, and of building them up in holiness and comfort through faith unto salvation" (Westminster, Q 89).

A Reformed piety teaches believers to live by faith. Men and women are creatures of need, and yet as Christians they are also children of God and live under the covenant promises of the people of God. To live by faith is to believe that these promises will be fulfilled. In prayer believers bring needs of both body and soul to God, and they are promised that whatever problems they meet in this life will turn out for good, "for [God] is able to do it being almighty God, and is determined to do it, being a faithful father" (Heidelberg, Q&A 26). To live by faith is to be ever thankful for the grace of God. It is constantly to remember his mighty acts of creation and redemption in prayer and to live in thankful obedience to his word. Faith believes that God's way is best and therefore follows that way, not in servitude but in gratitude.

A Reformed piety is a living out of baptism. Baptism stands at the beginning of the Christian life as a divinely given sign of the course of the believer's walk. It is a covenant sign to be received in faith. Through the washing of water believers are promised the washing away of all our sin and the purity of a new life. The outward washing by the minister is a promise of the inward baptism of the Holy Spirit, who renews us "in the whole man after the image of God and [enables us] more and more to die unto sin and live unto righteousness" (Westminster, Q 35). Baptism with water is a sign and a promise of the baptism of the Holy Spirit. It sets believers apart to the priestly service of the spiritual temple not made with human hands. Baptism is a promise of a variety of spiritual gifts. Not every Christian receives all of these gifts. The Spirit dispenses them when and where and how he pleases. He empowers believers to do God's work in the world and keeps Christians ever mindful that their burial with Christ implies their resurrection with him on the last day and their enjoyment of him forever.

A Reformed piety has a strong sense of the providence of God. Even in the wake of deism such Reformed theologians as Charles Hodge maintained that God still preserves and governs "all his creatures and all their actions" (Westminster, Q 11). It is because God is sovereign that believers can approach the future with confidence. As much as the Enlightenment may have opposed the doctrines of election and predestination, they are clearly taught in Scripture as Hodge, Louis *Berkhof and other Reformed theologians understood it. These doctrines went together with a strong moral discipline and a high sense of destiny. Those whom God calls to salvation he also calls to serve him by reflecting his holiness in this life and the building up of his eternal kingdom. Election entails service.

A Reformed piety teaches stewardship. Since God has so bountifully poured out his gifts upon his children, they must, as the parable of Jesus teaches, be good stewards of these gifts. Rather than deprecate the material things of life as Neo-Platonic asceticism had done, Reformed Christians understand that they are to be received with thanksgiving. The advantages of wealth, property and position should be used in the service of God's glory and for the welfare of neighbors. Fulfilling family responsibilities, as husband or wife, brother or sister, parent or child, has always been considered a major part of living the Christian life. A Reformed piety gives attention to vocation. Not only do those who serve the church professionally have a vocation, but also all Christians have a calling to spend their energies in the service of God. Farmers, merchants, engineers, nurses, teachers, corporation managers and secretaries serve God when they do their work well. Characteristic of Reformed churches is their understanding of deacons as ministers who lead the church in ministries of mercy. Relieving the need of the poor, the sick, the widowed and the orphaned is a traditional concern of Christian piety.

A Reformed piety has a special concern for the proclamation of the gospel. This has been particularly the case in America, where the Great Awakening shaped Protestant identity. The concern to preach the central message of our salvation in Christ has been characteristic of American Christianity ever since. It is a major responsibility of the church to be sure that every human being has an opportunity to hear the gospel. In the nineteenth century *revivalism often distorted true evangelism. *Old School theologians became very critical of the methods of evangelism used by the *New School. Still, the preaching of the message of salvation remained a primary concern of Reformed churches. This was especially evident in the great effort put into the *missionary movement.

A Reformed piety is eucharistic. Even if it is celebrated only a few times a year, the Lord's Supper is the feast day of the Christian life. At communion believers feast on the love of God. As Samuel *Davies taught, communion is a time to give thanks to God for his mighty acts of redemption and a time to renew covenant vows and reassert the Christian confession of faith. The *sacrament of communion is a covenant meal in which believers are united to Christ and to the whole household of God (Heidelberg, Q&A 75-77). There is great significance in the fact that the Reformed communion service is celebrated in such a way that the form of a meal is clearly discerned. The people sit around the table and serve one another with bread and wine. It is at the Lord's table that believers formally accept Christ. When Gilbert *Tennent preached at the Lord's Supper, he often took a text from the Song of Solomon to make the point that the communion is the wedding feast of the Lamb. Christ pledges his love to his church, and they in return pledge their love to him. The communion is a taste in this life of the consummation of God's blessings in the life to come.

Bibliography. A. Alexander, *On Religious Experience* (1844); J. W. Alexander, *Thoughts on Family Worship* (reprint, 1990); C. W. Baird, *Presbyterian Liturgies* (reprint, 1957); C. Hodge, *The Way of Life* (1841); B. M. Palmer, *Theology of Prayer* (1894); G. Tennent, *Sermons Preached on Sacramental Occasions* (1737); B. B. Warfield, *Faith and Life* (reprint, 1974); idem, *Perfectionism* (reprint, 1967).

H. O. Old

Plan of Union. Congregational-Presbyterian alliance. Sealed in 1801, the Plan of Union formally united Presbyterians and Connecticut Congregationalists in efforts to evangelize the western frontier. Close ties that had existed among the two groups for at least thirty-five years culminated in this plan designed to foster joint action rather than needless conflict in the home *missionary enterprise. Specifically it encouraged all missionaries toward mutual forbearance and a spirit of accommodation, allowed members of each persuasion in a frontier settlement to found separate or united congregations and permitted congregations to affiliate with either a presbytery or a congregational association.

In practice the plan contributed to the extension of evangelical faith into America's interior as missionaries, pastors and teachers made their way west under its auspices. Institutionally the Presbyterians benefitted most, due to their greater denominational consciousness and organizational assertiveness. Conversely, the *New England theology tended to dominate the doctrinal sympathies of union churches and pastors. Ironically, both developments contributed to the ultimate demise of the plan.

Presbyterian *Old School conservatives came to oppose the alliance because it prevented exclusive Presbyterian control over missionary endeavors and more importantly allowed for the influx of what they considered dangerous theological innovations from Congregationalists. When Old Schoolers gained control of the Presbyterian general assembly in 1837 (*see* Auburn Declaration), they revoked the Plan of Union and cut off four western synods that had developed from the union plan. Congregationalists eventually voided the accord at the Albany Convention of 1852 after becoming more denominationally self-conscious and realizing that Presbyterian gains had been made partially at their expense.

Bibliography. R. L. Ferm, *A Colonial Pastor: Jonathan Edwards the Younger* (1976); G. M. Marsden, *The Evangelical Mind and the New School Presbyterian Experience: A Case Study of Thought and Theology in Nineteenth-Century America* (1970); W. Walker, *A History of the Congregational Churches in the United States* (1894).

R. W. Pointer

Politics, Presbyterians and. Presbyterians' participation in American politics has been disproportionate to their numbers in the population in part because of the high vocation accorded to human government in Reformed theology. However, political action by the church as a corporate body has been a source of repeated conflict and debate among Presbyterians.

The origins of Presbyterians' political involvement and the debates that surround it reach back to the sixteenth-century Reformed theologian John *Calvin. Calvin recognized the state as a gift of God not only bringing order to a chaotic, sinful world but also upholding the church and Christian virtue in public life. He therefore commended civil office as an honorable Christian occupation and counseled obedience to the state. At the same time, Calvin introduced a critical, reformist edge into Calvinist political thinking by insisting the Christian's first allegiance is always to a sovereign God, not the state, for human governments are as subject to sin as are individuals. Thus when the state failed its high calling by contradicting the express will of God, it could in extreme cases be resisted under the leadership of lesser magistrates.

Most Presbyterians in colonial America enacted such political resistance by vigorously supporting the American *Revolution. King George III once referred to the conflict as "the Presbyterian War" because of the prominence of laypeople like William *Livingston and Benjamin *Rush as well as clergy like John *Witherspoon, the only minister to sign the Declaration of Independence, who agitated in the press or from the pulpit and served in the Continental Congress or army for the revolutionary cause.

Following the war, all except the Scottish Covenanters relinquished Calvin's claims on official state support for the church by accepting the new United States Constitution's official separation of church and state. Officially disestablished but informally privileged by public laws, nineteenth-century Presbyterians with other Protestants fostered new *missionary work and a complex network of voluntary benevolent societies to instill Christian morality into the political and social life of settled communities and the frontier. Sheldon *Jackson, both a Presbyterian missionary and the civil superintendent for public instruction in Alaska, personified the confluence of religious and political leadership responsibilities commonly assumed by Presbyterians of the period.

Nineteenth-century Presbyterians also campaigned actively for legal sanctions and politicians that would insure temperance and sabbath observance. But divisive political issues like slavery increasingly led Presbyterians into conflict over the propriety of the church placing its corporate weight behind political reform. *New School, *revival-oriented Presbyterians tended to pursue political remedies for slavery energetically because they assumed the church's call to effect as close an approximation of the kingdom of God on earth as possible. Their *Old School counterparts were less optimistic about political reforms' perfecting potential and wary about making pronouncements for the whole church on issues that were then considered biblically debatable.

With the outbreak of the *Civil War, a newly formed Southern, and largely Old School, *Presbyterian Church in the United States (PCUS) adopted the principle of the spirituality of the church. Formally framed by James Henley *Thornwell, this doctrine contended that the church is "exclusively a spiritual organization" and has "no mission . . . to become entangled with the kingdoms and policy, of this world." The PCUS still expected its members to participate in politics and, in such work, to be informed by their Christian consciences. But it rejected politics as a topic for the pulpit or for church governing bodies. Ironically, Southern Presbyterians frequently ignored this policy in their overseas missions. In 1909 the Southern church made a national political cause out of the Belgian Congo's prosecution of two PCUS missionaries who had challenged the oppression of native Congo tribes.

During the first half of the twentieth century, Presbyterians were well represented in American political power centers. Woodrow *Wilson served as president (1912-1920) and William Jennings *Bryan as his Secretary of State for a period. During the Eisenhower administration, John Foster *Dulles oversaw the State Department and introduced Reformed theologians like Reinhold *Niebuhr into the government's deliberations on national policy. By the 1950s Presbyterian political clout was sufficiently strong for the church to be jokingly referred to as the Republican Party at prayer.

Signals of a shift in Presbyterians' political agenda and activism began to appear in the early twentieth century, however. Peace and civil rights proved to be centers of this change in Presbyterian political action. Black Presbyterians had long demanded an end to racism within the church and the society. During the 1910s and 1920s, Francis *Grimké renewed this political advocacy to end the color line. When World War I began, most Presbyterians supported military efforts, as they would in World War II. The *Presbyterian Church in the U.S.A. (PCUSA) endorsed the war even while noting to President Wilson that it was an "irrational, inhuman and unchristian" war. But Bryan eventually broke with Wilson over involvement in World War I, and the Presbyterian minister Norman *Thomas led the formation of a Fellowship of Reconciliation to oppose the war and to promote pacifism.

The civil rights movement and protests against the Vietnam war during the 1960s and 1970s galvanized a major rethinking of the Presbyterian church's political role. This shift contributed to the 1973 secession from the PCUS and formation of the *Presbyterian Church in America (PCA), a communion that reasserted the doctrine of the spirituality of the church. Increasingly, Presbyterian clergy and their denominations' general assemblies advanced corporate church advocacy through ever more frequent proclamations across a widening range of political issues. Formal lobbying efforts to Congress were expanded, and acts of political nonviolent action were encouraged or at least condoned by first the *United Presbyterian Church U.S.A. general assembly and later the North-South merged Presbyterian Church (USA). Denominational pronouncements urged study by congregations and, in some cases, openly promoted civil disobedience for equal rights, conscientious objection to the Vietnam war in particular and the nuclear arms race in general, sanctuary for illegal immigrants and witness for peace demonstrations against military aid to oppressive regimes in Latin America.

These methods and issues have not been unanimously supported by Presbyterians, but the Christian's responsibility to transform the state through political action remains unquestioned throughout the largest Presbyterian communion, the PCUSA.

Recent research into Presbyterian political statements and action indicates that they have been most effective against hunger, but the effectiveness of the church's political lobbying is limited since general assembly statements are not binding on the Presbyterian membership, whose God alone is Lord of their conscience.

See also ABOLITION, PRESBYTERIANS AND; AMERICAN REVOLUTION, PRESBYTERIANS AND THE; CIVIL WAR, PRESBYTERIANS AND THE; SOCIAL REFORM, PRESBYTERIANS AND.

BIBLIOGRAPHY. A. M. Hallum, "Presbyterians as Political Amateurs," in *Religion in American Politics,* ed. C. W. Dunn (1989); A. D. Hertzke, "An Assessment of the Mainline Churches Since 1945," in *The Role of Religion in the Making of Public Policy,* ed. J. E. Wood Jr., and D. Davis (1991); B. Johnson, "From Old to New Agendas: Presbyterians and Social Issues in the Twentieth Century," in *The Confessional Mosaic,* ed. M. J. Coalter, J. M. Mulder and L. B. Weeks (1990); Presbyterian Church (U.S.A.), *God Alone Is Lord of the Conscience* (1988); C. Strout, "Religion and Politics Prior to World War II," in *The Role of Religion in the Making of Public Policy,* ed. J. E. Wood Jr., and D. Davis (1991); R. H. Stone, ed., *Reformed Faith and Politics* (1983).

M. J. Coalter Jr.

Polity, Presbyterian. The word *presbyter* is the Anglicized form of the Greek *presbytero,* meaning "elder." By definition presbyterian polity is government by elders. The basic elements of this polity are found in both the Old and New Testaments. Elders are found in the Bible, even before the establishment of Israel as a nation. The ideas of seniority and authority are closely joined in the patriarchal society. The heads of families and tribes exercised authority. There were elders in Egypt (Gen 50:7) and in other nations (Num 22:7), as well as Israel.

In addition to elders of a household, there were elders of the land (1 Kings 20:7-8), of cities (Deut 19:12; Josh 20:4), of Judah (1 Sam 20:26) and of Israel (Ex 12:21). The elders often represented the people. Moses gathered the elders and spoke to the people through them (Ex 3:16; 4:29). The elders spoke for the people in asking for a king (1 Sam 8:4). Moses and Joshua had elders associated with them as a governing council (Ex 3:18; Deut 27:1; Josh 8:10). In the exile the elders provided the Jews with a continuing government (Jer 29:1; Ezek 8:1; 14:1; 20:1, 3).

At the time of the exodus there was a body of elders who were recognized as authoritative. The Septuagint translates the "elders of Israel" as "the senate of Israel" (Ex 3:16-18; 4:29; 12:21). At Sinai seventy of the elders were called up to the mountain to feast in the presence of God (Ex 24:1, 9-11). Later a national eldership of seventy was formally organized to assist Moses in governance of the people (Num 11:16-17) and were given the Spirit to assist Moses in bearing the burden. They were representatives of the people, in being put forward by them and exercising authority over them. Traditionally the Jewish Sanhedrin was modeled after this body.

With the dispersion of the Jews, beginning with the Babylonian captivity, the eldership of each synagogue and a graduated court system culminating in the Sanhedrin became the primary form of government for Judaism. This became the pattern for the emerging Christian church in the book of Acts.

In accord with the custom in the synagogue and the biblical example of the election of the deacons in Acts 6, the elders are elected by the congregation. In this sense they are the representatives of the people; however, their governance was not primarily to represent the will of the people but to apply the law of God as representatives of Christ, the only King over the church. It is his law that they apply to the church. Acts 14:23 states that Paul and Barnabas appointed elders in each of the congregations established on the first missionary journey, thus establishing the principle that there should be a plurality of elders in every congregation. Based on Exodus 18, Numbers 11 and the graduated court system of the Jews, with the Sanhedrin in Jerusalem as the highest judicatory, the church at Antioch sent the question of circumcision to the apostles and elders at Jerusalem (Acts 15). This body met in an open session and settled the issue in accord with Scripture. This decision in turn was sent to all the churches (Acts 16:4).

In modern times Presbyterian polity is found in the Presbyterian and Reformed churches, with variations of detail in different denominations. Rule by elders and a graduated court system are common to all. John *Calvin developed Presbyterianism for the city of Geneva. The development of graduated assemblies or courts in a larger setting took place in France in 1560 and in Scotland with the adoption of the *Second Book of Discipline* in 1581 under Andrew Melville's leadership. The courts as developed in modern Presbyterianism are called, from the lowest to the highest: the session or consistory, the presbytery or classis, the synod or general assembly.

The session consists of a plurality of elders elected by the congregation. These are the teaching elders (pastors) and the ruling elders. The presbytery is made up of all teaching elders in a region and ruling elders representing each congregation within the region.

In Presbyterian churches the ministers or teaching elders hold their membership in the presbytery. This provides a body of elders, at least half of whom are teaching elders, to examine candidates for the ministry. In some Presbyterian churches ministers are reexamined as to their theological views when transferring to a new presbytery. The presbytery is also the court of original jurisdiction for any charges laid against a teaching elder, again providing a body of both teaching and ruling elders by whom the elder is to be judged.

Reformed churches from the Continent hold the membership of the ministers in the congregation. The examination for ordination is conducted by the general synod, and transfer to a new classis is without additional examination. The court of original jurisdiction is the consistory in the congregation where the minister holds membership. Larger Presbyterian churches have four levels of courts with regional synods and a general assembly as the highest court. Smaller churches may have just one court above the presbytery, designated as either general synod or general assembly. The membership of the highest court ordinarily is made up of teaching and ruling elder representatives elected by the presbyteries.

In distinction from a hierarchical system of government with different ranking officers at each level, all of the Presbyterian courts are constituted of the same kind of membership, namely, teaching and ruling elders. Christ is the head of each court, and thus as it acts in accord with the Word of God, it acts with his authority. The actions of each court are the actions of the whole church. For example, the reception of members by a session or of a minister by a presbytery is the reception by the universal church visible. The same is true for an act of discipline at any level. It is the act of the whole church visible. Essentially then, all of the courts are equal in authority, except on business assigned to the higher court or matters that are appealed to a higher court. The higher court has the prerogative of correcting a lower court.

The election of the elders is the only point in which the congregation enters into the governance of the church. In Presbyterian churches elders serve for life. Some churches provide for the possibility of rotation or resignation from the active session without the loss of the eldership. Reformed churches do not have lifetime elders but elect for specified terms of service. The elders govern as a joint power, meeting in council. Since the power of the church is not legislative or magisterial but declarative and ministerial, the governing councils are designated courts in the Scottish tradition. They are only to interpret the law of Christ and declare its meaning, not to make laws. The only lawbook in Zion is the Bible.

There are different views as to how many kinds of officers there should be in the church. Calvin spoke of four, namely, pastors, teachers, elders and deacons. The office of teacher has been understood in two senses. The Form of Government framed by the Westminster Assembly speaks of this function in both ways. The first is for one who teaches the Word in the local congregation in addition to the pastor of the congregation. These teachers join with the other elders of the congregation in the governance of the congregation. The second usage is with references to the teacher of the theological faculty of the church. These teachers do not sit as rulers in a consistory, classis or synod in Dutch churches but only as advisors.

Others see the pastors and teachers as descriptive of the minister of the Word, as distinguished from the ruling elder and the deacon. This is a three-office view. Charles *Hodge did not consider the ruling elders to be elders but rather governors, taken from the list of the gifts in 1 Corinthians 12:28. He held that the elder was a layman and the representative of the people.

James Henley *Thornwell maintained that the elders were the presbyters described by Paul in 1 Timothy 3 and Titus 1, and that the eldership is divided into two classes on the basis of 1 Timothy 5:17. They are teaching and ruling elders. Both classes of elders act equally as rulers in the church. All elders rule, and all rulers in the church are elders. The teaching elders are not of a higher rank but have the additional function of serving as ministers of the Word and *sacraments. As equal members of the presbytery the ruling elders participate in the ordaining of teaching elders with the laying on of the hands.

Presbyterians hold that Presbyterian polity is that which the Bible teaches, and thus it is essential for the well-being of the church but not for the being of the church.

Bibliography. D. Bannerman, *The Scripture Doctrine of the Church* (1887); J. Bannerman, *The Church of Christ* (1868); G. Gillespie, *Aaron's Rod Blossoming* (1646); D. W. Hall and J. H. Hall, eds., *Paradigms in Polity: Classic Readings in Reformed and Presbyterian Church Government* (1994); W. Heyns, *Handbook for Elders and Deacons, The Nature and the Duties of the Offices According to the Principles of Reformed Church Polity* (1928); C. Hodge, *Constitutional History of the Presbyterian Church in the United States of America* (1851); S. Miller, *An Essay on the Warrant, Nature and Duties of the Office of the Ruling Elder in the Presbyterian Church* (1832); idem, *The Primitive and Apostolic Order of the Church of Christ Vindicated* (1832); T. E. Peck, *Notes on Ecclesiology* (1892); J. L. Schaver, *Christian Reformed Church Order* (1937); idem, *The Polity of the Churches* (1939); M. H. Smith, *Commentary on the Book of Church Order of the Presbyterian Church in America* (1990).

M. H. Smith

Portland Deliverance (1892). A declaration by the 1892 General Assembly of the *Presbyterian Church in the U.S.A. (PCUSA), meeting in Portland, Oregon, that affirmed the inerrancy of Scripture and required all ministers in the church to adhere to this doctrine.

In the late nineteenth century, as higher-critical interpretations of the Bible began to threaten traditional understandings of the infallibility of the Scriptures, conservative Presbyterians, especially at Princeton Seminary, articulated a doctrine of scriptural inerrancy. Archibald Alexander *Hodge and Benjamin Breckinridge *Warfield gave classic expression to this view when they argued in 1881 that "the historical faith of the Church has always been that all the affirmations of Scripture of all kinds . . . are without any error when the *ipsissima verba* of the original autographs are ascertained and interpreted in their natural and intended sense."

In response to such views, Charles Augustus *Briggs, a Presbyterian minister and the foremost biblical scholar in America, declared, upon his inauguration into the chair of biblical theology at Union Seminary (New York) in 1891, that the Scriptures did contain errors. He went on in his inaugural address to deny the Mosaic authorship of the Pentateuch and the unitary authorship of the book of Isaiah.

An uproar over Briggs's views ensued, and Henry Preserved *Smith, professor at Lane Theological Seminary, defended Briggs in various articles, claiming that he too rejected biblical inerrancy. The 1892 general assembly responded to these events in part by adopting the Portland Deliverance, which stated that "the inspired Word, as it came from God, is without error." In order to clarify any ambiguity in this deliverance, the 1893 assembly further maintained "that the original Scriptures of the Old and New Testaments, being immediately inspired of God, were without error" and insisted that this had always been the view of the church. The assemblies thereby officially adopted the Princeton view of Scripture as that of the church.

The Portland Deliverance was instrumental in the suspension of Briggs and Smith from the ministry in 1893 and 1894, respectively. Moreover, the deliverance gave precedence for future assemblies of the church to define essential doctrines of the church by pronouncement. Thus in 1899 the general assembly, in response to the publications of Arthur Cushman *McGiffert, professor of church history at Union Seminary (New York), defined four "fundamental doctrines" of the church, including the inerrancy of the Scriptures, and enjoined lower judicatories to defend these doctrines. McGiffert resigned from the Presbyterian ministry in 1900.

In 1910 the general assembly, responding to concerns of conservatives about the ordination of liberal ministerial candidates, declared five doctrines, including the inerrancy of Scripture, to be "essential and necessary" articles of the faith that all candidates for ordination had to be able to affirm. These five points were reaffirmed by the general assemblies of 1916 and 1923.

In 1927, however, after years of intense and sustained struggle between *fundamentalists and modernists in the church, the general assembly declared that an assembly by itself could not declare any article of faith essential and necessary except by using the exact language of the *Westminster Confession. The doctrine of the inerrancy of Scripture that the Portland Deliverance as well as the five fundamentals had affirmed was thereby rejected as binding on the church.

Though a *neo-orthodox approach to Scripture dominated the church from the late 1930s to the 1960s, since that time a variety of understandings of biblical inspiration and authority has become prevalent in the denomination.

Bibliography. L. A. Loetscher, *The Broadening Church: A Study of Theological Issues in the Presbyterian Church Since 1869* (1954); B. J. Longfield, *The Presbyterian Controversy: Fundamentalists, Modernists, and Moderates* (1991); M. S. Massa, *Charles Augustus Briggs and the Crisis of Historical Criticism* (1990); M. A. Noll, ed., *The Princeton Theology, 1812-1929: Scripture, Science, and Theological Method from Archibald Alexander to Benjamin Breckinridge Warfield* (1983).

B. J. Longfield

Preaching. *See* WORSHIP, PRESBYTERIANS AND.

Predestination. In its normal and proper sense, the term refers to the foreordination of moral agents to their eternal ends. That is, the knowledge and choice made by God, before time began, of angels and men as to their final blessedness with God or damnation apart from him.

The doctrine was formulated by Augustine in his controversies with Pelagius (405-418). Augustine held that all persons were predestined either to belief, by the intervention of God's saving grace, or unbelief, by God's permitting them to follow their own ways (reprobation). Pelagius considered election to refer simply to God's foreknowledge of who would believe. He saw no need for God's intervention to cause belief because he denied that guilt was inherited from Adam's sin. The later dispute between *Calvinism and *Arminianism (1603-1619) was essentially the same (though Arminius did hold that original righteousness was taken away in the Fall).

Theologically this doctrine follows from the doctrine of God's eternal knowledge of all events in time and his eternally willing (in the same act, for his will and knowledge are only formally and not really separate) that they be as they are (his decree). The doctrine is also necessary for those who hold that human depravity makes it impossible for people to choose the good, as this would require that God initiate the response of every person who turns to him by giving each the grace to believe. As such, the doctrine is intimately connected with the other cardinal doctrines of soteriology: original sin, *election, limited/unlimited atonement, free will and grace.

Biblically the doctrine is derived from the Old Testament teaching of God's foreknowledge (Ps 139:4-6), his ordination of events (Is 14:26-27) and his choice of the nation Israel (Deut 10:15; Mal 1:2-3). In the New Testament God's foreknowledge (1 Pet 1:20) and ordination (Rom 9:11; 1 Cor 2:7; Eph 1:11; 3:11) are understood by some Christians to be specifically applied to individuals (Rom 11:2; Rev 13:8; 17:8). These terms are united in Romans 8:28-30. According to 1 Peter 1:2, predestination is in accordance with foreknowledge.

In American church traditions there is a broad spectrum of belief about this doctrine. While Catholicism has embraced a range of views on the question, for Protestant churches an understanding or denial of the doctrine has frequently formed an important part of their self-identity. Two views affirm both God's foreknowledge and his choice in predestination:

1. Dortian or Extreme Calvinism. The Reformed

tradition (including the Puritan Congregationalists, Presbyterians, Reformed churches and Particular Baptists) has generally held to an Augustinian Calvinism. Jonathan *Edwards, Charles *Hodge and B. B. *Warfield became its most important spokespersons. Here both predestination to eternal life and reprobation to eternal death are affirmed along with limited atonement and the need for irresistible grace.

2. *Moderate Calvinism.* Much of evangelicalism and some General Baptists affirm God's choice in election and each person's need for grace to choose God. However, they believe in unlimited atonement, stressing that salvation is hypothetically possible for all but that God has elected some actually to be saved. Some form of cooperation between people's wills and God's grace is seen. Some also hold that only predestination to life is made, denying any implication that God ordains people to hell.

Two views define predestination as foreknowledge only:

1. *Wesleyan Arminianism.* Methodism has generally held John Wesley's view that guilt was inherited from Adam, but that this did not affect people's ability to choose God. Hence, predestination is equated with divine foresight of people's free choice apart from any causal choosing by God.

2. *Arminianism.* Quakers, some General Baptists and much of the Holiness and Pentecostal traditions hold to a classic Arminianism. This position was nurtured by the modified Calvinism of the New Haven Theology of Nathaniel Taylor and the revivalism of Charles *Finney. It has penetrated a large and diverse segment of the nation's churches. The Fall is seen to negate persons' original righteousness but not to impair their ability to know and choose God.

Two views deny that God chooses individuals:

1. *Socianism or old Unitarianism.* This view maintains that God not only does not choose in predestination but is not able to know the actions of free agents in advance. To do so would be impossible, since freedom is understood to mean absolute random choice.

2. *Barthianism or Neo-orthodoxy.* This view has held that Christ was chosen by God, and the church was corporately chosen only because it is in Christ. This view avoids the entire issue of free will, determinism and original sin.

BIBLIOGRAPHY. B. G. Armstrong, *Calvinism and the Amyraut Heresy* (1969); L. Berkhof, *A History of Christian Doctrines* (1937); J. Edwards, *Freedom of the Will* (1754); F. H. Foster, *A Genetic History of the New England Theology* (1907); C. Hodge, *Systematic Theology*, vol. 3 (1873); C. Pinnock, ed., *Grace Unlimited* (1975). N. L. Geisler

Presbyterian Church (USA).‡ A mainline Presbyterian denomination formed from 1983 to 1987 by the union of the United Presbyterian Church in the United States of America (UPCUSA) and the *Presbyterian Church in the United States (PCUS), also known as the Southern Presbyterian Church.

The present-day PCUSA traces its roots to 1788 and the formation of the Presbyterian general assembly, and further yet to the presbytery, gathered in 1706. Representing the connectional side of *Puritanism and the Scottish Presbyterian traditions, the presbytery constituted itself a synod in 1716 and grew during colonial times to become a significant force in America. Throughout the varied fortunes of the Presbyterian church, the general assembly has remained the major judicatory body among Presbyterian bodies.

The Second Great Awakening (1800-1803) proved costly for the Presbyterians, whose leaders opposed the emotional demonstrations of conversion and the lack of attention to theology. Many members left to join the Restoration movement, which led to the forming of the Disciples of Christ and other Campbellite bodies. From 1803 to 1810, members of this body withdrew to form the *Cumberland Presbyterian Church (CPC), a separate body whose general assembly voted in 1906 to rejoin what had by then come to be called the *Presbyterian Church in the U.S.A. (PCUSA; about two-thirds of them did). In the 1830s, disputes in the PCUSA about theology, relations with other Christian bodies and *reform methods regarding slavery led to another split into *Old School and *New School assemblies. Generally more parochial in *missionary programs, Old School Presbyterians also proved less willing to work against slavery and were more closely tied to the *Westminster Confession of Faith.

Though Presbyterians in the South belonged to both New and Old School assemblies, most were Old School. Under the tensions that led to the Civil War, New School Presbyterians divided in 1857 into Northern and Southern denominations, but the Old School remained one until the secession of several states to form the Confederacy in 1861. The Old School in the South became the Presbyterian Church in the Confederate States of America, later taking the name Presbyterian Church in the United States (PCUS) in 1866. After the Civil War, Old and New School assemblies in the North reunited into the PCUSA (1870), and their mission work in the South among blacks soon led to the PCUSA's again being a truly national religious body.

The PCUSA, more than other Reformed denominations, was the scene of struggles between *fundamentalists and modernists. One major source of the struggle, the conservative *Princeton theology, had been taught at Princeton and other seminaries through much of the nineteenth century. Charles *Hodge, his son Archibald Alexander *Hodge and Benjamin Breckinridge *Warfield together enunciated principles, including a fully developed doctrine of the inerrancy of Scripture, that later characterized much of American Protestant thought. When J. Gresham *Machen, also a proponent of the Princeton theology, started an Independent Board for Presbyterian Foreign Missions, the general assembly suspended him from the ministry. In 1936 he founded the Presbyterian Church of America, later the *Orthodox Presbyterian Church (OPC). Soon the new denomination split, yielding the *Bible Presbyterian Church.

In the 1950s ecumenical impulses prompted merger discussions among the largest Presbyterian denominations. The fruit of these talks was the union in 1958 of the PCUSA and the *United Presbyterian Church of North America (UPCNA), a denomination formed in 1858 by Scottish Covenanter Presbyterians. This merger increased the size and stature of the mainline denomination, now calling itself the United Presbyterian Church in the United States of America. The PCUS, however, declined to join with the predominantly Northern Presbyterian communions. But a struggle in the 1960s among Southern Presbyterians similar to the fundamentalist controversy among Northerners in the 1920s led to the founding in 1973 of the *Presbyterian Church in America (PCA), a denomination started by conservatives. This division enabled the PCUS, which had rejected union with the Northern Presbyterians, to join with the Northern church on June 10, 1983, at which time the mainline denomination reverted to the name PCUSA. The gradual process of consolidating national offices, boards and agencies, as well as merging overlapping synods and presbyteries, continued into the late 1980s.

Bibliography. A. C. Piepkorn, *Profiles in Belief,* vol. 2 (1978); R. E. Thompson, *A History of the Presbyterian Churches in the United States* (1895); L. J. Trinterud, *The Forming of an American Tradition: A Reexamination of Colonial Presbyterianism* (1970); L. B. Weeks, *To Be a Presbyterian* (1983).

L. B. Weeks

Presbyterian Church in America.† A conservative Presbyterian denomination, organized December 1973 as the National Presbyterian Church. The present name dates from the second general assembly (1974). The denomination had its origin in the continuing church movement, a conservative effort in the *Presbyterian Church in the United States (PCUS; the Southern Presbyterian Church), originating in the 1950s, after Ernst Trice Thompson was acquitted of heresy charges for his liberal views. The ensuing outcry opposed the denomination's perceived departures from historic doctrines and the rise of higher criticism in the seminaries. Conservatives also objected to the membership of the PCUS in the National and World Councils of Churches and to social and *political pronouncements by church bodies.

The division that gave rise to the new denomination was encouraged mainly by four conservative organizations: the *Presbyterian Journal,* the Presbyterian Evangelistic Fellowship, Concerned Laymen and Presbyterian Churchmen United. As early as 1969 several hundred ministers and church sessions signed a Declaration of Commitment, opposing union with the United Presbyterian Church in the U.S.A. [the PCUSA], membership in the Consultation on Christian Union and substantial change in the doctrinal standards of the PCUS. In 1970 the executive committee of Presbyterian Churchmen United stated their goal for "A Church Reformed in Faith, Presbyterian in Polity, Evangelistic in outlook," hoping to promote a "Revival of true religion in our Southern Zion, and/or Realignment of Presbyterian and Reformed Churches" to create a national witness that would accomplish that goal. Several rallies and caucuses were held in the interest of the movement, and the leadership recommended that churches withdraw during 1973 (while the PCUS was engaged in union talks with the UPCUSA and was drafting a possible new confession of faith) by renouncing their membership in the PCUS. Many churches, however, requested and received dismissal.

After plans were laid at a convocation of sessions in Atlanta in May 1973, an advisory convention met in Asheville, North Carolina, in August 1973, and the first general assembly met in Augusta, Georgia, in December 1973. The first assembly adopted a "Message to All Churches of Jesus Christ throughout the World," which took issue with the PCUS regarding "a diluted theology, a gospel tending towards humanism, an unbiblical view of marriage and divorce, the ordination of women, financing of abortion . . . , and numerous other non-Biblical positions . . . all traceable to a different view of Scripture from that we hold and that which was held by the Southern Presbyterian forefathers." The assembly enunciated its stand for the inerrancy of the Bible, the Reformed faith of the *Westminster standards, the spirituality of the church, the historical Presbyterian view of church government and "the practice of the principle of purity in the Church visible."

Some independent churches and presbyteries, as well as congregations from other denominations, have joined the denomination. In the late 1970s and early 1980s, three-way union talks were held with the *Reformed Presbyterian Church, *Evangelical Synod and the *Orthodox Presbyterian Church (OPC). The PCA was augmented in 1982 by reception of the *Reformed Presbyterian Church, Evangelical Synod (RPC, ES; itself the result of a 1965 merger between the *Reformed Presbyterian Church, General Synod, and the *Evangelical Presbyterian Church). The union also brought Covenant College (Lookout Mountain, Tennessee) and Covenant Seminary (St. Louis, Missouri) into the denomination. Ecumenical efforts with the OPC have been unsuccessful. Both churches remain members of the North American Presbyterian and Reformed Council, a group of conservative Reformed denominations that promotes ecumenical endeavors among *Calvinist churches.

In recent years some debate has been raised surrounding the role of women, the propriety of certain church growth methods and the importance of subscription in the denomination. In 1994 several prominent ministers and seminary professors circulated a Proposed Statement of Identity in an attempt to reconcile the various perspectives.

The PCA is now a national church, the second largest Presbyterian denomination in the United States. The PCA is strongly committed to *missions, to the equality in position and authority of ministers and ruling elders and to the rights of local congregations. Its foreign missions agency, Mission to the World, sends career missionaries throughout the world, while its home missions counterpart, Mission to North America, has helped make the PCA one of the fastest-growing denominations in the United States. The offices of the church are in Atlanta, Georgia. *The PCA Messenger,* the denomination's official periodical, ceased publication by general assembly mandate in December 1994.

Bibliography. G. P. Hutchinson, *The History Behind the Reformed Presbyterian Church, Evangelical Synod* (1974); F. J. Smith, *The History of the Presbyterian Church in America* (1983); M. H. Smith, *How Is the Gold Become Dim* (1973); O. Whittaker, *Watchman, Tell It True* (1981).

A. H. Freundt Jr.

Presbyterian Church in Canada.† Canada's major Presbyterian denomination. *Canadian Presbyterianism arose first in Nova Scotia in the mid-eighteenth century. It followed the patterns of migration from the United States and the United Kingdom, but the predominant numbers and influence came from the Church of Scotland. Much of Canadian Presbyterian history mirrors that of the Scottish church. Several presbyteries were begun by both Church of Scotland and Seceder ministers during the late eighteenth and early nineteenth centuries. The former body eventually organized the Synod of the Presbyterian Church of Canada in 1831, and the United Presbyterians formed the United Synod of Upper Canada later that year, while the Presbytery of the Reformed Presbyterian Church was organized by Scottish Covenanters the following year. In 1844 the disruption of the Free Church (evangelical conservative) and Auld Kirk (traditional conservative) overflowed into Canada, resulting in the establishment of two separate Free Church synods.

Yet after the disruption noticeable changes occurred in the Canadian churches. The significant difference of the Canadian political climate from that of Scotland proved that many of the divisions between Presbyterians were no longer necessary, and by 1868 there were but four Presbyterian bodies in Canada: two synods in connection with the Church of Scotland and two independent synods comprised of Free Church, Seceder, Covenanter and some Auld Kirk churches. These four bodies united in 1875 on the basis of the infallible Scriptures, the *Westminster Confession and Catechisms (with liberty of conscience in matters of the sections on the civil magistrate) and the Form of Government and Directory of Worship that all four bodies had brought from Scotland. While still in contact with the Scottish Kirk, the general assembly of the Canadian body became an independent denomination.

Fifty years later, the formation of the United Church of Canada split the Presbyterian church into two groups. The larger one went into union with the major Methodist and Congregational bodies while about a third remained as continuing Presbyterians. No single motive directed all of these latter Presbyterians to remain outside the union. Some strongly preferred traditional Presbyterianism to any admixture with Methodism; others saw the Methodists and Congregationalists as adding harmfully to the growing presence already apparent within Presbyterianism of liberal theology and the social gospel; a few even saw the United Church as theologically too conservative in its Basis of Union and wanted Canadian Presbyterians to go well beyond it in a liberal direction. The United Church, for its part, saw the Presbyterian Church as having entered the union: those remaining outside were therefore schismatics. In 1939, however, the Canadian Parliament established the right of this latter group to the name Presbyterian Church in Canada as it amended the United Church of Canada Act of 1924.

Canadian Presbyterians have a long heritage of distinguished work in *missions, theology and social ministry. Within its ranks, however, there have been different conceptions and practices of each of these works. In the first place, missionaries like the well-known Jonathan *Goforth have gone out in traditional evangelical style; others have served the social gospel of the early twentieth century. In the second place, a number of theological traditions have found a home in Canadian Presbyterianism. Liberal theology, emerging in Presbyterian seminaries around the turn of the twentieth century, remained in those seminaries and increased its influence upon continuing Presbyterianism after the birth of the United Church. Traditional Presbyterian orthodoxy as well as evangelicalism have characterized other parts of the church. Evangelicalism in particular has been manifest in the recently organized Renewal Fellowship. And Canadian Presbyterianism saw the rise of an indigenous form of *neo-orthodox, or dialectical theology, preeminently in the work of W. W. Bryden, former professor and principal of Knox College in Toronto. In the third place, while some twentieth-century evangelicals and others have reacted against what they saw to be an overemphasis on social ministry among some other Presbyterians, the church has always sought to wrestle with the *social problems of the day, whether Prohibition, poor relief, preservation of the Lord's Day Act or the emancipation of women. To be sure, the church has comprised a variety of opinions about each of these issues, but it has maintained that involvement in such issues is a Christian duty.

Once the largest Protestant denomination in Canada, like the other mainline Canadian churches the Presbyterian Church has lost members steadily since the early 1960s. In the late 1980s it claimed more than one thousand churches and an inclusive membership of more than two hundred thousand. It is a member of the World Alliance of Reformed Churches (Presbyterian and Congregational) and of the Canadian and World Councils of Churches.

Bibliography. N. K. Clifford, *The Resistance to Church Union in Canada 1904-1939* (1985); J. S. Moir, *Enduring Witness: A History of the Presbyterian Church in Canada* (1974); N. G. Smith et al., *A Short History of the Presbyterian Church in Canada* (n.d.).

J. G. Stackhouse

Presbyterian Church in the United States (1861-1983).† Commonly known as the Southern Presbyterian Church, a Reformed denomination, formed by separation from the *Presbyterian Church in the U.S.A. (*Old School) in 1861. The Presbyterian Church in the Confederate States of America withdrew after the Old School general assembly declared that all Presbyterians owed political allegiance to the federal government during the Civil War. Receiving the tiny Independent Presbyterian Church in 1863 and the United Synod of the South (the Southern *New School body, which had left the Northern church in 1857) the following year, the denomination changed its name to the Presbyterian Church in the United States (PCUS) in 1866. Following the war, many Northern Old Schoolers joined the PCUS, including the synods of Kentucky (1869) and Missouri (1874), claiming that the Northern church had created unbiblical terms of communion and had departed from Old School theology and *polity.

In the 1880s the PCUS engaged in a vigorous controversy over evolution, due to the teaching of Columbia Theological Seminary professor James *Woodrow, who believed that Adam's body might have been formed through the evolutionary process (*see* Science, Presbyterians and). Opposed by Robert Lewis *Dabney, the leading theologian in the history of the church, Woodrow was never convicted of heresy, but the general assembly determined that his views were contrary to the received interpretation of the church, and he was removed from his position in 1886.

Like other Presbyterian denominations, the PCUS based its theology on Scripture, as interpreted through the *Westminster Confession of Faith and its accompanying catechisms (1648). In the twentieth century the church began to move away from its traditional *Calvinism, passing amendments to the Westminster standards that reflected changes in contemporary theology and liturgy.

In polity the PCUS followed received Presbyterian practices. Distinctive for the PCUS was the requirement that three-fourths of its presbyteries concur with any decision of general assemblies to change the *Book of Church Order.* The difficulty in having three-fourths of the presbyteries agree on anything assured a conservative stance on the part of the denomination.

In many respects the PCUS resembled other

Presbyterian denominations throughout the world. Emphasis on the sermon in *worship, on the celebration of infant baptism and at least quarterly communion and on the balance of power between teaching elders (ministers) and ruling elders (lay leaders) remained typical of connectional, Reformed Christianity.

The PCUS has also been characterized by engagements in foreign and domestic *missions throughout the nineteenth and into the twentieth centuries. Mission efforts in China and the Belgian Congo (now Zaire) have been especially significant, supplementing initial and important efforts in Brazil, where early missionaries also served ex-Confederate colonists for a time. Among home missions activities, those in the Appalachian highlands have proven particularly noteworthy.

During much of its existence, the PCUS stood for a doctrine of the spirituality of the church, contending that corporate church involvement in *social and *political issues was inappropriate (though individual Christians should vote and otherwise participate in moral and ethical matters). In fact many of the presbyteries and synods, as well as most general assemblies, did take stands on such issues as sabbath observance and temperance, which was condoned because of the religious character of such issues. Beginning in the 1930s, the assemblies began to speak and act more widely on such matters as patriotism and legislation concerning children. Issues like civil rights, women's rights and national foreign policy came to occupy more attention during the 1950s and thereafter.

Growing in numbers from 80,000 members in 1869 to more than 1,000,000 in 1962, the PCUS began to decline in part from the withdrawal of dissidents who formed the *Presbyterian Church in America (PCA) in 1973. Involvement of the church in civil rights and other political matters, the ordination of women and theological departures from strict Calvinism were reasons most often named for departures. These departures also enabled the PCUS, which had rejected union with the Presbyterian Church in the U.S.A. (PCUSA) and the *United Presbyterian Church in North America (UPCNA) in the 1950s to join with the *United Presbyterian Church in the U.S.A. to form the *Presbyterian Church (USA) in 1983.

See also SOUTH, PRESBYTERIANS IN THE.

BIBLIOGRAPHY. A. C. Piepkorn, *Profiles in Belief,* vol. 2 (1978); E. T. Thompson, *Presbyterians in the South,* 3 vols. (1965); R. E. Thompson, *A History of the Presbyterian Churches in the United States* (1895); L. J. Trinterud, *The Forming of an American Tradition: A Reexamination of Colonial Presbyterianism* (1949). L. B. Weeks

Presbyterian Church in the U.S.A. *See* PRESBYTERIAN CHURCH (USA)

Press, Samuel David (1875-1967). *Evangelical Synod theologian, seminary president and ecumenical pioneer. Born at Cambria, Wisconsin, Press was the son of an immigrant Swabian Evangelical pastor. He graduated from Elmhurst College (1893) and Eden Theological Seminary (1896), and in 1896 he was ordained by the Evangelical Synod. He served pastorates in Marlin, Gay Hill, and Houston, Texas, until 1908. In 1902 and 1903 he studied in Berlin.

In 1908 Press began teaching at Eden Seminary in St. Louis and became the first professor to teach in English. His lectures on Amos and Romans caused his students Reinhold *Niebuhr and Richard *Niebuhr to attribute fatherlike characteristics to him. From 1919 to 1941 Press was president of Eden Seminary.

Beginning in 1925, Press served on a denominational Committee on Closer Relations with Other Churches. In 1928 he began a dialogue with President George H. Richards of Reformed Seminary (Lancaster, Pennsylvania), from which developed formal negotiations leading to the Evangelical and Reformed Church union of 1934. Press was also instrumental in the 1957 merger of the Evangelical and Reformed Church with the Council of the Congregational Christian Churches to form the United Church of Christ. Passionate about church unity, Press believed that "the more the church grows in the knowledge of the Lord Jesus Christ . . . the more her catholicity will manifest itself." He died in St. Louis.

BIBLIOGRAPHY. W. G. Chrystal, "Samuel D. Press: Teacher of the Niebuhrs," *CH* 53 (December 1984) 504-21; S. D. Press, "The Church Union Memoirs of Samuel D. Press," *United Church Herald* (July 1, 1965) 20-22; idem, "Jesus the Christ, Our Lord," in *The Heritage of the Reformation: Essays Commemorating the Centennial of Eden Theological Seminary,* ed. E. J. F. Arndt (1950). L. H. Zuck

Presuppositionalism. A term describing a particular approach to philosophy and theology, it argues that all systems of knowledge are founded on unprovable assumptions about God, human nature and reality. Theoretical thought must therefore begin with a conscious appraisal of these assumptions. In this view, claims of objectivity as found in empiricism, rationalism or scientism are little more than pretensions resting on unexamined assumptions.

Among Christians, presuppositionalism began in the 1930s through the efforts of two *Calvinist thinkers, Herman *Dooyeweerd in the Netherlands and Cornelius *Van Til in the United States. They argued that Christians must radically reject all nonbiblical assumptions. In their voluminous writings they sought to demonstrate that most Christian thinkers had compromised their methodology by using nonbiblical assumptions in their theology, anthropology and epistemology. This practice, they argued, yields a distorted theology.

Perhaps the most crucial methodological factor for presuppositionalists is the question of authority. Their unequivocal answer is that the self-attesting triune God revealed in Scripture is the authority in all things. Believers must think analogically, thinking God's thoughts after him. This means that presuppositionalists consciously and constantly look to Scripture for norms in all theoretical matters. Presuppositionalists have therefore vigorously attacked reason and experience as principles of authority, arguing that they are merely human constructs. Rationalism and empiricism thus fail as viable methodological stances for Christians. As a practical matter, this means that presuppositionalists reject *Princeton theology and Thomism, maintaining that they are rooted in rationalistic assumptions.

BIBLIOGRAPHY. H. Dooyeweerd, *A New Critique of Theoretical Thought,* 4 vols. (1953-1958); C. Van Til, *A Christian Theory of Knowledge* (1969).

L. J. Van Til

Princeton Theology.‡ A Presbyterian theological tradition developed at Princeton Theological Seminary from its founding in 1812 until its reorganization in 1929. Princeton Theological Seminary was founded to provide ministerial training for Presbyterians. For more than a century Princeton was the domain of prominent professors— Archibald *Alexander, Charles *Hodge, Archibald Alexander *Hodge, Benjamin Breckinridge *Warfield and J. Gresham *Machen—who taught a demanding theological curriculum to more than six thousand students, defended Reformed interpretations of Scripture and laid intellectual and spiritual foundations for twentieth-century evangelicalism.

Princeton's theologians advocated Reformed confessionalism. In his famous remark that "a new idea never originated in this Seminary," Charles Hodge epitomized Princeton's claim to be merely a bearer of an unbroken and unaltered *Calvinism. The Princeton men treated Christian teaching as an unchanging whole by delineating their Calvinism back through the *Westminster standards, Swiss theologian Francois *Turretin (1623-1687), Augustine (354-430), early church fathers and ultimately to New Testament writers. While they displayed little sensitivity to historical conditions shaping doctrines and to the necessity of contextualizing faith for each generation, they were committed to retaining the Reformed biblical worldview as foundational for all Christian teaching.

As modern theologians mounted attacks against orthodoxy, each Princeton generation responded by refining its predecessors' view of Scripture. After Alexander defended the Bible against deism and Charles Hodge met the first onslaught of European biblical criticism, A. A. Hodge and Warfield taught that God's verbal and plenary inspiration produced a Scripture inerrant in the original autographs yet possessing human characteristics. While fully supporting critical inquiry of Scripture, Warfield adamantly opposed criticism predicated on naturalistic premises. Modern scholarship distorted Christianity's essence by denying biblical supernaturalism.

Princeton's defense of Scripture relied heavily on the principles of Scottish Common-Sense philosophy that empirical induction is the primary source of truth and that all reasonable people intuit moral absolutes. Princeton's apologists proposed to refute secularism by establishing God's existence, the Scripture's veracity and authenticity and the necessity of biblical religion. Critics have pointed out Princeton's failure to recognize the areligious nature of scientism and the conflict between Scottish philosophy's principles and John *Calvin's teaching that the noetic effect of sin precludes any natural theology. Usually, however, Princeton theologians evaluated philosophy through the lens of biblical revelation.

In practical matters the Princeton theologians taught Christian nurture as the basis for *piety, prayer and the *sacraments as means of grace, and Christian vocation as the means by which believers contribute to God's kingdom. Critical of the emotional excesses of American *revivals and the subjectivism of liberalism, Princetonians nevertheless pronounced regeneration and conversion as indispensable prerequisites of genuine piety.

The Princeton tradition altered when the *Presbyterian Church in the U.S.A. (PCUSA) instituted a more inclusive theological perspective by reorganizing the seminary board. Machen and several other conservatives resigned and founded Westminster

Theological Seminary in Philadelphia (1929), where the Princeton theology was continued with some modifications. Princeton Theological Seminary continued as the leading seminary of the PCUSA.

Bibliography. D. G. Hart, *Defending the Faith: J. Gresham Machen and the Crisis of Conservative Protestantism in Modern America* (1994); W. A. Hoffecker, *Piety and the Princeton Theologians* (1981); M. A. Noll, "The Founding of Princeton Seminary," *WTJ* 42 (fall 1979) 72-110; M. A. Noll, ed., *The Princeton Theology 1812-1921: Scripture, Science, and Theological Method from Archibald Alexander to Benjamin Breckinridge Warfield* (1983); J. C. VanderStelt, *Philosophy and Scripture: A Study in Old Princeton and Westminster Theology* (1978); D. F. Wells, ed., *Reformed Theology in America* (1985). W. A. Hoffecker

Protestant Reformed Churches in America, The. A denomination with roots in Reformed Churches in the Netherlands and the United States. On March 6, 1925, three consistories (bodies of ruling elders), with their pastors, signed an Act of Agreement that established them as an official denomination. The Protestant Reformed Churches (PRC) came out of the *Christian Reformed Church in North America (CRC) when that denomination officially adopted a doctrinal statement concerning the extent of God's grace. The statement asserted that in addition to God's saving grace, which is given to the elect alone, there is a grace of God that is common to and shared by all people. Common grace is especially evident in the general offer of the gospel, which expresses God's desire to save all who hear the gospel; but it is also evident in a general operation of the Holy Spirit in the hearts of all people that restrains sin and enables them to do some good. When three ministers refused to subscribe to these statements, they and their consistories were expelled from their offices.

In the years of their existence the PRC have maintained the doctrines of particular grace, believing that these doctrines constitute the essential teachings of the Protestant Reformation and the tradition of the Reformed faith in the Netherlands and in the United States.

The confessional basis of the denomination includes three creeds: the *Belgic Confession of Faith, the *Heidelberg Catechism and the *Canons of Dort. The liturgy is based upon the regulative principle of *worship and makes use of traditional forms, most of which were used throughout the history of the Reformed churches. Church government is presbyterian and emphasizes the rule of elders, the autonomy of local congregations and the necessity of federative unity among like-minded congregations.

From its beginning the denomination has maintained a theological school that is under the supervision of the synod, the broadest assembly of the churches. The school, staffed by three professors, has provided ministers for the denomination and has trained students from other denominations for the gospel ministry.

Under the supervision of the synod, a flourishing *mission program is carried on both in North America and abroad. The synod also supervises denominational contact with churches in Singapore, New Zealand, Australia and Great Britain.

The members of the denomination are active in *education and maintain a total of eleven elementary and junior high schools and one high school. These schools are parentally controlled and operated and have a total enrollment of about 1,475 students. Publishing and evangelistic work is performed by the congregations, which print brochures, pamphlets and/or books. A publishing organization called the Reformed Free Publishing Association publishes books and the denominational magazine, *The Standard Bearer.* One magazine, *Beacon Lights,* is produced by the young people.

A major split occurred in the denomination in the early 1950s, when more than half of the denomination left to establish a new church federation. The issue concerned whether faith and repentance are conditions on the basis of which God saves or whether the grace of God in salvation is applied, without any conditions, to those whom he elected from eternity according to his sovereign good pleasure. Those who left the PRC held to the former position and, after several years of separate existence, returned to the CRC.

See also Hoeksema, Herman.

Bibliography. H. Hoeksema, *The Protestant Reformed Churches in America: Their Origin, Early History and Doctrine* (1936). H. Hanko

Puritanism. Puritanism began in a time of religious upheaval in England. In 1534 King Henry VIII had broken with the Roman Catholic Church, primarily for nontheological reasons. The result of this break was a new church of which he, the English king, was the head. Because his quarrel with the Roman church had involved more personal than religious concerns, Henry did not seek to change significantly the theology or the ecclesiastical practices of the new English church.

Since the decade following Martin Luther's formal challenge to Rome in 1517, however, there had been Englishmen who had desired major theological reform of the church in England. As early as 1526, meetings were being held at the White Horse Inn in Cambridge to consider ways in which Christ's church in England could be made more scriptural in both its organization and teachings. Those who had participated in or who had approved those early Cambridge meetings saw in King Henry's action the beginnings of a great opportunity. But Henry's determination to leave most of the church as it had been for centuries brought frustration.

The frustration eased a bit during the reign of Edward, Henry's only surviving son. When Puritans produced in 1549 the First Book of Common Prayer, written largely by Thomas Cranmer, they made significant changes in the worship of the English church. But because he knew that for political reasons, liturgical reform had to be gradual, Cranmer had left significant elements of the old Roman Catholic liturgy in place. The response was predictable, and it mirrored attitudes that had developed during the two previous decades. Riots broke out in Cornwall to protest the making of any changes in the old liturgy, and sermons were preached primarily in London and East Anglia in which the failure to accomplish full biblical reform was lamented.

In reaction, John Hooper in 1550 called specifically for thoroughgoing, scriptural purification of the worship of the church. Thus was born one of the central aspects of the movement that became known as Puritanism—a biblical impatience with anything less than full reform of the church. Coupled with this impatience was the concomitant conviction that the Bible be the only source for reforming the faith and practices of the church.

Theologically, those who came to be regarded as Puritans were Calvinist. Their belief in the absolute sovereignty of God led them to the convictions described immediately above. No area of life was independent of the authority of Jehovah God, and therefore full obedience to God's revelation in every aspect of life, especially in the life of the church, was to be expected.

Linked closely to their *Calvinism was deep personal *piety. Again, because they knew that God's Word and God's moral expectations reach everywhere, the Puritans took their faith with utmost seriousness. They were not joyless or dull, as has been often asserted, but they did know that God requires and deserves obedience and *worship at all times and in all ways. They therefore scrutinized their own lives with the same diligence that they applied to the church.

But it was in the larger ecclesiastical and national matters that the specific identifying marks of Puritanism should be located. Other Christians shared the Puritans' theology and piety; their unique genius was their vision for total reform according to the inerrant, infallible Word of God.

The Puritan impulse within the Church of England was given significant boost by three crucial events that occurred in the thirteen years that followed Hooper's sermon. The first was the reign of Queen Mary from 1553 to 1558. A devout Roman Catholic and King Henry's oldest surviving child, Mary sought to return England to its pre-Henry ecclesiastical settlement. Some three hundred men, many of them Puritan in their leanings, died as martyrs to Mary's zeal. Many hundreds more escaped England to live on the Continent. Mary's successor and sister, Elizabeth I, wanted the Church of England to be a support to her reign, no more and no less. She opposed any reform that either threatened her supreme authority or seemed extreme. Elizabeth became the second crucial event to boost the Puritan impulse.

John Foxe, who had been born in Boston, England, in the year of Luther's break with Rome and who had spent the years of Mary's reign in Strasborg and Frankfurt, was the source of the third of these events. In 1563 Foxe published his *Book of Martyrs*, a book that powerfully described the lives of those who had died under Marian persecution and called Englishmen to live up to the sacrifice of these saints by seizing the opportunity to reform the English church thoroughly.

In this context the language of covenant theology increasingly defined Puritanism. Working from Foxe's insight, Puritans believed that every nation existed in implicit covenant with the Lord God. God set the terms of obedience, and every nation was expected to structure its affairs accordingly. While recognizing and affirming that personal eternal life is strictly the gift of God through faith, the distinctive conviction of Puritanism was that such national covenants were real and binding.

In spite of the efforts of the Puritans, Elizabeth remained recalcitrant. Neither the church nor the nation seemed to be moving toward the kind of full reformation Puritanism urged. This situation produced frustration, and a new, even more radical party arose. Known as Separatists, this group's origins may be traced to the publication in 1580 of Robert Browne's *Reformation Without Tarrying for Anie*. Abandoning the determination to bring church and state into full reformation, the Separatists left, sometimes literally, in order to bring individual, private reform immediately. Puritanism proper, however, maintained its conviction that all of church and all of society owed full obedience to the Lord of both.

A new Puritan strategy emerged with English colonization of the new world. In the spirit of many other Englishmen of the day, they would take their vision and would plant it in the new world, building there a holy commonwealth that conformed fully to the expectations of the Lord God. Known popularly as the Pilgrims and led by William Bradford, this group had ended up at Plymouth, there to live out their highly individualistic form of Christianity. Other Puritans, led by John Winthrop, went to the new world as Englishmen and as continuing members of the Church of England. The intention of this venture was to bring England to repentance so that the country would finally accept its responsibility to live in obedience to the Word of God in all aspects of church and society. Winthrop and those with him built a society in which the franchise was linked to church membership and church membership to visible sainthood.

When did Puritanism end? It ended as a distinct theological movement when the comprehensive Calvinistic determination to bring all of society into obedience to the Lord was abandoned. In England this might be traced to the Restoration in 1660, when the final dreams of the Commonwealth period evaporated with the return of the Stuarts, in the person of Charles II, to the throne of England. From this point, what had been Puritanism dissolved into the individualistic, privatized religion of Nonconformity. In New England, 1684 marked a significant end for Puritanism when the royal charter, which had allowed Winthrop and his associates to structure their colony as they saw fit, was revoked. Intense negotiations between the colonists and the English Crown finally produced in 1692 a new charter, but one that denied the colonists the right to use spiritual criteria in determining political rights.

After 1692 there were many American Calvinists, even many whose Calvinistic theology was married to an intense personal piety. But the vision of an entire society, church and state, living in purified, reformed, covenantal obedience to the Lord God had been abandoned, replaced, as in England, by an individualized, privatized form of the Christian faith. Puritanism as a distinct movement was gone. The spirit of separatism had prevailed and continues to dominate both English and American evangelicalism.

Bibliography. F. Bremer, *The Puritan Experiment* (1976); W. Haller, *The Rise of Puritanism* (1938); P. Miller, *The New England Mind: The Seventeenth Century* (1939); E. S. Morgan, *The Puritan Dilemma: The Story of John Winthrop* (1958); H. Stout, *The New England Soul: Preaching and Religious Culture in Colonial New England* (1986).

S. T. Logan

Q,R

Rauch, Frederick Augustus (1806-1841).† *German Reformed educator. Born the son of a Reformed pastor in Kirchbracht, Germany, Rauch was educated in the gymnasia of Hanau and Buedingen before entering the University of Giessen in 1824. In 1827 he was awarded the doctor of philosophy degree by the University of Marburg for a dissertation in classics on "The Electra of Sophocles." Later that year he began the study of philosophy at Heidelburg under the right-wing Hegelian Karl Daub, who left a permanent stamp upon Rauch. Reentering Giessen as a student in 1828, Rauch became a university lecturer in 1829. However, he became embroiled in a futile lawsuit against a senior faculty member that alienated his colleagues and threatened his academic career in Germany, precipitating his immigration to America in 1831.

Within two years Rauch had established himself as the one of the leading figures in the German Reformed Church. Arriving in Pennsylvania late in 1831, Rauch learned English and taught music in Easton before serving briefly as professor of German at Lafayette College. In need of a neutral party with solid academic credentials to resolve a troublesome division, the infant German Reformed Classical Preparatory School at York appointed Rauch as its first principal in 1832. Within months he was ordained to the ministry of the German Reformed Church as professor of biblical literature at the theological seminary. The scarcity of German academics in America made Rauch a highly desirable figure, and the frequent calls from other Pennsylvania colleges quickly stabilized his financial situation, enabling him to marry Phebe Moore in July 1833. The offer of a ten-thousand-dollar gift enticed the Classical School to move to Mercersburg in 1835, and the seminary followed two years later. When the Classical School became Marshall College in 1836, Rauch assumed the presidency, teaching intermittently in the seminary until the coming of John Williamson *Nevin in 1840.

As a teacher, Rauch was the first to introduce and popularize the philosophical idealism of G. W. F. Hegel (1770-1831) in the United States. His *Psychology* (1840) followed Daub's philosophical anthropology closely in its strict allegiance to Hegel's dialectical logic and mental philosophy, and it was used for more than a decade in several American schools and colleges. Upon its first appearance, it was endorsed by many reviewers, notably including the *Princeton Review,* but it also received severe criticism by those who felt that he was a "pantheist of the school of Hegel" and therefore hostile to orthodox Christianity. Rauch's early death left his defense to his students, such as Emmanuel Vogel *Gerhart, who insisted upon his mentor's fidelity to traditional Christian doctrine. In accordance with his Romantic philosophy of history, Rauch viewed Christ as the fullest expression of humanity in its organic development, primarily emphasizing Jesus' function as the example for humankind rather than the supernatural redeemer of humanity. Although Rauch showed little interest in the later *Mercersburg theologians' emphases on ecclesiology, liturgics and the *sacraments, his philosophical idealism and profound historical consciousness provided a substantial theoretical foundation for the work of Nevin and Gerhart.

Bibliography. *ANB* 18; *DAB* VIII; *DARB; NCAB* 11; J. H. Nichols, *Romanticism in American Theology: Nevin and Schaff at Mercersburg* (1961); H. J. B. Ziegler, *Frederick Augustus Rauch, American Hegelian* (1953). W. B. Evans

Rayburn, James C., Jr. (1909-1970).† Founder of Young Life. After studying engineering and mineralogy at Kansas State University and the University of Colorado, James and Maxine Rayburn were appointed home missionaries by the Presbyterian board of missions to New Mexico (1933-1936). Influenced by Lewis Sperry *Chafer, he attended Dallas Theological Seminary (1936-1939). Seminary field work requirements took Rayburn to the Presbyterian church of Gainesville, Florida, where the pastor told him to center his ministry on the campus of the local high school, reaching out to the unchurched teens. Through this challenge he developed "Good News Clubs," later "Miracle Book Clubs," which focused on ministering to them in their own language. By the end of his ministry in Gainesville he had 175 youngsters attending.

Back in Texas, with financial support from Herbert J. Taylor, Rayburn incorporated Young Life Ministries (1941), with Chafer as one of his first board members. As his ministry started to grow, he began *Young Life* magazine (1944), which reached a circulation of thirteen thousand within a decade. Taylor provided Star Ranch near Colorado Springs (1946), which became the national headquarters in 1965. A leadership training seminar called Young Life Institute (1951) and additional camps expanded the outreach of the highly pragmatic ministry to youth. Emphasizing that Christians can have fun too, Rayburn encouraged his staff workers to loosen up with high schoolers in order to win their trust. He retired from Young Life in 1964. Rayburn remained Presbyterian, but Young Life is a parachurch organization.

Bibliography. E. Cailliet, *Young Life* (1963).

D. D. Bundy

Reformed Church in America.‡ The Reformed Church in America (RCA) originated with the formation in 1628 of a *Dutch Reformed congregation in the colony of New Netherland by Jonas *Michaelius. Michaelius was followed in time by other pastors as the Dutch settlers moved west into New Jersey, north to Albany and east into Long Island. Once the English took control of the colony in 1664, Dutch immigration virtually ceased. But a number of Dutch Reformed congregations took root in New York and New Jersey.

With the coming of the English, Americanization was inevitable for the Dutch churches as well as for the French and *German Reformed congregations that joined the denomination in the later seventeenth and early eighteenth centuries. But the process led to conflict. The churches and pastors were divided between the conferentie, who wished to maintain Dutch ways and remain within the Classis of Amsterdam, and the coetus churches, who wished to organize an American body called a classis and educate ministers in America rather than sending them back to the Netherlands for theological education. John H. *Livingston, a promising young minister of the Dutch church in New York, succeeded in bringing the groups together in the Union Convention of 1772.

The *American Revolution eventually led to the autonomy of the Dutch-American church and its organization into a distinct body in 1792. Livingston was again a leader, contributing also to the establishment in 1784 of a theological seminary in Brooklyn. In 1810 Livingston moved to New Brunswick, New Jersey, and continued the program of theological education at Queens College (later Rutgers), which had been chartered by coetus pastors in 1766. In 1856 the seminary at New Brunswick separated from the college.

During the eighteenth and nineteenth centuries the church grew in New Jersey and New York despite ecclesiastical conflicts and a shortage of ministers. Beginning in 1762 in New York, Reformed congregations Americanized by using English in public worship. But the failure of the denomination to plant churches in the West meant that as Dutch Reformed settled in the Midwest they often joined Congregational and Presbyterian churches. Had it not been for the new Dutch migration in the mid-nineteenth century, which added many members and new congregations, the old Dutch Reformed Church might have merged with another denomination by the end of the century. As it was, in 1867 the Dutch Reformed Church dropped the word *Dutch* from its title and began to call itself the Reformed Church in America.

Beginning in 1847 a new surge of Dutch and German Reformed immigrants under the leadership of the Reverend Albertus C. Van Raalte settled in western Michigan. Another group of settlers under the direction of the Reverend Hendrik P. Scholte went to Pella, Iowa. Most of these new settlers had been members of the Afscheiding, or separatist movement, which seceded from the state church of the Netherlands in 1834. Strongly orthodox and pious, the newcomers immediately formed congregations, and some had already formed congregations in the Netherlands and emigrated en masse.

Under Van Raalte's effective leadership, separatists were encouraged to unite with the old Dutch church in the East. This injection of new Dutch congregations made a profound difference on the denomination. In time the Western churches were successful in establishing one seminary and three colleges: Western Theological Seminary and Hope College, in Holland, Michigan; Central College, in Pella, Iowa; and Northwestern College, in Orange City, Iowa.

However, the separatist spirit that many Afscheiding settlers brought to America became evident in 1857, when some members formed the *Christian Reformed Church (CRC). In 1882 a dispute over the issue of allowing Masons to be members of the Reformed Church resulted in a sizeable group leaving the denomination to join the CRC.

A confessional church since its formal organization in 1792, the denomination has adhered to the *Heidelberg Catechism, the *Belgic Confession and the *Canons of the Synod of Dort. Although the denomination holds a Reformed stance, the Americanization of the church also saw liberal, *fundamentalist and evangelical elements take root in the denomination, with evangelicalism making the greatest impact. Perhaps surprisingly, the contemporary positive thinking movement has been most visibly represented by two prominent Reformed ministers, Norman Vincent *Peale and Robert H. *Schuller.

See also DUTCH REFORMED IN AMERICA.

BIBLIOGRAPHY. J. D. Bratt, *Dutch Calvinism in Modern America: A History of a Conseravtive Subculture* (1984); A. R. Brouwer, *Reformed Church Roots: Thirty-five Formative Events* (1977); G. F. De Jong, *The Dutch Reformed Church in the American Colonies* (1978); E. M. Eenigenburg, *A Brief History of the Reformed Church in America* (1958); H. Harmelink III, *Ecumenism and the Reformed Church* (1968). E. J. Bruins

Reformed Church in the U.S., Eureka Classis. A classis, organized in 1911, in the Northwest Synod of the German Reformed Church in the United States, primarily in the Dakotas and northern Iowa. The classis refused to join the 1934 merger with the *Evangelical Synod of North America forming the Evangelical and Reformed Church and continued as a separate denomination. In 1934 the classis reported 1,400 communicant members in 26 congregations organized in nine charges.

German Reformed congregations were formed in the Great Lakes area beginning in the 1850s through the *mission of the Ohio Synod. Plans for theological education and the extension of the church west led to the establishment in 1862 of the Mission House in Sheboygan, Wisconsin, which evolved into an academy, college and seminary. In 1867 the Northwest Synod was organized, eventually including classes in Iowa and the upper Midwest, Canada and California. The Eureka Classis was formed as a nongeographical association of conservative churches, some of which had been influenced by the thought of Dutch theologian Hermann F. Kohlbruegge (1803-1875) through the periodical *Der Waechter.* While German Reformed theology was firmly tied to the doctrine and *piety of the *Heidelberg Catechism (1563), Kohlbruegge emphasized divine sovereignty and salvation through God's work in Christ to such an extreme that sanctification was subsumed into justification and the response of faith virtually eliminated.

Through much of the nineteenth century the *German Reformed Church was engaged in conflict over how to be the church in evangelical America. Churches served by the Mission House opposed what they viewed as the catholicizing theology of the seminary at Mercersburg (Lancaster after 1871), Pennsylvania. By century's end the denomination was effectively united by its universal allegiance to the Heidelberg Catechism. One legacy of the Mercersburg movement, however, rooted in Heidelberg's original irenic intent, was the involvement of the general synod in the ecumenical movement of the early twentieth century. In June 1934, the Reformed Church merged with the Evangelical Synod of North America, a Lutheran-Reformed unionist group that embraced Luther's Small Catechism and the Augsburg Confession alongside the Heidelberg Catechism, with the Constitution adopted in 1938. To Eureka's pastors this move abandoned the Reformed faith and the principle of having but one doctrinal base, Heidelberg.

A month before the 1938 general synod, the Eureka Classis adopted a resolution asserting its "right to continue to function as heretofore, as the legally constituted Reformed Church in the United States." It argued that all parts of the church that joined the new Evangelical and Reformed Church had "seceded" from the church. Eureka rejected general synod's authority to redistrict classes geographically. Indeed, since it was based on "a federation of confessions" the new denomination was "hardly entitled to be called a member of the body of Christ." The classis argued that "the Church should have a definite, unequivocal Confession which pledges its adherents and members to the doctrine of the entire Holy Scriptures, and to the Heidelberg Catechism in unmistakable words." It was on this basis that the classis became a denomination under the old name. A 1939 resolution renounced all Evangelical and Reformed efforts to discipline them. A number of court cases over property, and even over which denomination a congregation would affiliate with, continued until at least 1946.

Opposition to the merger's addition of Lutheran standards clothed a deeper concern of the Eureka Classis. The Evangelical Synod's unionist ecclesiology had always given it doctrinal flexibility, but by the early twentieth century its center at Eden Seminary, known for Reinhold *Niebuhr and H. Richard *Niebuhr, had become decidedly liberal and social gospel-oriented. To those within the enclave of Eureka's German-speaking and strictly conservative Reformed orthodoxy, far from Lancaster and Philadelphia, the merger represented a marriage with modernism. As "the remaining member of the Reformed Church in the U.S." this group understands itself as the guardian of the hyper-Calvinist faith. German was abandoned in worship and church business only in the period from 1940 to 1965. The church has no seminary but draws its pastors from Westminster and other orthodox Reformed seminaries. While not pietistic in terms of behavioral strictures, this is arguably the most doctrinally conservative of America's Reformed churches.

See also GERMAN REFORMED IN AMERICA.

BIBLIOGRAPHY. N. C. Hoeflinger and R. D. Stuebbe, eds., *History of the Eureka Classis, Reformed Church in the U.S.* (1985); *Minutes of the Eureka Classis, 1911-1939,* MS collection, Evangelical and Reformed Historical Society, Lancaster, Pennsylvania. C. E. Hambrick-Stowe

Reformed Ecumenical Synod, Council. An international body for Presbyterian and Reformed communions adhering to Reformed confessions in a strict manner. The RES was organized in 1946 when Dutch *Calvinist denominations in the Netherlands (the Reformed Churches in the Netherlands), South Africa (the Reformed Church in South Africa) and the United States (the *Christian Reformed Church [CRC]) sent delegates to Grand Rapids, Michigan, to affirm the unity of Reformed churches from around the world. The impetus for the body came as early as 1924, when the Reformed Church in South Africa took formal action to begin such a body. The churches belonging to the RES hold to one of the following Reformed confessions: the Second Helvetic Confession; the *Belgic Confession; the *Westminster Confession, the Gallican Confession; the *Heidelberg Catechism; the *Canons of Dort; and the Thirty-Nine Articles.

Since 1946 the RES has met once every three to five years to discuss matters of common interest and work toward joint actions. During the late 1950s and early 1960s the amount of activity and the expense involved in convening an international body resulted in a meager agenda and low levels of involvement. In 1988 at its gathering in Harare, South Africa, the RES changed its name to the Reformed Ecumenical Council. At the 1996 RES meeting in Grand Rapids delegates from twenty-three churches attended from sixteen nations.

The RES has provided an alternative to the more progressive World Alliance of Reformed Churches. Consequently, denominations from the United States that have sought membership in the RES have included Reformed and Presbyterian communions outside mainline Protestantism, such as the CRC, the *Orthodox Presbyterian Church (OPC), the *Reformed Presbyterian Church in North America, General Synod, the *Reformed Presbyterian Church of North America and the Associate Reformed Presbyterian Church. In 1980 RES adopted a report, "The Church and Its Social Relations," that advocated the reform of race relations throughout the world, but especially in South Africa. Some churches believed that the activist agenda of the RES was replacing its confessional identity. Compounding this perception was the RES's toleration of churches that ordained homosexuals and that were members of the World Council of Churches. Of the American denominations belonging to the RES only the CRC has retained its membership.

BIBLIOGRAPHY. *DSCHT* (1993); *RES Handbook* (issued after each meeting); P. G. Schrotenboer, *RES, A Venture in Confessional Ecumenism* (1965).

D. G. Hart

Reformed Presbyterian Church, Evangelical Synod.† A conservative denomination existing from 1965 to 1982, the result of a blending of dissenting American Presbyterians (the *Bible Presbyterian Church, renamed after 1961 the *Evangelical Presbyterian Church [EPC]) and former Scottish Covenanters (the *Reformed Presbyterian Church in North America, General Synod [RPC, GS]). The Bible Presbyterian Church (BPC) was a remnant of the 1936 departure of *fundamentalists from the inclusive theological trend within the *Presbyterian Church in the U.S.A. (PCUSA). Led by J. Oliver *Buswell Jr., and Carl *McIntire, the BPC separated first in 1937 from the Presbyterian Church of America (later the *Orthodox Presbyterian Church [OPC]). Then in 1955 it split over differences in goals, personalities and control of agencies.

The RPC, GS by 1965 had lost many of its covenanting distinctives, such as exclusive psalmody and nonparticipation in government, and it had dwindled in membership to the point that it recognized the need to join a larger body.

Each denomination maintained a genuine *piety, a testimony against unbelief and a commitment to Reformed ecumenism. In order to unite, each had to compromise: the EPC gave up its premillennial amendments to the *Westminster standards and returned to the pre-1903 confessional language. The RPC had already given up the *Reformation Principles Exhibited* in favor of the Westminster standards. In addition, the two sides agreed to neutralize the amillennial language of the Westminster Larger

Catechism, and the EPC toned down their language on the separated life as the united church produced a joint statement on "The Christian Life and Testimony" that eschewed the moral vices of the day, such as gambling, dancing, theater attendance, alcohol and tobacco, and advocated a mild form of separatism.

The union of the two denominations in 1965 merged their names, resulting in the Reformed Presbyterian Church, Evangelical Synod (RPC, ES). Feelings of euphoria surrounding the ceremonies at Covenant College in Lookout Mountain, Tennessee, soon gave way to the challenge of achieving a united Reformed *worship and testimony. The synod's first three acts were to reaffirm Reformed theology and the Westminster standards, call the church to support the *missionary and *educational programs of the new denomination and keep the Christian sabbath.

These three emphases were remarkably characteristic of the denomination during its brief history. The inerrant Bible was central for denominational life, with a subordinate allegiance to the Westminster standards. The RPC, ES stressed national and international missionary efforts, building on the world and national Presbyterian missions boards that the EPC had established. Emphasis was laid on local church autonomy and individual conscience. Higher educational institutions, such as Covenant College and Seminary, were promoted. Widely known men, such as J. Oliver *Buswell Jr., Gordon H. *Clark and Francis *Schaeffer, aided the testimony. After seventeen years, the RPC, ES merged with the *Presbyterian Church in America (PCA) in 1982.

BIBLIOGRAPHY. P. R. Gilchrist, *Documents of Synod* (1982); G. P. Hutchinson, *The History Behind the Reformed Presbyterian Church, Evangelical Synod* (1974). J. H. Hall

Reformed Presbyterian Church in North America, General Synod.† A Reformed denomination with roots in Scottish Presbyterian Covenanters and later absorbed into the *Reformed Presbyterian Church, Evangelical Synod (RPC, ES). Deriving mainly from dissenting Scottish Covenanters coming to America in the 1700s, the Reformed Presbytery, established in 1774, was characterized by exclusive psalm singing and nonparticipation in any civil government that refused to acknowledge the "crown rights" of Christ. After the majority of the RPs joined the Associate Reformed Presbyterian Church in 1782, the remaining Covenanters united in the Reformed Presbytery of the United States of North America in 1798.

The nineteenth century began with growth and optimism, with the 1809 formation of the synod, which adopted the 1806 *Reformed Presbyterian Testimony* as secondary standards alongside the *Westminster Confession and Catechisms. But, especially in light of the difference between the American and British political systems, some leaders began viewing nonparticipation in government (e.g., voting and jury duty) as a hindrance to evangelism. A division ensued in 1833, in which part of the denomination embraced the government-participation view and were called New Lights. This group adopted the name *Reformed Presbyterian Church in North America, General Synod (RPC, GS). More open to participation in American civil and religious life, the RPC, GS entered into fraternal relations with other Presbyterian churches in 1845 and encouraged close co-operation with orthodox *Calvinists, though they remained wary of any organic union that would compromise exclusive psalmody and closed communion.

Convinced that the United States was the best civil government since the time of Christ, the New Lights worked tirelessly to reform the evils still entrenched in the system. One of the earliest denominations to embrace *abolitionism, before and during the Civil War, the RPs engaged in vigorous antislavery polemics and were active in the freedmen's effort after the war. They were ardent Unionists but frequently criticized the government for failing to enforce the sabbath and for not properly promoting Christian morality, especially by permitting the liquor traffic. By the late 1880s the church had thrown its weight behind Prohibition and remained a vocal presence behind many *social reforms. Maintaining the Covenanter conviction that the Constitution should affirm and submit to the lordship of Christ, the RPC, GS promoted a constitutional amendment that would acknowledge the sovereignty of God over the state.

The church prospered until the 1860s, in the wake of the Civil War, during a time when church union was the rage throughout the churches. A group of ministers and laity who desired organic union with the *Presbyterian Church in the U.S.A. (PCUSA) or the *United Presbyterian Church of North America (UPCNA) openly questioned exclusive psalmody and closed communion, two issues they felt obstructed Christian unity. In 1867 elder George Stuart was charged with using "unauthorized psalmody" for using hymns in his sabbath school. A year later the general synod suspended him, resulting in the departure of several ministers and congregations. In 1870, after rejecting a union proposal with the UPCNA, the church was crippled by the Western Secession, in which seven congregations merged with the United Presbyterians out of frustration with the general synod. Loss of membership continued throughout the remainder of the nineteenth century. In 1873, after this decline, the church still had sixty-five congregations, but by 1902 only thirty-six remained. To try to stem the tide, the church sought to increase ministerial candidates for seminary by founding Cedarville College in 1894.

The twentieth century was marked by further progress in mission efforts but overall decline in the churches. Proposed plans of union in 1905 and 1906 with the PCUSA and UPCNA, respectively, were unanimously postponed due to the fear of *modernism in the larger churches. A growing disinterest among youth, laxity in sabbath keeping and church discipline, a relinquishing of closed communion and a neglect of tithing contributed to decline. After repeated abortive union efforts, in 1959 the church dropped one of its subordinate standards, *Reformation Principles Exhibited,* demonstrating that it had abandoned its Covenanter legacy. In the late 1950s several leading Presbyterian conservatives joined the RPC, GS, such as the Reformed philosopher Gordon H. *Clark, who, after departing from the PCUSA in 1936 with the *Orthodox Presbyterian Church (OPC), engaged in a losing battle with Cornelius *Van Til and the faculty of Westminster Theological Seminary. He proved to be a prominent figure in the 1965 union of the RPC, GS with the *Evangelical Presbyterian Church, becoming the *Reformed Presbyterian Church, Evangelical Synod.

BIBLIOGRAPHY. R. W. Chesnut, *A Historical Sketch of the Reformed Presbyterian Church, Evangelical Synod* (1945); G. P. Hutchinson, *The History Behind the Reformed Presbyterian Church, Evangelical Synod* (1974); *Reformation Principles Exhibited* (1807).

J. H. Hall

Reformed Presbyterian Church of North America, Covenanter Synod. A Reformed denomination with roots in Scottish Presbyterianism. The denomination originally grew out of dissent to the Revolution Settlement of 1689-1692 in the Church of Scotland, an arrangement that omitted the state church's adherence to the National Covenant of 1638 and the Solemn League and Covenant of 1643. For the next half century, these dissenters met in societies, something they had already been doing during the times of persecution under Charles II and James II. The groups were finally organized as a denomination on August 1, 1743, when the Reverend Thomas Nairn joined the Reverend John Macmillan to form the Reformed Presbytery in Braehead, Scotland.

Beginning with the Restoration in 1662 there was substantial migration to Ireland and then to the United States, and during the eighteenth century groups of Covenanters in America conducted themselves as societies in the pre-1643 fashion of Scotland because they were largely without an ordained ministry. The first organized congregation of the denomination was that of Middle Octorara, Lancaster County, Pennsylvania, organized by Alexander Craighead in 1742-1743. The Reformed Presbytery was constituted in 1774 but was dissolved in 1782 when its members united with the Associate Presbytery to form the Associate Reformed Synod. The Reformed Presbytery of the United States of North America was formed in 1798, and the Synod of the Reformed Presbyterian Church was constituted in 1809. The denomination distinguished itself from other Presbyterian denominations by not allowing its members to participate in civil government: members could neither vote nor hold office because Jesus Christ and his sovereignty was not recognized by the United States federal government.

In 1833 a major division occurred over the matter of the Christian's relationship to the civil authority, and the *Reformed Presbyterian Church, General Synod (RPC, GS) was formed. The Reformed Presbyterian Church of North America (RPCNA) continued to adhere to the traditional view of dissent to the civil government of the United States; they became known as the Old Lights. The RPC, GS took a more moderate view and declared that participation in the political system of the United States was not sinful even though the United States government did not explicitly recognize Jesus Christ as sovereign; they therefore became known as the New Lights. A further disruption in the RPCNA came in 1892, when a number of congregations split and a significant number of clergy went into other denominations, particularly the *United Presbyterian Church.

The RPCNA adheres to the *Westminster standards and maintains a written Testimony. The Testimony explains its distinctive beliefs in contrast to other Presbyterian and Reformed denominations and attempts to speak to questions that the original Westminster Confession of Faith did not address. The Testimony was most recently revised in 1980 and is placed in a parallel column to the original text of the Confession of Faith. The revisions of the Testimony over the years have led the denomination to place less emphasis on questions of church and state and more emphasis on adhering to classical Presbyterian beliefs and practices. Thus the RPCNA is committed to the regulative principle of *worship and therefore sings the psalms exclusively without instrumental accompaniment, using a psalter last revised in 1973. It holds to the inerrancy of Scripture in the original autographs and takes a prolife stance.

In 1800, under the leadership of one of its leading clergy, Alexander McLeod, the church took a position against slavery and would not allow its members to hold slaves; furthermore, many of its clergy and members were active in the *abolitionist movement. Consequently, during the westward expansion the denomination's center of gravity was always north of the Mason-Dixon Line, and various congregations participated in the Underground Railroad. It has continuously prohibited its members from participating in secret societies and has consistently stood for an amendment to the United States Constitution that would confess Jesus Christ as King and Lord over the United States of America and acknowledge his law and authority rather than popular sovereignty as the foundation for civil affairs. During and after the Civil War it was instrumental in the formation of the National Reform Association. In 1871 and 1954 it signed covenants that applied Reformed Presbyterian principles to the contemporary situation.

RPCNA congregations are generally located on an axis from Washington, D.C., and Ottawa, Ontario, to San Diego, California, but some are located also in Florida, Alabama, Arizona, Texas and Washington. The RPCNA sponsors Geneva College in Beaver Falls, Pennsylvania, the Reformed Presbyterian Theological Seminary in Pittsburgh, Pennsylvania, Ottawa Theological Hall in Ottawa, Ontario, a denominational magazine called the *Covenanter Witness,* a retirement/nursing home in Pittsburgh, Pennsylvania, and home *missions throughout North America. The denomination has conducted missions in Syria, Turkey and China and currently sponsors work in Kobe, Japan, and Larnaca, Cyprus.

BIBLIOGRAPHY. D. M. Carson, "A History of the Reformed Presbyterian Church in America to 1871" (Ph.D. diss., University of Pennsylvania, 1964); R. M. Copeland, *Spare No Exertions* (1986); W. M. Glasgow, *History of the Reformed Presbyterian Church in America* (1888); G. P. Hutchinson, *The History Behind the Reformed Presbyterian Church, Evangelical Synod* (1974). D. A. Weir

Reformed Tradition in America. The Reformed tradition has played a prominent role within American Christianity and has significantly affected both religious and cultural development in the United States. Its general principles such as the Protestant work ethic and the sovereignty of God have helped to shape the American character and ethos; its specific tenets such as total depravity, limited atonement and perseverance of the saints have powerfully influenced American theological understanding. Denominations and Christian leaders committed to Reformed theology have steadily proclaimed the gospel, labored diligently to develop congregations of dedicated Christians and worked fervently to improve social conditions in America.

The roots of the Reformed tradition lie in John *Calvin's (1509-1564) sixteenth-century Genevan Reformation and secondarily in the work of Theodore Beza (1519-1605), Calvin's successor in Geneva, and Heinrich Bullinger (1504-1575) of Zurich. Calvin's *Institutes of the Christian Religion* (first edition, 1536) expounded the central features of Reformed theology and helped shape its subsequent development. During the sixteenth and seventeenth centuries *Calvinism spread rapidly among the Swiss, French, Dutch and Germans on the European continent. In the 1550s John Knox (1505-1572) carried Reformed Christianity to Scotland, and in the 1590s Calvinism helped inspire the rise of *Puritanism in England. This broad movement of religious renovation sought to purify the institutional church by reviving New Testament forms of *worship and *polity, teaching Reformed doctrines and encouraging vital spirituality among clergy and laity. Reformed theological development has been guided by the *Heidelberg Catechism (1563), the Five Points of Calvinism, devised by the *Synod of Dort (1619) and especially the *Westminster standards, which English Puritans framed in the 1640s.

The Reformed Tradition in the New World. Most immigrants to the colonies during the first 150 years following the Puritan settlements at Plymouth and Massachusetts Bay in the 1620s were Reformed Christians from various denominational backgrounds. During these years hundreds of thousands of Dutch, German, Hungarian and Swiss Reformed as well as French *Huguenots streamed to the colonies. Different views of church organization divided English Puritans into Congregationalists and Presbyterians. These groups, along with Scottish and *Scots-Irish Presbyterians, came to America in increasing numbers in the years between 1650 and the American *Revolution.

The *New England Puritans sought to follow Christ's teachings in their individual lives, founding their congregations on scriptural principles and creating a thoroughly biblical commonwealth for the glory of God. In the Cambridge Platform of 1640 they adopted the Westminster standards as their theological basis. The Half-Way Covenant (1662) was a New England innovation devised to solve a crisis in their religious community. It permitted baptized individuals who had not yet demonstrated clear signs of saving faith (required for church membership) but had exhibited good behavior to have their children baptized. Neither they nor their children, however, were allowed to receive communion unless they displayed the marks of conversion.

The Sunday sermon was the center of intellectual life in Puritan New England. Preached in the plain style, Puritan sermons emphasized theological doctrines, used metaphors from agricultural and artisan life and attempted to apply biblical truth to everyday life. Many Puritan parents taught their children about the Reformed faith by using the Westminster standards. Contrary to common stereotypes, the Puritans were not glum, cold, stern and repressive. Their marriages were generally caring, compassionate and based on companionship. Many Puritans cultivated a deep and rich experiential *piety. Not without problems, they persecuted dissenters, poorly treated Indians, conducted witch trials and incorrectly identified themselves with Old Testament Israel. Nonetheless, in many ways their individual conduct and social practices were consistent with biblical teachings.

The Reformed Tradition and the Great Awakening. Reformed Christians contributed significantly to the Great Awakening of the 1730s and 1740s that helped to stamp evangelical Christian convictions and mores upon the colonies. Spreading from Georgia to Massachusetts, this *revival flowered especially among three Reformed communities: the *Dutch Reformed, Congregationalists and Presbyterians. In New Jersey the ministry of Theodore *Frelinghuysen brought spiritual renewal to many Dutch Reformed. Revival erupted at Northampton, Massachusetts, through the preaching of Congregationalist pastor Jonathan *Edwards and spread from there throughout New England.

Perhaps America's greatest theologian, Edwards chronicled the activities of the Awakening and defended it as thoroughly biblical. Convinced that human beings did not have the ability to choose Christ as their Savior, he stressed that the Holy Spirit produced conversions and that justification was by faith alone. His books describing the revival at Northampton, explaining the "distinguishing marks" of a revival and examining religious experience set forth a Reformed understanding of these issues. Also important in promoting revival were William *Tennent Sr. and his sons, John, *William Jr., and *Gilbert, who along with Jonathan *Dickinson fanned revival fires in Pennsylvania, New Jersey and New York. In the South, the dynamic preaching of Presbyterian pastors like Samuel *Davies of Virginia led to many conversions. The most spectacular aspect of the Awakening was the 1740 preaching tour of the Grand Itinerant, George Whitefield. Although an ordained minister in the Church of England and friend of the Wesleys, Whitefield was a committed Calvinist in theology. Thousands of those who came to hear his sermons in New England, New York, Philadelphia, Charleston and Savannah professed faith in Christ.

In the early eighteenth century Puritan theology had begun to depreciate God's sovereignty and accentuate more strongly human capabilities. Leaders such as Cotton Mather had sought to revive New England Puritanism through emphasizing broad evangelical piety. The Great Awakening, however, especially the work of Edwards and Whitefield, prompted a resurgence of commitment to and interest in Reformed theology. Edwards's many persuasive and powerful books restated Calvinist conceptions of salvation, while Whitefield's sermons stressed the role of God's irresistible grace in producing conversion.

At the same time the Awakening caused controversy among Reformed Christians. Conflict between Old Lights who opposed revival because of its socially disruptive effects, New Lights who supported revival and renewed evangelical zeal and Old Calvinists who were caught in the middle destroyed the Puritan synthesis of theology and spirituality. Dispute over revivalism produced temporary schisms among both Presbyterians and the Dutch Reformed in the mid-eighteenth century.

Reformed Denominations in the Eighteenth Century. Most Reformed denominations grew rapidly during the eighteenth century. Extensive immigration of Scots-Irish increased the number and vitality of Presbyterians who settled primarily in the Middle Colonies. In the *Adopting Act of 1729 Presbyterians declared the Westminster standards to be the theological basis of their denomination. By 1788, when Presbyterians established the general assembly, their communion consisted of at least 220 congregations organized in sixteen presbyteries, served by about 180 ministers.

From its founding in America in 1706 the Presbyterian church embraced two traditions: the Scots-Irish and Scottish desired precise theological formulations and orderly church government, while the English and Welsh emphasized religious experience and adaptability. Twice the dialectical tension between these two elements produced schisms in the denomination—in the *Old Side/*New Side division (1741-1758) and the *Old School/*New School division (1837-1869). Yet most of the time the communion was able to hold together those committed to pietist revivalism and those devoted to doctrinalist confessionalism.

Leaders of the *German Reformed Church met in 1747 in Philadelphia and adopted the Heidelberg Catechism as the doctrinal standard of their denomination. By 1791 the church had about 178 congregations scattered between New York City and Virginia. Throughout the eighteenth century most Baptists were committed to Reformed theology, especially because of the influence of the Philadelphia Baptist Confession of Faith (1742), a modified version of the *Westminster Confession adopted by the Philadelphia Baptist Association. During the 1700s Congregationalists, the *Reformed Church in America and two bodies with roots in Scotland—Reformed Presbyterians and Associate Reformed Presbyterians—also increased in size and influence.

The Reformed Tradition and the American Revolution. The teachings of the Reformed tradition helped to inspire the *American Revolution, and many proponents of Reformed theology supported the patriot cause. While Revolutionary leaders generally did not appeal directly to the Scriptures or to their religious heritage to justify their revolt against England, Reformed convictions about covenants, history, human nature and the connection between freedom and virtue helped to reinforce Whig arguments. Moreover, Presbyterian and Congregationalist clergy, especially Ezra Stiles, led efforts to keep an Anglican bishop out of the colonies. Numerous Reformed clergymen urged the colonists to sever their ties with England, described as the great Babylonian whore of the book of Revelation, so they could proclaim the light and liberty of the gospel to the world more effectively.

In the years following the Revolutionary War the complexion and character of American Christianity changed markedly. While Reformed tenets about human nature helped to shape important features of the new nation's constitution, such as the separation and balance of powers, America became much more pluralistic denominationally and theologically. During the early national period Baptists and Methodists grew much more rapidly than did Anglicans, Presbyterians and Congregationalists, who had dominated American religion during the colonial days. Revolt against Calvinism was widespread in the republican environment of the first half of the nineteenth century. Reformed commitments to the doctrines of total depravity, unconditional election, limited atonement, irresistible grace and perseverance of the saints has seemed to many Americans to deny human freedom and responsibility and contradict America's democratic principles. In 1776 about 85 percent of the colonists were affiliated with Reformed denominations; by 1850, 70 percent of Protestant church members were Baptists or Methodists.

The Reformed Tradition and the Second Awakening. Despite the changing religious environments, Reformed leaders such as President Timothy Dwight of Yale, Congregational evangelist Asahel Nettleton and Lyman *Beecher, the primary architect of the benevolent empire, helped inspire and direct the Second Great Awakening of the 1820s and 1830s. But the predominant theology of this Awakening as it was proclaimed by revivalist Charles Grandison *Finney, who was first a Presbyterian and later a Congregationalist, was more *Arminian than Calvinist in nature. Stressing the individual's right and ability to choose salvation, Finney promoted his new measures—techniques to be properly applied to sinners rather than awaiting what Calvinists regarded as God's sovereign and surprising work in conversion. Employing the tactics of a trial lawyer, Finney sought to convince sinners of their need of salvation. To foster conversions he introduced an anxious bench at the front of the sanctuary, community-wide revival campaigns that lasted several weeks and the use of teams to visit people in their homes. From 1801 to 1837 Congregationalists and Presbyterians operating under a *Plan of Union joined their forces in Western expansion. These two Reformed denominations supplied most of the leaders of the numerous societies the Awakening inspired to *abolish slavery and promote temperance, peace, *missions, *education, penal reform and many other good causes (see Social Reform, Presbyterians and).

During the mid-nineteenth century controversy erupted once again, especially among Presbyterians and Congregationalists, over the proper understanding of Reformed theology. Arguing that Calvinism was paralyzing evangelism, Nathaniel W. Taylor, professor of theology at Yale Divinity School, softened the traditional emphasis on total depravity and stressed humanity's free moral agency. Many Congregationalists and some Presbyterians accepted his New Haven theology. Building on Taylor, Finney argued that individuals had the power to choose salvation, avoid all evil acts and achieve entire sanctification. Old School Presbyterian theologian Charles *Hodge and German Reformed church historian Philip *Schaff spoke for the opponents of New Haven theology. Taylor's claim that people became sinful only by their own sinful acts, Hodge contended, contradicted the biblical teaching that all persons were born with original sin. Schaff, as a representative of the *Mercersburg theology, criticized Taylorism for focusing too little on the objective work of Christ in redemption and too much on people's own subjective experience. In 1837 the theological dispute over New Haven theology contributed to the dissolution of the Congregationalist-Presbyterian Plan of Union and to the division of the *Presbyterian Church in the U.S.A. (PCUSA), the largest American Presbyterian body, into two groups—the Old School and the New School.

From the Civil War to World War I evangelical Protestant institutions flourished in America despite intensifying secularization and the increasing religious diversity caused by the arrival of many Catholic and Jewish immigrants. During these years evangelical Protestants continued to use interdenominational voluntary organizations to promote missions and evangelism, distribute Bibles and tracts, wage moral crusades and improve social conditions. Reformed Christians still played a major, but no longer the leading, role in such enterprises. By 1930 commitment to Reformed orthodoxy and the influence of its theological tenets had reached an ebb in America.

The Rise of Four Reformed Schools, 1850-1930. While adherence to the Reformed faith declined between 1850 and 1930, four Reformed schools or emphases took shape during these years that are still influential within American Christianity. First, and probably most important, was the *Princeton theology of Archibald *Alexander, Charles Hodge, Archibald Alexander *Hodge and Benjamin Breckinridge *Warfield. Their teaching at Princeton Theological Seminary, their many books and pamphlets on diverse topics, their periodical articles and their ministry within the PCUSA significantly influenced the views of the Reformed community and, to a lesser degree, evangelical Protestantism in America. Issues such as biblical inspiration, the nature of religious experience and the work of the Holy Spirit were substantially shaped by Princeton theology.

Dutch Calvinists in the *Reformed Church of America (RCA) and the *Christian Reformed Church (CRC) comprise a second Reformed school. In general, Dutch Calvinists in America have emphasized strict adherence to the Reformed confessions and the lordship of Christ over all life. In addition, they have sought to establish Christian institutions that can serve as positive biblical models of love and righteousness in society. While the Eastern branch of the RCA has been less distinctly Reformed and more involved in broad American Protestant crusades, the CRC and the Western branch of the RCA have been more confessionally conscious. During the last one hundred years Dutch Calvinists in America have debated the nature of Christian *piety, the proper Christian approach to the world and the teachings of the neo-Calvinist revival in the Netherlands led by Abraham *Kuyper and Herman *Dooyeweerd.

A third discernable Reformed school is the Southern tradition. The Reformed faith was planted in the South during the colonial period by both Presbyterians and Baptists. In the early nineteenth century two groups—the *Cumberland Presbyterians and the Restoration movement—broke away from the Southern Presbyterians. Remaining essentially Old School in character during the nineteenth century, Southern Presbyterians guided by theologians James Henley *Thornwell and Robert Lewis *Dabney subscribed strictly to the Westminster standards. In 1861 Southern members left the Old School of the PCUSA, forming the *Presbyterian Church in the United States (PCUS). Prior to World War II members of this denomination remained strongly committed to orthodox *Calvinism, but in the postwar era a drift toward liberalism was detected by many conservatives within the denomination. Finally, in 1973 about one hundred thousand Southern Presbyterians left their denomination to form the *Presbyterian Church in America (PCA).

The fourth and final Reformed emphasis is the Westminster school. Arising in the midst of the *fundamentalist-modernist controversy of the 1920s and proposing to continue the Old School Presbyterian tradition of Princeton Theological Seminary, this school became centered at Westminster Theological Seminary in Philadelphia. In 1936 its chief proponent, J. Gresham *Machen, organized the *Orthodox Presbyterian Church (OPC), claiming the PCUSA had departed from historic Calvinism.

Reformed themes such as God's sovereignty, human sinfulness, salvation by grace, the significance of Scripture and the centrality of Christ are evident in the *neo-orthodoxy espoused by Reinhold *Niebuhr, H. Richard *Niebuhr and other theologians, pastors and denominational leaders of the post-World War II era. Neo-orthodoxy's use of Reformed theology, however, was highly selective.

The Continuing Legacy. There are today eighteen Presbyterian, Reformed and Congregationalist denominations in America, with a combined membership of about six million. Substantial numbers of Episcopalians, Baptists and members of independent churches also espouse Reformed theological convictions. In addition, the influence of the Reformed tradition is strong within the evangelical community because of the role Reformed and Reformed-oriented seminaries (most notably Calvin, Westminster, Biblical, Covenant, Reformed, Gordon-Conwell, Trinity and Fuller) have played in training evangelical leaders, as well as the influence of Reformed presses, periodicals and publications. While most contemporary American evangelicals reject Calvinist understandings of grace and salvation, many of them agree with the Reformed tradition's emphasis on experiential piety, its defense of biblical authority and inspiration and its commitment to transform culture.

From the founding of Plymouth to the present day, the Reformed tradition has strongly influenced American attitudes toward human nature, humanity's relationship with God, the authority of the Bible and engagement with culture, especially work. By championing the sovereignty and holiness of God, stressing the divine initiative in salvation, denouncing human pride and autonomy and exalting God's absolute standards for nations and individuals, Calvinists have done much to promote biblical Christianity in the United States.

Bibliography. F. Hood, *Reformed America: The Middle and Southern States, 1783-1837* (1980); B. Kuklick, *Churchman and Philosophers: From Jonathan Edwards to John Dewey* (1985); L. A. Loetscher, *The Broadening Church: A Study of Theological Issues in American Presbyterianism Since 1869* (1957); G. M. Marsden, *The Evangelical Mind and the New School Presbyterian Experience* (1970); P. Miller, *Errand into the Wilderness* (1956); L. Ryken, *Worldly Saints: The Puritans As They Really Were* (1986); G. S. Smith, *The Seeds of Secularization: Calvinism, Culture and Pluralism in America, 1870-1915* (1985); E. T. Thompson, *Presbyterians in the South*, 3 vols. (1963); D. F. Wells, ed., *The Reformed Tradition in America* (1985).

G. S. Smith

Revivals, Presbyterians and. On the surface revivalism and Presbyterianism would not appear to be a likely combination. Especially in the twentieth century as it has been associated with emotional *piety, non-Calvinistic theology and parachurch organizations, revivalism seems out of step with the staid spirituality, Augustinian soteriology and procedural church government that typifies Presbyterianism. Yet, since the revivals of the First Great Awakening in the eighteenth century, Presbyterians in America have been associated intimately with revivalism, and these associations have also generated a fair number of controversies in Presbyterian communions.

Beginnings of Revivalism. If by revivalism one means a concerted effort to win the unconverted to Christ and awaken believers from spiritual slumbers, then Presbyterians and Reformed were among the leaders in promoting revivals in the American colonies. Theodore *Frelinghuysen, a *Dutch Reformed minister in New Jersey, influenced by German pietism and *Puritanism, is generally cited as being one of the first revivalists. His direct preaching on the sinfulness of men and women, the curse of God that awaited unrepentant sinners and the need to believe in Christ as the only way of salvation prompted a greater number of conversions and a more vigorous *piety in several of the congregations where he ministered in the 1720s. Frelinghuysen's ways would have immediate effects upon the newly planted Presbyterian churches in New Jersey and Pennsylvania. Gilbert *Tennent and William *Tennent Jr., who saw the influence of Frelinghuysen's preaching and were similarly committed to Puritan piety, also led revivals among Presbyterians in the Philadelphia vicinity. Their father, William Tennent Sr., who had established the Log College as a way to train students for the Presbyterian ministry, also promoted the cause of revivals, and this school became the principal source for Presbyterian clergy dedicated to furthering revivalism.

Opposition to the new forms of preaching and piety, however, emerged within Presbyterian circles. Of particular concern was the question of theological education; was education at Tennent's Log College sufficient for ordination, or should candidates have a degree from a theological college in Scotland or Northern Ireland, the homeland of many recent Presbyterian immigrants to the colonies? Reluctance to ordain Log College graduates led to harsh judgments from revivalists. Gilbert Tennent's infamous and intemperate sermon, "The Dangers of an Unconverted Ministry" (1740), which charged opponents of revivalism with being unbelievers, showed how acrimonious revivals could become. When George Whitefield came to the colonies in 1739 and transformed revivalism from a local affair into a transcolonial and international phenomenon, the bonds uniting the Presbyterian Church in the colonies would no longer hold. In 1741 Presbyterians divided into *New Side and *Old Side branches with revivalism playing a major role in the division. The New Side advocated revivals and welcomed Whitefield's assistance. The Old Side, while sympathetic to the concerns of revivalists, wanted to preserve Presbyterian distinctives in theology and church government and so questioned the wholesomeness of revivalism. Both sides reunited in 1758 after the fires of revivalism had cooled and the animosities of church controversy had been overcome.

Revivalism in the New Nation. After the revivals associated with Whitefield and the Great Awakening, instances of greater numbers of conversions and renewed zeal among believers occurred sporadically and locally among Presbyterians and non-Presbyterians alike. In 1801, with the appearance of the camp meetings at Cane Ridge, Kentucky, revivalism again began to move beyond local churches and take on national proportions. Initiated by the Presbyterian James *McGready and bearing some resemblance to the *Scots-Irish Presbyterian practice of communion seasons when believers in a particular area would gather between two and four times per year for week-long services of preparation before receiving the Lord's Supper, the frontier revivalism associated with Cane Ridge did not directly affect Presbyterian churches. The Presbyterian ministers who promoted camp meetings in the upper South would eventually leave the Presbyterian Church to go into other denominations or to form their own, most notably the Disciples of Christ.

Not until the 1830s did revivalism again generate the kind of tensions that had split eighteenth-century Presbyterianism. Charles Grandison *Finney, ordained a Presbyterian minister in upstate New York, led a series of revivals throughout urban centers in the Northeast between 1824 and 1835. Finney's methods generated considerable controversy, especially since his rationale for many of them seemed to deny divine sovereignty in the work of salvation as taught by the *Westminster standards. But Finney had many Presbyterian supporters, and the revivals of this period added to the ranks of the Presbyterian Church, especially in western New York and the upper Midwest. During the 1830s a party emerged within Presbyterianism opposed to the new methods of Finney and like-minded ministers. In the Presbytery of Philadelphia strict Calvinists brought to trial Albert *Barnes, a popular minister whose preaching and writings denied such Reformed doctrines as the imputation of Adam's sin. Though conservatives failed to convict Barnes, opposition to the theology and methods of the Second Great Awakening among Presbyterians led to the 1837 split between *Old and *New School Presbyterians, with the former opposing revivalism and the latter encouraging if not promoting it. New School Presbyterians were strongest in those regions where Finney had been most successful, New York and the upper Midwest, while Old School Presbyterians had the greatest concentration in the Mid-Atlantic states and the South.

Yet despite the Presbyterian division and quieting of revival fires during the 1840s, another important manifestation of evangelistic fervor occurred during 1857 and 1858 with the Prayer Meeting Revival, begun in New York City and spreading throughout urban centers in the Northeast and Midwest. Like previous revivals, this one transcended denominational boundaries and depended greatly upon the network established by the newly founded Young Men's Christian Association. Yet many though not all Presbyterians from both the Old and New School denominations supported it in some fashion.

Modern Urban Revivals. The revivals of 1857 and 1858 turned out to be a precursor of the most recent period of revivalism, that associated with large-scale evangelistic crusades taking place primarily in urban centers. Here the names of Dwight L. Moody (1837-1899) and Billy Graham (1918-) stand as book ends on this period. Though historians have begun to argue that revivalists of the eighteenth and early nineteenth centuries used business methods to promote evangelism, scholars agree that the application of modern techniques of communication and advertising to revivalism has been particularly characteristic of the modern era. As such revivalism has been more of a parachurch phenomenon, with denominations acting in ancillary roles. Consequently, modern urban revivalism would appear to have less influence upon Presbyterian churches.

Still, one of the great modern revivalists, namely, Billy *Sunday, was ordained as an evangelist by the *Presbyterian Church in the U.S.A. (PCUSA). A major league baseball player who converted at a Chicago city mission, Sunday was ordained as an evangelist in 1903 and went on to be the leading American revivalist in the era between Moody and Graham. After starting in small Midwestern cities, Sunday went on to national fame during the 1910s and 1920s. Though his prominence coincided with the *fundamentalist-modernist controversy and though Sunday himself shared many of the fundamentalists' concerns, his methods and preaching had little to do with the divisions between liberal and conservative Protestants. Unlike the split between Old and New Side Presbyterians of the eighteenth century and that between Old and New School Presbyterians of the nineteenth century, the fundamentalist conflict had little to do with revivalism per se. And as Sunday's campaigns grew independent of the oversight and aegis of the church, his effort had no direct bearing upon the Presbyterian church.

This would even be more the case with Graham, who succeeded Sunday as the urban evangelist par excellence. Though Graham's cooperation with mainline denominations would eventually alienate fundamentalists, the various Presbyterian communions, whether mainline such as the PCUSA or sideline such as the *Presbyterian Church in America (PCA) and the *Orthodox Presbyterian Church (OPC), did not endorse or withhold support officially from Graham. Instead, cooperation with Graham and other evangelistic organizations was a matter for local congregations and presbyteries to decide.

To the extent that twentieth-century Presbyterians have sponsored their own programs of evangelism, they have usually chosen lay approaches rather than ordaining evangelists or promoting revivalistic crusades. For instance, the New Life Movement of the PCUSA, which ran from 1947 to 1950, was an effort by denominational leaders to encourage person-to-person outreach and bring new members into the church. But a decade later the program had been abandoned by most Presbyterian officials as the focus shifted to nurturing those already within the church.

Another form of lay evangelism promoted by Presbyterians, though without denominational imprimatur, is Evangelism Explosion, a program devised by the Presbyterian minister (PCA) D. James Kennedy. It began in 1961 at Kennedy's church in Fort Lauderdale, Florida, when the congregation counted only seventeen members. Within two decades the church had grown to more than five thousand members, and by 1978 Kennedy's method of door-to-door visitation and presentation of the gospel had blossomed into an international organization.

Conclusion. Because of the long history of American Presbyterian support for revivals as a means of evangelism rarely have questions surfaced about whether revivalism is wise or theologically appropriate. Yet, a careful reading of the Westminster standards reveals that the regular (what the Shorter Catechism calls "the outward and ordinary means") preaching of the Word, the administration of the *sacraments and the work of the ordained ministry were the ways Presbyterians in the seventeenth century believed God would reach the lost and nurture the faithful. Furthermore, the confession's teaching about human nature and the process of sanctification raises questions about the peak-and-valley Christian walk assumed by revivalism. That American Presbyterians have not been more critical and selective in appropriating the methods of revivalism may account for the ready identification in the minds of scholars and the laity alike of Presbyterianism, a confessional and formal expression of Protestantism, with evangelicalism, a historically anticreedal and antiformal variety of Protestantism.

See also FINNEY, CHARLES G.; NEW SCHOOL PRESBYTERIANS; SUNDAY, WILLIAM (ASHLEY).

BIBLIOGRAPHY. M. J. Coalter, *Gilbert Tennent, Son of Thunder* (1986); M. J. Coalter and V. Cruz, eds., *How Shall We Witness?* (1995); M. J. Coalter, J. M. Mulder and L. B. Weeks, eds., *The Diversity of Discipleship* (1991); P. Conkin, *Cane Ridge: America's Pentecost* (1990); L. Dorsett, *Billy Sunday and the Redemption of Urban America* (1991); C. Hambrick-Stowe, *Charles G. Finney and the Spirit of American Evangelicalism* (1996); G. M. Marsden, *The Evangelical Mind and the New School Presbyterian Experience: A Case Study of Thought and Theology in Nineteenth-Century America* (1970); L. E. Schmidt, *Holy Fairs: Scottish Communions and American Revivals in the Early Modern Period* (1989); L. J. Trinterud, *The Forming of an American Tradition: A Reexamination of Colonial Presbyterianism* (1949).
D. G. Hart

Revolutionary War. *See* AMERICAN REVOLUTION, PRESBYTERIANS AND THE.

Rice, ("Father") David (1733-1816).† Presbyterian minister and *abolitionist. Born in colonial Virginia, Rice became a Presbyterian under Samuel *Davies and followed him to the College of New Jersey, graduating in 1761. Licensed in 1762 by Hanover Presbytery and ordained in 1763, he married Mary Blair, daughter of Samuel *Blair, another prominent Presbyterian, and served congregations in Hanover and Bedford counties before pioneering in Kentucky in 1783. There Rice organized the Presbyterian congregations at Danville, Fork of Dix River and Cane Run. He also worked with other groups and congregations to form the Transylvania Presbytery (1796), the parent body of Presbyterianism in the Midwest. In 1798 he moved to southern Kentucky, where he organized several churches, before continuing west into Ohio.

Rice initiated higher education in Kentucky, working with members of his extended family and with close friends. He had been one of the founders of Hampden-Sydney College in Virginia, and the Transylvania Seminary (later Transylvania University) was begun in his house, with a son-in-law as its first professor.

Father Rice opposed slavery and *revivals alike. In 1792 he was elected to the convention to fashion a state constitution, solely to oppose the legalizing of slavery. He lost that vote and retired from active politics. When the Great Kentucky Revival began in 1799-1800, he criticized the emotional preaching and the "bodily agitations" that accompanied it.

Bibliography. *AAP* 3; ANB 18; R. H. Bishop, *An Outline of the History of the Church in the State of Kentucky . . . Together with the Memoirs of "Father" David Rice, D.D.* (1824); *DAB* VIII; L. B. Weeks, *Kentucky Presbyterians* (1983).

L. B. Weeks

Rice, John Holt (1777-1831).† Presbyterian minister and educator. Born in Bedford County, Virginia, Rice was educated under William Graham and George Baxter, and then, after teaching school and marrying Anne Smith Morton, read theology with Archibald *Alexander at Hampton-Sydney College. Licensed by Hanover Presbytery and ordained in 1804, Rice served the Cub Creek Presbyterian Church, farmed and formed a school for boys. He also raised funds for the beginning of a theological school at Hampden-Sydney, which began in 1808.

In 1812 Rice was called to Richmond, Virginia, and organized the First Presbyterian Church in that community. With others he founded the Virginia Bible Society in 1813 and the American Bible Society in 1816, to provide the Scriptures "without note or comment" for as many Americans as possible.

After experimenting with a biweekly religious paper, the *Christian Monitor,* from 1815 to 1817, Rice began in 1818 to publish the *Virginia Evangelical and Literary Magazine,* a significant religious monthly that continued for ten years. During this period Rice moved from an active, antislavery position to one that became quietly supportive of the South's peculiar institution. When the University of Virginia was founded in 1818, he successfully opposed Thomas Cooper's appointment to the faculty, which had been strongly supported by Thomas Jefferson, but failed in his bid to allow various religious groups to establish professorships of theology at the institution.

Elected moderator of the Presbyterian general assembly in 1819, Rice turned down an invitation to become the president of the College of New Jersey three years later. Firmly convinced of the necessity of regional seminaries for the theological training of Presbyterian ministers, he did accept the call in 1824 to be president of the Theological Seminary at Hampden-Sydney (later Union Theological Seminary in Virginia), and by the time of his death he was able to put the school on a sound intellectual and financial footing. His plan for the seminary focused on the centrality of the Scriptures, within the confessional framework of the *Westminster Confession but avoiding useless speculation.

Rice mixed orthodox *Calvinism with genuine respect for those who differed in Christian conviction. He especially directed his energies toward those who had not heard the gospel, establishing the Young Men's Missionary Society in 1819, and his lobbying for Presbyterian *missions led in part to the forming of the board of foreign missions by the denomination. He urged cooperation with the Scottish Presbyterians in world missions and preferred to avoid controversy with Christians from other denominations. Rice wrote several books and pamphlets, among them *Irenicum or the Peacemaker* (1820), and a series of letters to former president James Madison in the *Southern Religious Telegraph,* later republished as his *Historical and Philosophical Considerations on Religion* (1832). On a fundraising trip to New York, he caught a cold that led to a prolonged illness, from which he eventually died.

Bibliography. *AAP* 4; *ANB* 18; *DAB* VIII; W. Maxwell, *A Memoir of the Reverend John H. Rice, D.D.* (1835); *NCAB* 2; P. B. Price, *The Life of the Reverend John Holt Rice, D.D.* (1887).

L. B. Weeks

Richards, George Warren (1869-1955).† Reformed theologian and educator. Born in Farmington, Pennsylvania, Richards graduated from Franklin and Marshall College (B.A., 1887; M.A., 1890; D.D., 1902) and was ordained to the ministry of the Reformed Church in the United States (RCUS) in 1890. Following a pastorate in Allentown, Pennsylvania (1890-1899), he studied theology at the universities of Berlin and Erlangen and received the doctor of theology degree from Heidelberg (1925). Richards was appointed professor of church history of the Theological Seminary of the Reformed Church in the U.S. at Lancaster, Pennsylvania, in 1899 and later became its president (1920-1937). His major writings included *The Heidelberg Catechism—Historical and Doctrinal Studies* (1913), *Beyond Fundamentalism and Modernism: The Gospel of God* (1934) and *Creative Controversies in Christianity* (1938). He also wrote a history of the Lancaster seminary and edited the *Reformed Church Review* (1904-1911).

The son of a *German Reformed father and a Lutheran mother, Richards himself married a Lutheran, Mary Moser, prefiguring his later role in the blending of the two traditions. As a churchman Richards was involved with his own denomination at the national level and in the ecumenical movement. From 1905 to 1920 he participated in the unsuccessful merger attempts between the RCUS and the *Presbyterian Church in the U.S.A. (PCUSA), realizing in the end that the union would be nothing but the absorption of the RCUS into the larger body, which would strip it of its identity. Arguing that church union requires the organic merging of similar traditions in which both contribute to the common life of the new body, he was convinced that all ecumenical activity must wait upon God's time. He acknowledged that this may not always be possible until the far distant future, yet he pointed out that for humans to rush ahead without the Spirit of God would doom the whole movement to failure. He later oversaw the successful union of the Evangelical Synod of the West with the RCUS to form the Evangelical and Reformed Church in 1934, and he was instrumental in laying the foundation for the merger that would form the United Church of Christ after his death. He was a member of the continuation committee of the World Conference on Faith and Order and vice president of the Federal Council of Churches (1934-1936). A constant presence at the World Alliance of Reformed Churches from 1904 to 1948, he was unanimously elected president of that body in 1929.

Richards was an exponent of the *Mercersburg theology, which stemmed from John Williamson *Nevin, Philip *Schaff and Emanuel Vogel *Gerhart, whose emphasis on the organic nature of the church provided much of the stimulus for his ecumenical work. In the 1920s and 1930s, he quickly embraced Barthian, or *neo-orthodox theology, which he recognized as harmonious with his twentieth-century reformulation of the Mercersburg theologians and considered to be an alternative to both liberalism and *fundamentalism. Aside from his own historical and theological work, Richards helped introduce Karl *Barth to North Americans through his translations of many of Barth's sermons (*Come, Creator Spirit,* 1933; *God's Search for Man,* 1935).

Bibliography. M. C. Romig, "George Warren Richards: Architect of Church Union," *JPH* 55 (spring 1977) 74-99. J. F. Johnson

Riggs, Stephen Return (1812-1883).† Presbyterian *missionary and linguist. Born at Steubenville, Ohio, and educated at Jefferson College in Pennsylvania and at the Western Seminary in Allegheny, Pennsylvania, Riggs was ordained to the Presbyterian ministry in 1836 by the Chillicothe Presbytery. After preaching for a year in Hawley, Massachusetts, where he met and married Mary A. C. Longley, Riggs and his wife were called in 1837 by the American Board of Commissioners for Foreign Missions to the Lac qui Parle mission near Ft. Snelling, Minnesota.

Riggs utilized his outstanding linguistic ability to master the various Sioux languages, establishing two more mission stations, until the outbreak of the Sioux wars in 1862. Saved by his students from the massacre in which hundreds of settlers were killed, Riggs remained faithful to his flock, lobbying Congress on their behalf and continuing his work among the Dakotas imprisoned at Mankato, Minnesota, and later when they were confined to reservations in the Dakota Territory. Over the course of his forty-five years among the Dakotas, Riggs became an authority on their language, reducing it to written form and producing primers, grammars and a variety of educational and religious literature, including a Dakota catechism, *Dakota Wiwicawangapi Kin,* the New Testament in 1865 and the entire Bible in 1880. In his later years, he lived in Beloit, Wisconsin, and supervised the work of other missionaries, making frequent visits to the Dakota reservation. A tribute to his character and commitments, four of his nine children continued his work with the Dakota. He died in Beloit in 1883.

Bibliography. *ANB* 18; *DAB* VIII; *DARB; NCAB* 3; S. R. Riggs, *Mary and I: Forty Years with the Sioux* (1880); idem, *Tah-koo Wah-kan, or the Gospel Among the Dakotas* (1869). M. S. Joy

Rimmer, Harry (1890-1952). Presbyterian minister and Christian apologist. A native of San Francisco, Rimmer attended Hahnemann College of the Pacific, Whittier College and the Bible Institute of Los Angeles. He was ordained as a minister of the Society of Friends and served as pastor of the First Friends Church in Los Angeles and as a chaplain during World War I.

In 1920 Rimmer started the Research Science Bureau, Inc., in Denver, Colorado, through which he brought forward scientific evidence in support of the authenticity of the Bible. He undertook archaeological expeditions, studied manuscripts in British and Egyptian museums and lectured at hundreds of college and university campuses on the harmony of science and Scripture. He later became a Presbyterian and served as pastor of the First Presbyterian

Church in Duluth, Minnesota (1934-1939).

Rimmer was the author of twenty-nine books, among which were *The Harmony of Science and Scripture* (1938), *Modern Science and the Genesis Record* (1938) and *Internal Evidence of Inspiration* (1939). He also served as associate editor of *Christian Faith and Life,* as contributing editor of *Kings Business, Religious Digest, Northwest Pilot* and *Moody Monthly.* The recipient of several honorary degrees, he also served on the board of directors of John Brown University and radio station HCJB in Quito, Ecuador, where the Rimmer Memorial Hospital stands in honor of his fund-raising activity on behalf of Indian health care.

See also SCIENCE, PRESBYTERIANS AND.

BIBLIOGRAPHY. *ANB* 18; *NCAB* 41; R. L. Numbers, *The Creationists: The Evolution of Scientific Creationism* (1992).

D. G. Buss

Robertson, James (1839-1902).† Presbyterian *missions leader in Canada. Born in Scotland, Robertson immigrated to Woodstock, Canada, with his family in 1855. He taught school for several years and conducted worship services for the Gaelic-speaking settlers. He studied at the University of Toronto (B.A., 1866), Princeton Seminary and Union Theological Seminary (New York, B.D., 1869), returning to Canada to marry Betty Cowing. After ordination by the *Presbyterian Church of Canada in 1869, he ministered at Norwich in rural Ontario until he accepted a call in 1873 to the city of Winnipeg on the developing prairies of western Canada. There he taught theology and philosophy at Manitoba College and became intimately acquainted with the needs of the Canadian Northwest. In 1881 he became superintendent of Presbyterian missions on the prairies. Preaching widely throughout the West, Robertson spent twenty years ministering to the railroad workers, farmers and miners from Winnipeg to the Yukon. He was also instrumental in convincing dozens of young ministers and teachers to forsake the comforts of the eastern seaboard for the rough and demanding life of the frontier.

When Robertson began as "the Presbyterian bishop," the denomination had but four congregations. During his tenure the denominational presence increased to more than 140 established churches in addition to 226 mission charges that served more than a thousand communities. Robertson received a doctor of divinity degree from the Presbyterian College in Montreal in 1888, and in 1895 he was honored by election as the moderator of the Presbyterian church.

BIBLIOGRAPHY. C. W. Gordon, *The Life of James Robertson* (1908); I. McFadden, *He Belonged to the West: James Robertson* (1958).

B. A. McKenzie

Robinson, Stuart (1814-1881). Southern Presbyterian minister. Born in County Tyrone, Ireland, of *Scots-Irish parents, Robinson immigrated to the United States with his family when he was two, eventually settling in Virginia. Robinson was educated at Amherst College (B.A., 1836), Union Theological Seminary in Virginia (1836-1837) and Princeton Theological Seminary (1839-1840). Ordained into the Presbyterian ministry in 1842, he served as the pastor of the Presbyterian Church at Kanawha-Salines, Virginia (1842-1847); the Presbyterian Church at Frankfort, Kentucky (1847-1852); Fayette Street Church (Independent) in Baltimore (1852-1853); and Central Presbyterian Church in Baltimore (1853-1856). In 1856 he became professor of church government and pastoral theology at the Danville Theological Seminary in Danville, Kentucky. In 1858 he left his teaching post to become pastor of Second Presbyterian Church of Louisville, Kentucky, where he remained until his death. During his pastoral career he also edited *The True Presbyterian.*

A gifted preacher, noted for his exegetical, expository sermons, Robinson was an ardent defender of *Old School Presbyterianism. He was also a strong proponent of the distinctive Southern Presbyterian doctrine of the spirituality of the church, which asserted that the church should deal only with spiritual matters and avoid all political statements. He was suspected of Confederate sympathies and spent part of the *Civil War years in Canada. After the war he was active in relief work for the South. In 1869 he led the majority of the Synod of Kentucky out of the Northern church and into the Southern church. Robinson was an outspoken opponent of reunion with the Northern church. In addition to his sermons, he published several polemical theological works.

BIBLIOGRAPHY. *ANB* 18; *DAB* VIII; E. T. Thompson, *Presbyterians in the South,* vol. 2 (1965).

J. R. Wiers

Robinson, William (?-1746). Presbyterian evangelist to Virginia and North Carolina. Born near Carlisle, in England, Robinson immigrated to America out of fear of parental censure after having spent a period in youthful dissipation in London. In New Jersey he found employment as a teacher, but following Christian conversion he determined to take up the ministry and studied at the *Tennents' Log College on Neshaminy Creek.

Robinson was ordained to the Presbyterian ministry by the New Brunswick Presbytery on August 4, 1741. The following year he embarked as an evangelist to Presbyterian settlements in the Shenandoah Valley, on the south side of the James River in Virginia and along the Haw River in North Carolina. Persuaded to visit Hanover County, Virginia, Robinson's sermon of July 6, 1743, marked the first appearance of a Presbyterian minister in the eastern part of the colony and prefaced a triumphant four-day visitation. He then ministered along upper Chesapeake Bay, but his health rapidly declined, and he died in 1746 on the eve of taking up work in Delaware.

Robinson is said to have earlier been a victim of smallpox, which cost the sight of one eye and left his face badly scarred; hence the oft-used sobriquet "one-eyed Robinson." His importance to Presbyterianism rests almost entirely on the success of his Southern missionary journey in 1743, which paved the way for an extensive Presbyterian revival in Virginia and the larger work, beginning there in 1747, of his former pupil Samuel *Davies.

Bibliography. *AAP* 3; A. Alexander, *Biographical Sketches of the Founder and Principal Alumni of the Log College* (1845); W. H. Foote, *Sketches of Virginia* (first series) (1850).

W. J. Wade

Rodgers, James Burton (1865-1944).‡ Presbyterian *missionary. Born in Albany, New York, Rodgers received degrees from Hamilton College and Auburn Theological Seminary. After his marriage to Anna Van Vechten Bigelow and ordination in 1889, the *Presbyterian Church in the U.S.A. (PCUSA) sent Rodgers to Brazil and then transferred him to the Philippines in June 1898. On May 7, 1899, he preached his first sermon in the Philippines at the home of a Mr. Poblete. The congregation of seven included four members of the Paulino Zamora family, which would play a major role in the beginnings of Philippine Protestant churches.

Until his retirement in 1935 Rodgers participated actively in evangelistic, *educational and ecumenical endeavors. In addition to serving as head of the Presbyterian mission, Rodgers played instrumental roles in the founding of the Evangelical Union and the comity agreement in 1901; in the founding of Union Theological Seminary, Manila, in 1907; and in the founding of the United Evangelical Church in 1929. He also taught theology at Union Seminary, Manila, from 1908 to 1932.

His service beyond the Philippines included membership in the 1922 Presbyterian deputation visit to Mexico, the 1926 China Evaluation Conference and the 1936 deputation to Korea. After 1935 Rodgers lived in retirement in the Philippines. In 1940 he published *Forty Years in the Philippines.* He died in Baguio City during the Japanese occupation of World War II.

Bibliography. K. J. Clymer, *Protestant Missionaries in the Philippines, 1898-1916* (1986).

G. J. Bekker

Rowland, John (?-1745). Presbyterian *revivalist. He is supposed to have been a native of Wales, but little is known of his early years except that he studied at William *Tennent's Log College in Neshaminy, Pennsylvania, whose graduates became Great Awakening revivalists. He was licensed to preach by the *New Side (prorevival) New Brunswick Presbytery in 1738, in defiance of an act of the synod requiring those without a diploma from a *New England or European college to undergo a satisfactory examination by the synod. The presbytery regarded the rule an infringement of the traditional rights of presbyteries, and synod refused to recognize Rowland as a licentiate. Nonetheless Rowland was called by the Maidenhead and Hopewell congregations in New Jersey, within the bounds of Philadelphia Presbytery, and the nearby Amwell congregation in New Brunswick Presbytery. Despite some dissension in the former congregations, an extraordinary religious *revival occurred as a result of his powerful and effective preaching for conversion. His detractors called him "hell-fire Rowland" and managed to have him falsely accused of robbery and horse stealing. New Brunswick Presbytery, now part of the New Side Presbyterian Synod, sent him on evangelistic tours to New Side congregations in Pennsylvania and New Jersey; in 1742 he began the last pastorate of his short life at Charlestown and New Providence, in Chester County, Pennsylvania.

Rowland's effectiveness as an evangelist was recognized by George Whitefield and Gilbert *Tennent. Tennent preached Rowland's funeral sermon, referring to him as "a Boanerges, or a Son of Thunder." Rowland's narrative of the revivals that occurred in his ministry was printed as an appendix to the published funeral sermon.

Bibliography. A. Alexander, *The Log College* (1851); C. H. Maxson, *The Great Awakening in the Middle Colonies* (1920); R. Webster, *History of the Presbyterian Church in America* (1857).

A. H. Freundt Jr.

Ruffner, Henry (1789-1861).† Presbyterian minister and educator. Born to Mennonite parents in Page County, Virginia, Ruffner grew up in the western frontier of Virginia. In 1813, after graduating from Washington College in Lexington, Virginia, he studied theology with the college president and was licensed to preach in 1815. He was ordained in 1818 and shortly thereafter organized the first Presbyterian church in what is now Charleston, West Virginia. During his lifetime he served in a number of pastorates in the area.

Ruffner eventually returned to Washington College to teach, and over a thirty-year period he served twelve years as president (1836-1848) and taught nearly every subject offered by the college. His publications include *A Discourse on the Duration of Future Punishment* (1823) and *Against Universalism* (1833); a romance entitled *Judith Bensaddi,* published in the *Southern Literary Messenger* in 1839; and the two-volume *The Fathers of the Desert* (1850) on the origins and practice of monasticism.

In 1842, at a state *education convention, Ruffner submitted his comprehensive plan for a public school system. It drew praise from the U.S. Commissioner of Education as the most valuable piece on Virginia education since Thomas Jefferson's work. His detailed system was later implemented by his son. Ruffner's influential antislavery pamphlet was a dispassionate analysis, written by a slaveholder, detailing the system's evils and economic disadvantages while recommending gradual emancipation and colonization.

In 1848 Ruffner resigned under pressure from the presidency of Washington College, because of his views on slavery and other controversial issues. After an unsuccessful attempt at farming, Ruffner pastored the Presbyterian Church of Malden, in western Virginia, until his death.

Bibliography. T. C. Hunt, "Henry Ruffner and the Struggle for Public Schools in Antebellum Virginia," in *AP* 64 (Spring 1986): 18-26; E. T. Thompson, *Presbyterians in the South, 1607-1861,* vol. 1 (1963).

S. E. Berk

Rush, Benjamin (1745-1813). Physician, American revolutionary and reformer with lifelong Presbyterian connections. Rush was born in Byberry, Pennsylvania, near Philadelphia. Shortly after his father's death, when Rush was only five, his mother, Susanna Harvey Rush, joined the Philadelphia church of Gilbert *Tennent. Rush was decisively influenced by the revivalistic *New Side Presbyterianism of Tennent, Samuel *Finley (his academy teacher in West Nottingham, Maryland) and Samuel *Davies (Virginia Presbyterian *revivalist who became president of the College of New Jersey very soon after Rush entered as a student). From these New Side stalwarts, Rush received a seriousness about sin, a trust in divine revelation and a commitment to godly activity in the world. Following advice from Finley and Davies, Rush prepared for a career in medicine, studying in both Philadelphia and Britain. At the University of Edinburgh, under the influence of the Scottish Enlightenment, Rush added a great confidence in understanding secondary (or material) causes to his earlier belief in the supernatural. While in Britain, Rush also thoroughly imbibed radical Whig, or republican, political theory.

Upon returning to the new world, Rush became professor of chemistry at the College of Philadelphia and published the first set of lectures on chemistry to appear in the colonies. He eagerly joined the struggle for American independence and was a signer of the Declaration of Independence. He served as a physician in the *Revolutionary War but also revealed a talent for personal vendettas, including a lingering quarrel with George Washington. After the war, Rush established himself as the most important medical lecturer in the United States and put his controversial trust in bleeding to active use during Philadelphia's dreadful yellow fever epidemic of 1793. Always an active reformer, Rush helped found societies aimed at promoting temperance, ending slavery, starting colleges, establishing Sunday schools, founding churches for African-Americans and improving medical and psychological care for the mentally ill. He died in Philadelphia.

Rush left the Presbyterians in 1787. After briefly trying other churches, he abandoned denominational religion, calling himself rather a Christocrat—someone seeking the virtues of both Christian religion and republican politics. About the same time he also became a Universalist through the influence of contemporaries like Elhanan Winchester along with his own study of Scripture. Into the 1790s, Rush thought that the United States might inaugurate the millennium but then became disillusioned with current affairs, especially the deification of Washington, the financial policies of Alexander Hamilton, the nation's lust for money, the growth of political parties and the epidemics of yellow fever. His spirits revived briefly when his friend Thomas Jefferson became president in 1801, for Rush thought that Jefferson could restore republican innocence to the American experiment. Quickly, however, he relapsed into despair at the course of politics, though he continued to put great confidence in the ability of voluntary Christian activity to anticipate Christ's supernatural return. His religion illustrated how compatible Presbyterian emphases could be with many of the founding themes of the United States, but also how the American experience could undermine important principles of traditional Presbyterian belief.

BIBLIOGRAPHY. *ANB* 19; L. H. Butterfield, ed. *Letters of Benjamin Rush* (1951); G. W. Corner, ed., *The Autobiography of Benjamin Rush* (1948); *DAB* XVI; D. J. D'Elia, *Benjamin Rush: Philosopher of the American Revolution* (1974); J. M. Kloos Jr., *A Sense of Deity* (1991); *Princetonians: A Biographical Dictionary* (1976). M. A. Noll

S

Sacraments, Presbyterians and the. The doctrine and practice of baptism and the Lord's Supper in American Presbyterianism have been shaped by the Bible as the final authority for *worship; by the Protestant Reformation, especially as it developed in Zurich and Geneva; by the *Puritan emphasis on the Word of God and simplicity as expressed in the Westminster Directory (1644); and by the social context and demands of a new church on the frontier.

Many Presbyterian churches began as preaching points, often coming into existence on the initiative of Christian people, without the assistance of the presbytery. Preaching of the Word was the primary means of grace. The role of *revivals in American church life also added to this emphasis. No sacraments apart from the promise of God and preaching and teaching was a consistent Presbyterian emphasis. Presbyterian practice from the beginning fits Karl *Barth's formula of Word plus sacraments rather than the more traditional Word and sacraments.

Worship in early American Presbyterianism left much to the discretion of the minister. The first presbytery was organized in 1706. It was not until the synod of 1729 that the new church had an authoritative confession. This synod voted that "all the ministers . . . shall declare their agreement in and approbation of the Confession of Faith . . . as being in all the essential and necessary Articles, good Forms of sound words and systems of Christian Doctrine; and do also adopt said Confession and Catechisms as the Confession of our Faith." The synod declared the Directory of Worship to be agreeable in substance to the Word of God and "recommended the same to all their Members to be by them observed as near as Circumstances will allow and Christian Prudence direct." The directory, as a recommended guide, gave ministers and congregations great freedom in Christian worship.

The synod of 1786 again affirmed the directory as agreeable in substance to the New Testament. The movement toward a general assembly accentuated the need for a directory attuned to the needs of the American church and the appointment of a committee for this purpose. The committee moved in the direction of formal worship as it was practiced in urban areas. The synod, however, insisted upon freedom in worship, rejecting pattern prayers and providing guidelines and counsels for ministers. This directory, adopted in 1788, provided the guidelines and parameters of Presbyterian worship for 150 years.

The Lord's Supper. The directory states that the Lord's Supper shall follow a sermon. The minister is to introduce the sacrament with the words of the institution, which he is then to explain, a practice rooted in the teaching of John *Calvin. He is to warn the profane, the ignorant and the scandalous not to approach the table. The communicants may sit around the tables or in their seats. After the elements are set apart by prayer and thanksgiving they are distributed to the people with the minister repeating the words of the institution.

The sacrament ends with words of exhortation, a prayer of thanksgiving, a collection for the poor, a psalm or a hymn and a prayer and a gospel benediction. The basic structure is clear, but the directory does not prescribe the words of the minister.

The Lord's Supper is to be observed frequently, but frequently is not defined. The general pattern was quarterly communion or even annual communion. Infrequent communion enhanced the solemnity of the occasion. The Scottish practice of preparatory services and the communion season was brought to America. The communion season included revival preaching as well as preaching preparatory to the Lord's Supper. It was the occasion for receiving church members, catechizing, baptisms and congregational meetings. In rural situations the communion season made possible a form of church life that could not otherwise be sustained in geographically dispersed congregations with poor travel conditions. Preparatory services for the celebration of the Lord's Supper survived in some churches until recent years.

"Fencing the table," protecting the table from the scandalous and the ignorant, was an ancient tradition going back to Calvin. The fencing of the table included the minister's warning not to come to the table casually or unworthily and thus to drink damnation to oneself. The casual handling of sacred things always brings damnation. Those who heard the warning understood the solemnity of the occasion. This led to the use of communion tokens. These were sometimes slips of paper or metal pieces that were distributed by the minister or the elders to the members of the church certifying that they belonged at the table.

Fencing of the table, as well as discipline generally, could not be maintained in a diverse Christian community when those rejected by one church would be welcomed by another. As American society became more secular, the problem was not that of keeping the scandalous and those who would make mockery of the sacrament away from the table but of getting people from a secular society to come to the table.

Fencing the table conflicted with the doctrine that the sacrament was a means of grace and, as some insisted, "a converting ordinance." Yet the *New Side and Log College Presbyterians united in a unique way both the notion of fencing the table and the notion that the sacrament is a proclamation of the grace of God in Jesus Christ. They made the sacrament of the Lord's Supper an evangelistic opportunity by inviting those present to accept the faith and to come to the table. The Lord's Supper became for them an occasion for personal decision. The communion sermons of Samuel *Davies are an example of the Lord's Supper as proclamation of the gospel without diminishing the responsibility of participation.

Admission to the Lord's table, Presbyterians insisted, requires knowledge as well as faith. Calvin made catechetical study a condition for communion and ruled out any uncertainty as to whether children should commune. Knowledge was the precondition for participation in the sacrament. This practice held in American Presbyterianism until recent years, when admission to the table was separated from the personal assumption of membership in the life of the church.

Baptism. The practice of baptism as well as the Lord's Supper was modified by the uncertain and irregular services of the frontier churches and later by the enormous influence of revivals and the practice of believers' baptism. The Westminster Directory insisted that the service of baptism, like the Lord's Supper, is to be simple, prohibiting what Calvin called "theatrical trifles." Baptism is to take place in the presence of the congregation. The American directory of 1788 follows the Westminster Directory, but it allows baptism to take place in private houses when expedient, as judged by the minister. It also prohibits "adding any other service."

The American directory is more specific as to what the child is to be taught by the parents. It requires "that they teach the child to read the Word of God; that they instruct it in the principles of our holy religion, as contained in the Scriptures of the Old and New Testament; an excellent summary of which we have in the Confession of Faith of this church and in the Larger and Shorter Catechisms of the Westminster Assembly, which are to be recommended to them and adopted by this church for their direction." The directory adopted by the *Presbyterian Church in the United States (PCUS) in 1894 follows the early American directory in the instruction for baptism, as it does for the Lord's Supper.

The pervasive practice of believers' baptism in many American churches and the revivalist insistence on conversion as entrance into the church undermined the practice of baptism of infants even in Presbyterian churches. The baptism of infants is based on the conviction that children of believers are born into the membership of the church and thus are entitled to baptism. It takes seriously the significance of nature and of history, while the rejection of this practice emphasizes personal decision. The hope is that baptized infants will grow up in the church without a radical break before which they were not Christian and after which they are.

Many Presbyterians were confused about the meaning of the baptism of infants. Some continued to speak of joining the church with a public confession of faith and with admission to the Lord's table. Prominent Presbyterian theologians such as James Henley *Thornwell and Robert Lewis *Dabney were very uncomfortable with the baptism of infants and regarded it as an "ecclesiastical covenant" that placed the child in the context of the means of grace and instruction. The real moment of becoming a member of the church was the public profession of faith.

Liturgical Developments. The adequacy of a directory of worship with guidelines and counsels but with no set forms began to be challenged in the middle of the nineteenth century. The directory without a service book sometimes contributed to confusion and also to dullness and incompetence. Many ministers were poorly qualified to lead in prayer without reading the text. Yet there was opposition to read prayers and fixed forms in many Presbyterian churches until after World War II. An increasing awareness that the *Reformed tradition included books of services, especially the book that Calvin had prepared and used in Geneva, as well as the one that

John Knox had patterned on the Genevan Service for use in Scotland, contributed to discontent with the directory. Charles W. Baird published *Eutaxia, or The Presbyterian Liturgies: Historical Sketches* in 1855 and *A Book of Public Prayer Compiled from the Authorized Formularies of Worship of the Presbyterian Church As Prepared by the Reformers Calvin, Knox, Bucer and Others; with Supplementary Forms* in 1855. Many similar works would follow.

The liturgical movements of the last fifty years have emphasized the Christian year, greater openness to other traditions and a movement away from the simplicity of the Westminster Directory, more frequent celebrations of the Lord's Supper and an enhancement of baptism with services that the earlier Reformed tradition rejected. The liturgical emphasis and the decline of the revival tradition have also contributed to greater emphasis on the baptism of infants. It is not yet clear that the frequent celebration of the Lord's Supper or the new emphasis upon more elaborate baptismal services shall have greater impact on the life of the church than did the less frequent and more simple services of the earlier period.

The renewed emphasis on sacramental life in contemporary Presbyterianism comes at the same time the leading Reformed theologians of Europe, for example, Barth, Emil Brunner and Hendrikus Berkhof, have radically deemphasized the sacraments.

See also WORSHIP, PRESBYTERIANS AND.

BIBLIOGRAPHY. T. Leishman, *The Westminster Directory* (1901); J. Melton, *Presbyterian Worship in America: Changing Patterns Since 1787* (1967); H. Old, *The Shaping of the Reformed Baptismal Rite in the Sixteenth Century* (1992); L. B. Schenck, *The Presbyterian Doctrine of Children in the Covenant* (1940); L. E. Schmidt, *Holy Fairs: Scottish Communions and American Revivals in the Early Modern Period* (1989); L. J. Trinterud, *The Forming of an American Tradition: A Reexamination of Colonial Presbyterianism* (1959).

J. Leith

Schaeffer, Francis August (1912-1984).‡ Presbyterian *missionary and apologist. Born in Philadelphia, Pennsylvania, Schaeffer was reared in a nominally Lutheran family but during high school became an agnostic. While studying engineering at Drexel Institute he came to faith and completed his studies at Hampden-Sydney College (B.A., 1935). That same year he married Edith Seville, who would become a well-known evangelical author in her own right. Schaeffer attended seminary first at Westminster Theological Seminary, where he studied under the apologist Cornelius *Van Til, and then at Faith Theological Seminary (B.D., 1938). In 1938 Schaeffer became the first ordained minister of the *Bible Presbyterian Church and subsequently pastored churches in Pennsylvania and Missouri.

In 1948 the Schaeffers moved to Switzerland, serving under the Independent Board for Presbyterian Foreign Missions. In 1955 Schaeffer founded L'Abri, an international study center in the Swiss Alps. Over the years thousands of students and other seekers stayed with the Schaeffers, and through prayer, study and conversation many of them came to Christian faith. The ministry was greatly extended through Schaeffer's writings, and by the 1970s he was widely regarded among American evangelicals as a preeminent apologist for the faith.

In books such as *The God Who Is There* (1968) and *Escape from Reason* (1968) Schaeffer traced the decline of Western humanistic culture to a lack of intellectual and moral absolutes. He claimed that this decline began when the philosopher Hegel replaced the notion that truth is antithetical and therefore absolute with the idea that truth is synthetical and therefore relative. This shift from absolutism to relativism had spread three ways: geographically from Germany to the Continent, England and the United States; socially from intellectuals to the working class and then the middle class; and finally by disciplines from philosophy to art, music, general culture and then theology.

In his later writings, such as *How Should We Then Live? The Rise and Decline of Western Thought and Culture* (1976), Schaeffer detailed the political and moral consequences of abandoning absolute truth. Politically he held that without a Reformation base to unify form and freedom, freedom gives rise to chaos, which in turn leads to authoritarian government. In the area of morals, the belief that humankind was created in God's image has been replaced by a low view of humans, permitting the practice of abortion, infanticide and euthanasia. Schaeffer held that only a return to biblical absolutes can reverse these trends, and he admonished evangelicals to stand firm on the doctrine of inerrancy and take a public stand against social and moral evils.

While they are appreciative of his general argument, some evangelicals have argued that Schaeffer's analysis of modern thought bordered on superficiality. By any measure, Schaeffer was a leading figure in the resurgence of evangelicalism during the 1960s and 1970s.

BIBLIOGRAPHY. L. T. Dennis, ed., *Francis A. Schaeffer: Portraits of the Man and His Work* (1986);

R. W. Ruegsegger, ed., *Reflections on Francis Schaeffer* (1986); E. Schaeffer, *L'Abri* (1969); F. S. Schaeffer, *The Complete Works of Francis A. Schaeffer*, 5 vols. (1982). R. W. Ruegsegger

Schaff, Philip (1819-1893). *German Reformed church historian and ecumenist. Born in Chur, Switzerland, Schaff received his education at the universities of Tübingen (1837-1839), Halle (1839-1840) and Berlin (1840-1842), where he came under the influence of such notable scholars as Ferdinand Christian Baur, Friedrich A. G. Tholuck and Johann A. Neander. Upon completing his studies in 1842, Schaff became *privatdocent* at the University of Berlin. The next year Schaff accepted an invitation by representatives of the newly organized German Reformed Seminary at *Mercersburg, Pennsylvania, to become a professor there. He arrived to take up his duties in August 1844, and so began a career of nearly a half-century of scholarship at the forefront of the study of church history. Schaff taught at Mercersburg until 1865, lecturing occasionally at Drew and Hartford seminaries between 1868 and 1871, and in 1870 he accepted a professorship at Union Theological Seminary in New York, where he remained until his death.

In addition to his pioneering work in church history, Schaff served as secretary of the New York Sabbath Committee and was influential in the reorganization of the American branch of the Evangelical Alliance in 1866, serving as its corresponding secretary until 1873 and spending hundreds of hours and traveling thousands of miles to organize the World Conference of the Alliance held in New York City, October 2-12, 1873. From 1870 to 1885, Schaff was involved with the committee for the American Revised Bible translation project and served as president of that committee (1872-1885). He founded the American Society of Church History in 1888 and served as president of that organization until his death.

In addition to these many commitments, Schaff published an astounding number of books and articles. He edited *Der Deutsch Kirchenfreund* (1848-1854), wrote regularly for the *Mercersburg Review*, serving as its coeditor (1857-1861), and founded the German periodical *Evangelische Zeugnisse aus den Deutschen Kirchen in Amerika*, which was issued from 1863 to 1865. His first major work in America was *The Principle of Protestantism* (1845), an expansion of his inaugural address at Mercersburg Seminary. This work, which brought upon Schaff charges of heresy and Romanism, traced the development of the Christian church through history and emphasized the value of the church in every age. Schaff's assertion that the Reformation was "the legitimate offspring, the greatest act of the Catholic Church," provoked strong protest among the militantly Protestant wing of the German Reformed clergy. The next year Schaff published a summary of his theology of the history of the Christian church, *What Is Church History?*

After a decade in Mercersburg, Schaff took a sabbatical leave and returned to Europe, where he presented a series of addresses about his "adopted fatherland." Published in German as *Amerika* (1854), these addresses appeared in English the following year. There Schaff attempted to explain and defend the American system in which church and state were separated and complete religious liberty enjoyed. In 1858 Schaff published the first volume of his most ambitious work, his *History of the Christian Church*, which ultimately grew to eight volumes (the two on the Middle Ages were written by his son, David, after Schaff's death). On the centennial of the United States Constitution, he issued an interpretation of the constitutional guarantees of religious liberty entitled *Church and State in the United States*.

As an editor, Schaff presided over the translation of Johann Peter Lange's massive *Bibelwork*, a project finally completed in 1880, when the last of twenty-five volumes was published. From 1880 to 1886 Schaff edited the first series of fourteen volumes of *A Select Library of the Nicene and Post-Nicene Fathers of the Christian Church*, coediting with Henry Wace the first two volumes of the second series. In 1877 the first edition of Schaff's three-volume *Creeds of Christendom* appeared. The *Schaff-Herzog Encyclopedia of Religious Knowledge* was published in three volumes (1882-1884). Finally, he originated and organized the American Society of Church History's thirteen-volume *American Church History Series*. Inspiring all of his prodigious labors was Schaff's ultimate goal to heal the wounds caused by divisions in the church. His epitaph is apt: "He advocated the reunion of Christendom."

Bibliography. *ANB* 19; H. W. Bowden, *Church History in the Age of Science: Historiographical Patterns in the United States 1876-1918* (1971); *DAB* XVI; *DARB; NCAB* 3; J. H. Nichols, *Romanticism in American Theology: Nevin and Schaff at Mercersburg* (1961); J. H. Nichols, ed., *The Mercersburg Theology* (1966); D. S. Schaff, *The Life of Philip Schaff* (1897); G. H. Shriver, *Philip Schaff: Christian Scholar and Ecumenical Prophet* (1987).

S. R. Graham

Schlatter, Michael (1718-1790).† *German Reformed minister. Born at St. Gall, Switzerland, Schlatter's early spiritual mentor was his pastor, Christof Stähelin, who was widely known for his pietist publications. Comparatively little is known of Schlatter's early education at the local gymnasium. This study was interrupted by his matriculation at the University of Leyden in 1736, followed by study at Helmstedt in Germany. Three years later he was ordained in Switzerland. After serving as a private tutor in Holland, in 1744 he returned to Switzerland, serving as a vicar in Thurgau. Two years later he was recommended to the Dutch Reformed fathers at The Hague by John Caspar Crucinger as a worthy candidate for the German Reformed churches in the new world. Impressed by his gifts, his character and his fluency in both Dutch and German, the Classis of Amsterdam dispatched him to America with instructions that amounted to the task of overseeing the German Reformed congregations in the American colonies.

Arriving in September 1746, Schlatter focused on bringing some semblance of organization to the German Reformed churches. After strenuous efforts involving much travel by horseback, he succeeded in organizing the so-called coetus in 1747, consisting of four ordained ministers and twenty-eight elders who together represented twelve of the thirteen German Reformed congregations. Traveling widely for the next three years, he discovered or founded thirty more congregations throughout the Middle Colonies.

Commissioned by the coetus, Schlatter returned to Europe for the purpose of popularizing the spiritual and financial needs of the German Reformed people in America. Having been eminently successful in this endeavor he returned with six young ministers and a substantial sum of money (1752). A second trip to Europe in 1753-1754 resulted in another generous gift toward *education. The money was used to start a system of charity schools for the children of German immigrants, a work to which Schlatter gradually devoted most of his energies. Becoming superintendent of schools in Pennsylvania in 1754, he came into a close working relationship with William Smith, a leading Anglican educator in Philadelphia. Unfortunately, some misunderstandings between the German settlers and the English leadership, fueled by the German desire to maintain their heritage intact, ensured that these charity schools would be less and less appreciated, and Schlatter's relationship with the coetus, as well as with the Classis of Amsterdam, became strained. Schlatter resigned from his educational post in 1756.

For a time Schlatter held a chaplaincy in the Royal American Infantry of the British Army during the French and Indian War, participating in the siege of Halifax. After 1759 he ministered in some independent Reformed churches near Philadelphia and vocally supported the patriotic cause in the *American Revolutionary War, which resulted in his temporary imprisonment by the British. Though his relationship to the coetus was never to be restored, his early ministry and leadership were strategic in the organization and growth of the German Reformed churches in Pennsylvania. He died in Philadelphia.

BIBLIOGRAPHY. E. T. Corwin, *A Manual of the Reformed Church in America—1628-1902* (1902); *DAB* VIII; *DARB;* H. Harbaugh, *The Life of the Reverend Michael Schlatter* (1857); W. J. Hinke, *Ministers of the German Reformed Congregations in Pennsylvania and Other Colonies in the Eighteenth Century* (1951). F. E. Stoeffler

Schneder, David Bowman (1857-1938). *Missionary of the Reformed Church in the United States (*German Reformed). Born on a farm near Bowmansville, Pennsylvania, Schneder graduated from Franklin and Marshall College in 1880 and from the Theological Seminary of the Reformed Church at Lancaster, Pennsylvania, in 1883. Although he had applied to be a missionary to Japan before his graduation from seminary, he was not appointed by the mission board until 1887. In the meantime he served as pastor of the Reformed Church in Marietta, Pennsylvania. He and his bride of five weeks, Anna M. Schoenberger, sailed for Japan in late 1887.

Schneder joined the Sendai Theological Training School of the Reformed Church in the United States, which had been established in the previous year by his friend William E. *Hoy and the Japanese evangelist Masayoshi Oshikawa. After serving as professor of systematic theology and the history of philosophy at this school, which came to be known as Tohoku Gakuin (North Japan College), Schneder became its president in 1901 and remained in that position until his resignation in 1936. In spite of many difficulties—a shortage of funds from the mission board, a fire that destroyed a major school building, antagonism toward missionaries brought on by a growing nationalism in Japan—under Schneder's leadership Tohoku Gakuin grew to become the leading Christian school in the Tohoku region.

A man of strong will but irenic temperament, Schneder was deeply devoted not only to the cause of Christianity in Japan but also to the pursuit of peace between Japan and the United States. Before the United States Senate Committee on Immigration in 1924, he testified against the Johnson Immigration Bill intended to curtail immigration from Asia, especially from Japan. In a 1938 letter to President Franklin D. Roosevelt and Secretary of State Cordell Hull, he urged the United States not to intervene in Japan's war with China. His strong attachment to the Japanese people was reciprocated by their deep affection for him. He came to be regarded by the Japanese government as one of the most important educators among the missionaries. During the course of his fifty-one years in Japan, he was accorded four imperial awards for his service as an educator. He died in Sendai.

Bibliography. C. W. Mensendiek, *A Man for His Times: The Life and Thought of David Bowman Schneder: Missionary to Japan 1887-1938* (1972).

J. B. Payne

Scholasticism, Reformed. A methodology utilized by Reformed theologians to clarify, explicate and defend their faith. As Presbyterian and Reformed clergy and laity came to America, they brought the Reformed theology that had developed in Europe since the Reformation, and much of their technical theology utilized scholastic methodology and terminology. Because Reformed theologians all used and spoke Latin during the early modern period (1500-1800), they had a common language with which they could communicate throughout the European world and its colonies. Consequently Reformed scholasticism was also espoused by most Protestants in the New World.

Scholastic theology began in the medieval period, a time when scholastic methodology was used not only in theology but also in philosophy. The apogée of medieval scholastic theology and philosophy came with the work of Thomas Aquinas. Martin Luther vehemently denounced scholasticism and the schoolmen as heretics who confused the church and who distorted theology. But Luther's colleague Philip Melanchthon developed an educational system utilizing scholastic tools. The adoption of scholasticism to combat the Council of Trent (1545-1563) was a powerful impulse to use scholastic methods. As a result, Catholics and Protestants continued to be dependent on the medieval synthesis of the Greco-Roman philosophy and Christian theology. Scholars debate whether John *Calvin (1509-1564) was a scholastic or a humanist. After Calvin's death, however, his followers utilized the scholastic methodology in dogmatic theology and polemics against Roman Catholicism.

Reformed scholasticism is characterized by a great stress on the use of reason and logic in theology. Each theological topic was divided into discrete parts ("commonplaces," or *loci communes),* and the parts were defined and analyzed, usually utilizing biblical definitions. Contrary views concerning each of the sections were compared and errors refuted. Then scholastics treated a topic from the perspective of church history. Finally the question was resolved, often using syllogistic reasoning. The rules developed in the medieval period for academic disputation served as a backdrop to the entire exercise. This method relied heavily on the methodology and philosophy of Aristotle. It also tended to use Scripture as a collection of propositional truths detached from their historical setting.

In America the most influential Reformed scholastic theologian in the Presbyterian and Reformed world was Francis *Turretin, professor of theology at Geneva, Switzerland, from 1653 to 1687. His *Institutio Theologiae Elencticae* (1674) was the standard text in most theology classes in Presbyterian seminaries until Charles *Hodge published his *Systematic Theology* (1872-1873).

Reformed scholasticism, while continuing in many seminaries, was finally eclipsed by Protestant liberalism. Some Presbyterian theologians, such as Charles Hodge, tried to synthesize scholastic methodology with the techniques of modern science. Revived interest in scholastic theology and methodology emerged with the ascent of Karl *Barth (1886-1968) and *neo-orthodoxy to the forefront of the theological world in the middle of the twentieth century.

Reformed scholasticism shaped profoundly the development of Christian doctrine during the modern era. Among the topics that flow from it are predestination, the doctrine of Scripture, the *ordo salutis,* assurance, covenant theology, apologetics, the nature of sin, the nature and extent of the atonement, the church and the civil magistrate, baptism (its meaning, modes and subjects), the nature of the Lord's Supper and ecclesiastical *polity. Some have accused Reformed scholasticism of standing in the way of a proper understanding of the Scripture, while others have seen it as a helpful theological tool to explicate and defend biblical faith.

See also Turretin, Francis.

Bibliography. B. G. Armstrong, *Calvinism and the Amyraut Heresy: Protestant Scholasticism and Humanism in Seventeenth-Century France* (1969); J. W. Beardslee III, ed. and trans., *Reformed Dogmatics*

(1965); J. S. Bray, *Theodore Beza's Doctrine of Predestination* (1975); H. Heppe, *Reformed Dogmatics*, foreword by K. Barth (1950); R. T. Kendall, *Calvin and English Calvinism to 1649* (1979); R. A. Muller, *Christ and the Decree: Christology and Predestination in Reformed Theology from Calvin to Perkins* (1986); idem, *Post-Reformation Reformed Dogmatics* (1987) J. Platt, *Reformed Thought and Scholasticism: The Arguments for the Existence ofGod in Dutch Theology, 1575-1650* (1982); F. Turretin, *Institutes of Elenctic Theology*, trans. G. M. Giger and J. T. Dennison, 2 vols. (1992-1994); D. A. Weir, *The Origins of the Federal Theology in Sixteenth-Century Reformation Thought* (1990).

D. A. Weir

Schuller, Robert Harold (1926-).‡ *Reformed Church in America (RCA) minister. Born in Alton, Iowa, Schuller was nurtured in the RCA. He graduated from Hope College (B.A., 1947) and Western Theological Seminary (B.D., 1950) in Holland, Michigan. In June 1950, he married Arvella De Haan and was ordained to the ministry at Ivanhoe Reformed Church in Riverside, a Chicago suburb.

Having accepted a call to begin a mission church in Orange County, southern California, in 1955 and faced with a shortage of places for worship, Schuller decided to rent the Orange Drive-in Theater. After advertising by sign, brochures and newspaper, he held the first service of the Garden Grove Community Church on March 27, 1955. The early years brought little encouragement, but a guest appearance by Norman Vincent *Peale drew more than seventeen hundred cars and six thousand people and boosted the visibility of the church. By 1960 the congregation had grown to seven hundred and required new buildings, including the Tower of Hope (1968) and the Crystal Cathedral, completed in 1980 at a cost of nearly twenty million dollars.

Schuller maintains that he preaches the gospel by recasting it as a positive form that appeals to the desire for a positive self-image. For him the theme of possibility thinking is a modern restatement of the biblical principle of living by faith. Assailed by critics who accuse him of watering down the gospel, Schuller maintains that he is an evangelical with a faithful ministry relevant to modern Americans.

Bibliography. M. Nason and D. Nason, *Robert Schuller* (1983); D. Voskuil, *Mountains into Goldmines: Robert Schuller and the Gospel of Success* (1983).

D. G. Reid

Science, Presbyterians and. From the early 1700s to the present day Presbyterians have had an impact upon American thought, culture and society far beyond their numbers. This is especially true in the realm of science, where Presbyterian clergy, educators and scientists have played a major role in conducting scientific research, articulating a philosophy of science and explicating the relationship between science and religion. At the same time, the methods, principles and conclusions of modern science have profoundly affected the development of Presbyterianism in America.

John *Witherspoon, who emigrated from Scotland in 1768 to assume the presidency of the College of New Jersey (later Princeton), strongly influenced the Presbyterian response to science in the nineteenth century. He espoused Scottish Common-Sense realism as mediated through Francis Bacon's method of induction because he believed it provided intellectual justification for promoting virtue and for defending Christian convictions. Based upon the premise that truths about the world and religion must be grounded upon the facts of experience, this philosophy dominated Protestant thought during the antebellum years, permeating American classrooms and helping to shape the worldview of thousands of ministers, teachers, scientists and physicians. Led by Presbyterians, American Scottish realists adopted a thoroughgoing empiricism, rooted in confidence in the senses and belief that human reason, the natural world and the *Bible are all valid sources of knowledge. Deeply committed to induction, these Presbyterians urged scientists to base their theories solely on facts and argued that scientific explanations must incorporate all data, including that furnished by the Bible.

During the first half of the nineteenth century Presbyterians, like many other evangelical Protestants, were fascinated by natural science, and despite the challenges of new discoveries in geology and biology they remained convinced that scientific data could be reconciled with scriptural truth. Many Presbyterian ministers closely monitored new intellectual and scientific developments, the study of science flourished at many Presbyterian colleges, presbyteries often examined ministerial candidates directly on scientific subjects, and Presbyterian periodicals frequently discussed scientific issues.

Before the *Civil War Samuel *Miller, Archibald *Alexander, Charles *Hodge, Benjamin Morgan *Palmer, James Henley *Thornwell and many other *Old School Presbyterian proponents of Scottish realism contended that Christian conviction is essential to effective scientific research and to proper scientific conclusions. They produced a sophisticated natural theology based upon the proposition that nature displays compelling evidence of God's existence and attributes. Moreover, they applied Bacon's method of induction to the uses of biblical exegesis, penning hundreds of sermons, essays and addresses to present evidences, especially miracles and fulfilled prophecy, for Christianity. Because the Bible was inspired by God and factually accurate, they asserted, its data must be considered in scientific investigations. Through these efforts, Presbyterians developed a doxological science that testified to God's creating and sustaining power and a scientific theology that could be empirically verified. They participated intelligently in the scientific debates of this era, championed a holy alliance between science and religion and significantly influenced evangelical Protestant views of apologetics, natural theology and science.

The publication of Charles Darwin's *Origin of Species* in 1859 and the widespread discussion the book provoked significantly changed the perceived relationship between science and religion in the Anglo-American world. Darwin's apparent emphasis on random natural selection as the mechanism of evolution challenged long-standing Christian belief in teleology. Because some of their leaders were staunch opponents of Darwinism, it has often been assumed that almost all American Presbyterians, especially those connected with Princeton, repudiated organic evolution. In reality the Presbyterian response to Darwinism varied. Some did reject the concept of evolution; others tentatively endorsed it; and still others warmly embraced it.

Those who denounced Darwinism were led by Charles Hodge, Arnold Guyot, John William *Dawson, and numerous Southern Presbyterians, most notably Robert Lewis *Dabney. Hodge, who taught systematic theology at Princeton Theological Seminary from 1822 to 1878, concluded in *What Is Darwinism?* (1874) that it was atheism. Although Hodge rejected Darwinism on scientific grounds, his principal objection to Darwin's theory was that it overthrew the idea of design. He insisted that Darwin, by denying the concept of design in nature and making evolution a material process ruled by chance, had denied the existence of God. Guyot, a professor at Princeton College and America's leading geographer during the mid-nineteenth century, argued in *Creation: or, the Biblical Cosmogony in the Light of Modern Science* (1884) that the seven days of creation should be considered an ideal plan that revealed God's successive and progressive activity. Other Princetonians, however, including Archibald Alexander *Hodge, Francis Landey *Patton and Joseph Van Dyke, and theologian William Greenough Thayer *Shedd of Union Theological Seminary in New York expressed guarded approval of theistic evolution.

Meanwhile, Asa Gray, James *McCosh, George Macloskie, Henry Boynton *Smith and Benjamin Breckinridge *Warfield, among others, firmly supported the idea of evolution. Gray, a Presbyterian who joined a Congregationalist church when he moved to Boston, taught botany at Harvard from 1842 to 1873 and was America's premier botanist and the leading interpreter of Darwin. In many essays and reviews and in *Darwiniana* (1876) Gray labored to show that the mechanism of natural selection did not exclude the concept of design. McCosh, who served as the president of Princeton College from 1868 to 1888, contended in *Christianity and Positivism* (1871) and *The Developmental Hypothesis: Is It Sufficient?* (1876) that evolution was an organized process, guided by God, working toward one final end. In numerous publications McCosh and Macloskie, who taught biology at Princeton, insisted that order, design and beneficence could be observed in Darwin's scheme. Warfield, Princeton Seminary's renowned professor of systematic theology from 1887 to 1921, wrote and lectured widely on evolution, arguing that orderly natural laws are under God's supervision. While expressing some uneasiness about the antiteleological implications of evolutionary theory, he believed that the major tenets of evolution could be reconciled with his understanding of biblical inspiration.

Although disagreeing over the scientific support for Darwinism and over whether Darwin's theory could be reconciled with the traditional argument for design, members of all three of these groups strongly repudiated the various forms of scientific naturalism that emerged in the years following 1870. In general, though, in the years from 1860 to about 1915 many Presbyterians, especially those associated with Princeton, shifted from rejecting or doubting evolution to embracing or at least accommodating themselves to this view. To varying degrees they accepted a long history for the earth, the transmutation of species and the evolutionary development of humanity.

The situation in the Southern Presbyterian Church was quite different. Sharing the antievolutionary sentiment that prevailed much more in the South than in the North, denominational leaders forced James *Woodrow, a professor at Columbia Theological Seminary, from his position in 1886 because he espoused evolution as God's plan of creation. Two years later the communion's general assembly adopted a resolution declaring that "Adam's body was directly fashioned by Almighty God of the dust," and throughout the early years of the twentieth century most of the denomination's pastors, professors and laypeople continued to repudiate all forms of evolution.

Moreover, in the 1920s a reaction against evolution developed among conservative Presbyterians, including some Princetonians. During that decade the *Princeton Theological Review* published numerous articles that denounced evolutionary theory as godless and rehearsed its scientific deficiencies. The impact of various scientific attacks on Darwinism and the frequent association of evolution with higher criticism, with the quest for the historical Jesus and with an account of humans' progressive development from animism to monotheism made J. Gresham *Machen and other leading Presbyterian conservatives ambivalent at best toward the doctrine.

Meanwhile, many Presbyterians, most notably William Jennings *Bryan, participated actively in the crusade against evolution. Deeply concerned about the negative impact of Darwinism on morality and society, Bryan helped to lead a campaign to eliminate the teaching of evolution in the nation's public schools that culminated in the Scopes trial in Dayton, Tennessee, in 1925. The general assembly of the *Presbyterian Church in the U.S.A. (PCUSA, the nation's largest Presbyterian body), however, in 1923 rejected Bryan's request that the communion's judicatories be prohibited from giving funds to any school that taught evolutionary theories. Delegates instead passed a substitute resolution, declaring that the denomination would not approve schools that promoted a "materialistic evolutionary philosophy of life," indicating that the principal PCUSA objection was not to the concept of evolution but rather to scientific materialism.

Since 1930 some liberal Presbyterians have sought to reinterpret the Christian message in light of scientific conclusions, while conservatives continue to assert that a divinely inspired Bible conveys truth in all it discusses and allege that God's revelations in Scripture and nature, when properly understood, agree. Members of both camps have had to struggle with an increasingly positivistic natural science that has declared all religious teaching to be irrelevant to the scientific enterprise. Recently some conservative Presbyterians, including theologian Francis *Schaeffer, pastor James Montgomery Boice, televangelist D. James Kennedy and theonomist Rousas Rushdoony, joined the debate over scientific creationism that grew in intensity and publicity in the 1980s by arguing against evolution.

See also FUNDAMENTALIST-MODERNIST CONTROVERSY; INTELLECTUAL LIFE, PRESBYTERIANS AND.

BIBLIOGRAPHY. T. D. Bozeman, *Protestants in an Age of Science* (1977); A. H. Dupree, *Asa Gray* (1959); B. J. Gundlach, "The Evolution Question at Princeton, 1845-1929" (Ph.D. diss., University of Rochester, 1995); J. D. Hoeveler Jr., *James McCosh and the Scottish Intellectual Tradition: From Glasgow to Princeton* (1981); H. Hovenkamp, *Science and Religion in America, 1800-1860* (1978); J. E. Illick III, "The Reception of Darwinism at the Princeton Theological Seminary and the College at Princeton, New Jersey," *JPHS* 38 (1960) 152-65, 234-43; D. F. Johnson, "The Attitude of the Princeton Theologians Toward Darwinism and Evolution from 1859-1929" (Ph.D. diss., University of Iowa, 1968); D. N. Livingstone, *Darwin's Forgotten Defenders: The Encounter Between Evangelical Theology and Evolutionary Thought* (1987); G. M. Marsden, *The Evangelical Mind and the New School Presbyterian Experience: A Case Study of Thought and Theology in Nineteenth-Century America* (1970); J. R. Moore, *The Post-Darwinian Controversies: A Study of the Protestant Struggle to Come to Terms with Darwin in Great Britain and America, 1870-1900* (1979); W. E. Phipps, "Asa Gray's Theology of Nature," *AP* 66 (fall 1988) 167-75; G. S. Smith, *The Seeds of Secularization: Calvinism, Culture, and Pluralism in America, 1870-1915* (1985); T. W. Street, "The Evolution Controversy in the Southern Presbyterian Church," *JPHS* 37 (1959) 232-50; J. Wells, "Charles Hodge on the Bible and Science," *AP* 66 (fall 1988) 157-65.

G. S. Smith

Scots-Irish and Irish Presbyterians in America. In 1717 a group of passenger ships left the Irish province of Ulster, destined for British North America. Faced with occasional, haphazard persecution from the Anglican Church of Ireland, an increasingly restrictive economic environment and a series of droughts and poor harvests, these mostly Presbyterian emigrants sought greener and gentler pastures in the colonies. Throughout the century they migrated in response to economic distress and famine, with most headed for Pennsylvania, the "Best Poor Man's Country," and Carolina. Between 1717 and 1774, approximately two hundred thousand Ulster emigrants landed.

Scots-Irish colonists were themselves descended from colonists, lowland Scots, primarily from the counties in the west and those on the English border, who had settled in northern Ireland during the first two decades of the seventeenth century. Although not particularly religious, these Scots identified themselves with the Scottish Presbyterian Church founded by John Knox, and in Ireland they were pastored by dissenting Presbyterian clerics who had rejected the rituals of the newly established Anglicanism. Here, in 1625, the Six Mile Water Revival erupted, setting off eight years of religious enthusiasm that swept through the congregations of northern Ireland and western Scotland.

Within a Reformed tradition that valued learning, orthodox knowledge and understanding, this religiosity emphasized one's emotional, experiential connection with God. Through such communal rituals as open-air preaching, fast days, public confession and four- or five-day communion services, individual believers and communities were awakened to a sense of their sins, brought to repentance and led into the joy of union with Christ. While *revivalism may have been part of a conventicle tradition that began in sixteenth-century Scotland, throughout the rest of the seventeenth and eighteenth centuries this culture of *piety flourished and became identified with both Presbyterianism and Scottish nationalism.

While Scottish Presbyterians saw their communion established as the national church in 1690, Ireland's state church remained Anglican, so that Irish Presbyterians continued their precarious existence as dissenters. Congregants thus developed an ability to erect buildings and provide clerical maintenance without the assistance of tithes, while the clergy grew increasingly dependent upon maintaining good congregational relationships in order to sustain church unity and receive their salaries. These financial realities subtly changed the dynamics between clergy and laity, changes reflected in stronger and more insistent lay voices heard at congregational and synodical meetings. Such lessons prepared later generations for the exigencies of constructing churches in British North America.

From the moment that Ulsterman Francis *Makemie founded the first colonial presbytery in 1705, Scots-Irish clergy played a central role in American Presbyterianism. While church membership included significant numbers of Scots as well as many congregations of English settlers originally from *New England, from the 1720s until the *Revolutionary era the Scots-Irish set the agenda. For example, the New Englanders had endorsed a loosely organized ministerial consociation to ordain ministers and advise congregations, yet the Scots-Irish, with the Scots, convinced them to accept a hierarchical, legislative structure of congregation, presbytery, synod and, in 1789, national assembly, one that incorporated laymen at all levels. So too, although the English had a long tradition of refusing to honor any pro forma tests of orthodoxy, they were brought to accept subscription to the *Westminster Confession as a condition of ordination.

However, Irish Presbyterians had their greatest influence on Presbyterian piety. Among the early Irish immigrants was William *Tennent, who in 1726 opened a seminary at Neshaminy. Called the Log College by detractors, its students were prepared in languages, scriptural exegesis and theology. More importantly, Tennent emphasized the need for experiential piety, inculcating in his students a desire for a personal relationship with God.

Large numbers of Scots-Irish immigrants began to arrive in the late 1720s, and the first revivals among the Presbyterians occurred in 1729 in the congregation of Freehold, New Jersey, pastored by John Tennent. Revivals continued sporadically throughout the 1730s, with the Log College graduates, as itinerants, igniting revivalism across the countryside. Those same rituals of open-air preaching, public repentance and long communion services began to flourish as laypeople sought God and salvation. Not surprisingly, when the gifted George Whitefield appeared in 1739, preaching sin, damnation and repentance, the Presbyterian populace was enthusiastic, and the Great Awakening began in earnest. Yet it would be wrong to see Whitefield as the instigator of this enthusiasm. Among Presbyterians, he fueled fires that were already smoldering and then left the blazes to be tended by others in the field. In fact, Gilbert *Tennent was probably the most important of the revivalists. Called by Whitefield a "son of thunder," Tennent gathered congregations around himself and his peers, ardently defended his father's seminary against its detractors and published apologies of the Awakening as well as attacks upon its opponents.

As revivalism spread into English communities most of the congregations and their pastors embraced the Awakening. Some clergy, primarily Scots-Irish, opposed the enthusiasm of revival, particularly its impact upon the laity. Many congregants, excited by experiential piety, grew dissatisfied with pastors who did not support the movement or proved to be less gifted as preachers. They employed a variety of means to further the revivalist cause in their congregations, including persuading unwanted clergy to resign by withholding financial support, bringing charges against pastors in presbyterial courts and seceding from one congregation to organize another under a sympathetic minister. The laity proved immensely successful in their endeavors, prompting clergy to respond to their demands.

Opponents of revivals grew angry at what they saw as pandering to the laity. Believing that itinerants disrupted settled congregations and encouraged congregants to forsake their pastors, antirevivalists attempted to censor and control the advocates of revivals and their followers. In 1741 the church split into the prorevival *New Side Synod of New York and the antirevival *Old Side Synod of Philadelphia. Although these synods initially had roughly the same number of clerical and congregational members, within ten years the overwhelming majority of congregants and ministers were New Light. In 1758 the two synods reunited on terms generally favorable to the revivalists. It is important to note that at the moment of schism, almost all Presbyterians of the English descent were supporters of the Awakening, as were native-born descendants of the Scots-Irish, while Scots-Irish immigrants were evenly divided. Nevertheless the Scots-Irish were significant for first introducing revivalism into the area and remaining enthusiastic backers of the Awakening. They also rewarded the revivalist clergymen and provided clear models for establishing, rationalizing and maintaining the increased participation of laity.

In the 1750s and 1760s, Scots-Irish Presbyterians moved into Virginia and the Carolinas, and, after the Revolution, even further south and west. While the national Presbyterian Church fell under the magisterial influence of the Scots, initially the Scottish president of the College of New Jersey, John *Witherspoon, and discouraged the levels of enthusiasm of the previous generation, Scots-Irish in the west still promoted a lay-empowered, revivalistic culture. The Scots-Irish continued to influence the religious environment of the frontier, frequently within other denominations such as the Baptists and Methodists and despite the protests of an increasingly genteel Eastern clerical culture.

Overall, the Scots-Irish left an important legacy for American Presbyterianism and American Protestantism as a whole. While the democratic structure of the church judicatories, including the involvement of lay representatives, was characteristic of Scotland as well as Ireland, the extensive possibilities for the exercise of lay power were first broached within Ireland and later realized in the British colonies. Emigrants carried a nascent suspicion of clerical leadership and a willingness to reject the guidance of a highly educated clergy, even in matters of theology, if they believed that clerics were resisting the community's religious traditions. They displayed great skill in manipulating pastors and judicatures, skills picked up by other denominations. Additionally, the early abilities of colonial congregations to fend for themselves in frontier environments were first developed in the colonial environment of Ulster. Finally, Scots-Irish immigrants brought to British North America established practices of revivalism and experiential piety, traditions that would inform American evangelical culture for the next four centuries.

Bibliography. J. M. Barkley, *A Short History of the Presbyterian Church in Ireland* (1959); M. J. Coalter Jr., *Gilbert Tennent, Son of Thunder* (1986); N. Landsman, "Revivalism and Nativism in the Middle Colonies: The Great Awakening and the Scots Community in East Jersey," *American Quarterly* 34 (1982) 149-64; J. G. Leyburn, *The Scots-Irish: A Social History* (1962); M. E. Lodge, "The Great Awakening in the Middle Colonies" (Ph.D. diss., University of California, Berkeley, 1964); K. A. Miller, *Emigrants and Exiles* (1985); E. I. Nybakken, "New Light on the Old Side: Irish Influences on Colonial Presbyterianism," *Journal of American History* 68 (1982) 813-32; B. Schlenther, ed., *The Life and Writings of Francis Makemie* (1976); L. E. Schmidt, *Holy Fairs: Scottish Communions and American Revivals in the Early Modern Period* (1991); L. J. Trinterud, *The Forming of an American Tradition* (1949); R. Webster, *A History of the Presbyterian Church in America* (1857); M. J. Westerkamp, *Triumph of the Laity: Scots-Irish Peity and the Great Awakening, 1625-1760* (1988).

M. J. Westerkamp

Scott, William Anderson (1813-1885). Presbyterian pastor and *educator. Born in Rock Creek, Tennessee, Scott became a licensed preacher with the *Cumberland Presbyterian Church (CPC) at age seventeen. He pursued formal education intermittently between 1828 and 1833, graduating in the latter year from Cumberland College in Kentucky. The following year he attended Princeton Seminary, but financial constraints led him to leave after seven months. Ordained by the Cumberland Presbyterians in 1835, he transferred to the *Old School Presbyterian Church in 1838, attracted by their *Calvinist theology and educational ethos. He simultaneously served as principal of the Nashville Female Academy (1838-1840) and pastor of the congregation at Andrew Jackson's Hermitage. His reputation as an urbane pulpiteer increased during pastorates at First Presbyterian in Tuscaloosa, Alabama (1840-1842), and First Presbyterian in New Orleans, Louisiana (1842-1854).

Scott's reputation led to a call to leave the South and pastor Calvary Presbyterian Church in San Francisco (1854-1861). While he was in San Francisco, he became moderator of the Old School general assembly (1858). Also, he was twice hanged in effigy, first when his convictions on the spirituality of the church led him to oppose the San Francisco Committee of Vigilance of 1856, and again when he objected to what he considered church pro-Union partisanship in 1861. He also stirred controversy among regional Protestants by opposing a proposed law to require Bible reading in the public schools (1858). Moreover, he vigorously supported the establishment of Old School institutions in California, founding the *Pacific Expositor* (1859-1862) and City College (1859-1879).

Tired of controversy, Scott resigned from Calvary Church and left for Europe in 1861. He pastored Forty-Second Street Presbyterian Church in New York City (1863-1870) before returning to San Francisco, where still-loyal supporters organized St. John's Presbyterian Church for him. While serving St. John's (1870-1885), he also led in the founding of San Francisco Theological Seminary (1871). The seminary was the culmination of his educational goals for the region; it also expressed his commitment to a newly reunited Presbyterian denomination, the *Presbyterian Church in the U.S.A. (PCUSA). He was a member of the faculty and a director of the institution until his death.

Bibliography. *DAB* VIII; C. M. Drury, *William Anderson Scott* (1967). D. F. Anderson

Scudder, Ida Sophia (1870-1959).† Reared in India, Ida was the granddaughter of Dr. John *Scudder, one of a long line of Scudder medical missionaries to India who served under the *Reformed Church in America (RCA). Initially she scorned the idea of a missionary career for herself, yearning for more of life's luxuries than life in India offered. It was when she visited her parents as a young adult that she became burdened for the women of India who were deprived of medical services due to the lack of female physicians.

Returning to the United States, Scudder studied at Philadelphia Woman's Medical College before earning her medical degree at Cornell Medical College in 1899. Before leaving the United States, she raised more than ten thousand dollars for a women's hospital and for a woman evangelist to work with her. She rejoined her family in India in 1900, and her father died five months later, leaving her as the sole doctor in a culture that refused women doctors. Within a year people had softened, and she eventually established a medical complex at Vellore that included a clinic, a hospital and the Christian Medical School (1918), established to train women doctors to meet the vast medical needs of India. In all her efforts, Scudder worked closely with Annie Hancock, an evangelist who made contacts with patients after they left the clinic and hospital. Eventually the school became a university, and in 1947 it began to train men as well as women. In her Christian faith and service Scudder was an outstanding missionary of the twentieth century.

Bibliography. *ANB* 19; *NAWMP;* D. C. Wilson, *Dr. Ida: The Story of Dr. Ida Scudder of Vellore* (1959). R. A. Tucker

Scudder, John, Sr. (1793-1855).† Medical *missionary. After graduating from the College of New Jersey in 1811 and the New York College of Physicians and Surgeons in 1815, Scudder entered private practice in New York. The reading of a tract entitled "The Conversion of the World" so inspired Scudder that he committed himself to missions. In 1819 he and his wife left for Ceylon under the American Board of Commissioners for Foreign Missions. On Ceylon he founded a hospital and several schools. He was the first American foreign medical missionary. Himself a member of the *Dutch Reformed Church, he was ordained by a Congregationalist, a Methodist and a Baptist in 1821.

In 1835 Scudder moved to Madras, India, where he established one of the first medical missions in India, as well as a printing operation for publication of tracts and Tamil Bible translations. Preaching and healing extensively throughout the region, he himself became ill and exhausted. Following a period of service back in the United States (1842-1846), he moved to Chintodrepettah, near Madras, where he founded the Arcot mission. In 1852 this operation came under the care of the American board and later of the (Dutch) *Reformed Church in America.

Failing health led to a trip to South Africa, where Scudder died of a stroke at Wynberg. The Scudders had thirteen children, nine of whom lived to adulthood. Of these, seven became medical missionaries and pastors in India. Within three Scudder generations forty-three family members gave more than eleven hundred years of missionary service.

Bibliography. *AAP* 9; *ANB* 19.

G. J. Bekker

Shedd, William Greenough Thayer (1820-1894).† Presbyterian theologian and church historian. A sixth-generation descendant of Massachusetts *Puritans, Shedd appropriated many of the leading intellectual trends of the nineteenth century without sacrificing a commitment to Reformed orthodoxy. His speculative interests in Romanticism, historical consciousness and evolution made him remarkably sensitive to the powerful new thinking of his century. Yet Shedd did not create any controversy, for his firm, *Old School *Calvinist faith was never altered by his novel speculations.

While a student at the University of Vermont (B.A., 1839), Shedd was profoundly influenced by his philosophy professor, James Marsh. Thereafter his thinking reflected an intimate familiarity with the leading luminaries of European Romanticism. Upon his graduation from Andover Theological Seminary (B.D., 1843), Shedd served a Congregational church in Brandon, Vermont (1843-1845), and later he was copastor with Gardiner *Spring at the Brick Presbyterian Church in New York City (1862-1863). But his pastoral labors were brief, less than four years in all. The greater part of his career was devoted to teaching. His diversified appointments included seven years as professor of English literature at Vermont (1845-1852), two years as professor of sacred rhetoric at Auburn Theological Seminary (1852-1854) and eight years as professor of church history at Andover (1854-1862). In 1863 he was called to replace the late Edward Robinson as professor of New Testament literature at Union Theological Seminary in New York, beginning an affiliation with that institution that would continue for twenty-eight years. After 1874 he served as professor of systematic theology, succeeding Henry Boynton *Smith. His staunch defense of traditional Reformed understandings of original sin and the atonement were something of an anomaly among the Congregationalists of New England and New York, where the New Divinity was already giving way to liberalism. In 1862 he transferred his ministerial credentials to the Old School Presbyterian Church.

One of the eminent theologians of his era, Shedd exhibited literary gifts, historical interests and a speculative spirit in his many works, including a *History of Christian Doctrine* (1863), *Orthodoxy and Heterodoxy* (1893) and *Dogmatic Theology* (1889-1894). He was also known for his pastoral writings, such as *Sermons to the Natural Man* (1871) and *Sermons to the Spiritual Man* (1884). While developing a more Romantic understanding of history, he remained a great advocate of Baconianism and its inductive reasoning, arguing that purely naturalistic evolution was unscientific because it lacked sufficient evidence and could not adequately explain the facts. As an Old School Presbyterian he opposed any revision of the *Westminster standards, insisting that the confession's basic teachings were the teachings of Scripture and could not be softened without rejecting its Calvinism. Shedd was convinced that advances in theological understanding must always build upon the past. His progressive theology refused to break with traditional Calvinism but rather sought to develop it further in its organic wholeness. He actively opposed his colleague at Union, Charles Augustus *Briggs, who was attempting to introduce the higher-critical methods of German biblical scholarship, joining William Henry *Green and other faculty at Princeton Theological Seminary in their successful challenge to Briggs's efforts. He resigned due to failing health in 1893.

Bibliography. *ANB* 19; S. H. J. DeWitt, "William Greenough Thayer Shedd," *Presbyterian and Reformed Review* 21 (1895) 295-322; *DAB* IX; G. S. Smith, *The Seeds of Secularization: Calvinism, Culture, and Pluralism in America, 1870-1915* (1985); C. Strout, "Faith and History: The Mind of William G. T. Shedd," *JHI* 15 (1954) 153-62.

S. R. Pointer

Sherrill, Lewis Joseph (1882-1957).† Presbyterian *educator. Born and educated in Texas, Sherrill received the bachelor of arts degree from Austin College (1916) and, after serving in World War I, received his basic theological training at the Presbyterian Theological Seminary of Kentucky in Louisville. Married in 1921 immediately after graduation, he accepted a call to the First Presbyterian Church of Covington, Tennessee. Four years later Sherrill returned to Louisville as professor of religious education. Except for a leave to earn his doctorate at Yale (Ph.D., 1929), Sherrill spent the remainder of his career teaching at Louisville (1925-1950) and at Union Theological Seminary in New York (1950-1957).

Sherrill's major books include *Religious Education in the Small Church* (1932), *Guilt and Redemption* (1945) and *The Struggle of the Soul* (1951). These volumes reflect his changing theology of Christian experience. Originally viewing Christian nurture as the natural complement of evangelism, Sherrill came to believe that the process of Christian growth was more important than any single conversion experience. His preoccupation with process and his reliance on contemporary theories of depth psychology caused Sherrill to develop a view of Christian education that moved away from evangelical *revivalism. Rather than a humanistic liberalism, though, Sherrill's eclectic work demonstrated an appreciation for Reinhold *Niebuhr's theology of crisis.

In addition to his teaching and writing, Sherrill served as dean of Louisville Seminary (1930-1950) and as executive secretary (1935-1938) and president (1938-1940) of the American Association of Theological Schools. A popular preacher and lecturer, Sherrill emphasized the importance of the church as a transforming community in the Christian's growth in grace.

Bibliography. R. W. Fairchild, "The Contribution of Lewis Sherrill to Christian Education," *RelEd* 53 (1958) 403-10; L. B. Weeks, "Lewis Sherrill: Christian Educator," *JPH* 51 (1973) 235-48.

D. M. Strong

Shields, Charles Woodruff (1825-1904). Presbyterian minister and *educator. Born in New Albany, Indiana, to James Read, a Presbyterian minister, and Hannah Woodruff Shields, Shields graduated from the College of New Jersey (now Princeton University) in 1844 and Princeton Theological Seminary in 1847. After supplying several pulpits, he was ordained in 1849 as the pastor of the Presbyterian Church in Hempstead, Long Island, an *Old School congregation. In 1850 he became pastor of the prestigious Second Presbyterian Church in Philadelphia. Because of long-standing personality conflicts with certain members of his congregation, several friends endowed a chair for him at his alma mater, where he could better pursue his intellectual interests and be of more use to the church. In 1861 he became the professor of the harmony of science and revealed religion at Princeton College, where he remained until his death. It was the first faculty position at an American college specifically devoted to this subject. Shields was twice married: in 1848 to Charlotte Elizabeth Bain, who died in 1853, and in 1861 to Elizabeth Kane.

Shields devoted his entire academic career to expanding the seminal ideas first expressed in the pamphlet *Philosophia Ultima* (1861). In the *Final Philosophy* (1877), Shields, like other late-nineteenth-century educators, depicted the relationship between science and religion as one of unceasing conflict. Unlike others, however, it was a conflict that he proposed to resolve. He offered a final philosophy tethered between the extremes represented by the positivism of Comte and the absolutism of Hegel to serve as an "umpire" between science and religion. Upon the epistemology of Scottish Common-Sense Realism and armed with the Baconian method, Shields attempted to preserve the harmony between science and religion. Any conflict between the two realms, Shields argued, was "not because of any actual disagreement between natural facts and revealed truths, not even because of any essential defects in our instruments of knowledge, but simply because of some wrong induction from nature or some false interpretation of Scripture." In two subsequent volumes, *Philosophia Ultima* (1888-1905), Shields attempted to incorporate recent scientific discoveries into his natural theology and evidences for Christianity.

Alongside his academic pursuits, Shields had growing personal interest in finding some common ground for union among orthodox Protestant churches. In 1864 he published *Liturgia Expurgata, or the Book of Common Prayer Amended According to the Presbyterian Revision of 1661* and in 1893 the Presbyterian *Book of Common Prayer.* He created a brief controversy among Presbyterians in Princeton when he was ordained deacon of the Protestant Episcopal Church in 1898 and a priest in 1899.

Bibliography. *DAB* XVII; H. W. Rankin, "Charles Woodruff Shields and the Unity of Science," *Princeton Theological Review* 8 (1915) 49-91; W. M. Sloane, "Charles Woodruff Shields," *Philosophia Ultima,* vol. 3 (1905).

P. C. Kemeny

Shriver, Donald Wood, Jr. (1927-). Presbyterian theologian, *educator and minister. Born in Norfolk, Virginia, Shriver was educated at Davidson College (B.A., 1951), Union Theological Seminary in Virginia (B.D., 1955), Yale University (S.T.M., 1957) and Harvard University (Ph.D., 1963).

Ordained to the ministry in 1955, Shriver commenced his educational and pastoral ministry in the South. He was a Southern Presbyterian pastor at the Linwood Presbyterian Church in Gastonia, North Carolina, from 1956 to 1959. He served as university minister and professor of religion at North Carolina State in Raleigh from 1963 to 1972, where he also directed the program on science and sociology. In 1972 he accepted a position at Emory University in Atlanta as professor of ethics and society. Since 1975 he has been president of Union Theological Seminary in New York, where he also serves as the William E. Dodge professor of applied Christianity.

As a Christian ethicist, Shriver's research and writings reflect his interest in history and ethics, religion and society, science and society, and urban policy. His published works include *How Do You Do and Why* (1966), *Rich Man Poor Man* (with Dean D.

Knudsen and John R. Earle, 1972), *Spindles and Spires* (with Karl A. Ostrom, 1976), *Is There Hope for the City?* (1977), *The Social Ethics of the Lord's Prayer* (1980), *The Gospel, the Church and Social Change* (1980), *The Lord's Prayer* (1983), *Redeeming the City* (1982), *The Unsilent South* (editor, 1965) and *Medicine and Religion* (1979).

BIBLIOGRAPHY. R. T. Handy, *A History of Union Theological Seminary in New York* (1987); *Who's Who in America, 1988-1989,* vol. 2; *Who's Who in Religion, 1992-1993.* F. Heuser Jr.

Simonton, Ashbel Green (1833-1867).† Presbyterian *missionary. Born in West Hanover, Pennsylvania, near Harrisburg, Simonton was named for a distinguished clergyman and chaplain to Congress, Ashbel *Green. After graduating from the College of New Jersey (1852) he taught for eighteen months in Mississippi and briefly considered a legal career before studying at Princeton Theological Seminary (B.D., 1858), where under the preaching of Charles *Hodge he responded to the call to missionary service. The *Presbyterian Church in the U.S.A. (PCUSA, *Old School) ordained him, and in 1859 he became the first Presbyterian missionary in Brazil, under the Presbyterian board of foreign missions.

Settling in Rio de Janeiro, Simonton spent the first year mastering Portuguese and making initial contacts. In 1860 he held his first Portuguese service, and he spent much of his first four years struggling for religious toleration of Protestants, including legal recognition of Protestant marriages, which was obtained in 1863. He founded Brazil's first Presbyterian church in 1862, with only two members, but it grew quickly, in spite of constant opposition from the Catholic church. Simonton also founded an evangelical newspaper, the *Imprensa Evangelica,* in 1864 and, in cooperation with other Presbyterians, engaged in extensive evangelistic campaigns throughout the country. In 1865 he and two other missionaries organized the first presbytery in Brazil, ordaining an ex-Catholic priest as the first native minister, and two years later he founded the first Protestant seminary in that country. His wife, Helen Murdoch, shared his mission work for a short time before she died in giving birth to their only child. Simonton himself died of yellow fever at the age of thirty-seven.

BIBLIOGRAPHY. P. S. Landes, *Ashbel Green Simonton* (1956). J. M. Smylie

Skinner, Thomas Harvey, Jr. (1820-1892). Presbyterian minister and theological *educator. Skinner studied at Yale and the University of New York (B.A. 1840), then served in various pastorates from 1843 until 1881, when he was appointed to the faculty of McCormick Seminary. There he served as professor of didactic and polemical theology from 1881 until 1891 and as professor of divinity until his death. Though he was the son of one of the founders of Union Seminary in New York and thoroughly trained in the *New School traditions, Skinner was a consistent advocate of *Old School Presbyterianism. In one of the early postreunion heresy trials in the ongoing conflict between New and Old School, Skinner led disciplinary proceedings against William C. McCune in 1877 in Cincinnati. His Old School views brought him to the attention of the McCormick family, who supported his call to the Chicago seminary in 1881. His teaching career was marked by a heavy reliance on seventeenth-century *Puritan writers and an intense interest in *missions. Skinner's allies at McCormick, Western and Princeton stood firmly against any forms of biblical higher criticism. At McCormick, Skinner's successors showed a greater willingness to appropriate contemporary methods in the discussion of theology and biblical studies.

BIBLIOGRAPHY. L. Halsey, *History of McCormick Theological Seminary in the Presbyterian Church* (1893); L. A. Loetscher, *The Broadening Church: A Study of Theological Issues in the Presbyterian Church Since 1869* (1954); A. Nevin, ed., *Encyclopedia of the Presbyterian Church* (1884).
K. S. Sawyer

Slavery. *See* ABOLITION, PRESBYTERIANS AND.

Smith, Asa Dodge (1804-1877). Presbyterian minister and *educator. Smith was born in Amherst, New Hampshire, the son of a doctor. Originally apprenticed as a printer, Smith only slowly acquired a classical education and was finally graduated by Dartmouth College in 1830. He taught briefly before entering Andover Theological Seminary (1831-1834). In 1834 he was ordained by the predominantly *New School Third Presbytery of New York City and installed as the minister of the Brainerd (after 1851, the Fourteenth Street) Presbyterian Church in New York. He served this congregation for twenty-nine years. During this time it became one of the largest and most important congregations in the city. In addition to his pastoral work, he served Union Theological Seminary in New York as a trustee (1841-1864). He also served on several denominational and interdenominational boards, including the American Board of Commissioners of Foreign Missions (ABCFM) and the American Home Missionary Society (AHMS).

In 1863 Smith was elected president of Dartmouth College at a time when the fortunes of the school were low. His tact and energetic fundraising quickly restored public confidence. Like other Protestant evangelical scholars of his era, Smith believed in the harmony of biblical revelation and the results of scientific discovery. He eventually doubled the college's attendance and added two new departments and several new buildings to the campus, but he made no changes in the traditional classical curriculum. Smith's health broke in 1876. He resigned the presidency only a few months before his death.

Bibliography. *DAB* IX; L. B. Richardson, *History of Dartmouth College*, 2 vols. (1932).

K. J. Ross

Smith, Henry Boynton (1815-1877).† Presbyterian theologian and educator. Born of Unitarian parents in Portland, Maine, Smith attended Bowdoin College (1834), where as a senior he was converted during a revival. He later prepared for the ministry by spending a year each at Andover and Bangor seminaries. After teaching at Bowdoin for a year, he studied in Germany from 1838 to 1840, where he was heavily influenced by German philosophy and theology, especially that of Georg W. F. Hegel and the mediating theology of Friedrich A. G. Tholuck, E. W. Hengstenberg and Johann A. W. Neander. He returned to Bowdoin, but in 1842 he was ordained as the pastor of the Congregational church in West Amesbury, Massachusetts, where he remained until 1847. He married Elizabeth Lee Allen (daughter of Bowdoin's president) in 1843, and from 1845 to 1847 he taught occasionally at Andover Seminary. Smith was appointed professor of mental and moral philosophy at Amherst College in 1847, but after vigorously challenging the views of Horace Bushnell in 1849, he was invited to become professor of church history at Union Theological Seminary in New York City in 1850. Here he spent the rest of his career as a professor, later switching to the chair of systematic theology (1854-1874), and also librarian.

Smith exercised his greatest influence through his efforts to reconcile the principles of Edwardsean theology and German-inspired philosophy for an American audience. As a historian, he encouraged the teaching of the history of doctrine and discussed the nature of historical progress, consciously modeling himself on German historical thought but also on Jonathan *Edwards's *History of the Work of Redemption.* As a theologian, he disagreed sharply with Bushnell's dismissal of theology as an enterprise irrelevant to faith. However, he conceded that New England theology had wasted its energies on abstractions, and he shifted the center of his theological attention away from freedom of the will and other Edwardsean questions to christology as the only way to stave off rationalism.

Smith was a major factor in the *New School's move away from the speculative emphases of the New England theology toward a christocentric model. Wanting to affirm traditional Reformed theology while avoiding the dangers of falling into a mechanistic system, Smith agreed with the classical Protestant *scholastics in positing God as the principle of being and Scripture as the principle of knowledge, but he insisted that Christ is to be seen as the "constructive principle," the center around which all theology revolves. He refused, however, to follow the trend in most German theology to let christology become the determinative doctrine from which all other doctrines are deduced. Arguing that God's decrees must be seen in the light of the incarnation, he saw the covenant theology of the seventeenth century as a reminder to dogmaticians of the historical and organic nature of the sovereign plan of God. Smith remained an orthodox and conservative Reformed theologian who did not desire revision in theology but renewal based on constructive dialogue and critical appropriation of the best in contemporary German thinking.

At Union, Smith transferred his ministerial credentials to the Presbyterian Church (New School), and he became deeply involved in the affairs of his new denomination. Selected moderator of the New School general assembly in 1863, Smith sought to reestablish ties with the *Old School Presbyterians. A significant force behind the reunion of 1869, Smith vigorously defended the orthodoxy of the New School, and his movement back toward traditional *Calvinism softened the fears of many in the Old School, like Charles *Hodge (who still remained mildly opposed), convincing the majority that the New School had successfully eliminated the *Arminian errors of the New Divinity.

Smith disseminated his vision for theology and the church as editor of the *American Theological Review* (later the *American Presbyterian Theological Review* and other titles) from 1859 to 1874. In 1864, through the *Review,* he chastised the British government and the press—secular as well as religious—for their refusal to support the Union during the *Civil War. He took the *North British Review,* the organ of the Free Church of Scotland, to task for Southern sympathies, responding to British charges that the United States was a failed experiment in democracy.

His essays on the New England theology, as collected in *Faith and Philosophy* (1877), are among the most prescient examples of theological criticism in nineteenth-century Calvinism. His lecture notes were published posthumously by W. S. Karr as *Introduction to Christian Theology* (1883), *Apologetics* (1885) and *System of Christian Theology* (1886). Retiring in 1874 due to a prolonged illness, he died three years later at the age of sixty-two.

Bibliography. *ANB* 20; *DAB* IX; B. Kuklick, *Churchmen and Philosophers: From Jonathan Edwards to John Dewey* (1985); R. A. Muller, "Henry Boynton Smith: Christocentric Theologian," *JPH* 61,4 (1983) 429-44; S. Stearns, *Henry Boynton Smith* (1892).

A. C. Guelzo

Smith, Henry Preserved (1847-1927).‡ Presbyterian minister and *educator. Born in Troy, Ohio, Smith attended Amherst College (B.A., 1869) and studied theology at Lane Theological Seminary in Cincinnati and at the University of Berlin. In 1874 Smith taught church history for one year at Lane Seminary before becoming professor of Hebrew. He returned to Germany to study at the University of Leipzig from 1876 to 1877 to prepare more adequately for his new duties at Lane. His efforts were rewarded with his appointment as professor of Old Testament, a position he held until 1893.

Smith's scholarship questioned received understandings of biblical infallibility. Although he rarely published these ideas, Smith defended Charles Augustus *Briggs, a leading protagonist of the new biblical scholarship, before the Presbyterian general assembly of 1891. Alarmed by his remarks, the Presbytery of Cincinnati tried Smith for heresy, found him guilty of denying the verbal inspiration and inerrancy of the Bible, and in 1892 suspended him from the ministry. His views were subsequently published in *Inspiration and Inerrancy* (1893).

In 1898 Smith became professor of biblical literature at Amherst College. In 1907 he moved to Meadville Theological Seminary to teach the history of religions, and from 1915 to 1925 he served as librarian at New York's Union Theological Seminary. Among his publications in Old Testament studies were *A Critical and Exegetical Commentary on the Books of Samuel* (1899), *Old Testament History* (1903) and *The Religion of Israel* (1914).

Bibliography. *ANB* 20; *DAB* IX; *DARB;* M. A. Noll, *Between Faith and Criticism: Evangelicals, Scholarship, and the Bible in America* (1986); *NCAB* 23.

D. G. Hart

Smith, Oswald J(effrey) (1889-1986).† Presbyterian minister and *missionary statesman. A native of rural Ontario, Smith was converted at age sixteen under the ministry of R. A. Torrey. His decision to become a missionary was thwarted as the *Presbyterian Church of Canada repeatedly rejected him as a candidate on academic and health grounds. He turned to preaching and personal evangelism in western Canada and Alaska, including a year of evangelism and teaching among the Native Americans, before returning for further training at Toronto Bible College (graduate, 1912) and McCormick Theological Seminary in Chicago (B.D., 1915). While he was at McCormick, he pastored a Presbyterian church with great success.

Ordained in 1915, Smith returned as an assistant pastor to his home congregation, the second largest Presbyterian church in Canada, Dale Presbyterian Church in Toronto. The next year he became interim pastor, but his evangelistic and missionary zeal, combined with his preference for gospel songs over traditional hymns, did not sit well with his congregation, and he resigned. Smith started a church in a Toronto YMCA, and in 1921 merged it with a struggling Christian and Missionary Alliance church. Anxious to promote missions, Smith began traveling overseas in 1924, returning home to raise funds and recruit missionaries. In 1928 he began The People's Church, a large, independent, mission-oriented church in downtown Toronto. A powerful preacher, Smith was a leading figure in Canadian *fundamentalism who wrote thirty-five books and had more than one hundred of his poems set to music.

Bibliography. L. Neely, *Fire in His Bones: The Official Biography of Oswald J. Smith* (1982).

D. M. Lewis

Smith, Samuel Stanhope (1751-1819). Presbyterian minister and *educator. Smith was born in Pequea, Pennsylvania. His father, Robert, was an able preacher, an ardent patriot and a long-time trustee of the College of New Jersey (later Princeton University). His mother, Elizabeth (née Blair), was the daughter of a Presbyterian *revivalist and teacher. Smith excelled at his father's academy and at Princeton, where he graduated in 1769 as one of the first students to benefit fully from the teaching of John *Witherspoon. Smith especially took to heart Witherspoon's effort to show the common-sense rationality of supernatural religion; he did not absorb as much of the old Scot's traditional *piety. After his graduation, Smith tutored at Princeton and helped in his father's church. In 1773 he accepted a call to itinerate in Virginia, where he was immediately successful as a preacher. He actively supported Virginia's independence in the *Revolutionary War, and soon he was involved in educational activities, especially the founding of Hampden-Sydney College. In 1779 Smith was recalled to Princeton as professor of moral philosophy. He succeeded his father-in-law as president in 1795 and remained in Princeton after his retirement (1812) until his death. Smith was a major figure—a powerful orator along classical rather than revivalistic lines and the most systematic philosopher in the early history of American Presbyterianism.

Smith's significance as a thinker arose from the way he tried to unite traditional *Calvinist faith with both the scientific precepts of the Scottish Enlightenment and the *political republicanism of the new nation. As a preacher, Smith was a model of eloquence who stressed the gospel's compatibility with the finest precepts of modern reason more than its supernatural power. His reliance on common-sense morality led him to abandon traditional Calvinistic teachings, like the internal testimony of the Spirit to Scripture and the bondage of the human will to a sinful nature. Smith's ideas earned him the respect of many students but the suspicion of conservative ministers.

Bibliography. *ANB* 20; F. Beasley, "An Account of the Life and Writings of the Reverend Samuel Stanhope Smith," with Smith's *Sermons* (1821); M. A. Noll, *Princeton and the Republic, 1768-1822: The Search for a Christian Enlightenment in the Era of Samuel Stanhope Smith* (1989); *Princetonians 1769-1775* (1980); D. Sloan, *The Scottish Enlightenment and the American College Ideal* (1971); S. S. Smith, *An Essay on the Causes of the Variety of Complexion and Figure in the Human Species* (1810); idem, *Lectures . . . on the Subjects of Moral and Political Philosophy* (1812).

M. A. Noll

Smith, Wilbur M(oorehead) (1894-1976). Presbyterian *fundamentalist *educator. Born in Chicago to parents who were personal friends of the early fundamentalist leaders, Smith studied at the Moody Bible Institute for one year (1913-1914) and then at the College of Wooster (Ohio) for three years after that, but he earned no academic degrees. He left Wooster in 1917 to assist the pastor of the West Presbyterian Church in Wilmington, Delaware. For the next twenty years Smith pastored Presbyterian congregations in Maryland, Virginia and Pennsylvania.

From 1937 to 1947, Smith taught at the Moody Bible Institute. In 1947 he helped design Fuller Theological Seminary and then joined its faculty. He departed in 1963 following a controversy over biblical inerrancy, but he was recruited to serve half-time at the Trinity Evangelical Divinity School. Smith finally retired from teaching in 1971.

Smith was a very popular Bible lecturer and a tireless author. He wrote more than two dozen books, several hundred short magazine pieces and pamphlets and thirty-eight annual volumes (1934-1971) of *Peloubet's Select Notes on the International Bible Lessons for Christian Living.* Smith served on the revision committee of the Scofield Reference Bible from 1954 to 1963, and he was at one time or another a contributing editor or columnist for *The Sunday School Times, Moody Monthly, Revelation, Bibliotheca Sacra, His* and *Christianity Today.* Smith's love of books (twenty-five thousand in his personal library) and bibliographic talents were without peer in the fundamentalist-evangelical movement of the mid-twentieth century. As a champion of scholarship among fundamentalists, he was an inspiration to a younger generation of scholars who sought to reform fundamentalism.

Bibliography. G. M. Marsden, *Reforming Fundamentalism: Fuller Seminar and the New Evangelicalism* (1987); W. M. Smith, *Before I Forget* (1971).

J. A. Carpenter

Smith, William Robertson (1846-1894). Scottish biblical scholar and mediator to the English-speaking world of Continental assumptions and methods of Old Testament criticism. Born in Aberdeenshire, Smith was educated in Scotland and Germany before assuming the Hebrew post at the Aberdeen Free Church College in 1870 at the precocious age of twenty-three. His subsequent academic career was unusually turbulent and influential.

Smith wrote a series of articles for the ninth edition of the *Encyclopaedia Britannica* in which he expounded the Wellhausen interpretation of the Pentateuch as a composite document and Israel's law and cultus as the culmination of naturalistic evolution. Smith's article on the Bible (1875) specifically precipitated considerable controversy. A subsequent *EB* article on "Hebrew Language and Literature" (1880) added to the debates. Brilliant, articulate and pugnacious, Smith continued both to affirm evangelical conviction and to argue that his view of the Old Testament made it more, rather than less, credible. Though his views were never officially declared heretical, in 1881 he was removed from his chair at the Free Church College.

The extended controversy associated with the Smith case intrigued and educated the public. Smith's lecture series before huge audiences in Glasgow and Edinburgh were published for wider circulation as *The Old Testament and the Jewish Church* (1881) and *The Prophets of Israel* (1882). The protracted debates were a turning point in the popularization of the newer views in the English-speaking world, and nowhere outside of Scotland were developments followed with more interest than in the United States, especially among Presbyterians. Under Charles Augustus *Briggs's editorship, for example, the *Presbyterian Review* published from 1881 to 1883 an extended colloquium of eight major articles evaluating the Smith affair and the implications of his views for the faith and future of the church.

Smith influenced the course of biblical criticism in American Presbyterianism in at least three ways. First, he fostered among the clergy and laity both an awareness of issues in higher criticism and a climate of plausibility for his reconstructed understanding of the Old Testament since he appeared to blend his critical views with an intact evangelical reverence for the Bible. Second, Smith exercised a direct and personal influence on Briggs (of Union Seminary in New York), an important voice in Presbyterian circles. Third, advocates of conservative Old Testament scholarship and theology recognized Smith as a worthy opponent and a serious threat to orthodoxy. His case and the issues he raised compelled such senior American scholars as Francis Landey *Patton, William Henry *Green and Benjamin Breckinridge *Warfield to stake out and defend more conservative positions. In this sense Smith served as an early catalyst for debates about theology and the Bible that would ultimately divide American Presbyterianism.

Following his deposition from the Free Church of Scotland, Smith became a coeditor of the *Encyclopaedia Britannica* (1881) and moved south to a series of prestigious teaching positions at Cambridge University. There his growing interest in the emerging field of comparative religious studies found expression in *Kinship and Marriage in Early Arabia* (1885) and *Lectures on the Religion of the Semites* (1889; 2d ed., 1894). His fundamental assumption of immanent development, what he called "the organic unity of all history," became a paradigm for interpreting and understanding the history of all religious behavior and institutions. On this point Smith's influence extended to Emile Durkheim, Sigmund Freud and Smith's protege, Sir James Frazer, author of *The Golden Bough*. Smith died in Cambridge after a protracted illness.

Bibliography. W. M. Bailey, "William Robertson Smith and American Biblical Studies," *JPH* 51 (1980) 285-308; T. O. Beidelman, *W. Robertson Smith and the Sociological Study of Religion* (1974); J. S. Black and G. W. Crystal, *The Life of William Robertson Smith* (1912); *DSCHT; HHMBI*; R. R. Nelson, *The Life and Thought of William Robertson Smith* (1980). G. G. Scorgie

Smyth, Thomas (1808-1873).† Southern Presbyterian minister. Born in Belfast, Ireland, Smyth spent his youth in northern Ireland and began his higher education at Belfast College (1827-1829), where he took the highest prize. In 1829 he entered Highbury College, London, where he continued his studies in classics and theology. Due to financial setbacks, his family immigrated to the United States, and he continued his theological education at Princeton Theological Seminary (1830-1831). Ordained in 1831, he became pastor of Second Presbyterian Church in Charleston, South Carolina, where he remained the rest of his life.

Smyth was famous as a scholarly pastor, amassing one of the largest private collections of theological books in the United States, containing more than twenty thousand volumes. A staunch *Old School Presbyterian, Smyth wrote a number of theological works, many of them polemical. The majority of these were in the area of ecclesiology. His love of scholarship induced him to leave an endowment for the Smyth Lectureship at Columbia Theological Seminary, where he also left the majority of his library. An ardent Confederate, he saw the early Northern defeats in the Civil War as evidence of divine judgment and predicted a speedy victory for the South. He supported the foundation of the Perkins Professorship of Natural Science in Connection with Revelation at Columbia Seminary in 1859, believing that the pursuit of science could not ultimately compromise the Christian faith. His *Complete Works* have been collected in ten volumes (1908-1912).

Bibliography. *ANB* 20; *DAB* IX; T. Smyth, *Autobiographical Notes, Letters and Reflections* (1914). J. R. Wiers

Social Reform, Presbyterians and. Several aspects of their heritage and theology suggest that Presbyterians might have been likely to play a leading role in the persistent Christian attempt to reform American institutions and cultural practices. Their forebears did much to shape the political, economic and social life of Protestant Europe and colonial America in the years before 1776. John *Calvin, John Knox and the

*Puritans labored diligently to create Christian commonwealths in Switzerland, Scotland, England and America during the sixteenth and seventeenth centuries and profoundly influenced the development of government and society on both sides of the Atlantic. *Calvinism's emphasis on God's sovereignty over all countries, obedience to the law of God, the doctrine of calling and civic duty strongly affected the cultural life of these and other nations. Max Weber and R. H. Tawney have argued that Calvinism generated an ideology and inspired a set of business practices that contributed significantly to the rise of *capitalism. Robert Merton has contended that Reformed belief in an orderly universe subject to the laws of its Creator helped to give birth to modern science. H. Richard *Niebuhr has insisted that Calvinism, more than other theological tradition, has taught that Christ is the transformer of culture.

Despite this theological and historical heritage, however, Presbyterians have generally not been in the forefront of efforts to reform American culture and to remedy the nation's social ills. Their conservatism, their concentration on defending biblical orthodoxy, promoting scholarship, saving souls and producing intellectually sophisticated sermons, and in many cases, their privileged socioeconomic status, premillennialism, insulation from social problems and stress on moral issues (sabbath observance, gambling, card playing, etc.) all limited Presbyterian participation in campaigns to redeem American society. Nevertheless, Presbyterians played a larger role in shaping American public life and in helping to achieve specific reforms than is usually recognized. Through their advocacy of the American *Revolution, participation in antebellum reform movements, involvement in varied social gospel crusades during the years from 1880 to 1925 and social activism during the second half of the twentieth century Presbyterians promoted many positive social changes.

During the eighteenth century America's largest Presbyterian denomination, the *Presbyterian Church in the U.S.A. (PCUSA), founded numerous *educational institutions, strongly supported the American Revolution and, through the constitution and organizational structure it adopted in 1788, influenced the foundation and form of the new United States government. Especially significant Presbyterian proponents of independence were Benjamin *Rush, a Pennsylvania physician, David Caldwell, a North Carolina pastor, and John *Witherspoon, the president of the College of New Jersey. Witherspoon served several terms in the Continental Congress, stirred sentiment for revolt through a sermon preached to the Congress in May 1776 and was the only clergyman to sign the Declaration of Independence. In May 1775 Presbyterians in Charlotte, North Carolina, adopted the Mecklenburg Resolves, which challenged the authority of George III and the British Parliament to enact laws for America and enumerated some of the same grievances as did the Declaration of Independence. Many Presbyterian ministers promoted the American cause from their pulpits, and some of them organized regiments and led them into battle.

During the antebellum years Presbyterians worked closely with other Protestants to create a wide array of interdenominational organizations whose members distributed Bibles and tracts, promoted education, peace, prison reform, temperance, sabbath observance and home and foreign *missions, aided sailors, the insane, domestic servants and the poor, and labored to *abolish slavery. During the first half of the nineteenth century Presbyterians founded, administered and taught in hundreds of colleges, academies and common schools, edited numerous literary, political and religious newspapers, and published many influential books. Through its educational, charitable and missionary enterprises and the ministry of its local congregations, the PCUSA, Charles Beecher argued, had "a power rivaling, if not really surpassing, that of Congress, and affecting not merely the religious, but the civil interests of the nation." Stephen *Colwell's *New Themes for the Protestant Clergy* (1852) was the most compelling and influential call for Christian social action published during the antebellum years. A manufacturer, philanthropist and active Presbyterian layman, Colwell sharply criticized America's churches for failing to help the victims of the nation's rapid social change and urged Christians to apply the teaching of Jesus to a variety of social questions.

In the years between 1880 and 1925 many American Protestants championed the social gospel, which sought to remedy a wide assortment of industrial, political and social ills. While Congregationalists and Episcopalians led the crusade to reform the nation's institutions and practices, members of the PCUSA and the *United Presbyterian Church in North America (UPCNA) as well as Reformed Presbyterians, Southern Presbyterians and Associate Reformed Presbyterians contributed significantly to the effort to meliorate the nation's social evils. In 1903 the PCUSA created a Department of Church and Labor, the first denominational agency specifically concerned with industrial problems. Under the direction of Charles *Stelzle, the department conducted a wide range of ministries to workers during the next ten years.

Around 1900 the PCUSA, like many other Protestant communions, established numerous institutional churches to provide shelter, employment counseling, education, recreation and other social services to urban residents. Paul Strayer's Third Presbyterian Church in Rochester, Samuel Holmes's Westminster Presbyterian Church in Buffalo, A. T. Pierson's Bethany Presbyterian Church in Philadelphia, Mark *Matthews's First Presbyterian Church in Seattle, and other PCUSA congregations developed extensive programs in these areas. At the same time, Holmes, Matthews, Charles Parkhurst, and other PCUSA pastors helped to lead urban crusades to reform civic conditions and achieve social justice.

During the Progressive era many members of the PCUSA worked to remedy social problems through other fields: John *Wanamaker, Robert Odgen, H. J. Heinz and John Converse established and operated businesses upon biblical principles and supported civic and educational reforms; through their political service William Jennings *Bryan and Woodrow *Wilson worked to accomplish various reforms; and numerous professors at colleges and seminaries promoted social reform through classes they taught and books they wrote.

Other Presbyterian communions also joined the fight against social evil in the late nineteenth and early twentieth centuries. Although small in number, Reformed Presbyterians diligently worked to abolish child labor, improve treatment of immigrants, reform prisons, resolve labor problems, aid the poor and promote temperance and international peace. United Presbyterians, centered primarily in New York, Pennsylvania and Ohio, campaigned vigorously for women's suffrage, racial equality, civil service reform, better factory conditions and a more just distribution of wealth.

Their conservatism, largely rural locations and belief that the church was a spiritual body that should not interfere with the civil relations of society hindered the social ministry of Southern Presbyterians (*Presbyterian Church in the United States [PCUS]). Nevertheless individuals, congregations and the denomination itself sponsored or supported a wide variety of reforms in the years from 1890 to 1925. Editor Alexander *McKelway led Southern efforts to pass child labor laws. Seminary professor Walter Lingle promoted the social gospel through many courses and publications. Businessman John Eagan sought to base all the activities of his foundry in Birmingham, Alabama, on the teachings of Jesus. Abandoning the doctrine of the spirituality of the church, many Southern Presbyterians worked to promote temperance, to improve race relations and to establish schools, medical facilities, social settlements and institutional churches.

In 1914 the PCUS, UPCNA, PCUSA and the Associate Reformed Presbyterian Synod issued a "United Declaration of Christian Faith and Social Service" that delineated a distinctly Reformed basis for social reform, rooted in traditional *Calvinist understandings of creation, fall, redemption and the work of the church. It exhorted religious bodies to oppose "the sins of social injustice and tyranny" and urged individuals to practice "love, justice and truth" in all their social, economic and political relations. Expressing a widely held Presbyterian conviction, the declaration counseled congregations not to adopt definite positions on political or social issues or to promote particular social reforms. Presbyterians should instead remedy social ills through participating in voluntary organizations created specifically for this purpose.

In the years following 1925 most theologically conservative Presbyterians reacted to the increased connection of social action with liberal theology and what they perceived to be a neglect of evangelism among liberal Protestants by retreating from social involvement and intensifying their own efforts to save souls. This action was consistent with the longstanding belief of American Presbyterians that redeeming the social order depended first and foremost on converting individuals. Since the mid-1920s most evangelical Presbyterians have concentrated on promoting moral reforms (most recently centering around opposition to homosexuality, abortion and pornography). During this same period, liberal Presbyterians, especially through their control of the PCUSA's denominational agencies, have emphasized the need for structural reforms and have made pronouncements and developed programs on a wide variety of sociopolitical issues, including war and peace, economic justice, human rights, poverty, racism, sexism and hunger. The amount, scope and leftist nature of these initiatives undertaken by PCUSA leaders since the mid-1960s have significantly contributed to dispute and dissension in the denomination.

See also ABOLITION, PRESBYTERIANS AND; AMERICAN REVOLUTION, PRESBYTERIANS AND; CAPITALISM, PRESBYTERIANS AND; POLITICS, PRESBYTERIANS AND.

BIBLIOGRAPHY. J. W. Flynt, " 'Feeding the Hungry and Ministering to the Broken Hearted': The

Presbyterian Church in the United States and the Social Gospel, 1900-1920," in *Religion in the South,* ed. C. R. Wilson (1985); C. I. Foster, *An Errand of Mercy: The Evangelical United Front, 1790-1837* (1960); W. R. Glass, "Liberal Means to Conservative Ends: Bethany Presbyterian Church, John Wanamaker and the Institutional Church Movement," *AP* 68 (fall 1990) 181-92; D. T. Hessel, "Conscience and Justice: Interpreting the Social Teachings of the Presbyterian Church," *Church and Society* 81 (1990) 1-129; P. H. Hobbie, "Walter Lingle, Presbyterians and the Enigma of the Social Gospel in the South," *AP* 69 (fall 1991) 191-202; B. Johnson, "From Old to New Agendas: Presbyterians and Social Issues in the Twentieth Century," in *The Confessional Mosaic: Presbyterians and Twentieth-Century Theology,* ed. M. J. Coalter et al. (1990); B. Morgan, "Stephen Colwell (1800-1871): Social Prophet Before the Social Gospel," in *Sons of the Prophets,* ed. H. T. Kerr (1963); G. S. Smith, "Conservative Presbyterians: The Gospel, Social Reform and the Church in the Progressive Era," *AP* 70 (summer 1992) 93-110; idem, *The Seeds of Secularization: Calvinism, Culture, and Pluralism in America, 1870-1915* (1985); W. H. Smith, "William Jennings Bryan and the Social Gospel," *Journal of American History* 53 (1966) 41-60; J. H. Smylie, ed., "Presbyterians and the American Revolution: An Interpretive Account," *JPH* 54 (spring 1976) 5-199; L. B. Weeks, "Faith and Political Action in American Presbyterianism, 1776-1918," in *Reformed Faith and Politics,* ed. R. H. Stone (1983). G. S. Smith

South, Presbyterians in the. The history of Presbyterianism in the South is a story of Presbyterianism with Southern accents. This story, which is both Presbyterian and Southern, reflects the complex interaction of an evolving religious tradition with a dynamic social and cultural context over a three-hundred-year period.

Southern Presbyterianism had its origins in the colonial period with the arrival of European people who were by background and theological commitment *Calvinists—*Puritans from England and *New England, French *Huguenots, Scottish, and above all, *Scots-Irish Presbyterians. The earliest to arrive were Puritans in Virginia and Maryland, but the most numerous by the first decade of the eighteenth century were the Presbyterians in the South Carolina Low Country. Under the leadership of Archibald Stobo they established in 1718 Charlestown Presbytery, the first in the South. By the 1730s Scots-Irish were beginning to move into the Southern backcountry by way of the Great Philadelphia Wagon Road. Arriving in Philadelphia, these immigrants moved South through the Valley of Virginia into North Carolina and down the Catawba River Valley into the Piedmont of South Carolina. Along this route Scots-Irish settlers established what would become for generations the most important region for Presbyterianism in the South.

During the revivals of the Great Awakening, African-Americans began joining Presbyterian churches for the first time in any numbers. While they remained a small part of the total Presbyterian population in the South, by 1860 they did represent a significant part of the Presbyterian membership in certain influential regions of North and South Carolina. For example, in 1860 the Johns' Island Presbyterian Church, south of Charleston, had 60 white members and 510 African-American members. When freedom came, African-American Presbyterians, in the midst of their struggles against racism, established numerous schools and represented an elite class among African-Americans in the South.

During the years between the *Revolution and the American *Civil War, white Presbyterians in the South became more Presbyterian and more Southern. A distinct Southern Presbyterian church began to emerge as presbyteries and synods were organized as a part of the *Presbyterian Church in the U.S.A. (PCUSA), colleges and seminaries of the church were established and theological and ecclesiastical positions were articulated. At the same time, white Presbyterians moved more clearly into a social location that would largely mark them: an upper-middle-class people often associated with a conservative ideology that sought a middle way in religion, *politics and the great social issues of the day. In the *Old School/*New School division in the 1830s, Southern Presbyterians were overwhelmingly Old School.

The Second Great Awakening that swept across the country during the early decades of the nineteenth century encouraged the rapid growth of Presbyterianism in the South. While the growth was not so rapid as that of the Methodists or Baptists, it did exceed the growth of the general population as new churches were built and frontier presbyteries were organized. *Cumberland Presbyterians, who separated from the PCUSA, became an important denomination in parts of Appalachia and among people in the piney woods and the expanding Southern frontier. They generally represented a different social class from that of the main body of Presbyterians in the South and reflected alternative social and theological perspectives. The small Associate Reformed Presbyterian Church was confined primarily to isolated communities of significant social and cultural strength.

The Old School ministers of the South were gentlemen theologians who were largely committed to building "our Southern Zion"—a Southern society ruled by Christian values and by a hierarchical social order that they hoped would keep at bay what they regarded as the emerging chaos of the modern world with its radical individualism. The primary metaphor that shaped their social and cultural imagination was a middle way between extremes in matters social, political and theological. Informed by natural law, common sense and *scholastic traditions, this middle way was the bridge over great rifts in their experience—between being American and being Southern, between an impulse toward modern democracy and a competing impulse toward a paternalistic hierarchy, between Protestant individualism and an ancient belief in the organic character of human life.

Surrounding and influencing the life of Southern Presbyterianism during these years was the institution of slavery. Presbyterian theologians, especially James Henley *Thornwell, developed theological defenses of slavery and served an important ideological function in the South. In spite of this defense, these theologians thought of themselves as moderates standing between the extremes of *abolitionism and the radical proslavery advocates of the South. Their moderate position expressed itself in attempts to make slavery a more humane institution—masters were to provide good food, housing and sabbath rest and were not to divide slave families.

As a part of their defense of slavery, theologians developed a doctrine of the spirituality of the church. This doctrine, which had roots deep in some streams of Reformed thought, insisted that the church and state are separate spheres: the state is designed to realize the idea of justice; the church is designed to realize the idea of grace. This doctrine did not mean that Presbyterians were not interested in the great issues of slavery and race that confronted Southern culture. On the contrary, they were profoundly interested and were committed to help maintain a white hegemony in the South by keeping the church silent on social issues. States rights, as developed by John C. Calhoun, was intended to ensure no outside interference in the South's peculiar institution. The spirituality of the church, as developed by Thornwell—called the Calhoun of the Southern church—was to ensure that there be no interference from the church with slavery.

Unlike Southern Baptists and Methodists, who formed in the 1840s separate Southern denominations, Old School Presbyterians seeking a more moderated course remained united North and South until after the Civil War had begun. The Presbyterian Church in the Confederate States of America was organized in Augusta, Georgia, in 1861. After the war, the name was changed to the *Presbyterian Church in the United States (PCUS). This church used the name Southern Presbyterian, although there were other Presbyterian churches in the South.

The PCUS did not reunite with Northern Presbyterians after the war for several reasons. Northern Presbyterians were regarded as having abandoned important elements of the *Reformed tradition, especially in regard to the spirituality of the church. The bitterness left by the war and by Reconstruction was intensified by what many Southern whites regarded as the self-righteousness of Northern Presbyterians, leaving little enthusiasm for reunion. And perhaps most important, a separate white Southern Presbyterian Church provided an important institution to transmit a distinct Southern identity and to nurture values associated with a Southern way of life. Central to that way of life was the task of keeping African-Americans "in their place."

The Civil War left the South and most Southern Presbyterians impoverished. As Presbyterians sought to regain some prosperity during the closing decades of the nineteenth century, they gave themselves vigorously to both home and foreign *missions. At home, Presbyterian growth exceeded the growth of the general population, especially in Texas. Abroad, missions were established in a number of countries, eventually being concentrated in China, Korea, Japan, Brazil, Mexico and the Congo (present-day Zaire).

Women had long constituted the majority of members in Southern Presbyterian churches. They had, however, no direct participation in church government and no denomination-wide organization of women. Under the leadership of Hallie Paxon Winsborough, the Women's Auxiliary was organized early in the twentieth century. Conservative in its structure as a separate organization for women, the auxiliary nevertheless functioned as an important means of leadership development for women and as a forum for addressing women's concerns. The Birthday Offering of the auxiliary became in time one of the most important promoters of progressive causes within the PCUS. In 1965 Rachel Henderlite became the denomination's first women minister.

Southern Presbyterianism was characterized during the first six decades of this century by its social cohesion—a cousin system played an important role in the calling of ministers—and by the denomination's long struggle to move out of the old South and into the new. The driving assumptions of this movement, encouraged by commercial and industrial developments in the South, are revealed in the subtitles of the third volume of Ernst Trice Thompson's monumental study of Southern Presbyterians: "Part I: Out of the Backwaters"; "Part II: Into the Mainstream." By 1983 much of the South had moved through the new South and into the mainstream of the Sunbelt—an amorphous region marked by economic growth, population expansion and a decided tendency toward hedonism and the pursuit of the good life. With the old ideological reasons for a separate Southern Presbyterian church rapidly losing their power in such a context, reunion with the UPCUSA was achieved. The formation in 1973 of the *Presbyterian Church in America (PCA) by those most closely associated with the old South and its social system helped clear the way for reunion. Since the mid-1960s, the PCUS and its successor presbyteries in the PCUSA have shared, with some notable exceptions among the presbyteries, the mainstream Protestant experience of losing members.

See also PRESBYTERIAN CHURCH IN THE UNITED STATES.

BIBLIOGRAPHY. J. O. Farmer, *The Metaphysical Confederacy: James Henley Thornwell and the Synthesis of Southern Values* (1986); E. D. Genovese, *Slavery Ordained by God* (1985); B. E. Holifield, *The Gentlemen Theologians: American Theology in Southern Culture, 1795-1860* (1978); F. J. Hood, *Reformed America: The Middle and Southern States, 1783-1837* (1980); A. C. Loveland, *Southern Evangelicals and the Social Order, 1800-1860* (1980); E. T. Thompson, *Presbyterians in the South,* 3 vols. (1963-1973).

E. Clarke

Southern Presbyterians. *See* PRESBYTERIAN CHURCH IN THE UNITED STATES; SOUTH, PRESBYTERIANS IN THE.

Spalding, Eliza Hart (1807-1851). Presbyterian *missionary. Born in Berlin, Connecticut, Hart moved with her family to western New York when she was thirteen. There she joined the Holland Patent Presbyterian Church (1826) and taught school. Upon the advice of a friend, in 1830 she and Henry Harmon *Spalding began to correspond with each other. They were married in 1833. While Henry attended Lane Theological Seminary in Cincinnati, Ohio, Eliza not only supplemented the couple's income by taking in boarders but also found time to attend classes at the seminary.

The Spaldings desired to become missionaries, and Marcus *Whitman and Narcissa Prentiss *Whitman persuaded the Spaldings to join them in establishing the Oregon Territory mission of the American Board of Commissioners for Foreign Missions (ABCFM) in 1836. The Spaldings settled among the Nez Perce people, working from their station at Lapwai in what is now Idaho (1836-1847). Eliza's diary and letters are rich sources for perspectives on antebellum feminine evangelical experience and sensibilities. Eliza reared four children while on the mission field, and she joined the other women of the Oregon mission in founding the Columbia Maternal Association in 1838. Further, she learned the native language and taught in the mission school, handwriting her books and drawing her own pictures until a printing press became available. Following the killing of the Whitmans in 1847, Eliza and her family were forced to leave Lapwai. The Spaldings settled in Oregon, where Eliza's deteriorating health led to her death in Brownsville.

See also SPALDING, HENRY HARMON.

BIBLIOGRAPHY. *ANB* 20; C. M. Drury, *Henry Harmon Spalding* (1936); C. M. Drury, ed., *First White Women Over the Rockies,* vol. 1 (1963); *NAW.*

D. F. Anderson

Spalding, Henry Harmon (1803-1874). Presbyterian *missionary. Born out of wedlock in Wheeler, New York, Spalding had a difficult youth. Starting his formal education in his twenties, he graduated from Western Reserve College, Ohio, in 1833. That same year he married Eliza Hart. The Spaldings then moved to Cincinnati, where Henry attended Lane Theological Seminary.

Henry was ordained in 1835, and the Spaldings committed themselves to mission work among the Osage Indians of Kansas. However, Marcus *Whitman and Narcissa Prentiss *Whitman prevailed upon the Spaldings to join them in heading for the Oregon Territory to establish a mission work among the Indians of the region on behalf of the American Board of Commissioners for Foreign Missions (ABCFM). Following their overland journey in 1836, the Spaldings chose to work among the Nez Perce tribe at Lapwai in what is today Idaho.

The Spaldings's part of the Oregon mission progressed as they mastered the Nez Perce language. By 1839, some one hundred families were gathered around the mission station, where they not only heard the preaching of the gospel but also were taught American farming and domestic skills as part of the "civilizing" mission the Spaldings deemed essential.

The year before, the Spaldings and the Whitmans had organized the First Presbyterian Church in the Oregon Territory, which was the first Protestant congregation on the Pacific slope. Of the twenty-one Indian members baptized in the church between 1836 and 1847, twenty were from Lapwai. However, dissension among the mission personnel and policy differences between the missionaries and the ABCFM kept the mission's viability in doubt. The Lapwai station was closed in 1847 along with the rest of the ABCFM mission after a band of Cayuse Indians killed the Whitmans and others at the Waiilatpu station.

The Spaldings then moved to Oregon, where Henry organized and pastored a Congregational church at Calapooya (1848-1859). Two years after Eliza died (1851), Henry remarried. Meanwhile, he helped create the myth of the Whitmans as martyrs for Protestantism and American settlement. The Spaldings moved back to Nez Perce country in 1859. Eventually Henry became the reservation's interpreter and, for a time, schoolteacher, but not without tension with both government and church officials. Dedicated to evangelizing the Nez Perce, he fostered a *revival in 1872 that led to the baptism and reception into membership of more than six hundred of the tribe. He died at Lapwai.

See also SPALDING, ELIZA HART.

BIBLIOGRAPHY. C. M. Drury, *Henry Harmon Spalding* (1936); H. R. Lamar, ed., *The Reader's Encyclopedia of the American West* (1977); J. H. Webster, "The ABCFM and the First Presbyterian Missions in the Northwest," *AP* 65 (1987) 173-85.

D. F. Anderson

Speer, Robert Elliott (1867-1947).† Presbyterian *missionary statesman. Born in Pennsylvania and educated at Phillips Academy in Andover, Massachusetts, he graduated from Princeton University in 1889. Speer then worked for the Student Volunteer Movement before attending Princeton Theological Seminary (1889-1891). From 1891 until his retirement in 1937 he served as a lay secretary of the Presbyterian board of foreign missions in New York. In 1893 he married Emma Doll Bailey, later a leader in the Presbyterian church and in the Young Men's Christian Association.

Speer's interest in missions was shaped by attending Dwight L. Moody's Northfield Conferences and by his friend John R. Mott. His own thinking is well illustrated in *The Unfinished Task of Foreign Missions* (1926). For Speer the purpose of foreign missions was "to plant and set in the way to autonomy and self-maintenance the Christian Church in nations where it [does] not exist." He also wrote about the social conditions in Asia and Latin America during the period of 1890 to 1930 and the work of the Presbyterian missions and churches in those areas. An advocate of the unique authority of Christ amid the religions of the world, his book *The Finality of Jesus Christ* (1933) was widely influential. A prolific author, he wrote more than sixty-seven books and pamphlets and numerous articles.

In his early years Speer remained in conservative circles with Arthur Pierson and Moody, even writing articles for *The Fundamentals,* but by World War I he began moving in a broader orbit. Combining a personally conservative stance on issues such as the virgin birth and the person and work of Christ with a strong emphasis on Christian unity, Speer stood as a theological centrist in the Presbyterian debates of the 1920s and 1930s. As a trustee of Princeton Seminary, he strongly encouraged the reorganization of the seminary in 1929, believing that the institution needed to reflect the position of the whole church, not merely the conservative faction.

An ecumenist, Speer was a leader in the Federal Council of Churches—elected as its president in 1920—as well as in the Foreign Missionary Conference of North America and the International Missionary Council, a parent body of the World Council of Churches. His early interest in the Student Volunteer Movement continued throughout his life, primarily as a regular speaker at national meetings. His own denomination, the *Presbyterian Church in the U.S.A. (PCUSA), elected him moderator of the general assembly in 1927. However, conservatives within his own denomination were not happy with his policies, and he was sharply criticized by J. Gresham *Machen for sending theologically liberal missionaries overseas. In 1933 a liberal interdenominational report, *Re-Thinking Missions,* caused a furor among conservatives, who claimed that Speer's critique (*The Finality of Jesus Christ,* 1933) was inadequate. Believing that doctrinal conflict inhibited missionary endeavors, Speer argued that only a united church could unite the world in Christ.

BIBLIOGRAPHY. *ANB* 20; *DAB* 4; *DARB;* H. M. Goodpasture, "Robert E. Speer's Legacy," *IBMR* 2 (1978) 38-41; B. J. Longfield, *The Presbyterian Controversy: Fundamentalists, Modernists, and Moderates* (1991); *NCAB* 36; W. R. Wheeler, *A Man Sent from God: A Biography of Robert E. Speer* (1956).

H. M. Goodpasture

Spirituality. *See* PIETY, PRESBYTERIAN AND REFORMED.

Sprague, William B(uell) (1795-1876).† Presbyterian minister and biographer. Born in Andover, Connecticut, Sprague was educated at Yale College (M.A., 1815) and Princeton Theological Seminary (B.D., 1819). Ordained to minister at the Congregational church in West Springfield, Massachusetts, he served there from 1820 to 1829, first as a colleague of Joseph Lathrop and then as Lathrop's successor as senior minister. First married in 1820, he lost two wives and three infant children to premature deaths. He was called to Second Presbyterian Church in Albany, New York, in 1829 and remained there until 1869.

Known as an outstanding preacher throughout America and Europe, Sprague was also a prolific author. Among his many books was his *Life of Timothy Dwight* of Yale (1844), but his greatest achievement was his nine-volume *Annals of the American Pulpit* (1857-1869), an interdenominational collection of memoranda of American clergymen up to 1855. *Old School in his theology and twice serving on the board of directors at Princeton Seminary, Sprague preferred to avoid controversy, and he held the respect of all parties. The only controversy he became embroiled in revolved around his support for the usage of wine in the celebration of the Lord's Supper.

One of the first significant collectors in American history, Sprague amassed a large library of manuscripts, addresses, pamphlets and books, but his greatest penchant was for autographs. His collection, numbering in the tens of thousands, was donated to several libraries, but especially Princeton Theological Seminary.

Bibliography. *ANB* 20; *DAB* IX; J. M. Mulder and I. Stouffer, "William Buell Sprague: Patriarch of American Collectors," *AP* (1986) 1-17.

D. Macleod

Spring, Gardiner (1785-1873). Presbyterian minister. Born in Newburyport, Massachusetts, Spring attended Berwick Academy in Maine and Yale University (B.A., 1805). He studied law, taking two years off to teach school in Bermuda, before being admitted to the bar in Connecticut in 1808. In 1806 he married Susan Barney, and together they had fifteen children. Soon, however, he became convinced that he should enter the ministry and attended Andover Seminary (1809-1810). In 1810 Spring was called as pastor to Brick Church (old First Presbyterian Church) in New York City, where he was ordained in early August. He remained there for sixty-three years, until his death.

Spring was very active in denominational politics. He objected to the Excision Act of 1837, which precipitated the *New School-*Old School split. Nonetheless, Spring kept his church in the Old School, always seeking to be a voice of moderation within that body. Preaching was his first concern, and he believed that sermons ought to result in genuine and thorough conversions. Spring published many of his sermons and addresses, most notably *The Power of the Pulpit* (1848), and his autobiographical *Personal Reminiscences of the Life and Times of Gardiner Spring* (1866). In New York, he was active in numerous religious and charitable associations, particularly *missions. Spring also led Brick Church to a major move from downtown to a magnificent new building at Fifth Avenue and 37th Street in 1858.

Spring is perhaps best known for the so-called Spring Resolutions that he presented at the general assembly of 1861. This assembly, meeting in an atmosphere of national tension, was divided along sectional lines over the question of supporting the federal government in its suppression of secession, but due to the rising hostility, very few of the Southern delegates were in attendance. While Spring was convinced that the Constitution recognized the legal existence of slavery and had been opposed to antislavery agitation, which he considered extreme, he nonetheless felt strongly that the lawful government in Washington should be supported now that a crisis was at hand. Spring's resolutions affirmed that churches should "do all in their power to strengthen, uphold, and encourage the federal government." Not merely individuals but the church as a whole must commit itself to the Union cause. His opponents, including Charles *Hodge of Princeton Theological Seminary, argued that under normal circumstances that might be tolerable, but that here it was improper for the general assembly to force Southern Presbyterian ministers to swear allegiance to the federal government, because the church was not the proper court in which to try the Confederacy's grievances. By adopting the Spring Resolutions by a narrow margin, the Old School assembly broke its traditional silence on political issues and declared that the entire church should support the federal government. Consequently, the Southern group withdrew and formed its own assembly.

During the war, the Old School-New School dispute in the North lost much of its urgency. In 1869, with the general assembly meeting in his own Brick Presbyterian Church in New York City, Spring pleaded powerfully for reunion and was pleased to see it accomplished before his death, four years later.

Bibliography. *ANB* 20; *DAB* IX; *DARB; NCAB* 5; G. Spring, *Personal Reminiscences of the Life and Times of Gardiner Spring,* 2 vols. (1866); L. G. VanderVelde, *The Presbyterian Churches and the Federal Union, 1861-1869* (1932).

D. M. Strong

Stanton, Robert Livingston (1810-1885). Presbyterian minister, church statesman, *educator and writer. Born at Griswold, Connecticut, Stanton attended Lane Seminary, graduating in 1836. He was ordained by the Mississippi Presbytery and served pastorates at Pine Ridge and Woodville, Mississippi, and Second Church of New Orleans, Louisiana. From 1851 to 1854 he was president of Oakland College in Mississippi and then pastor at Chillicothe, Ohio. In 1862 he became professor of pastoral theology and homiletics at Danville Theological Seminary in Kentucky.

An advisor to Abraham Lincoln on Southern affairs, Stanton emerged during the *Civil War as a leader of the strongly nationalistic Midwestern faction of Presbyterian clergymen. In *The Church and the Rebellion* (1864) they argued the responsibility of church leaders in promoting the spirit of secession. Stanton's own election as moderator of the 1866 *Old School general assembly in St. Louis signaled the triumph of radical forces in the church, especially in regard to postwar policies for Southern congregations.

In 1866 Stanton assumed the presidency of Miami University in Ohio, an institution faltering for lack of students and financial support. Unable to increase the enrollment or strengthen its finances, he left in 1871 to become an editor of the New York *Independent,* followed by the Cincinnati *Herald and Presbyter* (1872-1878). Later he moved to Washington, D.C., was attracted to faith healing and wrote *Gospel Parallelisms: Illustrated in the Healing of Body and Soul* (1884). Ill with malaria, Stanton sailed for England in 1885 to attend a faith healing conference and died on the voyage. He was buried at sea.

Bibliography. *NCAB* 26; L. G. VanderVelde, *The Presbyterian Churches and the Federal Union, 1861-1869* (1932).

W. J. Wade

Stearns, Lewis French (1847-1892). Congregational theologian. Born in Newburyport, Massachusetts, Stearns graduated from Princeton College (B.A., 1867) and later studied at the Columbia School of Law (1867-1869). In preparing for the ministry he attended Princeton Theological Seminary (1869-1870) and Union Theological Seminary in New York (1871- 1872), with a year at the universities of Leipzig and Berlin (1870-1871). After a few years as a Presbyterian minister in Norwood, New Jersey (1873-1876), he taught history and literature at Albion College, Michigan (1876-1879). Resigning from the faculty because of eye trouble, he turned his energies toward theological reconstruction while recuperating. That reconstruction involved rejecting the *Calvinist emphasis on divine sovereignty and election and the adoption of a distinctively liberal christology that highlighted the humanity of Jesus while not denying his divinity. In the experience of the human Jesus, Stearns believed, one had a way to interpret human suffering, a model for recognizing that all were part of one human family and a basis for the liberal Protestant insistence on the immanence of God and progress in human social development. Stearns resumed teaching in 1880, this time at Bangor Theological Seminary, a Congregationalist institution in Maine, where he remained until his death.

Bibliography. *ANB* 20; *DARB;* G. L. Prentiss, "Biographical Sketch" in L. F. Stearns, *Present Day Theology* (1893).

C. H. Lippy

Stelzle, Charles (1869-1941).‡ Presbyterian minister. Born in New York City, Stelzle grew up in the Bowery, a poor, tenement area on the Lower East Side of Manhattan, working in a sweatshop as a child and as a machinist during his teens. He joined the International Association of Machinists. These experiences prompted Stelzle to work for better relations between the church and the working classes. After attending Moody Bible Institute (1894-1895) he served in several churches, first as a lay worker at Hope Chapel in Minneapolis (1895-1897) and Hope Chapel in New York (1897-1899), and then as pastor of Markham Memorial Church in St. Louis (1899-1903). He was ordained in 1900.

In 1903 Stelzle began a special mission to workers under the auspices of the Presbyterian board of home missions. The project became the Department of Church and Labor in 1906. Stelzle served as superintendent of this agency, the first established by any denomination to implement social Christianity. In 1910 he organized the Labor Temple on the East Side. He also worked for the Men and Religion Forward Movement. Stelzle resigned his position in 1913 when budget cuts and reorganization threatened to limit his activities. From then on he did public relations work, was a social service field secretary for the Federal Council of Churches and worked for the Red Cross in Washington, D.C. He wrote several books, including *The Workingman and Social Problems* (1903).

Bibliography. *ANB* 20; *DAB* II; *DARB; NCAB* C; C. Stelzle, *A Son of the Bowery* (1926).

L. M. Japinga

Stevenson, Joseph Ross (1866-1939).† Presbyterian minister and Princeton Seminary president. Born at Ligonier, Pennsylvania, Stevenson graduated from Washington and Jefferson College (1886) and McCormick Theological Seminary (1889), studying briefly the following year at the University of Berlin. After pastoring in Sedalia, Missouri, in 1894 he returned to McCormick as professor of church history. He pastored Fifth Avenue Church in New York City from 1902 until 1909 and then went to Baltimore's Brown Memorial Church for five years. He was elected moderator of the general assembly in 1915.

Stevenson is best known for serving as Princeton Seminary president from 1914 to 1936—tumultuous years in the school's history. Immediately attempting to assert his authority in what had traditionally been a faculty-run institution, his efforts to broaden the seminary's approach met with stiff resistance. While theologically conservative, Stevenson had an irenic approach toward the presence of liberalism within Presbyterianism, believing the seminary should concentrate on preparing ministers for the entire denomination. To more militant faculty members, including conservative leader J. Gresham *Machen, this smacked of an unacceptable inclusivism and a betrayal of Princeton's confessional heritage. After years of conflict and a denominational investigation, in 1929 the seminary government was reorganized to ensure broader representation of theological views and to increase the president's powers. This was a major victory for Stevenson, which led to the withdrawal of Machen and his supporters to found Westminster Theological Seminary. Working with the new board of trustees, Stevenson hired new professors who would be more representative of the whole *Presbyterian Church in the U.S.A. (PCUSA). By 1936, when Stevenson retired, only two members of the Old Princeton faculty remained.

Bibliography. R. T. Clutter, "The Reorientation of Princeton Theological Seminary, 1900-1929" (Th.D. diss., Dallas Theological Seminary, 1982); L. A. Loetscher, *The Broadening Church: A Study of Theological Issues in the Presbyterian Church Since 1869* (1954).

W. V. Trollinger

Stockton, Richard (1730-1781). Presbyterian lawyer and politician. Born to a wealthy family in Princeton, New Jersey, Richard Stockton was sent by his parents to study with Samuel *Finley in Nottingham, Maryland, for two years before entering the College of New Jersey (now Princeton), then situated in Elizabethtown, New Jersey. After graduating from college in 1748, Stockton read law in the office of the Honorable David Ogden in Newark, New Jersey. He was licensed to practice law in 1754 and built up a very successful practice in Newark, New York City and Philadelphia. After his father's death in 1757, Stockton moved with his new wife, Annis Boudinot, into the family estate in Princeton. Annis named their new home Morven, and both Annis and Richard spent a considerable amount of time and money developing the estate.

At first hesitant to enter public life, Stockton swiftly rose to a position of great prominence in both New Jersey and the nation. Already a trustee of the College of New Jersey (1757-1781), Stockton was appointed a member of New Jersey's governor's council in 1768, became a justice of the New Jersey Supreme Court in 1774, was elected to the Continental Congress in 1776 and soon thereafter became a signatory of the Declaration of Independence. During the *Revolutionary War, the British imprisoned Stockton, treated him horribly and nearly destroyed Morven. Among Presbyterians, Stockton is perhaps best known for his role (supported considerably by Benjamin *Rush) in securing the services of John *Witherspoon as president of the College of New Jersey in 1766-1767. Stockton died of cancer at Morven.

Bibliography. *ANB* 20; R. Balmer and J. R. Fitzmier, *The Presbyterians* (1993); J. McLachlan, ed., *Princetonians, 1748-1768* (1976); M. A. Noll, *Princeton and the Republic, 1768-1822: The Search for a Christian Enlightenment in the Era of Samuel Stanhope Smith* (1989).

D. A. Sweeney

Stone, Barton W. (1772-1844).‡ Leader of Stonite wing of the early Restoration Movement. Born near Port Tobacco, Maryland, Stone converted at age nineteen and dedicated his life to the ministry. After a short period of preaching in North Carolina, Virginia and Tennessee, Stone began preaching for Presbyterian congregations at Cane Ridge and Concord, Kentucky. The congregations in 1790 issued a call to ministry.

In 1801 Stone visited a *revival in Logan County and was impressed by the "religious exercises" he observed (falling, jerking, dancing, barking, running, laughing and singing), believing them to be authentic manifestations of God's presence. These religious exercises were increasingly seen in his own famous revival at Cane Ridge.

Stone's revival methods generated tension between him and the Presbyterian Synod of Kentucky. In turn, he and several other revivalists organized in 1804 the Springfield Presbytery. Within a few months they began questioning the validity of presbyteries and dissolved theirs. The group then agreed to be known as Christians only and to follow only the Bible. In 1807 they adopted the practice of baptism by immersion for the remission of sins.

From 1826 until his death, Stone extended his influence through his monthly journal, *Christian Messenger.* In 1830 Stone met Alexander Campbell and, finding a common ground, Stone and most of his followers united with the Campbellites to form a group that became known as the Christian Church (Disciples of Christ).

Bibliography. *ANB* 20; *DAB* IX; *DARB;* B. W. Stone, *The Biography of Eld. Barton Warren Stone* (1847); C. C. Ware, *Barton Warren Stone* (1932).

T. L. Miethe

Stone, John Timothy (1868-1954). Presbyterian minister and theological *educator. Stone studied at Amherst (B.A., 1891) and Auburn Seminary (B.D., 1894). Following pastorates in New York City and Baltimore, Stone was appointed pastor of Fourth Presbyterian Church in Chicago, where he served from 1909 until 1930. Stone was moderator of the general assembly of the *Presbyterian Church in the U.S.A. (PCUSA, 1913-1914); chairman of the Committee of Fifteen (1921-1923) and president of McCormick Seminary (1928-1940).

Stone's robust faith strode confidently through many of the conflicts of twentieth-century Presbyterianism. While his own creed was evangelical, he rejected strict doctrinal definitions and subscriptionism. His popular preaching and writing encouraged conversion and social engagement, though his view of church and society favored Republican politics and looked away from labor issues. Stone led Chicago's affluent Fourth Presbyterian Church to new buildings, new programs and new political and social prominence as a center of urban ministry, with the congregation supporting a broad program of *missions, evangelism and church planting. As moderator of the PCUSA general assembly, Stone advocated an aggressive mix of urban and world missions, focusing on the work of the church rather than the issues that would divide the denomination in the next decade.

Stone's contribution to *The Fundamentals* was characteristic: upbeat, christocentric and devoted to evangelism. Though Stone encouraged support of conservative evangelist Billy *Sunday's Chicago crusade in 1918 and welcomed *fundamentalists at Fourth Church, he was clear about his loyalties to a gospel that was conservative but generous, more readily verified in a life of service than in propositions and doctrinal ultimatums. Stone's advocacy of the *Auburn Affirmation during the Presbyterian conflict was an effort to maintain and enlarge a vital middle ground between fundamentalists and modernists. During his presidency of McCormick Theological Seminary, Stone pursued a building program during the course of the Depression years, secured the affiliation of Cincinnati's Lane Theological Seminary, admitted women to degree programs and supported high standards for faculty and for institutional accreditation through the American Association of Theological Schools.

Bibliography. *ANB* 20; M. M. Scroggs, *A Light in the City: Fourth Presbyterian Church of Chicago* (1990); idem, "Making a Difference: Fourth Presbyterian Church of Chicago," in *American Congregations,* ed. J. P. Wind and J. W. Lewis, vol. 1 (1994); O. R. Sellers, *The Fifth Quarter Century of McCormick* (1955).

K. S. Sawyer

Stonehouse, Ned Bernard (1902-1962).† Presbyterian biblical scholar. Born in Grand Rapids, Michigan, and educated at Calvin College (B.A. 1924), Princeton Seminary (Th.B. and Th.M., 1927), the University of Tübingen and the Free University of Amsterdam (Th.D. in New Testament, 1929), Stonehouse was a member of the original faculty of Westminster Theological Seminary in Philadelphia, where he remained until his death. Ordained by the Presbytery of Philadelphia of the *Presbyterian Church in the U.S.A. (PCUSA), he was prominent in the formation of the *Orthodox Presbyterian Church (OPC) in 1936, and in time became one of its most highly regarded leaders, with a special concern for its ecumenical vision. In *J. Gresham Machen: A Biographical Memoir* (1954), he told the story of the eminent founder of both Westminster and the OPC.

Combining a cordial commitment to Reformed theology with breadth of learning, Stonehouse was among the more widely respected New Testament scholars of his day. He wrote on a wide range of New Testament topics, but his particular area of expertise was the Synoptic Gospels, as demonstrated in his *Origin of the Synoptic Gospels* (1963). Perhaps his most enduring contribution, as expressed in *The Witness of Matthew and Mark to Christ* (1944) and *The*

Witness of Luke to Christ (1951), was his anticipation of the rise of redaction criticism. Basing his work on a high view of Scripture, he drew attention to the theologically distinctive editorial activity of each of the Synoptic writers. Arguing that both liberals and conservatives usually read modern ideas into the ancient text, Stonehouse attempted to uncover the theological purposes of the Evangelists.

Bibliography. M. A. Noll, *Between Faith and Criticism: Evangelicals, Scholarship, and the Bible in America* (1986); M. Silva, "Ned B. Stonehouse and Redaction Criticism," *WTJ* 40 (fall 1977) 77-88; (spring 1978) 281-303. R. B. Gaffin

Sunday, William (Billy) Ashley (1862-1935).† Presbyterian evangelist. Born on a farm near Ames, Iowa, Sunday was known in his lifetime as the baseball evangelist. Receiving little formal schooling, he lived in an orphanage for two years, and when he was fourteen he went out on his own. After attending high school and working odd jobs, Sunday began a career as a major league baseball player in 1883. Three years later he surrendered his life to Christ at Chicago's Pacific Garden Rescue Mission. By 1891 the talented ball player walked away from his sports career to devote his full time to Christian ministry. In 1896, after working for the Young Men's Christian Association (YMCA) and two traveling evangelists, including John Wilbur *Chapman, Sunday was invited to Garner, Iowa, to conduct a revival. From that time on he was never without invitations to preach.

Sunday was licensed by the Presbyterian church in 1898, and in 1903 he was ordained. During the early years of his ministry his campaigns were held in small Midwestern towns. By the eve of World War I, however, he was preaching in larger cities all over the United States, including Chicago, Boston and New York City. By the time of his death the itinerant evangelist had preached thousands of sermons in more than two hundred campaigns. Millions of people heard his message and approximately three hundred thousand men and women were led to faith in Christ in his meetings.

Until the advent of Billy Graham, no American evangelist ever preached to as many people and counted as many conversions for his efforts as did Sunday. His unorthodox preaching style—flamboyant antics, theatrical poses and impassioned gestures—attracted the attention of the press and helped make him a household name. For him, virtually nothing was too extreme if it brought people to Jesus Christ. He tried to avoid overdoing the altar call, because he wanted people to come forward only if they were serious about committing their lives to Christ. But much of his success was due to the organizational talents of his wife, Helen Amelia Thompson, whom he married in 1888. Despite the fact that she reared four children, she found time to select the cities where he preached, arrange the precampaign machinery and organize the campaigns themselves.

Thanks to his preaching skill and Mrs. Sunday's managerial talent, Sunday went from obscurity to national prominence and from poverty to modest wealth. The common people admired his pluck and no doubt took vicarious delight in his popularity and success. To be sure he made enemies. Many in the church loathed his down-home style, especially his backwoods vocabulary. And ultraconservatives found his promulgation of women's rights and his outreach to blacks to be as distasteful as the liquor interests found his battle for prohibition.

Sunday is credited with making Prohibition a popular cause. He is also remembered for helping raise millions of dollars for the American military effort in World War I. What cannot be measured is his impact on the nation's morality, let alone his effectiveness as an evangelist. Nevertheless the evidence is overwhelming that Sunday left countless changed lives in the wake of his campaigns.

Bibliography. *ANB* 21; *DAB* IX; L. W. Dorsett, *Billy Sunday and the Redemption of Urban America* (1991); W. T. Ellis, *Billy Sunday, the Man and His Message* (1936); W. G. McLaughlin Jr., *Billy Sunday Was His Real Name* (1955); H. Rodeheaver, *Twenty Years with Billy Sunday* (1936). L. W. Dorsett

Swing, David (1830-1894).‡ Presbyterian and independent pastor. Born in Cincinnati, Ohio, Swing graduated in 1852 from Miami University in Ohio, studied theology under Nathan Lewis Rice in Cincinnati and taught classical languages at Miami from 1854 to 1866. In 1866 he went to Chicago to pastor Westminster Presbyterian Church, which in 1869 consolidated with North Church to form Fourth Presbyterian Church.

A popular preacher who attracted several thousand worshipers every Sunday, Swing came to national attention in 1874, when Francis Landey *Patton accused him of heresy. Patton's main charge was that Swing's sermons and his book *Truths for Today* (1874) denied the teachings of the *Westminster standards. Swing's defense rested principally on his argument that creeds as human expressions are necessarily imperfect and therefore must be constantly revised to keep pace with cultural circumstances. The Presbytery of Chicago acquitted Swing of all charges, but when Patton threatened to appeal to the Northern Illinois Synod, Swing withdrew from the denomination.

In 1875 Swing became the pastor of the newly organized and independent Central Church of Chicago. For nearly two decades Swing preached weekly to three thousand or more worshipers and was widely respected across the nation. His views helped give rise to the theological liberalism of the latter years of the nineteenth century. And his pulpit eloquence made him one of the most celebrated and controversial preachers of the second half of the nineteenth century.

Bibliography. *ANB* 21; *DAB* IX; *DARB;* W. R. Hutchison, *The Modernist Impulse in American Protestantism* (1976); *NCAB* 3; J. F. Newton, *David Swing* (1909).

G. S. Smith

T

Talbot, Louis Thomson (1889-1976).† Presbyterian minister and president of the Bible Institute of Los Angeles. Born the sixth of eight children to John and Elizabeth Freyling Talbot, Louis grew up near Sydney, Australia. He was a graduate of Newington College in Australia and Moody Bible Institute in Chicago. Talbot served as pastor of the First Congregational Church of Paris, Texas, before and after he studied at McCormick Seminary.

During his seminary years Talbot started the Madison Street Church in Oak Park, Illinois. Then Talbot took pastorates in Presbyterian churches at Keokuk, Iowa (1921-1925), and Minneapolis, Minnesota (1925-1929). In 1929 he was called to the Philpott Tabernacle in Hamilton, Ontario. From 1932 to 1948 he was pastor of the Church of the Open Door and president of the Bible Institute of Los Angeles (1932-1952). At that time both institutions were in one location at the corner of Hope and Sixth Street in Los Angeles. Talbot rescued the work from bankruptcy in 1938 through a radio fund drive. After 1953 he served as chancellor of Biola College (now Biola University), and the board named the newly founded Talbot Seminary in his honor.

Among Talbot's publications were *God's Plan of the Ages* (1936), *The Prophecies of Daniel in the Light of the Past, Present and Future Events* (1940) and *Christ in the Tabernacle* (1942). He received a doctor of divinity degree from Wheaton College in Illinois and a doctor of laws from John Brown University in Arkansas. During his later years Talbot actively promoted evangelical foreign mission endeavors through his extensive travels in Asia, Africa and Latin America.

Bibliography. C. Talbot, *For This I Was Born: The Captivating Story of Louis T. Talbot* (1977).

D. G. Buss

Talmage, T(homas) DeWitt (1832-1902).† *Dutch Reformed and Presbyterian minister. Talmage was born near Bound Brook, New Jersey, and was the son of a farmer. He had three brothers, a brother-in-law and two uncles who were ministers in the Dutch Reformed Church. After attending school in New Brunswick, New Jersey, at the age of nineteen he entered the University of the City of New York to study law. Talmage never completed his law course, turning instead to the study of theology at the New Brunswick Theological Seminary of the Dutch Reformed Church, from which he graduated in 1856.

Ordained in 1856, Talmage pastored the Dutch Reformed Church at Belleville, New Jersey, until 1859. He then served the Dutch Reformed Church in Syracuse, New York (1859-1862), followed by a pastorate at the Second Dutch Reformed Church of Philadelphia (1862-1869). Accepting a call from the badly divided Central Presbyterian Church in Brooklyn, New York (1869), he remained there until 1895, developing it into one of the largest churches in the United States. During his tenure there he attracted considerable attention and became involved in lecturing and journalism, in addition to his preaching. Three times during his Brooklyn pastorate the church building burned down, and each time his middle- and upper-class congregation replaced it with a larger and more impressive edifice, the final two with seating in excess of five thousand. It was said that his was the largest Protestant church in the world. Shortly after the last building burned, he moved to Washington, D.C., where he pastored the First Presbyterian Church (1895-1899). A popular lecturer, he delivered an average of fifty lectures a year during the peak of his career.

Talmage was probably the most popular preacher during the last quarter of the nineteenth century, and his sermons were published in thirty-five hundred newspapers. They also appeared in the journals *Christian at Work* (1874-1876), *Frank Leslie's Sunday Magazine* (1881-1889) and *Christian Herald* (1890-1902), all of which were edited by Talmage. Considered a master of sensational rhetoric and having an unconventional style of organizing and delivering his sermons, he was both strongly admired and criticized. The substance of the criticism was that he mishandled texts by badly pulling them out of context and that he mistook assertion for proof. He preached to the contemporary issues of the day, taking strong stands against divorce, gambling and liquor, rather than explicating a particular text, and he often ignored doctrinal issues. His admirers appreciated his florid rhetoric and his ability to communicate to the cultured urban dwellers of the Gilded Age. Not an innovator in theology and an outspoken critic of Darwinism, he was nonetheless accused in 1879 before the Brooklyn Presbytery "of falsehood and deceit and . . . using improper methods of preaching which tend to bring religion into contempt." Talmage was acquitted of these charges by a close vote, but the fact that he was charged demonstrates the controversial nature of his preaching. His collected sermons fill twenty volumes.

Bibliography. *ANB* 21; C. E. Banks, *Authorized and Authentic Life and Works of T. DeWitt Talmage* (1902); *DAB* IX; *DARB; NCAB* 4; J. Rusk, *The Authentic Life of T. DeWitt Talmage* (1902); M. Talmage, ed., *Five Hundred Selected Sermons,* 20 vols. (1900).

J. R. Wiers

Templin, Terah (1742?-1818). Pioneer Presbyterian minister of Kentucky. Reared on a farm near Peaks of Otter, Bedford County, Virginia, Templin was attracted to the ministry by David *Rice, a Presbyterian evangelist who had settled in the vicinity. Given a basic education by Rice, Templin attended Liberty Hall Academy and was licensed to preach by Hanover Presbytery in 1780. He followed Rice in immigrating to Kentucky and in 1785 was ordained *sine titulo* by a commission of Hanover Presbytery. On October 17, 1786, he was admitted to Transylvania Presbytery at its formative meeting. Settling in Washington County and making his home with General John Caldwell, a benefactor, Templin ministered in central Kentucky for some fifteen years, preaching and establishing churches. About 1800 he moved with General Caldwell to Livingston County in western Kentucky, but upon the general's death Templin returned to Washington County, where he died.

Neither a powerful intellect nor a charismatic preacher, Templin instead consistently and sacrificially dedicated his service to the church. He never received a regular salary and was regarded by his colleagues as a "plain practical preacher," orthodox in theology and respected for his integrity and unassuming modesty. In the controversies surrounding the Cumberland Presbytery, Templin was staunch in his loyalty to the orthodox party. He never married; it is conjectured that he remained celibate in loyalty to the memory of a fiancee who died.

Bibliography. R. Davidson, *History of the Presbyterian Church in the State of Kentucky* (1847).

W. J. Wade

Tennent, Gilbert (1703-1764).† Presbyterian minister and *revivalist during the Great Awakening. Born in County Armagh, Ireland, Gilbert was the eldest son of William *Tennent. The Tennent family immigrated to the American colonies in 1718. Gilbert studied at Yale, receiving his master of arts degree in 1725. In that same year he was licensed by the Presbytery of Philadelphia. Later that year he briefly served a church in Newcastle, Delaware, and in 1726 he assumed a pastorate in New Brunswick, New Jersey.

In New Brunswick Tennent met the *Dutch Reformed minister Theodorus *Frelinghuysen, whose emphasis on personal *piety and evangelistic fervor had a dramatic and lasting impact on young Tennent. In the late 1720s and early 1730s Tennent was involved with his father's efforts at the Log College, and this involvement, coupled with his revival zeal, made him the leader of a vigorous minority within the Presbyterian church. When conflicts between pro- and antirevivalists came to a head, the revivalists formed a separate presbytery within the Synod of Philadelphia, which temporarily soothed the tension. Tennent's influence was such that George Whitefield sought him out when he arrived in the Middle Colonies, bringing the Great Awakening with him. Whitefield first preached for Tennent in New Brunswick in 1739.

Tennent became the chief spokesman for supporters of the Great Awakening and is frequently remembered for "The Danger of an Unconverted Ministry" (1740), preached at Nottingham, Pennsylvania. This sermon assailed opponents of the Awakening, calling congregations to insist that their ministers had experienced what the revivalists considered a proper conversion experience. Naturally this contributed to the spirit of animosity that produced the first split in the Presbyterian church between the *Old Side and the *New Side in 1741. In 1743 Tennent moved to Philadelphia to become pastor of a New Side congregation. While continuing to support the Awakening, he thereafter led the attempt to bring reconciliation, admitting publicly in 1742 that his own censoriousness had contributed to the schism in the church. After retracting his virulent sermon and working diligently to repair the breach, his efforts finally paid off. In 1758 the two sides were reunited, and the united synod elected him moderator in honor of his labors. In tribute Francis *Alison, one of the most influential Old Side ministers, wrote, "Gilbert Tennent . . . has written more and suffered more for his writings, to promote peace and union, than any member of this divided church."

Another factor in Tennent's change of heart was his encounter with Count Nicholas Von Zinzendorf. The radical pietism and emotionalism of the Moravians convinced Tennent that revivalism could go too far and that the Old Side was not as great a danger. He continued the Scottish tradition of preaching revival sermons during the annual sacramental seasons, but by the late 1740s he had switched from extemporaneous jeremiads on the terror of the wrath of God to writing out manuscript sermons focusing both on the revival of the heart toward God and on sound doctrine as the only way to maintain the true piety and warmth of the revival.

See also TENNENT, WILLIAM, JR.; TENNENT, WILLIAM, SR.

BIBLIOGRAPHY. *ANB* 21; *AAP* 3; *DAB* IX; *DARB;* M. J. Coalter Jr., *Gilbert Tennent, Son of Thunder* (1986); L. J. Trinterud, *The Forming of an American Tradition: A Re-Examination of Colonial Presbyterianism* (1949). S. T. Logan

Tennent, William, Jr. (1705-1777). Presbyterian pastor. Born in northern Ireland, Tennent immigrated with his family to America in 1718. His father, *William Sr., educated William and his three brothers for the ministry.

Between 1727 and 1729, William Jr. and his brother John apprenticed under their older brother, *Gilbert, at his parish in New Brunswick, New Jersey. During a period of severe soul searching while preparing for his examination for ordination before presbytery, William fell ill and lapsed into a coma. Mistaken for dead, he was about to be buried when he suddenly awoke. He later recounted a vision during his trance in which he encountered a great multitude singing before an indescribable glory. Before he could join the group, a celestial being laid his hand upon Tennent's shoulder and insisted that he must return to life.

Tennent was ordained in the Presbyterian church in 1733, and he became the pastor of his brother John's Freehold, New Jersey, congregation after John's death in 1732. He served this congregation until his death.

In 1738 Tennent married Catherine Van Brugh Noble. Three years later Tennent, who was known for his aversion to lying even in jest, was embarrassed by a much publicized trial in which he was accused of perjuring himself in behalf of a fellow revivalist, John *Rowland. The court case occurred at the height of the Great Awakening, a revival movement that swept British North America in the late 1730s and early 1740s and one in which the entire Tennent family played a major role. Many of his contemporaries believed that the charges had been intentionally created by opponents of the awakening to humiliate the prorevival party in the Presbyterian church. Tennent was eventually exonerated.

Tennent's father and older brother, Gilbert, were more prominent leaders of this spiritual awakening than was William Jr., but William itinerated in the South in behalf of the revival movement, and as late as 1753, he and Gilbert sparked a major revival in Pennsylvania.

Tennent was recognized as a particularly effective pastor, a powerful preacher of new birth and practical *piety, as well as an unusually gifted peacemaker. Members of his congregation noted the care with which he instructed the young in the *Westminster Catechisms and, during his regular visits to parishioners, examined their souls for the season or stage that they had attained in their journey to salvation. Students of the College of New Jersey, where Tennent became a trustee in 1746, were known to walk the twenty miles from Princeton to Freehold to hear his sermons. But Tennent was best remembered for his strong sense of humor and his irenic attitude toward those with whom he disagreed. Both qualities earned him frequent requests to serve as peacemaker for congregations in conflict.

Tennent's published works include Benjamin Coleman, Gilbert Tennent and William Tennent, *Three Letters to the Reverend Mr. George Whitefield* (1739); Gilbert Tennent, William Tennent and Samuel Blair, *Sermons on Sacramental Occasions* (1739); William Tennent, *An Exhortation to Walk in Christ* (1739); and William Tennent, *A Sermon Upon Matthew 5:23-24* (1769).

See also TENNENT, GILBERT; TENNENT, WILLIAM, SR.

BIBLIOGRAPHY. *AAP* 3; A. Alexander, *Biographical Sketches of the Founders and Principal Alumni of the Log College* (1851); E. Boudinot, *Memoirs of the Life of the Reverend William Tennent* (1807); *DAB* XVIII; T. Murphy, *The Presbytery of the Log College* (1889). M. J. Coalter Jr.

Tennent, William, Sr. (1673-1746).† Presbyterian minister and *educator. Tennent was probably born in Ireland, although inadequate records leave open the possibility that he was born in Scotland. He was trained at the University of Edinburgh, from which he received his master of arts degree (1693). Formally received by the general synod of Ulster in 1701, he married in 1702 and took orders in the Church of England in 1704. In 1718 he immigrated to Pennsylvania and on September 16 of that year applied for admission to the Presbyterian church, the synod of which was then meeting in Philadelphia. After Tennent declared his belief that episcopacy was "a mere human invention" and his commitment to the Presbyterian church, the synod accepted him and encouraged him to labor within its bounds. Between 1720 and 1727 he served pastorates in New York, and in 1727 he moved to Neshaminy, Pennsylvania, to assume a pastorate there.

In the late 1720s, with controversy building in the Presbyterian church over ministerial subscription to the *Westminster Confession and out of concern for "experimental orthodoxy," Tennent became convinced of the need for theological education in the Middle Colonies. The dearth of Presbyterian ministers was in part caused by the high educational standards that Presbyterians expected from their pastors, which was exacerbated by the expense of traveling to Scotland or to Yale or Harvard in *New England. So Tennent began tutoring young men, including his four sons, who were preparing to enter the Presbyterian ministry. By 1735 these efforts had become sufficiently formalized that Tennent built a simple log building that became known as the Log College. Tennent was a fluent Latin scholar and well-versed in Greek, Hebrew and philosophy; his students proved to have been given a thorough classical education, passing licensure examinations with flying colors.

George Whitefield, upon his visit in 1739, was favorably impressed by the school, comparing it with the ancient schools of the prophets for the godly preachers it produced but also for the primitive conditions under which they labored. Others, however, were less kind. Many British and New England trained ministers felt that Tennent's private college was academically deficient and pointed to the fact that the Log College graduates, such as Tennent's son *Gilbert, were primarily responsible for provoking the irresponsible enthusiasm that was overtaking the colonies during the Great Awakening. Even a minority in his church at Neshaminy were dissatisfied, and in 1740 they tried to argue that since Tennent had never been officially installed, he was not their pastor. The synod overruled them, reminding them that they had invited him thirteen years previously.

After the *Old Side had forced the *New Side out of the synod in 1741, Tennent continued until his death to be influential in the work of the New Side New Brunswick Presbytery. In 1742, due to his advanced years, he requested that the presbytery send an assistant, and in 1743 his former student Charles Beatty replaced him. His son Gilbert and several other former students, including Samuel *Finley, Benjamin *Rush and Samuel *Blair, were noted leaders of the New Side Presbyterians.

See also TENNENT, GILBERT; TENNENT, WILLIAM, JR.

BIBLIOGRAPHY. *ANB* 21; *AAP* 3; A. Alexander, *The Log College* (1845); *DAB* IX; *DARB;* L. J. Trinterud, *The Forming of an American Tradition: A Re-Examination of Colonial Presbyterianism* (1949).

S. T. Logan

Thomas, Norman M(attoon) (1884-1968).† Presbyterian minister and leader of the Socialist Party in America. Born in Marion, Ohio, the son of a Presbyterian minister, Thomas was educated at Bucknell University (1901-1902), Princeton University (B.A., 1905) and the Union Theological Seminary in New York (B.D., 1911). While studying at Union, Thomas served as an assistant minister and social worker in New York City and became well acquainted with the slum conditions of the city's Little Italy. After a controversial ordination examination in 1911 he ministered at the East Harlem Presbyterian Church and was director of the American Parish, a federation of Presbyterian churches that addressed social issues in the city.

Convinced that Christians could not be involved in war, Thomas formed the Association of Pacifist Ministers in 1914, and in 1917 he joined the Fellowship of Reconciliation, serving as its executive secretary and editor of *The World Tomorrow* (1918-1922). Perceiving conscientious objection as a watershed issue, since the draft seemed to repress the freedom of conscience and civil liberties, he became one of the founders of the American Civil Liberties Union. In 1918 Thomas resigned his pastorate under pressure and joined the Socialist Party, assuming leadership from 1926 to 1950. He ran for governor of New York in 1924 and mayor of the city of New York in 1925 and 1929. He was six times a presidential candidate for the Socialist Party from 1928 to 1948. His best showing was in 1932, during the Great Depression, when he received nearly a million votes, but most of these voters cast their lot with Franklin Delano Roosevelt's New Deal in the mid-1930s, and the Socialist Party declined. Thomas remained unconvinced by the New Deal, believing that a more systematic and complete reform was still necessary to bring about moral change. Nonetheless, many of the ideas he championed, such as minimum wage laws, pensions and health and unemployment insurance, were implemented by the major parties, due at least in part to the constant pressure that he maintained.

Before and during World War II, Thomas fought to keep the United States out of any entanglements, believing that involvement in a European war would move the country irrevocably toward fascism. Opposed to communism for its crass materialism and extreme measures, he removed communists from important positions in the ACLU in 1940 but defended their civil liberties against the extreme attacks of the McCarthy era. His public efforts in the 1960s were directed against racial inequality and the mounting conflict in Vietnam.

Intellectually Thomas was eclectic, borrowing from the social gospel, progressivism and moderate socialist thinkers. His early years in the slums convinced him that *capitalism was unable to address properly the growing problem of poverty in American cities. Building on the work of Walter Rauschenbusch and John H. Holmes, he spoke out for the poor and the oppressed, proclaiming a gospel of social reform and economic justice. Even after stepping down from the pulpit, he had remained a minister in the *Presbyterian Church in the U.S.A. (PCUSA) until 1931, but he abandoned organized religion soon thereafter. He articulated his new religious views in *A Socialist's Faith* (1951).

Bibliography. *ANB* 21; *DARB;* J. C. Duran, "In Defense of Conscience: Norman Thomas as an Exponent of Christian Pacifism During WWI," *JPH* 52 (1974) 19-32; H. Fleischman, *Norman Thomas: A Biography* (1969). C. E. Stockwell

Thompson, Charles Lemuel (1839-1924).‡ Presbyterian minister and denominational executive. Born in Lehigh County, Pennsylvania, Thompson was reared in Wisconsin. He attended Carroll College (B.A., 1858) and studied theology at Princeton Theological Seminary (1858-1860) and the Theological Seminary of the Northwest (later McCormick; B.D., 1861). Ordained by the *Presbyterian Church in the U.S.A. (PCUSA) in 1861, from then until 1888 he served churches in Wisconsin, Ohio, Illinois, Pennsylvania and Missouri. In 1888 he was called to the Madison Avenue Presbyterian Church in New York City. He served as moderator of the general assembly in 1888 and 1898, and eventually he left his pastorate to become secretary of the board of home missions, a position he held until 1914.

Thompson championed ministries to Native Americans, immigrants, rural churches and Hispanics. Though evangelical in conviction, Thompson was more interested in *mission than in doctrine and deplored the heresy trials of his time. His concern for cooperation and comity among various denominations involved him in the Home Missions Council (chairman, 1908-1914) and the Federal Council of Churches of Christ. He interpreted his work in his various writings, including *The Soul of America* (1919) and *The Religious Foundations of America* (1917). At the time of his death he was recognized as the home missionary statesman of his generation.

Bibliography. DARB; NCAB 10; E. O. Thompson, ed., *Charles Lemuel Thompson* (1924).

J. M. Smylie

Thomson, John (c. 1690-1753). Presbyterian minister. Born around 1690 in northern Ireland, Thomson graduated from the University of Glasgow (1706) and soon after licensure crossed the Atlantic in 1715. He was ordained and settled at Lewes, Delaware, in 1717, and quickly rising in the estimation of his colleagues, he was chosen moderator of synod twice in the first six years of its existence (1719 and 1722) and of New Castle Presbytery three times (1718, 1722 and 1730). He was the first moderator of Donegal Presbytery when it was founded in 1732. From 1730 to 1744 Thomson pastored in and around Middle Octarora and Chestnut Level, Pennsylvania. His wife (whose name is unknown), the mother of twelve of his children, died around 1734, and within a couple of years he married Mary McKean Reid, a widow, who bore him one more daughter. Before he remarried, he wrote a tender volume of fatherly advice, *The Poor Orphan's Legacy* (1734), in which he entreated his children "to make serious practical religion your main and principal work and business while you are in the world."

Thomson is perhaps best known for proposing subscription to the *Westminster standards, which, after considerable debate and discussion, was unanimously approved in 1729. One point that is often forgotten, however, is that Thomson's original proposal allowed for scruples, as he suggested that if any minister should teach or preach contrary to the confession and catechisms, "unless, first, he propose the said point to the Presbytery or the Synod to be by them discussed, he shall be censured so and so."

During the Great Awakening, Thomson opposed the extremes of the *revivalists and therefore was accused of being unregenerate and a "minister of Satan" by Gilbert *Tennent and his associates. In later years the *New Side realized that it had spoken too harshly, and both Samuel *Davies and Gilbert Tennent lauded Thomson for his charity and humility. Nevertheless the damage to Thomson's reputation was done, and even 250 years later he is still often considered a representative of dead orthodoxy and repressive church government. His controversial works *The Doctrine of Convictions Set in a Clear Light* (1741) and *The Government of the Church of Christ* (1741) articulated an even- tempered response to the excesses of New Side revivalism, setting forth an evangelical Presbyterian doctrine of conversion and pleading for Christian charity and humility on both sides. Maintaining a clearer head than most during the schism of 1741, he supported the exclusion of the revivalists on the grounds of their disorderly conduct and teaching but was eager to resolve differences and restore unity.

In 1738 Thomson began regular preaching tours among the *Scots-Irish settlers in the backwoods of Virginia. Six years later he moved there, later removing to Carolina, establishing a series of preaching stations that he regularly supplied. Due to the scarcity of gospel ministers and good books for the edification and training of the people of Virginia, Thomson prepared *An Explication of the Shorter Catechism* (1749) for the use of families and individuals.

Bibliography. J. G. Herndon, "The Reverend John Thomson," *JPHS* 21, no. 1 (1943) 34-59; W. H. T. Squires, "John Thomson: Presbyterian Pioneer," *Union Seminary Review* 32, no. 2 (1924) 149-61.

P. J. Wallace

Thornwell, James Henley (1812-1862).† Southern Presbyterian theologian and educator. Born in the Malborough District of South Carolina, Thornwell graduated from South Carolina College with top honors (1831) and served as a schoolteacher for two years. During that time he experienced a dramatic conversion and a call to the ministry. He studied theology at Andover and briefly at Harvard (1834); after being ordained by Bethel Presbytery, he pastored churches in and around Lancaster, South Carolina (1835-1838), where he married Nancy White. He then accepted a call as professor of philosophy at South Carolina College (1838-1839). Returning to the pastorate for a brief period (First Presbyterian Church, Columbia, 1839-1841), he soon returned to the college as chaplain and professor of sacred literature and Christian evidences (1841-1851). After another brief stint in the pastorate at Glebe Street Church in Charleston, he served as president of the college, as well as chaplain and professor, from 1852 to 1855. While at South Carolina College he worked to counter the influence of his predecessor, Thomas Cooper, whose liberal views on religion Thornwell strongly opposed. From 1855 to 1862 Thornwell occupied the chair of theology at Columbia Theological Seminary and served as supply pastor of the Columbia Church during most of this time.

A leader in the formation of the Presbyterian Church in the Confederate (later United) States (1861), he wrote the "Address to All the Churches of Jesus Christ Throughout the Earth" justifying its separation from the Northern church. Thornwell argued that one church could not exist in two separate and hostile countries, especially after the Spring Resolutions (*see* Spring, Gardiner) of the general assembly of 1861 had mandated that all *Old School Presbyterians were to render obedience to the federal government in Washington. Thornwell was founding editor of the *Southern Presbyterian Review* (1847) and editor of the *Southern Quarterly Review* (1855-1857). Most of his writings appear in his *Collected Writings* (4 vols., 1871-1873).

Thornwell had a passion for orthodoxy and a sense of duty to truth, and he sought to defend traditional institutions and standards against liberal and ungodly assaults. He defended the South and its institutions, including slavery. He was a unionist until the election of Abraham Lincoln, after which he championed the Confederacy. His theology, which he supported with immense learning, was essentially that of the *Westminster standards. He defined theology as "the system of doctrine in its logical connection and dependence, which, when spiritually discerned, produces true piety." Following Scottish Common-Sense philosophy and Old School Presbyterian orthodoxy, Thornwell believed that the task of theological scholarship was to show the complete harmony of sound philosophy and theology as one system of truth. He had few views not shared with other Old School theologians, unless it was in making justification the central principle of all theology and in the large place he gave to Christian ethics as a section of systematic theology. He died before he could develop a complete systematic theology.

Thornwell's influence was more lasting in the area of ecclesiology. In 1857 he was selected as the chairman of the committee devoted to revising the rules of discipline. In the debates that followed, he articulated a *jure divino* view of Presbyterianism, which Charles *Hodge called "hyper-High Church Presbyterianism," to which Thornwell responded by claiming that Hodge's view contained "a touch of democracy and a touch of prelacy, a large slice of Quakerism, but no Presbyterianism." Thornwell believed that the *polity of the church as well as its doctrine is limited to scriptural teaching. He viewed the lay elder as just as much a presbyter in the biblical sense as the minister. Elders should share equally with ministers in the government of the church and in the ordination of ministers. Since the church cannot surrender the discharge of its own divinely assigned responsibilities, it should not use boards or voluntary societies to carry out its mission. The church is the only missionary society with divine authority, and it alone is competent for the task. This should be done through committees subject to church courts. Nor should the church become embroiled in political controversies or give its endorsement to movements for *social reform. The church can only enforce scriptural duties, and slavery was considered a political matter that the church could neither enjoin nor condemn.

A brilliant Old School preacher, theologian and churchman, Thornwell was the youngest general assembly moderator ever (1847) and perhaps the most influential Southern minister before the *Civil War. He died prematurely of consumption and overwork.

Bibliography. *ANB* 21; *DAB* IX; *DARB;* J. O. Farmer Jr., *The Metaphysical Confederacy: James Henley Thornwell and the Synthesis of Southern Values* (1986); P. L. Garber, "A Centennial Appraisal of James Henley Thornwell," in *A Miscellany of American Christianity,* ed. S. C. Henry (1963); E. B. Holifield, *The Gentlemen Theologians: American Theology in Southern Culture,* 1795-1860 (1978); B. M. Palmer, *The Life and Letters of James Henley Thornwell* (1875); J. H. Thornwell, *The Collected Writings of J. H. Thornwell,* ed. J. B. Adger and J. L. Girardeau, 4 vols. (1871-1873).

A. H. Freundt Jr.

Towner, Margaret Ellen (1925-). Presbyterian minister. Born in Columbia, Missouri, Towner was educated at Carleton College (B.S., 1948) and began her career as a medical photographer at the Mayo Clinic. She attended Syracuse University and served as director of Christian *education at the East Genesee Presbyterian Church in New York from 1950 to 1951.

In 1951 Towner enrolled at Union Theological Seminary (B.D., 1954) to pursue a three-year course of study in preparation for her work as a Christian educator. Following graduation from seminary, she accepted a call to the Tacoma Park Presbyterian Church, Maryland, where she served as director of Christian education. In 1955 she served in a similar position at the First Presbyterian Church of Allentown, Pennsylvania.

Towner became the first woman in the *Presbyterian Church in the U.S.A. (PCUSA) to be ordained as a minister of the Word and sacrament. As a seminary-trained commissioned church worker, she typified both the background and vocational interests of the majority of Presbyterian women who entered the ministry in the 1950s and 1960s.

After her ordination in 1956, Towner continued her ministry at the First Presbyterian Church of Allentown, where she was installed as assistant pastor. In 1961 she was called as associate pastor to the First Presbyterian Church in Kalamazoo, Michigan. From 1973 until 1978, she served several smaller congregations at the Kettle Moraine parish in Wisconsin. Until her retirement in 1990, she continued to copastor several small churches (Delafield, Zion United and Bethesda) in Wisconsin.

Throughout her ministry, Towner served on various presbytery and synod-level committees that were involved with Christian education, including radio and television work and children's and young adult work.

Bibliography. L. A. Boyd and R. D. Brackenridge, *Presbyterian Women in America: Two Centuries of a Quest for Status* (1983); J. D. Krugler and D. Weinberg-Kinsey, "Equality of Leadership: The Ordinations of Sarah E. Dickson and Margaret E. Towner in the Presbyterian Church in the USA," *AP* 68 (1990) 245-57.

F. Heuser Jr.

Trumbull, David (1819-1889).† First Protestant American *missionary to Chile. A Congregational minister and son of a governor of Connecticut, Trumbull completed studies at Yale (1842) and Princeton Seminary (1845) before responding to an appeal from the foreign residents of Valparaiso for a resident Protestant pastor. He was sent jointly by the Foreign Evangelical Society and the Seaman's Friend Society, arriving in 1845.

For more than fifteen years Trumbull was not officially permitted to evangelize native Chileans, but his arguments for religious liberty, as well as the increasingly liberal attitude of the Chilean authorities, eventually allowed him to work freely even among the Roman Catholic population. A church in his home resulted in the acquisition of property and completion of a chapel by 1856. His efforts to influence legislation contributed to the granting of limited religious toleration in 1865, the opening of cemeteries to Protestants in 1883 and civil marriage in 1884. Due to financial difficulties, the mission was transferred to the *Presbyterian Church in the U.S.A. (PCUSA), and in 1872 Trumbull was instrumental in founding the Presbyterian Church in Chile, even though he himself remained a Congregationalist. A vigorous defender of evangelical Christianity against what he considered the yoke of Catholicism, his cooperation with all Protestants has been credited with the absence of sectarian divisions in Chile that afflicted missionary work in the neighboring republics. Trumbull took Chilean citizenship in 1886, and when he died three years later the Chilean congress rose for a moment of silence in a display of respect.

Bibliography. H. M. Goodpasture, "David Trumbull: Missionary Journalist and Liberty in Chile, 1845-1889," *JPH* 56 (1978) 149-65; J. B. A. Kessler Jr., *A Study of the Older Protestant Missions and Churches in Peru and Chile* (1967); W. R. Wheeler et al., *Modern Missions in Chile and Brazil* (1926). E. A. Wilson

Turretin, Francis (1623-1687). Teacher and pastor at Geneva. Turretin was a leading Reformed covenant theologian, vigilant in combating the rationalistic and humanistic trends appearing in the late 1600s that culminated in the Enlightenment. Observing similar inclinations in the French Reformed Academy at Saumur, Turretin promoted the Helvetic Consensus Formula (1675). Even though the *Canons of Dort could be interpreted in Saumur's liberal direction, through this formulary Turretin championed a "safer" and "purer" tradition at Geneva. His *Institutio Theologiae Elencticae* (1679- 1685) is a classic summation of strict *Calvinism, refuting all challengers in its three volumes. Each *questio* in this polemics displays an unusual ability to uncover false options with historically aware and logically rigorous arguments.

When traditional Calvinism was in retreat during the eighteenth century, the conservative interpreters of the *Westminster Confession zealously studied Turretin's *Institutio,* believing this rigorous work equipped diligent students for future challenges. Cotton Mather and Jonathan *Edwards recommended Turretin as without equal and excellent on the five points of Calvinism and other controversial matters. His *Institutio* was widely used in nineteenth-century America. It was the primary text at Union Seminary in Virginia until it was replaced by Robert Lewis *Dabney's *Lectures* and at Princeton Seminary until the publication of Charles *Hodge's *Systematic Theology* (1872-1873).

Since Princeton trained more seminarians than did any other school in the nineteenth century, Turretin's theology helped define the American theological landscape. Charles Hodge represents the height of Turretin's influence at Princeton. However, Hodge had to adjust Turretin's scholastic theology to Scottish Common-Sense philosophy. This framework devalued and flattened such scholastic categories as *habitus,* first and second act and spiritual presence. While lacking the creativity to counter this reductionism successfully, Hodge was a faithful disciple. Resisting Archibald *Alexander's evidentialism, Hodge reinstated Turretin's defense of Scripture's self-authenticating authority in *The Way of Life.* Unlike James Henley *Thornwell and Dabney, Hodge never openly criticized Turretin.

Hodge's combative zeal for a pure orthodoxy emulated Turretin. American *revivalistic tendencies as well as the culture's elevation of human concerns and abilities led the *New School Presbyterians toward *Arminianism and others into subjectivism. Hodge noted the parallels with Turretin's day: the "New School system adopted in this country, lies between the Arminian and the French scheme, containing more truth than the former, and less than the latter," he wrote. Turretin's core concerns defined the Princetonians' battle lines: an infallible Bible, God's particular grace, immediate imputation of Adam's sin, natural inability, Christ's substitutionary atonement, an immediate preceding regeneration and justification as imputed righteousness. While influenced by other theologians, Turretin played a prominent role in helping Princeton keep a version of traditional Calvinism alive well into the twentieth century. The charge that Turretin distorted the Westminster standards overlooks Westminster's advocacy of a generic Calvinism and frequently misunderstands Turretin's scholastic terminology.

Since the *fundamentalist-modernist controversies in the twentieth century, only the more conservative schools even mention Turretin.

See also Scholasticism, Reformed.

Bibliography. C. Briggs, *Whither?* (1889); P. Helm, "Introduction," in J. Edwards, *Treatise on Grace* (1971); M. A. Noll, ed., *The Princeton Theology 1812-1921: Scripture, Science, and Theological Method from Archibald Alexander to Benjamin Breckinridge Warfield* (1983); T. R. Phillips, "Francis Turretin's Idea of Theology and Its Bearing upon His Doctrine of Scripture" (Ph.D. dissertation, Vanderbilt University 1986); J. Rogers and D. McKim, eds., *The Authority and Interpretation of the Bible* (1979); F. Turretin, *Institutes of Elentic Theology,* tran. M. Giger, ed. J. Dennison (1992); B. B. Warfield, *The Westminster Assembly and Its Work* (1931); J. D. Woodbridge, *Biblical Authority: A Critique of the Rogers/McKim Proposal* (1982). T. R. Phillips

U

Underwood, Horace Grant (1859-1916). Presbyterian *missionary. Underwood was born in London, England, and reared in New Durham, New Jersey. He graduated from the University of the City of New York (now New York University) in 1881 and New Brunswick Theological Seminary in 1884.

First ordained by the *Dutch Reformed Church in 1884, Underwood became a Presbyterian and was commissioned as a missionary for the Presbyterian board of foreign missions. Amid the postbellum period of missionary expansion, he pioneered the Presbyterian missionary enterprise in Korea. Arriving in 1885, he established an orphanage and school that later became the John D. Wells Academy for Christian Workers in Chemulpo. After learning Korean, he wrote a dictionary and an introductory grammar, founded the Korean Religious Tract Society and helped translate the Bible and various religious works. He married Lillias Stirling Horton, M.D., in 1889. That same year he established the Sai Mun An Church. On one itinerant trip he crossed into Manchuria and baptized thirty converts despite a governmental edict that forbade missionaries from proselytizing.

Underwood was a confidant of the Korean king, and on several occasions he acted as an translator for foreign governments. While on furloughs, he spoke at churches and conferences, including those sponsored by the Student Volunteer Movement and the Young Men's Christian Association (YMCA), key organizations in rallying support for missions. In 1903 he established a YMCA in Seoul. He wrote dozens of articles and two books, *The Call of Korea* (1908) and *The Religions of Eastern Asia* (1910).

Bibliography. *DAB* XIX; M. Huntley, *To Start a Work: The Foundations of Protestant Missions in Korea (1884-1919)* (1987) ; L. H. Underwood, *Underwood of Korea* (1918). P. C. Kemeny

United Presbyterian Church of North America. The origins of the United Presbyterian Church of North America (UPCNA) lie in post-Reformation Scotland, when a high church party asserted the authority of the church over civil magistrates and clashed with the episcopal forms of church government favored by the Scottish Crown. These tensions exploded in 1638, when the critics of royal policy signed their famous National Covenant, agreeing never to lay down arms until the bishops were driven out of Scotland. In 1643 the Covenanters made an alliance with the Parliament in England against Charles I, resulting in the Solemn League and Covenant and the *Westminster Confession, undertaking to establish a Presbyterian form of church government throughout the British Isles.

From their high-water mark of Covenanter power, the majority of Scots gradually retreated into a moderate stance of mutual toleration with the Anglican establishment in England, but a slowly dwindling minority resisted any deviation from the total authority of the Covenants of 1638 and 1643. During the Restoration of the Stuarts from 1660 to 1688 this minority conducted desultory rebellion against the Crown and acquired a folk memory of its sufferings during "the killing times." A small remnant that refused any compromise with the authority of the government even after the Glorious Revolution organized itself as the Reformed Presbyterian church. Many of its adherents emigrated to northern Ireland and the American colonies, especially Pennsylvania and the Carolinas.

In Scotland the religious antipathies of the Covenanter era smoldered on into a major secession from the church of Scotland in 1733. The Seceders, or the Associate Synod, objected to lay patronage, the customary selection of parish ministers by the landlords of the parish. Beneath this grievance ran a deep suspicion that the philosophical ideas of the Enlightenment were undermining the authority of the Westminster standards in the Church of Scotland. The Associate Synod gained adherents in Ireland and contributed many immigrants to the colonies. In 1782 the very similar Covenanters and Seceders buried their minor theological differences and united to form the Associate Reformed denomination. A fragment of both bodies remained out of the union, so that from 1782 to 1858 there were three minor Presbyterian denominations in America. In 1858 the Associate Reformed denomination, with 31,000 members in 367 congregations, joined with the Associate Synod's 23,000 members in 293 congregations to become the United Presbyterian Church in North America (UPCNA).

Between 1858 and 1958 the new denomination evolved from an ethnic *Scots-Irish denomination into an American church. While generally espousing a conservative theology it gradually modified some of the tenets cherished by its antecedent denominations. For example, in the early twentieth century it abandoned its insistence on the exclusive use of the psalms is public worship. Its ethnic character enabled it to enjoy increments in membership from Scottish and Northern Irish immigration until the tide of immigration dried up after 1920.

The UPCNA benefited from sound administrative practices. It advanced its work by means of a number of well-run church boards, among which were home *missions, foreign missions, church extension, mission to the freedmen and *education. The foreign mission board established missions in Egypt and northern India that contributed to the evangelization and modernization of both regions. The Egyptian mission eventually extended into the Sudan and Ethiopia. The board of church extension methodologically ringed the suburbs of American cities with new United Presbyterian congregations. The response of the church to the needs of the freedmen continued into the twentieth century with programs directed to the changing needs of black people. The board of education helped support six denominational colleges and the theological seminaries of the denomination.

By 1958 the UPCNA could no longer discern differences between itself and the *Presbyterian Church in the U.S.A. (PCUSA) large enough to warrant the continuation of its separate denominational existence. Merger with the larger body came with minimal opposition but not without expressions of nostalgia for the Scots-Irish ethnic ties of the United Presbyterians.

BIBLIOGRAPHY. W. N. Jamison, *The United Presbyterian Story: A Centennial Study, 1858-1958* (1958).

W. L. Fisk

V

Van Dusen, Henry Pitney (1897-1975).† Presbyterian *educator and ecumenical leader. Born in Philadelphia, Pennsylvania, Van Dusen was educated at Princeton University (B.A., 1919), Union Theological Seminary in New York (B.D., 1924) and the University of Edinburgh (Ph.D., 1932). Ordained a Presbyterian minister in 1924 during the midst of the *fundamentalist-modernist debate, Van Dusen argued that belief in the virgin birth was not necessary for ordination in the *Presbyterian Church in the U.S.A. (PCUSA) and was defended by a young lawyer and Presbyterian layman, John Foster *Dulles, a long-time friend and associate. After serving as secretary of the student division of the Young Men's Christian Association (YMCA), Van Dusen returned to Union Seminary in 1926, serving as instructor and then as assistant professor of philosophy of religion and systematic theology, as Roosevelt Professor of Systematic Theology, as dean of students and, from 1945 to 1963, as president.

Van Dusen's tenure as president of Union was marked by a significant expansion and diversification of the seminary's faculty, student body and curriculum. Van Dusen led Union to a position of great prominence and prestige among Protestant seminaries. He was a leading American Protestant advocate of the ecumenical movement and a delegate to the world conference of the Life and Work Movement at Oxford in 1937. Van Dusen actively promoted the formation of the World Council of Churches (WCC), serving as chair of the WCC study commission and as a member of its executive committee. He attended the first WCC assembly in Amsterdam in 1948 and six years later was appointed chair of a joint committee of the International Missionary Council and the WCC for the purpose of merging the two bodies, which was accomplished at the New Delhi WCC in 1961.

Following the Oxford Conference in 1937, Van Dusen became one of the few churchmen to favor intervention in the growing global crisis preceding World War II. Admitting that war is a manifestation of the power of sin, he insisted that it may sometimes be necessary to preserve a just society. He warned that Japanese and German aggression in the late 1930s would engulf America sooner or later and chastised Christian pacifism as "bad politics and debased religion." Claiming that liberal theological ethics tended to create a false dichotomy between the "Christian way" and the "way of power," he believed that the viewpoints espoused by the *Christian Century* were idealistic and naive, which led him, with Reinhold *Niebuhr and others, to found the journal *Christianity and Crisis* in 1941 to encourage the mainline churches toward a more interventionist position.

Van Dusen defined religion as "the experience of the soul's communion with Ultimate Reality" and sought to train churchmen who would provide "world-minded" leadership. Serving on the editorial board of several journals of American Protestantism, Van Dusen was an important proponent of Protestant missions, an interest which, along with his concern for Christian unity, was reflected in his many publications. Long supporters of euthanasia, he and his wife chose to overdose on sleeping pills after both of them had concluded that their physical condition had deteriorated past the point of possible recovery.

Bibliography. *DARB;* R. T. Handy, *A History of Union Theological Seminary in New York* (1987); *NCAB* H; D. K. Thompson, "Henry Pitney Van Dusen: Ecumenical Statesman" (Ph.D. diss., Union Theological Seminary, Richmond, Virginia, 1974).

W. A. Silva

Van Dyke, Henry (1852-1933).‡ Presbyterian minister, *educator and diplomat. Born in Germantown, Pennsylvania, Van Dyke was educated at the Brooklyn Polytechnic Institute, Princeton University (B.A., 1873) and Princeton Theological Seminary (B.D., 1877). He also studied with Isaak Dorner at the University of Berlin. He returned to the United States to pastor the United Congregational Church in Newport, Rhode Island (1879-1883). From 1883 to 1899 he was the pastor of Brick Presbyterian Church in New York City.

Van Dyke's literary career began in 1884 with the publication of *The Reality of Religion,* followed by a great variety of works, including poetry, short stories, literary criticism and outdoor life (he was an avid fisherman). His most famous work is *The Story of the Other Wise Man* (1896), which was subsequently translated into twenty-eight languages. His literary renown led to his appointment as Murray Professor of English Literature at Princeton University (1899-1913; 1919-1923). During Woodrow *Wilson's administration Van Dyke served as ambassador to the Netherlands and Luxembourg (1913-1916).

Van Dyke's crowning achievement was his leadership in the production of *The Book of Common Worship of the Presbyterian Church* (1906; rev. ed. 1932). He was moderator of the general assembly in 1902.

Van Dyke's theology can best be described as moderately liberal. A leader in the movement for creedal revision, he particularly opposed the traditional Reformed doctrine of reprobation. Nevertheless he retained the language of evangelical *piety even while displaying doctrinal imprecision.

Bibliography. *ANB* 22; *DAB* X; *DARB;* H. T. Kerr, *Sons of the Prophets* (1963); *NCAB* 25; T. Van Dyke, *Henry Van Dyke* (1935). J. R. Wiers

Van Til, Cornelius (1895-1987).† Presbyterian *educator and apologist. Born at Grootegast, the Netherlands, Van Til emigrated with his family to America in 1905. As a member of the *Christian Reformed Church (CRC), Van Til attended Calvin College and Calvin Seminary in Grand Rapids, Michigan, followed by studies at Princeton Theological Seminary and Princeton University. Ordained in the CRC (1927), he ministered briefly in Michigan and then taught apologetics for one year at Princeton Seminary, until its reorganization in 1929, when he was persuaded to join the faculty of the newly founded Westminster Theological Seminary in Philadelphia. Van Til joined the *Orthodox Presbyterian Church (OPC) soon after its inception in 1936 and remained professor of apologetics at Westminster until his retirement in 1975 at the age of eighty.

Van Til built his apologetics around an original application of traditional Reformed theology. Joining two streams of the *Reformed tradition, the *Princeton theology of Benjamin Breckinridge *Warfield and Geerhardus *Vos, and the Dutch contributions of Abraham *Kuyper and Herman *Bavinck, he constructed a presuppositional apologetic based on two fundamental assertions: the Creator-creature distinction that demands human beings presuppose the self-attesting triune God in all their thinking; the reality that unbelievers will resist this obligation in every aspect of life and thought, seeking to be autonomous from God. All reasoning processes are circular since they must begin with an ultimate, prior religious norm, either for God or against him. Autonomy is self-defeating since its circular reasoning rejects the only basis for its claims, the Word of the living God. Thus Christian apologetics must not yield to any autonomous principle, such as a framework of philosophy or logic abstracted from the Creator God of the Scriptures.

This apologetic quickly became controversial when Van Til challenged philosopher Gordon H. *Clark on his overly rigorous usage of the principle of noncontradiction as a virtually autonomous standard. Believing that finite ways of knowing are inevitably limited, Van Til rejected Clark's assertion that human knowledge can be identical to God's, even qualitatively. Rather, human knowledge is analogical to God's, and in order to be true knowledge, it must be self-consciously dependent on the reality of the biblical God and the authority of his revelation.

One of Karl *Barth's most vocal opponents, Van Til published three critiques, *The New Modernism* (1946), *Has Karl Barth Become Orthodox?* (1954) and *Christianity and Barthianism* (1962), in which he challenged the fundamental assumptions of *neo-orthodoxy. Claiming that neo-orthodoxy was merely the old *modernism in new clothes (and hence neo-modernism, rather than neo-orthodoxy), Van Til argued that Barth's underlying philosophical standpoint rested too much on a Kantian epistemology, undermining his stated intent to return to a reformational theology. Admitting that Barth frequently used words in an orthodox fashion, Van Til pointed out that Barth's meaning was far from confessional orthodoxy and even remained worlds apart from historic evangelicalism.

Van Til wrote more than twenty books during his teaching career, in addition to more than thirty unpublished class syllabi that were widely circulated. Perhaps best known is *The Defense of the Faith* (1955). His views were widely known and debated among evangelical and conservative Reformed theologians and apologists and have been developed by some of his students.

Bibliography. J. Frame, *Van Til: The Theologian* (1976); E. F. Geehan, ed., *Jerusalem and Athens* (1971); W. White Jr., *Van Til, Defender of the Faith* (1979). H. M. Conn

Vassady, Bela (1902-1992). Reformed theologian and *educator. Born at Arad, Hungary, Vassady studied at the University of Debrecen in Debrecen, Hungary (1920-1922). At the invitation of the historian of the Reformed Church in the United States, James I. *Good, he attended Central Theological Seminary from 1922 to 1924 (B.D., 1924). In 1925 he received the master of theology degree from Princeton Theological Seminary.

In Hungary Vassady had an illustrious career as a professor of theology at three Reformed theological seminaries: Papa (1925-1928), Sarospatak (1928-1934) and Debrecen (1934-1948). While he was in the United States on a speaking tour in 1946, the communists took over Hungary, and Vassady chose to remain in this country. For the next five years he served briefly on the faculty of four seminaries: visiting professor at McCormick Theological Seminary in Chicago (1947); Princeton Theological Seminary (1947-1949); Presbyterian Theological Seminary in Dubuque, Iowa (1951-1952); and professor of biblical theology and ethics at Fuller Theological Seminary (1949-1951). Vassady's tenure at Fuller Theological Seminary was terminated because of a conflict with the institution concerning his ecumenical views and because of his refusal to sign a statement propounding verbal inspiration of Scripture. In 1952 he obtained a position as professor of systematic theology at Lancaster Theological Seminary in Lancaster, Pennsylvania, where he remained until his retirement in 1973.

Through much of his career Vassady was active in the ecumenical movement: executive secretary of the Ecumenical Council of the Churches in Hungary (1942-1946); delegate of the Reformed Church of Hungary to the Life and Work Conference (Oxford, England, 1937) and to the Faith and Order Conference (Edinburgh, Scotland, 1937); member of the continuation committee of the Faith and Order Movement (1938-1952); delegate of the Reformed Church of Hungary to the first assembly of the World Council of Churches (Amsterdam, 1948); and a delegate to the Reformed and Presbyterian World Alliance (1948, 1954, 1959, 1964).

The editor of several theological journals in Hungary and of *Theology and Life* (1958-1963) at Lancaster, Pennsylvania, Vassady contributed more than three hundred articles to Hungarian and English periodicals and wrote several books in Hungarian. His principal books in English are *Light Against Darkness* (1961), *Christ's Church: Evangelical, Catholic and Reformed* (1965) and a theological autobiography, *Limping Along: Confessions of a Pilgrim Theologian* (1985). He died in Ann Arbor, Michigan.

J. B. Payne

Veenstra, Johanna (1894-1933). Christian Reformed *missionary. Veenstra was born in Paterson, New Jersey, and her family attended the *Christian Reformed Church (CRC). When she was two years old she moved with her family to Grand Rapids, Michigan, so that her carpenter father could attend Calvin College and Seminary. Eight months after he was ordained, he died of typhoid fever, and his widow and six children returned to Paterson, where Veenstra's mother opened a general store. Veenstra attended a Christian school until she was twelve; after two years in business school, she went to work as a stenographer in New York City. For five years she commuted to the city from Paterson, experiencing first-hand the pleasures and temptations of city life.

At the age of nineteen, having become committed to mission work, Veenstra entered the Union Missionary Training Institute in New York. While studying there, she applied to the Sudan United Mission (SUM) to work in Africa. Because she was only twenty-two years old, she had to wait three years to be sent overseas. She returned to Grand Rapids and went to work for a city mission. She also attended classes at Calvin College, where she became the first female member of the Student Volunteer Movement. Her final year in the United States was spent in New York City, studying midwifery at Bellevue Maternity Hospital.

In 1919 Veenstra left for Lagos, Nigeria. From Lagos, she traveled three hundred miles by train to Minna. From Minna she was poled up the Benue River to Ibi. The trip took two weeks, and no one on the flat-bottom boat spoke English. From Ibi she pedaled a bicycle twenty-five miles to Wukan and later another twenty-five miles to Donga, where she studied the Hausa language. In February 1921 she arrived on bicycle at Lupwe, which became her home base.

Close to several villages in the foothills of the Cameroon Mountains, Veenstra lived among the Dzompere ("to eat a man") tribe. There was danger everywhere: disease, snakes, mosquitos, wild animals and angry tribal chiefs. At Lupwe she established a boarding school and organized a medical dispensary; she trained young converts to become evangelists and showed farmers how to increase their crop yield. During the dry season, some two hundred days of the year, Veenstra traveled on bicycle, visiting the people of her district and preaching.

Veenstra wrote of her experiences for publication in *De Heidenwereld*, which was later called the *Missionary Monthly*. In 1926 her autobiography, *Pioneering for Christ in the Sudan*, was published. Her views on missions caused considerable debate. She frequently asserted that she did not want "to swamp the district with white workers." She believed strongly in a self-supporting, self-governing and self-propagating Nigerian church. Veenstra worked at a furious pace, both when at Lupwe and when traveling around her district. Even when she was home on furlough, she did not rest but traveled around the United States, talking about her work on the foreign mission field. Her schedule was demanding; her work arduous and emotionally draining. Her health was seriously undermined and when, in April 1933, she suffered an attack of appendicitis, her heart was not strong enough to survive the surgery.

Veenstra's work at Lupwe was continued after her death. The boarding school and the medical dispensary continued to teach young converts and provide medical care respectively for the district. In 1939 SUM offered the Lupwe field to the CRC, because by that time most of the SUM missionaries in Nigeria were from the CRC. In 1940 SUM/CRC was created, and the Lupwe field became part of the CRC's mission effort.

BIBLIOGRAPHY. H. Beets, *Johanna of Nigeria* (1937); *A Memorial Tribute to Miss Johanna Veenstra* (1933); E. Stuart-Watt, *Aflame for God* (1938).

S. H. Goliber

Verbeck, Guido Herman Fridolin (1830-1898).† Dutch-American Reformed *missionary. Born to Moravian parents and educated at the Polytechnic Institute of Utrecht in Holland, Verbeck emigrated to America in 1852. He received theological training at Auburn Seminary in New York to prepare for the mission field. In 1859 he was ordained, and he and his new wife went to Japan under the mission board of the *Dutch Reformed Church. Verbeck was one of the first six Protestant missionaries to arrive in Japan in 1859, the year that four ports were opened to foreigners for trade and residence.

At Nagasaki, in addition to evangelizing, Verbeck taught English and western technology. Many of his students later held influential positions in the Meiji government. Not long after the Restoration (1868), Verbeck was invited to Tokyo by the new government to help in setting up a new school. There he served as the first president of the school, which developed into what is now Tokyo University. As one of the *oyatoi gaikokujin* (hired foreigners), Verbeck had a prominent role as an adviser to the government. In his position he influenced many promising young men to study in the United States.

In 1878 Verbeck officially severed his government responsibilities and returned to missionary work. For his services to the government, he was decorated by the emperor. Verbeck gave the last twenty years of his life to evangelism, training pastors and Bible translation. He died in Japan and was buried in a plot deeded to his family by officials of the city of Tokyo.

BIBLIOGRAPHY. *ANB* 22; *DAB* X; W. E. Griffis, *Verbeck of Japan* (1901); H. Sato, "Verbeck, Guido Herman Fridolin," in *Kodansha Encyclopedia of Japan,* vol. 8 (1983).

W. N. Browning

Vos, Geerhardus (1862-1949). Presbyterian theologian and author. Born in Heerenveen, the Netherlands, Vos emigrated to the United States as a young man. Following study at Calvin Theological Seminary and Princeton Theological Seminary, he studied at the University of Berlin and the University of Strasburg (Ph.D. in Arabic). In 1893 Vos became the first professor of biblical theology at Princeton Theological Seminary, where he remained until retirement in 1932.

Vos was significant for his pioneering work in the discipline of biblical theology, based on a firm commitment to Scripture as God's inerrant Word. Among American orthodox Protestant theologians, Vos was among the first to grasp the fundamental significance of the progressive character of God's special, redemptive revelation and to begin drawing methodological consequences for interpreting Scripture. A controlling emphasis of his work was that the Bible is not a catalog of truths about God, humans and the world but that postfall verbal revelation accompanies and interprets redemption. Revelation, as an ongoing process, is invariably focused on the history of God's redemptive acts, that redemptive history that reaches its consummation in the coming of Christ. Vos made enduring contributions in both Old Testament and New Testament theology in his *Biblical Theology* (1948), but probably his most important work was on the kingdom teaching of Jesus in *The Teaching of Jesus Concerning the Kingdom of God and the Church* (1903) and on the theology of Paul in *The Pauline Eschatology* (1930). His writings continue to have an influence on conservative Reformed scholarship in America.

BIBLIOGRAPHY. R. B. Gaffin Jr., ed., *Redemptive History and Biblical Interpretation: The Shorter Writings of Geerhardus Vos* (1980); M. A. Noll, *Between Faith and Criticism* (1986).

R. B. Gaffin Jr

W

Waddel, Moses (1770-1840).† Presbyterian *educator. Born in Iredell County, North Carolina, of *Scots-Irish parentage, Waddell was first educated at Clio's Nursery, a school conducted by the Reverend James Hall, and then, after teaching for six years, Hampden-Sydney College (B.A., 1791). Waddel moved to South Carolina, where he was ordained and served several Presbyterian churches near Charleston. But soon he went to Appling, in northeastern Georgia, and opened a school. In 1804 Waddel established at Willington, in South Carolina near the Savannah River, a distinguished college-preparatory school, what some called the American Eton. Samuel Stanhope *Smith of Princeton considered its program equal to any.

In 1819 Waddel became president of Franklin College at Athens, Georgia, a moribund institution of seven students, but he built its enrollment and laid the foundations for what would become the University of Georgia. In opposition to the "infidelity" of many contemporary educators, his goal was to train godly ministers and teachers. Retiring in 1829, Waddel continued to preach regularly until he suffered a paralytic stroke in 1836 and died at Athens, July 21, 1840. During his lifetime he taught nearly four thousand students, including a dozen members of Congress as well as state governors and numerous lawyers, teachers, ministers and authors. Among the more notable were John C. Calhoun, William H. Crawford, Hugh S. Legare and Augustus Baldwin Longstreet, who described his teacher in the novel *Master William Mitten* (1864).

Bibliography. *AAP* 4; *ANB* 22; *DAB* X; J. N. Waddel, *Memorials of an Academic Life* (1891).

W. J. Wade

Wadsworth, Charles (1814-1882). Presbyterian minister. A native of Litchfield, Connecticut, Wadsworth studied at Union College and then at Princeton Seminary from 1838 to 1840. That same year the Troy Presbytery in New York licensed him, and two years later he was ordained to pastor Second Presbyterian Church of Troy. This was the beginning of Wadsworth's successful preaching career.

From 1850 until 1862 Wadsworth ministered at Arch Street Presbyterian Church in Philadelphia. By 1860 he was one of the most celebrated preachers in the United States and was compared with no less a figure than Henry Ward Beecher. In less than a decade he had taken a small congregation of twelve families and made it nationally prominent. In 1850 a New York newspaper reported that Wadsworth's "church is besieged by persons anxious to hear, long before the hour for the services to commence" and claimed that the minister was able to take even the shortest of texts, such as "Jesus wept," and move his congregation through "the plaintive wail of his tremulous voice." Mark Twain, never a great admirer of preachers or their sermons, admitted that Wadsworth "never fails to preach an able sermon."

After serving on the East Coast, Wadsworth moved to San Francisco to pastor Calvary Church in until 1869. The final years of his life were spent in Philadelphia, where Wadsworth served as minister at Third Dutch Reformed Church until 1879, and then at Clinton Street Immanuel Church until his death.

Wadsworth's greatest claim to fame may have been as the mysterious man in the life of one of America's greatest poets, Emily Dickinson. As a young woman the poet from Amherst, Massachusetts, heard Wadsworth in the spring of 1855 and developed a lasting attachment to him. Dickinson and Wadsworth corresponded, he visited her twice (in 1860 and 1880), and she owned a volume of his sermons. The exact nature of their relationship remains a mystery, but Dickinson clearly prized him as a spiritual confidant, calling him "my Shepherd from 'Little Girlhood.'"

Bibliography. A. Nevin, ed., *Encyclopedia of the Presbyterian Church* (1884); C. Wadsworth, *Sermons* (1883).

R. Lundin

Wagner, James Edgar (1900-1985). Pastor and president of the Evangelical and Reformed Church, copresident of the United Church of Christ. Born near Williamsburg, Pennsylvania, Wagner received his higher education at Findlay College (A.B., 1921) in Ohio and at Lancaster Theological Seminary

(B.D., 1931) in Pennsylvania.

Ordained into the Churches of God in North America at Shippensburg, Pennsylvania, Wagner served as pastor of the North Street Church of God in Harrisburg, Pennsylvania, from 1922 to 1931. During the course of his studies at Lancaster Theological Seminary he transferred his allegiance to the *Reformed Church in the United States and was received into the ministry of that body by the Lancaster Classis on October 26, 1931. From 1931 to 1953 he served as pastor of St. Peter's Reformed (from 1934, Evangelical and Reformed) Church.

Having become well-known as a pastor, speaker and writer within the denomination, Wagner was elected first vice president of the Evangelical and Reformed Church in 1950. He served as the last president of that church from 1953 to 1957. In 1957, when the Evangelical and Reformed Church united with the Congregational-Christian Churches to form the United Church of Christ, Wagner was elected copresident of the new denomination and held that position until 1961. From 1961 to 1968 he was vice president of Ursinus College in Collegeville, Pennsylvania.

In the 1950s and early 1960s Wagner played a prominent role in ecumenical affairs at the national and international levels. A member of the general board of the National Council of Churches from 1950 to 1961, he was its vice president from 1954 to 1957. He was likewise a member of the central committee of the World Council of Churches from 1954 to 1961 and a member of the executive committee of the World Alliance of Reformed Churches from 1954 to 1964, serving as vice president from 1959 to 1964.

Wagner wrote three books: *So You're a Consistoryman* (1949), *Incarnation to Ascension—A Pastoral Interpretation* (1962) and *Perspectives for a Local Church Officer in the United Church of Christ* (1965). He died in Wyncote, Pennsylvania.

J. B. Payne

Wall, Georg Wendelin (1811-1867). Evangelical Synod minister. Born at Owen bei Kirchheim unterem Teck, Württemberg, Wall graduated in 1835 from the Basel Mission House in Switzerland. Immediately following ordination in February 1836, he was sent to America with the Reverend Joseph Rieger to serve German Protestant immigrants in the Midwest.

After a few months of orientation in Hartford, Connecticut, Wall arrived in St. Louis, then a frontier town of eleven thousand people, and became the fourth pastor of the Evangelical Protestant Church of the Holy Ghost, where he served from 1836 to 1843. Holy Ghost was the first German Protestant church in St. Louis, founded in 1834. Wall succeeded in erecting a large new building in 1840, but after conflict between the pastor and his congregation, Wall resigned from his post in 1843. From there he became the leader of the organization of the Evangelical Church Association of the West, which had begun at Mehlville, Missouri, in 1840. Afflicted with health problems, Wall in 1845 became pastor of what was then a rural Evangelical congregation, St. John's, in Mehlville, the mother congregation of the Evangelical Synod, where he served happily until 1850. He then returned as pastor of St. Marcus in St. Louis, where he steadily upheld the Evangelical cause until his early death.

Wall was a steadying influence in founding the Evangelical Synod of the West, becoming its vice president and finding support in Germany for the synod and what became Eden Theological Seminary. He combined pietist and church-forming commitments in a powerful way.

Bibliography. J. W. Flucke, *Evangelical Pioneers* (1931) 21-32; C. E. Schneider, *The German Church on the American Frontier: A Study in the Rise of Religion Among the Germans of the West* (1939).

L. H. Zuck

Wanamaker, John (1838-1922).† Presbyterian businessman, Sunday school leader and supporter of evangelical ministries. Born in Philadelphia, the son of a brickmaker, Wanamaker had little formal education but grew up in a religious atmosphere. He was converted at age eighteen at Philadelphia's First Independent Church. There he taught Sunday school and participated in the 1857 prayer meeting *revival. In 1858 he launched out on his own, founding Bethany Sunday School in a rough neighborhood of the city. By 1865 that group was organized as Bethany Presbyterian Church, with 100 members, although membership at the Sunday school was 900. Sunday school attendance would peak in 1897 at 6,097, while the church topped off at 4,239 five years later.

Hired in 1858 as the first full-time paid secretary in the history of the Young Men's Christian Association (YMCA), Wanamaker resigned his paid secretaryship in 1861 and began his famous mercantile business. The stores grew into an immense business enterprise, but Wanamaker never relinquished his Christian work—in fact, his religious undertakings grew as well as his secular ones.

Wanamaker is perhaps best known for promoting the Sunday-school movement. At Bethany, Wanamaker was a dedicated and concerned Sunday-school superintendent for more than sixty years. He introduced a standard curriculum that improved the efficiency and interest level in the Sunday school. Through his efforts Bethany became the largest Sunday school in America and provided numerous social and recreational activities for people of all ages and economic levels. A model of an institutional church program, Bethany made full use of educational, reformatory and philanthropic activities as a means of evangelism. All the social programs were explicitly designed to bring people into contact with the message of the gospel. Emphasizing personal conversion and revival preaching, one of Bethany's early pastors, John Wilbur *Chapman, was to become one of the leading evangelists of the era.

By 1901 Bethany had developed—largely on the initiative and finances of Wanamaker—a college, kindergarten, dispensary, home for unemployed men, a savings bank for the poor and a men's brotherhood that not only provided for the entertainment and recreation of the members but also involved them in evangelism and social welfare. A lifelong elder at Bethany, Wanamaker served regularly on the board of trustees and around the turn of the century was honored by the brotherhood when he was made president. As in all his religious endeavors, Wanamaker employed many of the same promotional tactics and entrepreneurial skills that made him one of the nation's most successful retail merchants.

Conservative in temperament, Wanamaker lived by strict sabbatarian and temperance principles. Conservative in *politics, he was active in the Republican party. He served as president of the YMCA from 1870 to 1887 and encouraged many of the same programs he had initiated at Bethany. He bought the *Sunday School Times* in the 1860s and established it as the standard source of Sunday school materials in the nation. Through the years, Wanamaker was instrumental in supporting the Philadelphia revivals of Dwight L. Moody and Billy *Sunday and was a national figure in the Presbyterian church.

Bibliography. *ANB* 22; *DAB* X; H. A. Gibbons, *John Wanamaker,* 2 vols. (1926); W. R. Glass, "Liberal Means to Conservative Ends: Bethany Presbyterian Church, John Wanamaker and the Institutional Church Movement," *AP* 68 (1990) 181-92; L. A. Loetscher, "Presbyterians and Political Reform in Philadelphia from 1870 to 1917," *JPHS* 23 (1945) 2-18, 119-36. D. M. Strong

Warfield, Benjamin Breckinridge (1851-1921).† Princeton theologian and *educator. Born near Lexington, Kentucky, the grandson of Robert J. Breckinridge, Warfield graduated from the College of New Jersey with highest honors in 1871. Entering Princeton Theological Seminary, he studied under Charles *Hodge (B.D., 1876). After traveling and studying in Europe (1876-1877), Warfield ministered at Baltimore's First Presbyterian Church (1877-1878) and then began his teaching career in New Testament at Western Seminary in Allegheny, Pennsylvania (1878-1887). When Archibald Alexander *Hodge died in 1887, Warfield succeeded him as professor of didactic and polemic theology at Princeton. After the resignation of Francis Landey *Patton, Warfield served as acting president of the seminary from 1913 to 1914.

Unlike his predecessors, Warfield was not an active churchman, but he maintained Princeton's reputation for demanding scholarship. Although he did not write a systematic theology, he left behind a considerable intellectual legacy for Reformed Christianity. Besides monographs and collections of sermons, his reviews and articles written for learned journals, encyclopedias, dictionaries and the popular press fill more than ten volumes. For more than ten years (1890-1903) he was editor of *The Presbyterian and Reformed Review,* and he was a constant contributor to that journal's successor, *The Princeton Theological Review.*

After his wife, Annie Pearce Kinkead, whom he married in 1876, suffered from a debilitating injury that left her an life-long invalid, Warfield refrained from engaging in ecclesiastical battles that Hodge had tackled. He faithfully cared for his wife, avoiding prolonged absences from Princeton for her sake. Yet he expressed opposition to the revisions of the *Westminster Confession in 1903 in a series of articles, claiming that since the committee insisted that it was not changing the substance of the confession, there was no reason to change the confession at all. Himself fully committed to the Westminster standards, Warfield on several occasions expressed his conviction that the Presbyterian church was slipping from its *Calvinist roots.

Warfield's most lasting contribution was his exposure and refutation of liberalism's naturalistic worldview and reinterpretation of traditional Christian teaching. To the liberals' acceptance of human autonomy and skepticism of the uniqueness of Christian revelation, Warfield responded by buttressing Princeton's main themes: an authoritative Scripture and its supernaturalistic worldview and a strict Calvinistic theology. Warfield honed a rigorous apologetic method as a prolegomenon to theology. Since

Christianity's mission was nothing less than to "reason its way to its dominion," Warfield subjected major schools and thinkers both in Europe and in America to trenchant criticism. He argued that critics' denial of biblical miracles and reinterpretation of the text were without any factual foundation. Their radical conclusions were based on mere hypothetical naturalistic premises that render the Bible's supernaturalism impossible a priori. In denying the biblical worldview, which is the only perspective by which Scripture can be correctly interpreted, liberals devalued Christ, overestimated human nature and eliminated biblical teaching on atonement. In lengthy articles he defended traditional doctrines of the person and work of Christ and the distinctive teachings of Augustine, Calvin and the Westminster standards.

Warfield also developed a rigorous apologetic for Scripture. In the 1881 article "Inspiration," written in collaboration with A. A. Hodge, Warfield defended a totally trustworthy and inerrant Scripture. In numerous articles and reviews he described carefully reasoned nuances of the Princeton view by examining biblical data and demonstrating that conservative teaching rested on the Reformed confessions.

In an age preoccupied with religious consciousness, Warfield opposed its multiform subjectivism. He esteemed Augustine's *Confessions* as a model of religious consciousness and John *Calvin as the theologian of the Holy Spirit. In place of Friedrich Schleiermacher's speculative dependence, he proposed Augustine's religion of dependence on an absolutely sovereign God and Calvin's view that Christian piety is living constantly in the attitude of prayer. He also denounced Immanuel Kant's Copernican Revolution for putting categories of human reason in the place of God's revelation and denounced varieties of Protestant perfectionism for substituting individual revelatory experiences and "counterfeit miracles" for the completed objective revelation of Scripture. Warfield's most positive reaction to modern thought was his attempt to correlate Calvin's doctrine of God's providence in creation with Charles Darwin's teaching on evolution. Repudiating Darwin's principle of natural selection, Warfield admitted the possibility that a historical Adam and Eve might have had animal forebears.

See also PRINCETON THEOLOGY.

BIBLIOGRAPHY. *ANB* 22; *DAB* X; *DARB;* W. A. Hoffecker, "Benjamin B. Warfield," in *Reformed Theology in America,* ed. D. F. Wells (1985) 68-86; idem, *Piety and the Princeton Theologians* (1981); J. E. Meeter, ed., *The Works of Benjamin B. Warfield,* 10 vols. (1927-1932); *NCAB* 20; M. A. Noll, ed., *The Princeton Theology, 1812-1921: Scripture, Science, and Theological Method from Archibald Alexander to Benjamin Breckinridge Warfield* (1983).

W. A. Hoffecker

West, Nathaniel (1826-1906).† Presbyterian Bible conference leader. Born in England, West immigrated to America as a boy and graduated from the University of Michigan in 1846. He pastored Presbyterian congregations in Cincinnati, Ohio (1855-1862); Brooklyn, New York (1862-1869); Detroit, Michigan (1883-1884); and Louisville, Kentucky (1884-c. 1898), and taught at Danville Theological Seminary in Kentucky (1869-1875) and briefly at Moody Bible Institute in Chicago.

West was one of the founders of the Niagara Bible Conference, the first and best known of many Bible and prophecy conferences in the United States. A regular speaker throughout its two decades, he was widely admired for his *piety, knowledge of the Scriptures and theological understanding. By the mid-1880s he had also become a fixture at Northfield, Dwight L. Moody's annual conference, and spoke at the first conference of the Student Volunteer Movement in 1886. In 1892, after being challenged to reconsider his position on the rapture by a younger member of the executive committee of the Niagara conference, West came to the conclusion that the Niagara conference had been wrong in its traditional claim that Jesus could return at any moment. His charge that the secret rapture of the church lacked biblical support provoked a major controversy among premillennialists, and many, including William Gallogly *Moorehead and William Jacob *Erdman came to support him. Nonetheless, the furor eventually split the Niagara leadership, and the conference came to an end at the turn of the twentieth century. His numerous writings, especially *The Thousand Years in Both Testaments* (1889), won many to premillennial eschatological views in the late nineteenth century.

BIBLIOGRAPHY. E. R. Sandeen, *The Roots of Fundamentalism: British and American Millenarianism, 1800-1930* (1970). G. S. Smith

West, Presbyterians and the. The western United States of America needs to be understood as more than an appendage of the East in religious history. When President Thomas Jefferson sent Lewis and Clark (1804-1806) to explore the recently purchased Louisiana Territory, the West that would eventually become a part of the United States was varied not only in climate, terrain, flora and fauna but also in peoples and religion. Polynesians, Inuit and Native American peoples had their traditional religions, though European culture and Christianity had already been introduced through Russian Orthodox outposts in Alaska and Spanish Catholic missions in the borderlands north of Mexico.

Presbyterians were, like other Anglo-American Protestant denominations of the nineteenth century, concerned to win converts, organize churches and promote a Protestant Christian civilization in western regions. What came to be called the *Presbyterian Church in the U.S.A. (PCUSA) by 1870 was by far the most important Presbyterian denomination in the West. The exception to this was Texas, where the *Cumberland Presbyterian Church (CPC) and the *Presbyterian Church in the United States (PCUS), or Southern Presbyterians, were more important in the nineteenth century.

Prior to 1845, Presbyterian presence in the West was tentative, reflective in large part of the then uncertain prospects of United States settlement. Presbyterians supported the American Board of Commissioners for Foreign Missions (ABCFM) mission to Hawaii begun in 1820, but they largely deferred to the dominance of the Congregationalists in shaping the work and the legacy.

The most significant work begun by Presbyterians before 1845 was with Native Americans. Moreover, ministering among various Indian tribes continued to be an important Presbyterian commitment in the West until the present. Prior to the reunion of 1870, both *Old School and *New School Presbyterians engaged in such missions, and in a few cases the work in the West was a continuation of what had begun in the East before the removal of tribes to Indian Territory.

Presbyterian presence in the West, including missions among Native Americans, emerged most noticeably after 1845, since, with the exception of Texas, significant westward migration did not take place before that time. While zeal for "christianizing" and "civilizing" the society of the West was plentiful among nineteenth-century Presbyterians, supporting institutions were at best loosely structured until well into the twentieth century. Conventional theological training was deemed sufficient preparation for what was called home mission work. Official support in the field often meant little more than occasional funds and communications that were seldom enough to encourage the missionary in addressing the needs of the work. Understandably, mission work in Western cities and large towns tended to become self-supporting much sooner than did works in the more sparsely settled areas that formed the major part of the West. Even the urban West, though, was more unsettled than the urban East because of the boom-and-bust cycles endemic to the economy of many of the West's locales. Further, the nature of the West as a meeting ground of cultures distant from the power centers of United States society meant that more often than not Presbyterians found their aspirations to cultural custodianship frustrated.

More than anyone else, Sheldon *Jackson came to symbolize Presbyterian home missions in the latter nineteenth century. Jackson indefatigably boosted the missionary needs of the West. Between 1869 and 1884, he prodded a board of home missions (BHM) that was hesitant to overextend Presbyterian resources or begin work that was not assured of stability by recruiting missionaries, organizing churches, publicizing needs through his speaking and his Denver-based *Rocky Mountain Presbyterian* and by raising some of his own funds to use when BHM money was not enough. His territory, his title and his official authority were at times vague, but Jackson was never one to allow such things to stand in the way of the missionary imperative. By 1884 he left the Great Plains-Rocky Mountain-Southwest region in order to concentrate on Alaska, where he led in the establishment of churches and schools, including what is now Sheldon Jackson College in Sitka.

Given the conventional nineteenth-century assumptions of women's subordinate place in church and society, it is not surprising that Presbyterian women tended to be less visible than men in the Western home missionary effort. Less visibility does not mean less historically significant, however. Many, perhaps most, Presbyterian congregations depended on what were usually called Ladies Aid societies for their founding and their ongoing viability, and the wives of missionary clergymen were more often than not leaders in work with women and children in church and local community if not also in other realms such as temperance and medical care. What was new after the *Civil War was the increased role of Presbyterian women, particularly single women, in formal lay ministry through new institutions. What became the Woman's Board of Home Missions was formed in 1878, and in addition to providing financial support to the work of the BHM, it assumed not only the support of but also the oversight and staffing of Presbyterian day and boarding schools in the West for so-called exceptional populations: Indians, Mormons and Hispanic New Mexicans. Since the West faced the Pacific rather than the Atlantic, it was the region where Presbyterians and Asian immigrants first met. The West was also, as has been alluded to, the area where Presbyterian ministry among Hispanic peoples and Native Americans has been primarily focused. Thus the West became an important context for racial/ethnic diversification among Presbyterians.

By the 1920s, the home missionary era of Presbyterianism in the West was fading. Denominational corporatization had by then brought about the demise of a regionally distinctive Presbyterian press as well as the women's mission boards. Structural centralization, however, was paralleled by theological decentralization. At the same time, the West in general and California in particular were socially and culturally developed enough not merely to reflect widespread trends but in some cases significantly shape them.

California was the most populous Western state in the nineteenth century, and as such, Presbyterian strength was visible there in institutions such as the San Francisco Theological Seminary (1871) and Occidental College (1887), and in church membership, leadership and social involvement. Indeed, for a time during the early twentieth century, Presbyterians in the Los Angeles area were an important group in sustaining a general Anglo-American Protestant cultural dominance in the subregion. This dominance crumbled, though, under the pressures of the shifting composition of immigration. On the whole, even as Americans old and new have continued to move to the West in the twentieth century, especially during the boom years of federal investment in the Western economy during the Depression, World War II and the Cold War eras, Presbyterian membership in California and the West has remained proportionally small. The Protestant dream of a Christian America has tended to be, more often than not, fitful, even nightmarish, in the face of a highly mobile, culturally diverse and religiously uncommitted Western populace.

Furthermore, as the twentieth century has gone forward, California Presbyterianism has come to typify, with regional nuances, the broader national trends of Presbyterian and Protestant polarization. On the one hand, the San Francisco Theological Seminary reflected old-line Protestant trends of denominational centralization (e.g., in 1913, a year after the Thomas Franklin *Day case was resolved, the seminary was removed from the control of the Synod of California and placed under the authority of the general assembly) and theological pluralism (e.g., the school is a charter member [1962] of the Graduate Theological Union, a consortium of Protestant, Catholic and other religious educational institutions). On the other hand, today's thriving Biola University was founded in 1908 as the Bible Institute of Los Angeles by two wealthy southern California Presbyterian laymen, Lyman (1840-1923) and Milton (1838-1923) Stewart, who were concerned about the growth of theological *modernism and who also sponsored the publication of a series of antimodernist booklets entitled *The Fundamentals* (1910-1915). Moreover, Presbyterians were active in the founding of Fuller Theological Seminary in Pasadena in 1947. Originally conceived of as a new Princeton theologically, Fuller has become a major center of neo-evangelicalism. The continued support and involvement of Presbyterians in the school has been a point of tension with local and national denominational structures.

Thus, what has been called the fragmentation of twentieth-century Presbyterianism is salient in the development of that denomination in the contemporary West. Further attention to the history of religion in the West will probably highlight other things of significance. In any ongoing consideration of Presbyterians and the West, a paraphrase of the Western writer Wallace Stegner might prove useful: Presbyterians in the West are American, only more so.

See also DEMOGRAPHICS, PRESBYTERIANS AND; NEW ENGLAND, PRESBYTERIANS IN; SOUTH, PRESBYTERIANS IN THE.

BIBLIOGRAPHY. D. F. Anderson, "Through Fire and Fair by the Golden Gate: Progressive Era Protestantism and Regional Culture," (Ph.D. diss., Graduate Theological Union, 1988); M. C. Coleman, *Presbyterian Mission Attitudes Toward American Indians, 1837-1893* (1985); C. M. Drury, *Presbyterian Panorama: One Hundred and Fifty Years of National Missions History* (1952); E. G. Ernst with D. F. Anderson, *Pilgrim Progression: The Protestant Experience in California* (1993); S. S. Frankiel, *California's Spiritual Frontiers: Religious Alternatives in Anglo-Protestantism, 1850-1910* (1988); L. F. Maffly-Kipp, *Religion and Society in Frontier California* (1994); G. M. Marsden, *Reforming Fundamentalism: Fuller Seminary and the New Evangelicalism* (1987); P. Pascoe, *Relations of Rescue: The Search for Female Moral Authority in the American West, 1874-1939* (1990); G. H. Singleton, *Religion in the City of Angels: American Protestant Culture and Urbanization, Los Angeles, 1850-1930* (1977); F. M. Szasz, *The Protestant Clergy in the Great Plains and Mountain West, 1865-1915* (1988); R. S. Warner,

New Wine in Old Wineskins: Evangelicals and Liberals in a Small-Town Church (1988).

D. F. Anderson

Westminster Catechism. *See* WESTMINSTER CONFESSION OF FAITH.

Westminster Confession of Faith.† A Reformed confessional document. Composed by an Assembly of Divines convened at Westminster Abbey by the Long Parliament (1643-1648), the confession was designed to unite the English and Scottish churches in their theology. Other projects of the assembly included the production of a directory for worship (public and private), a form of government and two catechisms. The final draft of the confession was presented to Parliament on December 3, 1646, and it was adopted by both houses of Parliament on February 7, 1649. The General Assembly of the Church of Scotland gave its approbation August 27, 1647, quickly becoming the chief patron and promulgator of the document.

Most of the British colonists until 1776, and most American churches through much of the nineteenth century, were significantly influenced by the Westminster Confession of Faith (WCF). Presbyterians, Congregationalists and Baptists all subscribed to the WCF with slight variations. Presbyterians, beginning with the *Adopting Act of 1729, differed only on the WCF state-over-church posture, which was changed after the *Revolution. Congregationalists, in their 1648 Cambridge Platform, excepted only matters of church government and discipline; the Baptists, following the London Confession of 1677, took issue only with church government and infant baptism.

Historically, Presbyterians firmly subscribed to the WCF until the 1880s, although there were occasional controversies over the extent of subscription. During the 1880s, however, Charles Augustus *Briggs, through rejecting the inerrancy of the Bible, cast doubt on the biblical basis of the WCF and, during the next decade, sought to revise the document. These broadening efforts of Briggs and others were opposed by professors Archibald Alexander *Hodge and Benjamin Breckinridge *Warfield of Princeton Theological Seminary but eventuated in the revisions of the WCF in 1903, which enabled part of the *Cumberland Presbyterian Church (CPC) to unite with the *Presbyterian Church in the U.S.A. (PCUSA).

The influence of the WCF continued to erode, despite the efforts of the conservative majority of the PCUSA general assemblies of 1910, 1916 and 1923, which declared certain doctrines as salvifically "necessary and essential." An opposing document, the *Auburn Affirmation, signed in 1923 by thirteen hundred ministers, decried these doctrines as adding to the WCF, arguing for a broader interpretation of such doctrines as the deity of Christ, the virgin birth and the substitutionary atonement. Upon the victory of the signers of the Auburn Affirmation, J. Gresham *Machen led many conservatives in the formation of the *Orthodox Presbyterian Church (OPC) in 1936.

In the middle of the twentieth century, the PCUSA recognized that it needed a new confession, since the majority of its ministers no longer held as firmly to the WCF. In 1967 it adopted a Book of Confessions, including several traditional Reformed documents, along with the Barmen Declaration (1934) and a new composition. This *Confession of 1967 introduced elements regarded by conservatives as *neo-orthodox.

Today the broadened PCUSA gives allegiance to both the WCF and other documents, while several smaller conservative Presbyterian bodies, such as the *Reformed Presbyterian Church in North America, the OPC and the *Presbyterian Church in America (PCA) continue to maintain a traditional confession of the WCF.

See also DORT, CANONS OF; HEIDELBERG CATECHISM.

BIBLIOGRAPHY. C. Hodge, *The Constitutional History of the Presbyterian Church in the United States of America* (1839-1840); J. H. Leith, "The Westminster Confession in American Presbyterianism," in the *Westminster Confession in the Church Today,* ed. A. I. C. Heron (1982); L. A. Loetscher, *The Broadening Church: A Study of Theological Issues in the Presbyterian Church Since 1869* (1954).

J. H. Hall

Whitman, Marcus (1802-1847). Presbyterian *missionary physician to the Cayuse Indians. Born in Rushville, New York, Whitman experienced conversion at age seventeen while attending the Congregational church and academy in Plainfield, Massachusetts, but his family gave him no encouragement to follow his interest in the ministry. Instead, he took up medicine, studying at the College of Physicians and Surgeons of the Western District of New York in Fairfield (1825-1826, 1831-1832).

As a physician practicing in Wheeler, New York, in 1834 Whitman responded to the challenge of Samuel Parker to become a missionary of the American Board of Commissioners for Foreign Missions (ABCFM) to Native Americans in the Oregon Territory. He accompanied Parker in an exploratory trip west of St. Louis in 1835. The following year, Whitman and Narcissa Prentiss, a missionary-minded schoolteacher who had also been moved in hearing Parker, married. They journeyed by wagon that same year with Henry Harmon *Spalding and Eliza Hart *Spalding as Presbyterian missionaries of the ABCFM to establish the Oregon mission in what is now the Washington-Idaho region. Incidentally, the trip established the feasibility of overland immigration to the Oregon Territory, and Narcissa *Whitman and Eliza Spalding became the first white women to cross the Rocky Mountains.

The Whitmans established a mission station among the Cayuse people at Waiilatpu, Washington, while the Spaldings worked among the Nez Perce at Lapwai, Idaho. Competent as a physician but uneasy with his lack of theological training, Whitman sought to instruct the Cayuse in Christianity and agriculture. In 1838 the Whitmans and Spaldings organized the First Presbyterian Church in the Oregon Territory, the earliest Protestant church on the Pacific slope. Worship services were well attended, but by 1847 only one Cayuse from Waiilatpu had become a baptized member. Dissension among the missionaries together with the scant number of conversions made among the Indians led the ABCFM to order the closing of the Oregon mission in 1842. On behalf of the mission, Whitman traveled east and persuaded the ABCFM to rescind its directive. He returned in 1843, leading a wagon train of hundreds of American settlers. Between 1843 and 1847, Waiilatpu served as an important way station for Oregon immigrants.

Whitman was encouraged by the inrush of Anglo-American settlers. He had hopes that they would provide the economic and Protestant moral base to model "Christian civilization" to the Cayuse and thereby aid Whitman in his mission goals. Ironically, it was the settlers who brought an epidemic of measles in 1847. This led some Cayuse, frustrated with the escalating change in the region launched by the coming of the Whitmans, to blame the physician for the deaths of Indians. Marcus, Narcissa and twelve others died at the mission station on November 29, 1847, as a result of an attack by a party of Cayuse. The earnestness and sincerity of Whitman's motives and his fortitude on the mission field need to be balanced with his persistent cultural naivete and rigidity in dealing with the Cayuse in assessing his historical significance.

See also WHITMAN, NARCISSA PRENTISS.

BIBLIOGRAPHY. *ANB* 23; *DAB* X; *DARB;* C. M. Drury, *Marcus and Narcissa Whitman,* 2 vols. (1973); J. H. Webster, "The ABCFM and the First Presbyterian Missions in the Northwest," *AP* 65 (1987) 173-85.

D. F. Anderson

Whitman, Narcissa Prentiss (1808-1847).† Pioneer Presbyterian *missionary in the Oregon Territory. Narcissa Prentiss was born in Prattsburg, New York, and from her childhood was an energetic participant in *revivals and prayer meetings in the Prattsburg, and later, Amity Presbyterian Church. After studying at the Female Seminary in Troy, New York, she taught school in nearby Bath. About this time she declined the marriage proposal of Henry Harmon *Spalding, who would later join the Whitmans on the mission field.

In response to an appeal for missionaries for the Oregon Territory, Prentiss offered her services but was rejected as a missionary candidate in December 1834 because she was single. Three months later Marcus *Whitman, a doctor who was equally dedicated to missionary work, proposed marriage to her and was accepted. After traveling to Oregon to explore the area, he returned to New York, and on February 18, 1836, they were married. Two weeks later they left as pioneer missionaries to the Oregon Territory under the American Board of Commissioners for Foreign Missions (ABCFM), traveling westward with the American Fur Company. Accompanying them on the long, hard journey were Henry and Eliza Hart *Spalding. On December 10, they finally settled in to their new home. Plans called for a team enterprise, but discord between the two men led to a separation as soon as they arrived at their destination—the Whitmans settling in the lush green valley in Waiilatpu among the Cayuse Indians, and the Spaldings at Lapwai, among the Nez Perce Indians.

The Whitmans initially met with a favorable response from the Cayuse, but sorrow and tragedy haunted their steps. Two years after their arrival, the Whitmans' only child, Alice, drowned in a nearby stream. After Alice's death, Narcissa became foster mother to at least sixteen children—usually of mixed race and born out of wedlock—and later opened a school for mission children. As the mission compound grew and expanded, it soon became a rest stop for weary travelers. Yet in the long run, this began to work against the Whitmans. Because the Oregon Trail ran straight through their territory, the Cayuse Indians came to bitterly resent the incursion of the whites, and the Whitman mission compound was a symbol of this incursion. Although her husband offered his healing ministry to the Native Americans, misfortune struck when even mild vaccinations brought unexpected death to Native Americans, thus confirming their suspicions that Marcus Whitman practiced witchcraft. Moreover, their assistance to white immigrants was seen by the Cayuse as giving aid to the enemy, and many Indians concluded that the Whitmans were more interested in civilized society than the condition of the natives.

In November 1847, less than twelve years after their work in Oregon was initiated, the mission compound was attacked by a small group of Cayuse Indians, and fourteen residents were killed, including Marcus and Narcissa. The five Native Americans involved in the murders were hanged, and all the mission work in the region was suspended on government orders for more than two decades.

See also WHITMAN, MARCUS.

BIBLIOGRAPHY. *ANB* 23; O. S. Allen, *Narcissa Whitman* (1959); *DAB* X; *DARB;* C. M. Drury, *Marcus and Narcissa Whitman and the Opening of Old Oregon,* 2 vols. (1973); N. Jones, *The Great Command: The Story of Marcus and Narcissa Whitman and the Oregon Country Pioneers* (1959); *NAW* 3; *NCAB* 11.

R. A. Tucker

Wilson, Robert Dick (1856-1930).† Presbyterian Old Testament scholar and *educator. Born in western Pennsylvania, Wilson received his undergraduate education at the College of New Jersey (now Princeton University) and graduated in 1876. From Princeton, he went on to study and teach at Western Theological Seminary in Pittsburgh before attending the University of Berlin (1881-1883), where Wilson did research in Semitic languages. Following his studies in Berlin, Wilson returned to teach at Western for fifteen years, producing grammars in Syriac and Hebrew. In 1900 Wilson accepted an appointment at Princeton Seminary in Semitic philology and Old Testament criticism.

At Princeton, Wilson devoted his scholarship to defending the historical character of the Old Testament in general (*Is the Higher Criticism Scholarly?* 1922) and of the book of Daniel specifically (*Studies in the Book of Daniel,* 1917). Utilizing his linguistic and philological expertise in *A Scientific Investigation of the Old Testament* (1926), Wilson outlined an objectivist and evidentialist approach to defending the conservative positions on historicity and authorship. In 1929, at the age of seventy-four, Wilson joined his younger colleague, J. Gresham *Machen, in the establishment of Westminster Theological Seminary in Philadelphia as a response to the controversial reorganization of Princeton Seminary. He died after only one year with the new seminary, taking with him a significant measure of the Old Princeton legacy of biblical scholarship.

BIBLIOGRAPHY. G. L. Haines, "The Princeton Theological Seminary, 1925-1960" (Ph.D. diss., New York University, 1966); J. W. Hart, "Princeton Theological Seminary: The Reorganization of 1929," *JPH* 58 (1980) 124-40; M. A. Noll, *Between Faith and Criticism: Evangelicals, Scholarship, and the Bible in America* (1986); M. A. Taylor, *The Old Testament in the Old Princeton School (1812-1929)* (1992).

D. G. Hart

Wilson, Thomas Woodrow (1856-1924).‡ Presbyterian churchman, *educator and twenty-eighth president of the United States. Born in Staunton, Virginia, the son of Presbyterian minister Dr. Joseph Ruggles Wilson, Wilson was educated at Princeton University (B.A., 1879; M.A., 1882) before launching an unsuccessful law practice in Atlanta, Georgia. In 1885 he married Ellen Louise Axson of Rome, Georgia, who bore three children, all daughters. In 1883 Wilson began graduate study in history at the Johns Hopkins University (Ph.D. 1886). From there he taught at Bryn Mawr (1885-1888), Wesleyan (1888-1890) and Princeton (1890-1902). At Princeton, he became a popular lecturer and published his major work, *A History of the American People* (1902). From 1902 until 1910 he served as president of Princeton, the first layperson ever to fill that office.

Wilson's statewide reputation as a dynamic educator, his oratorical ability and his abiding interest in *politics conjoined to make him the Democratic Party's gubernatorial candidate in 1910. After winning an impressive victory, Wilson launched a successful program of progressive reforms that brought him national attention and made him a leading contender for the Democratic presidential nomination in 1912. Wilson was nominated and won election by enunciating his proposed New Freedom—a program to liberate American economic energies by drastically reducing tariffs, strengthening antitrust laws and reorganizing the banking and credit system.

Wilson's world was shattered in the summer of 1914 by two tragedies: the outbreak in July of a general war in Europe (World War I, 1914-1918) and the death of his wife on August 6. He won reelection in 1916, largely because of his successful progressive reforms and by keeping America out of the European conflict. However, Wilson finally asked for a declaration of war against Germany and its allies in 1917.

Wilson made his greatest contribution by formulating war aims in his Fourteen Points of 1918, which unveiled plans for a just and lasting peace. It was largely on the basis of Wilson's pronouncements that the Germans finally agreed to an armistice on November 11, 1918. The Versailles Peace Conference, which followed in 1919, betrayed Wilson's program; in order to save his plan for a League of Nations with responsibility for executing the treaty and preventing future wars, he had to compromise other peace aims. This disappointment was followed by the rejection of the Versailles Treaty with its provision for Wilson's league by a Republican-controlled Congress. Wilson's heroic efforts to save his peace plan were primarily responsible for the debilitating stroke he suffered on October 2, 1919, in Washington after an extensive tour of the Western states. He suffered the further indignity of seeing his proposals rejected when in the 1920 presidential election the nation chose Republican Warren G. Harding, who had pledged never to join the league. The events of 1919-1920 permanently broke Wilson's health. He retired to his Washington home, where he lived the remainder of his days in seclusion.

Some scholars consider Wilson to have been "the most God-centered man" ever to be president, while New Jersey Democratic Party boss James Smith once derisively called him "a Presbyterian priest." Whatever the case, there is no doubt that Wilson's political philosophy rested firmly on his understanding of Christianity and that throughout his life he drew his greatest strength from the resources of his Presbyterian faith. A Presbyterian elder, he had a superb command of Reformed theology, read the Bible and prayed daily and attended church regularly. It was no accident that he never thought about public matters, as well as private ones, without first trying to decide what the teachings of Jesus dictated in such circumstances.

The mainspring of Wilson's public life was a crusading idealism that grew out of his faith. He represented the last gasp of both the evangelical urge to reform the nation and the progressive movement in American politics. He was at heart a political missionary who believed that humans could improve the world in which they lived and that America, because of its unique history and place in the divine plan, could serve as the vehicle for world reform.

Bibliography. *ANB* 23; J. M. Blum, *Woodrow Wilson and the Politics of American Morality* (1956); J. M. Cooper, *The Warrior and the Priest* (1983); *DAB* XX; E. Fuller and D. E. Green, *God in the White House* (1968); C. T. Grayson, *Woodrow Wilson, An Intimate Memoir* (1960); A. S. Link, *The Higher Realism of Woodrow Wilson and Other Essays* (1971); idem, *Wilson,* 5 vols. (1947-1965); J. M. Mulder, *Woodrow Wilson: The Years of Preparation* (1978); R. V. Pierard and R. D. Linder, *Civil Religion and the Presidency* (1988). R. D. Linder

Witherspoon, John (1723-1794). Presbyterian minister and *educator. Born in Yester, Scotland, Witherspoon received his university education at the University of Edinburgh (M.A., 1739), where he also studied theology (1739-1743). A parish minister in Beith (1745-1757) and Paisley (1757-1768), Scotland, Witherspoon became known as an opponent of the trend in the Scottish Church known as moderatism, which tended to deemphasize the distinctive theological dogmas of the church. In his defense of traditional, Reformed orthodoxy, Witherspoon made extensive use of Scottish Common-Sense Realism, a brand of philosophy that had been developed by Thomas Reid at the University of Glasgow. Reid had realized that the fundamental truths of Christianity are consistent with common sense and that those truths are clearly based on "self-evident axioms."

In 1768 Witherspoon accepted the invitation of *New Side Presbyterians to serve as president of the College of New Jersey. With him he brought Scottish Common-Sense realism and from that perspective sought to train his students, specifically opposing the lingering elements of New Light *Edwardseanism in the curriculum. Through Witherspoon's influence the Scottish philosophy entered the mainstream of American thought. After the *Revolution Witherspoon helped reorganize the Presbyterian church and was instrumental in the establishment of its general assembly (1789), of which he was the first moderator. Witherspoon's influence was not limited to the ecclesiastical sphere, however. He was a delegate to the Continental Congress (1776-1782), the only clergyman to sign the Declaration of Independence and a member of the New Jersey state legislature (1783, 1789).

Bibliography. *AAP* 3; *ANB* 23; L. B. Butterfield, *John Witherspoon Comes to America* (1953); V. L. Collins, *President Witherspoon,* 2 vols. (1925); *DAB* X; *DARB; NCAB* 5; R. Fechner, "The Godly and Virtuous Commonwealth of John Witherspoon" in *Ideas in America's Cultures,* ed. H. Cravens (1982); J. Scott, ed., *An Annotated Edition of Lectures on Moral Philosophy of John Witherspoon* (1982); M. L. Stohlman, *John Witherspoon: Parson, Politician, Patriot* (1976). S. T. Logan

Woodrow, James (1828-1907).† Presbyterian theologian and scientist. Born in Carlisle, England, the son of a Presbyterian minister who immigrated to Canada and then Ohio, Woodrow graduated from Jefferson College, Pennsylvania (B.A., 1849), and then taught school in Alabama. He later pursued graduate studies in science at Harvard (1853) and became professor of natural science at Oglethorpe University in Georgia (1853-1861). During this time he pursued further graduate studies at Heidelberg, earning his doctorate in 1856. He was ordained a minister in the Presbyterian church in 1860.

In 1861 Woodrow was made professor of Natural Science in Connexion with Revelation at the Presbyterian seminary in Columbia, South Carolina, in order "to evince the harmony of science with the records of our faith, and to refute the objections of infidel naturalists." When the *Civil War came, Woodrow served as a chemist for the Confederate army. During many of his years at the seminary he served simultaneously as professor of science (1869-1872, 1880-1897) at South Carolina College and later as president (1891-1897) of that institution. Woodrow was coeditor of the *Southern Presbyterian Review* (1861-1885), the publisher and editor of the weekly *Southern Presbyterian* (1865-1893) and the denomination's treasurer of foreign *missions (1861-1872).

Woodrow held that God's Word and the world both reveal divine truth and that there is no contradiction between them when they are each rightly interpreted. The true teacher of all things is God, and the Christian student must not only do rigorous academic work but also pray for God's guidance. We are to interpret nature rationally but in dependence upon revelation as well. He accepted the inerrancy of the Bible but believed that it gave no technical explanation of the origin of Adam's body, because its purpose is not to give scientific details. After some years of opposition to the evolutionary hypothesis, Woodrow came to hold that theistic evolution—what he called mediate creation—was probably true. An address published in 1884 and approved by the board of the seminary publicized his views and brought about a storm of protest within the Southern Presbyterian denomination. Woodrow argued that the church should neither wholeheartedly support nor condemn evolutionary theory because it is not within its jurisdiction.

In the furor that resulted, the four synods that controlled the seminary board replaced Woodrow's supporters with opponents, who dismissed him in 1884 without a trial. After he was reinstated, his presbytery acquitted him of the charge of heresy in 1886. The majority of the denomination, however, was not satisfied with this resolution, so the 1886 general assembly pronounced that "Adam's body was directly fashioned by Almighty God, without any natural animal parentage," by a vote of 137-13. Following this decision, Woodrow was permanently removed from the faculty. Although he differed with the traditional interpretations of the Bible and the *Westminster Confession of Faith, he was never convicted of heresy and remained a minister in good standing. Woodrow was the uncle of President Woodrow *Wilson.

See also SCIENCE, PRESBYTERIANS AND.

BIBLIOGRAPHY. *ANB* 23; *DAB* X; C. Eaton, "Professor James Woodrow and the Freedom of Teaching in the South," *JSH* 28 (1962) 3-17; T. W. Street, "The Evolutionary Controversy in the Southern Presbyterian Church," *JPHS* 37 (1959) 232-50; M. W. Woodrow, ed., *Dr. James Woodrow as Seen by His Friends* (1909). A. H. Freundt Jr.

World Alliance of Reformed Churches. International organization of Presbyterian, Reformed and Congregationalist denominations. The World Alliance of Reformed Churches was formed in 1970 at Nairobi, Kenya, from a union of two organizations: the World Alliance of Reformed Churches throughout the World Holding the Presbyterian System, and the International Congregational Council. The roots of the denominations comprising the Alliance are in the Protestant Reformation, especially the theology of John Calvin and Ulrich Zwingli. Member denominations affirm the supreme authority of the Bible in matters of faith and morals and hold to classic Reformed creeds. The parent World Alliance was established in 1875 to further cooperation among Presbyterian and Reformed communions and to promote their common interests and joint endeavors, making its successor the oldest international Protestant confessional body. Today about 160 denominations with congregations in more than eighty countries and approximately 70 million members belong to the Alliance.

A general council, which first met in 1877 and ordinarily meets every five years, makes and administers the policies and programs of the Alliance. Between assemblies an executive committee, which meets annually, directs the work of the Alliance. The headquarters of the Alliance is in Geneva, Switzerland. The Alliance has promoted better understanding among Reformed denominations, held many theological discussions and conducted relief work. Since the mid 1960s Alliance leaders have held conversations with both Roman Catholic and Lutheran representatives. In recent years area organizations, including a Caribbean and North American branch, have been formed within the Alliance to provide fellowship, encourage cooperation and foster study. The Alliance publishes a journal, *The Reformed World*, to promote its activities and views.

BIBLIOGRAPHY. M. Pradervand, *A Century of Service: A History of the World Alliance of Reformed Churches, 1875-1975* (1975). G. S. Smith

Worship, Presbyterians and. What makes Reformed worship distinctive is theology rather than particular practices. The Presbyterian/*Reformed tradition worships God for God's sake. Our "chief end" is to glorify God. Thus worship in the Reformed churches is often termed objective—the focus is God rather than religious affections.

If the purpose of worship is to glorify God, according to the Continental Reformers, the substance of worship is gratitude. We are grateful for election, for creation, for God's providential leading and for the promise of salvation. Above all, we are grateful for a Savior who "while we still were sinners, . . . died for us" (Rom 5:8 NRSV). Thus Presbyterian hymnody has been strong on hymns of praise that celebrate God's remarkable goodness—Old Hundredth is a Reformed theology of worship. Of course, if the substance of worship is gratitude, then inevitably it will be eucharistic.

In Reformed theology, worship is ordered by Word and Spirit. Both John *Calvin and Ulrich Zwingli supposed that God addressed people through the preaching of Scripture. The Second Helvetic Confession echoes their confidence: "The Preaching of the Word of God is the Word of God." Thus preachers must be well-trained theologians and Scripture scholars. But reception of the Word is by the so-called inner testimony of the Spirit. Word and Spirit are bound together, as in the Trinity, so that Reformed worship cannot be turned into a *fundamentalist court or a charismatic rally.

All worship in the Presbyterian/Reformed tradition is worship of the people, a "royal priesthood." Worship is corporate. For Calvin nothing was more useful in the praise of God than music where voices could be joined into one voice. Calvin regarded the psalms as divinely provided for common praise. No wonder that the metrical psalm has always been a crucial feature of Reformed praise.

The Origins of Reformed Worship. Reformed worship begins with Zwingli in Zurich, moves to Calvin's Geneva and finally is repackaged in Heidelberg by Zacharias Ursinus and Kaspar Olevianus for churches of the Palatinate.

Zwinglian worship was not derived from the structure of the Mass but was based on the *prone,* a brief, vernacular preaching service that sometimes preceded the Mass. In Zurich the service commenced with a Scripture reading, followed by the Our Father and the Ave Maria. Then a sermon was delivered and, after the sermon, bidding prayers, a commemoration of the recent dead and again, the Our Father and Ave Maria. The service concluded with the Apostles' Creed, the Decalogue and a final confession with an absolution. Though Zwingli modified the *prone,* Zwinglian worship was a framework for preaching. Communion was observed quarterly with a separate, different order for worship. For Zwingli, the "this" in "this is my body" meant "this signifies." Elements in the Lord's Supper could not convey grace because, according to Zwingli, Spirit and matter can never be one. Thus the real presence of Christ is in the shared faith of the community. Zwinglian worship was biblical, perhaps to a fault, and fiercely iconoclastic.

In Calvin's Geneva, worship was a pattern of Word and sacrament; it was an antecommunion. Worship opened with the familiar "Our help is in the name of the Lord, who made heaven and earth." Immediately there was a general prayer of confession, followed by a bold declaration of pardon. The congregation would then sing the commandments, expressing a "third use of the law." Thereafter there was the preaching of a scriptural passage, often *lectio continua.* The sermon was preceded by a prayer of illumination—a distinctive feature of Reformed worship—and followed by intercessions, often in the form of a bidding prayer, concluding with the Lord's Prayer.

Of course, Calvin wanted the preached Word to lead to a regular celebration of the Lord's Supper. But in Geneva, under the influence of nearby Zurich, he managed only quarterly communion. Calvin never ceased to complain. He saw the refusal of what God wished to give as a surly form of sin. In the Lord's Supper, we are joined to the risen Christ by faith and receive all the benefits of Christ's saving death for us. Calvin instituted services of preparation before the Eucharist so that people could welcome the Supper with repentance and a proper resolve.

Thus, in Reformed communities during the Reformation, worship was either a Zwinglian preaching service or a *Calvinistic antecommunion. Zwinglian worship spread among the Waldensians and influenced Dutch, Hungarian and Bohemian communities. John Knox of Scotland was taught by Calvin's Geneva services, as were some French parishes. In 1563, the Palatinate Liturgy drew together Calvinist and Zwinglian patterns along with Lutheran influences. In sixteenth-century Europe, worship was conducted in set liturgical patterns with set liturgical forms.

Reformed Worship in the New World. Reformed worship came to America in damaged condition. Tides of *Puritanism, pietism and rationalism swept Reformed churches and radically changed patterns of worship. In Scotland, after a scrap with England ousted Knox's *Book of Common Order,* Scottish practice tumbled into chaos. In 1645, the Westminster Divines produced *A Directory for the Public Worship . . . ,* which offered rubrics to guide worship but, out of deference to Puritans, no actual forms. In Scotland, worship gradually became an opening exercise for prodigious sermons.

Puritanism was powerful in England and welcomed in Holland, where Mennonite pietism had formed congregations. Pietism moved through the Reformed churches of Europe. Exponents supposed that as regenerate children of God we should speak from the heart without liturgical aids. So both Puritan and pietist edged toward a free church position. Rationalism in turn tended to accommodate orthodoxy to Enlightenment, thus dulling the theological rigor of liturgical texts. In the midst of such movements, Reformed liturgy drifted into the new world.

Reformed worship came to America along with the Puritans who settled New England. Puritans seemed radically Zwinglian. The Bible was their textbook, and what was not specifically mentioned in Scripture was banished from Sunday assemblies—God should be worshiped God's way. So *New England Puritans preached often and prayed at length in their stark meeting houses. Worship in Puritan places was dominated by the didactic sermon. Fortunately, Puritan preachers were not unintelligent.

In the Middle Colonies, where Presbyterians came ashore, the situation was scarcely better. Worship involved high-built pulpits, rational sermons and infrequent celebration of the Lord's Supper. Because of a shortage of ordained clergy, frontier communities seldom received the sacraments. In remote places, a sacramental season was sometimes observed with devotions, confessions, sermons and scriptural study preparing for the solemn if occasional observance of the Supper. In 1788 American Presbyterians drew up a new *Directory for the Worship of God.* The document displays the rising influence of *New School energies by endorsing acts of devotion and tacitly permitting the singing of hymns in addition to psalms. Yet, in deference to *Old School sensibilities, the directory also attempted to tame the hoopla of the sacramental seasons. The pattern of worship endorsed by the directory included opening prayer, Scripture reading, singing praise, a long prayer (often fifteen to twenty minutes) and the Lord's Prayer, a sermon, another prayer related to the sermon, the singing of a psalm, offering and a blessing. The German churches that moved into the Middle Colonies were in much the same state. While a few retained touches of a half-forgotten Palatinate tradition, for the most part pietism ruled.

Nineteenth- and Twentieth-Century Liturgical Recovery. In the nineteenth century, Reformed churches began to rediscover their heritage. The movement could be described as a return to Geneva. Though the period has been labeled a Gothic Revival, it featured liturgical research as well as aesthetic concern. Under the leadership of George W. Bethune, the *Dutch Reformed Church issued a partial, revised liturgical book in 1857. The *German Reformed Church published a provisional study in the same year. Also in 1857, Presbyterian Charles W. Baird put out his *Eutaxia,* a description of the liturgies of Calvin and Knox as well as some representative prayers. A rash of prayer collections and liturgical books followed. Toward the end of the century, under the influence of a Scottish liturgical collection, the *Euchologion,* Presbyterians produced a fledgling prayer book, *Presbyterian Forms of Service,* and in 1898 a revised *A New Directory for Public Worship.* Liturgy returned but often without theology.

The *Mercersburg movement deserves special mention. In 1849 the German Reformed Church moved to revise liturgy. Two able professors were instrumental, Philip *Schaff and John Williamson *Nevin. Their efforts led to the publication of a new *Order of Worship* in 1866, perhaps the finest Reformed liturgical production of the century. The liturgy restores Calvin's eucharistic theology to the Lord's Supper. Nevin's major work, *Mystical Presence,* had a huge impact on subsequent Reformed and Presbyterian worship.

In the twentieth century, along with Reformed churches all over the world, American denominations issued a series of prayer books. The period between 1950 and 1990 was unusually productive. Presbyterians managed two different revisions of *The Directory for Worship* and as many books of worship, culminating in a new *Book of Common Worship* (1993). Presbyterians also published two new hymn collections. Likewise, the *Reformed Church in America (RCA) produced both a new liturgy and a fine new hymnal. The United Church of Christ, which in 1957 merged several branches of the Reformed tradition, joined New England Congregationalism and Mercersburg *Calvinism in its *Book of Worship* and followed recently with a second hymn collection (1994). Newer hymn books in the Reformed tradition draw on the pluralism of congregations by providing African-American, Spanish and Hawaiian hymns as well as contemporary settings for the psalms.

If liturgical revision in the 1960s and 1970s recovered the Reformation heritage, worship books in the 1990s appear to be more catholic and ecumenical.

See also SACRAMENTS, PRESBYTERIANS AND THE.

BIBLIOGRAPHY. B. A. Gerrish, *Grace and Gratitude: The Eucharistic Theology of John Calvin* (1993); H. G. Hageman, *Pulpit and Table: Some Chapters in the History of Worship in the Reformed Churches* (1962); A. I. C. Heron, *Table and Tradition* (1983); D. K. McKim, ed., *Major Themes in the Reformed Tradition* (1992); J. Melton, *Presbyterian Worship in America: Changing Patterns Since 1787* (1967); J. H. Nichols, *Corporate Worship in the Reformed Tradition* (1968); H. O. Old, *Worship That Is Reformed According to Scripture* (1984); T. H. L. Parker, *Calvin's Preaching* (1992); J. F. White, *Protestant Worship: Traditions in Transition* (1989).

D. G. Buttrick

Wright, G(eorge) Ernest (1909-1974). Presbyterian Old Testament scholar and archaeologist. Born in Zanesville, Ohio, Wright graduated from Wooster College (B.A., 1931), studied theology at McCormick Theological Seminary in Chicago (B.D., 1934) and was ordained a Presbyterian minister (1934). After pursuing graduate studies under William F. Albright at Johns Hopkins University (Ph.D., 1937), he returned to McCormick to teach Old Testament for the next two decades (1939-1958). From 1958 until his death he was Parkman Professor of Divinity at Harvard Divinity School. In addition to directing excavations at Shechem (1956-1964) and Gezer (1964-1965), Wright was founding editor of *The Biblical Archaeologist* and served as president of the American Schools of Oriental Research (1966-1974) and curator of the Harvard Semitic Museum.

Wright figured prominently in the biblical theology movement and was active in the early post-World War II ecumenical movement. His own perspective was characterized by a concern for archaeological and historical reconstruction of biblical history. The objective reality of the events described in the Bible was seen by Wright as essential, but the burden of theology was to interpret these events. For Wright the Bible was not primarily the Word of God but the record of the acts of God accompanied by the human response.

BIBLIOGRAPHY. *ANB* 24; F. M. Cross Jr. et al., *Magnalia Dei—The Mighty Acts of God* (1976); *HHMBI*; R. L. Hicks, "G. Ernest Wright and Old Testament Theology," *ATR* 58 (1976) 158-78.

S. Meier

Wright, Theodore Sedgewick (1797-1847). Presbyterian minister and *social reformer. A free black from birth, Wright was educated under the direction of Samuel Eli *Cornish, a prominent African-American clergyman, at the New York City African Free Boys School. After being refused admission to several collegiate institutions on racial grounds, and with the encouragement of Cornish and the support of DeWitt Clinton and Arthur Tappan, Wright attended Princeton Theological Seminary from 1825 to 1828 and became the first African-American to graduate from an American theological seminary. He then succeeded his mentor Cornish as pastor the First Colored Presbyterian Church (also called Shiloh Presbyterian Church) of New York City, remaining there until his early death.

During his tenure at Shiloh Presbyterian Church, Wright's congregation grew from seventy-five to more than four hundred members, and Wright became a key figure in the *abolitionist movement. A founder of the American Anti-Slavery Society in 1833, he served various other local and regional antislavery societies throughout the 1830s. In May 1840, Wright withdrew from the American Anti-Slavery Society and helped to found the American and Foreign Anti-Slavery Society, an alternative abolitionist organization that avoided the radicalism of the Garrisonians within the American Anti-Slavery Society. Providing leadership for a wide variety of efforts to expand the rights and enhance the quality of life of African-Americans, Wright was also active in temperance, *missions work and other manifestations of Christian benevolence. In 1840 he coauthored (with Cornish) *The Colonization Scheme Considered.*

BIBLIOGRAPHY. *ANB* 24; R. Balmer and J. R. Fitzmier, *The Presbyterians* (1993) 251-52; *Dictionary of American Negro Biography;* B. Gross, "Life and Times of Theodore S. Wright, 1797-1847," *Negro History Bulletin* (1940) 13-38. D. Sweeney

X,Y,Z

Young, Edward Joseph (1907-1968).† Presbyterian minister and Old Testament scholar. Born in San Francisco to a Presbyterian elder, Young was educated at Stanford University (B.A., 1929) and San Francisco Theological Seminary before transferring to Westminster Theological Seminary to study under J. Gresham *Machen. He then studied under Albrecht Alt at Leipzig and eventually earned his doctoral degree (1943) at Dropsie College in Philadelphia. Young joined the Old Testament department of Westminster Theological Seminary in 1936, where he taught until his death. A minister in the *Orthodox Presbyterian Church (OPC), he was extensively involved in its life and became one of its most admired leaders.

Young combined a deep commitment to Reformed theology with a phenomenal linguistic talent, which extended through thirty languages. He was widely regarded as the leading evangelical Old Testament scholar of his day, giving direction especially to the reasoned defense of the authority and integrity of Scripture (*Thy Word Is Truth,* 1957) against liberal critical views. His extensive writings, whether scholarly or popular, blended careful exegesis and theological insight with pastoral sensitivity. His *Introduction to the Old Testament* (1949; rev. ed., 1960) was widely used by evangelicals, but his area of expertise was Isaiah, on which he published a three-volume commentary, *The Book of Isaiah* (1965, 1969, 1972). Young was widely in demand, particularly within the North American evangelical community, as a lecturer, preacher and conference speaker. He died of a heart attack at the age of sixty.

R. B. Gaffin Jr.

Zahniser, Charles Reed (1873-1955). Presbyterian pastor and *educator. Born in Mercer County, Pennsylvania, Zahniser received his bachelor of arts degree from Grove City College in 1896 and both his S.T.B. in 1900 and his doctoral degree in 1909 from the University of Chicago. He was ordained as a *Presbyterian Church in the U.S.A. (PCUSA) minister in 1899 and in 1901 organized the Lemington Presbyterian Church near Pittsburgh. After pastoring this congregation for thirteen years and playing a leading role in the work of the Anti-Saloon League in the Pittsburgh area, Zahniser became the executive secretary of the newly created Christian Social Service Union in 1914. As the chief administrator of an organization formed by fourteen different denominations, he oversaw programs designed to curb drunkenness, graft, prostitution and poverty in the city. Under his leadership, the union worked to improve the quality of the city's police force, reform its judicial system and educate its residents about social problems. Its members persuaded the mayor to appoint a morals bureau to suppress vice, conducted several social and religious surveys and promoted social evangelism.

In 1917 Zahniser became the first executive secretary of the Pittsburgh Council of Churches, created that year by the merger of the Christian Social Service Union with two other interdenominational organizations. He helped to spearhead an investigation of the city's industrial, social, moral, physical and religious conditions, which led to the 1917 publication of *The Challenge of Pittsburgh,* a book designed to call attention to the city's problems and suggest remedies for them. For twelve years he directed the cooperative venture of the council in sponsoring evangelistic campaigns, encouraging missions to immigrants, blacks and the poor, reforming social conditions, inspiring civic action and promoting Christian education. In 1929 Zahniser accepted a position as professor of social science and applied Christianity at Boston University, where he remained until 1940. During these years he also lectured on social issues in seminaries and universities throughout the nation under the auspices of the Federal Council of Churches.

In addition to his work as an administrator and educator, Zahniser wrote several important books. His *Social Christianity* (1911) analyzed the causes and results of America's social and industrial problems, the insufficiency of the old evangelism and the inadequacy of socialism and outlined how congregations could develop extensive programs for social service. A pioneer in applying the principles of casework to evangelism, he penned *Casework Evangelism: Studies in the Art of Christian Personal Work* (1927). Drawing primarily upon his years of ministry in Pittsburgh, Zahniser issued *Interchurch Community Programs* in 1932 to explain how churches could combine their resources to evangelize the unsaved, educate children and adults and improve social conditions. In *The Soul Doctor* (1938) he sought to teach ministers how to use ideas derived from social work and psychology in their work.

As a crusader for civic righteousness, an efficient executive of two ecumenical bodies, a director of numerous local and national boards and agencies, a seminary professor and an author, Zahniser did much to promote both evangelism and social service.

See also Social Reform, Presbyterians and.

Bibliography. C. C. Johnson, "The Testimonial Dinner," *The Pittsburgh Christian Outlook* 1 (May 1924) 7-8; "The Local Anti-Saloon League," *The Presbyterian Banner* 31 (January 30, 1908); C. Sheldon, introduction to *Casework Evangelism* (1927); G. S. Smith, "Pittsburgh and the Social Gospel," paper presented at the Duquesne History Forum, October 21, 1994. G. S. Smith

Zenos, Andrew Constantinides (1855-1942). Presbyterian pastor and theologian. Born in Constantinople, Turkey, he studied there at Robert College and in 1872 graduated. After studying in Athens he moved to America in 1877. Zenos's early thinking developed under *Old School Presbyterian teachers at Princeton Theological Seminary (B.D., 1880). He entered the Presbyterian ministry in 1881 and pastored in Brandt, Pennsylvania, before embarking on a teaching career. He taught Greek at Lake Forest University (1883-1888) and New Testament exegesis at Hartford Theological Seminary (1888-1891). In 1891 he was inaugurated professor of biblical and ecclesiastical history at McCormick Theological Seminary, where he taught until resigning his professorship in 1931. He served as dean from 1920 to 1934.

A transitional figure, Zenos moved McCormick and his denomination toward theological liberalism during the *fundamentalist-modernist controversy. While never jettisoning his evangelical convictions, Zenos championed the autonomy of biblical theology from dogmatics. In his Hartford inaugural, he criticized German higher criticism for contradicting biblical teaching. But he also opposed confessionalists who allowed only lower criticism and opposed theological innovation. Theology must evolve but slowly and within narrow limits.

In the aftermath of heresy trials, Zenos not only approved of changes in the *Westminster Confession but also edged the denomination toward a progressive *Calvinism. By proposing "liberty, open-mindedness and catholicity," Zenos advocated a "plastic theology," which he believed imitated developments in the New Testament age. In so doing he anticipated Presbyterianism's ready participation in the ecumenical movement. Among his important writings are *The Plastic Age of the Gospel* (1927) and *Presbyterianism in America* (1937).

Bibliography. L. A. Loetscher, *The Broadening Church: A Study of Theological Issues in the Presbyterian Church Since 1869* (1954).

W. A. Hoffecker

Zwemer, Samuel Marinus (1867-1952).† Reformed *missionary. Born near Vriesland, Michigan, Zwemer was of *Huguenot and *Dutch parentage, and the thirteenth of fifteen children. He graduated from Hope College (1887) and the Theological Seminary of the Reformed Church at New Brunswick, New Jersey (1890). Zwemer resolved to become a missionary, due to the influence of Robert P. Wilder of the Student Volunteer Movement.

Ordained by the Classis of Iowa in 1890, Zwemer went to Arabia, "the hardest country, the hardest climate, the hardest language, the hardest everything on earth," on an independent Arabian mission, which came under the board of foreign missions of the *Reformed Church in America (RCA) in 1894. After a year of travel around the Arabian peninsula, he and his colleague James Cantine chose Basra for their mission base. Establishing a second medical base in Bahrain in 1892, which became his primary base of operations, Zwemer evangelized the Gulf from Basra to Muscat, where he started a third station. While in Basra, he met and eventually married Amy Wilkes, a young Australian missionary nurse.

In 1907, while receiving medical treatment for an eye infection, Zwemer accepted a three-year appointment as a traveling secretary for the Student Volunteer Movement, simultaneously accepting a position as field secretary for the Reformed board of foreign missions. Although he returned to Bahrain in 1911, he was called the following year to Cairo by the United Presbyterian Mission, where he became the recognized leader of Christian missions to the Muslim world through his prodigious labors, cooperating with several mission organizations throughout Asia and Africa. He was constantly in demand as a conference speaker, and his desire to see the gospel spread to Muslims everywhere took him as far as

China and South Africa.

After seventeen years in Cairo, Zwemer accepted a position as professor of missions and the history of religion at Princeton Theological Seminary in 1929. Energetic and stately (six feet, 160 pounds), Zwemer was known as "a steam engine in breeches." A prodigious author and editor, Zwemer founded *The Moslem World* (1911), editing it for thirty-six years, and wrote such classics as *Arabia, the Cradle of Islam* (4 eds., 1900-1912), *The Cross Above the Crescent* (1941) and *Islam, a Challenge to Faith* (1907). In *The Origin of Religion* (1935), he challenged the evolutionary paradigm, arguing that monotheism was the first religion and that all other forms of religion have degenerated from that. He was elected president of the General Synod of the Reformed Church of America in 1923.

An indefatigable traveler, in 1927 and 1928 Zwemer covered 15,262 miles and once gave 151 addresses in 113 days. Appropriately he died while at work, following a lecture to InterVarsity Christian Fellowship in New York. Revered as the apostle to Arabia, Zwemer, wrote Sherwood Eddy, was "unique in our generation . . . a voice in the wilderness calling for the evangelization of Islam."

Bibliography. *ANB* 24; C. G. Fry and J. P. Fry, "Samuel Marinus Zwemer, Pioneer Missionary to the Muslims," *Missionary Monthly* 83 (1978) 3-5; J. C. Wilson, *Apostle to Islam: A Biography of Samuel M. Zwemer* (1938).

C. G. Fry